CBH
956

D1832888

R
375

THE LIFE
OF
LORD CLIVE

LORD CLIVE

From the portrait by George Dance, R.A., in the possession of Earl Powis.

THE LIFE

OF

LORD CLIVE

BY
SIR GEORGE FORREST

IN TWO VOLUMES

VOLUME - I

Gian Publishing House

29/6 SHAKTI NAGAR · DELHI-110007 · INDIA

GIAN PUBLISHING HOUSE
PUBLISHERS OF BOOKS ON HUMAN CIVILIZATION
29/6 SHAKTI NAGAR, DELHI-110007

First Reprint in India, 1986

Printed at Goyal Offset Printers, Delhi-110035
and published by Smt. Gayatri Garg
for Gian Publishing House, Delhi-110007

To

The Memory of
Percy Robert Herbert
VISCOUNT CLIVE
Elder Son of the 4th Earl of Powis
He died Fighting for England
her Wide-spread Dominions and
her Indian Empire
Whose foundations were laid firm
and deep by his Lineal Ancestor
ROBERT LORD CLIVE

PREFACE

THE SOURCES OF THE NARRATIVE

This biography concerns the actions and character of a soldier who won great victories, and a statesman who effected brilliant triumphs of policy and legislation. The materials on which it is founded consist mainly of original documents obtained by me from Public Archives in India and Europe, and from the vast accumulation of private papers at Walcot, the fine country house which Sir Robert Chambers built for Clive.

The duties of my office as Director of Records of the Government of India led me to pay sundry visits to Madras—the scene of Clive's earliest service—and I took advantage of my opportunities to select from the archives in Fort St. George the documents which threw light on Clive's career when, in the full freshness of youth, he took part as a gallant soldier and victorious commander in the struggle between the English and French for establishing a solid dominion in India. In order to gather fresh material and to revise impressions produced by the study of contemporary documents written by Englishmen, I made frequent journeys to Pondicherry. Through the courtesy of the Governor, I was enabled to search the ancient records in the official archives, and considerable work was devoted to mastering their contents. A number of the despatches and letters written by French soldiers, giving accounts of the Homeric combats which occupy this page of history, were copied for me. They illustrate the chivalry of the French race. A judge of the Pondicherry High Court, who took a deep interest in the history of his countrymen in India, informed me that there was in the archives some important evidence as to La Bourdonnais having taken a bribe from the English to conclude an unauthorised treaty for the ransom of Madras. He also gave me an authentic copy of the document, a translation of which is printed in the Appendix.

During one of my visits to Pondicherry, General Macleod, R.A., the Consular Agent, informed me that Ranga Pillai, the chief broker who transacted business with the natives for the Pondicherry Government, and was on intimate terms with Dupleix and his wife, had left a most important diary. In 1892 General Macleod and myself brought to the notice of the Madras Government the existence of the diary, and it was suggested that the matter which it contained was of such interest and value that it was highly desirable that a copy of it should be obtained, and a translation made of this and published. The Madras Government, which was then presided over by Lord Wenlock, readily adopted the suggestion, and after considerable research the undoubted originals of volumes i. and ii. and the last volume were discovered. They have been transcribed, and five volumes of translation published. This diary, from which I have often quoted. is of considerable historical value.

The work begun by me at Pondicherry was continued at Paris, and I desire to tender the expression of my gratitude to the French officials for their constant kindness and assistance. I am also deeply grateful to French Ministers for the indulgence accorded me to copy a certain number of documents. The limit of space has allowed me to print only two of them in the Appendix.

During a term of special duty in England, I was employed in examining and summarising the State Papers relating to Clive and the epoch covered by his career in India, kept in the Archives of the India Office. A large number of most important original documents—some of them extracts from the Orme Manuscripts—were copied and forwarded to me when I returned to India. My intention was to use them to illustrate the Introduction to a selection of State Papers dealing with Clive. But, before I could mould the Introduction into form, General Sir George Chesney, K.C.B., at that time Military Member of the Government of India, requested me to examine and arrange systematically, with a view to publication, all the State papers relating to the revolt of the Bengal Native Army in 1857 deposited in the different military offices of the Imperial Government. The editing of the Selections from the Letters, Despatches, and other State Papers relating to the Indian Mutiny proved a more difficult and laborious task than I anticipated, and the publication was delayed considerably beyond the date at which I hoped to conclude the work.

During the time I was engaged in writing the History of the Indian Mutiny, derived from these sources, it was a relief to withdraw from the difficult task of composition, and employ moments of leisure in arranging and exploring a huge mass of authentic materials which Clive had accumulated during his lifetime. On his death these documents passed into the possession of his son, Edward Clive, who succeeded to the Irish Barony, and for twenty years sat in the House of Commons as Member for Ludlow. In 1784 he married Henrietta, sister of George, the last Herbert, Earl of Powis, and, ten years after, he was created Baron Clive of Walcot in the British peerage. In 1799 he was appointed Governor of Madras, and landed at that port about the end of August. Three months before, Richard, Lord Mornington, the brilliant scholar and great statesman, who has stamped the name Marquess Wellesley upon the pages of the history of our Indian Empire, had assumed the office of Governor-General. The second Lord Clive had inherited some of his father's capacity for government. Soon after he arrived at Madras, Colonel Arthur Wellesley (afterwards Duke of Wellington) wrote: "The truth is, he does not want talents, but he is very diffident of himself; and now that he has begun to find out there is no conjuration in transacting the business of Government, he improves daily, takes more upon himself, and will very shortly have less confidence and reliance than he must have at present upon the opinion and abilities of those who have long done the business of the country." During the campaign against Tippoo he rendered substantial aid by pushing on the preparations for supplying the infinite wants of an army in the field. At the close of the war he conducted with firmness and tact the negotiations which led to the treaty by which the territories of Arcot and of the Carnatic Payen Ghaut passed into the possession of the British Government, " perhaps," wrote the Great Marquess, " the most salutary and useful measure which has been adopted since the acquisition of the *dewanny* of Bengal." Lord Clive was a sound administrator, desirous to extirpate every abuse, and on the watch for every improvement. He appointed a Committee of Reform, and his long Minute, based on their reports, is worthy to rank with the State Papers of his father. Many of the reforms he proposed were at once introduced. In the work of administration he had received loyal and able support from Mr. Webbe, Secretary to the Government, and when the Court of Directors requested him to remove that official from his post he remonstrated. The Court persisted in their order, and he resigned the Governorship. " The result," said Wellesley, " had been to drive that honest, diligent, prudent and able public servant from India." On his return to England, Lord Clive received the thanks of both Houses of Parliament for his services, and was created Earl of Powis. He was succeeded in 1839 by his son Edward, who took the arms and surname of Herbert only, in lieu of Clive, by royal licence, in accordance with the will of his maternal uncle, George, Earl of Powis. The present Earl is the grandson of the second Earl, the direct male descendant of Clive, and the fifth to hold the proud title Baron Clive of Plassey.

When the second Lord Clive was governing Madras he became acquainted with Sir John Malcolm, and their acquaintance in due course ripened into a close friendship. On Malcolm's return to England he was often a welcome guest at Powis Castle and Walcot. Malcolm suggested that he should write the Biography of Clive, and Lord Powis entrusted to his care the vast collection of political papers and correspondence brought together by his father—the founder of the Indian Empire. The collection is characterised by animated variety, and it would be difficult to exaggerate its value for historical and biographical purposes. It is not practicable in this place to give a full account of the papers Clive had stored during his strenuous lifetime. The collection consists of Minutes on important administrative measures which he laid before the Council, and the drafts of the more important Despatches to be forwarded to the Court of Directors. There are Memoranda on miscellaneous subjects of importance, and a mountain of bills. Clive had, as a Factor, before he became a soldier, been trained in the accuracy of mercantile method, and he kept his accounts with the greatest precision, and filed his bills with the utmost care. The Company obliged their servants to keep duplicates of their letters, and Clive acquired his lifelong custom of keeping copies, often written by himself, of his own letters. Among them is a copy of the first letter he sent to his father, when he landed at Madras, written in a firm, clear hand, and there are a few illegible lines written shortly before his tragic death. The letters written to him constitute numerous bundles, and those written by Stringer Lawrence, Eyre Coote, Forde, Watts, Scrafton, and other colleagues, are of the highest interest and importance. A number of letters written by Warren Hastings have come to light, and they supply an important gap in the biography of the great statesman who built the stately fabric whose wide foundations his great chief laid. There are also letters written by the leading statesmen of the day, and a multitude of epistles from all sorts and conditions of men, seeking his counsel, or his patronage, or his pecuniary aid.

Soon after these abundant materials were placed at the disposal of Sir John Malcolm he was appointed Governor of Bombay, and his biographer informs us that "he thought that he might turn the leisure afforded to him by the long sea-voyage to profitable account, by digesting his materials, and commencing the actual composition of the biography. He employed some of his young friends in copying his manuscripts." Malcolm embarked for Bombay on July 5th, 1827, and he arrived there on October 26th. On November 30th he wrote to his friend Sir Charles Metcalfe, afterwards Lord Metcalfe, " I have been busy during the voyage with the Life of Lord Clive—all his papers, public and private, having recently been discovered and given to me. I have finished about one thousand pages, and Elphinstone, who is fastidious enough about such works, is quite delighted—not with my composition, but with the admirable letters of Clive, whom he thinks I have managed to make tell his own story in a way that is both instructive and entertaining. I may have to refer upon some points that may require looking into old public records, or inquiries from natives." The Introduction and early chapters, written during the leisure of a long sea voyage, are the best in the Life. But Malcolm did not continue to make sufficient use of the materials placed at his disposal. As Governor of Bombay, he had to make extensive tours through the Presidency, besides performing the multifarious duties of his high office. He wrote to Sir Walter Scott : " I am toiling from dawn to sunset to bring to a good finish the labours of my public life." It is a marvel that he had been able to finish thirteen chapters when he departed from Bombay. On his return to England, Malcolm allowed himself to be lured into the strife of politics, and he had a restless longing to write a great work on the Government of India. The Life of Clive was neglected, and only two more chapters were written when Malcolm died, in 1833. The work was finished by a friend, and published in 1836. It exhibits the defects of the author and the conditions under which it was written. The narrative is often dull, and intermingled with disquisition ; the valuable matter is ill-arranged, the style that of the official report, and the biography remains an important work with intrinsic weaknesses.

The collection of papers consigned to Malcolm's care was returned in a state of hopeless confusion. Some of the original bundles appear never to have been opened, others to have been broken up, and the correspondence and papers extracted for publication in Malcolm's work were not put back.

The present Earl, who takes a deep interest in the career

of his direct ancestor Robert Clive, has rendered a service to the student of history by undertaking the difficult task of replacing the folios and bundles as nearly as could be ascertained in chronological order. I am specially indebted to him for the liberality with which he placed these muniments, in which he delights, under my care, in order that a more thorough examination should be made of their contents for the purpose of this work.

Other sources, besides the Powis MSS. have been freely drawn upon, and it may be well to indicate briefly the authorities on which I have relied for specially important or interesting episodes in Clive's life. The story of the first siege of Pondicherry, which gave Clive—a young subaltern—his first insight into the practical difficulties of the business of war, is told by himself in a modest and distinct narrative, which is now put in print for the first time. The tale of the "first fruitless expedition" to Tanjore is told in a memorandum written by Clive for Orme, and here printed for the first time.

In devoting a chapter to "The Political State of Southern India" I may have made the preponderance of history seem excessive in the story of Clive's life. But it is almost an impossible task to draw a line between history and biography in writing about a soldier-statesman whose career covers two of the most critical periods in the history of British Dominion in India, and who played so vital a part in fashioning them. The feature which distinguishes the first period is the long struggle between the French and English in the Carnatic, and it is impossible to form a just or discriminating estimate of the character and measures of Dupleix, or the conduct of the British, without a knowledge of the political state of India at that time. Without this knowledge the campaigns in which Clive took a leading part cannot be followed with interest and utility.

My account of the Valconda disaster is founded on the contemporary Journal of Captain John Dalton, whose narrative differs considerably from that given by Orme. The tale of

Clive's capture and defence of Arcot is derived from a journal which Orme, who became possessed of it in 1752, says was written by a Serjeant who served in the operations of which he gives such a simple, clear, and accurate account. Besides being a contemporary narrative of a most animating military episode, it has a strong attraction as a revelation of the character of the British soldier.

The Serjeant's account of Arni, Clive's first important victory in the open field, is here printed in its integrity. The history of the siege of Trichinopoly and the stern contests around it is mainly told from the Madras MS. Records, the Fort St. David MS. Records, Stringer Lawrence's own modest narrative, Clive's account of "Several Events," and the correspondence of Clive and Lawrence. These letters illustrate the beautiful and father-like interest taken in Clive's career by Stringer Lawrence, who had fired Clive's imagination to be a soldier, and had told him that Trichinopoly was the Gibraltar of India. Among the many memoranda which Clive sent Orme is a narrative of the siege of Covelong, and the surrender of Chingleput, which Orme embellished and incorporated in his work. It is now printed in its original state.

The account of the expedition made by the Royal Squadron under Watson and the King's troops under Clive, against Gheria, the stronghold of Angria the pirate chief, is constructed from the records in the Bombay archives, and from an Introduction to the present writer's Selections from the Bombay State Papers. The origin, progress and loss of the settlements and factories in Bengal have been traced, in order that the subsequent narrative may be intelligible and instructive. The substance of the account appeared in three papers—"Job Charnock," "The Siege of Calcutta," and "The Tragedy of the Black Hole," contributed by the present writer to *Blackwood's Edinburgh Magazine.* The sketch of the career of Job Charnock was drawn from "The Diary of William Hedges," illustrated and illuminated by Sir Henry Yule, and fresh material gathered from the archives of Madras. The account of the siege and capture of Fort William, and the dismal catastrophe that followed, was mainly told from the narratives and other writings of those engaged in the siege. The second volume of Orme's history deals with the important and interesting period of the annals of our Indian Empire from "The calamity which befel the English settlements in 1756 to the peace of 1763." In his account of the calamities which befel the English settlements Orme omits materials for forming a fair judgment as to the causes which led to the siege; he enhances the errors and crimes of Surajah Dowla, and suppresses facts which bear on individual characters. Eighteen years after the siege of Calcutta, John Zephaniah Holwell, who had so gallantly defended the fort after the dastardly flight of the Governor, published "A Genuine Narrative of the Deplorable Deaths of the English Gentlemen and Others who were suffocated in the Black Hole in Fort William, at Calcutta, in the kingdom of Bengal, in the night succeeding the 10th day of June, 1756. In a Letter to a Friend." The friend was "W. Davis, Esq.," and the letter was written "from on board the *Syren* sloop, the 28th of February, 1757." In a short preface Holwell informs the reader that "the narrative has been freely communicated to several, and amongst them to persons of the first distinction; who thought it might gratify public expectation, more especially if it appeared in the same natural and undignified dress in which they had seen it."

Nothing in Defoe's "History of the Plague" is more life-like nor more appalling than Holwell's natural and matter-of-fact narrative of what took place in the Black Hole. It was from Holwell that Orme took his account of the horrors of that night, and Macaulay borrowed from Orme. Besides Holwell, two other survivors of the tragedy have left notices of what occurred that night. The last four pages of the "Account of John Cooke, Esq., who was in the Black Hole, June, 1756," refer to events after the surrender; and there is a very brief mention of the tragedy in "The Journal of Captain Mill, who was in the Black Hole, from the 7th of

June to the 1st of July, 1756." The last half-page of "Mr. Grey, jun.'s Account of the Siege of Calcutta," refers to the catastrophe; and Mr. William Lindsay, in his letter to Orme, dated Fulta, July, 1756, mentions it. William Tooke also refers to it. We have a further account of the tragedy by Watts and others from hearsay; and Captain Alexander Grant, Adjutant-General of the Forces engaged in the defence of Calcutta, briefly notices it. It has been argued that it would be wiser to let that "great crime" fall under the shadow of the great power oblivion. But that crime cannot, any more than the Massacres of St. Bartholomew, Drogheda, and Glencoe, be effaced from the page of history. The contemporary evidence proves that Surajah Dowla was not guilty of that great crime. He was sleeping far from the fort when the deed was perpetrated. Holwell mainly attributes the severity with which he himself was treated to Omichund, the Punjabi banker. It was, indeed, a common belief at the time that the English owed their sufferings to the intrigue and resentment of Omichund; and letters in the old records show that when, after the battle of Plassey, the money sent to Calcutta as compensation was about to be distributed, a vigorous protest was raised against any restitution to Omichund, "because it is well known he was the chief instigator of the massacre of the Black Hole."

The circumstances that led to the formation of a conspiracy to dethrone Surajah Dowla amongst the Mohammedan officers and Hindu capitalists who were his subjects have been reviewed, and the urgency of the case that pressed the Bengal Council to accept the overtures of the chiefs and nobles of the Nawab's court to enter into a compact to deprive him of the rulership has been explained. The conduct of the intrigue was confided by the conspirators to Omichund. The fabrication of the fictitious treaty to deceive Omichund has been regarded as "an indelible stain" on the memory of Clive. The whole transaction is here discussed by the light of contemporary evidence, fortified by contemporary documents. No full discussion of the sources of the incident has been attempted by any historian, but there has been no lack of criticism. The chief basis of our historical knowledge must rest upon the statements of those who had good means of knowing the truth. The evidence reproduced in this book has lain buried in the Report from the Select Committee appointed by the House of Commons on April 13th, 1772.

The account of the march to Plassey and of that famous victory is constructed from fresh material of interest and importance. An exact transcription of the original record of the Proceedings of the Council of War, signed by the Officers present, from the Powis MSS., is given. The incidents of Eyre Coote's fruitless pursuit of Law after the battle of Plassey depend on a correspondence between Clive and Eyre Coote, preserved in the Powis MSS., which not only reveals a half-forgotten episode, but throws light on the characters of Clive and Eyre Coote. The narrative of the disastrous campaign of the brave and impulsive Lally is illustrated by a memorandum by John Call, the able engineer of Fort St. George. It contains much fresh material for the historian.

The story how the Dutch were defeated by land and water is taken from a straightforward "Narrative of the Disputes with the French in Bengal," Grosse's "Voyages," Clive's "Evidence," the Report of the House of Commons, and Forde's Letters. The account of Clive's residence in England in Chapter IV. of Vol. II. is illustrated by letters from Clive, Eyre Coote, Lawrence Sulivan, and by extracts from an original memorandum—"Memorials as to the East Indies by Lord Clive"—written by Clive for Lord Bute. The letters of Eyre Coote, which are printed in the same chapter, give a vivid description of the final contest between France and England in India.

An account is given of Clive's voyage to India, from June, 1764, to April, 1765, from a paper in a hand which resembles that of Strachey, the letters of Edmund Maskelyne to his sister, and Clive's letters to his wife. The survey of Clive's second Governorship of Bengal—the last as it was also the most arduous work of administration he was to engage in—

has been chiefly derived from his Minutes and Despatches. A study of his despatches shows that his foresight was clear and far-reaching, his judgment sane and sure, and his knowledge of the facts with which he dealt comprehensive and solid. The true man is, however, not made known to us in his seasons of victory and supreme power, but in the last record of his years of persecution and of the bitter moments of taunts and false charges. The courage did not sink, and he was still stirred with a zeal for the service of the kingdom he had governed and for causes and policies now beyond his control. He replied to his assailants in a speech which Lord Chatham, who was present during the debate, declared was "one of the most finished pieces of eloquence he had ever heard in the House of Commons." In a last speech, setting forth the services he had rendered his country, there is no trace of egotism. It is a great man's satisfaction at the great work he had done.

Clive's actions and his inmost thoughts are now given in their integrity to all who read our English. History, which seeks first to know what was done before delivering a verdict, has ample original authentic materials to judge critically and calmly the conduct and character of the man. Men of his race will remember him as a man of boundless devotion and charity, as a soldier of dauntless courage, a sound and brilliant commander of victorious armies, as a wielder, by sympathy, of great influence over alien races, as a statesman who, by the power of an unfaltering will, founded a mighty Empire.

G. W. FORREST.

Iffley,
Oxon.

NOTE

My thanks are due to the Warden and Fellows of All Souls' College for affording the Powis MSS. shelter, and granting me the privilege of conducting my work in their splendid Library. In the early chapters of the work I have had the great advantage of the advice of Mr. C. H. Firth, Regius Professor of Modern History, Oxford, and I also owe my warmest acknowledgments to Mr. R. S. Rait, Professor of Scottish History in the University of Glasgow, for his helpful corrections and important suggestions while the sheets were passing through the press. I desire to record my obligations to Mr. Rushbrook Williams, Fellow of All Souls, for the generous assistance he gave me, and to Miss L. M. Anstey for her explorations in the archives of the India Office for fresh material. My friend Mr. F. G. Stokes has rendered me willing and valuable help in the correction of the proof sheets—a difficult and tedious task, owing to the multitude of Oriental words and names, and the infinite inconsistencies in their transliteration. After careful consideration I determined to make no alteration in the spelling of words and names in the passages quoted, but, in order to maintain some uniformity, and that they should not be a non-conductor of interest to English readers, the forms which have become familiar to them have been adopted in the text, as far as possible. Complete uniformity is neither desirable nor practicable.

G. W. F.

CONTENTS

LIST OF PLATES

The Life of Lord Clive

CHAPTER I

1725–44: EARLY LIFE—ARRIVAL IN INDIA

MARKET DRAYTON is a small town in a sequestered corner of Shropshire, not many miles from the Staffordshire border. The ancient timber houses convey a sense of prosperity and comfort befitting a town which has been for centuries a focus of agrarian commerce. On a wooded height above the sloping street stands the ancient church, built of red sandstone, whose square sentinel tower has lightness, strength, and dignity. About two miles from Market Drayton nestles amongst its trees the hamlet of Moreton Say. Near it is one of the gates which open on the wide, undulating grounds of Styche, and on the brow of a slight eminence is situated the house which has long been in the possession of the Clives. The old seat commands a perfect English prospect—wide green meadows where the cattle love to browse and the stout oaks delight to grow, cultivated fields, wooded uplands, and, in the distance, the blue barrier which cuts off Shropshire from Staffordshire.

A pleasant mansion, built in the Georgian style, has taken the place of the black-and-white timber house with projecting wings in which was born, on September 29, 1725, one of England's greatest and most resolute sons. On October 2 the babe was baptized in the parish church of Moreton Say. He was given the name of Robert, for his grandfather and great-grandfather had been "Robert Clive, of Styche, in

Shropshire." His father, Richard Clive, was so called after Richard Clive, of Huxley, in Chester, who also owned the small estate of Styche, and who lived in the days of Henry VII. The second Richard Clive inherited a long pedigree and a short rent-roll of some five hundred pounds a year, and, thinking this too small a provision, he followed the profession of the law. His letters show him a man of an affectionate nature, not lacking in ability, but wanting in those sterner qualities which are necessary for success in the actual business of the profession he embraced. His wife, daughter of a Mr. Gaskell, of Manchester, was, unlike her husband, endowed with homely sense and force of character, and Clive always said he owed more to his mother than to any school.

Robert Clive was a delicate child, and though he grew energetic and fearless, there never came to him through the length of days the voice of joy and health. Before he was three years old he was sent away from home to live with one of his mother's sisters who had married a Mr. Bayley, of Hope Hall, Manchester. The vigorous air of Styche may have proved unfavourable to so frail a constitution. He had not been long at Hope Hall when he had a severe attack of illness. On December 22, 1728, Mr. Bayley writes:

"If I were given to be superstitious, and to believe things ominous I think I should omit writing to you, for it has been poor Bob's Fate to grow worse just after I have finished my Letters; from the Time of Andrew's leaving us till yesterday about five o'clock, He was worse than at any Time yet, and the Dr discovered by all his Behaviour that he apprehended full as much danger as ever, but since that time He has been much better, and we hope that then was the Crisis of the Fever. He slept pretty well last night, and when awake talked with his usual chearfullness, and I can say is now better, and in a more hopeful way to recover than hitherto, if no Relapse come upon him. He is (as you may well imagine) very weak, but the Dr doubts not his getting more Strength if the Fever continues (as it has began) to go off and leave him."[1]

Two days later he sends more hopeful news:

"I thank God I can now inform you that Bob continues better, and is in a very likely way to recover. We hope that the Crisis of

[1] Powis MSS.

the Fever was on Saturday Last about Noon, it having abated ever since. His exceeding patience is also exchanged for an eminent Degree of Crossness, which we take as a good Omen of his mending."

The fever, however, returned with great violence, was attended with convulsions, and there was grave danger that the child would not recover. But death was not awaiting him. On January 26, 1729, Mr. Bayley writes:

> "Yesterday Bob came down into the Parlour the first time, he goes on successfully with the Bark and is very merry and good as it is possible. He is poor and thin, but in a brave way, and has a stomach for more meat than we dare give him. He can run about, and chatters continually and is always asking Questions."

The worthy man adds: "This afternoon Bob with some reluctance suffered Aunt Bay to go to Chappel."[1] The boy recovered, but the fever was the cause, or the result, of some constitutional weakness that made him liable to fits of despondency, only overcome by the instincts of action and of command. Very early did the imperative instinct display itself. Clive was only seven when his uncle Bayley wrote:

> "I hope I have made a little further Conquest over Bob, and that he regards me in some Degree as well as his Aunt Bay. He has just had a fine new suit of Cloths, and promises by this Reformation to deserve them. I am satisfyed that his fighting (to which he is out of measure addicted) gives his temper a fierceness and Imperiousness that he flies out upon every trifling occasion, for this Reason I do what I can to suppress the Heroic that I may help forward the more valuable Qualities of Meekness, Benevolence and Patience. I assure you Sr it is matter of Concern to us, as it is of Importance to himself that he may be a good and virtuous man to which no care of Ours shall be wanting."[2]

The heroic was never suppressed, and the quality of meekness never acquired, but the benevolent and affectionate nature shone forth through the dark clouds of contention and battle.

While still a mere child, Clive was sent to a private school kept by Dr. Eaton, of Lostock, in Cheshire, evidently a shrewd man, able to gauge character. He observed that in courage and sagacity Clive surpassed his fellows. "If," said he, "that lad should live to be a man, and an opportunity

[1] Powis MSS. [2] *Ibid.*

be given for the exertion of his talents, few names will be greater than his." [1] From Lostock, Clive returned to Market Drayton, where he was placed under the Rev. Mr. Burslem, the master of the grammar school, who was "eminently skilled in the Latin tongue." How long Clive remained at the grammar school, and what proficiency he attained in study, we do not know, but many anecdotes have been related as to how he spent his playtime. He is said to have been the leader of a little band in all their mischievous tricks, now levying black-mail on anxious shopkeepers trembling for the security of their windows; now turning his body into a temporary dam across the street gutter to flood the shop of an offending tradesman.

The stories of Clive's wild youth must, however, be received with caution. The tale of his seating himself on a gargoyle of the parish church is the one which rests on the most credible traditional evidence. It has, however, been altered and embellished by successive writers. Clive's first biographer wrote:

> "In that town there stands, on the edge of a high hill, an antient Gothic Church, from the lofty steeple of which, at the distance of a few feet from the top, there projects an old stone spout in the form of a dragon's head. On this head he once seated himself, to the great astonishment and terror of his schoolfellows." [2]

Sir John Malcolm relates the incident thus:

> "One well-authenticated and extraordinary instance is recorded of his boldness as a boy. The church at Market Drayton, which stands on the side of a hill, has a lofty steeple, near the top of which is a stone spout of the form of a dragon's head. It was with no slight surprise and alarm, his companions, and some of the inhabitants, saw young Clive seated on this spout, and evincing by his manner an indifference, if not insensibility, to the danger of his situation."

Malcolm adds that

> "several of the oldest inhabitants of Market Drayton not only confirm this fact, but add, on the testimony of their parents, that Clive

[1] A. Kippis: "Biographia Britannica" (2nd edit.), art. Clive, p. 645.

[2] "His object was to get a smooth stone which lay on the projecting stone spout, for the pleasure of jerking it." "The writer has heard this anecdote related by several of the inhabitants of Drayton."—"Biographia Britannica" (2nd edit.), art. Clive, p. 645.

OLD STYCHE: THE BIRTHPLACE OF LORD CLIVE

(*From a Drawing made before the year* 1754)

was wont to levy from some of the shopkeepers contributions in pence and trifling articles, in compensation to himself, and the little band he led, for abstaining from breaking their windows . . ."[1]

Macaulay, in his essay on Clive, gives, however, an exaggerated impression of the boy's daring:

> "The old people of the neighbourhood," he writes, "still remember to have heard from their parents how Bob Clive climbed to the top of the lofty steeple of Market Drayton, and with what terror the inhabitants saw him seated on a stone spout near the summit."[2]

But we have no reason for assuming that Clive did not ascend the steeple—or rather tower, for such it is—of Market Drayton by the stairs in the ordinary way. In any case, to sit astride the gargoyle was a daring feat for the lad to perform; but Clive, like Nelson, never saw fear.

From the grammar school at Market Drayton, Clive was sent, in 1737, to Merchant Taylors' in London,[3] and he was one of the first of the many illustrious men who, by the life and discipline of a public school, were prepared for the work of founding and governing an empire. In 1739 he was removed to a private school, kept by Mr. Sterling, at Hemel Hempstead, in Hertfordshire, in order, as we may reasonably conjecture, to be taught the science of book-keeping and the fine art of penmanship—accomplishments which the directors of a trading company considered of far greater importance than an acquaintance with the authors of Greece and Rome.[4]

Clive's father had always formed great hopes of the high destiny of his eldest son. At first he was desirous that the boy should follow his own profession. But the younger sons of squires had begun to come home with large fortunes made in a few years in India. To a boy of good understanding

[1] "Life of Robert, Lord Clive," Vol. I., p. 35 (1836).

[2] "Critical and Historical Essays," Vol. III., p. 112 (1843).

[3] "Robert Clive, born 29th September, 1725. . . . The usual date assigned to his birth is 24th February, 1726, but the Probation Lists give the above. . . . Left the school in 1739."—C. J. Robinson: "A Register of the Scholars admitted into Merchant Taylors' School from A.D. 1562 to 1874."

[4] Warren Hastings was removed from Westminster and placed for a time under the tuition of Mr. Smith, the teacher of writing and accounts at Christ's Hospital.—"Memoirs of Warren Hastings," by the Rev. G. R. Gleig, Vol. I., p. 13.

and strong will it offered the best field of enterprise. A post in the service of the East India Company was sought, and we find the following entries in their Court Minutes :—

"At a Court of Directors holden on Wednesday the 15th December, 1742 * * *

"The Court proceeded to the Choice of Writers for Fort St. George, Bombay, and Bengal, and the following Persons being ballotted for were chosen accordingly, vizt.—

William Smith King	For Fort St. George
Robert Clive	
Henry Cope	
John Walsh	
Samuel Bankes	
John William Speck	
John Andrews	
John Pybus	

"And they being called in were acquainted therewith * * *

"At a Court of Directors holden on Wednesday the 5th January, 1742 [1743]—

"The following Securitys were approved of, vizt.—Richard Clive, of Copthall Court, Gentleman;

"Mr. George Wapple, of Ladd Lane, Merchant; for Robert Clive, Writer, for Fort St. George, in £500."[1]

The foundation of Fort St. George, the presidency to which Robert Clive was appointed, was due to the struggle between the Portuguese, the Dutch, and the English, as to who should enjoy the trade between India and the Spice Islands. In 1611, eleven years after Elizabeth had granted the first charter to "the Governor and Company of Merchants of London trading into the East Indies," Captain Hippon was dispatched by the directors of the India Company in the ship *Globe* to open a trade with the Coromandel Coast. He was accompanied by two Dutch merchants, Peter Floris and Lucas Antheunis.[2] The English and Dutch were both attracted to the eastern coast of Hindustan by the same object. They wished to purchase painted cloths, or Indian cotton goods, and take them to the Moluccas in exchange for spices to be sold in Europe. The *Globe* touched at Pulicat, where the Dutch had established a

[1] Court Minutes, Vol. LX., pp. 182, 202.

[2] The Journal of Peter Floris is in the India Office. Extracts from it were printed by Purchas.

factory and built a fort. The Dutch governor refused to allow the English to trade. Hippon, therefore, left Pulicat and coasted up the Bay of Bengal till he reached Masulipatam, at the mouth of the Kistna, then the principal port of that part of India. At Masulipatam the English managed to establish a small agency, which was put under a chief, and a council was chosen from the merchants. Fifteen years later, in 1626, a factory was established and fortified at Armagon, a roadstead south of Masulipatam, and about forty miles north of Pulicat. It was the first fortification erected by the English in India. In the year 1628–9 Armagon is described as defended by twelve pieces of cannon mounted round the factory, and by a guard of twenty-three factors and soldiers. The factory at Masulipatam was transferred in 1629 to this fortress owing to the oppression of the native governor. But Armagon was not a good entrepôt for the supply of cotton goods, and three years later the agency was again established at Masulipatam.

In 1639, Francis Day, one of the council at Masulipatam, was sent to examine the country in the vicinity of the station which the Portuguese, who were then friendly to us, had established at St. Thomé.[1] Day

> "was Inordered to goe towards St. Thomay to see what payntings[2] those parts doth afford, as alsoe to see whether any place were fitt to fortifie upon."

In August of the same year, three years before the outbreak of the Civil War in England, Day, "haveinge Dispatcht what hee was sent about," returned to Masulipatam and told his colleagues what he had done.

> "And, first, hee makes it appeare to us that at a place Called Madraspatam, neare St. Thomay, the best paintings are made, or

[1] Alfred the Great sent an embassy, under Bishop Sighelm of Sherborne, to do honour to the tomb of a Holy Thomas. Gibbon hints that the envoys got no farther than Alexandria, the great centre-point of the East and West, where they collected their cargo and invented a legend. According to this legend of antiquity the Gospel was preached in India by St. Thomas. Recent research has shown that it was preached in the eighth century by Thomas Canam, an Armenian merchant, as Marco Polo was informed on the spot, at Meliapur (*Mayillapur*), the native name for St. Thomé.

[2] Payntings, painted cloths, i.e. chintz.

as good as anywhere on this Coast, likewise Exellant long Cloath, Morrees,[1] and percalla[2] (of which wee have seene Musters), and better Cheape by 20 per cent. then anywhere Else. The Nague[3] of that place is very Desirous of our residence there, for hee hath made us very fayre proffers to that Effect; for, first, hee proffers to build a forte, in what manner wee please, upon a high plott of ground adjoyneinge to the sea, where a ship of any Burthen may Ride within Muskett shott, Close by a river which is Capeable of a Vessel of 50 Tonns; and, upon possession given us by him, and not before, to pay what Charges hee shall have disbursed."[4]

Day was "dispeeded" back to Madraspatam, and so important was the new acquisition considered that the agency at Masulipatam directed him to begin building "the Forte" without waiting for the orders of the Court from England.

The fort, as first erected, was but a small place, not a quarter of a mile long, only a hundred yards wide from east to west, and situated in the north-east corner of the present fort. Five years after its first erection its total cost had been only Rs. 23,000, and the highest estimate of a sufficient garrison was one hundred soldiers. In 1652, thirteen years after its foundation, it was considered safe with a garrison of twenty men. No great change was made in it for a century.

Clive sailed "from England towards Madrass" on board the *Winchester*, a vessel of about 500 tons, one of the Company's ships. This was only her third voyage. Gabriel Steward was commander and John Samson chief mate. The log kept by them[5] is among the "Marine Records" at the India Office, and the water-stained and almost illegible pages tell a story as exciting as any embodied in "The Principal Navigations, Voyages, Traffiques and Discoveries of the English Nation," compiled by Richard Hakluyt. On March 10, 1743, the *Winchester* left the Thames, and on "Sunday, 20 March 1742/3 . . . . Lay too for the fleet and some Mercht. Ships to come out of Plymouth. In

[1] Morrees, murry (*muri*), purple-red cloth.
[2] Percalla (*parkala*), spangled cotton cloth.
[3] Naik, naique (*nayak*), a ruler, provincial governor.
[4] "The Founding of Fort St. George, Madras," by William Foster, p. 10.
[5] Log of the *Winchester*, Captain Gabriel Steward, succeeded by John Samson. To Madras, Calcutta and Tellicherry. Log begins 1 Dec., 1742, and ends 18 March, 1746.

Company with the *Stirling Castle* of 70 Guns, Capt. Clealand, the *Princess Louisa,* Capt. Pinson, and 26 Sail of small Merchantmen, unbent our Cables and Stowed our Anchors."

When the *Winchester* sailed, England and France had begun to contend against each other in the War of the Austrian Succession, and it was to protect them from French privateers that the fleet was convoyed by H.M.S. *Stirling Castle.* The two Indiamen were soon left to make their voyage to the Eastern seas. But they did not long pursue their way together.

On Monday, April 18, 1743, at 8 P.M., the *Princess Louisa* fired a gun as a signal to the *Winchester* to alter her course.

> " We shortned Sail and went under an Easy Sail, Vizt. our topsails on the Caps, till ½ past 12 A.M., at which time we saw the land bearing S.W. upon which we wore Ship fired a Gun hung four lights up the Mizen Shrouds and fired false fires as a Proper Signal of Danger."

At 1 A.M., finding the *Princess Louisa* drew from them very fast,

> " we Wore Ship and stood to the N.Wd. after her, at two Do. she fired two Gunns."

It was the last they heard.

> " At 4 A.M. the body of the Isle of May[1] bore S.W. b S. distance about four Miles; at Break of day could not see the *Louisa,* upon which we Tack'd and stood to the Shoals again, soon after we saw her among the Rocks without ever a Mast Standing and the Sea making a free Passage over her."

They stood as near her as they thought they could do with safety, tacked and lay to. The pinnace and yawl were hoisted out, and the captain sent them, " to go to Endeavour to save the men if Possible."

> " I went within hail of them, but found the Sea Run so high & Break that we could not venture any further, they waved their Hatts and Call'd to us but we could not distinguish what they said. We went on board our own Ship again, took two Coyles of small Rope and a Grapnail . . . so as to take some of the men out, but when we Came there her upper works was all wash'd away, nothing to be seen but the Bowsprit, some of her Top Timbers, and not a man to be seen, then we went on board, hoisted our Pinnance in, and

[1] One of the Cape Verd Islands.

made Sail, there being no possibility of saving anything. And am Affraid there is not a man alive of them to tell their Tale."

Some, however, lived to tell the tale, though the ocean swallowed seventy. After spending three days at Santiago (another of the Cape Verd Islands), the *Winchester* sailed from "St. Jago towards Madrass." It was the constant practice of vessels bound for the Indies to use the North-East trade wind to carry them right across the Southern Atlantic until they could pick up the South-East trade wind which would take them round the Cape. The North-East trade blew merrily, and the *Winchester* sailed across the Southern Atlantic for Brazil. For twenty-four days all went well with them. Then, "Tuesday May 17th 1743. Between 3 and 4 o Clock A.M. to our great surprize found the Ship to Strike. When notwithstanding all our Endeavours she was so fast a Ground that she would neither veer nor stay." At daylight they saw "severall small Vessels in Shore at an Anchor, and a place which seemed to be a large Town to the S.W. of us. We hoisted our Collours, when there came on board a small boat and several Catamarans with some Portuguize who informed us the Governour livd at a place call'd Pernambuco." About 9 A.M. there came to them "the most experianced Pylot of the coast." Acting on his orders they landed all their sails and all the "Treasure" belonging to "the Honble. Company." "Made a tent upon the Sand in which the Treasure was putt, and guarded by a Company of Soldiers. Struck Yards and Topmast." A week passed before the lightened ship was got into 6 fathoms of water, where they moored. The pilot informed them that they must lie where they were until the month of September or October before they could get the ship up to Pernambuco "on account of the bad weather they generally have between this and that time." In June the wild gales compelled them to "go back," and they "hired some Portuguize and set them to work to build a house to put our Masts, Yards, Rigging, &c. out of the weather." The battered ship had to be repaired from stem to stern, and the crew found it hard, monotonous work in the damp heat.

At length, on September 22, 1743, "the Pylott came on board to Carry us into the Harbour." There was still much to do, and two months passed before they "began to heave the ship down: in about 2 hours had her keel out, find she makes but little Water, so as to keep her free with one Pump, if she continues so till to-morrow morning the Carpenters will begin on her bottom." The work now progressed fairly rapidly, and on Saturday, February 11, 1744, the *Winchester* weighed anchor, and "saluted the Fort with 9 Gunns which number they returned. Stood to the No. Ward." During the nine months he was detained at Pernambuco Clive acquired a knowledge of Portuguese, which was afterwards of service to him. After leaving the Brazils a storm fell upon them, and they had to put in "att Cape Bona Esprance," and "found riding here His Majesties Ship the *Centurion* of 60 Gunns, Commadore Anson, the *Warwick*, Captain Mizner, and the *Salisbury*, Captain Burrows, all for England, and Eleven Sail of Dutch Indiamen." Eleven days later they again weighed (7th April 1744) and sailed north-eastward, till on

"*Friday* 1 *June* 1744. Att 7 P.M. came too in Madrass Road with the B Bower in 10 fathoms Water & ¼. Found Riding here, the *Montague,* Captain Freeman; the *Prince of Wales*, Captain Pelley; and the *Winchelsea,* Captain Baron. At Sun Rise Saluted the Fort with 9 Gunns, and the Governour with 21. Was Saluted by the *Montague* and *Winchelsea* with 7 Gunns each, for which we returned 13."

The landing of Clive at Fort St. George as a writer, at the age of 17, marks the first point of a career which was to shape the destiny of the whole continent. There was little brightness in the dawn at Fort St. George to awaken hope. He was in an alien land, without money or friends, and sick for home. Frequent correspondence between the exile and the loved ones whom he had left at home did not in those days mitigate cruel separation. Clive landed on the southern coast of India at the time when the monsoon or season of southwest storm was approaching, and only a few coasting ships anchored in the open roadstead some miles off the dangerous coast. The homeward bound East Indiamen had sailed, and it was not till September, when the monsoon began to lose its force, that he had an opportunity of sending his first letter[1] announcing his arrival. It was written to his father in the stiff old style :—

Hon^{D} S^{R}—It is with no small Satisfaction that I can inform you of my safe Arrival at Fort St. George, after the long and Dangerous Passage, and the many Inconveniencies which by that means we have met with. I can also acquaint you of my enjoying a perfect State of Health ever since my Departure from England, which I think is something remarkable, considering the different Change of Climates, and so many Misfortunes which generally from thence ensue, especially as I have been accustomed to live in one of the most moderate Climates in the World. I shall now make it my Duty to inform you in what Manner I have acted with respect to my Expences, which indeed are very considerable, tho I used all the Prudence and Frugality I was then Master off ; I must confess at my first setting out from England was a little Careless and lost several of my Things on the Coast of Brasil, tho I can assure you I am not the only Person by many who have met with the like Misfortune, it being impossible to avoid it considering the fright and Confusion we were all in at the Ships first running on Shore. I hope you'll be so candid as to excuse me and impute it to want of Experience rather than any careless Extravagant habit in my Nature ; since I can assure you I have so much instructed myself in the Way of the World, as easily to foresee the bad Consequences that must attend such misdemeanours, and am willing to undergo your Displeasure If ever I am guilty of the like Folly : We lay at the Brasils upwards of nine Months, during which time I receivd of Captain Stewart, Necesarys to the Value of ten Pounds, £10 and about forty 40 Shillings in Money, the p^{r} Centage being charged makes it more, of which I gave you an Account at the Cape of Good Hope ; I found my own Brakefast almost all the time since our first Arrival on that Coast, and what with the Expence of Washing, and lining for my Cloaths, I persuade myself you wont think I have been Extravagant. Upon my Arrival at this Place I immediately waited on the Governour and had the Honour to dine with him also deliver'd him my Letters of Recommendation, but when I enquir'd after Mr. Benyon, was inform'd he had embark'd from this Place towards England about 4 Months ago, upon which I advis'd with the Captain, also made bold to open the Letter directed to Mr. Benyon,

[1] Malcolm gives a brief summary of this letter in his "Memoirs of Lord Clive." He writes, p. 40 : "The whole of the last part of this letter being lost, we are left in the dark as to its date, and such other particulars as he may have communicated." A complete copy of the letter, written by Clive himself, was, however, discovered by me among the Powis MSS., in an old packet of bills dated 1752 and 1753.

where I found a Letter of yours inclos'd with Orders for him to receive the Bag of Dollars, upon which Account I waited on Governour Morse, and enquir'd if he had receiv'd any Letters relaiting to the Money, which I thought not improbable, as Mr. Benyon was gone home, and our Passage had been so much prolong'd, but finding myself mistaken, I receiv'd the Money of Captain Stewart, and have given him a Receipt for the same. Some of the Factors and Writers were so good as to inform me of the Customs and Manners of the Place, and with their Advice, I sold the Silver for one hundred thirty seven Pagodas thirteen Fanams sixty Cash $\overset{\text{Pag}^{s}}{137} : \overset{\text{F}}{13} : \overset{\text{C}}{60}$ which in Stirling Money is valued at about fifty four Pounds Sixteen Shillings and Sixpence $\overset{£}{54} : \overset{s}{16} : \overset{d}{6}$. You must needs think that so long a Passage has made me very bare of all Wearing Apparrel, as for the Cloaths brought out of England, I have none that are of any Service to me except my double Alepine[1] Coat, my laced Wastecoat is long enough, but cannot button it, so have taken the Lace of, and put it on a Wastecoat made of this Country Silk ; and in respect to Linnen was so greatly reduc'd, that I have been oblig'd to get Shirts and Stockings of some of the Gentlemen on board, and thought myself very lucky in being provided, else shou^{d} have been oblig'd to go naked, and have paid them at my Arrival on this Place, eight Pagodas, thirty two Fanams, $\overset{\text{P}}{8} : \overset{\text{F}}{32}$ wch is about three Pounds ten Shillings $\overset{£}{3} : \overset{s}{10}$ Stirling Money: When I had computed the Expence that it wou'd stand me in providing Furniture for my Rooms, Linnen and other wearing Apparel, I found it woud amount to the full if not more, than the Sum you sent out with me, so found it impossible to avoid taking some things of Captain Stewart, and he has not only charg'd me a very extroardinary Price upon them, but also fifty p^{r} Cent on the Money, so that what with the Percentage, and what with the Advantage gain'd on the Goods, it amounts to thirty Pounds one Shilling and Sixpence $\overset{£}{30} : \overset{s}{1} : \overset{d}{6}$. I think he has acted a very ungenerous Part in charging me such extraordinary Prizes, as I am persuaded no other Capt but himself wou'd have been so unreasonable, and I realy believe had these things been bought in England at prime Cost, without the percentage, both this Bill, and that drawn at the Cape, woud not am^{t} to above fifteen Pounds, $\overset{£}{15}$. But when I had consider'd that I had not yet heard from you, and that it was very probable I shou'd not till next Year at the furthest, as all the Ships bound to this Place are arriv'd excepting two, as we are inform'd there is a french War, and an Invasion intended, it is every Persons Opinion that there is an Embargo laid on these two Ships, especially as they are not yet Arrivd, so that before I can have the Pleasure of hearing from you, it will be almost

[1] Alepine, a material made of wool and silk, or of mohair and cotton.

three Years, from my departure from England: so thought it the most prudent and safe Way to do as before mention'd, tho upon such disadvantageous terms, rather than any Way detriment myself, by running in Dept, which wou'd not only be a means of incurring the Companys Displeasure, but very likely of being turn'd out of their Service, there being many Instances of the like Nature wch have happen'd to several Gentlemen in this Place by such imprudent Practizes; Mr. Stratton fourth of Council is at this present time suspended, only upon the bare Report of a Man wh° did it with a Design to ruin him: The Company have given strict Orders to enquire, whether we are Persons to whose Conduct they may entrust their Affairs, and have impower'd them, either to degrade, or turn out, such Persons as dont behave consistent with their Promises; and indeed most of them seem to be a set of very prudent and Industrious People, some few excepted: I think myself not only very happy, but infinitely oblig'd to you for my Education, and as it has render'd me in a fair Way of improving my Talent, I flatter myself with ye Hopes of enlarging tenfold: I have sent you an Account of the things I receivd of Captain Stewart; You may very reasonably conjecture that I have been very negligent with Respect to my Buckles, as Mr. Vere was so kind as to make me a Present of a set of Silver ones, which I had the Misfortune to loose by a very unforseen Accident, which had nigh cost me my Life, having tumbl'd overboard, whilst I was standing on the Poop of the Ship as she was laying at an Anchor on the Coast of Brasil, and shoud certainly have been drowned, there being a very great Sea and much Wind, if the Capt had not Accidentally met with a Bucket and a Rope tied unto it, which he threw out of the Balcony to me, I having the good fortune to lay hold of it; I then lost my Shoes off my Feet, and with them my Silver Buckles, also a Hat and Wigg. With respect to my Wiggs two of them are too little, which I have not as yet dispos'd of, one I wore out on the Coast of Brasil, and having but one left, thought it necessary to take one of the Capt. I hope you'll be so kind as not to take Exception at the Wine, as there are no other Sort of Drinkables here but that, and Punch, and as I always shall drink it with Water, intend to make it serve me a whole Year. As for the Glasses Knifes Pewter Spoons &c^t^ I tooke them for the Reasons above mention'd, which I persuade myself You'll think was absolutely necessary; I also took ten Yards of Camlet to make me a Shewt of Cloaths, as I had none left but my Allepine Coat and one Duroy[1] D° I have sent you inclos'd a List of things which I bought upon my Arrival at this Place, and I fancy you'll be surpris'd at the Quantity of Linnen &c^t^ mention'd in the Bill, there being a greater Stock than is needful in England, for in this Place there are none but what put clean Linnen on every Day, and indeed the greatest Part shift twice, upon Account of the intollerable Heat, which sweats them to that Degree, that

[1] A coarse woollen fabric.

they are just as if they had been dipt in a River, with all their Cloaths on, and upon that Account they generally wear such things as can be wash'd again, besides the Washmen live three or four Miles in the Country, and bring the Linnen but once a Month, they make no use of soap here, but beat the Shirts till they are clean against a Stone, so that in eight or ten times washing they are all in rags. As for Furniture I flatter myself you wont think I have acted with any Extravangancy, as the Companys Rooms allow'd us are entirely bear of all Manner of Such sort of things, and it was as much as even I cou'd do to get them clean'd out and Whitewash'd at the Companys Expence, being oblig'd to live at a publick House upon that Account for seven Days, which stood me in half a Pagoda a Day only the bear Victuals being Allow'd but one Boul of Punch, and one Bottle of Wine, let there be ever so many. The Companys Allowance is eight Pagodas twenty three Fanams p^r^ Month, out of which ye Money paid for Servants Wages, Washing, Candles, and many other Necessarys belonging to Housekeeping, together with the Dearness and Scarcity of Provisions, makes it as much as ever we can do to live upon that Allowance ; I have sent you a short Account of the Money deducted for Servants Wages and other Particulars ; As I have nothing more to add on this Subject, I shall only make it my Request that in what I have acted amiss, You'll be so good as to excuse, as it is upon such an Extroardinary Occasion & which I hope will never happen again. If you shou'd think it Adviseable to advance me some Money, I cou'd not only make considerable Advantages by it, by saving wherewithall out of the Interest to defray Expences in Cloathing and other Necessarys, but cou'd also increase the Principal very considerably, I can Assure you we have equaly the same Priviledges when Writers, as Factors, and I dont doubt but you'll take it into your Consideration ; Money is let out here at Respondentia from 16 to 32 p^r^ Cent, besides many other Advantages by Private Trade &c^t^ and if you shoud think proper to favour my request, by entrusting it eighter into the Hands of some of the Gentlemen of this Place, or any other Way which you shall judge most convenient, I shall think myself infinitely in Duty bound to you, and shall thankfully acknowledge the Favour. I have sent you an exact Account of all the Companys Covenanted Servants as they are station'd. I shall always make it my Duty to behave worthy & deserving of your Confidence, and Esteem, and am willing to give up all Pretensions to your Favour in case I dont behave with that Sobriety and Diligence which is expected. As a Recommendation to some of the Gentlemen in this Place woud be a means of being better acquainted, and more fully instructed of the Customs and Advantages of this Country, I shoud be very glad If you cou'd get me recommended to some of them for that Purpose : When I was in England I remember you entertain'd Hopes, of removing me to Bengal, which wou'd be much more Advantageous to me, as it wou'd not only reduce my Expences, as all Manner of

Provisions are much cheaper, but also allows greater Liberty of Merchandizing, & trade is in a much more flourishing Condition, than at Fort St. George, there being three times the Number of Ships always in constant Employ, and any of the Company Servants may trade as largely as they please, therefore make it my Request you'll make all the Interest you can to remove me, there has been two Writers remov'd there very lately, so flatter myself wth the Hopes of Succeeding. I can acquaint you of the Agreable News of my time being Accounted for Since the Arrival of the first Writers, in the Year 1743, and as I have thoroughly instructed myself in the Portugeese Language, it will something alleviate my unfortunate Stay at the Brasils. as we have Dayly several Instances of Persons being made Factors, whereof we hear two are coming out this Year, I don't doubt but you'll make use of all possible means for my Advancement. The World seems to be vastly debas'd of late, and Interest carries it entirely before Merit, especially in this Service, tho I shoud think myself very undeserving of any Favour, were I only to build my Foundation on the Strength of the former : I have been contriving a Scheme concerning my Cousin Bobby, but whether it may take Effect, or whether my Uncle may care to entrust him in these Parts, I am entirely at a Loss to know. The Company keep two Clergymen at this Presidency at one hundred Pounds p^{r} Annum each $\overset{\pounds}{100}$, besides twelve Pagodas p^{r} Month, which is about fifty Seven Pounds twelve Shill^{s} $\overset{\pounds}{57}$: $\overset{s}{12}$ more, together with other Perquisites, now as their is a Vacancy of one of them if you coud get him chose for this Place, I cant foresee any better Provision that can be made for him in England, they have equally the same Priviledge of trading, as the Companys Covenanted Servants, and indeed if we had nothing more to depend on but their Allowance, it woud be to very little purpose for us to spend our time here, of which Truth I believe you may be very easily convinc'd, when you peruse the List I have sent you. I beg leave to recommend Mr. Simson to your Favour, he having behav'd with a great deal of Conduct and Prudence, and seems to be thoroughly reform'd of all past Misdemeaners, being well persuaded of the bad Consequences that attend a Debauch'd and extravagant Life ; He's a Man of exceeding good Sense, & I think it a great Pity that persons endow'd with such Qualifications, shou'd make so bad a use of them : I believe Capt Stewart will give you such an Account of him, as you may venture to employ him in any Affair of Confidence and Trust, & if you cou'd make interest to get him out Purser, with your Assistance we cou'd drive on a very considerable Traffick : for my part I shall let no Opportunity slip of improving myself in everything where I can have the least View of Proffit : I can Assure you my stay in this Place is in every respect pleasant, & satisfactory to me, as it is back'd with the Hopes, (if it please God to preserve my Life) of being able to provide for myself, & also of being of Service to my Relations, and shou'd at this time as much as lies in my Power, be glad of serving You in this Part of the World, if my Mother, Sisters, or any of the Family, shou'd want any Silks, Stuffs, Tea, Callicoes, or any other Productions which the Country Affords, upon Notice given I will be sure to provide and send them by the first Opportunity. I shou'd be glad if you wou'd send me some Europe Stuffs for Cloaths with their Trimmings, also some Wigs, Shoes, and Hats, and I shall thankfully acknowledge the Favour. Camblets, Barragons,[1] and Duroys tu[rn] to a very good account in the Place, especially those of a Gaudy Colour; My not hearing from you makes me very uneasy, and were it not for some little Hopes that these two latter Ships which are expected, have pass't this Place, and gone to Bengal, my time wou'd be very burthensome to me, as there is a great Part of the Year in which we have no Employment, and having no manner of Acquaintance, but with my Brother Writers, I find it of great disadvantage to me, however shall endeavour to employ my Time in reading, and all other Diversions, which may be of Service to me, & if you'll indulge me so far as to send me out some Books for that Purpose, I shall be very much oblig'd to you, a little News wou'd be also very agreable to me. I beg the Favour of you when you write me, that you'll be so good as to send the Letters, to the India House to be put in the Packet, transcrib'd at the Bottom p^{r} first Ship, as they very often neglect the first opportunity unless reminded by such Memorials: I wou'd Advise not to entrust any of them on Board, as the Gentlemen very often either through Carelessness loose them, or else by neglect forget to deliver them; If you shoud think proper to send me out any Money, wou'd advise you to send it to the India House, and there by paying into the Company's Cash I or any other into whose Hands you please to entrust it, may receive the Value of it either in Pagodas, or Rupees, the currant Coin of this Place, or else by paying two & and half p^{r} Cent, you may send it in any Species you please, of which that you sent out with me is the best being old Pillar [dollars]; This latter Method is the most generally made use of because it is the most advantageous, the former (or first) being us'd by Persons who pay their Money in this Place, receive the Value of it in England; I shall send Duplicate of this Letter, lest by any Misfortune the Original shoud miscarry together with all Occurrences that in the Interim may happen in the Postscript. I beg leave to remember my Duty to my Mother, Love to my Sisters, & Service to all distant relatives and [Friends . . . and Mr. Bayley . . . ?] of whom I shall always retain a thorough Sense of Gratitude for the many Favours I stand indepted to him for, and so conclude heartily wishing You, my Mother, all Relations & Friends length of Days, Prosperity, and Success in all your, and their Undertakings, and am in the meantime studious to be thought

Your most Ob^{t} & Dutiful Son

FORT ST. GEORGE ROB^{T} CLIVE.
10th September 1744.

[1] Coarse camlets.

P.S.—I have just now receiv'd the News of Captain Stewarts Death, by the *Mercury*, who died at Bengal three days after his Arrival in that Place and was always a very noted Man for a strong Constitution but had the Misfortune to get a Fever which in these hot Countries are sure either to recover or die in three or four days.

The next letter,[1] full of warm feeling, was written to his uncle.

Dear Uncle,—The concern that it gives me to think that I have neglected so necessary a Branch of my Duty, in not writing to you before, has stamped on my mind no small impression, and should esteem myself very happy, if a sincere and hearty acknowledgement of my fault might be accepted of: I do assure you it did not proceed from any Slight or Contempt, but rather from a Lightness and Instability of Mind, which naturally attends all School Boys, who have not the least thought of time past, or to come, and as I am well persuaded, no one understands the Frailties and Imperfections of Youth better than yourself. I flatter myself you'll be so candid as to impute it to that cause: I shall always retain a due sense of Gratitude for the Many Obligations & Favours you have laid me under, & the pleasant and delightfull days I have spent with my kind Relations and Friends in Lancashire, refreshes & entertains my mind, with very Agreeable Ideas. I must confess at Intervals when I think of my dear Native England, it affects me in a very particular manner, however knowing it to be for my own Welfare, rest content and patient, wishing the views for which my Father sent me here, may in all Respects be fully accomplished. If I should be so far blest as to revisit again my own Country, but more especially Manchester (the centre of all my Wishes), all that I could hope or desire for would be presented before me in one view.

If you'll favour me with a Letter, I shall thankfully acknowledge the same. I desire to remember my Respects to Mrs. Bailey & service to all Friends, wishing you and them length of Days, prosperity and success in all your and their Undertakings, and am in the mean time studious to be thought Dear Uncle

Your Dutiful Nephew,

Robt Clive.

Fort St. George.
10*th December*, 1744.

[1] An extract from this letter is given by Malcolm, *op. cit.*, p. 40.

CHAPTER II

1744–6: CAPTURE OF MADRAS BY THE FRENCH

MADRAS proved, as Day had prophesied, "as good as the best." A large number of natives sought protection of the English, and thus a prosperous settlement arose outside the English bounds, which part was styled "the Black Town"; the original settlement, where none but Europeans were allowed to reside, being known as "the White Town." When Clive landed at Madras in 1744, the town had, owing to the trade from England to the coast of Coromandel, "to the great returnes it makes in callicoes and muslins," to its considerable trade with China, Persia and Mocha, and to its "not being a great way from the diamond mines of Golconda," risen "to a degree of opulence and reputation which rendered it inferior to none of the European establishments in India excepting Goa and Batavia."[1] There were 250,000 inhabitants in the Company's territory, of which the greater part were natives of India of various castes and religions. The English in the colony, however, did not exceed the number of 300 men, and 200 of these were soldiers who composed the garrison, "but none of them, excepting two or three of their officers, had ever seen any other service than that of the parade." Fort St. George "was surrounded with a slender wall, defended with four bastions and as many batteries," but these were very slight and defective in their construction, nor had they any outworks to defend them. The principal buildings inside were fifty good houses in which the chief Europeans resided, an English and a Roman Catholic church, the warehouse of the Company, and the factory in which their servants lived.

[1] R. Orme: "History of the Military Transactions of the British Nation in Indostan," ed. 1763, Vol. I., p. 66.

The servants of the Company at Madras were divided into four classes—Senior Merchants, Junior Merchants, Factors and Writers. The ten writers were the clerks and book-keepers, and their wages were small. In September, 1744, Robert Clive, an entry in the diary states, drew his first quarter's pay, £1 5s., a writer's salary being £5 per annum. The five factors, who had annual salaries of £15, received and dispatched the commodities. The senior and two junior merchants, who had £40 and £30 a year, dealt with the native merchants, who bought their broadcloths, kersies, lead, vermilion, sword-blades and looking-glasses, whilst they purchased silks, muslins, coloured calicoes, indigo, and drugs brought from the inland. The senior merchants, having been writers for five years, factors for three, and junior merchants for three, were qualified to be members of Council, with the chance of being governor. The governor had the modest salary of £200 a year with a gratuity of £100; of the six councillors the chief had £100 a year; the others in proportion, £70, £50 and £40 a year. Two chaplains on £100 a year, a surgeon £36, two "essay masters" £120, one judge £100, and the attorney-general fifty pagodas[1] completed the civil European establishment. Married men received from five to ten pagodas a month as diet money, according to their quality; inferior servants dining at the general table had no other allowance beyond their salaries than a very trifling sum for washing and oil for lamps.

The governor and Council superintended the civil departments, had chief control of the military and maintained order. They managed the relations with native powers and they conducted the correspondence home. On Wednesday and Thursday they met in the spacious Council Chamber at eight in the morning, and the secretary entered, in the book kept for the purpose, their consultations, together with all other occurrences and observations after the manner of

[1] Pagoda—a southern Indian coin, and the standard coin of Madras up to 1818. In one of Clive's accounts, dated Dec. 11, 1752, we find the pagoda reckoned as 4 Rs.

a diary. A duplicate copy was afterwards sent home to the directors.

In these old silent "Consultation Books" preserved at Bombay, Madras and Calcutta lies buried the history of the rise of British dominion in India. From the old records and the early travellers we gain some knowledge of the daily life in the factory at Madras. At dawn the morning gun fired, and first all the writers and factors attended service in the church; for every Protestant that lodged "within the house" who was absent from public prayer morning and evening on week days, "without lawful excuse," had "to pay twelve pence for the poore or be confined one whole weeke within the house for every such default." After prayers, business was transacted with the natives, the sales of European and the purchase of Oriental goods registered, bales packed, and the accounts audited. At twelve the "Inferior Servants" had their dinner in the Refection Room. Business was again transacted from four, when the great heat of the day had passed, till the sun began to set.

> "On certain afternoons in the week the younger men were taught some one or other of the languages of the country, being stimulated thereunto by the promise of large rewards for proficiency—twenty pounds being given for the knowledge of an Indian language, and ten pounds for a knowledge of Persian." [1]

Clive never became, like Warren Hastings, a proficient Persian scholar, but he had a good colloquial knowledge of the vernacular languages which enabled him to acquire that intimate knowledge of the politics and character of the natives, without which the career of an Indian soldier or administrator can never be really successful. Clive declared in after years that much of his success in securing the fidelity of the sepoys was owing to his care "to entwine his laurels round the opinions and prejudices of the natives."

Towards evening, when the sea breeze made it comparatively cool and pleasant, the inmates of the fort went abroad and watched the country boats ride over the tumbling

[1] J. Talboys-Wheeler: "Madras in the Olden Time," Vol. I., p. 49.

surf and looked across the sea to catch the first glimpse of the vessel which brought news from home. The tolling of the church bell for another service brought them back to the fort. Evening prayers over, there was supper in the Refection Room. So one day telleth another. Their pleasures were few. They killed their leisure time in the tavern, drinking and playing at cards. Clive's dreary leisure in Fort St. George however was not idle. He read the books in the governor's library and his early classical training went with him. It is stated that he "became so good a Latin scholar that a particular friend of his remembers to have heard him in 1753 translate an Ode of Horace into very proper English extempore." Impatience of control also went with him. A companion at the time describes the lad as "short, inclined to be corpulent, awkward and unmannerly, his aspect was gloomy, his temper morose and untractable." There is some exaggeration doubtless in this, but it is also certain there is some truth in it. No man had a frame so little like an ideal hero. Another contemporary tells us: "His person was the largest of the middle size, his countenance inclined to sadness, and the heaviness of his brow imparted an unpleasing expression to his features."

Some months passed before Clive saw on the horizon the long-expected ships from Europe, and in the fervour of his youth he tells his father of his great joy and heart-breaking disappointment.[1]

HON^{D} SIR,—When I wrote my Last to You I was impatiently waiting the long expected Ships from Europe, and on the 11th December arrived here under Convoy of two Men of War, five of the Company's Ships, Viz. The Scarborough, Royal George, Lincoln, Kent, and Admiral Vernon. I had for a long time kept up hope with the pleasing Pleasure of what was to come, and I do declare never in my Life, did I enjoy such real Happiness, as upon Sight of the five abovementioned Ships, not all the Riches of the Indies, could have satisfied my desires more fully than News from my Native Country, but it seems Fortune had elevated me to this high Summit of expectation, that I might in a greater degree experience so heavy a disappointment, in short I was the only sorrowful Person in Madrass, but as I cannot

[1] Powis MSS.

think You have forgot me, so shall I with Patience wait the Arrival of the London and Princess Mary, by one or both of whom, I don't in the least doubt of being honoured with your Favour: The London we hear lost her Main Mast 70 Leagues to the Westward of the Cape, so that it is conjectured she must either be at the Brasils, or Madagascar; the Princess Mary as Yet we have heard nothing of, and if not at Batavia is concluded either lost or taken, so that in case of their Arrival here, it is not at all unlikely, but before that time I may be favoured with Letters from You, of this Years date. I take the Liberty to say that as things have fallen out so unluckily, the Assistance I received from Captain Stewart was very serviceable to me, without which I must have been driven to the Necessity of borrowing Money here, and am even as it is almost reduced to my last Shift. I assure You I have managed my Expences with the greatest Frugality, and shall always endeavour to act so as to merit your Approbation. I beg leave to renew my request for some shoes, Hats, and Wiggs, and in regard to other Matters, what over you shall deem necessary or for my Advantage, shall be acknowledged by me as a particular Favour. I promised in my Letter by the Benjamin, to send Duplicate of it by Dolphin, but was disappointed by a violent Feaver, so bad, that it was undetermined for some time, whether Death or Life would be my Lot, however by the strength of my constitution, I got the better of my disease, and am now perfectly well recover'd; from the latter end of May to the Beginning of November, have died here, no less than twelve Persons, most of them Young Men, which has reduced our Number (which did not then exceed fifty at the furthest) very Considerably, and the Major Part of the rest have been visited with very severe Feavers. These Intemperate Climates demand a particular Care in the Preservation of our Constitutions, and as I have very little fault to find with myself upon that Subject, hope I shall still continue it as my Opinion, that Health is the greatest Blessing I can enjoy, at least I am sure it is by that means only, that I can revisit again my Relations and Friends in England. A great many of our Inhabitants are removed to Bengal, and more intend it, and I am persuaded it would conduce greatly to my Advantage, could I thro' your means procure Interest, to be removed likewise, I beg leave to recommend it in a particular manner to your Consideration. This Duplicate will wait on you by the Admiral Vernon as mentioned &c[t]

I am

Your most dutiful & Obed[t] Son

ROBERT CLIVE.

FORT S[T] GEORGE

31*st January* 1745–6

P.S.—I desire to remember Duty to my Mother and Service to all Friends. I must beg you'll dispence with my not writing the Duplicates Better as upon the dispatch of these Ships, I have scarce an Hour that I can call my own.

Clive landed at the hottest season of the year and the climate affected his melancholic temperament. The gloom found expression in a letter which he wrote to one of his cousins: [1]

Dear Cousin,—The want of a proper conveyance is the only Plea I can offer for not addressing you sooner, it is a long time since I enjoyed the Pleasure of your Company and Conversation, and as both Parties have been equally culpable, I beg that from henceforth the strictest amity may subsist between us: the Bond of Friendship, especially when united by the Ties of Blood aught not to be dissolved on any consideration whatever, and I believe you'll agree with me, that the only effectual Means to preserve it entire, must be by Letters, since the vast Ocean which divides us so far asunder won't admit of it by Word of Mouth, and which I heartily wish may turn out to the mutual Satisfaction of both of us. If there is any such thing which may properly be called Happiness here below, I am persuaded it is in the Union of two Friends who each love each other without the least Guile or Deceit, who are united by a real Inclination, and satisfied with each others merits. Their Hearts are full, and leave no Vacancy for any other Passion, they enjoy perpetual tranquillity, because they enjoy content, for my part I can't ascribe my Neglect to any other cause than the Frailties and Imperfections of Youth, who at those years postpone the greatest advantage to their own private pleasures. I shan't persist in excusing my Error, since it is so evident, and will admit of but a very bad Construction when drest in its finest colours, yet give me leave to justify myself, so far as to assure you it did not proceed from the least slight, or Contempt of your Person.

I should take a particular Delight in giving you a short Description of the Country, was I not assured that you may quote many Historians, who can afford you much more accurate account than can be expected from me, whose Habitation here hath been of so short a date. I shall only add, that the Intemperance of the Climate together with the excessive heat of the Sun, are very obnoxious to our Health, and I really think the advantages which accrue to us here are greatly overballanced by the Sacrifices we make of our Constitutions; I have not been unacquainted with the Fickleness of Fortune, and may safely say I have not enjoyed one happy day since I left my Native Country; I am not acquainted with any one Family in the Place, and have not Assurance enough to introduce myself without being asked. If the state I am now in will admit of any Happiness it must be when I am writing to my Friends. Letters were surely first invented for the Comfort of such solitary Wretches as myself. Having lost the substantial pleasure of seeing them, I shall in some measure compensate this Loss by the satisfaction I

[1] Powis MSS.

shall find in their Writings; When you write me, I beg it may be carelessly and without study, for I had much rather read the Dictates of the Heart than those of the Understanding. The Paquet is just now going to be closed, which hastens me to a Conclusion sooner than I designed; I desire you to tender my Duty to my Uncle and Aunt. Love to my Cousins, and service to all Friends, and it will greatly add to the Obligations of him who esteems it his greatest Happiness to be thought

Your Kind & loving Cousin

ROB^T CLIVE.

FORT S^T GEORGE
16 *February* 1744/5

The time of monotonous toil and isolation was nearly out; war and glory were at hand.

On September 24, 1744, "at a Consultation, Present Nicholas Morse, Esqr., Governour President,"

It was "Agreed to dispatch a Pattamar[1] this evening to Bombay, to advise of the war with France lest any accident should have befallen the *King William.*" It was further agreed, "The war with France being broke out, and it being therefore highly proper to have our garrison in the best order we can, and as it happened that for some months past there have not been less than forty to fifty of the Military on the Sick Roll, which, with the servants hitherto allowed the officers, Reduces considerably the number of Mounting Men, it is agreed that in lieu of servants each Lieutenant have Five (5) Pagodas[2] per month, and Each Ensign four (4), and that this be continued to them only so long as the Board shall think it necessary."[3]

This is the first mention in the records of that long combat which was to determine the issue whether France or England should win an empire in Asia.

On August 27, 1664, twenty-five years after Francis Day had obtained permission to form the settlement of Madras, Louis XIV., induced by Colbert, issued an edict founding the French East India Company.[4] The French, setting to work with considerable zeal, established factories at Surat and other places on the Malabar coast. In 1672 they took from the

[1] Pattamar (*pathmar*), a foot-runner, messenger.

[2] *See* note, p. 20.

[3] The Consultations and Diary Book of the President and Governour, &c., Council of Fort St. George, pp. 293, 294.

[4] "*L'Inde française avant Dupleix,*" par H. Castonnet des Fosses (1887), pp. 48-9.

Dutch, with whom they were at war, the splendid harbour of Trincomalee; but the Dutch soon retook it. The French then passed over to the Coromandel Coast and obtained possession of St. Thomé; two years later they were compelled to restore it also to the Dutch. The fortune of the French East India Company, now at its lowest ebb, was revived by the far sight, courage and administrative capacity of François Martin, whose name shines with a fair and honest lustre in an age of intrigue and corruption.

Martin had lent the governor of Gingee, the great mountain fortress sixty miles from Pondicherry, money he could not repay, and in return received a village[1] near the coast, and permission to fortify a strip of land by the sea. Here, in 1676, Martin brought sixty Frenchmen, all that remained of the factories at Ceylon and St. Thomé. The fortification that Martin erected could not have been of any great extent, seeing that it cost only the modest sum of seven hundred crowns. Beneath the shelter of the slender walls he, however, proceeded to lay out streets and to build houses for the native weavers, whom he wished to attract to his new settlement. The aim of his policy was to gather at Pondicherry a thrifty, loyal population, and he was wise enough to see that the best way of doing this was by respecting the manners, customs and religion of the people, and so winning their love and confidence. His policy proved eminently successful. However, just as Martin's little colony began to rise and flourish, a grave danger menaced it. The Mahratta chief Shivaji seized Gingee and threatened an attack on the new settlement. But Martin pacified the great freebooter by a present of 500 pagodas, and obtained from him a grant for the French to reside at Pondicherry in perpetuity, on condition that they did not interfere in the wars of the neighbouring states. Shivaji, however, insisted that the French should pay him a heavy tax on the imports and exports of the little colony, which continued to grow in wealth and importance. To protect it

[1] It was called by the natives Puducheri, which, by degrees, was corrupted to Pondicherry.

still further, Martin now threw around the town a wall, which was flanked by four towers, each of which mounted six guns.

He had hardly finished the new fortifications when war broke out between France and Holland, and in 1693 Pondicherry was attacked by a Dutch fleet consisting of nineteen ships of war. Martin, who had only forty European soldiers to defend the place, was compelled to surrender. The Dutch, fully realising the value of their new possession, proceeded to improve the town and fortification, and make it the capital of their Indian possessions. But, five years after it had come into their hands, the Treaty of Ryswick restored Pondicherry to the French. Martin hastened from France to resume possession of the city which he had founded, but the Dutch refused to restore it until they had been handsomely compensated for the improvements they had made. A French writer with patriotic indignation says: "The sale, characteristic of a nation of traders, took place on the 17th September, 1699, when Martin paid 16,000 pagodas to the Director of the Dutch Company as the price of the improvements and fortifications they had made." [1]

Under the wise and vigorous administration of Martin, the town rapidly grew in prosperity. He mapped out new streets on the lines of an important European capital, erected substantial houses, warehouses and shops, and built a palace for the governor. When the English had only a small factory at Calcutta, and Chowringhee (Chaurangi) was a malarious swamp, Pondicherry was a flourishing town with fifty thousand inhabitants. For the greater protection of the city, Martin proceeded to construct a citadel after the model of Tournay. When finished, the new fortress was consecrated with great pomp and ceremony. On August 25, 1706, a stately procession of laymen and priests, chanting the *Te Deum* and *Exaudiat*, wended its way around the town, and as it reached the bastion, the cannons sent forth a roar of triumph and joy.

[1] "*L'Inde française avant Dupleix*," par H. Castonnet des Fosses (1887), p. 143.

This was the crowning day of François Martin's life. A few months later the patriot's manly heart ceased to beat.

After the death of François Martin, two of his successors, Lenoir and Dumas, managed the Company's affairs with prudence and sagacity. Mahé and Karikal were acquired by France, and Pondicherry soon rose to distinguished importance among the European settlements in India. Dumas was succeeded by Dupleix, who, after being first member of the Supreme Council at Pondicherry for ten years, was appointed chief of the French factory at Chandernagore in Bengal. By his knowledge of Orientals, by his strong business capacity, he not only amassed a fortune for himself, due to the coast trade which he introduced, but he raised Chandernagore from an insignificant village on the Hugli to a rich and populous colony. The success at Chandernagore led to his being appointed governor of Pondicherry and *ex officio* director-general of the affairs of the French East Company. On arriving at Pondicherry he found there La Bourdonnais, whom he had known in former years. They were of the same age, both endowed with extraordinary abilities, but dissimilar in their talents and their character.

Born at the ancient town of St. Malo, a nursery for hardy mariners, La Bourdonnais made several voyages to different parts of the world. He entered, when he was twenty, the service of the French East India Company. After having served as lieutenant and second captain, he left the Company in 1727, and commanded, as "captain and supercargo," the *Pondichéry*, a special vessel which had been commissioned by Lenoir and the Council of Pondicherry. For five years he traded on the coast. Then he quarrelled with Lenoir and entered the Portuguese service, in which he remained for two years. In 1733 he returned to France. He sent to the Ministry a report on the situation in India, and was appointed, in 1735, governor of the Isles of France (Mauritius) and Bourbon. By his constant supervision, and the healthy stimulus of his strong character, the islands became, during the eleven years of his rule, flourishing colonies, and the naval arsenal in the East.

In 1739,[1] La Bourdonnais returned to France. He saw that war with England must shortly arise, and he proposed to certain friends that they should subscribe to equip a fleet to cruise in search of English merchantmen. But the Ministry proposed to send out a fleet composed partly of the king's ships and partly of the Company's ships, with La Bourdonnais in command, and La Bourdonnais gives us no explanation of this change of plans. On April 5, 1741, he sailed from L'Orient with five of the Company's ships, and arrived at the Isle of France on August 14. He there learnt that the Mahrattas had invaded the Carnatic and that the garrison had left the islands, summoned by Dumas, the governor of Pondicherry, who feared a siege. La Bourdonnais, when he reached Pondicherry, found the danger had blown over, but that Mahé had been eight months blockaded.

On January 14, 1742, Dupleix reached Pondicherry and succeeded Dumas as governor. To him La Bourdonnais explained his project of capturing Madras when war was declared. Dupleix approved of it and sent Paradis, an able Swiss soldier and engineer, on a secret mission to Madras, who examined the place with sufficient precision to enable him to draw up a memorandum and prepare a plan of attack. La Bourdonnais proceeded to Mahé, chastised the enemy, re-established the factory, and then returned to Mauritius, ready to prey upon the English commerce. But the finances of the French Company did not admit of their keeping ships without some commercial profit, and, hoping that neutrality would be maintained in India, they recalled the fleet. It was a grave error.

When the Ministers in England heard of the preparations made by the French, they sent a squadron of men-of-war in 1744 under Commander Barnet to India. It consisted of two sixty-gun ships, one of fifty, and a frigate of twenty guns. In July, 1745, the squadron appeared upon the coast of Coromandel, at which time the garrison of Pondicherry consisted of no more than 436 Europeans, and its fortifications

[1] Mill, Vol. III., p. 58, says 1740.

were still incomplete. This was due to no fault of Dupleix, for as soon as he took charge he began to reform the administration, to discipline the soldiers, to recruit sepoys and to build fortifications. But, on September 18, 1743, he received a dispatch from the Company which told him "to make a point of reducing all expenses by at least one half, and to suspend all outlay on buildings and fortifications." He obeyed the first order. But he continued with renewed vigour the construction of the fortifications. He advanced to the treasury of the Company "cinq cent mille livres"; a part of it he employed on the fortifications, and the remainder in supplying cargoes for two ships, which he sent post-haste to France for arms, munitions of war, and men. But before reinforcements could reach him or the fortifications be completed, the English squadron anchored off Fort St. David. Pondicherry was now at their mercy. Happily for the French, the Nawab of the Carnatic informed the Madras Government that their ships of war must not "commit any hostilities by land against the French possessions" within his territories. At the same time he assured the English that "he would oblige the French to observe the same law of neutrality, if their force should hereafter become superior to that of the English."[1]

Moved by these threats, the authorities at Madras persuaded Barnet to suspend his attack. He sent one of the sixty-gun ships to cruise at the entrance of the Ganges, where he took several ships returning to Bengal. Soon after, the approach of the monsoon compelled him to leave the coast.

In the beginning of 1746 the squadron returned to the coast of Coromandel, and was reinforced by two fifty-gun ships and a frigate of twenty guns from England. The sixty-gun ship, however, in which Barnet hoisted his flag, was found unfit for action and, together with the frigate, was sent back to England. The French squadron was now daily expected. But months went on and no French ships could be seen. "The 29th April [1746] Mr. Barnet departed this life at this place

[1] Orme, *op. cit.*, Vol. I., p. 61.

[Fort St. David] when all the ships were here or near us."[1] His death was generally regretted as a public loss, "and indeed he was a man of great abilities in public affairs."

Captain Peyton then commanded the squadron as senior captain. On June 9 the *Princess Mary*, laden with bales and treasure, "sailed for Madrass, under convoy of his Majesty's ship the *Lively*, as did the rest of the squadron for Trancomalay."[2] But just as they were getting to the Bay, the *Preston's* bowsprit was sprung, and they had to bear away to Negapatam.[3] "On the 25th at day break, from the mast head in Negapatam Road, they made several ships" in the offing to which they went out "and found them to be nine (9) French ships."

On September 18, 1744, the frigate *La Fière* had arrived at Mauritius with the news that war had been declared. She also brought a message from the directors of the French Company to La Bourdonnais forbidding him to commence hostilities; he was only to oppose them. La Bourdonnais began at once to arm all the Company's ships he could collect, and he wrote to Dupleix that he could assemble six vessels and 1,500 to 1,800 men. These, with 300 to 400 furnished by Dupleix, would make a little army with which they might carry out some enterprise that would repair their losses. He proposed that he should send half of his ships to cruise for the Company and half for Dupleix and himself. He further suggested that the vessels should cruise between the Cape and St. Helena, because, in all probability, the Indian Seas would be a neutral region. Dupleix replied that he had approached the English governor, and therefore counted on the maintenance of peace. He added that he had very few soldiers, barely enough to guard Pondicherry. He also disapproved of the cruise in the Atlantic, as it would be contrary to the

[1] Dispatch from Fort St. David, 17th October, 1746 (Madras Records).

[2] *Ibid.*

[3] Negapatam—seaport town in Tanjore district; the modern spelling of Nagapatnam, snake (seaport) town, or the seaport town of the Nagas. One of the earliest settlements of the Portuguese on the east coast, and called by them the City of Choramandel. Captured by the Dutch in 1660, it was their chief Indian possession until captured by the English in 1781. It was finally ceded in 1799.

wishes of the Company, who could not authorise their officers to sail under the conditions proposed by La Bourdonnais without running the risk of ruining their ordinary commerce, which was less protected than that of the English. But the capture of the China ships by Barnet, in some of which Dupleix had a pecuniary interest, roused his wrath, and drove from his mind all thoughts of neutrality. He set about equipping the country ships to follow the squadron.

La Bourdonnais now sent him a plan of his voyage, and inquired if the scheme of 1741 for taking Madras was still feasible. He asked for the service of Paradis and a body of sepoys. He was certain that, with the aid of Dupleix, he could easily take and retain Madras. He had studied Paradis's plan, and he sent Dupleix the result of his study. It was, he said, "the only means of repairing our loss."[1] A little later he asked Dupleix to send him clothes for his troops, arms, and the munitions of war. Dupleix complied with the greatest good-nature with these requests. He was full of zeal for the enterprise, and burning to have his revenge for the loss of the China ships. He once more had Madras thoroughly explored, and procured an account of the place from Madame Barneval, his wife's daughter, who was married to a merchant resident there named Barnewall or Coyle de Barneval.[2] "He even had scaling ladders made, of various lengths, in accordance with the measurements given by Paradis in his memorandum."[3]

Meanwhile the departure of the ships which La Bourdonnais had equipped was delayed by the news that a fleet was being sent from France. La Bourdonnais was appointed to the command, and it was suggested to him that, after having landed the treasure on board the ships at Pondicherry, he should proceed to the Bay of Bengal. He might, if he wished, return to Mauritius about June, 1746, and start for France with the fleet in 1747. But the French fleet, which

[1] *See* "Dupleix," by Prosper Cultru, pp. 202-203.
[2] French writers describe him as a British subject. But in the English records he is mentioned as a Frenchman.
[3] *See* "Dupleix," by Prosper Cultru, *loc. cit.*

was expected in October, 1745, did not reach Mauritius till January, 1746. They arrived in bad order, and only one was armed. La Bourdonnais, with characteristic energy, proceeded to repair and equip them, and as soon as they were ready he sent them to Madagascar. On March 24 he sailed in the last ship from Mauritius. Before the ships left Madagascar they were driven from their anchorage and scattered by a hurricane. One was lost and the rest greatly damaged. La Bourdonnais, collecting them in the bay of a desert island on the coast of Madagascar, refitted them, "overcoming the greatest difficulties with such indefatigable perseverance and activity as intitles him to a reputation equal to that of the ablest marine officer his country has produced." [1]

In forty-eight days the fleet was again ready for sea. It now consisted of nine sail containing 3,342 men, among whom were 720 blacks, and from three to four hundred sick. In passing the island of Ceylon they heard that the English fleet was at hand, and on June 25 [2] the British ships appeared to windward, advancing in full sail towards them.

La Bourdonnais knew that he was superior to the English in number of men, but greatly inferior in weight of cannon. He therefore determined to gain, if possible, the wind and to board. But Peyton, seeing his design, kept the wind and so frustrated it. The breeze was also light, and it was not till four in the afternoon that a distant fight began and lasted till about seven, when it grew dark. "In the English squadron," wrote the Council at Fort St. David, "were fourteen killed and forty six wounded, but not one killed or wounded in the *Medway*." The *Medway* was Peyton's ship.[3]

[1] Orme, Vol. I., p. 63. Mill writes: "Here the operations of repairing were to be renewed; and in still more unfavourable circumstances. To get the wood they required, a road was made across a marsh, a league in circumference; the rains were incessant; disease broke out among the people; and many of the officers showed a bad disposition; yet the work was prosecuted with so much efficiency, that in forty-eight days the fleet was ready for sea."—"Hist. of British India" (1840), Vol. III., p. 62.

[2] Mill says July 6, *ibid.*, p. 63.

[3] Dispatch from Fort St. David, October 17, 1746 (Madras Records). Orme states: "The fight finished with the entrance of the night; about 35 men were killed in the English squadron, and the greatest part of these on board the *Medway's* Prize. We are not exactly informed of the loss sustained by the

The next morning the two squadrons were near one another, according to the dispatch, and continued so all the day. "At four in the afternoon Capt. Peyton summoned a Councell of Warr where it was agreed not to engage the enemy but to proceed to Trancomalay Bay." The resolution was mainly due to the sixty-gun ship being extremely leaky. The English ships made sail for the harbour of Trincomalee, and in the evening lost sight of the French squadron, which had lain to the whole day as if challenging the English, who were to windward, to bear down and renew the fight. "This appearance of resolution in Mr. De La Bourdonnais," writes Orme, "was no more than a feint, practised to deter the English from doing what he most dreaded; for most of his ships had expended the greatest part of their ammunition, and several of them had not victuals on board for twenty-four hours." [1] La Bourdonnais in his "Memoirs" states that it was not a feint, and that it was with supreme regret that he saw the English escape him.

It was on the evening of Saturday, July 9, 1746, that the French fleet rode off Pondicherry, and as soon as La Bourdonnais stepped from his boat a salute of fifteen guns was fired from his ship.

> "Another salute of fifteen guns was fired on his arrival at the sea-gate," says Ranga Pillai, "where he was met by the Deputy Governor and other members of the Council, and by the captains and other officers—M. Dupleix alone excepted—and was escorted by them to the Governor's residence. On M. de la Bourdonnais entering this, the Governor received him at the sentinel's post, with an embrace, and conducted him into the court-yard, when a salute of fifteen guns was again fired. They afterwards conversed together for a while in the open space on the other side of the verandah." [2]

It was a mere exchange of civilities. The two men could never be friends. La Bourdonnais was a gallant sailor, re-

French; but it was believed that the killed and wounded together did not amount to less than 300. One of their ships, which mounted 30 guns, was in less than half an hour dismasted, and so much shattered, that immediately after the action, Mr. De la Bourdonnais ordered her to proceed to Bengal to be refitted in the Ganges."—Vol. I., p. 63.

[1] Orme, *ibid.*

[2] "The Private Diary of Ananda Ranga Pillai," edited by Sir J. Frederick Price, Vol. II., p. 114.

markable for his grasp and capacity of mind, but he had the privateer's sordid desire of gain. Dupleix was a far-seeing statesman with a fierce thirst for power and for glory. They both had quick tempers, and they both were arrogant and insolent. The feeling that had long existed between them swiftly grew worse. La Bourdonnais considered he should be received with the same honour as Dupleix. The Governor of the Islands, he held, was equal, if not superior, to the Governor of Pondicherry.

Ranga Pillai, a shrewd observer, states:

"The Governor and he entertain a mutual dislike for one another. The former is aggrieved because M. de la Bourdonnais does not regard himself as his subordinate, maintains a guard of honour of troopers, keeps at his residence a party of soldiers and troopers, and conducts everything independently, and without consultation with him; whilst M. de la Bourdonnais holds that he is on a par with the Governor, and is consequently entitled to all the honours accorded to that functionary; and that the control of military operations resting wholly with him, he is not bound to consult the Governor in matters connected therewith. Thus business is transacted between them with but little cordiality. The future development of this remains to be seen."

The disputes worked to produce a delay in carrying out their common object. It was not till August 4[1] that La Bourdonnais set sail with his fleet to discover the English squadron. Mill writes: "On the 17th (August) he (La Bourdonnais) descried the English fleet off Negapatnam[2] and hoisted Dutch colours as a decoy. The English understood the stratagem, changed their course and fled." According to Ranga Pillai, La Bourdonnais landed at the Dutch settlement of Negapatam, had a grand banquet given in his honour and, whilst he was at the table, news reached him that five English men-of-war were at hand. He immediately embarked, but before he had cleared for action darkness had begun to fall and he waited for the morning to engage the enemy. When the day dawned

[1] "Ranga Pillai's Diary." Orme, who uses the old style, says the French squadron sailed from Pondicherry on July 24th, "working to the southward against the southern monsoon, and on the 6th of August discovered the English [squadron], which had been refitted at Trincanomalee."

[2] Negapatam.

no English ships were to be seen. La Bourdonnais says he pursued them all that day and the next, when having the wind they escaped.

On August 18, the French squadron appeared before Madras and opened fire on the *Princess Mary*, which was returned from the ship and from the fort.

> "Each ship gave her a broadside as she stood to the northward and another as she returned, and then stood to the southward again. We are since informed that they have two motives for this expedition. One was to make a plea with the country government that the English committed the first hostillitics ashoar and the other to see if Captain Peyton wou'd come to our assistance or not."[1]

The inhabitants of Madras anxiously watched for the appearance of the English squadron on which their safety depended, and they were struck with consternation when they heard that—

> "on the 23rd Captain Peyton with the squadron stood in Pullicat Road, where he sent his Lieutenant Mr. Weeims, on board a vessel in the Road, who was there told of all the circumstances of their attacking the *Princess Mary*, and of their being between Madras and Pondicherry, on which he disappeared and has never since been heard of,[2] or from, by any of the English, though there has been no cost or pains spar'd for that purpose as may easily be imagined from the since mellancholly situation of affairs on the Coast. The last letter that was received from anyone belonging to the squadron was from Captain Peyton to Governor Morse dated the 4th August when he was just come out from refitting. This unhappy conduct so animated our enemy that they determined on attacking Fort St. George. We call it unhappy because it has truely been so in its consequences, though what reasone Captain Peyton could have had for this Proceeding we know not."[3]

Morse, the Governor of Madras, now called on the Nawab of the Carnatic to fulfil his promise of restraining the French from committing hostilities against them by land. But he omitted to forward a present of money, and consequently the Nawab took no steps to prevent them from attacking Madras.

[1] Dispatch from Fort St. David, October 17, 1746.

[2] Orme states: "They proceeded to Bengal; for the 60 gun ship was now so leaky, that it was feared the shock of firing her own cannon would sink her, if she should be brought into an engagement."—Vol. I., p. 67.

[3] Dispatch from Fort St. David, October 17, 1746.

When war became imminent, the French governors, Dumas and Dupleix, made all possible preparation for the struggle; the English, according to a well-established custom, did nothing. The day after news reached them that war had been declared, they chose a safe site for a powder magazine. But it was never built. The fort was entirely unfit to stand a siege.

"The principal officer among the garrison was one Peter Eckman, an ignorant, superannuated Swede, who had been a common soldier, and now bore the rank of a first lieutenant: he was assisted by two other lieutenants, and seven ensigns. To all which may be farther added, that though the garrison had near 200 pieces of cannon, yet they wanted men that were capable of playing them; besides that, the want of military stores was equal to the paucity of military men." [1]

Long before the war with France, the English Company had promised to augment the garrison of Madras to 600 Europeans, "exclusive of the gun-room crew," but they never sent the recruits. The time had now come when European soldiers were sorely needed.

On the night of August 23, 1746, the French fleet anchored in the roads of Pondicherry. La Bourdonnais landed so enfeebled by fever and diarrhœa that he had to be supported by two men. On arriving at Government House Dupleix "came forward to meet him, embraced him, and took him into a room, where they had a conference, in which M. Paradis took part." [2] The quarrel between the two men soon blazed forth fiercer than ever. The most ungracious pretext was chosen by Dupleix for a rupture. "M. Dupleix tried very hard to have M. Paradis appointed commander, in the place of M. de la Bourdonnais, who is now ill; but the latter would not assent to this." [3] The bitter conflict of the belated antagonists further delayed the attack on Madras, and it was not till Monday, September 12, 1746, that Ranga Pillai enters in his Diary—

"At half-past 8 this night, all the ships of the expedition against Madras set sail. The fleet consisted of M. de la Bourdonnais' squadron

[1] J. H. Grose: "A Voyage to the East Indies" (ed. 1772), Vol. II., p. xxvi.
[2] "Ranga Pillai's Diary," Vol. II., p. 234.
[3] *Ibid.*, p. 254.

of seven ships, two country craft, and a number of sloops and boats. When it stood out to sea, a gun was fired to intimate this to the Governor" (Vol. II., p. 299).[1]

A letter from Madras dated October 17, 1746, states: "They came in sight the 2nd. Nine sail, and landed 800 Europeans at Covalong; marched to St. Thomé, there landed more." The neighbourhood covered with country houses was given up to pillage, and the French Commissary-General states that La Bourdonnais and his brother La Villebague harassed the town of St. Thomé for loot. On September 7/18 the French

"began to play their mortars being 15 in number from behind the garden house, 10 and 5 from across the Bar: their strength on shore I compute 2,000 Europeans, Seapiahs, and 300 Coffrees: they have when all on board 3,000 Europeans, 600 of which were Pondicherry troops: their intent was to have stormed us by escalade which we were in no condition to prevent, 1,000 Bombs having prevented our sleeping for 3 days and nights. Yet we had more to dread from our own disorder within and want of Government and Council than from the enemy without."

On September 9/20 William Monson, ensign, and John Hallyburton, ensign, were sent as deputies to treat with La Bourdonnais. He received them with all courtesy, and, after a consultation, he offered them the following conditions: "That the town should be delivered up, and all the English remain prisoners of war: that the articles of capitulation being settled, those of the ransom should be regulated amicably: that the garrison should be conducted to Fort St. David; and the sailors sent to Cuddalore."[2] The deputies pressed for more explicit explanation as to the ransom being regulated in a friendly manner. La Bourdonnais replied, "Gentlemen, I do not sell honor: the flag of my king shall fly over Madrass,

[1] Mill writes (Vol. III., p. 69): "He left Pondicherry on the 12th of September and on the 14th commenced the operations which ended, as we have seen, in the surrender of the place." Orme, who uses the old style, says (Vol. I., p. 67): "On the 3rd of September [3rd/14th] the French squadron anchored four leagues to the south of Madrass, having on board the troops, artillery and stores intended for the siege." Grose uses the same words as Orme.—"A Voyage to the East Indies," Vol. II., p. xxv.

[2] J. H. Grose: "A Voyage to the East Indies," Vol. II., p. xxvii.

or I will die at the foot of the walls. In regard to the ransom of the town, and in every thing that is interesting, you shall be satisfied with me; (and, taking the hat of one of the deputies, he said) here is nearly the manner how we will regulate matters: this hat is worth six rupees, you shall give me three or four for it, and so of the rest."[1] The capitulation was signed the next day, and in the afternoon La Bourdonnais, at the head of a large body of troops, marched to the gates, where he received the keys from the Governor. The French flag was immediately hoisted and the boats of the French squadron took possession of the Company's ships.

The letter from Madras adds that:

"The French hitherto have been extremely civil with respects to the Inhabitants, and have come to a treaty with the Governor and Council for the ransome of the place at eleven Laack of Pagodas, payable in 3 years, half in India and half in Europe; they to carry off all the Company's goods and ½ the Cannon and Warlike Stores: but here's to be a garrison of 400 French till January and I dont much trust to their faith."

The value of the Company's goods was about "four lacks of pagodas" in silver, broadcloth, etc., and

"it is generally believed that Monsr. L. Bourdonnie in Diaminds, Jewells, etca., Screwd Us a purse of about 150,000 Pagodas, so Altogether makes up the Sum of 1,650,000, One million six hundred and fifty thousand Pagodas.[2] For security of which hostages were to be delivered to Monsr. L. Bourdonnie, the Governor's two Children, Mr Stratton and family, Mr Harris and wife, and Messrs Strake and Walsh. The first capitulation was according to the above terms, and the town was to be delivered to the English on the 1st October."

The terms did not suit Dupleix. He had agreed with La Bourdonnais that they should levy a large sum from Madras, either before the assault or in case the French were too weak to hold it. But a few days after the fleet set sail for Madras, Dupleix learnt that a squadron of three large vessels of the French Company had touched at Mahé. This reinforcement would enable him to hold both Madras and Pondicherry against

[1] J. H. Grose: "A Voyage to the East Indies," Vol. II., p. xxvii.

[2] Grose states (Vol. II., pp. xxvii.-xxviii.): "The governor and council settled the price of the ransom with the French Commodore at 1,100,000 pagodas, or 421,666*l.* sterling."

any attacks made by the English, and he at once declared that the arrangement of restoring it on the payment of a ransom must be altered. He determined to keep the town or have it at his mercy. He had, however, to consider the native power. A few days before the fleet sailed, Dupleix received a letter from the Nawab of the Carnatic, which was to the following effect:

> "In spite of our explicit instructions that you should forbear from attacking Madras, you have dispatched an expedition thither. We are therefore not disposed to allow Pondicherry to continue in your possession. We accordingly propose to advance against your town. You transgress all bounds; this is improper."[1]

Dupleix was not the man to be duped or frightened. He replied: "The captains of the ships of war of France are bound by the orders of their King; and will not care to listen to the counsels of others."[2] The next day he sent a letter to the Viceroy of the Deccan through the Nawab informing him that the King of France had heard of the capture of French ships by the English and he had therefore "despatched a few men-of-war to take Madras and to hoist the white flag over it."[3]

On September 19, when La Bourdonnais was bombarding Fort St. George,[4] Dupleix received a letter from the Nawab sent by camel-post expressing surprise that the French should have sent, contrary to his remonstrance, an expedition against Madras. He trusted that they would "in future refrain from affording ground for similar complaints." Dupleix sent the evasive answer that "No harm will be done to the merchants of Madras."[5] He fully realised the necessity of conciliating the Nawab. But he was also determined to build up solidly a French dominion in India, and in order to do that Madras, the rival of Pondicherry, must be destroyed. Dupleix met the difficulty with his usual resourcefulness. He determined that he would sack Fort St. George, dismantle the fortifications and

[1] "Ranga Pillai's Diary," Vol. II., p. 291. [2] *Ibid.* [3] *Ibid.*, p. 292.

[4] Orme states (Vol. I., p. 69): "On the day in which Madrass was surrendered."

[5] "Ranga Pillai's Diary," Vol. II., pp. 311, 312.

hand the place over to the Nawab. He wrote to La Bourdonnais:

> " I believe I have found the means of keeping him quiet by telling him we will give up Madras, you understand, in the condition that we think suitable. This warning should induce you to press the attack briskly and not to listen to any propositions for ransoming the place after it is taken, as this would be deceiving the Nawab and causing him to unite with our enemies. After all, when you are master of this place, I do not see where the English can find the means to pay the ransom. I beg you to reflect suitably on this subject." [1]

On September 23, two days after the capitulation, La Bourdonnais wrote to Dupleix a long letter in which he announced his intention of carrying off the goods taken, and making the English pay first a ransom for the town, and second for the pillage he had stopped. The first of these two contributions was to be for the Company, the second for the soldiers. He asked advice from the Council as to whether he should seize the goods of the Armenians and Malabars. On the 24th he wrote again to Dupleix, asking him to send a scheme of how he thought Madras should be treated. All this time he was acting as if he were independent of any control. He was accompanied on the expedition by two commissioners, Messieurs d'Espréménil and Bonneau, who were charged with the duty of taking over the captured property. The former was appointed by Dupleix, the latter by La Bourdonnais. D'Espréménil was the head of the Supreme Council and second in authority only to Dupleix. La Bourdonnais, however, proceeded to act as if he were sole master of Madras. In reply to the letter in which he had asked the advice of the Council, Dupleix boldly put to him the question whether he recognised the superior authority of the Supreme Council and of the Governor-General of the Indian settlements, which were founded on the permanent orders of the King passed before the special letter that La Bourdonnais received conferring on him the naval command. La Bourdonnais promptly replied that he had never been forewarned of the supremacy of the

[1] *See* Prosper Cultru: "Dupleix," p. 212.

Council, that he had come to Madras as a man in full authority, and as a man possessed of full authority he must keep to the terms of his engagement. From this position he would not depart:

> "Whether I am right or wrong," he said, "I believe myself to be acting within my powers in granting a capitulation to the Governor of this place. I have pledged my honour to the English deputies that I will treat favourably the ransom of the fort and city."[1]

Dupleix sent four more commissioners to Madras, and on Sunday, October 2, the six deputies had an interview with La Bourdonnais and demanded an explanation of the restoration of Madras to the English. La Bourdonnais replied that he had restored the town to the English because the capture of Madras was planned and effected by them all, without any authority from the King of France to wage war on land, and also because he had seized all the treasure that he found in the fort, and had settled with the English for the payment of eleven lakhs of pagodas, as a condition of restoring the fort to them. The officers then burst out into undisguised insolence and declared that a fresh order of the Council at Pondicherry conferred the supreme authority on d'Espréménil. They drew their swords and called upon the ships' crews, the officers, the captains and all others, to swear fealty to the King of France, and take an oath of allegiance to M. d'Espréménil. The order of the Council at Pondicherry was next read and proclaimed. M. La Bourdonnais was called upon to surrender his sword and to take the oath. They threatened that if he did not, he would, in accordance with the instructions which they said they had received, be taken into custody. The captains and officers of the ships remained silent. M. d'Espréménil took charge of the keys of the fort, and issued his orders. Mr. Morse, the Governor of Madras, and the other Englishmen, were next summoned, and informed that they were prisoners, and that the restoration of the fort to them was cancelled.

But the power of the French officials was of short duration.

[1] *See* Prosper Cultru: "Dupleix," p 216.

A few days later was the celebration of La Bourdonnais' saint's day. He ordered the guns at Madras to be fired at sunrise, and he invited the commissioners and other leading men to dine with him at midday. When the guests were seated at table, La Bourdonnais addressed them and said, "I have received a report that the English ships are approaching. You must permit me to embark all the soldiers from Pondicherry on board my fleet." "No, no," cried de Bury, Paradis, and their companions. La Bourdonnais frowned on them, and ordered twenty-four of his men, who were under arms, to seize de Bury, Paradis, and de la Tour, and to keep them in custody. He deprived d'Espréménil of his authority, and assumed the sole power. He next ordered that the soldiers be embarked on board his ships, and directed that the merchandise in fort and town should be conveyed on board.

La Bourdonnais was most anxious to put an end to his quarrel with Dupleix and to set sail with his ships for France. He had in former years traded on the coast, and he knew well the danger of remaining in the Madras roadstead when the northern monsoon burst, which it does about October 15. He, however, did not wish to leave until his treaty had been ratified by the Superior Council at Pondicherry. He therefore opened negotiations with Dupleix and informed him of the conditions on which he would leave Madras. But before the reply of Dupleix and the Council could reach him, his fleet was destroyed. On October 13,[1] the weather at Madras, Orme tells us, was remarkably fine and moderate all day.

"About midnight a furious storm arose, and continued with the greatest violence until the noon of the next day. Six of the French ships were in the road when the storm began, and not one of them was to be seen at day-break. One put before the wind, and was driven so much to the southward, that she was not able to gain the coast again: the 70 gun ship lost all her masts: three others of the squadron were likewise dismasted, and had so much water in the hold that the people on board expected every minute to perish, notwithstanding they had thrown overboard all the cannon of the lower tier; the other ship, during the few moments of a whirlwind which

[1] Orme, who uses the old style, says October 2nd (2nd/13th).

happened in the most furious part of the storm, was covered by the waves, and foundered in an instant, and only six of the crew escaped alive. Twenty other vessels belonging to different nations were either drove on shore, or perished at sea." [1]

La Bourdonnais was no longer able to face the English or to continue on the coast of Coromandel. On October 21, a treaty, which he asserted had been assented to at Pondicherry, was signed by him and Governor Morse and five of the English Council. All the merchandise, part of the military stores of the East India Company, all the naval stores belonging to the Company or private persons became the property of the French Company. La Bourdonnais gave up to the English and the other inhabitants all the effects and merchandise belonging to them except the naval stores. It was agreed that the French should evacuate the town before the end of the ensuing January, after which the English were to remain in possession of it without being attacked by them again during the war. Upon these conditions the Governor and Council of Madras agreed to pay the sum of 1,100,000 pagodas, or £440,000 sterling. Of this sum £240,000 was to be paid at Pondicherry, by six equal payments, before the month of October in the year 1749: and for the remaining £200,000 bills were drawn on the East India Company in London, payable a few months after they should be presented. The English gave hostages for the performance of this treaty.

On October 23, having made over the governorship of Madras to the senior member of Council sent by Dupleix, La Bourdonnais sailed for the roads of Pondicherry. He anchored there the following day but did not land. After an angry discussion with the Pondicherry Council he acquiesced in their desire that the fleet, consisting of seven ships, should proceed to Achin in Sumatra. For that port he accordingly set sail; the three ships which had arrived last from Europe, with another that had escaped from the storm, made good their destination in spite of a contrary wind; but La Bourdonnais' seventy-gun ship and two others which had suffered in the

[1] Orme, Vol. I., p. 71.

storm were forced to give way and sail before the wind to Mauritius where they arrived in the beginning of December. Here he took charge of a squadron and was directed to proceed to France, taking Martinique on the way. Owing to a storm which he encountered, he put in for shelter at St. Paul de Loanda, the Portuguese colony. As has been stated, he had been some time in the Portuguese service in India, and it was reported at Madras that he meant to send gold, silver, diamonds and merchandise to Goa. At St. Paul he chartered a small vessel, which carried his wife, his children (and, it was said, the riches that he had gotten), to Brazil and thence to Lisbon. On reaching Martinique, with only four of his ships, he found his homeward voyage was barred by English cruisers. He proceeded to St. Eustache, one of the islands forming the colony of Curaçoa, lying north from the coast of Venezuela, and took a passage to France in a Dutch ship. War, however, had now been declared between France and Holland, and the Dutch vessel was forced into an English harbour. La Bourdonnais was recognised and made prisoner. Grose states that the

> "ship was taken by an English privateer, and carried into Falmouth in December 1747. . . . But the Commodore's lady, with most of the jewels, arrived in a Portugueze ship at Lisbon." [1]

He adds—

> "The commodore was confined some days in Pendennis castle, from whence he was conducted to London in the custody of two messengers."

He was treated with the utmost politeness and afterwards sent to France. As is well known, on reaching France he was imprisoned in the Bastille and remained there for three years in the most rigorous confinement. He was charged, in addition to his political offences, with corruption, embezzlement and extortion, but was at length acquitted by a committee of the Private Council to whom his case was referred.

The chief accusation brought against La Bourdonnais is that he received a large sum of money from the English to

[1] Grose, Vol. II., p. xxxi.

conclude an unauthorised treaty for the ransom of Madras, and little doubt can exist from the evidence[1] that he was guilty of the charge. But in condemning him for the act it is necessary to consider that La Bourdonnais was a corsair of the same stuff as Drake and Hawkins. He regarded the capture of Madras as a prize in a privateering cruise, and he considered he was entitled to a share of it, as Drake did when he captured the Spanish cities and held them to ransom. It must also be remembered that La Bourdonnais was instructed not to form any new settlements, and the only alternatives in his power with regard to Madras were to restore or destroy it. The capture of Madras was but a part of his general plan to destroy the prestige and power of all the English settlements. By the capture of Madras he had dealt a severe blow to the reputation of the English, but the hurricane which destroyed his ships altered his prospects. He was no longer able to continue on the coast of Coromandel, and he had to settle with all expedition the affairs of Madras. He was obliged to leave the Indian Ocean for want of ships, but he left at Pondicherry 900 Europeans and 300 " Caffres " : " 1,200 disciplined men," says Orme, who were of the utmost service to Dupleix in his future operations. Resolution, daring, and professional skill historians allow to La Bourdonnais, and he must have a place among the fighting heroes of France.[2]

Dupleix had written to La Bourdonnais : " I believe I have found the means of keeping him (the Nawab) quiet by telling him we will give him up Madras." But Dupleix did not mention that he had also found another means of keeping the Nawab quiet. Clive states that " when Dupleix obtained the old Nabob's consent for attacking Madras upon paying a

[1] *See* Appendix I.

[2] Orme writes : " His knowledge in mechanics rendered him capable of building a ship from the keel : his skill in navigation, of conducting her to any part of the globe : and his courage, of defending her against any equal force. In the conduct of an expedition, he superintended all the details of the service, without being perplexed either with the variety or number of them. His plans were simple, his orders precise, and both the best adapted to the service in which he was engaged. His application was incessant ; and difficulties served only to encrease his activity, which always gave the example of zeal to those he commanded."—Orme, Vol. I., p. 73.

certain sum of money, the one half down the rest when the place was taken, as soon as Madras fell the rest of the money was demanded and refused, upon which the Nabob sent his eldest son Maphuze Cawn to punish the French and retake Madras."[1] The army his son commanded consisted of 8,000 or 10,000, of whom 4,000 were cavalry. Mahfuz Khan[2] on reaching Madras proceeded to invest the town on all sides, and the two deputies who were sent to treat with him he made prisoners. Dupleix had sent orders to d'Espréménil not to assume the offensive. The Oriental, as is his wont, regarded inaction as entirely due to fear. The native commander, having learnt the dispositions which La Bourdonnais had made, endeavoured to copy them. At the spot where the French had erected one of the batteries of mortars they began to construct a battery of their cannon "which were so old as not to be fired without risk to those who managed them."[3]

La Bourdonnais intended to escalade the Black Town, whose walls were very low and the bastions of very little strength, and Mahfuz Khan determined to do the same. In order to facilitate the assault he let off a piece of water which covered the south face of the fort by cutting through a sand-bank. At the same time a large body of his troops took possession of a spring lying about three miles to the north of the town, which was the only source from which the inhabitants were supplied with good water. Without good water he knew the multitude in the settlement could not exist. D'Espréménil was now compelled to assume the offensive. On the following morning (October 22, 1746) the guns from the bastions of the Black and White Towns opened fire, and a small body of 400 men, with two field-pieces, marched out of the northern gate and formed on the plain, concealing their two field-pieces behind their line. The Nawab's cavalry, on seeing them, threw

[1] Orme MSS.: India, Vol. I., pp. 108–11.

[2] Orme spells it Maphuze Khan. Wilks, a Persian scholar, writes Maphuz Khan, Vol. I., p. 261. According to the official system of transliteration, it should be written Mahfūz Khān.

[3] Orme, Vol. I., p. 74.

themselves into their saddles, united their squadrons and swept down like an avalanche. The French waited. The horsemen were within a few paces. The line opened to the right and left, and the two guns sent forth their shot. Men and horses went down. The cavalry bravely stood their ground. They expected the sudden fire would quickly cease. They knew not the skill of European artillerymen. More men and horses fell to the ground. Panic struck them and, wheeling round, they galloped away. The French took possession of their tents and baggage and "two pieces of cannon" which they found "so little fit for service that they flung them into a well."[1] They killed about "70 Moors" in the attack, and returned into the town without the loss of a man.

Mahfuz Khan was surprised and alarmed at the sudden attack made on his cavalry. He immediately recalled his troops from the outlying posts and concentrated his forces about two miles westward of Madras. His alarm was increased by the news which now reached him—a French force was advancing rapidly from Pondicherry. The next day he broke up his camp and moved to St. Thomé, which had so recently been pillaged by the French. The town had no defence excepting here and there the remains of a ruined wall, but the River Adyar, flowing from the west to the sea, afforded it some protection from an invading force advancing from the south. On the strand between the town and river Mahfuz Khan placed in position his 10,000 men and planted his cannon along the bank of the river.

Orme's graphic account of the defeat of the Nawab's army has been accepted by English and French historians. He states that the French detachment arrived by break of day. They crossed the river under a fire of the enemy's guns and, on reaching the other bank, they gave a general fire of their small arms and charged them with their bayonets. The "Moors" retreated into the town, their horse and foot got jammed in the narrow streets and they suffered severe loss before they could extricate themselves and gain the plain to the west-

[1] Orme, Vol. I., p. 75.

ward. "Their general, Maphuze Khan, mounted on an elephant, on which the great standard of the Carnatic was displayed, was one of the first who made his escape." Orme adds that the "Moors" were scarcely fled out of the town before the detachment from Madras arrived.[1] Clive in his answers (which have never been printed) to "a paper of queries" sent to him by Orme, stated:

> "The French contrived to send a party of 300 Men from Pondicherry by land, and, as soon as they had notice of the arrival of those troops at St. Thomé, they made a Sortie from Madrass in the night time, at the same time with the other from St. Thomé and surprized the Moorish Camp consisting of about 10,000 Men, took all the Baggage, killed and wounded many and drove the rest up into the Country."[2]

One thing is, however, clear amid the differences in the two accounts; it is that a small number of French soldiers defeated a whole army. The fight on the banks of the Adyar destroyed the belief that the Moors were a brave and formidable enemy, and produced far-reaching political and military results.

After the victory Paradis, who was in command of the detachment, proceeded to Madras and assumed charge of the government. On October 30, 1746, the garrison were drawn up under arms and a manifesto was read to the inhabitants who had assembled. The treaty, which the Government of Pondicherry had engaged themselves and given their parole on October 13 to keep, was declared null and void.

> "The English were enjoined to deliver up the keys of all magazines without exception: all merchandize, plate, provisions, warlike stores, and horses, were declared the property of the French Company; but the English were permitted to dispose of their moveables, cloaths, and the jewels of the women: they were required to give their parole not to serve against the French nation until they should be exchanged; and it was declared that those who refused to obey this injunction would be arrested and sent to Pondicherry. All, excepting such as were willing to take the oath of allegiance to the French King, were ordered to quit the town in four days, and were prohibited from taking up their residence within the bounds of

[1] Orme, Vol. I., p. 76.
[2] Orme MSS.: India, Vol. I., pp. 108–11.

Madrass, or in any of the country houses belonging to the English without those bounds." [1]

The French put their manifesto into execution with the utmost rigour. Most of the English inhabitants were ruined. Many of them not only refused to give the parole, but justly considered that they were absolved from the parole which they had given by the bad faith of Dupleix. They made their escape out of the town by night, and, travelling by various routes through the country, arrived at the English settlement of Fort St. David. Among those who escaped was Clive. "I made my escape," he wrote to Orme, "the beginning of October, disguised in the habit of a Dubosh [2] and black'd and arrived at St. David the same month." [3]

[1] Orme, Vol. I., p. 78.
[2] Dubash (*Dabashi*, *dubashiya*), an interpreter.
[3] Orme MSS.: India, Vol. I.

CHAPTER III

1746–8: CLIVE AT FORT ST. DAVID

FORT ST. DAVID, situated on the sea twelve miles from Pondicherry, associated with the great names of Lawrence and Clive, must always be, to Englishmen who take pride in the brave deeds of their forefathers, one of the most memorable places in the Empire. It was in the year 1690 that we purchased it from the Mahrattas, and one Mr. Hatsell was ordered "to go and to receive possession of the fort and pay the money," and with him were to be sent "some factors to be of councel there, also a lieutenant, two ensigns, gunners, &c., officers, 100 soldiers, 20 matrosses, 20 laskars, 30 great guns, 100 barrels of powder, 200 musquets, 100 cartouches, 100 swords, and ammunition, &c., necessary for such a garrison and settlement," and it was resolved that "the guns, stores, and household stuff be removed from Conemier and the southern factories thither."

The cession included not only the fort but the adjacent towns and villages "within ye randome shott of a piece of ordnance." The best brass gun at Madras was sent with Mr. Hatsell, and he was informed that it "lyes in the gunner's art to load and fire it to the best advantage." The gunner was evidently skilled in his art, for on September 23, 1690,[1] at the time when Dutch William was busy establishing his power in Ireland, the "randome shott" was fired, and it fell beyond Cuddalore. And to this day the villages included within the range of that "randome shott" are known as "Gundu Gramam" or "Cannon Ball Villages."

The English proceeded at once to introduce law and order into their new possession. Mr. Haynes, Mr. Walls, and Macee-

[1] Malleson says 1691—"French in India," p. 195.

dum Nina were appointed "justices of the Choultry[1] to try and determine causes civill and criminal and to execute according to sentence, lyfe only excepted, which must be done by another court of judicature." "All tryalls of moment" were to be registered by "an English Clerk of said Court," and "the differences amongst black merchants" to be decided by members of their own caste. Under the powers, judicial, executive and military, which the governor in Council wielded, the merchants plied their trades and tended their shops, and Cuddalore became a busy and opulent place. A traveller of the time has left us a pleasant picture of the settlement:

"Fort St. David is a small, but strong and regular fortification, built on a rising ground, about a mile from the Black-Town, which is called Cuddalore. This last has a wall running round it, with the addition of a few bastions, but is too large even for all the English troops on the coast properly to defend. In it, reside the greatest part of the native Indian inhabitants of Fort St. David's boundaries. Both the town, and the fort, are situated near the sea side; Cuddalore lying almost due south from the fort. The extent of this settlement's boundaries, are, towards the land, about four miles, and three along the sea side: the former are pointed out by a thick hedge of the aloe plant and cocoa-nut tree, having bastions of six or eight guns, at about three-fourths of a mile from each other. In one of these little forts Deputy Governor Starke had fitted up a pleasant apartment, and to which he frequently retired from Fort St. David.

"The country within the boundaries is very pleasant, and the air fine, having seldom any fogs. In the district are many neat houses with gardens; the latter were laid out with much good taste by the gentlemen, who either had been, or were in the company's service. These gardens produce fruits of different sorts, such as pine-apples, oranges, limes, pomegranates, plantaines, bananoes, mangoes, guavas, (red and white,) bedams (a sort of almond), pimple-nose, called in the West Indies, chadocks, a very fine large fruit of the citron-kind, but of four or five times it's size, and many others. At the end of each gentleman's garden there is generally a shady grove of cocoa-nut trees. . . .

"In the neighbourhood of the agreeable retreats before mentioned, are many pleasant rows of the ever-green tulip tree, which are planted through great part of the boundaries, in the same manner

[1] *Choultry*—"A hall, a shed, or a simple *loggia*, used by travellers as a resting-place, and also intended for the transaction of public business. . . . A building of this kind seems to have formed the early Court-House."—Yule and Burnett; "Hobson-Jobson" (1903), p. 211.

as the elms in St. James's Park. At some little distance from one of these walks, is a building, belonging to the company, and designed for the governor, and called 'the garden-house.' It is roomy, handsome and well built; and has a very good and large garden belonging to it, with long and pleasant avenues of trees in the back and front." [1]

The writer omits to mention that the large garden "was inclosed with a brick wall, and before the house, to the south, [was] a court with buildings on each side of it." [2] The Governor of Fort St. David has long since passed away, but Garden House, "roomy, handsome and well built," stands at the end of a stately avenue and is the appointed residence of his successor, the modest Collector. The garden with its old trees still exists and the buildings on each side of the court have been converted into Government offices.

Clive in a letter to the Court (8th March, 1755) states that when he and his two companions "came safe to Fort St. David" they found themselves

"for some time under the disagreable Circumstances of being unprovided for, till at last the Gentlemen of St. David offer'd a Monthly writership to all those in our Condition, which was accepted of by all but us three; We were of Opinion that acting in a Military Sphere (tho then at a very low Ebb) was the most honourable of the two and most conducive to the Company's Interest." [3]

Besides the cankering inaction to which he was condemned, there were other factors which made life in the small fort far from pleasant. There was little amusement. As it was a time of war, no shooting excursions, no pleasant trips up the river, no ships from home broke the monotony of life. Gambling was the chief method of passing away the tedious hours. There was no military discipline, and the few officers were soldiers of fortune. It is therefore not strange that Fort St. David should be the scene of murderous brawls. Malcolm mentions one of these brawls. He states that Clive formed one of a party at play, whom two officers, by the grossest cheating, contrived to fleece. The winners were noted duellists, and all the party paid their losses except Clive. He told the winners

[1] E. Ives: "A Voyage from England to India, etc.," ed. 1773, pp. 18–21.
[2] Orme, Vol. I., p. 83.
[3] "Miscellaneous Letters Received," Vol. 38, No. 120 (India Office Records).

that they had cheated and strictly refused to pay. He was challenged by one of them, went out without seconds, gave his fire and missed. His adversary marched up to him, put his pistol to Clive's head and desired him to ask his life. Clive did so. Then the bravo demanded that Clive should pay the sum of which he had been cheated, and retract what he had said. "And what if I refuse?" demanded Clive. "Then I fire," replied the other. "Fire and be damned!" said Clive; "I said you cheated, I say so still, nor will I ever pay you." The bully, finding his threats useless, called him a madman and threw the pistol away. Clive's young companions complimented him on his behaviour, but he refused to discuss the matter and would never again breathe a word against the officer. "He has given me my life," he said, "and though I am resolved on never paying money which was unfairly won, or again associating with him, I shall never do him an injury." [1]

Clive was now merely acting in a "military sphere," but the time was at hand when he would join a service which disciplines and directs the stubborn, indomitable courage he had shown.

When Fort St. George fell, the eyes of Dupleix were turned towards Fort St. David. It was the chief obstacle to the complete subjection of the English. In the month of December he recalled Paradis from Madras to command an expedition against it. Paradis set forth with a detachment of 300 Europeans and a long train of coolies carrying the chests which contained the treasure he had acquired in the administration of his government. When he had proceeded thirty miles from Madras, he was surprised by a division of the Nawab's commanded by Mahfuz Khan, who had publicly sworn to revenge the defeat of St. Thomé. Fired on by the enemy's infantry concealed in the thickets, their rear and flanks threatened by clouds of cavalry, his oppressed troops with their encumbrance made their way with the utmost difficulty to Sadras, a Dutch settlement forty-two miles from Madras. Several of the French soldiers were wounded during the march, and twelve or fourteen

[1] Malcolm: "Memoirs of Lord Clive," Vol. I., p. 47. Taken from the "Biographia Britannica" (2nd ed.), art. "Clive," p. 646.

Europeans were made prisoners. Mahfuz Khan gave out that he had won a great victory, and showed his prisoners as an incontestable mark of his triumph. The moral effect of the French success at St. Thomé was destroyed.

Paradis, when reinforcements from Pondicherry reached him, marched to Ariancopang (Arian Kuppam), a small fort built by the French about two miles to the south-west of Pondicherry and about one mile and a half from the sea. Here the force for the capture of Fort St. David was assembled. It "consisted of 1,700 men, for the most part Europeans, of which 50 were cavalry: they had one or two companies of Caffre slaves, natives of Madagascar and one of the eastern coast of Africa: these had been disciplined, and were brought into India by Mr. De la Bourdonnais. Their artillery consisted of six field pieces and as many mortars."[1] Dupleix had summoned Paradis, the able Swiss engineer, to command the expedition, but, owing to the petty jealousy of the French officers and their vigorous opposition, the command was given to Bury, without talent and without energy, old and infirm, the senior officer of the French troops in India.

The garrison of Fort St. David numbered 200 Europeans and 100 half-caste Portuguese infantry called "Topasses," perhaps on account of wearing a *topi* or hat.[2] When La Bourdonnais laid siege to Madras the government of Fort St. David hired 2,000 "Peons" (a species of irregular infantry, armed with swords and spears or matchlocks) for the defence of Cuddalore and their seven miles of territory. But, though the numerical strength of their forces was small and their efficiency slight, Hinde, the governor, and his colleagues were men formed by nature to fight against difficulties. They wrote to the Court that "this for us most Fortunate Storm, which we look upon as a distinguish-

[1] Orme, Vol. I., p. 82.

[2] "The Christians, who call themselves Portuguese, form part of a garrison: they are little superior in courage to the lowest casts of Indians, and greatly inferior to the higher casts, as well as to the northern Moors of Indostan; but because they learn the manual exercise, and the duties of a parade with sufficient readiness, and are clad like Europeans, they are incorporated into the companies of European troops. From wearing a hat, these pretended Portuguese obtained amongst the natives of India the name of Topasses; by which name the Europeans likewise distinguish them."—*Ibid.*, p. 81.

ing mark of Providence in our favour," had prevented the French from attacking "this Place" by sea. "Though it is the opinion of most of our officers that, had they come, we should have taken up more of their time than they had to spare." They added:

> "We have about Twenty of the Kings people that were left ashoar sick who have put our Gun room in Excellent order, some of the people came to us from Madras, though not many. The additions and alterations to our Fort within this Twelve month have made it Infinitely more secure than it was. We have full six months Provisions of all Kinds in the Fort, so that we doubt not but we should have been able to make a defence for a considerable Time had they come; they now Talk of coming to us by Land, in which case We Bless God we are no ways apprehensive but with the Common protection of Providence we shall be able to Defend and Secure this Place till we are releived, for which purpose We assure your Honours our Utmost Endeavours shall be used." [1]

Their dependence on Heaven did not prevent Hinde, the governor, from applying to the Nawab for his assistance against the French when he learnt that a force had been collected to attack Fort St. David. The Nawab, exasperated at the defeat of his son, readily engaged to send his army to their aid. Clive, in the memorandum mentioned, states that "under the command of Maphuze Cawn and Mahomed Ally Cawn [the Nawab's sons] these forces, who were encamped on the plain by Chemundalum [three miles from the fort] arrived the day before Major Bury took Possession of the Garden House." [2]

On December 8, 1746, the French troops set out at night from Ariancopang, and as the scarlet shafts of sunshine broke above the palms they arrived at the Panar River and crossed at a ford about a quarter of a mile from the Garden House. They moved quickly forward and took possession of the walled garden. "There might be," says Clive, "a few scattering shot fired from some of the points on the Enemy when they were advancing towards the Bound Hedge, and they might have received some trifling Molestation from a Body of about 600 Peons commanded by one Malrauze and

[1] Dispatch from Fort St. David, 17th October, 1746 (Madras Records).
[2] Orme MSS.: India, Vol. I., pp. 108–11.

who were posted in and about the Thicketts near the Garden House."[1] Weary with their long night march, the French intended to rest at the Garden House during the day. They had no reason to expect an attack. The scanty garrison would not leave their fortifications, and Dupleix had told Bury that the English had not been able to prevail with the Nawab to send more than 1,500 men to their assistance. The slight resistance offered to their advance confirmed them in the belief that they had no formidable foe to fight. Bury, who expected a detachment of native troops, suddenly found an army. But Clive, who served that day as a volunteer, must tell the story of his first action:

"The French commander as soon as in possession of the Garden House and Plantation thought he had nothing to fear and gave leave to all the troops without exception to lay down their arms to look for Pots and wood to dress their Victuals and to refresh themselves after the fatigue of their march: in this unSoldierlike and scattered condition were the French when the whole Moorish Army were descried marching towards the Plantation and Garden House: the Enemy had just time to lay hold of their arms but not to form and their panick was so great that instead of making a disposition for defending themselves in their naturally strong Situation they began to retreat towards Pondicherry in an unformed Heap and did not recover their Order or fears for the first three miles: had the Moors been good for any thing and made a Charge upon them in that condition they must every man have been cut off: on seeing the Enemy retreat from the Garden House we made a Sortie from the fort, with 200 men 50 of which were Topasses and marched after them for about 6 miles before we overtook them but then they were in too good order and too much recovered for us with our small force to attempt any thing against them: however they lost a great many men by the random Shot of the Moorish infantry and our Peons: what military Stores were lodged in the Garden House were all abandoned and we found there a great many Chests of small arms: the Moors also took great quantities of Stores and Baggage, in short the French arrived at Pondicherry the Evening of the same day greatly fatigued and frightened."[2]

Dupleix now set himself to surmount the hostility of the Nawab and Mahfuz Khan by bribes and blandishments. At the same time he formed a project to take Cuddalore by

[1] Letter from Lord Clive, Cundover, July 19, 1762 (Orme MSS.: India, Vol. I., pp. 137–41).

[2] Orme MSS.: India, Vol. I., pp. 108–11.

surprise. The Government of Fort St. David wrote to the Court:

"The 20th [December 1746]. We are advised they fitted out a Force by sea to surprize us that day but Providence disappointed them, some of their Boats were drove ashoar and their ammunition all spoiled which reduced them to a necessity of laying aside their Design and putting back into Aria Copang River: The 31st We had a skirmish by Land, we again obtained an advantage over them, and had we even then been succoured your Honours Affairs would have been in all humain probabillity Restored in a great measure, if not altogether. The Nabob was so well disposed towards us, but as yet we had not had a line or any assistance from Bengall since Madrass was taken, now 4 months. . . . We shall only add we think it somewhat unkind in our Countrymen and Fellow Servants to have abandoned us, and that we will do all wee can under these discourageing Circumstances, and Trust to Providence for the Events. Hitherto we have been [at] but a small Expence, our Presents to the Country Government not Exceeding above Three thousand 3,000 Pagodas, Triffle not worth mentioning in Proportion to the Expence they are at, and the Desquiet it has given our Enemys, who are trying every possible method to make up Affairs with them, and the above Circumstance[s] greatly Facillitate their Negotiation as they clog the Wheels of ours. We have in General Terms promised in your Honours' name that we will not be ungrateful for any favours the Nabob may show us." [1]

Hinde and his Council were persecuted with sordid importunity by the Nawab, who had a great appetite for subsidies. But they had not the money to gratify his "extreme lucrative disposition." Their treasury was almost exhausted when a gallant sailor anchored his ship in the road and landed £60,000 in silver, and twenty recruits. Dupleix had all the plunder of Madras at his command. He spared no art which could withdraw the Nawab from the English. He appealed to his avarice by offering him lakhs of pagodas. He aroused his fears as to the fate of his kingdom by sending a detachment from Madras which burnt his villages and threatened his capital. Just at that time the four ships of La Bourdonnais' squadron, which had made their way to Achin, returned to Pondicherry. Dupleix informed the Nawab of their arrival, and he exaggerated the strength of the reinforcement they brought. The English at Fort St. David were, he urged, a handful of men

[1] Dispatch from Fort St. David, January 10, 1746–7 (Madras Records).

deserted by their countrymen. His statement was supported by the long absence of the English squadron. The Nawab became convinced that the English cause was the losing cause. The inevitable result followed. The Government of Fort St. David wrote to their masters:

" Since our last account of the melancholy Situation of this Settlement which must Certainly have appeared to be very Precarious, We had the misfortune to be reduced to almost inevitable Danger, for as our security chiefly depended on the assistance of the Moors, We were soon brought to the utmost Extremity by being abandoned by them, notwithstanding all the arguments and Persuasions that could possibly be used on our parts to Continue them in our Interest; but the long delay of our ships with the uncertainty of their coming at all, and the frequent offers and proposals they received from the French, which arose to five Lack of Rupees, made all our endeavours prove fruitless, as we could by no means think of making such offers, and if we could, they would have still outbid us, having this advantage of us, that if they did not perform their Promises, they could not be on worse Terms than they were, whereas We must literally have performed all ours upon the whole. On the 4th February, both their armies decamp'd, leaving us wholly to ourselves; In which destitute Circumstances the French, on the last of February, came out of Pondicherry, and on the 1st March made another attempt upon us by Land, bringing with them a Force considerably superior to any yet sent or we could equal in more than a Quarter part." [1]

Clive gives an account of the second attempt to capture Fort St. David, March 2/13, 1747.

" Soon after Dupleix bought Maphuze Ally Cawn off, who went and paid him a visit at Pondicherry, But Mahomed Ally Cawn returned to Arcot with the greatest part of the forces seemingly much disgusted at the treacherous behaviour of his Brother: by the latter end of February the French had recovered their spirits and began their march a second time against Fort St. David with 1200 Europeans a body of Caffrays [*kafir*, negro soldier] and a troop of horse all under the command of Paradis. To this great force we could not oppose near the 200 Men; however we marched out with 2 or 3 field pieces to oppose the French in crossing the Peneer River. About a mile to the North of Shoemakers and Patchere Points the French were drawn up on the other side of the river at the distance of about 600 yards. We Cannonaded one another the whole day without the Enemy ever attempting to cross the River; but as the Evening came on we could perceive the Enemy were making dispositions to cut off our retreat upon which we re-

[1] Dispatch from Fort St. David, May 2, 1747 (Madras Records).

turned to the Fort; in this Cannonadement we lost 8 Men and the French 22; the next morning at daybreak the 3rd of March we could discover from the Fort that the French had taken Possession of the Garden House but we shortly after discovered something of a much more agreeable nature, which was the sight of Mr. Griffins squadron and as soon as the French had made the same discovery they retreated a second time to Pondicherry with great precipitation." [1]

Soon after the repulse of the second attack, Robert Clive received his first commission. The document marks the very outset of a military career, distinguished by a series of successes that laid great foundations:

John Hinde Esqr, Deputy Governor for All Affairs of the United Company of Merchants of England trading to the East Indies at Fort St. David, and the Towns of Tevenapatam, and Cuddalore in the Chinie [? Gingee] Country, and the Territories thereto belonging. To all to whom these presents shall come. Greeting.

Seal of the Company

BY VIRTUE of the Power given to the President of Fort St. George by the Court of Directors for Affairs of the United Company of Merchants of England trading to the East Indies, which power is derived by Charter from our late Sovereign Lord George, and is now devolv'd on me, I do hereby Constitute and Appoint you Robert Clive Gent^{n} Ensign of the Second Company of Foot Soldiers at Fort St. David, giving and Granting you full power and Authority to call together, train, conduct and to Battle lead them according to military and martial Discipline, strictly willing and Commanding all your Inferior Officers and Soldiers to obey you as such, and You Yourself are strictly Enjoyned to obey all Orders You shall receive from me, or the Deputy Governor of this place for the time being, or from any your Superior Officers for the time being.

GIVEN under my hand, and the United Company's Seal this Sixteenth day of March, in the twentieth Year of the Reign of our Sovereign Lord George the Second by the Grace of God of Great Britain, France and Ireland King Defender of Faith, and in the Year of our Lord one thousand, Seven hundred Forty and six/seven

Witness (Sgd) *John Hinde.*

(Sgd) *Thomas Cooke Junr*
Secry.

[1] Orme MSS.: India, Vol. I., pp. 108–11.

In a dispatch to the Court, dated May 2, 1747, the Governor in Council writes :

"Mr. Robert Clive, Writer in the Service, being of a martial disposition and having acted as a volunteer in our late engagements we have granted him an Ensign's Commission upon his application for the same."[1]

The Court in their letter of December 4, 1747, remark :

"Be sure to encourage Ensign Clive in his martial pursuits, according to his merit : any improvement he shall make therein shall be duly regarded by us."

On January 1, 1748, there arrived at Fort St. David a veteran commander who fostered the military ardour of the young soldier and taught him all the details of the profession. It was from Stringer Lawrence Clive learnt that by discipline and a training in details soldiers can be made with whom battles are won.

Stringer, the son of John Lawrence of Hereford, and Mary his wife, was born March 6, 1697. Little is known of his ancestry or his early life. At the age of thirty he was appointed ensign in General Jasper Clayton's regiment (afterwards the 14th Foot, and now the West Yorkshire), then stationed at Gibraltar, and there is some reason to suppose that he served in the ranks of some regiment during the previous siege. Clayton's regiment was at Gibraltar for several years, and was employed as marines in Wager's fleet on the coast of Italy. Legend states that Lawrence was taken prisoner by an Italian pirate vessel, and was for some time on board it. In 1746 he became lieutenant. He was present when the column, headed by the King's son, broke the heart of the French line at Fontenoy ; and he heard the wild yell with which the Highlanders threw themselves on our ranks at Culloden. On December 17, 1746, the Court of Directors

"Resolved that the garrison of Fort St. George be strengthened with a number of recruits, sergeants, and ensigns, and that an able officer be sent from hence as Major thereof, at the salary of £250 per annum, and one hundred guineas for his charges out. And

[1] Dispatch from Fort St. David, May 2, 1747 (Madras Records).

Captain Lawrence being recommended as a person qualified for the post, Resolved by the Ballot that the said Captain Lawrence be appointed Major of the Garrison on the terms above mentioned, and being called in, he was acquainted therewith." [1]

On February 18, 1747, Stringer Lawrence took the usual oath, and set sail in the *Winchelsea.* His appointment was notified to the Governor of Madras in the following terms:

"Stringer Lawrence Esq., is entertained by us to be Major of our Garrison at Fort St. George upon the same terms as Major Knipe, viz., two hundred and fifty pounds sterling per annum and one of the Companies." [2]

But before the notification reached India, Madras had surrendered to the French, and the Government of Madras had ceased to exist. In January, 1748, Stringer Lawrence, a "stout hale man of fifty," landed at Fort St. David.

When Lawrence assumed command of the garrison, it had been reinforced by 100 men from the Bombay European regiments, 150 recruits from England, and 400 sepoys from the English settlement of Tellicherry on the Malabar coast. Griffin's squadron of "Nine sails" had landed 100 Europeans from Bengal, and the admiral had lent 500 sailors and 150 marines "as a temporary augmentation of the garrison." [3] Clive tells us that soon after the arrival of Lawrence a report reached the garrison that the French intended to make a third attempt on Fort St. David.

"Being 7[00] or 800 Strong Major Laurence encamped with these forces between the Garden House and the River Pennar; in this Camp we continued some time till we had discovered a Conspiracy formed by the Commander of the Tellicherry Seapoys to desert with all his men to the French in the day of Battle; this discovery led us to many others and by seizing the Papers of Mr. Morse's Dubash it appeared that Mr. Dupleix and he had carried on a constant Correspondence together in the Country Language. Mr. Dupleix got acquainted with him during the time Mr. and Mrs. Morse were at Pondicherry and upon examining his Papers it appeared by numbers of Letters from Mr. Dupleix that he had received exact intelligence of the most minute Transactions and that all our Counsels were betrayed. In one

[1] "Court Minutes," Vol. 62, quoted by Col. S. Biddulph: "Stringer Lawrence," p. 18.

[2] "Letter Book," Vol. 26, quoted *op. cit., loc. cit.*

[3] Orme, Vol. I., p. 89.

of Mr. Dupleix's Letters he says to the Dubash, You write me the English have pulled down your House and that you desire I would send you Money to build you a new one; if I was to comply with your request the English knowing you are poor would immediately inquire how you came by the money and by that means discover the Correspondence between us and put you to death. I make no doubt but by your means we shall soon be in possession of St. Davids and then I will build you a house of double the Value at Pondicherry.

"A General Court Martial being held upon these Traytors, the Dubash and his Second were hanged, the Commander and others of the Tellicherry Seapoy Officers were banished to St. Helena and the West Coast: the Dubash at the Gallows declared his Master's Mr. Morse's Innocence of his intrigues with Mr. Dupleix: this Plot being unravelled the French gave over their designs and we returned to Garrison." [1]

The treachery of the Tellicherry sepoys showed the necessity of stricter discipline, and led to the introduction of a Military Code. Lawrence also knew that to carry on a campaign with success you must place your army on a systematic footing. He formed the different companies of the European Corps into a regular battalion of seven companies, one of them being a grenadier company. Each company consisted of one captain-lieutenant, one lieutenant, one ensign, four sergeants, four corporals, three drummers, and seventy privates. All the men of the battalion, except the grenadiers, ceased to wear swords. The officers carried in addition to their swords light fusils, the sergeants halberds. The peons were formed into companies and were trained in the manœuvres and evolutions practised in the Royal Army. Lawrence had learnt the value of cavalry in war, and the first troop of horse in the Madras Presidency was raised at this time.

The Government of Fort St. David wrote to the Court:

"As our enemies are furnished with a troop of horse, by which they have greatly the advantage of us in sending out parties thereof, that make frequent incursions near our limits, and the adjacent villages, we have thought it absolutely necessary, with the opinion of Major Lawrence and several of the officers, to raise a troop also in your service, and have granted commissions to Lieutenant Gengins and Mr. Hallyburton to act as Lieutenants, and one to Ensign

[1] Letter from Lord Clive, Cundover, July 19, 1762 (Orme MSS.: India, Vol. I., pp. 139–40).

Cheseborough to be a Cornett, these being the properest persons. We have only been able to provide horses and accoutrements for 30 men, but we daily expect more horses from the country, and hope in a short time to make up this number, one hundred." [1]

Lawrence had also under his command a company of artillery which consisted of a hundred gunners commanded by a First Captain and Chief Engineer.[2] The little force, disciplined and trained by Stringer Lawrence, was the germ of the army that won an empire for England.

On the night of June 9, 1747, an English 20-gun ship, returning from a cruise, brought the intelligence to Fort St. David that she had discovered seven large ships to the south. Next day at noon the French squadron was discerned in the south-east. The sea-wind was set in, and they were sailing directly before it towards St. David. The English squadron was at anchor near the land, and during the sea-breeze could not get near the enemy. At four in the afternoon, the French squadron, "being within three leagues of the road," altered their course, and as they kept to the windward the English admiral thought their intention was to make Pondicherry at all events. About midnight the English fleet put to sea with the land-wind. In the morning they shortened sail, in expectation every minute of seeing the French squadron again to the south. But when evening came, and no ships were seen, Admiral Griffin, feeling that he had been deceived, made sail for Madras, where he arrived the next evening and found no French ships in the road. Bouves, the commander of the French squadron, an able and experienced mariner, had reached Pondicherry in the morning, and having landed 400 soldiers and £200,000 in silver, immediately put out to sea on his return to Mauritius.

[1] Dispatch from Fort St. David, February 13, 1747–8 (Madras Records).

[2] The Artillery Company . . . was of the following strength:

1 First Captain and Chief Engineer.	1 Ensign Fireworker.
1 Second Captain and Engineer.	4 Sergeant Bombardiers.
1 Captain-Lieutenant and Director of Laboratory.	4 Corporal Bombardiers.
	2 Drummers.
1 First Lieutenant Fireworker.	100 Gunners.
1 Second Lieutenant Fireworker.	

—Vibart's "Military History of the Madras Engineers," Vol. I., p. 9.

MAJOR-GENERAL STRINGER LAWRENCE

From the mezzotint by R. Houston after a painting by Sir Joshua Reynolds

When Dupleix at Pondicherry saw that the English squadron had sailed to Madras, he determined to attack Cuddalore at once by night and capture it by surprise. Master of Cuddalore, he could deprive the garrison of Fort St. David of their direct communication with the English squadron. Lawrence met his plan with a dexterous move. What took place Clive has described:

> "Some time after this Mr. Floyer and Major Laurence received intelligence that the French intended to attack Cuddalore by Scalade: to encourage them in the attempt they artfully withdrew all the forces and Cannon from Cuddalore in the day time and as soon as it was dark sent them back with a strong Reinforcement. The next morning the French force consisting of 800 Europeans at least began their March and marching a good deal inland possessed themselves of [Bandiopollam] Hills and march[ed] down towards Cuddalore between 10 and 11 o'clock and immediately began the Attack by planting Ladders against the Walls: the Garrison being prepared for them they were readily repulsed with considerable loss, and they made the best of their way back again overwhelmed with Fatigue and disgrace: their Ignorance was plainly discovered by their attacking the only place which was fortified and had a Wall for to the North and South it was quite open and they might have entered with ease and overpowered our Numbers." [1]

Three times had the French endeavoured to take the fort, and three times they had been gallantly repelled by the small garrison. The outlook for Dupleix was grave. Early in the year 1747 the Governor and Council at Fort St. David had received advice that a strong armament was fitting out under the command of Admiral Boscawen for the attack of Pondicherry.[2] Letters received from the French Ministry had also informed Dupleix that the English armament had left England in November. It might now appear at any moment. Dupleix, who had been confident about capturing Fort St. David, became anxious for the security of Pondicherry. He proceeded, with the expert advice of Paradis, to strengthen its defences. The preparations were being actively carried on when a native courier brought Dupleix the news that the great English fleet was come at last.

[1] Letter from Lord Clive, Cundover, July 19, 1762 (Orme MSS: India, Vol. I., pp. 140–1).

[2] Orme MSS.: India, Vol. I., pp. 111–20. Siege of Pondicherry.

CHAPTER IV

1748–9: THE FIRST SIEGE OF PONDICHERRY

On November 4, 1747, the squadron under the command of Admiral Boscawen sailed from St. Helena "with a fair wind which only served for that day." On March 29, 1748, the fleet came to anchor in Table Bay.

> "On the 30th, the ground was pitched on to encamp, and men were ordered on shore to clear it; but the wind blowed so fresh, that the forces could not land till April 6th, when the whole encamped in good order and discipline, being three battalions, with artillery; on the right were 400 marines, making one battalion: six English independent companies, of 112 men each, were on the left; and six Scotch companies were in the centre. The men made a good appearance, and no pains were spared, as to discipline and refreshment, in order to fit them for their better performance in action."[1]

On May 8 Boscawen sailed from the Cape with his squadron, together with six ships belonging to the Dutch East India Company, on board of which were 400 soldiers. Owing to the stormy weather the fleet did not make the Mauritius till June 23. Boscawen had been ordered to attack the island. But he found the landing, owing to the rocks and breakers, dangerous, and the coast strongly defended by the fortification which La Bourdonnais had erected during his administration. Port Louis was protected by forts; across the harbour lay moored a large ship of two decks, "and there were besides twelve ships at anchor within the harbour, four of which were of considerable force, and ready for sea." A council of war was held to consider what should be done next. They thought themselves sufficiently strong to reduce the island, "yet the loss, they would probably sustain in the attack, and the number of men which would be requisite to

[1] "Asiatic Annual Register," 1802 (Characters, p. 35).

garrison the fortifications, would necessarily so much weaken their force, that it would certainly retard them, and might, perhaps, entirely prevent them from undertaking the siege of Pondicherry, which Boscawen was instructed to consider as the principal object of his command."[1] It was determined to run on to the coast of Coromandel without delay. On June 27, Boscawen "sailed from the Mauritius, when the Dutch ships parted with the fleet, and steered for Batavia."

On July 29, 1748, Boscawen arrived at Fort St. David, and Admiral Griffin resigned the command of his squadron to him, and a few days after proceeded with a 60-gun ship and two frigates to Trincomalee.

"The junction of these fleets," writes an English officer who had sailed with Boscawen from England, "formed the greatest marine force belonging to any one European nation that had ever been seen in the Indian seas; it consisted of more than thirty ships, of which thirteen were of the line. The English at Fort St. David, and all the native powers attached to their cause, beheld this formidable armament with a joy proportioned to the success which was naturally looked for from its operations."[2]

Boscawen carried a commission from the King as General and Commander-in-Chief of the land forces employed in the expedition. Stringer Lawrence was actively engaged in preparing his men for the business of war, when they were called upon to undertake an arduous siege under a commander who, being a sailor, knew nothing whatever of soldiering. Boscawen's object was to capture Pondicherry. He regarded it in the same light as an enemy's fleet. He would go straight in and win. He had not a moment to lose. He must strike a decisive blow before the French called in their ally the Rajah of Tanjore to their assistance. As soon as his troops were landed, he dispatched three line-of-battle ships and a sloop of war to Pondicherry in order to blockade the place by sea. On August 8 the army under his command began

[1] "Asiatic Annual Register," 1802, p. 36.
[2] Orme, Vol. I., p. 100. "Asiatic Annual Register," 1802, pp. 36–7.

their march. But Clive must tell the story of the siege, in which he distinguished himself by his daring and obstinate determination. His narrative, which is now put in print for the first time, is modest and distinct.

"If there be any Officers or Soldiers in India remaining of those who were at the Siege of Pondicherry, 12 or 13 years experience must have convinced them how very ignorant we were of the art of war in those days. Some of the Engineers were Masters of the Theory without the Practice, and those seemed wanting in resolution; others there were who understood neither, yet were possessed of courage sufficient to have gone on with the undertaking if they had known how to go about it. There was scarce an Officer who knew whether the Engineers were acting right or wrong till it was too late in the Season, and we had lost too many men, to begin an Approach again; in another (*sic*) the duty of the Engineer was in a great measure performed by the Office of Artillery and they seemed to be the only people who knew something of what they were about during this memorable Siege.

"We received advice early in the year 1747 that an Expedition was fitting out under the command of Admiral Boscowen for the attack of Pondicherry. In August the Admiral arrived himself in the *Namur*, and was soon after followed by the rest of the Squadron and Transports. On board the Fleet were embarked 1200 Independants under the command of Major Mompesson. As soon as the forces were disembarked and had refreshed themselves, being joined to the Company's troops, they consisted in Numbers as nearly as I can remember as follows: 1200 Independants, about 7 or 800 Marines, 750 Company's troops, Topasses included, two Companies of artillery (one was belonging to the King the other to the Company), and about 1100 Seapoys, or rather Peons in those days, for they knew little of Discipline and were of little Service in comparison to what they are now.

"The Regulars amounted to about 3000 men. The Independants were formed into two Battalions commanded by Majors Muir and Peppe, the Marines by the oldest Captain, the Company's troops by Major Laurence, and the Train by Major Goodere; the whole was commanded by Major Mompesson, under Admiral Boscowen who was Commander-in-Chief by Sea and Land and had the rank given him of Major General.

"With this Force we began our March towards Pondicherry, and our first Mistake in my Opinion and one principal cause of our miscarriage was the resolving to attack Ariocopang. Their little fortifications were not to be defended against Battering Cannon or a bombardment, but was not to be taken by a Coup-de-main, for it had a very good deep dry ditch full of Pittsell, a covered way, and Cavaliers in each of the Angles, and many other advantages which made it necessary to attack the place with heavy Cannon. The Engineers were ordered to reconnoitre this fortification, and make their report to the General; their Report was that the Enemy had thrown up an Entrenchment and manned it a few Yards in front of the Place, and that this Entrenchment must be stormed first, and afterwards the Fort of Ariocopang might easily be taken. Accordingly a detachment of Marines, Independants, with part of the artillery under the direction of Major Goodere, were ordered upon this service. The troops marched up to the Entrenchment, as they thought it, at day-break, with great Spirits and resolution, but how great was their disappointment to find, instead of an Entrenchment full of Frenchmen, only a heap of rubbish consisting of a few old bricks, and a Fortification (not to be taken by a coup-de-main) fraught with all those advantages before described. The Troops finding themselves exposed to a terrible fire of both Musketry and Cannon loaded with grape Shot, from the Walls, all within Pistol Shot, without a possibility of doing any thing, had no Choice left but that of surrend'ring or making a precipitate retreat. They chose the latter, and we had near 180 Gallant Men and officers killed and wounded to no manner of purpose; 3 or 4 Officers were killed outright, and many desperately wounded, among the rest was Major Goodere who lost his leg, and soon after his life. On this Officer's experience the General chiefly depended for the Operations of the Siege. This unfortunate blundering Disaster affected the Spirits of the Troops in such a manner that it was a long time before they recovered themselves, and I believe never after entertained any great hope of Success against Pondicherry.

"Grown wise by fatal experience, they began now to find it necessary to bring on them some heavy Cannon for the reduction of the place. The French finding us resolutely bent upon carrying this Point, very judiciously threw every Obstacle in our Way, well knowing that by employing us at 3 miles distance from Pondicherry we lost both time and men, and should be nothing nearer to the taking the Place when Ariocopang should fall.

"To the Northward and about the Fort ran a broad deep river called Areacopang River. On the banks of this river the French erected a Battery of heavy Cannon to obstruct and enfilade our approaches to the Fort. Our Engineer[s] erected a Counter Battery to this, but with so little judgment that when they came to open it in the Morning at day-break, there was a thick wood between ours and that of the Enemy. This blunder must be owing to their great caution in reconnoitring. As soon as the Mistake was set to rights, the Batteries played upon one another to little purpose. An entrenchment was thrown up in front of this Battery for its greater Security, and a strong detachment posted there. It was usual for the French Seapoys to fire a few popping Shot at the distance of 4 or 500 yards; one of these random Shot happened to kill one of the Sailors in the Entrenchment; this, added to the appearance of the French Troop of Horse, struck the others with such a panick that they all abandoned the Entrenchments. The Example of the Sailors was followed by all the Military in spight of the Exhortations of their Officers to the contrary; this unaccountable panick was immediately observed by the Enemy, and taken advantage of by them. They advanced with some Seapoys and the Troop of Horse, took possession of the Entrenchments, and afterwards pursued the fugitives to the Battery, who were there assembled in a confused Heap of at least 15 Deep; however, in this confusion they fired upon the Horse, killed 6 or 7 of them, dropp'd the Horse of the Commanding Officer, and took the Officer Prisoner. This obliged the French to turn tail, and thus ended this curious Exploit. If our loss had only ended here, it had been nothing, [but] this Action was rendered truly unfortunate by the Loss of Major Laurence, who commanded the Entrenchment that day, and sooner than follow the Troops in their ignominious flight, chose rather to be killed or taken Prisoner, as did Captn. Bruce, a very gallant Officer." [1]

In announcing this incident to the Court of Directors, and how "very unfortunately our brave Major [was] made prisoner," the Governor and Council of Fort St. David state, "We have since received a letter from the Major, who says he received no hurt in the action, and that they meet with extream good treatment." [2] In their next letter mention is made of their attempt to exchange him. But Dupleix was "very ready to exchange all but Major Lawrance, as he is pretty well acquainted with the use that gentleman is of to us; but as the General has returned him for answer that unless he is exchanged none of the rest shall, but be sent to Europe, we hope that may have an effect upon him, and induce him to favour us with the Major again." [3] But Dupleix was too wise to favour them with the major again, and it was owing to his absence and Boscawen's want of knowledge of the art of war that the siege proved so disastrous a failure.

Clive proceeds to relate how an accident caused the French to blow up the fort at Ariancopang:—

"Our operations before Areocopang went on very slowly, and no appearance of its being reduced, when, very fortunately for us, the French Battery by some accident blew up and with it the whole Guard, consisting of 100 Europeans. This had such an Effect that the Enemy to our great Joy and

[1] Orme MSS.: India, I., pp. 111–20. Siege of Pondicherry, 1748, by Lord Clive.
[2] Dispatch from Fort St. David, September 2, 1748 (Madras Records).
[3] Dispatch from Fort St. David, October 17, 1748 (Madras Records).

surprize blew up the Fort of Areacopang themselves the same day, and abandoned it, which we took possession of. In the Undertaking we lost a fortnight of time, which was irrecoverable, and a great many brave Officers and Men, in my Opinion to no purpose, for there was not the least necessity for attacking this place; being 3 miles from Pondicherry we had only to avoid it, and the Enemy as soon as they had seen us marching between them and Pondicherry would immediately have abandoned it, or if they had not, a Detachment of 200 Men, while we were forming the Siege, would have kept open our Communication with Fort St. David and kept the Enemy within the Fort, for it was not capable of holding above 100 men, neither did the Garrison ever consist of more.

"Areacopang being taken we began our march for Pondicherry with great Caution and circumspection, and encamped on the heights about 2 miles from the town, and took possession of Mr. Dupleix's House and Garden and the Village of Wolgary, which consisted of houses built by the French like our Mount houses. In this Camp we were reinforced with 1100 Sailors from the Ships, under the Command of Captn. Lloyd, and about 150 Dutch from Negapatam.

"The same Evening a strong detachment was sent to possess themselves of the French bounds, which was effected with little or no opposition, but so prevailing was the panick amongst the Men that in the night time the advanced Sentries were constantly firing without seeing any body, and very often at one another: this kept the whole detachment in continual alarm the whole night, and I am persuaded the appearance of 50 of the Enemy would have put us all to flight.

"Having made some preparations for the Siege we began it by opening of ground at the distance of about 1500 Yards; in the night time we threw up one Trench in front which contained 100 Men, and another in the rear which we called the Grand Trench, containing 300 men. These Trenches were neither of them compleated, being without Epaulements, and the lesser Trench had many Hutts in front at the distance of about 10 yards, which we could not level or destroy in the day time without being exposed to the fire from the Town. At about one o'Clock we could perceive the Enemy advancing with a large body of men and field-pieces to drive us out of the Trenches; notice was immediately sent to the General, but before Succours came the sally was decided. Paradis who commanded, ordered the French Grenadier Company and some Seapoys to attack the lesser Trench, whilst he with the main Body advanced to attack the large one. Fortunately for us, whilst he was advancing with his Field pieces to enfilade the Grand Trench, he was mortally wounded in the head by a Random Shot; this put an end to the Design, and the Detachment retreated back to the Town unobserved by the French Grenadier Company and Seapoys, who according to Orders attacked the Front Trench, where Captn. Brown, who commanded, was mortally wounded, and his Platoon fled and abandoned the Trenches, as did the Platoon belonging to Ensign Greenville, so that there remained only one Platoon consisting of about 30 Men belonging to the Independants, with Ensign Clive. The French Grenadier Company could approach under cover of the huts within 10 yards of the Trench, which they did, and fired upon the Men in the Trenches for about 3 or 4 Minutes, when they attempted to force the Trench, but were received with such a heavy fire from Ensign Clive's Platoon that they immediately went to the right about. In this Affair Captain Le Roche and 27 French were killed upon the Spot; of Ensign Clive's Platoon, 8 Men were shot through the head." [1]

An English officer who was present at the siege remarks in his journal that Clive on this occasion "by his gallant conduct gave the first prognostic of that high military spirit which was the spring of his future actions." [2] But the valour of veterans instead of the rawest of recruits would not have counteracted the extraordinary series of blunders made by those who guided the operations. Clive criticises them with clear touch: [3]

[1] Orme MSS.: India, Vol. I., pp. 115–17.
[2] "Asiatic Annual Register," 1802, p. 40.
[3] Orme MSS.: India, Vol. I., pp. 117–20.

"The disappointment of the Enemy in this Sally, together with the loss of Paradis, dispirited the Garrison in such a manner that it was some time before they recovered themselves. In the mean time we continued carrying on our approaches, very ignorantly and very slowly; a Battery of 3 Pieces of Cannon was erected by the Train at the distance of about 1200 Yards, to cover our Trenches and check the Enemy in their future Sallies, but they never made another upon our Trenches, tho' they had many Opportunities given them from the heavy Rains which had fallen in the Night time and destroyed all our Ammunition.

"After some Weeks hard labour we carried on our Approaches to the distance of about 850 yards, tho' the Engineer assured the General we were within 500 yards. Here we began to erect our Batteries in Breach, and here in fact we were much too far from even destroying the Defences; after several days Labour we finished one Battery of Eight 24-Pounders and one of four 24-Pounders, besides one or two Mortar Batteries. From these Batteries we began to play upon the Town, and attempted to make a Breach in the Courtain at the distance of 850 yards, without even destroying the least of the Enemies Defences. In this useless work we continued for several days, one half of our Cannon dismounted, and our Batteries torn to Pieces every day by the superior fire of the Enemy. In short, the Enemy increased their fire every day and ours diminished every day, until at last the Enemy had 37 Pieces of heavy Cannon playing upon our Batteries, and we not more than 5 or 6 upon theirs. To have seen a Plan of this Siege an Experienced Officer would have thought the Besiegers were the Besieged, so much were we beset by the Enemies Batteries without the Walls of the Town.

"In short the General, finding he had been deceived by the Engineers, and that the Monsoon was too far advanced to make an Attempt in another Place, came to a resolution of withdrawing the Cannon, burning the Batteries, and raising the Siege, which he accordingly put in Execution without any Opposition from the Enemy, and arrived at St. Davids after having first destroyed the fortifications of Areacopang. In this expedition we lost between 5 and 600 Men by Death and Sickness.

" During the Siege we had several skirmishes to the Northward of the Town, in escorting our military Stores, in most of which we were unsuccessful, particularly in one when they sallied from the Town, defeated the Escort, and took two of our 24-Pounders, Transports and all, and carried them in Triumph to Pondicherry before our Forces who were in the Trenches. A Detachment from the Camp was sent to intercept them, but they met with so warm a fire from the Enemy, who lay concealed in a Wood, that they were oblidged to retire with considerable loss.

" Reasons without number may be assigned for our ill Success against Pondicherry. In the first place, the Engineers made a very injudicious choice, for they pitched upon a Spot of ground fraught with every disadvantage which could attend a Siege ; by being to the Westward we could receive no advantage from our ships, but were oblidged to send strong Parties every day the distance of 7 Miles to Escort all our military Stores, while the French had not half that Distance to march to intercept them. Our communication with the Sea and with the Ships was by this means continually interrupted, and our Numbers for the attack of the Place greatly lessened by the men which were constantly employed upon this service. I need not represent the many ill consequences besides the loss of time which must attend transporting such an infinite quantity of Stores 7 Miles. Had we opened ground to the Northward, or even to the Southward, all these Inconveniences had been avoided, all our Stores would have been at hand and could have been landed and made use of in half the time, several hundreds of Men could have been spared for the Siege which were employed to guard the Stores, besides the ground where we carried on our approaches was so low in itself that the Trenches were quickly filled with water, and by the time we had finished our Batteries the French let out such a quantity of pent-up Water from the Paddy Field that a great part of the ground between the Front of our Batteries and the Town was overflowed, so that it was impossible for us to carry on our approaches any further in that Place.

"We ought to have encamped on the Northwest of the Town, and opened ground, if possible, within 6 or 700 yards of the Walls. Our first Batteries should have been so constructed as to have ruined all the Defences which could have annoyed our Batteries or have obstructed the carrying on of our approaches. The Defences once destroyed, we might have continued our approaches to within 2 or 300 yards, where we might (as there was no Glacis) have erected other Batteries for Battering in Breach, [and] during this time have advanced near enough to fill the Ditch; then it would have been soon decided whether the Place could be taken or not. None of these Steps were taken by us, for which reason we could not have succeeded, without the Enemy, more ignorant than ourselves, had been frightened into a Surrender at our appearance. It is esteemed next to impossible to master a place till the fire of the Besiegers becomes superior to the fire of the Besieged; the contrary being our case, we could not succeed, and this the Engineer as well as every Officer ought to have known if they had known ought of the Matter. Brohier, who saw the French return, informed me the Garrison of Pondicherry consisted of about 1400 Europeans and 1500 Blacks."

Clive's estimate of the loss sustained by the English at the siege of Pondicherry does not tally with the figures given by an English officer. He writes: [1]

"On a review of the army it was found, that during the siege there had perished in action and by sickness 757 soldiers, forty-three artillery men, and 265 seamen, in all 1065 Europeans: of the sepoys very few were killed, for they had only been employed to guard the skirts of the camp, and being altogether undisciplined, generally took flight at the approach of danger. The French garrison, commanded by M. Dupleix (a man justly distinguished for his spirit and sagacity), consisted of 1800 Europeans and 3000 sepoys, of which 200 Europeans and about fifty sepoys were killed."

[1] "Asiatic Annual Register," 1802, pp. 41–2.

Among those killed on the English side was John Hallyburton, who had specially devoted himself to converting the peons into disciplined soldiers. But he did not fall in fair fight. The Governor and Council wrote to the Court:

"We have also been so unfortunate as to loose Mr. John Hallyburton to whom, as we before acquainted your Honours, we had given a Commission to be Lieutenant of the Troop of Horse, and of which he was very deserving, for he took infinite trouble in disciplining the Troop and shewed himself very active in the field. It was by one of our own Sepoys that he had the misfortune to be killed, who shot him upon his reprimanding him for some offence, of which the poor Gentleman died the next day, And the Villain did not live so long, for his Comrades that stood by him cut him to picess (*sic*) immediately." [1]

The defence of Pondicherry reflects equal honour on the courage of the garrison and on the conduct of their governor. When Paradis was mortally wounded the details of the defence fell entirely on Dupleix. Then, as he wrote, the study of mathematics and especially of fortification, which his father had impressed upon him, became of great assistance to him. He showed his skill in strengthening the weak places and in repairing the ravages to the works. Every day, regardless of the fire from the trenches, Dupleix, accompanied by his wife, walked on the summit of the ramparts giving orders to the officers and encouraging the French soldiers by his presence. Macaulay states [2] that Dupleix "was not qualified to direct in person military operations. He had not been bred a soldier, and had no inclination to become one. His enemies accused him of personal cowardice; and he defended himself in a strain worthy of Captain Bobadil. He kept away from shot, he said, because silence and tranquillity were propitious to his genius, and he found it difficult to pursue his meditations amidst the noise of fire-arms." The basis for the statement appears to be a note in Mill's "History," which states:

"The memoir drawn up by the French East India Company, in answer to Dupleix, alleges more than once that Dupleix was defective in personal courage; and says he apologized for the care with which

[1] Dispatch from Fort St. David, September 2, 1748 (Madras Records).
[2] "Essay on Clive" ("Essays," Vol. III., p. 135).

he kept at a distance from shot, by acknowledging 'que le bruit des armes suspendoit ses réflexions, et que le calme seul convenoit à son génie.'"[1]

The "memoir, drawn up by the French East India Company," is merely the testimony of the Company which, as Mill himself states, "ruined in the space of a few years the only eminent men she had placed at the head of her affairs in India—Labourdonnais, Dupleix and Lally." On Monday, September 10, Ranga Pillai writes:[2]

"This morning at half past seven o'clock, while the Governor was inspecting the battery on the sea shore a bomb fell near him . . . . thanks to God, it did not burst but buried itself in the earth. The Governor immediately returned to the citadel . . ."

Dupleix was forty-four years of age when he married the widow of M. Vincens, an intimate friend who had been his colleague in the Pondicherry Council. Her father was a Frenchman, by name Albert, who had passed his life in India, and her mother was Elizabeth de Castro, the daughter of Thomas Lopes de Castro, who had married a native woman.[3] As the wife of Vincens, Mme. Dupleix had been distinguished for her beauty, her ready wit and her keen interest in affairs. She was the mother of eleven children, five of whom were alive when she was left a widow. Dupleix invited her to come to Bengal in order that he might act as guardian to the children of his old friend, and he took the most effectual step for carrying out his intention. He married their mother on April 17, 1741, the year he was appointed Governor of Pondicherry. The following year was born the only child of the marriage—a son who died the day of his birth, October 10, 1742. Ranga Pillai writes:[4]

[1] Mill: "History of British India (1840)," Vol. III., p. 83.
[2] *See* Vinson: "Les Français dans l'Inde," p. 216.
[3] The grandmother of Mme. Dupleix was a native woman (see below).—Eugène Guerrin: "Dupleix d'après des Documents inédits."

Thomas Lopes de Castro = a native
|
Jacques-Theodore Albert = Elizabeth Rose de C.
|
Dupleix = Jeanne = M. Vincens
| |
(son) 11 children

[4] "Ranga Pillai's Diary," Vol. I., p. 201.

"About half past 12 this afternoon, the Governor, M. Dupleix, was blessed with a son. As soon as he was born, each ship in the roads fired a salute of twenty-one guns and the church bells rang peals for half an Indian hour. But the life of the infant was limited to this period, and his soul then retired to the feet of God."

Mme. Dupleix was well qualified to be the consort of Dupleix. She was endowed, as Stringer Lawrence states, "with as much spirit, art and pride as himself." Born and educated in Pondicherry, she was well skilled in the vernacular languages and conducted her husband's negotiations with the native princes. She had Eastern blood in her veins and was Oriental in her tastes and feelings. Ranga Pillai lays bare her political machinations, her money-lending transactions, her bribery, her corruption. During the siege, however, she proved herself to be a woman of virile energy and determination. She not only encouraged by her firm attitude the French ladies, whose privations she shared, but revived the drooping courage of the native inhabitants. She took an important part in the councils of the defence. It was she who pointed out to Dupleix and Paradis, while they were on the summit of a bastion, the plan of the sortie which cost Paradis his life. Fifteen days later she ordered, on her own authority, a company of sepoys and peons to make a sortie. As an active instrument in the defence, to her must be given with good reason some of the credit for its complete success. Dupleix and the French garrison had every right to be proud of their victory, and the day the siege was raised was a day of joy.

So ended the first siege of Pondicherry. The failure to reduce the city gave Clive, a young subaltern, his first insight into the practical difficulties of war. He had seen in the trenches how easily panics may be generated, he had marked the fatal weakness inherent in half-trained troops and he had realised the advantage of a vigorous attack. He had learnt the value of war as a school of character. "Few men," says Wolfe, to whom Clive may be aptly compared, "are acquainted with the degrees of their own courage till danger has proved them." Danger had proved that Clive possessed in the highest degree physical courage and at critical moments self-control absolute and judgment clear and prompt. That a young lad, who had recently been a civilian, should display these high military qualities aroused the envy of some of his comrades. Malicious anecdotes were spread, as they always will be spread about anyone who raises himself in a slight degree above his fellows. They reached the ears of Clive; he traced them to their chief source and took decisive action. At a Consultation, held February 28, 1749,[1] at which Charles Floyer, President and Governor, and six Councillors, including Stringer Lawrence, were present, the following letter from Robert Clive was read:—

To—THE HON'BLE CHARLES FLOYER, ESQ., *President & Governour, &ca Council of Fort St. David.*

HON'BLE SIR & SIRS,—I have been informed that the Reverend Mr. Fordyce some days ago preferr'd a Complaint against me to your Honour, &ca., this therefore is to request that your Honour, &ca., will be pleased to examine into the Cause of the Said Complaint for the Justification of

Your most obedt. humble Servant,
Signed ROBERT CLIVE.

FORT,
28*th February* 1748–9.

The Secretary was ordered "to Summons the Reverend Mr. Fordyce to attend on Friday next at 9 o'Clock in the Forenoon, when its agreed to hold a Consultation to examine into this Affair, and that he brings with him such Persons as he thinks necessary to prove what he has to Alledge against Mr. Clive who is also ordered to give his attendance at that time." On Friday, March 3, the Council again met, and the following letter from the Reverend Mr. Fordyce was read:—

To—THE HON'BLE CHARLES FLOYER, ESQR., *President & Governour of Fort St. David, &ca., Council.*

SIRS,—I have received Mr. Bourchier's Letter of yesterday's date signifying your direction that I should attend you next Friday to prove my Allegation against Mr. Robert Clive for Assaulting me, and in answer thereto, I beg leave to acquaint you that it never was nor is my Intention to give you any trouble in that affair, having

[1] "Consultations at Fort St. David, 1749" (Madras Records).

only mentioned it to the Governour and Major Lawrance, as I then thought and do now that their knowing of it might be somewhat Conducive to favour a further Prosecution of Mr. Clive and his accomplices, since I apprehend there is not a proper Court of Judicature in these parts, wherein to try it, and as I conceive that no part of the Laws of England can justify Mr. Robert Clive or any other person in assaulting a Laick much less a Clergyman. However as it is your orders I shall attend at the Appointed Time, who am with Respect, Sirs,

Your most obedient & most
Humble Servant,
Signed FRAN. FORDYCE.

CUDDALORE,
1*st March* 1748–9

Mr. Fordyce being then called before the Board, he handed to the Secretary a paper forbidding

"this Cause to be heard or try'd Directly or Indirectly before the Honourable The Governour and Council of Fort St. David for special reasons I need not name they being well known."

After the protest was read,

"The Board having directed it to be enter'd and an attested Copy to be delivered to Mr. Fordyce, then asked him if he disputed their Authority, to which he gave them no direct answer, but being ask'd the same a second time, he rudely replied he would answer no Questions, and so left the room abruptly, which so extraordinary Behaviour being taken into consideration, the Gentlemen are Unanimously of Opinion, that as it is Evident he disputes their Authority, and for his Insolent Behaviour, he is no longer worthy to be entertained in the Service of the Hon'ble Company, from which Its agreed he be dismiss'd and the Secretary is ordered to acquaint him therewith, and that his allowances will cease from this day."

The Board then

"directed Mr. Clive to be call'd in, as also Messrs. Dalton and Worth, whom Mr. Fordyce in his protest accuses of being his accomplices, and the said protest being read to them, Mr. Clive is desired to acquaint the Board with the particulars of the Affair, when he replied as follows :—

"That being at Dinner with Messrs. Dalton & Worth on or about the 16th day of February at Bandipollam, they told him Mr. Fordyce had said to a Gentleman in publick Compy. that he was a Scoundrel and a Coward, and that he had shook his Cane over him in the presence of Mr. Levy Moses. Mr. Clive further says that some time before this he had been inform'd by Capt. Cope that Mr. Fordyce did in Conversation with him threaten to break every Bone in his Skin, and he says that these repeated abuses so irritated him that he could not forbear on meeting Mr. Fordyce in Cuddalore to reproach him with his Behaviour which he told him was so injurious he could bear it no longer, and therefore struck him two or three times with his Cane, which at last Mr. Fordyce returned and then clos'd in with him, but that they were presently parted by Captain Lucas who happen'd to be by. Mr. Clive further observes that he is not the only person who has been abus'd and Calumniated by Mr. Fordyce, who had also aspers'd the Character of Mr. Joseph Fowke, by saying he was a dark designing Villain, that he would slit his Nose the first time he met him, and that he had knock'd him under the Table at the Governours. He further says Mr. Fordyce had told Capt. Dalton at Mr. Belsches's that if every body would discourse the Governour in the manner he had done, it would alter affairs greatly, and that he had talk'd to him till he made him quake or shake in his Shoes, or words to that effect. Mr. Clive also says Mr. Lindsay told him he had heard Mr. Fordyce say that Mr. Bulkley was a Scoundrel and a Coward, and that he had shook his Cane at him as he had done at Mr. Clive. Mr. Clive further says he threaten'd to thrash Mr. Bouchier, and that he had declar'd to several people, he had taken away Gentlemen's Swords before now, and would pull off his Canonicals at any time to do himself Justice ; and lastly Mr. Clive says Mr. Lennox told him that Mr. Fordyce was generally shunn'd & detested both at St. Helena and the West Coast on account of his medling Disposition wch render'd him disagreeable and obnoxious to every one.

" Signed ROBERT CLIVE."

The Governor in Council in their dispatch referring to this matter wrote, on November 22, 1749:

" A complaint having been brought before us by Mr. Francis Fordyce for an Assault that was made on him by Mr. Robert Clive, due Enquiry was made by us into the same. In the Course of which it appearing that Mr. Fordyce had given great Provocation for such Proceeding, by having frequently scandalized his Character in a most unsufferable manner, and being further acquainted that he had at several times taken great Libertys in his Conversation in making use of many unbecoming Reflections on the President and all the Members of the Board, In Consequence of this his Aggressions and Disrespect together with the many Instances we have had of his Insolent and Medling disposition, We came to a Resolution of suspending him your Honours Service, And besides the reasons already given for our so doing, We might still add that He was in General remark'd to be extreamly Negligent and remiss in the several Duties of his Functions, particularly in the Burial of the Soldiers and Seamen, which part of his Office he scarce ever attended, notwithstanding he had been twice or thrice Rebuk'd by the President for not doing, and which neglect had at length began to Create great Discontent in our Military. We therefore presume that upon a due consideration of all these Circumstances, your honours will concur with us in the measures We have taken herein. In which dependance we shall only add, as It is not to be doubted but Mr. Fordyce will set forth his own Story to your Honours, and least the same should be to Mr. Clive's Prejudice, We think it not improper to assure you that he is Generally Esteem'd a very quiet Person, and no ways guilty of Disturbances." [1]

Mill, in his sketch of Clive, states: "His turbulence, though he was not ill-natured, engaged him in quarrels with his equals." [2] It appears, however, according to the evidence of his superiors who were in constant contact with him, that he "was generally esteemed a very quiet person and no ways guilty of disturbances." Clive was stern and imperious, but "turbulent" is the last word that with justice could be applied to him. No man had a greater love of order and of discipline.

Dupleix "sent letters to all the princes of Coromandel, and even to the great Mogul himself, acquainting them that he had repulsed the most formidable attack that had ever been made in India; and he received from them the highest compliments on his own prowess and on the military character of his nation: this indeed was now regarded throughout Indostan as greatly superior to that of the English." [3] Dupleix at once determined to act on the offensive. He was busy making preparations for another attack on Fort St. David when an official intimation from Paris reached him, which disconcerted for the moment his plan of expelling the English from Southern India and converting the Deccan into a French dependency—a cessation of arms between Great Britain and France had been proclaimed in the preceding April.

[1] The foregoing papers were discovered by me in the Madras Archives and a brief extract given from them in a Memorandum printed in 1890. No mention of this quarrel is made by biographers or historians. It is, however, possible that the account of a fracas between Clive and an officer given in the "Biographia Britannica" is a distorted version of this affair.

[2] Mill: "History of British India," Vol. IV., p. 116.

[3] Orme, Vol. I., p. 110.

CHAPTER V

1748–9: THE TANJORE EXPEDITION

In December, 1748, hostilities ceased between the English and French in India. A few months later, however, circumstances occurred which led to Clive being again employed on active service. South of Cuddalore, separated from it by the River Coleroon, lies the province of Tanjore, which extends seventy miles along the sea and sixty inland.[1] It is not what Burke called it, "the most exquisite spot on earth," but its ancient reservoirs and canals have so husbanded its many streams and fructified the whole country that it has become a well-watered garden, vying in fertility with the delta of the Nile. Two or three years after the English had obtained their first settlement at Madras, Shahaji, the father of Shivaji the founder of the great Mahratta Confederacy, was appointed by the independent Mohammedan king of Bejāpur to administer his possessions in the Carnatic. It was the Mohammedan custom to bestow on men for distinguished service to the Crown a jaghire (*jagir*), or hereditary assignment of land and of its rent as an annuity, and a large territory which included part of Mysore was conferred on Shahaji as a jaghire. He introduced into his new domain a large number of Mahratta Brahmans for establishing a new system of revenue administration and for suppressing the universal anarchy which prevailed. From that day the Mahratta Brahman has played an important part in the politics and administration of Southern India. His influence at the time for evil or for good was great. Shahaji's aim was to establish an independent Mahratta Kingdom in

[1] The present Collectorate of Tanjore.

Southern India. But it was his son Venkoji (or Eccojee), half brother of Shivaji, who carried out his design.

About 1675 the Naicks or Hindu Rajahs of Tanjore and Trichinopoly, according to the normal course of things in India, began to wage war one against another. The Rajah of Tanjore, being hard pressed by the superior force of his neighbour, sent envoys to the king of Bejāpur to solicit protection and aid for his vassal. The monarch sent two Mohammedan agents with an order addressed to Venkoji at Bangalore, directing him to march for the relief of Tanjore. Venkoji set forth on the expedition, and having raised the siege of Tanjore, "made the customary demand of the expenses of the expedition; the account of which, as usual, doubled the actual amount."[1] This the Tanjore Rajah was unable or unwilling to satisfy.

It was Shahaji, the grandson of the founder of the Mahratta dynasty of Tanjore, who, not long after the return of the troops from Pondicherry, asked the Government of Cuddalore to assist him in regaining the Tanjore throne from which he had been expelled by his natural brother Pratap Singh. Pratap Singh had before and during the siege of Pondicherry proved himself to be an active ally of the French and an active enemy to the English. Boscawen was burning to punish him and wipe out the disgrace of the failure of the siege of Pondicherry. He was a usurper. The cause of Shahaji seemed just, and it was asserted with great confidence that he should no sooner appear in the kingdom, supported even by a moderate force, than his standard would be joined by numbers, and his title acknowledged by thousands. It was stipulated that he would give the Company the Fort of Devicotah at the mouth of the River Coleroon.

"The Fort of Devi-Cotah is," says Orme, "situated in a populous country, in which manufactures of linnen proper for the company's trade are fabricated; and the territory in its neighbourhood is the most fertile part of the coast of Coromandel. On this coast, from Masulipatnam to Cape Comorin, there is no port capable of receiving

[1] Wilks: "Historical Sketches of the South of India in an attempt to trace the History of Mysoor," Vol. I., p. 79 (ed. 1810).

a ship of 300 tons burden ; which defect subjects the navigation of these parts to great risques at particular seasons. The mouth of the river Coleroon, near Devi-Cotah, is indeed generally obstructed by sands, but the channel within the bar is deep enough to receive ships of the largest burden ; and it was thought that the bar itself might with some labour and expence be removed : if this should be effected, the coast of Coromandel would be no longer without a harbour, and the greatest advantages would accrue to the European nation which should obtain the exclusive possession of it." [1]

Shahaji also agreed to pay all the expenses of the campaign. The Governor and Council of Fort St. David accepted these terms, and in the early days of April, 1749, they sent a small force under the command of Captain Cope to replace him on the throne of Tanjore.

Clive, who had been appointed on March 1, 1749, to be Lieutenant of a Company of Foot in the Honourable Company's Service at Fort St. David, took part in our first frontier expedition as the commander of a company. The story of "this fruitless expedition" is told in a memorandum which Clive wrote for Orme : [2]

" Early in the beginning of the year 1749, a young man who had resided some time at Fort St. David, under the English protection, asserted that he was the lawful heir to the Crown of Tanjore, and accompanied this assertion with a very probable story, which being laid before Admiral Boscawen and Governor Floyer they resolved to support him with a military force to recover his right, and accordingly in the month of March, 4 Companies of Europeans, a detachment of Artillery with 4 field pieces, some cohorns and 1000 sepoys were ordered upon this service under the command of Captain Cope. The young Pretender accompanied this little army, with great promises that as soon as it entered the Tanjore Country it would be joined by great numbers and his Right to the Throne acknowledged by thousands. The forces being encamped on the banks of Porto Novo River, about 12 miles inland of that Town, we were overtaken with such a dreadful Storm, which began at about 8 o'Clock in the Evening and continued till 4 o'Clock the next morning, as entirely disconcerted the expedition for some days. The tents were all blown to rags, many of the Tumbrills were overset by the violence of the storm, and the military stores in general much damaged ; this obliged the Commanding Officer to make the best of his way with the Troops to Porto Novo. To remember (*sic*) the ravages of the storm at this

[1] Orme, Vol. I., p. 116.
[2] Orme MSS. : India, Vol. I., pp. 219 *sqq.*

place we received the melancholy News of the loss of the *Namur*, *Pembroke*, and *Apollo*. A few days having put the army in condition, it resumed its march for Tanjore, passed Chellambrum, and arrived on the Banks of the Calderoon, where the Commanding Officer encamped and entrenched waiting for Intelligence from the opposite shore, which not being satisfactory, and there not being the least appearance of our being joined by any of the forces on the opposite shore, numbers of which we saw constantly in motion on the banks of the river, the Commanding Officer did not think himself strong enough, and wrote for another reinforcement which was accordingly sent him. Being joined by this reinforcement we crossed the River in sight of the Enemy without much opposition; the object of this first Expedition was the taking of the Fort of Devi Cotah, in order to make it a Place of Arms for carrying on our future designs against the Capital of Tanjore. As we entered further into the Country our difficulties seemed to increase, the Country became very woody and the Enemy annoyed us very much from the Bushes; the Enemy's army now appeared in full view in our Rear and Flank upon the Plains, being very numerous; this being our first Expedition the Men and Officers were a little staggered at the appearance of so great an Army; however, the brisk firing of our field Pieces kept them at some distance and gave us time to recover that confusion which we were thrown in by our situation. We then changed our situation and drew up on the Banks of the river; our flanks were covered by our Field pieces and our Rear by the river. The Commanding Officer then held a Council of War whether to proceed or wait for better advice, when he received orders from Mr. Boscawen to continue his march and attempt the Fort of Dave Cotah, let what would be the Consequence. Fortunately for us we discovered a Road by the river side which at the same [time] that it covered our left flank disengaged us from a very close and woody Country through which we must have marched 10 or 12 miles back, frightened and harrassed most of the way. We met little or no interruption on this road and encamped near a Pagoda at the distance of about a mile from Dave Cotah. Here we expected to have heard of the ships with more forces and military stores, in order for the attack of the Fort, but such was the singularity of our condition, and so totally ignorant were we of the Country, that we could not receive the least intelligence of them or they of us, altho they were at Anchor near the mouth of the river at the distance of about 4 miles from us. We had not three days Provisions with us, all supplies by land being cut off by the Enemy, and by sea we could not receive any for the Reasons recited above: our Artillery were only Field pieces, so that we could only try the Effect of a few Cohorn Shells, which we threw into the Fort all night, which had no manner of Effect. It was proposed to advance the field Pieces and endeavour to batter the Gates, but this was disapproved of by the Commanding Officer as attended with too much risque, and two days after we came before the place the

Forces began their march back again, which the Enemy being apprized of, took possession of some woods which lay upon our flank, and fired upon us with artillery and musquetry; this obliged us to advance some platoons of Europeans to dislodge them, or keep them at a distance, that the army might pass a Nullah which, tho not breast high when we passed it, was now by the rising of the Tide above our heads. This inconveniency was not foreseen till the Cooleys with the Baggage had entered into the Nullah, and those in front being prest upon by those in the rear and fired upon by the Enemy from the adjacent Wood near 400 of these poor wretches were drowned and with them we lost great part of the Baggage. The Nulla falling, we passed over without further interruption from the Enemy and continued our retreat all that day, passed the Calderoon in the afternoon, and arrived at Chellambram much fatigued late at night. The next day we continued our march to Fort St. David, and thus ended this fruitless Expedition by Land."

Clive does not mention that it was he who urged blowing the gates open and delivering an assault. The storm he mentions was the violent hurricane in which the *Namur* of 74 guns (the admiral's flag-ship), the *Pembroke*, and the *Apollo*, hospital ship, together with the greater part of their crews, were unhappily lost. It was on April 13 that the hurricane arose.

"When the gale commenced, the *Namur* was at anchor in the road of Fort St. David. The admiral was on shore, but the officer in command of the ship immediately cut the cables and put to sea, though the impetuosity of the tempest and the uncommon height of the sea were such, as to offer little prospect of being able to save the ship; and, after struggling for some hours in the endeavour to get off the coast, she foundered in nine fathom water, Captain Marshall, Mr. Gilchrist the third lieutenant, the captain of marines, the surgeon, purser, chaplain, boatswain, and about forty seamen, being all that were saved out of six hundred." [1]

Boscawen was not inclined to sit down in patience under a second failure. He at once began to make preparations for another expedition, and the whole of the Company's troops under the command of Major Lawrence, who had again assumed charge of the garrison, were ordered for this service. [2]

[1] "Asiatic Annual Register," 1802, p. 42.

[2] "The day after the receipt of the News of the Cessation of Arms, &c. and His Majesty's Proclamation thereof, General Boscawen sent an account of the same to Mr. Dupleix, whereupon Major Lawrance and Captain Bruce that was taken Prisoner with him were permitted to give their Parole, and

The operations under Lawrence were carried on with vigour. But Clive, who volunteered to lead the attack at the storm of Devicotah, must be allowed to tell the tale:

" It was now determined to attempt the reduction of Dave-Cotah by Sea, as it was found inpracticable to attempt it by land on account of its Situation. Accordingly, all the Company's Forces under the command of Major Lawrence, amounting to 800 Europeans, Artillery included, and about 1,500 Sepoys, embarked on board the men-of-war and Company's ships. The Sepoys were mostly in boats. Captain Paulet of the *Exeter* commanded the Expedition. Having landed all our forces near the mouth of the River without seeing any of the Enemy, we immediately encamped, and Officers sent to reconnoitre reported that we were upon an Island, that a branch of the river Calderoon, being about 300 yards broad and very deep, separated us from the Fort of Dave Cotah. The heavy artillery being landed, it was agreed to erect a Battery of four 24-pounders to batter in and breach the Fort, which was at the distance of about 400 yards; accordingly a Battery was erected, and after three days a practicable Breach was made, which the Enemy did not attempt to repair, but threw up a Trench from one angle of the Fort quite across the Breach, which trench they filled with musquetry and gingalls. The difficulty now was to cross the River, when John Moor, the King's Carpenter, offered to make a stage which should carry over 400 men at a time: this stage being made was brought up the river in a very dark night, and a rope was carried across the River and fastened to some trees within 50 Yards of the Enemy, who were in possession of the opposite ground which was very woody; the rope was sunk in the water that the Enemy might not discover it. Every thing being ready for the attack, the first division of 400 men passed the river at 2 o'Clock in the Afternoon, and by 4 the whole Army was landed on the opposite shore: this was not effected without considerable loss from the enemy, who fired briskly from the Trenches and the walls of the Fort all the time. It was agreed [1] should be first stormed: for this service Lieut. Clive offered himself voluntarily; a platoon of 30 Europeans and 700 Sepoys were allotted him for this attempt, and as soon as the trenches were carried, the grenadiers and the rest of the Europeans were to attack the Breach. Lieut. Clive, at the head of his party, advanced, being followed by the rest of his Army, till he came to a Nullah which was very deep and muddy: this Nullah he passed with much difficulty, having lost 4 or 5 of his Platoon in passing it,

come hither, and upon the Arrival of the *Favourete* with them the 7th. instant, who brought a Confirmation of the same, all the Prisoners they had there belonging to us were sent hither, and the Major has again taken Charge of the Garrison."—Dispatch from Fort St. David, January 16, 1748–9 (Madras Records.)

[1] Some words seem to be omitted here.

for the Enemy's trench was not at the distance of more than 50 yards, and he was fired upon the whole time. As soon as he had formed his Platoon, and the Sepoys who were to support him and cover his Rear had begun to pass the Nullah, he marched up briskly close upon one of the flanks of the intrenchments, and ordered the front ranks to kneel in order to give his fire; but before he could effect this, a body of the enemies Cavalry having turned the corner, and the Sepoys not doing their duty in covering his Rear, all his platoon, excepting 3 or 4 men in front, were in an instant cut to pieces by the Horse. Lieut. Clive was just upon the point of falling a Sacrifice to one of the Horsemen, who had his sword uplifted to cut him down, which he avoided by slipping on one side, and seeing himself abandoned by the Sepoys and all his platoon cut off, he had nothing for it but flight to the Nullah, where he found the rest of the forces drawn up, waiting the Event of his attack of the trenches. Upon this disaster, a Platoon of Grenadiers were ordered to attack the trenches, supported by the whole army, and the men being seconded, the trenches were easily carried: the breach was then mounted, and no resistance made, the Fort being abandoned. In marching to the breach, a body of Cavalry attempted to make a Charge, but were received with so warm a fire by 1 or 2 Platoons that they were obliged to retire with very considerable loss.

"As soon as we were in possession of the Ramparts, we could perceive the Enemy's army retreating over the plains which was very numerous, being not less than 15 or 20,000 men, but their chief strength being Cavalry, they did not chuse to shut themselves within the walls of a fortification.

"The Breach being repaired, Major Lawrence detached a Party under the command of Capt. Cope to take possession of Acheveram Pagoda, a fortified place at the distance of 5 miles from the Pagoda [*sic*], which he easily effected: here the Enemy attempted out of zeal for their religion what they could not be prevailed upon to do for Pay or from a principle of honour, for as soon as night came they made many desperate attempts to make themselves masters of the Pagoda by scalade and by piling up great bundles of straw against the gate and setting fire to it, in order to burn it down. While this was transacting, the Soldiers opened the wicket of the gate and fired upon the Enemy, and the Serjeants with their halberts tumbled down the straw, notwithstanding which, and a very severe loss sustained, they persevered in their attack, tho' they were always repulsed, until day break, when they retired. Major Lawrence receiving intelligence from Capt. Cope of his condition, immediately marched to his relief with all the forces, but before he could arrive, the Enemy had abandoned the enterprize.

"By this time Admiral Boscawen and Mr. Floyer had sufficient reason to distrust the Pretender to the crown, and to us there was little prospect of success in any future undertaking. They therefore agreed to a Peace with the King of Tanjore upon the following terms:

That the fort of Dave Cotah with as much land as would produce 9,000 [? Rs.] Per Annum should be ceded to the English East India Company for ever, and that the King of Tanjore should defray all the expence of the whole Expedition against him, also that the King of Tanjore should allow the Pretender an Annual Income of R.... Per Annum, and that the English should be accountable for his Person, and that he should never give any more disturbance to the Kingdom. These articles being ratified and fulfilled on the part of the King of Tanjore, Major Lawrence returned to Fort St. David with the army, leaving a sufficient garrison for the defence of the Fort." [1]

The high military qualities, daring, courage, sound judgment and quickness of apprehension which Clive showed at the siege of Pondicherry and the storming of Devicotah won the confidence and friendship of the veteran commander. "This young man's early genius surprised and engaged my attention," wrote Lawrence, "as well before as at the siege of Davecottah, where he behaved in courage and judgment, much beyond what could be expected from his years, and his success afterwards confirmed what I had said to many people concerning him." [2]

[1] Orme MSS.: India, Vol., I. pp. 222–5.
[2] R. O. Cambridge: "Account of the War in India," 1750–60, p. 14.

CHAPTER VI

POLITICAL STATE OF SOUTHERN INDIA

It has often been stated that in supporting the cause of Shahaji the English first set the example of taking part in the quarrels of the native rulers. But the Tanjore intervention was due to the active influence which the French had acquired in that state, and before the Tanjore expedition Dupleix had matured a scheme for establishing by the aid of French arms a ruler dependent on the French connection. It is, however, impossible to form a just or discriminating estimate of the character and measures of Dupleix, or the conduct of the British, without a knowledge of the political state of South India at this time. Without this knowledge the campaigns in which Clive took a leading part cannot be followed with interest and utility.

When the long and splendid reign of Aurangzib, the ablest of the Mogul emperors, was drawing to a close, South India, or The Deccan, came under the Mogul government. Twenty-three years before Clive landed (1721), a Turki nobleman—best known by the title of Nizam-al-Mulk [1] or "regulator of the state," bestowed on him by the Mogul Emperor—assumed the subahdarship or viceroyship of Hyderabad, one of the six *subahs* or provinces into which the Empire had been divided. A man of great ability and greater cunning, a brave and capable soldier, he converted a large territory in Southern Central India into an independent kingdom with Hyderabad as its capital, and his descendants are known as the Nizams of Hyderabad. Each *subah*, or province, was

[1] His name was Chin Kilich Khan. He received the honorary title of Asaf Jah, which according to Mohammedan tradition was the name of the minister of Solomon, and hence he is often called Asaf Jah.

formed of a number of territories varying in size, governed by nawabs or deputies under the subahdar or viceroy, and of native states under rajahs who had been allowed to survive, subject to the payment of tribute to the Emperor, which was collected by the viceroy, or his deputy the nawab. The nawab was appointed by the Emperor, or, in the case of a death vacancy, by the viceroy, but the appointment, it is important to remember, was not valid until it had been confirmed by royal letter and insignia or investiture. The viceroy and the nawab were, so far as the people of Southern India were concerned, foreigners. The mass of the people were Hindus; the small minority who conducted the administration were Moslem, the descendants of the Afghans, Mongols, and Turks who had come to India with every successive wave of Mohammedan conquest. A contemporary native authority states that the government of provinces was now held by nobles of inferior rank, poor and rapacious, who oppressed the people. Contributions were collected in lieu of the regular revenue, and "collectors of the *odious religious capitation* forced millions from the farmers." He adds, "The farmers thus oppressed left off cultivating more ground than would barely subsist them, and in their turns became plunderers for want of employment."[1]

The most important of the principalities under the suzerainty of the Viceroy of Hyderabad was the Carnatic (Black Country) below the Ghauts,[2] a stretch of land between the mountains and the sea which extended from the Kistna to the Coleroon. It was bounded on the north by the province of Orissa and on the south by the Mahratta state of Tanjore and the Hindu kingdom of Trichinopoly. The two chief towns of the Payanghat, or Lower Carnatic, were Arcot and Vellore (*Vêlûr*, javelin town), and when Arcot became the capital the principality became better known as the province of Arcot, and the Nawab of the Carnatic was called Nawab

[1] Wilks: "History of Mysoor," Vol. I., pp. 221–222.

[2] For the boundaries of the true Carnatic, or Karnatika-desa, *see* "Imperial Gazetteer of India," new ed., ix., 301.

of Arcot. In the year 1708 the Viceroy of the Deccan appointed one of his officers, whose name was Saadat Ali Khan, to be the Faujdar, or military commander of the Carnatic. He fixed the seat of his government at Arcot about the year 1716, and he founded the first dynasty of the Nawabs of Arcot. He died in 1732, leaving a will appointing his nephew Dóst Ali to succeed him in his government; but the strong fort and territory of Vellore he bequeathed to Murtaza Ali, married to one of his daughters. Another daughter was married to Husain Dost Khan, known in history by his nickname Chanda Saheb. Soon after the accession of Dóst Ali the Rajah of Trichinopoly died without issue. What followed is a very Eastern tale. The first wife became regent by the help of the confidential minister to the government. The Commander-in-chief supplied another heir, and with the aid of the Rajah of Tanjore he organised so powerful a party that the Rani was driven to solicit the aid of the Nawab of Arcot. Dóst Ali, under the pretext of collecting the revenue, sent a force into the province of Trichinopoly commanded by his eldest son, with Chanda Saheb as his chief civil and military officer. The city of Trichinopoly was well fortified, but the Rani was induced by Chanda Saheb—swearing by "a false oath on a false Koran"[1] that they should be employed only for her protection—to admit some of the Moslem troops within the walls.

Chanda Saheb, master of the capital and the provincial towns, imprisoned the queen and hoisted the flag of Islam. The Hindu kingdom of Trichinopoly was brought under the rule of a Mohammedan power, and Chanda Saheb was appointed its first governor. He was a bold, dashing soldier, who added to the qualities of a warrior a power of political organisation and an infinite capacity for intrigue. High above the intellectual level of the princes of the time, he was acquainted not only with the classical languages of the East but with the French tongue, and had a great admiration for

[1] It was actually a *brick* wrapped round with the same splendid covering in which a Koran is usually enveloped.—Wilks: "Mysoor," Vol. I., p. 250, footnote.

the French nation. In 1739 he took from the Rajah of Tanjore the town of Karikal and the adjacent territory, and handed it over to the French. The following year a host of Mahrattas spread like locusts over the face of the Deccan. By a series of rapid marches they reached the mountain barrier, and, entering through an unfrequented pass the lower Carnatic, took by surprise the Nawab's army and defeated it. Dóst Ali was slain in the battle, and Safdar Ali, who succeeded him, made a treaty with the Mahratta chief that he should evacuate the province on the payment of a large sum of money. There was, however, a second agreement that these freebooters, who lived on the pillage of India, should return to capture Trichinopoly, and retain a large portion of the territory in the possession of Chanda Saheb as the price of his effectual removal.[1] The Mahrattas quitted the province, stating they were going to seek for richer plunder in another quarter of the continent. The two brothers-in-law, seemingly reconciled, went down together to Pondicherry, where they had sent their wives, children and treasure to remain in safety during the war. After a stay of several days Chanda Saheb, leaving the women of his family and one of his sons in the French settlement, proceeded to Trichinopoly. In December the Mahrattas suddenly returned and invested the city. "After a gallant resistance of three months, Chanda Saheb reduced by famine alone surrendered at discretion; and with his eldest son, was sent a prisoner to Satara, now the declared capital of the Mahratta Empire and the prison of its prince, whose authority his minister had usurped."[2] A Mahratta general named Morari Rao was left as governor of the conquered province, which comprised the whole of the lower countries south of the Coleroon.

[1] Wilks: "Mysoor," Vol. I., p. 253.

[2] *Ibid.* From the time of Báláji Bísvanátte Bhatta (1718–1720), a Konkun Brahmin, the Brahmin Peshwa or Chief Minister, became the real head of the Mahratta Confederacy, the Rajahs, the descendants of the great Shivāji being merely nominal rulers living in splendour as state prisoners in Satara. Báláji caused the office to be made hereditary in his family. It was his son Baji Rao Peshwa who made the Mahrattas the greatest power in India. He died in 1740.

During the siege of Trichinopoly the Mahratta commander wrote to Dumas, the Governor of Pondicherry, and demanded the surrender of Chanda Saheb's wife and family and the delivery of the treasure, the jewels, the horses, and the elephants which he had sent to the French settlement. "I send my cavalry," he said, "to whom you can make them over. If you decline to do so, we shall be compelled to force you to it as well as to the payment of tribute which you have kept back for forty years." The demand of the Mahratta chief was an insult to the honour of his nation, and Dumas replied, "The wife of Chanda Saheb is in Pondicherry under the protection of the King of France, my master, and all the French in India would die rather than deliver her to you." On December 24, 1741, two thousand Mahratta horsemen, after having made a march "of 110 miles in a day and a half," appeared before Porto Novo, a town about thirty-two miles south of Pondicherry used as a depot by the Dutch, French, and English. As soon as the inhabitants heard of the approach of the marauders they flocked with their movables into the factory. Those who could not find shelter there took refuge in the boats lying near the river bank. "Every one of these was calculated to hold some forty or fifty persons, but this being a time of peril, between 200 and 300 entered each, so that they grounded and could not be moved." The Mahrattas entering the town from all sides pillaged every house. "Those who remained in their dwellings were beaten, and plundered of everything. Only a cubit length of cloth was given to them to cover their nakedness. Some were forced to hold the horses of their captors, whilst others were made to carry the spoils of their conquerors on their heads."[1] The gates of the factory were burst open and the Mahratta horse rushed into the courtyard. "Every one there was seized and stripped stark naked. Some received sword-cuts, and others were scourged with whips. They were each given two cubits length of cloth, and driven out of the fort."[2] That evening the Mahrattas encamped two miles outside the town. The

[1] "Ranga Pillai's Diary," Vol. I., pp. 142–3.

[2] *Ibid.*, p. 144.

next day they appeared in the neighbourhood of Pondicherry. Dumas had strengthened the fortifications and the Mahrattas soon discovered that any attempt to capture it must fail. Dumas had also on the approach of the Mahratta force imprisoned all the Mahratta merchants who were residing in the town. The freebooters, seeing they had no chance of taking Pondicherry, proceeded in small parties to ravage the country and collect plunder.

"They pillaged the villages," says Ranga Pillai, "violated many women, and committed numerous other outrages." On March 30 a letter from the Mahratta camp announced that Chanda Saheb and his son had surrendered, and were "in honourable custody." "Such was the news of the war contained in the letter which was received by the Governor, and read by him with sorrow." On April 18 some Mahrattas appeared at Ranga Pillai's garden-house with presents from their chief, Raghuji Bhónsla, to Dumas. A large cavalcade was sent out "with two empty palanquins" to convey them to the Governor. As the gifts were being brought into the town in this stately fashion "nine guns were fired from the gate, and there was a further salute of eleven guns when they were set down at the Governor's house."[1] The Mahratta envoy asked for the release of his countrymen, and his request was granted. The resolute action of Dumas greatly increased the prestige of the French among the native princes, and this prestige his successor, Dupleix, inherited.

When his formidable rival had been removed to Satara, Safdar Ali, having sent the women and children of his family to Madras to be protected by the English from any sudden Mahratta raid, proceeded to Arcot and had himself proclaimed Nawab. But he was not strong enough to wield the power which passed into his hands. "The late calamities," says Orme, "left such an impression of terror upon his mind that he did not venture to keep his court in the open and defenceless city of Arcot but took up his residence in Vellore which was well fortified and its citadel built two hundred years ago

[1] "Ranga Pillai's Diary," pp. 150, 162, 165.

by the Morattoes, the strongest in the Carnatic."[1] The citadel had been bequeathed to his cousin and brother-in-law Murtaza Ali,[2] but the government of Vellore was a fief subject to the Nawab of Arcot. Safdar Ali wounded the avarice of his host by demanding that he should pay him a portion of the tribute due to the Mahrattas, and he roused his fierce resentment by threatening in public to remove him from his government.

On October 16 the Company's peons brought the news to Dupleix that on the night of the 13th Safdar Ali had supped in the house of Murtaza Ali at Vellore, "who stabbed him to death when he was in a deep sleep at about 2 in the morning."[3] Next day, the army, who were encamped outside the citadel, threatened to storm it and avenge the murder of the Nawab. But their rage was quickly appeased by a promise that the arrears of pay due to them would be settled by instalments, "and the whole army, officers as well as soldiers, agreed to acknowledge Mortiz-ally Nabob of the Carnatic within two days after the murder of Subder-ally Khan."[4] Murtaza "now pitched his tents without the gates of Vellore, and caused himself to be proclaimed Nabob of the Carnatic. In November he made his entry with pomp into the city of Arcot."[5] The chief men of the province had, however, a contempt for the cowardly assassin, and three months later the army at their instigation mutinied, and Murtaza Ali, disguised in the habits of a woman, "quitted Arcot in the night, in a covered Pallankin, accompanied by several female attendants, and in this equipage gained his fort of Velore without interruption."[6] The young son of Safdar Ali, who was residing with his mother at Madras, was proclaimed Nawab of the Carnatic.

Whilst the Carnatic was being distracted by these dynastic struggles, the Viceroy of the Deccan was at the Imperial Court

[1] Orme, Vol. I., p. 45.

[2] Wilks calls him Murteza Khan; Orme, Mortiz-ally. It should be Murtaza Ali—One with whom God is pleased.

[3] "Ranga Pillai's Diary," Vol. I., p. 202. This account differs from the story given by Orme. His History was published twenty years after the account of the murder was recorded in "Ranga Pillai's Diary." Orme, Vol. I., pp. 47–8.

[4] Orme, Vol. I., p. 49. [5] *Ibid.*, pp. 49–50. [6] *Ibid.*, p. 50.

of Delhi working, as Chief Minister, with a resolute purpose to reform a government which had since the death of Aurangzib (February 21, 1707) fallen rapidly into a state of helplessness and corruption. Nizam-al-Mulk was now stricken in age, and the old warrior in 1738 had allowed the Mahrattas by skilful and rapid evolutions to surround his army, cut off its supplies, and extort from him a convention by which he engaged to procure from the Emperor a cession of the chout (*chauth*) for Malwa and Gujerat. Baji Rao Peshwa took possession of Malwa and divided it between his generals, Ranaji Sindhia and Mulhar Rao; and the dynasties which they founded still rule Malwa as feudatories of the British Empire.

The rise of the Mahrattas was one of the main causes which led to the fall of the Mogul Empire, but it was the Turki freebooter Nadir Kuli (Slave to the Wonderful [1]) who, on assuming the throne of Persia, had taken the title Nadir Shah (the Wonderful King). He crossed the Indus towards the close of 1738, and sacked Delhi in March, 1739. After a stay of two months Nadir Shah went back home, taking with him the wealth which the trade of the world had brought to the Imperial city. Before leaving Delhi he replaced Mohammed Shah, the Emperor, on the throne, after having extracted from him all his provinces west of the Indus. Nadir, with grim irony, informed the Emperor that if he ever were disturbed by intrigues at his court and required his assistance, he could return from Kandahar in forty days. He also sent to the Rajah at Satara, Baji Rao the Peshwa, and other great Hindu chiefs, circular letters bidding them "walk in the path of submission and obedience to our dear brother" and threatening in the event of their rebellion to return and "blot them out of the pages of the book of creation." But the Nadir had struck a fatal blow at the central authority of the empire, and a chaos of devastation, plunder and massacre followed. He also revealed to the free lances of the north that the power of the Great Moguls had vanished.

Asaf Jah, having secured the continuance of power at

[1] Slave to the Divine, "Wonderful" being a title of Divinity.

the Imperial Court by the appointment of his eldest son Ghazi-ud-din to the high office of captain-general of the Mogul army, proceeded in the year 1741 to the Deccan, where his presence was greatly needed owing to the rebellion of his second son Nasir Jang, whom he had left in charge of the province. On July 23, 1742, the Nizam defeated the troops of Nasir at Aurangabad, took him prisoner and had him confined in a hill fort as a precautionary measure. He then proceeded to Hyderabad and thence to the southern part of the province. He reached Arcot with an army of eighty thousand men in March, 1743 (two months before Clive sailed from England), and he who was accustomed to the Mogul government was surprised at the anarchy which prevailed. Every petty governor and the officer of every mud fort or town affected the designation of Nawab as a step towards independence. At the first levée the Viceroy was so enraged at this assumption of rank that he exclaimed to his guards, "I have seen this day eighteen nawabs, in a country where there should be but one; scourge the next fellow who comes with that title."

Among those who came to do homage was Mohammed Said, the young son of Safdar Ali, who had been proclaimed Nawab of the Carnatic and was residing at Wandiwash for safety. Nizam-al-Mulk refused him permission to return, and ordered some of his own officers to take charge of his person, directing them to treat him with lenity and respect, but in view of his extreme youth he appointed the general of his army Nawab of Arcot and all its dependencies. Nizam-al-Mulk, after settling the administration of the Carnatic, returned with his army and its commander, the newly appointed Nawab of the Carnatic, to Hyderabad. The morning this officer was about to return to Arcot he was found dead in his bed, poisoned, it was supposed, at the instigation of Anwar-ud-din, a native of Hindostan, who was appointed to succeed him as administrator of the Carnatic during the minority of the young Nawab. In April, 1744, Anwar-ud-din[1] arrived at Arcot, and his young charge, who had been received

[1] Wilks spells it Anwar-u Deen; Orme, An'war-adean Khan.

with general joy, took up his residence in the palace in the fort. Three months later Mohammed Said presided at the wedding of one of his relations, and among the guests was Murtaza Ali, the murderer of his father. "Such are," writes Orme, "the manners of a court in Indostan."[1] Anwar-ud-din was also invited, and when his approach was announced the young prince, attended by his officers and guards, went into the vestibule of the hall to meet his guardian. At the foot of the staircase were thirteen Pathans or Afghans who had been in his father's service. They saluted him with the utmost respect. The captain of the band advanced as if he was desirous to throw himself at the young man's feet. When he got within reach the Afghan drew a dagger and stabbed him to the heart. No sooner did the lad fall than the assassin was cut to pieces by the guard, and ten of his accomplices were slain by the enraged multitude below.

Anwar-ud-din and Murtaza Ali were generally supposed to have been the instigators of the foul deed. An old man who was present at the murder as a personal attendant of the young prince told Colonel Wilks: "People of different parties invented different tales; but according to the general opinion, those persons were engaged in the murder who were most interested in effecting it; namely, Murteza Khan, who knew that Mohammed Saeed would retaliate for the murder of his father, and Anwar-u Deen, who wanted to be Nabob without a future rival."[2] The Nizam, regardless of the wishes of the people who had an affection for the family that had governed them for thirty years, confirmed Anwar-ud-din in his post of Nawab of the Carnatic.

Such was the state of things in the Carnatic when war was declared between England and France (March, 1744).

[1] Orme, Vol. I., p. 56.
[2] Wilks: "History of Mysoor," Vol. I., p. 255, note.

CHAPTER VII

1749: RESTORATION OF MADRAS

THE Nizam, who was a vigorous administrator, soon established his complete authority over his vast territory in the Deccan. It was his strong support which enabled his deputy, Anwar-ud-din, to exercise control over the Carnatic. They both behaved to the English and French as " a sovereign to his subjects." We have seen how Dupleix spared no art which could withdraw the Nawab from the English; how he appealed to his avarice by offering him lakhs of rupees; how he aroused his fears as to the fate of his kingdom by sending a detachment from Madras, which burnt his villages and threatened his capital; how the Nawab abandoned the English when they made their second attempt on Fort St. David; how the French retreated to Pondicherry when Griffin's squadron appeared in sight on March 4, 1747. Two days later Admiral Griffin wrote to the Nizam regarding " all robberies, cruelties and depredations " committed on shore " by that insolent perfidious nation the French," and entreating him, " in the name of the King of Great Britain, my Royal Master, to call the Nabob to account for his past transactions and interpose your power to restore, as near as possible in its original state, what has been so unjustly taken from us." The Nizam sent a favourable answer to the admiral, and at the same time sent a mandate to his vassal of the Carnatic, commanding him to use his best endeavours " that the French may be severely chastised and rooted off, that his Majesty's sea-port town may be recovered, and that the English nation may be restored to their right, establish themselves in their former place, as before, and carry on their trade and commerce for the flourishment of the place." [1]

[1] Mill: "History of British India," Vol. III., pp. 104–5.

Dupleix was not a mere ambitious visionary, as he has so often been represented, but a politician fertile in expedients who grappled with events as they arose. The wife of Dupleix carried on a continuous correspondence with the native princes and the confidential agents of the French at every court. The negotiations of the English with the Nizam were no secret to her and her husband. The orders issued to Anwar-ud-din were fatal to the first great design of Dupleix, the expulsion of the English from the coast. He could not declare war against the Nizam and Anwar-ud-din. He determined to conciliate them, while at the same time he overthrew their authority by making use of the opinions and forces which existed in the Carnatic. A brave soldier, Anwar-ud-din was able to maintain order, but he could not win the liking and esteem of his subjects. He was mean and avaricious. The Nawab, said a native writer at the time, " is but a *Renter*, he does not much regard the distress of the people of this Province." [1] They longed for the restoration of the old dynasty. Chanda Saheb was the popular hero. He was esteemed the ablest soldier that had of late years appeared in the Carnatic, uniting in every military enterprise " the spirit of a volunteer with the liberality of a prince." The relations and connections of Chanda Saheb were the governors of most of the strong places in the province of Arcot. The prospect of a revolution in the Carnatic headed by his ablest and most formidable opponents would prevent Anwar-ud-din from venturing to commit himself to open hostilities with the French.

When Dupleix became Governor of Pondicherry, Chanda Saheb was being carried away to his Mahratta prison. Madame Dupleix became an intimate of his wife's, and so there was frequent communication between Dupleix and the exile. At the close of 1747 there came a communication from Chanda Saheb informing them that he had come to an arrangement with the Mahrattas, but he had not the money demanded for his release. Anwar-ud-din had declined to continue the payment of the sum exacted by the Mahrattas as the price of his

[1] Mill: " History of British India," Vol. III., p. 105.

perpetual imprisonment. It was a grave blunder. Dupleix was wiser. He advanced seventy thousand pounds to the wife of Chanda Saheb, which she conveyed secretly to her husband, and he was set at liberty.

Early in 1748 Chanda Saheb left Satara attended by his eldest son, eight of his faithful adherents "and a decent but not numerous train."[1] They slowly made their way to the south. They were free lances, and Chanda Saheb on reaching the River Kistna put his band at the disposal of the Poligar[2] of Chitledroog, who was at war with the Rani of Bednore. Soon after a bloody and obstinate battle was fought. The troops of Bednore were gaining some ground when the Rajah "ordered his elephant to be picketed on the spot, thereby indicating to his troops his fixed determination not to retreat." Chanda Saheb, while directing the operations in another part of the line, encountered the elephant of the Bednore general. They discharged at the same moment their respective pistols. The Bednore general was killed, "and Chunda Saheb, in the fall of his son Aabid by his side, felt for a moment a pang more grievous than the loss of victory; his exertions were enfeebled and the day was lost." The Rajah "was slain surrounded by a heap of his faithful adherents," the bravest troops of the south; and Chanda Saheb was taken and conducted in triumph to Bednore. The Rani was desirous of detaining him as a prisoner, but he was still in the custody of two Mohammedan officers, to whose fifteen hundred horse he had surrendered, "and having opened his views" to them, "they not only resisted the orders of the Ranee, but marched off under the command of their prisoner, to whom a recent event had opened new and unexpected means of pursuing his objects at Arcot."[3]

The recent event was the death of Nizam-al-Mulk, the ablest man the court of Delhi had produced since the death of Aurangzib. His eldest son was, as previously stated, acting as his father's deputy at the Imperial Court. His second son Nasir Jang ("Victorious in War"), who, having been forgiven, had

[1] Wilks: "History of Mysoor," Vol. I., p. 256. [2] *See* note, p. 135.
[3] Wilks: "History of Mysoor," Vol. I., pp. 257–8.

during the latter part of his father's life taken an active part in affairs, assumed the government. Another competitor for the succession swiftly arose. Muzaffar Jang ("Triumphant in War"), the child of a favourite daughter, who was governor of Bijapur, and had possession of the strong fortress of Adoni,[1] produced an alleged will of his grandfather bequeathing to him his treasures and his dominions. Chanda Saheb swiftly seized his opportunity. He proceeded to the court of the prince, and pointed out to him that by the aid of the French they might first conquer the Carnatic and then the Deccan. He would be the faithful vassal of Muzaffar Jang, Viceroy of the Deccan. Muzaffar readily adopted his ambitious schemes, but the arrival of Admiral Boscawen with a large force, and the siege of Pondicherry, prevented the two allies from putting them at once into execution. It was not till the English were occupied in Tanjore (June, 1749) that Muzaffar Jang and Chanda Saheb, at the head of forty thousand horse, reached the frontier of the Carnatic. In July, Dupleix informed his Council that Chanda Saheb had arrived in the neighbourhood of the hill fort of Ambur, which commanded one of the principal passes leading into the Carnatic.[2] He also told them that Chanda had agreed to subsidise two thousand of the French sepoys, and to grant them on favourable conditions forty villages when he was master of the province.

Dupleix, on hearing that the allies were on the frontier of Arcot, at once sent 400 Europeans, together with 2,000 sepoys, to the support of the two chiefs. By crossing the western mountains at some distance from Anwar-ud-din's army this force, under the command of M. D'Auteuil, joined the invaders without opposition. The Nawab had thrown up across the pass a strong entrenchment defended by cannon,

[1] Adoni (Adhvani), a town in the Bellary District, Madras. "The fort, built on the top of a precipitous cluster of rocky hills, was considered impregnable, being fortified with eleven ramparts one within another. Commanding the frontier tract between the Kistna and the Tungabhadra, it was a stronghold of great importance from the time of the Vijayanagar kings."

[2] Ambur is situated on the south bank of the Pular, about 30 miles from Vellore, and commands the Kadapanattam Pass leading into Salem.—*See* "New Imperial Gazetteer," Vol. V., p. 291.

which was served by about 60 Europeans. In front of the entrenchment was a ditch, which he filled with water from a neighbouring lake. The French soldiers advanced with the sepoys, regardless of the heavy sodden ground, to storm the entrenchment. The Nawab's artillerymen poured their shot with deadly aim into the advancing ranks, and they had to fall back. The fiery pride of the French soldiers was roused; again they rushed forward; they mounted the breastwork, but they were thrown back by numbers. Auteuil, their commander, was wounded. M. de Bussy was now the senior officer and, led by that gallant soldier, the French flung themselves a third time on the entrenchment and captured it. "Although this achievement evidently decided the fortune of the day, Anwar-u Deen continued with great personal bravery to animate his troops, and was at length slain, in pushing forward his elephant too close to the standards of his rival, on the twenty-third July, 1749." [1] The Nawab's eldest son was taken prisoner and his youngest and illegitimate son Mohammed Ali, afterwards the Nawab of Arcot, so well known in our Parliamentary history, fled with a few troops to Trichinopoly, of which place he was governor. The victors marched to Arcot, and Muzaffar Jang, after proclaiming himself Subahdar of the Deccan, invested Chanda Saheb with the government of the Carnatic.

Instead of laying siege at once to Trichinopoly the victors proceeded in pomp to Pondicherry, and were received with great magnificence by Dupleix. Orme states that "Chunda-saheb presented Mr. Dupleix with the sovereignty of 81 villages in the neighbourhood of Pondicherry." The Government of Madras in a letter to the Court, after mentioning that Chanda Saheb had taken "upon him the Government of this Province as Nabob by an illegal Fermaund procured from Mustapa Jung without the knowledge or consent of Nazar Jung," adds:

"The first act he did after arriving at this dignity was the recompensing his good allies by granting them 42 villages of the Villanour

[1] Wilks: "History of Mysoor," Vol. I., p. 259.

country which lay all around this Settlement; and by way of reward to Mr. Dupleix in particular the following towns and their revenues have been given to him and his Relations, viz.

Corbelong to Mr. Dupleix,
Porto Novo to Madame Dupleix,
Alempara to Monsieur D'Autel (*sic*) his brother-in-law,
St. Thome to Padrie D'[la Purification] a relation of Madame Dupleixes.[1]

"So that, we are surrounded in such a manner as for the French to have it entirely in their power to stop our trade or debar us from any supplies of provision from the country and we have great reason to believe, from what has already happened they will not be wanting to make use of this advantage."[2]

Mohammed Ali, on reaching Trichinopoly, at once applied to the Cuddalore Government for assistance. Boscawen was in favour of granting it, but Mr. Floyer, the governor, did not wish to embark on any enterprise which might give Dupleix an excuse for not restoring Madras, which he was bound to do by the Treaty of Aix-la-Chapelle, the conditions of which were now officially known. In August, Boscawen, with a part of the squadron, sailed to take possession of Fort St. George. A letter to the Court stated:[3]

"As we imagine an address by the way of Bussorah may possibly reach your Honours before any of the shipping that will proceed for Europe next month, we therefore now dispatch this to Bombay to be forwarded from thence by the first opportunity, and have the great satisfaction to acquaint Your Honours that General Boscawen took possession of Fort St. George on the 21st instant, which occasioned universal joy among the late inhabitants of that place, who thronged there in great numbers immediately on hoisting the English Flag, though all the art the French made use of could not induce them to return while they were in possession, and the attachment they now shew to the English gives them no little mortification."

Mountstuart Elphinstone, in his "Rise of the British Power in the East," states (p. 131) that the French restored Madras in a condition very different, "greatly strengthened and improved since the time when it fell into their hands." The destruction

[1] Alamparida, north of Pondicherry; Covelong, farther north; St. Thomé, farther north still.
[2] Dispatch from Fort St. David, October 18, 1749 (Madras Records).
[3] *Ibid.*, August 30, 1749.

of a part of the Black Town, which Orme mentions, may have been, from the point of view of the European inhabitants, an improvement, but the fortifications were certainly not returned greatly strengthened. The Government of Fort St. David writes:

"Your Honours have been already informed in an address we made you overland the 30th August that your Settlement of Fort St. George was restored to us on the 21st of that month, We have therefore here only to acquaint you that the condition in which it was delivered was so extreamly bad that we apprehend it will require to be entirely new fortified, all the walls and bastions being undermined in such a manner that they must in all probability fall down in the ensuing Moonsoon, and it is represented by His Majesty's Engineers and all the bricklayers that they are no ways to be repaired, neither are they the least capable of bearing any cannon upon them, on which last circumstances We have been obliged so far to deviate from your directions as to permit a platform that was began by the French to be finished, as we are informed it tends greatly to the present security of the place, and we hope your Honours will not be displeased thereat, as we conceive it to be absolutely necessary. As our Engineer is gone, we cannot at this time send you a plan thereof, but will endeavour to get one prepared with an estimate of the expense in readiness to send by the January ship." [1]

The English, soon after the restoration of Madras, took possession of the settlement of St. Thomé. The priest to whom it had been assigned had, the Government of Fort St. David wrote home, forbidden

"on the severest penalties any sort of refreshments going to Madrass through or out of his Dependances, and by insulting us in other respects, insomuch that at last we were obliged to apply to General Boscawen for his assistance, who immediately sent and took the Padre prisoner, and is bringing him to England to be disposed of as His Majesty shall think proper." [2]

The English flag was hoisted in the town of St. Thomé, and a small redoubt capable of containing about thirty men was raised at the mouth of the river.

On October 21 Admiral Boscawen sailed from Fort St. David, leaving 300 men to reinforce the garrison. The gallant sailor was anxious to take vigorous measures in defence of

[1] Dispatch from Fort St. David, November 2, 1749 (Madras Records).
[2] *Ibid.*, October 18, 1749.

English interests, and he declared that he would remain if the Government publicly requested him not to depart at this critical juncture.[1] Mr. Floyer and his colleagues were, however, incapable of estimating political problems and of dealing firmly with them. "They were at that time," wrote Clive afterwards, "entirely attached to mercantile ideas." Peace was indispensable to the prosperity of trade, "and the prospect of a firm and lasting peace very agreeable to the wishes of the Province at this juncture of time." The augmentation of the military establishment during the period of war had been a severe drain on their finances. They determined to reduce it. Soon after the restoration of Fort St. George, Clive and his two most intimate friends, Bulkeley and Maskelyne, who also were present at the siege of Pondicherry and took part in the Tanjore expedition,[1] "received," says Clive, "a letter from the Governor and Council insisting upon a Categorical Answer whether we would return to the Civil or continue in the Military. Messrs. Bulkeley and Maskelyne's Circumstances were too indifferent to accept the Offer, and were under a Necessity of forfeiting a certain future Advantage for the sake of a present comfortable Subsistence; as this was not my Case I return'd to the Civil." To this date, apparently, belongs the Memorandum addressed by Clive to his employers. In the Fort St. David Consultations, dated November 30, 1749, we have the following:

> "Mr. Robert Clive having returned a few days past from Fort St. George whither his Quarter Masters employ obliged him to proceed with the Commissarys, his travelling charges are therefore ordered to be paid and as he is desirous of resigning his Commission and being entertain'd in some Civil Employ, Its agreed that he be appointed Steward and to take charge of that Post the 1st of next month and that Messrs. Westcott and Wynch accompanied by Messrs. Smith and Clive examine the account remains of Provisions and Garrison Stores, and Report to us the Condition they may find them in." [2]

[1] "In the attack upon Daeve Cotah Mr. Maskelyne was wounded in the groin and owed his life entirely to the knot of his sash."—Letter of Clive to the Court of Directors, March 8, 1755 ("Miscellaneous Letters Received," Vol. 38, No. 120, India Office Records).

[2] "Factory Records, Fort St. David" (Vol. 6, India Office Records).

CHAPTER VIII

1749–51: WAR IN THE CARNATIC

THE day after Admiral Boscawen sailed for Europe, Chanda Saheb left Pondicherry with a large native force and "800 Europeans, 300 Caffres and Topanes with a train of artillery," under M. Duquesne. His destination was Trichinopoly. It was of vital importance that he should capture the key of Southern India, now the last refuge of his only rival. But Chanda Saheb was in need of money to maintain his numerous army, and he turned aside to plunder the Rajah of Tanjore. The Rajah, upon the approach of the enemy, shut himself up in his capital and offered to pay a ransom. He at the same time entered into correspondence with Mohammed Ali and joined with him in exhorting Nasir Jang at Golconda to come and settle the affairs of the Carnatic. "He likewise solicited the assistance of the English, who exhorted him to defend himself to the last extremity; but sent to his assistance no more than 20 Europeans, who were detached from Trichanopoly, and entered the city of Tanjore in the night."[1] Chanda Saheb, weary of negotiating, proceeded to bombard the town, and when one of the gates of the city was carried the frightened Rajah agreed to pay Chanda Saheb as Nawab 7,000,000 rupees, and 200,000 immediately in hand to the French troops. He likewise ceded to the French Company the sovereignty of 81 villages in the neighbourhood of Karikal. But the resources of Oriental craft had not been exhausted.

"The king," says Orme, "paid the money with the same spirit of procrastination that he had employed in making the agreement. One day he sent gold and silver plate, and his officers wrangled like pedlars for the prices at which it should be valued; another day

[1] Orme, Vol. I., p. 139.

he sent old and obsolete coins, such as he knew would require strict and tedious examination; and then he sent jewels and precious stones, of which the value was still more difficult to ascertain. Chunda-saheb saw the drift of these artifices, and knowing them to be common practices, submitted to wait, rather than lose the money, of which he was so much in want."[1]

Several weeks passed, and the first instalment had not been paid, when Dupleix with a touch of irony informed Chanda Saheb that he ought at all events to take possession of Tanjore as a place of refuge, as Nasir Jang with an overwhelming army was approaching from the north. Muzaffar Jang and Chanda Saheb at once broke up their camp and marched back upon Pondicherry, harassed by a large body of Mahratta horse which had suddenly appeared from the south.

From the north Nasir Jang advanced slowly towards Pondicherry. All the chiefs whose possessions were adjacent to his route joined him with their forces. He summoned Mohammed Ali to join his standard, and requested the English to send him a body of Europeans. Mohammed Ali, with a nominal six thousand horse, and the English detachment commanded by Captain Cope, reached his camp at Vilnier, a fort some miles west of Pondicherry, in February, 1750. When the Nawab waited on the Viceroy, Nasir Jang asked him what he had brought as the customary present. "The Nabob took Captain Cope by the hand and presenting him said he had brought that gentleman and the assistance of the English nation."[2] The Viceroy was so pleased with the answer that he conferred some honours on Cope, and appointed Mohammed Ali to succeed his father as Nawab of Arcot.

Meanwhile, Dupleix, finding that his letters to Nasir Jang were of no avail, made strenuous efforts to meet the advancing foe. At the end of March, Muzaffar Jang and Chanda Saheb marched out of Pondicherry with their army and 2,000 Europeans under D'Auteuil, and took up a strong position in front of Vilnier. On April 2, Lawrence, with six hundred Europeans, reached the camp of Nasir Jang, which was in sight of the enemy's lines. The Viceroy received him with every mark

[1] Orme, Vol. I., p. 140. [2] Cambridge: "War in India," p. 5.

of honour, and with Oriental courtesy declared him Generalissimo.

> "He proposed to me to attack the enemy immediately: I told him, in the Eastern stile, that he might be sure of victory wherever he fought, yet the attack might be attended with some difficulty, and cost him the lives of many brave men, as the enemy were strongly posted, and had with them a large train of artillery. But that, if he pleased to march between them and Pondichery, he might, by cutting off their communication, oblige them to fight at a greater disadvantage."

The Viceroy replied, "What! shall the great Nazirzing, the son of Nizam al Mulk, even for an advantage, seem to retreat before so despicable an enemy? No, he would march and attack them in front. I told him he might do as he pleased, I was ready to support him." [1]

The next morning the two armies were drawn out to engage. Lawrence states:

> "A messenger came to me from Mr. Dauteuil, to acquaint me, 'That although we were engaged in different causes, yet it was not his design nor inclination, that any European blood should be spilt: but as he did not know our post, should any of his shot come that way, and hurt the English, he could not be blamed.' I sent him for answer, 'That I had the honour of carrying the English colours on my flag gun, which if he pleased to look out for, he might know from thence where the English were posted;' and I assured him, I should also be very loth to spill European blood, but if any shot came that way, he might be assured I would return them." [2]

A shot was fired from the French battery over the English troops, and Lawrence ordered three guns to answer it, "and saw them well pointed." D'Auteuil, owing to the desertion of some of his officers and a panic among his troops, thought it more prudent to retreat in the night, leaving his guns behind him. The retreat of the French was soon known, and

[1] Lawrence's Narrative, in Cambridge's "War in India," pp. 5–6. Lawrence gives the following in a note: "The French were entrenched, and had 20 pieces of cannon. Nazarzing had 800: but his principal officer of artillery was an Irishman, for the natives, in general, think every European an engineer. I happened to find fault with this gentleman's disposition of his artillery, which was in a hollow, where his cannon were hid. He gravely replied, 'What, did I think him mad, or foolish enough, to expose his excellency's cannon, by placing them on a rising ground?'"

[2] *Ibid.*, p. 6.

Morari Rao, the Mahratta leader,[1] set off in pursuit of D'Auteuil.

"They came up with him the next day. Mr. Dauteuil formed his men into a square. Morarow attacked and broke it with only fifteen men, imagining his whole party in the rear; but feeling his danger, he with that handful, when surrounded boldly pushed for it; and breaking through the opposite side, cleared his way with six men, having lost nine in the attack."[2]

Chanda Saheb and a few horsemen who were still true to him retreated with the French, and it was due in a great measure to his dash and bravery that the retreating force got within the bound hedge at Pondicherry. The Mahratta horse fell in with some French gunners that had been left behind, "and cut most of them to pieces." "We saved as many as we could," says Lawrence, "taking them by force out of the hands of the Moors, got their wounds dressed by our surgeons, and took all the care of them that humanity required of us."[3]

Muzaffar Jang's army had vanished, Muzaffar Jang himself had surrendered to his uncle. No calamity more agitating could have overtaken Dupleix. But Dupleix was always most himself in the moments of adversity and danger. He lost no time in ordering the army to return and encamp beyond the bound hedge and so show a bold front to the Mahratta horse. He commanded that D'Auteuil should be tried for retreating without orders, and he placed the mutinous officers under arrest. He swiftly restored discipline among the men, and inspired them with his own confidence and his burning desire to wipe out the disgrace of the disaster. Finding himself,

[1] Stringer Lawrence writes: "Moraraw, whose name often occurs in this narrative, is a Maratta, who by supporting the divisions in the country, has made himself considerable from a small beginning; he sides with no party but as he finds his advantage in it, and as easily changes sides; he commands about 3000 very good horse. When he is not employed or paid by any prince, he scours the country for himself, and raises contributions where he can get most, and with least risque. His real master is the Nanah Shaw Raja; but he obeys his orders just as they are conducive to his own interest."—R. O. Cambridge: "An Account of the War in India," etc. (1761), p. 7 n.

[2] *Ibid.*, p. 7.

[3] Lawrence adds: "In return, Mr. Dupleix wrote a long protest against me, for making French subjects prisoners in time of peace; but the poor fellows, more sensible of the obligations they were under to us very gratefully acknowledged our tender usage, and confessed it was entirely owing to us that they were saved."—*Op. cit.*, p. 7.

however, too weak to risk at once a battle, Dupleix had recourse to intrigue. He sent an embassy consisting of two members of the Pondicherry Council, one of them "well versed in the Indostan and Persic languages," to Nasir Jang's camp. After an official audience the envoys conferred with the council of ministers. Notwithstanding the critical position of their affairs, the French envoys put forward exaggerated claims which were debated for several days. Then they proposed the final terms. The estates of Muzaffar Jang should be invested in his son until Nasir Jang could be prevailed on to reconcile himself to the father, and Chanda Saheb should become Nawab of the Carnatic. Dupleix had already in a letter to the Viceroy insisted that none of the family of Anwar-ud-din should ever succeed to that office. The ministers dared not even put before their sovereign the French demands. The negotiations came to an end.

> "The French deputies left the camp, after having remained in it eight days; but although they failed in gaining the apparent ends of their mission, they obtained the real advantages Mr. Dupleix proposed from it, by making themselves acquainted with the state of Nazir-jing's court, and by establishing the means of carrying on a correspondence with the discontented Nabobs of Cudapa, Canoul, and Savanore."[1]

These three Pathan chiefs had joined the army of the Viceroy, and were discontented because he would not gratify their vanity and their avarice.

Soon after the return of the envoys to Pondicherry, Dupleix determined that the prestige of the French Government required that some active measures should be taken, and he sent three hundred Europeans, under M. de la Touche, who boldly surprised a quarter of the enemy's camp by night. The Viceroy was thrown into the utmost alarm, and he determined to return to a safer residence at Arcot. So great was his fear that he did not care to be separated from the English troops. Lawrence had been instructed to obtain an enlargement of the territory round Madras, and Nasir Jang promised to comply with the request, but his chief minister prevented

[1] Orme, Vol. I., pp. 148–9.

the phirmaund or patent from being issued from his office. Lawrence was now assured that his request would be immediately granted if he would march with the Viceroy to Arcot, "a proposal we could by no means consent to, as it would have left our settlements and frontier bounds exposed to the insults of 2,000 French, and Chunda Saheb, who at the time was raising another army. We also endeavoured to make him sensible that his march to Arcot removed him too far from his enemies, who were only waiting for a favourable opportunity to renew the troubles."[1] Lawrence, finding that all his arguments were of no avail, returned with his troops to Fort St. David, and, in the latter end of April, Nasir Jang broke up his camp and marched to Arcot.

Dupleix snatched at the opportunity of the departure of the enemy to pursue his designs with vigour. The Viceroy's officers, acting under his orders, had seized the horses and effects of the French Company at Masulipatam. Dupleix determined to be revenged. He knew the strategical and commercial value of that city, and in the beginning of July he embarked on board two large ships a small detachment of 200 Europeans and 300 sepoys with a battery train, and directed the commander to sail direct for Masulipatam. After a passage of three days they anchored in the roads. "The troops landed in the night, and attacking the city by surprize, took it with very little loss. They kept possession of it, and immediately began to put it in a better posture of defence." Before the Masulipatam expedition Dupleix had sent 500 Europeans to attack the pagoda of Trivadi, lying about fifteen miles to the west of Fort St. David. "The pagoda served as a citadel to a large pettah, by which name the people on the coast of Coromandel call every town contiguous to a fortress. Trivadi made no resistance, and the French, having garrisoned it with 50 Europeans and 100 Sepoys, began to collect the revenues of the district."[2]

Mohammed Ali now requested Nasir Jang to permit him

[1] R. O. Cambridge: "An Account of the War in India," etc. (1761), p. 8.
[2] *Ibid.*

to take the field; the Viceroy consented, and sent him a reinforcement, which raised the number of his troops to twenty thousand men. At the same time he applied to the English for a body of Europeans and a train of artillery. It was of the utmost importance to the settlement of Fort St. David that the French should not hold Trivadi, so near to them, and Lawrence sent Captain Cope with 400 Europeans and 1,500 sepoys to his assistance. Lawrence would himself have taken the field, "but the chair being vacant by the removal of Mr. Floyer, I was obliged to take the government till Mr. Saunders, who was appointed to succeed, could come from Vizagapatam." [1] Mohammed Ali now marched to Trivadi and discovered the French encamped in a grove, enclosed by strong entrenchments mounted with ten pieces of cannon. Cope advised Mohammed Ali that the best way of moving the French from their strong position would be to continue their march and attack Trivadi. The next day they appeared before the pagoda, but the Nawab's troops refused to storm the lofty walls, and the following morning they marched back towards the French encampment, "and halting, formed for battle within gun-shot of their entrenchments."

"The commander of the French troops sent a messenger to ask the reason why the English came so near their posts, and declared that if they did not immediately march away, he shall in his own defence be obliged to fire on them. Captain Cope replied, that the English acting as allies to the Nabob, were determined to accompany him into all parts of his dominions, and to assist him against all who should oppose his authority. The messenger was scarcely returned when a shot from the French entrenchment struck down some of the English soldiers. It was answered by two 18 pounders and four field pieces; and a cannonade ensued, which lasted from noon till night, when the English quitted their ground with the loss of 10 Europeans and 50 sepoys, and 200 of the Nabob's troops were likewise killed: the French, secured by their entrenchments, suffered much less." [2]

Mohammed Ali, disheartened by this repulse, proposed to march towards Arcot; Cope was desirous that they should cut the French off from Pondicherry, but he refused to listen

[1] Cambridge: "War in India," pp. 9–10. [2] Orme, Vol. I., p. 152–3.

to his advice. Mohammed Ali had promised to defray all the expenses of the English troops in the field, but when Cope demanded the money he, either from anger or necessity, declined to pay "unless they (the English) should consent to degrade their reputation, and sacrifice their own possessions by marching away from the enemy to a distant part of the province." Lawrence, annoyed at the prevaricating conduct of the Nawab, ordered the English troops to return to Fort St. David. It was not a wise step, and Dupleix took immediate advantage of it. He commanded the main body under D'Auteuil at Vilnier to march and join the camp under La Touche near Trivadi. D'Auteuil instantly repaired to it, and "the whole force when united consisted of 1,800 Europeans, 2,500 Sepoys and 1,000 horse levied by Chunda-saheb together with twelve field pieces." [1] The army of Mohammed Ali consisted of 5,000 foot and 15,000 horse variously armed, lacking in discipline and badly posted. On September 1, 1750, D'Auteuil and Chanda Saheb attacked and entirely routed Mohammed Ali, who fled to Arcot with two or three attendants. Dupleix followed up the blow with his usual spirit and decision. He sent Bussy with a small detachment to take by surprise the great mountain fortress of Gingee, sixty miles from Pondicherry; Orme, who gives a good plan of the town and surrounding mountains, writes: [2]

> "A strong wall, flanked with towers, and extending near three miles, incloses three mountains, which form nearly an equilateral triangle; they are steep and craggy, and on the top of each are built large and strong forts; besides there are many other fortifications upon the declivities: On the plain between the three mountains is a large town. The Indians, who esteem no fortifications very strong, unless placed upon high and difficult eminences, have always regarded Gingee as the strongest fortress in the Carnatic."

By petarding one of the gates the young French general gained possession of the town at sunset, and proceeded to erect a barricade of baggage wagons in the streets. But his position was one of great peril, for from the heights above the enemy poured down a deadly shower of shot and grape

[1] Orme, Vol. I., p. 154. [2] *Ibid.*, p. 155.

The French returned their fire with the mortars and guns till the moon set, which was the signal to storm the fortifications.

> " None but the Europeans were destined to this hardy enterprize, who attacked all the three mountains at the same time, and found on each redoubts above redoubts, which they carried successively sword in hand, until they came to the summits, where the fortifications were stronger than those they had surmounted; they nevertheless pushed on and petarded the gates, and by day-break were in possession of them all." [1]

Of the many heroic deeds by which the French attempted to found an Empire in the East, few equal and none surpass the storming of Gingee.

Nasir Jang was now at last roused to action, and leaving Arcot, he advanced towards Gingee, but his progress was slow, as his camp consisted of 60,000 foot, 45,000 horse, 700 elephants, and 360 pieces of cannon, and the usual multitude of attendants which accompanied an Indian army. When sixteen miles from Gingee, owing to the monsoon setting in with great violence, the country was completely inundated and his army was enclosed between two swollen rivers. Before his departure from Arcot the Viceroy had sent two of his officers to Pondicherry to treat with the French. Dupleix saw that the enterprise on which his soul was intent would be successful if the Pathan Nawabs and Mahrattas were won over to his side, and he raised his terms. Not only was Muzaffar Jang to be restored to his liberty and estates, and Chanda Saheb invested as Nawab of the Carnatic, but Masulipatam and its dependencies must be ceded to the French. Nasir Jang resisted these hard terms.

Two months rolled on. Dupleix employed the time in carrying on his intrigues with the Pathan Nawabs and some chief officers in the Viceroy's service. Provisions became scarce and sickness began to spread among the troops. Nasir Jang renewed his correspondence with Dupleix, and promised to give patents for all his demands on condition that the French should hold them as his vassals. He sent deputies to Pondi-

[1] Orme, Vol. I., p. 156.

cherry, who affirmed that Nasir Jang would sign the treaty, break up his camp, and march out of the Carnatic. But Dupleix had no substantial assurance that the treaty would be signed. He demanded that the deputies should produce the treaty ratified by their sovereign. Wearied by the delays of the envoys, pressed by the confederates to act, he at the same time ordered an advance of his forces at Gingee as soon as there came the concerted call from the traitors. "The summons from the Pitan Nabobs arrived at Gingee before the ratification of the treaty at Pondicherry." [1]

On the night of December 16, 565 French soldiers and 2,000 sepoys, with ten field-pieces, under the command of M. de La Touche, were on the move. They entered the encampment straggling over eighteen miles of ground, and, led by a guide from the confederates, they made their way in firm and compact order through a host of enemy by means of their field-pieces. When the day broke they found themselves in that part of the camp occupied by Nasir Jang, and saw in the distance a vast body of horse and foot drawn up in order. For the moment the small body of French troops felt that the odds of numbers were heavy. Then was seen in the centre of the living line an elephant bearing a large white flag. This was the signal of the confederates. It was immediately recognised by M. de la Touche, and explained to the troops, who expressed their joy by repeated shouts. Soon after the French commander had word of a tragic event, and there quickly followed a ghastly proof of its truth.

When Nasir Jang first heard of the attack on the camp he thought it was an affair of a few drunken French soldiers, and he told his officers to go and cut them to pieces. Messengers now arrived in hot haste with the evil tidings that

[1] Orme, Vol. I., p. 158. In his *Mémoire,* Dupleix affirms that he wrote immediately to inform the commander at Gingee of the conclusion of the treaty, and to prevent further hostilities, but that his letter arrived not till after the revolution was performed. Wilks states that the ratification of the treaty by Nasir Jang, and the summons of the insurgents, were determined on one and the same day; but the latter arrived at Gingee before the former had reached Pondicherry.—M. Wilks: "Hist. Sketches of the South of India" (1810), Vol. I., p. 266; "Mémoire pour le Sieur Dupleix," p. 60.

the attack was serious. A native author, who was in the train of Nasir Jang at the time, states that the Viceroy prepared with cheerfulness for the combat.[1]

"As he approached the mirror to adjust his dress and perceived the reflection of his own figure, he addressed it in the following words:—'O Meer Mohammed,[2] the Almighty is thy protector'; and proceeded to mount his elephant without being induced by the hurry of the moment to omit any one of the religious observances prescribed by the sacred law: that it was his general practice on the day of battle to be clothed in armour from head to foot, but, on this occasion, he put on a simple muslin robe; and in this state fulfilled his destiny, and attained the crown of martyrdom."

Nasir Jang, accompanied by his bodyguard, went direct to that part of the line where the troops of the Pathan Nawabs were stationed.[3]

"Approaching the elephant of the Nabob of Curpa, he anticipated his salutation by first raising his hand; it was not yet clear day-light, and thinking the Nabob did not recognise him, he raised himself up in the houda and repeated the salutation, when two carbine shots from the opposite elephant pierced his body, and he instantly expired. The Patans cutting off his head, and fixing it on the end of a spear, exhibited to their associates in the conspiracy this ultimate and direct evidence of complete success."[4]

The death of Nasir Jang put an end to the conflict. By nine o'clock Muzaffar Jang was acknowledged by the

[1] Wilks: "History of Mysoor," Vol. I., p. 267 n.

[2] His original name; Nasir Jang, "Victorious in War," being a title.

[3] Orme states that Nasir Jang "was told that the troops of Cudapah, Canoul Candanore, of Mysore, together with 20,000 of the Morattoes, were drawn up in order of battle, but had not yet advanced to repulse the French. Enraged at this inaction of so large a part of his army, he mounted his elephant, and accompanied by his body-guard advanced toward these troops." Wilks, who took his narrative from the "Servi Azad," states: "Nasir Jung, unsuspicious of treason, directed his elephant to that part of his army, with the intention of giving orders." Mountstuart Elphinstone, who took his narrative from the "Servi Azad" and the "Moasir-ul-Umra," writes: "Warning was given to him of the intended perfidy of the Afghans, but from his unsuspecting temper he refused to credit it, and went straight to their part of the line to satisfy himself of their fidelity."—M. Wilks: "History of Mysoor," Vol. I., p. 267 n.; Orme, Vol. I., p. 160; Mountstuart Elphinstone: "Rise of the British Power in the East" (1887), p. 146.

[4] Wilks: "History of Mysoor," Vol. I., pp. 267-8. Wilks remarks: "And it is only useful to add, as a feature of the manners of the people, that after the confusion of the day, the troops reunited the head and the trunk of the corpse, and preserving them with pious care in a chest or spacious coffin filled with *Abeer*, a powder formed of various perfumes and the filings of odoriferous woods, dispatched these remains of their late chief to be deposited in the tomb of his ancestors."—*Op. cit.*, Vol. I., pp. 268–9.

whole army Viceroy of the Deccan. Mohammed Ali, when he heard the news, mounted his fleetest horse and, accompanied only by two or three attendants, made for Trichinopoly.

News of the successful revolution was brought to Chanda Saheb the same afternoon. He quitted his house alone, ran to Government House, and gave the first news of the great event to Dupleix. "They embraced with the agitations of two friends escaped from a shipwreck; the news was proclaimed to the town by a general discharge of the artillery; and in the evening Mr. Dupleix held a court" and . . . "the next day a Te Deum was sung in all the Churches, and three deputies were sent to compliment Murzafa-jing,"[1] and to invite him to visit Pondicherry. The ulterior object of the policy of Dupleix was that the French should be the suzerain power in India. He was, therefore, anxious that the successor of Nizam-al-Mulk, who had gained his throne by the valour of the French, should attend a durbar at the French capital. Muzaffar Jang, who knew that his tenure was mainly dependent on the French, consented. On the evening of December 26, attended by the principal lords of his Court, he arrived at the bounds of Pondicherry. Dupleix and Chanda Saheb received him in a tent without the city. "It was intended in deference to his rank that he should have entered the town on his elephant; but the animal was too large to pass under the beam to which the draw-bridge was suspended; whereupon he politely desired to go in the same palankin with Mr. Dupleix to the palar." On arriving there they had a brief conference, and then Muzaffar Jang "retired to the house appointed for his reception, where he was expected with impatience by his mother, his wife, and his son."

The next day the durbar was held, and gave Dupleix an opportunity of displaying his love of magnificence. In the wide *place* was erected a tent of immense proportions, whose sides were hung with silk of divers colours and the rich tapestries of the East. In the centre, facing each other, were two *musnuds*, or thrones of cushions, covered with the delicate

[1] Orme, Vol. I., p. 163.

fabrics of Cashmere, and cloth of gold embroidered with jewels. In the morning a royal procession set forward from Government House. A squadron of horse, twelve lancers, and twenty foot soldiers, each carrying a flag, gold on white ground, led the way. After them came Dupleix and his chamberlaim followed by two elephants of enormous size; one of them bore the standard of France unfurled to the wind, the other a banner of golden ground with the insignia of "the fish," the Garter of the Mogul Court. Then followed twelve elephants carrying kettle-drums and musicians, succeeded by battalions of sepoys, companies of European infantry, batteries of artillery, and lastly a squadron of horse. In this state the procession moved through the street lined by the victors of Gingee. Arrived at the reception tent, Dupleix entered amidst the roar of artillery and the sound of drums, trumpets, and fifes. He saluted the Subahdar and offered the usual presents. A short pause, and Muzaffar Jang took him by the hand and seated him on the other *musnud*. A long line of nobles and chief officers, apparelled in silk and velvet sparkling with diamonds, filed by the two thrones and presented their *nuzzers*.[1] Muzaffar Jang then rose and, after arraying Dupleix in a *khil'at*, or robe of honour, the same that Aurangzib gave to Nizam-al-Mulk, he proclaimed Dupleix Nawab of all the region south of the River Kistna to Cape Comorin. Following the custom of Eastern monarchs he bestowed on him the title "Zafar Jang Bahadur" (The always brave and victorious Lord), and created him "an officer with rank" (Mansabidar) in the army, with permission to bear the ensign of the fish which had been carried in the procession. He bestowed upon him as a personal gift the fortress of Valdore with the villages and land dependent upon it, as well as a separate jaghire (*jagir*) of 100,000 rupees.[2] He confirmed the possession by the French Company of the city of Masulipatam and its dependencies, and the territory near Karikal. He gave to the French Company 1,250,000 livres in payment of what they

[1] Nuzzer—Ar. *nazr*, or *nazar*, a ceremonial present.
[2] "Mémoire pour le Sieur Dupleix," p. 61.

had advanced to him, and he bestowed the same sum on the French troops which had rendered such signal service. He directed that the Pondicherry currency should be the sole currency of Southern India, which in an Oriental land was a direct symbol of sovereignty. He elected Chanda Saheb to be Nawab of Arcot under the authority of Dupleix.

The durbar ended with redoubled professions of friendship; Dupleix took his leave, and the French pomp returned to Government House. On that day the fortunes of Dupleix reached their culminating point. By his masterly genius, by his patience, his courage, his indefatigable labour, he had realised his most ambitious dreams. He had acquired the position and power of a sovereign, and he invested his new dignity with all the gorgeous ceremonial of an Oriental court. This was not due, as it has been so often represented, to mere vulgar vanity. His tastes were high and splendid as his glowing mind, and as in the case of Wellesley his love of magnificence was rooted in a nature which aspired to build an empire for his nation. In order to celebrate a victory which had raised the fame of his country to the highest degree, and to impress the Oriental mind, he followed an Eastern custom, and decreed that a town should be built on the battlefield, to be called Dupleix-Futtehabad, "the place of the victory of Dupleix."

The rejoicings of the hour were, however, overshadowed by an ominous cloud. The wages of the traitors remained to be paid, and their demands were exorbitant. They amounted, as Dupleix says, to being put in possession of half the Deccan. He employed his infinite diplomatic skill to induce the chiefs to moderate their claims. But even so expert an intriguer as Dupleix was no match for an Afghan. They agreed among themselves to appear satisfied with the terms; they signed an agreement accepting them; and they swore on the Koran that they would be faithful to the Viceroy. Dupleix was deceived. Muzaffar Jang knew the value of an Afghan oath; he would not undertake his long homeward journey without a French escort. Bussy—"excellent officer," says

Dupleix—was appointed to command a detachment of 300 Europeans and 4,000 sepoys which was to accompany him to Hyderabad. They left Pondicherry in January, 1751, and at the end of the month they reached the territory of the Nawab of Cuddapah. Some slight skirmishes now took place, but they were attributed to accident. Soon, however, it was discovered that the three Pathan chiefs intended to oppose their advance, and their troops were posted in a defile through which the road to Hyderabad ran. The Viceroy's force resumed its march, and on sighting the enemy Muzaffar Jang, at the head of his cavalry, hurried forward and attacked them. After a murderous conflict they were beaten back. The French troops came to his aid and their disciplined valour and the quick fire of their artillery cleared the gorge. Muzaffar Jang with his cavalry again dashed forward and hotly pursued the fugitive foe. The Nawab of Savanore had been cut to pieces, the Nawab of Cuddapah had fled from the field, and in pursuing him Muzaffar Jang came upon the Nawab of Kurnool.[1] Finding escape impossible, the Nawab turned with the handful of troops which surrounded him, and charged the elephant of his pursuers.

"Exasperated by this defiance, the young prince made a sign to the troops to leave the person of the Nabob to be attacked by himself. The two elephants were driven up close to each other, and Murzafa-jing had his sword uplifted to strike, when his antagonist thrust his javelin, which pierced his forehead with so much force that the point entered the brain; he fell back dead: a thousand arms were aimed at the Nabob, who was in the same instant mortally wounded; and the troops, not satisfied with this atonement, fell with fury on those of the Nabob, whom they soon overpowered, and cut to pieces."[2]

The news of the death of Muzaffar Jang struck the French with the greatest consternation. Whom would the army

[1] Kurnool, one of the four *Ceded Districts* in the Madras Presidency. It is bounded on the north by the Tungabhadra and Kistna rivers (which separate it from the Nizam's dominions); on the north-east by Guntūr District; on the east by Nellore; on the south by Cuddapah and Anantapar. By the Partition Treaty of Mysore the Nizam secured it. He ceded it in 1800 to the British, but the Nawab of Kurnool was left in possession of his jaghire. In 1838, having been found guilty of treason, his territories were annexed.

[2] Orme, Vol. I., pp. 168–9.

acknowledge as his successor? Bussy was a man of great ability and of a bold and daring spirit; he acted with promptitude and decision. The only son of Muzaffar Jang was an infant, unable to exercise power, and his father's title to sovereignty was far inferior to the claims of the sons of Nizam-al-Mulk. Three of these were prisoners in the camp, and by a superiority of tact and resolution Bussy had Salabat Jang, the eldest, proclaimed Viceroy, with the consent of the chiefs and army. In February, 1751, the new Viceroy, with his army and the French troops, quitted Cuddapah territory, and on March 15 they came to Kurnool, the capital of the Pathan Nawab who had slain Muzaffar Jang. "It was determined that the city should atone for the treachery and rebellion of its Lord." The place was stormed by the French troops, led by M. Kirjean, a nephew of Dupleix; all the garrison was put to the sword, and many of the inhabitants were massacred. The territories of Kurnool and Cuddapah were annexed to Adoni, the jaghire of Muzaffar Jang, and the government of the whole principality conferred on his son.[1]

On April 2, 1751, Salabat Jang entered the capital, Hyderabad, with Eastern pomp, and was welcomed by the inhabitants, pleased at seeing a Viceroy return to their city, next to Delhi the most populous and wealthy in the Mogul dominions. He "went through the ceremony of sitting on the musnud or throne in public, and of receiving homage not only from his own immediate officers, but also from most of the governors of the neighbouring provinces." He confirmed all the privileges which his predecessors had granted to Dupleix and his nation, and he amply rewarded the French battalion. The French troops, whose strength had been increased by reinforcements from Masulipatam to 500 Europeans and 5,000 sepoys, took up their quarters in the capital. Bussy was the

[1] Orme writes: "He received the investiture of the government of Adoni, which had been the patrimony of his father, and as a just reparation for the treachery that caused his death, the territory of the Nabob of Cudapah who planned the conspiracy, and of Kanoul, by whose arm he fell, were added to the sovereignty of the young prince, which by the French accounts produced altogether an annual revenue of near a million of pounds sterling."—Orme, Vol. I., p. 253.

real master of the wide domain of the Deccan. Dupleix was the absolute ruler of a region as large as France, inhabited by thirty millions of people and defended by a large and victorious force. The power and glory of France was at its height; the prestige of England at its lowest depth. Dupleix had effected this great change in the fortunes of his country, but the time had come when the tide of success was soon to be checked by a young man five-and-twenty years of age, a civilian serving as a commissary.

In the summer of 1750 Thomas Saunders, a man of a sound and vigorous judgment, a clear and quick perception, a constancy of mind not to be disturbed by danger,[1] assumed the government of Fort St. David. He saw at once the far-reaching effects of the French victory and the death of Nasir Jang. If the French rule became supreme the English must perish out of the land. Stringer Lawrence had gone home disgusted by the perpetual interference of civil authority in military details, and dissatisfied at not being allowed to have the definite authority which a commander ought to have over his army.[2] Though the British force had no competent commander, though it was lacking in discipline and inferior to the French in numbers, Saunders decided to support Mohammed Ali. In January, 1751, 280 Europeans and 300 sepoys, under the command of Captain Cope, were sent to Trichinopoly. Not long after their arrival Mohammed Ali, in order to establish his power, sent 6,000 of his own troops, with 30 Europeans, "to settle the government of Tinavelly, a city lying 160 miles to the south of Trichenopoly and capital of a territory which extends to Cape Comorin."[3]

Meanwhile, the garrison of Madura, the capital of a vast territory lying between Trichinopoly and Tinnevelly, revolted

[1] Wilks: "History of Mysoor," Vol. I., p. 273—"Mr. Thomas Saunders, a man inferior perhaps to M. Dupleix in splendour of talents, and in all that constitutes the decoration of character, but not yielding to that distinguished statesman in the possession of a sound and vigorous judgment, a clear and quick perception, a constancy of mind not to be disturbed by danger, and a devotion to the cause of his country no less ardent and sincere than that of M. Dupleix."

[2] Mountstuart Elphinstone: "Rise of the British Power in the East," p. 141.

[3] Orme, Vol. I., p. 173.

and declared for Chanda Saheb. Captain Cope offered to retake the town. But the attempt to storm its lofty walls ended in disaster, though the sepoys " went to the attack with as much spirit as the Europeans." [1] A large body of Mohammed Ali's troops deserted to the enemy, and at the same time he heard that Chanda Saheb, with a force consisting of 12,000 horse, 5,000 sepoys, and the French battalion, was about to march from Arcot to besiege Trichinopoly. He again applied to the English to help him in his distress. Saunders with the utmost exertion was able to dispatch only a detachment consisting of 500 Europeans, 100 Caffres, and 1,000 sepoys with eight field-pieces under the command of Captain Gingen, a Swiss officer in the Company's service. Clive accompanied the detachment as commissary. The English and French were at peace, and Gingen was commanded to remain near Fort St. David until he should be joined by some of Mohammed Ali's men, for the Madras Government was determined not to appear as principals in the war. About the middle of May a small party of the Nawab's troops arrived, and Gingen, vested with the somewhat transparent disguise of an auxiliary, advanced to the large and strong pagoda of Verdachellum, about forty miles from the coast, which commanded the most direct communications between Fort St. David and Trichinopoly. The governor, after a show of resistance, surrendered. Gingen had been sent to watch the movements of Chanda Saheb and the French; finding their intentions were to attack Trichinopoly, he, leaving a small garrison at the pagoda, moved that way also, and on his march was " joined by 100 Europeans detached by Captain Cope from Tritchanopoly, and 2,000 horse, with 2,000 foot, the remainder of the Nabob's troops, under the command of his brother Abdul-wahab Khan." [2] Soon after this junction Gingen discovered that the army of Chanda Saheb was encamped in the neighbourhood of Valconda, a consider-

[1] Orme, Vol. I., p. 174.

[2] *Ibid.*, p. 176. Stringer Lawrence states that the party from Trichinopoly joined him at the pagoda.—Cambridge: " War in India," p. 13. Captain Dalton writes that the Nawab's force joined them at Valconda.—" Memoir of Captain Dalton," p. 89.

able town ninety miles from the coast and forty-five from Trichinopoly. It was also of considerable strategic importance, as its citadel, built on a rock some two hundred feet high and a mile in circumference at the base, commanded the great road which ran directly between Arcot and Trichinopoly and also joined the best road to Fort St. David.

"The citadel of Volconda," says Dalton, "has round towers and some small pieces of cannon mounted on it; the town below joins to it, and is surrounded with a pretty good stone wall of about 16 feet high, flank'd with round towers, but has no ditch. In this place the Moors and all the people of distinction reside, and without all is the *petta*, or village, where the poorer sort have their habitations, inclos'd with a mud wall and a ditch." [1]

Gingen encamped in a large grove about a mile and a half to the southward of the town: the camp of Chanda Saheb lay about four miles to the north, separated from the British by a long range of hills and a river which lay near the western side of the citadel and town.[2] Besides his own large force, Chanda Saheb had the French detachment, mustering about 600 Europeans and 5,000 sepoys, under D'Auteuil. He had in vain endeavoured to persuade the Mogul governor to admit his troops into the fort. The English made the same request. "He gave us for answer that the fort was his family estate, which we could not blame him for taking care of, and that he could not admit one party in without giving umbrage to the other." [3] The English commander asked leave of the Nawab's brother to attack the place, but this was refused as the governor was a relative and he was certain that "his relation was not in any interest but his." [4] A fortnight was spent in fruitless negotiations. The Council at Fort St. David grew impatient at the delay, and there is the following entry in the records:

"June —? 1751. Mr. Robins volunteers to go to Volcondah, but is not allowed; he and the Board concur that Captain De Gingins

[1] C. Dalton: "Memoir of Captain Dalton, H.E.I.C.S." (1886), p. 92.

[2] Orme in his description of Valconda speaks of the fortified town as a fort built of stone, and he calls the village "a town slenderly fortified with a mud wall."—Orme, Vol. I., p. 176.

[3] Dalton, p. 90. [4] *Ibid.*

be ordered to seek the enemy, and use his utmost endeavour to bring to an engagement, and this as soon as possible, their strength increasing daily by the arrival of their supplies from Europe, and the President is now ordered to write to Captain De Gingins to that purpose." [1]

On the receipt of the President's letter Gingen determined to commence at once military operations. He was a brave man who had, as a subaltern, seen much active service in Europe, but he was without ability and without enterprise. He thought a few shells thrown into the fort would lead to its surrender. Some of the officers suggested that instead of throwing away bombs, which would be visible to Chanda Saheb's army, they should in the night " scalade the lower town where all the principal men liv'd." Gingen was, however, says Dalton, " of an unfortunately jealous temper which made him mistrust the good will of any who offer'd to give him advice." [2] He rejected the suggestion, adhered to his scheme of bombardment, and gave orders that as soon as the first shell was fired the village should be attacked and burnt, " in order to increase the confusion." About 8 P.M. the mortars opened fire, and " the whole village, which was a very fine one, plunder'd and set in flames." [3] This stupid and barbarous deed was followed by its natural consequences. " The governor, as was foreseen, immediately sent a messenger to acquaint Chundasaheb that he was ready to admit his troops into the place." [4] All night the bombardment continued, but when daylight came, as the garrison showed no sign of surrendering, " we drew off our mortars and join'd our army which was lying on the plain drawn up out of cannonshot of the fort." [5] Soon after Chanda Saheb's army, " with the French battalion of about 500 men in their front," [6] were seen marching pretty fast to gain the deep bed of the river that led directly to the gate of the town and was almost dry. The English battalions and the sepoys were posted a mile northward of the citadel near the river, and might have seized it before the French. " But we lay

[1] Dalton, p. 99.
[2] *Ibid.*, pp. 93–4.
[3] *Ibid.*, p. 94.
[4] Orme, Vol. I., p. 177.
[5] Dalton, p. 94.
[6] *Ibid.*, pp. 94–5.

still in a state of stupefaction and saw 'em all enter the watercourse and pushing hard along it to the fort."[1] The English stood to their arms. Gingen, instead of sending his men forward, consulted his officers as to whether it was possible to check the French advance; "I believe this beginning gave none a very extraordinary idea of our success. Notwithstanding which some gave it their opinion that a brisk push might still doe it, as the fire from the fort was very inconsiderable." The officer "commanding the negroes, showing great readiness,"[2] was ordered to advance and engage the enemy's front and if possible stop them till the English main body could come up.

I march'd after him as fast as I could," Dalton enters in his journal, "in any order, with the grenadiers, 3 companys of Sipoys from the right, and a company of Topasses belonging to the Nabob. The Coffreys ran all the way as fast as they could and attacked the French Grenadiers and Sipoys who led their van in so daring a manner, that (assisted by the fire of the artillery from the left of the Battallion, and 3 guns of the Nabob's) they made 'em give way, and abandon their two advanced guns, so precipitately, that they threw the French main body into confusion and they all got for shelter into the bottom of the watercourse firing from thence up in the air, without doing us the least harm. Never was there a finer prospect of a compleat victory, and the French saw it so plainly themselves, that giving over thoughts of relieving the fort, they suffer'd us to stop 'em, and with much adoe got 2 field pieces up on the bank to bear upon our battallion which was marching down in all appearance with a great deal of resolution, to support us, but on receiving about 20 shot which killed a Lieut. and 8 or 9 men the whole went to the right about and march'd towards camp in great disorder without giving us who were advanced the least notice to retire in time."[3]

Dalton's account differs from that given by the historian of "The War of Coromandel." Orme states that the English troops advanced against the enemy with resolution.

"As they approached a cannonade ensued, and a shot struck one of the French tumbrils, which blowing up wounded some of their Europeans, and frightened so much a hundred more, who were posted near it, that they ran away with Mr. d'Auteuil at their head to the fort of Vol-kondah, where they were admitted; and from hence they immediately began to fire from 14 pieces of cannon upon

[1] Dalton, p. 95. [2] *Ibid.* [3] *Ibid.*, pp. 95–6.

the English battalion. This unexpected cannonade, notwithstanding that most of their shot flew too high, flung the troops into disorder, and some of the officers likewise discovering fear, the whole battalion were seized with a panic. The captains Gingen, Dalton, Kirkpatrick, and lieutenant Clive, endeavoured to rally them, but in vain; for they retreated in great confusion, without stopping until they reached the camp."

Orme also mentions that

"Abdul-wahab Khan had prevailed on one of their generals, who commanded 4000 horse, to come over to him on the field of battle, which body was observed to separate from the rest as the enemy approached; and this appearance of defection flung Chunda-saheb into such perplexity, that he did not venture to pursue the English, over whom he would otherwise have had every advantage." [1]

Some of Orme's statements are founded on a memorandum which Clive sent to him. Clive wrote: [2]

"A Moors Officer in Chunda saheib's army commanding 2000 men had agreed to come over. This party was observed to be detached from the main body, ready. If the English had not, the French would have retired first—Explosion of a Tumbril threw them into confusion—In this first action the Nabob's troops behaved better than ever they did afterwards, & even in the field of battle reproached the English with their want of spirit."

As soon as it was dark Gingen broke up his camp, and, marching with great expedition, arrived the next morning at "the streights of Utatoor," about twenty miles from Valconda, and the same distance from Trichinopoly. Captain Dalton with a small force and two field-pieces was left in a village to guard the entrance of the pass, and the main body made their camp in the valley. At a meeting of the Council held at Fort St. David on July 22, 1751,

"The President acquaints the Board that Lieut. Maskelyne, who came in from Camp a few days ago, gives an account that Captain De Gingins having advice that a Body of the Enemy's Horse was moving towards our army, then encamped at Wootatore, went out attended by Captains Dalton and Kilpatrick and himself, with about 100 Sepoys and a few troopers to reconnoitre, but advancing too far, they were all surrounded by a party of the Enemy's Horse that were lying in Ambuscade. That Captain De Gingins, Dalton and Kilpatrick thereupon mounting their horses made their way

[1] Orme, Vol. I., pp. 177–8. [2] Orme MSS.: India, Vol. II., p. 297.

thro' them by the assistance of the troopers, and arrived safe in camp, but he (Lieut. Maskelyne) not having a horse was obliged to surrender to the Sepoys, that he was carried prisoner to Chunda Saib who gave him leave to come here on his parole, but not till he had received an answer from Mr. Dupleix to a letter he wrote on this subject. The President further informs the Board that he has advice that a few days after the above accident, the Enemy made a great attack on our advanced guard at Wootatore, which was so bravely defended by Captain Dalton that they were obliged to retreat with a considerable loss without effecting anything. That our troops have nevertheless quitted that Post and retreated across the river very near Trichinopoly, whither the Enemy have followed them, and encamped on the Banks. Captain De Gingins writes that the reasons of his taking this step were the want of provisions, and his apprehensions that the Nabob's people would leave us." [1]

The town of Trichinopoly was at that time rectangular in form and nearly six miles in circumference. A double enceinte of masonry with flanking towers and a wet ditch thirty feet wide and twelve deep protected it. In the north quarter of the town rises sheer up a broad mass of dark grey gneiss that bears on its topmost pinnacle a small shrine. Looking from the platform northward the eye rests on two bright rivers winding serpentine, and left between them a fair champaign covered with the dark mango, the feathery tamarind, and the lovely green banian. Amidst the varied foliage may be faintly seen red battlements high towered; they are the walls and the gate-towers of the stupendous temple of Seringham, which has for centuries been a centre of Hindu religious life. Seven enclosures surrounded by seven lofty and solid walls, the outermost of which was four miles in circumference, protected the inmost sacred shrine containing the image of Vishnu, the maintainer of existence, and the treasury containing the dedicated silver and gold and the jewels of the gods, necklaces of diamonds, emeralds, and rubies, charms of gold, armlets and rings for the toes wrought with much cunning work. About a mile and a half from the great pagoda is a smaller one with four quadrangles dedicated to Shiva, the destroyer and the healer. The two temples so well fortified afforded good posts for an invading army, and the sacred

[1] Dalton, pp. 107-9.

place is charged with history. Men call it an island, but it is, in fact, a peninsula, two miles broad at its western extremity, but growing narrower until at about the end of thirteen miles it joins a large and strong mound of earth which prevents the union of the two branches of the river Caveri, and sends the northern stream, which takes the name of Coleroon, rolling farther north-west until it reaches the sea near Devicotah, while the Caveri, retaining the name, spreads out into many channels and fertilises the green rice fields of Tanjore. A king of Tanjore, realising that the prosperity of his kingdom depended on the ancient dam, erected for its protection at a distance of a mile the mud fort of Coilady.

Looking southward, instead of bright river, gardens, courts, and cloisters, lie stretched below a vast veldt full of hollow ways and studded with kopjes. Due south of the town are two conspicuous heights, the Golden Rock and the Sugar Loaf Rock, both rising a hundred feet above the plain. Almost east, about two miles from the town, there is a ridge of rocks and sand not more than forty feet high, known as the French Rocks, and three miles farther to the east is the almost inaccessible rock of Elsemeram with a fortified pagoda on the summit. On this wide veldt the French and English struggled for two years for the mastery of India. Many gallant deeds of arms did these old rocks witness.

On July 13 Gingen's force left the valley of Utatoor, and after a march of eighteen hours, "without refreshment in the hottest season of this sultry climate,"[1] the English battalion took possession of "Pitchandah, a fortified pagoda situated on the northern bank of the Coleroon, about a mile to the east of Seringham: the rest of the army encamped along the river."[2] During the night they crossed the rapid stream in boats, and occupied "three of the first enclosures, which affording room much more than sufficient for their reception, they complied with the earnest solicitations of the Bramins, imploring them to carry the stain of their pollutions no nearer the habitation of the idol." The post might easily have been held against the

[1] Dalton, p. 114. [2] Orme, Vol. I., p. 183.

enemy's whole force, but "the spirit of retreat still so strongly possessed the army," says Orme, that two days later they took "shelter under the walls of Tritchanopoly." "The English battalion encamped on the west side of the city close to the ditch, and the Nabob's troops on the southern side: captain Cope with 100 of the Europeans sent thither in the beginning of the year remained within the walls."[1] Chanda Saheb and the French at once crossed the Coleroon, occupied the pagodas, and in the beginning of August they sent a strong detachment to attack the fort of Coilady. Gingen, on hearing of their movement, "detached 20 Europeans and 100 Sepoys, under the command of Ensign Trusler, to reinforce the garrison. This officer defended the fort very gallantly for several days, until it was so shattered as to be no longer tenable: he then received orders to draw off his men in the night."[2] The fort was evacuated. Chanda Saheb having obtained a post which protected the "island" at its most vulnerable point, left a small detachment to guard the pagodas, and crossing the Caveri, encamped on the east side of the town at the French Rock.[3]

When Gingen began his retreat from Valconda, Clive returned to Fort St. David and told the tale of beaten troops. The attempt to relieve Trichinopoly had ended in disaster. Mohammed Ali no longer possessed a single district in the Carnatic. Verdachellum was the only fort north of the Coleroon which acknowledged his rule, and it was invested by the troops of a neighbouring chief. Saunders was a resolute man, and disaster did not prevent him from directing with his usual energy the slender resources which he possessed. The ships from Europe had brought a few recruits. In July he sent a detachment of Europeans and 300 sepoys with a large convoy of stores to the relief of Verdachellum,

"but every officer of established character being already in the field, there remained none in the garrison to whom such a command could be prudently entrusted. The governor, Mr. Saunders, there-

[1] Orme, Vol. I., p. 184. [2] *Ibid.*, p. 185.
[3] Cambridge: "War in India," pp. 13–14.

fore requested Mr. Pigot, one of the council, to proceed with the detachment until it should be out of reach of enemies, and then to send it forward under the command of the military officer at Trichenopoly."

Clive again accompanied the detachment as commissary of the troops. The small band surprised the forces of the hostile chief at midnight, and the convoy entered Verdachellum without any loss. From thence Mr. Pigot sent it forward "under the command of the military officer at Trichenopoly," and the convoy reached that fort without interruption. After having delivered over their charges, Pigot and Clive set out from Verdachellum, accompanied by twelve sepoys and the same number of servants, to return to Fort St. David. On the march they were surrounded by the Poligar's[1] troops, who with matchlocks harassed them for some hours, and killed seven of the sepoys and several of the attendants. The ammunition of the rest of the party being expended, they were ordered to disperse. Pigot and Clive galloped off, with the enemy's cavalry thundering after them for several miles. It was a close race, and Clive's fighting nearly came to an end. Many a fierce contest, however, lay before him.

In the difficult vocation of commissary to an army in the field, Clive, who was now a civilian, had to meet great demands upon his organising and administrative powers. He had to keep marching columns supplied with food and forage in a country which had been devastated by successive invaders. He had to find oxen, camels, and elephants to convey the supplies and the guns through a country where roads were few and great rivers had to be crossed. He had to keep together the motley elements that compose the staff of an Indian convoy, by patience, firmness, and tact. He knew how to win his way into the affections of the native drivers and sepoys, and he was rewarded by their great fidelity when in service. As commissary, Clive had to find the money for the troops.

[1] *Poligar.* "This term is peculiar to the Madras Presidency. The persons so called were properly subordinate feudal chiefs, occupying tracts more or less wild, and generally of predatory habits in former days; they are now much the same as *Zemindars* in the highest use of that term."—Yule and Burnell: "Hobson-Jobson," p. 718.

He obtained loans from the native merchants in order to meet the bills drawn upon him in the field. The position which he had previously held in the mercantile service of the Company enabled him to deal with these matters. In the "Account Salary due to the Hon. Co.'s covenanted Servants," Clive is entered for September 25, 1750, at the head of the factors at a salary of £15 per annum. He is also mentioned as "Steward." In May, 1751, John Smith appears to be acting as steward, and on the 21st of that month Clive is entered as Junior Merchant at £30. As a Junior Merchant, Clive had the privilege of private trade, and he had ample opportunity of making a fortune in legitimate business. He had those qualities which make a man a great merchant—foresight, calm judgment, and a temperament not to be discomposed by success or failure; but mercantile ambition did not satisfy the fiery temper. He had left the army because he thought the Treaty of Aix-la-Chapelle had secured a lasting peace. The clash of arms awoke again the desire to command, to fight, to win, or to die as a soldier. He asked that he should be restored to the army, and the request was readily granted. Among the proceedings of a Consultation held on July 22, 1751, we find the following:

"Mr. Robert Clive, who has lately been very serviceable in conducting several parties to camp, offering to go without any consideration of pay, provided we will give him a Brevet to entitle him to the rank of a captain, as he was an officer at the siege of Pondicherry and almost the whole time of the war, and distinguished himself on many occasions, it is conceived that this Officer may be of some service and, therefore, now ordered that a Brevet be drawn out and given him." [1]

[1] Clive's commission appointing him captain runs: "Given under our hands, and the seal of the Honble United Company of Merchants of England trading to the East Indies in Fort St. David this first day of January in the Twenty-fifth year of the reign of our Sovereign Lord George the second, by the Grace of God, of Great Britain, France and Ireland, King defender of the faith, &c, and in the year of our Lord one thousand Seven hundred and fifty-one." —Powis MSS.

CHAPTER IX

1751: CLIVE'S CAPTURE AND DEFENCE OF ARCOT

Soon after Clive had been made a captain for the skill and gallantry he had shown in the field "on many occasions," he was sent in command of a detachment consisting of only 100 Europeans and 50 sepoys, with one small field-piece, to make his way through the Tanjore country to Trichinopoly. After a smart skirmish with the French he entered the besieged city. He soon realised the critical condition of the garrison. There was the grave disparity in numerical strength between them and the besiegers; "the English battalion did not exceed 600 men; whereas the French had 900, and the troops of Chunda-saheb outnumbered the Nabob's ten to one." But this was not the chief evil. "Disagreement and Caballs among the officers (the usual consequence of bad success) ensued," says Dalton, "and never was a more unhappy set of people got together, nor from whom less good could be expected."

Clive returned at once to Fort St. David, and informed the governor that Trichinopoly, the safety of which was vital, was in instant peril. He also made a proposal which was an example of daring and military sagacity. Chanda Saheb and his French allies had, in their desire to capture Trichinopoly, left Arcot, the capital of the Carnatic, without a sufficient garrison. If a bold, swift dash was made for it, Chanda Saheb would be bound either to lose the seat of his government or send a large portion of his besieging force from Trichinopoly to protect it or retake it. Clive offered to lead the expedition. Saunders had been struck with the young officer, ardent, void of fear, who had shown such a precocious faculty for commanding men, and he approved of the proposal. On Monday, August 19,

"The board being of opinion that a diversion in the Arcot country will oblige the enemy to withdraw part of their forces from Trichinopoly and put it in our power to attempt something that way, now agree that Captain Clive be sent with a party of all the Europeans we can possibly spare & some sepoys for this purpose, and that he proceed on the *Wager* to Fort St. George, where he is to be reinforced by all the men they can any ways furnish, and march immediately towards Arcot, and the President is now desired to write to the Deputy Governor to acquaint him with the intent of their coming, and to recommend it to him to dispatch letters to the several Killadars [commandants of forts], &c., to engage them to bring in their troops to his assistance, and to forward the design all in their power." [1]

But all the Europeans and all the sepoys they could spare at Fort St. David, and all the men they could furnish at Fort St. George, amounted only to 200 Europeans and 600 sepoys. To command the men they could find only eight officers, "six of whom had never before been in action, and four of these six were young men in the mercantile service of the company, who, inflamed by his [Clive's] example, took up the sword to follow him." [2] With a handful of men lacking in discipline, and four trained officers, and "only three field pieces for their artillery," Clive marched from Madras on August 26 (September 6 N.S.) to lay the first stone of the foundation of our Indian Empire.

The town of Arcot, which was his goal, lies sixty-four miles to the southward of Madras. Surrounded by a barren country and granite hills, it was chosen by the Mohammedan Nawabs of the Carnatic to be their capital on account of its healthy climate and its great strategic situation. It was only fifteen miles from Vellore, the strongest fortress in India, which commanded the main communication from and to Mysore, then a powerful Hindu kingdom. The city stands upon the left bank of the River Pálár, whose bed at the dry season of the year is a stretch of sand some three thousand feet wide. It was surrounded by a broad high rampart nearly five miles in circuit, faced with a thick masonry wall, gates and bastions, and five gateways. The Delhi Gateway, with its two

[1] Minutes of Consultation, Fort St. David, August 15 (Madras Records).
[2] Orme, Vol. I., p. 187.

arches, is the only one that has defied war and time, and from a small chamber which surmounts it the traveller looks down upon the river flowing through a wide plain bounded by brown hills. Tradition states that the chamber was a favourite resort of Clive's. Inside the city wall, about half a mile from the river, was the citadel, a rectangular fortress of considerable size, surrounded by a very broad moat about a mile in circumference.[1]

It was the gallant Pathan officer Daud Khan who, when he was administering the affairs of the Carnatic (1706–13), with Arcot as his headquarters, built or improved the fort, and laid out the town in eighteen streets named after illustrious commanders. The Nawabs of the Carnatic erected a palace outside the fort on the verge of a large tank, and their new capital grew rapidly in prosperity and became a chief seat of the manufacture of chintz and gold lace for the nobles of the court. When the city came into the possession of Chanda Saheb the population was estimated to have exceeded 100,000 souls, and the strength of the garrison of his troops to have amounted to 1,100 men. The capture of this fortified city with a strong citadel by 200 Europeans and 600 sepoys was certainly a hazardous game. But Clive was never unwilling to run a risk or to fight against odds when a great result was to be achieved.

Two days after he marched from Madras, Clive arrived at Conjeveram (Kanchipuram), a considerable town, with a large pagoda, lying about 40 miles inland, and hearing of the strength of the garrison at Arcot he sent back to Fort St. George for two eighteen-pounders. But he did not wait for them to reach him. On August 31 (September 11 N.S.) the detachment marched on, and they had gone but a short distance when one of the monsoon storms which sweep over the Carnatic at that season of the year burst upon them. The heat was stifling, the wind sent billows of sand over them; there was a lull, and lightnings illuminated the sky, and the thick clouds,

[1] *See* "Madras District Manual, North Arcot," pp. 306–307. Orme, however, states that the city "had no walls or defences."—Orme, Vol. I., p. 187.

"with the big stores of steaming oceans charged," poured out water. Soon the small band was marching through a liquid plain. But on they went, and they did not halt till they arrived within ten miles of Arcot. The spies ran in hot haste to the town and spread the marvellous tidings that, unchecked by the prodigies of heaven and earth and the mutterings of the thunder, the English had continued their march. The populace, always inclined, like Orientals, to be superstitious, believed that a terrible disaster was in store for them, and the garrison during the night abandoned the fort.

At ten, next morning the detachment marched, says a sergeant who was with them,

> "without opposition through the town, amidst a million Spectators whose looks betrayed them traytors notwithstanding their pretended friendship and dirty presents. We then took possession of the fort where we found great quantities of Rockets and lead, with some gunpowder, which afterwards was of infinite service to us."[1]

Clive also found in the fort goods belonging to merchants to the value of five lacs of rupees, which he restored to their owners, "and this judicious generosity conciliated many of the principal inhabitants to the English interest."[2] He also insisted that the populace should be treated with consideration, and they remained neutral throughout the operations. He allowed the residents of the fort, some three or four hundred in number, to remain undisturbed in their dwellings. He collected provisions and materials for a siege, for he felt certain that when the garrison, who were encamped within a few miles of the town, recovered from their panic and were reinforced, they would attempt to recover the fort. In order to prevent them, as long as possible, from returning, he determined to take every opportunity for offensive action. He therefore, on September 4, went with the greater part of his men and four field-pieces in quest of the fugitive garrison. About three in the afternoon he found them drawn up near Timary, a fort situated six miles south of the city. The sergeant enters in his diary:

[1] Orme MSS.: India, Vol. II., pp. 277–92. "Siege and Defence of Arcot, by a Serjeant."

[2] Orme, Vol. I., p. 188.

"4th [September 1751] We marched towards Timmerie, a fort of no inconsiderable force in possession of the enemy, and about six miles distant from Arcot. About three in the afternoon the enemy's horse to the number of 500, & about 300 foot, made their appearance about a mile distant from us then on the march. Without hesitation we turned to the left, and as they advanced soon came near enough to cannonade, which they begun from one field piece on the left where their foot were posted. Capt. Clive ordered one of our field pieces to advance towards them under care of Lieut. Bulkley's platoon, and attacked their horse himself with the Seapoys. As they advanced upon the right, he soon put them to flight, as had Mr. Bulkley's platoon done the same on the left by advancing on their foot and cannon which they carried off precipitately & disappeared under cover of the rocky hills and some tops (*sic*) [1] about a mile in their rear. Night coming on, we buried one [(*sic*) ? some] of their dead and returned to Arcot having had only one Seapoy wounded and [a] Camel killed. The loss sustained by the enemy could not be considerable, as they did not stand fire at proper distance, but several horses were seen without their riders."

Two days later Clive again marched out and found the enemy in considerable strength formed up in a tope, protected by the guns of the fort of Timary. A bank and a ditch gave cover and concealment to them. About fifty yards in front was a large tank, almost dry, surrounded by a bank much higher than that of the grove, which also sheltered them.

"6th [September]. We again marched towards Timmerie, and as we came within a mile of the fort, upon a rising ground, saw the enemy (who had been considerably reinforced) drawn up in a top [tope] under the protection of the fort guns. We continued our march towards 'em, and as we came near they fired from two field pieces very briskly, and killed 3 of our Europeans. Mr. Bulkley was immediately ordered to dislodge them if possible, and take possession of the top which their men lay under cover of, a bank which made a good breast work for them. Notwithstanding which, the undaunted manner in which our people ran up to them intimidated them so much that they retired to the side of a tank, in front of the top and within musket shot of it. Being now under command of the fort guns, they fired very briskly upon us from the fort field pieces and musketry; from Tank (*sic*) we cannonaded them in the tank but with little execution, not more of a man to be seen than his head and musket. Captain Clive, finding our situation very disadvantageous, ordered the men under cover of a house, and ordered Mr. Glass's platoon with some

[1] Tops; characteristic of the British soldier for topes, groves or orchards.

Seapoys to go round upon the flank of the enemy, who no sooner made their appearance in flank but Mr. Bulkley advanced upon them in front, and put them to the rout without losing one man ; we immediately marched into the village adjoining the fort which they had left in flames. Several messages were interchanged, and we fired a few shot and Shells from the Houbitz but the fort being strong and well surrounded with a wet ditch (*sic*). As we could do nothing by bullying were sensible nothing could be attempted with hopes of success by force of arms, having no battering cannon with us and our force short one platoon (left at Arcot) of the number brought out with us, we returned to Arcot in the Evening; attended great part of the way by the enemy's horse, who carefully avoided coming within cannon shot of us. We lost in this fray 3 Europeans, some blacks & whites ; can't compute the loss of the Enemy."

During the next few days Clive employed his troops in repairing the defences of the fort and constructing new works. The enemy, regarding the intermission of sallies from the fort as due to fear, and being reinforced by 5,000 men, advanced and encamped within three miles of Arcot. They boasted that they were about to besiege the fort. On the night of September 14 Clive stole out with the greater part of his garrison and attacked their camp. The sergeant must tell the tale :

"14th [September]. The enemy now being very strong ventured to encamp within 3 miles of Arcot, which we having intelligence of, about 12 at night marched out with 3 platoons & the Seapoys, observing the most profound silence, well knowing the success of a handfull of men against such numbers entirely depended on not being discovered. The attempt succeeded to wish, for unobserved we arrived in their camp and alarmed them by firing platoons. So great was their confusion that tho' we went through the middle of 'em they fired very few shot amongst us, & those few to no purpose. We made no stay, but returned to Arcot immediately. So privately was this affair conducted that the Inhabitants knowing nothing of our being out upon our return imagined it to be a reinforcement for the garrison. We can no otherwise judge of the enemy's loss than by the terrible shreiks and groans all over the camp. As our people were strictly order'd to keep their ranks less plunder was got than perhaps might have been expected from such an exploit. From this time till the 24th little worth notice happened, only as the enemy increased in numbers they did in audacity, now and then coming into the town and cutting our people, who for that reason were denied port liberty."

The enemy, hearing that the two eighteen-pounders which Clive had sent for from Madras were on their way, escorted by a few sepoys, determined to interrupt them by the occupation of the great pagoda, Conjeveram. Clive sent 30 Europeans and 50 sepoys to dislodge them, and two days later, urged by the importance of being strengthened by the two eighteen-pounders, he took the bold measure of sending the rest of the garrison to meet and escort them, leaving, says the sergeant, "only a few men besides the sick to take care of the fort."

"16th Sept. Some stores being on the road from Madrass and having intelligence that the enemy had possessed themselves of Conjeveram Pagoda in order to intercept our communication Lieut[s]. Revel and Trenwith, with Ensign Dawson, one platoon, & some Seapoys and field pieces, were ordered to escort the stores. The enemy on their approach deserted the Pagoda and retired to Matchulavaum, a fort six miles distant. Captain Clive, somewhat dissatisfied with the proceedings of Lieut. Trenwith, on the 18th ordered Lieut: Bulkley with the rest of the garrison to march towards him, leaving only a few men besides the sick to take care of the fort. This party was joined [on] the 20th on the road by Lieut. Trenwith's and marched back for Arcot. But the men being fatigued they halted about six miles distant. The enemy sensible of the incapacity of the fort for a defence, came into the town and attacked the fort about ten at night, flushed with hopes of our non-resistance and of an insurrection amongst their friends within. The number of our men would not admit even of centries [*sic*] upon the proper posts round the walls, so that we were oblidged to divide into parties and keep moving round. The enemy did little else but pop at us from the houses on the side of the ditch (by which we had 1 or 2 wounded) till about two o'clock when a great number of horse and foot came close up to the gate and were received by all the fire we had, and some Grenades, which put them into confusion and obliged them to retire, the horse riding over the foot. They then went to the other gate, called the back gate, but retired in the same manner, as we were apprized of the place they intended to attack by the hideous shouts and noise they made. They made no further attempts at the gates but kept a brisk fire all round our walls till six in the morning, when Lieut. Bulkley appearing on the banks of the river they betook themselves to flight. Our men saw several dead in the streets, and brought in some prisoners and near 300 Cattle which they picked up in their march.

"This attack of the enemy with small arms and horse against stone walls may seem trifling, but we look upon it in a different light, there being above 2000 men in the fort, every one of them attached to Chawndas interest, and willing to cut our throats had not their dastardly spirits hindered them from the attempt."

The capture of Arcot produced the effect which Clive predicted. Chanda Saheb must relax his hold on Trichinopoly. On hearing that Clive was in possession of his capital, he sent 4,000 of the best troops from his force to recover it, and entrusted the command to his son, Rezza (Razia) Saheb, who was joined in his march by 150 French soldiers from Pondicherry. On the night of the 23rd they came into the town, the sergeant tells us, and took possession of the palace and streets adjacent to the fort. On the 24th,

" Captain Clive with the whole garrison sallied forth, only a few left in the fort. The enemy began firing on us before we had got 50 yards from the gate, but we kept so brisk a fire from our musketry & field-pieces with grape as obliged them to retire into the palace and houses, from whence they kept a continual fire, wounding many of our people. The only people of theirs remaining in the street were the french artillery who played their guns upon us with great execution. Our people got into a Choultry which proved a good shelter from the enemy's shot. Our train by this time had advanced their foremost gun within ten yards of the Enemy's two and oblidged them to desert them (having killed most of the gunners) upon which Capt. Clive ordered Lieut. Tre[n]with's platoon to bring off the guns, but the men not showing the greatest readiness, and the loss it must necessarily be attended with, made us decline it as the taking of guns is at best but a nominal victory and dearly purchased by the loss of even a few Europeans where they are so scarce. Lieut. Glass with his platoon was stationed at a street on the other side of the palace and was ordered to come upon the enemy's rear, but by some mistake the orders miscarried. The enemy, not a man of 'em to be seen in the street, & their shot falling in great quantities, was the only reason we had to think they were not gone, for they were all in the palace and house windows under cover. How to retreat now became the question, and as the doing it in a regular manner must have been attended with the loss of many, Captain Clive ordered the field pieces to be fired till they ran back to the corner of a street when the men followed and carried them off. The loss on our side was very considerable, having a great number both Europeans and Blacks wounded, of which some afterwards died Viz: Lieut: Trenwith and some 1 or 2 of the train, besides blacks. The loss of the enemy must likewise be great, most of their Train being killed or wounded, as were a good many blacks by Mr. Glass, who ordered his platoon to fire over a wall into a square where 200 of them were."

The loss was most serious when we consider the number of the garrison. Fifteen Europeans were either killed on the spot or died afterwards of their wounds. Clive himself very nearly lost his life in the street fight. Trenwith, one of the officers sent out to escort the guns, "perceiving a Sepoy from a window taking aim at Captain Clive, pulled him on one side, upon which the Sepoy, changing his aim, shot Lieutenant Trenwith through the body."[1] Lieutenant Revel, the only artillery officer, with sixteen other men was likewise disabled. Clive had been foiled and frustrated; his small force had suffered severely in men but not in *moral.* They had shown the enemy how they could fight.[2]

The next day Rezza Saheb was joined by Murtaza Ali with 2,000 men, and he completed the investment. His force now consisted of 150 Europeans, 2,000 sepoys, 3,000 horse, and 5,000 irregular infantry. Clive's force had been reduced to 120 Europeans and 200 sepoys fit for duty. Of the eight officers who had set out on the expedition only four were left to guide, encourage and command. The fort which the little band had to defend was a mile in circumference, and how little the fortifications were capable of defence is shown in the plain, matter-of-fact narrative of the sergeant, a narrative of which Englishmen may well be proud:

"24th [September]. The enemy now in possession of the town hindered all manner of supplies of provisions, cut off the communication for the waters coming into the fort, and we had nothing before our eyes but the dismal prospect of either being starved out by blockade or being obliged to stand a storm in case of their bringing battering cannon to make a breach, which the unshaken fortitude of our officers made us chearfully resolve upon rather than meanly to submit to any terms could be proposed us. Great were the disadvantages we laboured under from the mal situation & condition of the fort. The town houses close to the walls, the ditch in many places easily fordable and in some dry. The walls in many places tumbled down, and those standing ready to fall; the parapet afforded but little cover for our men. The bastions ill contrived and of no service till made so by the hard labour of our men who were constantly annoyed

[1] Orme, Vol. I., p. 191.

[2] Orme writes: "This sally would be condemned by the rules of war established in Europe, for they forbid the besieged to run such a risque, unless they are assured of greatly outnumbering the party they attack; but it is not reasonable to strain the rules calculated for one system to the service of another differing so widely from it, as the modes of war in Indostan differ from those in Europe."—*Ibid.*, p. 192.

by the enemy's fire from the houses, whilst we could not see so much as one of them. The inhabitants gave us to understand the use of the water would be destructive to our men, and the hopes of fresh supplies intirely cut off, besides our quantity of ammunition far short of what would be judged sufficient for our defence.

"The enemy intirely surrounded our walls, placing their men in the houses upon the side of the ditch and kept a continual fire all round, so that our people could no sooner look over the parapet but they had a whole volley of small shot fired at them from the houses not thirty yards distant, by which we lost a good many men."

The sergeant omits to mention that "three serjeants were killed, who at different times singly accompanied Captain Clive in visiting the works."[1] The enemy at first had no battering guns, and the sergeant tells us that nothing more remarkable than the throwing of a few shells into the fort happened till October 7:

"7th October. When they dismounted one of our two eighteen pounders by the first shot they fired, which was the knowledge we had of their having battering cannon, and by another shot intirely disabled her, which gave them an opportunity to beat down the parapet and destroy our defences before we could have the other gun mounted to oppose them; however we had been provident enough to have fascines ready, with which we made a battery in the night and endeavoured to retaliate our misfortune by dismounting theirs, but our train Officer being ill of his wounds our shot were badly aimed and the enemy soon dismounted this gun likewise. The place of the wall they began to batter the stone-work was already tumbled down, so that they had little difficulty in making a breach, which Captain Clive being resolved to defend, endeavoured to raise with fascinery on the inside, and filling up with earth, ordering a deep trench to be dug that their design might be as difficult as possible. On the inside this trench was the whole length of the breach, which he made the best use of by taking down the upper part of its wall and leaving enough standing for a breast work for our men, supporting the roof on pillars for a protection from the weather, and kept a strong guard in it, at the same time ordering pickets to be drove on the ramparts at the ends of the breach to hinder the enemy's running along the curtain. And got one six pounder on the flank and two on the terras of a house in front.

"14th. The enemy kept so hot a fire from their cannon that they split their only 18 pounder, the rest being only 6s & 3s."

On October 21 the President at Fort St. David laid before the Board a letter from Captain Clive:

[1] Orme, Vol. I., p. 193.

"Advising that he is invested in the fort of Arcot, where the enemy are cannonading him. That unfortunately two of his 18-pounders are disabled by the shot from their battery; he was going to mount the last he has. That he has three months' provisions and thinks himself able to defend a breach should the enemy make one. His only apprehension, therefore, are his peoples falling down through fatigue; that he thinks no less force than 1,000 Blacks and 200 Europeans can attempt to relieve him, as the enemy's situation is strong and their number increase daily; if therefore we cannot furnish such a body he gives it as his opinion the place should be evacuated as soon as possible, as it must fall when his provisions are expended. Mr. Prince writing that if he can have fifty men more from hence he shall be able to send out the party Captain Clive thinks necessary. Ordered that number be immediately detached to Madras with some sepoys. And the President is desired to direct the Deputy Governor to dispatch the reinforcement to Arcot as expeditiously as possible."[1]

The enemy grew nearer and nearer every day, and two wide breaches were now nearly practicable. The sergeant enters in his diary:

"24th [October]. They opened a Battery of 1.18, and 1.9 pounder on the S.W. of the fort. Our parapet being pretty good in this place, we drove them several times from their guns by our small arms, killing several of their gunners. But they by degrees beat down that defence and breached without any other opposition than from a 6 pounder we had mounted in a fascine battery on one of the Cavaliers, which they soon disabled, and made a practicable breach of forty yards wide. Our defences at this breach were contrived nearly in the same manner as at the other."

Thus October wore away. The courage of the garrison never faltered, but it was sorely tried. The deficiency in all articles of food grew serious as the month advanced. Strange and insufficient diet increased the sickness.[2]

[1] Memorandum on the Madras Records (1891), by G. W. Forrest, Director of Records, Government of India.

[2] Malcolm writes: "I have it in my power, from authority I cannot doubt, to add to the account of this celebrated siege an anecdote, singularly illustrative of the character of the native troops of India. When provisions became so scarce that there was a fear that famine might compel them to surrender, the sepoys proposed to Clive to limit them to the water in which the rice was boiled." "This water," says Malcolm in a note, "is called Canjee, and contains a sufficient infusion of the grain to be nutritive, resembling thin gruel." "'It is,' they said, 'sufficient for our support: the Europeans require the grain.'"—"Memoirs of Lord Clive," Vol. I., pp. 96–7. Macaulay (Essays, Vol. III., p. 130) converts this into the following well-known passage: "The sepoys came to Clive, not to complain of their scanty fare, but to propose that all the grain should be given to the Europeans, who required more nourishment than the natives of Asia. The thin gruel, they said,

Early in November, the sergeant says, "Our people sickly, not above 80 military fit for duty." They had daily watched with anxious eyes to see some sign of the reinforcement which had left Madras. A spy brought the evil tidings that it had been compelled to fall back. But Clive was ever full of resource. Morari Rao, the Mahratta chief, was encamped with 6,000 horsemen thirty miles from Arcot. He had been paid by the kingdom of Mysore to render assistance to Mohammed Ali. But he had heard of the retreat of Gingen's force, and he remained inactive on the frontier of the Carnatic awaiting the issue of the siege of Trichinopoly. He would then take part with the victor. Clive now sent a messenger to the Mahratta to inform him of his critical situation, and requesting that he would approach to his relief.

"The messenger returning safely to the fort, brought a letter from Morari-row, in which he said that he would not delay a moment to send a detachment of his troops to the assistance of such brave men as the defenders of Arcot, whose behaviour had now convinced him that the English could fight."[1]

On this exchange of communication between Clive and the Mahratta chief becoming known to Rezza Saheb he began

which was strained away from the rice, would suffice for themselves. History contains no more touching instance of military fidelity, or of the influence of a commanding mind." Malcolm first mentioned the incident in a "Short Account of the Rise, Progress, and Character of the Native Army of India, written in 1816, at the desire of the late Lord Buckinghamshire." He states: "The particulars of that siege, which forms a remarkable feature in the life of the celebrated Clive, have been given by an eloquent and faithful historian (Orme), but he has not informed us of one occurrence that took place, and which, as it illustrates the character of the Indian soldier, well merited to be preserved. When provisions were very low the Hindoo sepoys entreated their commander to allow them to boil the rice (the only food left) for the whole garrison. 'Your English soldiers,' they said, 'can eat from our hands though we cannot from theirs; we will allot as their share every grain of rice, and subsist ourselves by drinking the water in which it has been boiled.' I state this remarkable anecdote from an authority I cannot doubt, as it refers to the most unexceptionable contemporary witness." "The authority I cannot doubt," we may presume, was the second Lord Clive, created Earl of Powis, eldest son of Robert Clive, who was Governor of Madras (1798–1803), and with whom Malcolm was on intimate terms of friendship. "The most unexceptionable contemporary witness," I presume, was Clive himself. But why were these words omitted in the Life? It was right to omit the words "the only food left," as that was absolutely incorrect, for the sepoys could not have existed on the gruel alone nor the soldiers on the rice. The second version of the anecdote is greatly impaired by the omission of the main circumstance—the entrance of caste considerations into the case. The sepoys could not eat the food cooked by Christians, and therefore they made the offer.

[1] Orme, Vol. I., p. 196.

to consider whether it were not possible to gain his ends by negotiations instead of war. He accordingly sent a messenger, who, under a flag of truce, obtained admission into the fort. On being conducted into the presence of Clive he delivered his message. Rezza Saheb "offered honourable terms to the garrison and a large sum of money to Captain Clive; and if his offers were not accepted he threatened to storm the fort immediately and put every man to the sword."[1] Clive calmly listened, and when the speaker had ended he treated the threat to storm with scorn, and the offer of money with contempt. He wrote to the President at Fort St. David and to the Deputy Governor at Madras,

> "giving a description of his situation and that the enemy had made two large breaches in the walls which he was fortifying in the best manner he could, and was not under the least apprehension from them unless they should make a breach of one-half the fort. That he had received a summons from young Chunda, to whom he returned an answer and let him know that neither threats nor bribery should hinder him from doing his duty."[2]

News now reached Arcot that the reinforcements from Madras, increased in numbers, were again on the march, and on November 9 "the Morattoes . . . coming to our assistance, took some of the enemy's ammunition and burnt some of the skirts of the town."[3] There was now no alternative for Rezza Saheb but to storm the fort.

"About 2 in the morning 24 November 1751, a Harcarry [or spy] who had been sent out to watch the motions of the enemy," says the sergeant, "came in and informed us they intended to storm. But as our people were night and day on their posts we made no alteration in our disposition." Clive having given orders that he should be awakened at the first alarm, lay down to sleep. "About half an hour before day-break they made the signal for a general attack."

The day that came was one of the great days of the Mohurram, the period of fasting and public mourning observed by the

[1] Orme, Vol. I., p. 196.

[2] Memorandum on the Madras Records (1891), by G. W. Forrest, Director of Records, Government of India.

[3] "Siege and Defence of Arcot, by a Serjeant."

Mohammedans in commemoration of the murder of Hassan and the cruel death on the plains of Kerbela of his brother Hosain—the sons of Ali, and the grandsons of the Prophet. On the annual festival of their martyrdom the Mussulmans abandon their souls to religious frenzy, and a peculiar blessing rests on those who die in holy war during that mournful period. It was at such a time that the Moslem soldier at Arcot felt and obeyed the impetus that paradise was the swift and sure reward of him who fell in battle against the infidel. The stormers, their hot blood inflamed to madness by arrack, by opium, and by religious fury, moved swiftly forward to the attack. A formidable host that carried ladders strove with considerable courage to "scalade all round." Two large divisions preceded by elephants, which the princes of India kept for the service of war, advanced against the two gates. The beasts had for battering purposes a protecting pike fastened by an iron band round the head. Their drivers drove them against the ponderous gates. A supreme moment. The gates stood firm. The unwieldy brutes presented an easy mark to the besieged, who shot at them from the loop-holes in the walls. Terrified at the sound of the muskets and galled by the bullets, they soon turned round, and dashing through the advancing troops trampled down many of them and threw all into disorder.[1]

Meanwhile, the other columns attacked the two breaches.

"The ditch before the breach to the north-west was fordable; and as many as the breach would admit, mounted it with a mad kind of intrepidity, whilst numbers came and sat down with great com-

[1] It was from the pages of Orme that Macaulay took his famous account of the storming of Arcot fort. Orme wrote (Vol., I., p. 198): "Captain Clive, awakened by the alarm, found his garrison at their posts, according to the dispositions he had made. The parties who attacked the gates drove before them several elephants, who, with large plates of iron fixed to their foreheads, were intended to break them down; but the elephants, wounded by the musketry, soon turned, and trampled on those who escorted them." Macaulay wrote (Essays, Vol. III., p. 131): "He was awakened by the alarm, and was instantly at his post. The enemy advanced, driving before them elephants whose foreheads were armed with iron plates. It was expected that the gates would yield to the shock of these living battering-rams. But the huge beasts no sooner felt the English musket-balls than they turned round and rushed furiously away, trampling on the multitude which had urged them forward." The conversion of elephants into living battering-rams is characteristic.

posure in the fausse-braye under the tower where the field piece was planted, and waited here to relieve those who were employed in the attack: these passed the breach, and some of them even got over the first trench before the defenders gave fire; it fell heavily, and every shot did execution; and a number of muskets were loaded in readiness, which those behind delivered to the first rank as fast as they could discharge them. The two pieces of cannon from the top of the house fired likewise on the assailants, who in a few minutes abandoned the attack, when another body, and then another succeeded, who were driven off in the same manner: in the mean time mortars with short fusees, which had been prepared and lodged on the adjacent rampart, were thrown into the fausse-braye, and by their explosion drove the crowd, who had seated themselves there, back again over the ditch."[1]

At the breach to the south-west, "the ditch being deep," says the sergeant, "they attempted to come over on floats, but were so warmly opposed by the fire of our well pointed grape that only two of them got over, the rest being drove into the water or killed. They fired very hot to cover their retreat, and we did great execution among them by our hand granades and musketry." The sergeant does not mention that Clive himself laid one of the field-pieces with his own hand and sent "the well pointed grape."

After a stiff struggle the enemy were repulsed at every point. How stiff it was is revealed in the sergeant's simple and faithful record:

"Our men fit for duty, Europeans and Blacks, did not exceed 240, of which 4 whites were killed and 2 Blacks wounded, and there were 12,000 cartridges expended during the action, which lasted not an hour, so that it will be readily allowed we were not idle. The loss of the enemy on this occasion we can [know] no otherwise than that there were a great many dead in the streets, ditch and breaches, and the deserters and inhabitants affirmed their loss to be near 200 killed and wounded, among which was one Abdul Codah [Khan] a leading man among their Seapoys, which afterwards occasioned many disturbances among 'em. It was reported that one of their Seapoys shot a french Serjeant who commanded the party to the attack, the Serjeant having left them in the lurch."

Abdul Codah Khan, the commander of the enemy's sepoys, had shown conspicuous bravery in the attack. When he

[1] Orme, Vol. I., p. 198.

received his mortal wound a gallant exploit was performed. A sepoy, seeing his beloved commander fall in the breach, crossed the ditch and carried off the body, "exposing himself during the attempt to the fire of 40 muskets, from which he had the good fortune to escape."[1] The assailants continued their fire upon the breach till three in the evening, when they requested a short truce that they might bury their dead. This was granted and hostilities ceased; "the enemy carried off their dead and we their arms."[2] The truce lasted till four, "at which time they began and continued till 2 in the morning [of] the 15th (26 November N.S.), when they broke up the siege, going away in the greatest confusion, leaving behind them most of their guns, some shot, shells and powder. This agreeable news was soon communicated to the inexpressable satisfaction of everybody."

Soon after more "agreeable news" came to them,

> "and gave us unbounded joy when we heard Captain Kilpatrick was within a few hours march with only a handfull of men, with which he must have encountered 6 or 7,000, had he attempted to relieve us, under the most insurmountable difficulties. The enemy having barricaded every street and passage in such manner that it was impossible for us ever to have joined had the enemy kept possession, and equally impracticable for the Morrattoes to be of any service to him or us. Thus did providence disapoint our fears, and relieve us from the dread necessity of starving or submitting to the terms of merciless barbarians. And Captain Kilpatrick's command joined us in the afternoon. We fully and unmolested enjoyed the fruits of the earth so long denied us, tho every day in our sight, and solaced ourselves with the pleasing reflection of having maintained the character of Britons in a Clime so remote from our own."

So ended the memorable siege of Arcot. For fifty days, amidst fatigue, hunger, disease, and imminent danger, 320 men in all, commanded by four officers, held a vast fortress invested by 10,000 men before the little band had time to repair the dilapidated defences. The enemy from their "18 pound shot besides many more from their smaller cannon" showered shots and bombs on the working parties, but they

[1] Orme, Vol. I., p. 199.

[2] The Sergeant's Diary.

toiled on. They poured on those who manned the ramparts volleys of musketry; "a good many men" fell "owing to the unlucky nearness of the houses to the walls," but they held on. The spirit of the garrison answered to that of their youthful commander. They admired and trusted a leader who surmounted every obstacle, whose energy was untiring, who with calm equanimity was ever ready to face the bullets of the enemy. The same feeling stirred Clive and the sergeant, and it was one which must be well understood and well remembered if we are to hold the noble Empire whose foundation stone was laid at Arcot—the conscious motive of maintaining "the character of Britons in a clime so remote from our own." [1]

Clive had sustained a siege with conspicuous success, but defensive fighting had been forced on him. He had no love for it; the chief aim of his strategy in all his campaigns was to secure the offensive, however inferior his force. Four days after the siege had been raised and reinforcements had reached him, he, leaving a small garrison under the command of Kilpatrick in the fort, took the field with 200 Europeans, 700 sepoys, and three field-pieces. He had been invited by the Governor of Timary to take possession of its fort, "which we accordingly did on the 18th." "We found in Timmerie a few horses, a few pieces of cannon, some arms, shot, gunpowder, a little money, and other things of value." [2] Leaving a few men to guard the fort, Clive returned and encamped in a grove on the skirts of Arcot.

[1] Orme concludes his narrative of the defence as follows: "Thus ended this siege, maintained 50 days, under every disadvantage of situation and force, by a handful of men in their first campaign, with a spirit worthy of the most veteran troops; and conducted by their young commander with indefatigable activity, unshaken constancy, and undaunted courage: and notwithstanding he had at this time neither read books, or conversed with men capable of giving him much instruction in the military art; all the resources which he employed in the defence of Arcot, were such as are dictated by the best masters in the science of war."—Vol. I., p. 200. Wilks writes: "In a siege of fifty days, which terminated on the 14th November, Captain Clive, infusing his own spirit into the remnant of his little party, displayed in the defence of this place that ready perception of the best possible resources, under every varied emergency, which men of ordinary talents are contented to acquire as the result of study, long experience, and attentive observation."—Vol. I., p. 275.

[2] The Sergeant's Diary.

"This top [tope] commanded the three Roads into the town on the side of Velour where the enemy were encamped. Here we remained a few days, judging it inconsistent with the rules of prudence to leave the fort guardless, well knowing the disadvantages we must be under if the enemy should repossess themselves of the town, and we thought it too daring to attempt attacking so numerous an enemy in a camp where their fears had entrenched them up to the eyes, besides being under cover of Velour guns, till we were joined by the Morrattoes, who were then some 20 miles beyond the enemy to secure their booty. Marched out and encamped in a top about 3 miles distant from the fort, where we remained inactive for two or three days, being in expectations the Morrattoes would join us. At length, tired with their ill timed delays, we marched towards Velour, but by the villany of our Harcarrys were misconducted and returned to our encampment." [1]

The next day it was rumoured that the French had surprised the Mahratta camp. The report was swiftly confirmed by the arrival of the Mahratta commander and his thousand horse, "who tho they had about 20 men killed and wounded, besides some horse and furniture taken, were more frightened than hurt, and agreable to our wishes were filled with sentiments of revenge, intreating Captain Clive to march towards Chuckley droganm, the place the French had used 'em so ill in as to come upon them without preadvising them of their intention." Clive complied with their request and marched to the place, "when the Morrattoes made a vain search for what they had lost." [2]

On Clive's return, a letter from the French commander was intercepted, in which he complained to Dupleix that the reinforcements from Pondicherry had not approached nearer to him. Clive resolved at once to march to Arni, a strong fort situated about twenty miles south of Arcot, in order to intercept them. "But the Morrattoes would not stir that way." A few days later spies brought news that the French party were at Chittaput and intended to march to Vellore with the greatest expedition. "Captain Clive intreated the Morrattoes to march with him, and meeting with a flat denial, begged them to lend him 200 horse or even bullocks; but these mercenary wretches expected no plunder, a reason

[1] The Sergeant's Diary. [2] *Ibid.*

sufficient to hinder them from assisting us with anything in their power."[1] The next day the Mahratta commander heard from his spies that the reinforcement had encamped near Arni, and that they escorted a large amount of treasure. He immediately went to Clive and urged him to march against them, "which he did immediately, and to the Morrattoes great disappointment on our arrival at Pandavocam found the enemy had marched off in the night."[2] The troops returned to their encampment near Arcot, where Clive awaited the movements of the enemy. On December 13 news reached him that Rezza Saheb, who had with his whole force quitted Vellore in the night and made a forced march to Arni, had been joined by the French reinforcement. He had determined to strike them on the march to Vellore. The sergeant's account of Clive's first important victory in the open field bears printing in integrity:

"We immediately marched towards them, and our advanced party came in sight of them about eight o'clock in the morning; we continued our march till near ten when Captain Clive ordered to halt in full sight of the enemy. This he did as well to refresh the men, who had marched most of the night as to wait the motions of the enemy (then 2 miles distant) who seemed on their march towards us. The place we encamped in was an eminence in front of which were Paddy fields reaching more than musket shot from the encampment. On the right flank was situate a village with a wet trench on one side of it. On the left flank was a Palmira top. Between the trench which ran down by the side of the Paddy fields on the right was a hard road that would not admit of above six men abreast. We were soon satisfied the enemy intended to attack us, by their continuing to march in order of battle towards us, and began to be much pleased with the situation Captain Clive had pitched upon, and more so when we found the numbers of the enemy so far exceed our expectations and that the Morrattoes had left at Arcot 1000 of their nominal three. At twelve at noon the enemy began cannonading out of distance. Upon which Captain Clive ordered a party of Seapoys to advance down the trench side on the right with a small pop gun. The three 6 pounders and Howbitz were on the eminence in rear of the Paddy fields. Behind them was a Tank in rear of which [were] posted the Europeans. On the left the Morrattoes advanced into the top as did the Enemy's horse the same.

[1] The Sergeant's Diary.

[2] Orme's account differs from that of the Sergeant. Orme, Vol. I., pp. 201–2.

" The enemy by continuing their march soon came near enough to cannonade at proper distance, which we returned to more purpose. The ground they were upon was a gradual descent, hard and channelly, which carried our shot a vast way. The Paddy fields in front buried their shot at once, so that they did little execution. Our advanced Seapoys at first retreated, but it was only to a Bank from behind which they kept the enemy from advancing that way. On the left the Morrattoes charged the Moor horse, but they being interlined with musketry the Morattoes retreated, having a great aversion to small arms since their being surprized. Captain Clive observing that the warmth of our cannonadement made the enemy incline towards the top on the left, ordered Messrs. Bulkley and Morrice with three platoons and field piece over into the top, and Messrs. Dawson and Turner to advance on the right with one platoon to a little Choultry near where the Seapoys were. When Lieut: Bulkley and party arrived, very unluckily there were no shot with the gun, which as soon as Captain Clive got notice of, he ordered the party back to their ground, strictly charging the officer to march as slow as were he on a parade, which retreat, so far from appearing an advantage to the enemy, that they began to retire from the top leaving only their horse, imagining we intended to carry off their artillery and baggage by advancing to the right. The Moor horse now deserted by their foot, the Morattoes at several different charges dislodged them from the top. Captain Clive observing the French advance behind a Choultry and fustrees [*sic*] ordered the Europeans with two of the 6 pounders to advance upon them, but they scattered and ran off in the greatest confusion. Their horse were retreated near a mile, and by sunset Capt. Clive with some Seapoys had drove them [into] three different Choultry's and a pagoda, where we encamped that night. About 60 yards distant from this pagoda was a very deep ditch naturally hollowed out by the declivity on each side and being difficult to transport our carriages over it together with the night coming made it certainly the most prudent step to halt, especially as had we attempted a pursuit we must have laboured under the same and greater disadvantages than the enemy did in attacking us, as they were by this time got over Aroni river the banks of which being very steep made it a difficult task to convey carriages and baggage, besides being under the cover of the fort. In the night the enemy betook themselves to flight leaving behind them most of their baggage some horses, and, it was said, two of their cannon, the carriages being broke in the engagement. Their flight was in a manner the most unguarded, for except the body of French there were not above 20 or 30 of them in one place, this gave the Morrattoes an opportunity of making a capture of many of their horses, Muskets and baggage. Themselves acknowledged to have got 200 Horses. We were well satisfied of many more, and the Braminy Kelledar of the fort assured us the Morrattoes had got 7000 gold Moors, Nazajines, fan [ams ?] and other things to the value of 40000 Pagodas. The loss on our side killed and wounded did not exceed 10 or 12, And those only Topasses and Seapoys. That of the enemy was more numerous, and, by the report of deserters & the Braminy of the fort, was above 200 killed and wounded, of which were a good many French. We encamped between the fort and river and next day a great many of their Seapoys (almost a number equal to the whole of ours) offered their service to us. Those who had muskets we entertained, and dismissed the others. As we were informed the enemy had left most of their baggage in the fort we summoned the Braminy to deliver them up. But he denied our allegiance and we marched up to his gates and either by persuading him he had some horses & an Elephant of the enemy's, or by his fears, he came upon terms & sent us 15 horse, one Elephant and a bill for 2000 Rupees which I can't say whether accepted or not. It was Captain Clive's opinion we should go to Chittaput where the scattered remains of their army were collecting, but the Morrattoes would not stir that way, being of opinion little plunder was to be got where the french had been and Conjevaram being a rich place they advised and insisted on going to it, which we afterwards did, and after their having got every thing of value in the town and adjacent country deserted us in a most rascally manner.

"In the time of the engagement our Seapoys, excepting about 250, all were behind the horse on the left and into the village on the right." [1]

Thus, by a good use of his artillery and skilful tactics, Clive defeated a force superior to his own in numbers and artillery. Of his own share in this or any other battle Clive said but little. At the request of Orme he in after years sent the following brief memorandum:

"BATTLE OF ARANI

"The Seapoys and horse in Raja Saheib's army behaved much better than the french. Platoons of Seapoys were interspersed with the horse, and by their fire dispersed the Marattas in four or five charges they made upon them. When observing the retreat of the french, & being annoyed by the fire of two field pieces which were just brought to play upon them, retreated into the Village with the Marattas at their heels. The french did not think themselves safe till they got to Gingee.

"The fort of Arani is very strong—The Kelledar was a Brahmin. After the victory in sight of his walls he sent an Elephant as a compliment of submission to Captain Clive, & assured him of his fidelity to Mahomed Ally, having hitherto acted a neutral part between Mahomed Ally and Chunda Saheib." [2]

[1] The Sergeant's Diary.
[2] Orme MSS.: India, Vol. II., p. 297.

Clive immediately followed up his success. The French, in order to intercept communications between Arcot and Madras, had again taken possession of the great pagoda of Conjeveram and placed a garrison in it. From this stronghold they sallied forth and cut off convoys. In one of these raids they surprised a body of men who, having been disabled at Arcot, were proceeding to Madras. Amongst these were Ensigns Revel and Glass. Clive determined to reduce the pagoda, and two or three days after the battle he marched rapidly on it.

"The French officer at Conjevaram was summoned to surrender; and none of the garrison understanding the English language, he ordered his prisoners, Revel and Glass, to write a letter, and acquaint captain Clive, that he intended to expose them on the walls, if the pagoda was attacked. They wrote this, but added, that they hoped no regard to their safety would induce him to discontinue his operations against the place." [1]

Two eighteen-pounders were brought from Madras and began to batter in the walls at a distance of two hundred yards. "The enemy had no cannon, but fired very smartly with their musketry, which killed several men." Clive had another miraculous escape. He and Bulkley were reconnoitring the pagoda over a garden wall, when the latter was shot through the head by his side. For two days the stout walls resisted, and then they began to crumble away; the garrison slipped away in the cover of darkness, but left behind the two prisoners.

"After ruining the defences of Conjevaram, captain Clive sent 200 Europeans and 500 Sepoys to Arcot, and returned in the middle of December with the rest to Madrass; from whence he went to Fort St. David to give an account of his campaign to the presidency." [2]

He also went to arrange further operations for the relief of Trichinopoly.

[1] Orme, Vol. I., p. 203. [2] *Ibid.*

CHAPTER X

1751–2: THE SIEGE OF TRICHINOPOLY

WHILE Clive was being besieged at Arcot the French persistently carried on the regular operations of the siege of Trichinopoly. In the beginning of September, 1751, they raised a battery, which they afterwards converted into a regular redoubt, twelve hundred yards from the city wall. It consisted of three 18-pounders and three mortars. They mounted two 18-pounders on the sand-hill which has ever since been known as "the French Rock." They also raised a battery of two guns on the island of Seringham "from which they fired across the Caveri at the northern gate of the city, to interrupt the communication of the inhabitants with the river." [1] But these guns, as well as those on the French Rock, were at too great a distance to be of any real service.

D'Auteuil had been succeeded in the command of the French detachment by Mr. Law, nephew of the famous Scottish financier. He had displayed considerable personal courage and energy during the siege of Pondicherry, but he was not one of those men who grow greater with the increase of responsibility. He was not lacking in ability, but in judgment and character. He was full of ideas, and was able to express them with considerable skill and fluency, but he could not weigh them. He regarded them as inspirations, and adhered to them with tenacity. As is the case with most vulgar natures, his determination was mere obstinacy. From the moment he arrived at Trichinopoly, Law determined to take it by siege or blockade. Dupleix sent him every soldier that came from France. He sent him letter after letter directing, beseeching him to storm the town while the enemy were demoralised. It

[1] Orme, Vol. I., pp. 204–5.

was all in vain. Law wrote to Dupleix and argued that it was impossible to take by storm a city so well fortified, and defended, not by Indians, but by British soldiers. He preferred winning his way into it by the slow process of sap and mine. Thus week passed after week, and at the end of October the French had done no more than surprise the English entrenchments opposite the French Rock and carry off "the captain of nine Coffres." Gingen, knowing that an attack on the strong French posts was too hazardous, and seeing that the besiegers did little harm to the town, kept the British troops out of the reach of annoyance.

During the month of November the French continued to bombard the town, but, as Law did not change the position of his guns, he met with no greater success. He hoped that the constant bombardment would keep the garrison in check while the native levies of Chanda Saheb, 15,000 horse and 20,000 foot, would, by cutting off communications, compel the town to surrender from want of supplies. Week after week he informed Dupleix that the capitulation could not be long delayed. But his own strategy and the diplomacy of Mohammed Ali proved a bar to the fulfilment of his hopes. When Mohammed Ali found that he had no money to pay his troops and that provisions grew scarce, he sent an ambassador to the Rajah of Mysore, whose territory lay on the tableland between the Eastern and Western Ghats. The extent of the territory was not great—about 200 miles in length and 150 in breadth—but its physical features, deep ravines and lofty mountains, were favourable to protection and to dominion. On the west it extended to within 30 miles of the coast of Malabar, on the east its frontier was protected by the strong fortress of Carour (Karur),[1] within 40 miles of Trichinopoly.

When Aurangzib contemplated subduing the whole of the Deccan and actually brought it back once more under the

[1] "Carour, situated about 50 miles from Tritchanopoly and close to the bank of the Coleroon."—Orme, Vol. I., p. 207. It was one of the most important posts of the Mysore kingdom. In "The Imperial Gazetteer" it is written "Karur," but in history it will always be Carour, so often thus mentioned on account of its different sieges.

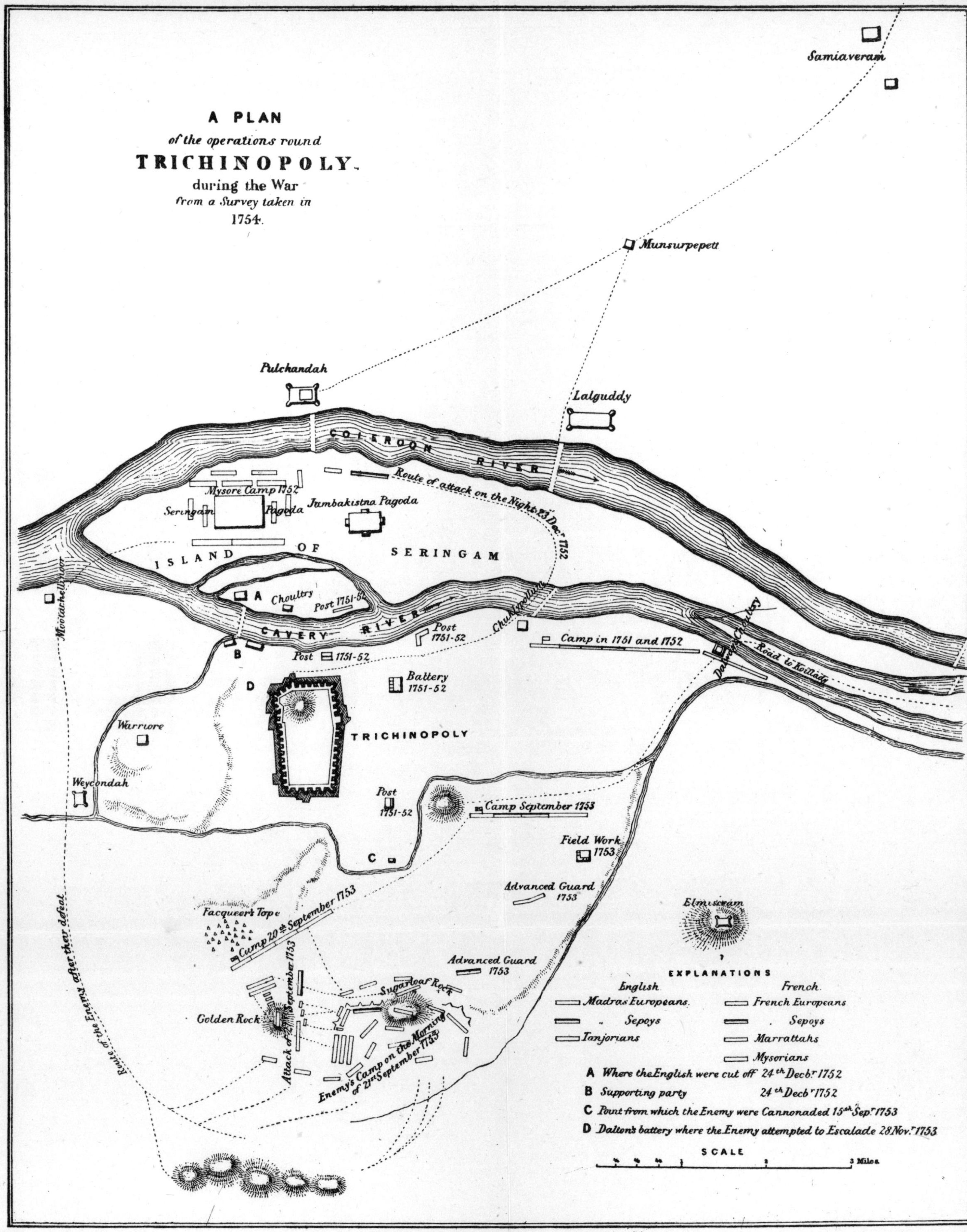
A PLAN
of the operations round
TRICHINOPOLY.
during the War
from a Survey taken in
1754.
Samiaveram
Munsurpepett
Pulchandah
Lalguddy
COLEROON RIVER
Route of attack on the Night 23 Decr. 1752
Mysore Camp 1752
Seringam Pagoda
Jambakistna Pagoda
ISLAND OF SERINGAM
Mootachellinoor
A
Choultry
Post 1751-52
CAVERY RIVER
Post 1751-52
Chucklypollam
Camp in 1751 and 1752
Dalton's Choultry
Road to Koiladdy
B
Post 1751-52
Battery 1751-52
D
Warriore
TRICHINOPOLY
Weycondah
Post 1751-52
Camp September 1753
Field Work 1753
C
Advanced Guard 1753
Elmiseram
Facqueer's Tope
Camp 20th September 1753
Attack of 21st September 1753
Advanced Guard 1753
Sugarloaf Rock
Golden Rock
Enemy's Camp on the Morning of 21st September 1753
Route of the Enemy after their defeat
EXPLANATIONS
English
French
Madras Europeans
French Europeans
Sepoys
Sepoys
Tanjorians
Marrattahs
Mysorians
A Where the English were cut off 24th Decbr. 1752
B Supporting party 24th Decbr. 1752
C Point from which the Enemy were Cannonaded 15th Sepr. 1753
D Dalton's battery where the Enemy attempted to Escalade 28 Novr. 1753
SCALE
1
2
3 Miles

allegiance of Delhi, Mysore escaped under its wise ruler, Chikka Devaraj, who was advanced by the Mogul Emperor. With Devaraj the greatness of the house ended, and he was succeeded by incompetent princes who rapidly lost all authority. Under them all real authority passed to the Mayor of the Palace, who was in this case the *dhalavay* or Commander-in-Chief.

When Mohammed Ali sent his envoy to the capital of Mysore, the *dhalavay* was Nanj Raj, an uncle of the young king, a man of unbounded ambition but lacking in many of the qualities which command success. Quick and cunning, he was a master in the art of intrigue, but at a critical moment he lacked decision and boldness. Nothing could be more gratifying to Nanj Raj than to learn that Mohammed Ali needed his help, and that the price he was willing to pay for his successful assistance was the cession of Trichinopoly and all its dependencies down to Cape Comorin, constituting a dominion little inferior to that of Mysore itself. All that Mohammed Ali asked for himself was a personal jaghire to which he might retire. It is not easy to believe that any Oriental prince ever thought that Mohammed Ali would voluntarily fulfil these terms. What is more easy to believe is that Nanj Raj hoped that, once in possession of the fort of Trichinopoly, he would have him in his power. By lending Mohammed Ali pecuniary and military aid he was taking a course by which he might gain, and could not lose, a great deal. There was also another strong motive, based not on probability but on facts, which prompted Nanj Raj. During the time that Chanda Saheb governed Trichinopoly he formed a design of conquering Mysore and had besieged Carour for several months. The time for revenge had come, and Nanj Raj entered into the compact. About the same time that Morari Rao, the Mahratta chief, marched towards Arcot, Nanj Raj set forth from Seringapatam and arrived towards the latter end of the year in the district of Carour. His force consisted of 5,000 horse and 10,000 infantry, of which the only regular troops were a small body in the corps of Hyder Naick.

Hyder Naick, or Hyder Ali, who lived to convert the Hindu kingdom of Mysore into a Mohammedan empire and to endanger the very existence of the British power in India, was the grandson of a wandering dervish from the Punjab who is said to have founded, in a little town about a hundred miles from Hyderabad, a small mosque and rest house for fakirs and to have accumulated some property by this pious speculation. His two sons proceeded to the south in search of service. Hyder was only seven years of age when his father, a gallant soldier, fell in battle, and he, with his brother aged nine, were put to the torture for a pretended debt of their parent. This monstrous act of cruelty made a lasting impression on a nature inclined to be savage and morose. He "sought his revenge after the lapse of thirty-two years with all the virulence belonging to the memory of a recent injury."[1] Hyder grew up without learning to read or write any language, but he received from Nature excellent parts, vast muscular strength and unflinching courage.[2] He was a bold and skilful horseman, and no one outdid him as a marksman.

It was at the siege of Deonhully (1749), a strong fort about one hundred miles from Bangalore, that Hyder first saw active service as a volunteer horseman who was also occasionally entrusted with the command of parties of infantry in the trenches. "He was observed on every service of danger to lead the way, and to conduct himself with a coolness and self-possession seldom found in a young soldier."[3] By his valour, energy, and self-possession he won the favour of Nanj Raj, who, at the close of the siege, raised him at once to the command of fifty horse and two hundred infantry, with orders to recruit and augment his corps. The following year he was present when the French attacked the encampment of Nasir Jang, and was foremost in an unsuccessful attempt on the flank of the French column. During the confusion of the day his select

[1] Wilks: "History of Mysoor," Vol. I., p. 246.

[2] Selections from the State Papers of the Governors-General, edited by G. W. Forrest (Warren Hastings), Vol. I., p. 282.

[3] Wilks: "History of Mysoor," Vol. I., p. 247

band of "brave and faithful thieves" secured 500 muskets. Hyder armed his infantry with these, and he employed a few French sepoy deserters to drill his recruits: and he "was much advanced in the favour of Nunjeraj by exhibiting to him these invincibles who were to conquer Trichinopoly."[1] Early in February, 1752, Nanj Raj with his force arrived at that famous stronghold of the south.

The disappointment and distress which Dupleix endured at Law's refusal to act with vigour were increased when he heard the news of Clive's victory at Arni. The siege of Arcot revealed that the English had got a new leader of rare courage and resource; the operations after the siege proved that they had found a commander with dash and vigour who could lead a small force to victory. When Dupleix heard that Clive had sent the main portion of his force to Trichinopoly and had himself proceeded to Fort St. David, he was too clear-sighted not to see the next move—a fresh expedition to Trichinopoly under the command of Clive. He determined to checkmate it by playing Clive's own game. Clive had lessened the pressure on Trichinopoly by his dash at Arcot. Dupleix would prevent him from relieving the beleaguered garrison by threatening Madras. In a dispatch, dated January 25, 1752, the Governor in Council at Fort St. David informed the Court that "Captain Clive with the Morattas" had routed the enemy in the field near Arni with "many killed and made prisoners." The defeated army

> "took the advantage of the night and each shifted for himself, their next rendezvouse was at Chittaput about twenty miles nearer Pondicherry, where they have gather'd their scatter'd Troops again, taken the Field and are near Covelong; it is said their design is against St. Thomé but judged they are not in a condition to do it."[2]

The Presidency soon discovered the error. Rezza Saheb, at the instigation of Dupleix, invaded the Company's territory, burnt several villages, and plundered the country houses built by the English at the foot of St. Thomas's Mount.

[1] Wilks: "History of Mysoor," Vol. I., pp. 269–70, 278–9.
[2] Madras MS. Records.

Clive was ordered to return at once to Madras and assume command. At a Consultation held on February 17, 1752, the President produced to the Board two letters from Captain Clive, dated 10th and 11th,

"advising that he had taken upon him the Command of the Army at Madrass and had been joined by part of the Bengal Detachment that were arriv'd from thence on the Ship *Fort St. David*, but was apprehensive of not meeting with any Arms, therefore requests a supply, having rais'd about five hundred Sepoys for whom he is in want of them. That he was then encamped in a very strong situation at the little Mount, and the enemy were about seven miles distant, whose strength, from an exact account he had procur'd, consisted of about fourteen hundred Sepoy's Matchlocks, &c, and about the same number of Horse, though only six hundred were esteem'd good, thirty Europeans, eighty Topasses, with eight small Field Pieces and two Tomans."

At a Consultation held seven days later (February 24)

"The President lays before the Board two Letters he has received from Captain Clive dated the 15th & 20th Instant, the most material part of which is vizt, that he has received a Letter from Captain D^{e} Gingins representing how necessary a Step his proceeding to Trichinopoly will be; that Captain Kilpatrick had joined him from Arcot by which with the Bengal Detachment his party consisted of four hundred Military and Train, Thirteen hundred Sepoys besides Matchlocks and 120 horse which last he found great difficulty in raising as money would not do it; that he should do his utmost to bring the enemy to an engagement, if the strength of their situation did not render it imprudent to attack them in it, in which case he thinks he will be best to come this way in order to proceed to Trichinopoly to join Captain D^{e} Gingins, and if he can be strongly reinforced with Military from hence, Deve Cottah and Chellambrum, is of opinion it will soon put an end to the disturbances of the Province, and that he designs leaving behind him for the protection of Madrass about sixty Military, some Horse and Sepoys." [1]

The strong situation to which Clive referred was an entrenched camp at Vendalore, about seventeen miles south-west of Madras, where the enemy lay with a force far superior in numerical strength to his own. It consisted of 400 Europeans, 2,000 sepoys, 2,500 native cavalry, and a large train of artillery. Clive did his utmost to bring the enemy to an

[1] Madras MS. Records. Orme states: "His whole force united consisted of 380 Europeans, 1,300 Sepoys, with 6 field pieces."—Orme Vol. I., p. 213.

engagement. He received intelligence that this camp was not so strongly secured behind as it was in front, on which he took the resolution of making a circuit to attack them in the rear,

"When he was informed that they had very precipitately broke up their camp, and dispersed, with all the appearance of people greatly alarmed. Captain Clive attributed this to their having received bad news from Tritchanopoly, but immediately advanced and took possession of the camp they had deserted. Here 12 hours afterwards he received intelligence that all the dispersed parties had rejoined at Conjevaram. He immediately conjectured their intention was against Arcot, & in this persuasion made a forced march of 20 miles to Conjavaram that evening. Here he found the breach he had made in that place repaired and a garrison of 300 Seapoys left in it who surrendered on the first Summons and here likewise he found his conjectures of the enemy's intentions confirmed by a letter from the commanding officer of Arcot who acquainted him that the enemy were in full march towards that place intending as he supposed to attack him immediately, depending upon the weakness of his garrison. Captain Clive as soon as his men were refreshed proceeded for Arcot, & on his march received a second letter which acquainted him that the french had entered the town in which they had skirmished against the walls, in expectation that their appearance would immediately produce the effect of a piece of treachery they had been carrying on with two Seapoy Officers in the garrison to open one of the gates to them which he had discovered. But that now they had as suddenly disappeared, and he could give no farther account of them. About Six in the Evening near the village of Coverypauck the situation of the enemy was discovered by the fire of 9 pieces of cannon, but not till Captn. Clive's advanced guard was within 250 yards of their entrenchment." [1]

Clive, "for want of horse," as he says, "could not receive intelligence to be depended upon," and he had been entrapped. The enemy were in a strong position, and had the advantage of guns, foot and cavalry. When Clive saw he was surprised and found battle imminent, courageously, aware of the danger round him, with calm diligence and decision he disposed his troops for action. Here is the story of this memorable fight told by the victor with terseness, modesty, and faithfulness of detail:

"The French Infantry and artillery were drawn up in an

[1] Orme MSS.: India, Vol. II., p. 298.

Orchard with a breastwork in front. Their fire did great mischief before it could be avoided but fortunately there was a deep water course to the left of the road into which Captain Clive immediately threw both military and Seapoys, ordering at the same time the baggage with a guard 4 or 500 yards back again: it was the close of evening when this battle began and the enemy began to extend themselves on the plain to the left of the water course & to advance fast upon us: this obliged us to oppose them with two field pieces on the other side of the watercourse which with our musketry kept them at a distance. The French also were in possession of the upper part of the watercourse and fired several platoons which were returned by us in such manner as to prevent their advancing or gaining any ground upon us. Our field pieces drawn up in the road fired upon the French cannon, but their fire was greatly superior to ours. Hitherto we had effected nothing but what was to our disadvantage and our loss was greatly beyond that of the enemy. This made Captain Clive determine either to attack the orchard or so far give up the point as to endeavour to find out some other Road which might enable Captain Clive with the army to throw themselves between the French and Arcot, and by that means engage the enemy at his leasure and under less disagreeable circumstances. At about 10 o'clock he sent one Shaulur, a Mustee [1] Serjeant who spoke the language, with some trusty Seapoys to reconnoitre who shortly after returned with a report that the enemy's infantry and artillery were entirely uncovered in the rear and might all be surprized killed and taken. Captain Clive rejoyced at such an opportunity, immediately ordered 200 Europeans and 4 or 5 Companies of Seapoys under the command of Lieutenant Keene with Serjeant Shaulur the guide to undertake this enterprize & accompanied them part of the way himself. On his return he found the remainder of the forces left in the watercourse had quitted it and were retreating in spite of all the efforts made by their officers. It was with great difficulty Capt. Clive led them on to the

[1] Mustees, *Mestiz*, Portuguese half-caste.

attack to the place from whence they came, where Captain Clive continued in great suspence till past eleven o'clock, when he received advice from Lieutenant Keene that he had surprized and routed all the french infantry and taken their cannon. Captain Clive then immediately joined Lieutenant Keene with the rest of the forces and in the morning found we had taken 9 pieces of cannon & 3 mortars with 50 french prisoners, & had killed upwards of 60 more with a great many Seapoys, & soon after Captain Clive had left Lieut: Keene he continued his march in great silence till he could very plainly discover the rear of the french artillery & forces, when he thought proper to halt in order to get further intelligence. Accordingly Ensign Symmons advanced alone. His first obstruction was a deep trench full of Seapoys some of which offered to shoot him: them he deceived by speaking french & pretending to be a french man. Having got clear of them, he advanced to within a very few yards where the french infantry & cannon were drawn up firing upon the party commanded by Captain Clive in the water course. After he had made these observations, he luckily returned safe to his party & conducted the party in such manner that they marched between the Seapoys in the Trench & the French infantry & cannon in the orchard so as to come directly in their rear & without being discovered from the darkness of the night & the noise and confusion arising from the firing of the Cannon and Musketry. At the opposite party Lieutenant Keene gave them a general volley from 200 Europeans at the distance of 50 yards which at one firing gained this battle." [1]

The battle of Coverepauk (Kaveripak), won by the skill and insight of Clive, deserves the dignity of an historical event. It destroyed the organised force which Dupleix had raised with so much difficulty; it increased the reputation of British arms, and it changed the balance of French and English influence in Southern India. After their defeat "a very considerable body" [2] of Rezza's troops retired into the fort of Coverepauk.

[1] Orme MSS.: India, Vol. II., pp. 299–300.
[2] *Ibid.*, p. 301. Orme states (Vol. I., p. 216): "Part of the fugitives."

Clive "sent a summons to the governor, who was a Moor man, who answered that he was ready to submit to Mahomad Ally, but that the great numbers of Raja Saheib's forces which were in the fort would not suffer him to surrender." A party was sent to invest the fort, "but before these got there, the enemy had retired and the governor submitted." [1]

On February 29 Clive wrote to Saunders and informed him that

> "the enemy having possessed themselves of a strong spot of ground near Coverepauk, an engagement ensued wherein they were entirely defeated, an Aid Major, thirty nine French and eighteen Topasses made prisoners, all their Cannon, eight large Tumbrills of Ammunition, above two hundred Barrels of Gunpowder taken with a Number of Carriage Bullocks and every thing else they had belonging to them, and had it not been late in the evening not a single Man would have escap'd. That the Head Jemidar of Chunda's Horse was killed and a great many French, and our loss had been pretty considerable, besides Ensign Keene, and Mr. Preston, a Volunteer wounded." [2]

On March 2 Clive wrote that

> "he had left a party to watch the Prisoners at Coverepauk, that having intelligence some money, Elephants and all young Chunda's Baggage was left at Vellour Pettah, he had sent to demand them of Moortaz Ally Caun and intended proceeding thither the next morning to look after them, and after refreshing his People a little should set out for this place." [3]

Five days later he informed the governor

> "that he is on his march hither, and on his approaching Chetteput, young Chunda retir'd to Gingee and from thence to Pondicherry, that he was encamped to the Eastward of Gingee, and hop'd to be within ten or twelve miles of Pondicherry to-day." [4]

The "young Chunda" did not receive a pleasant welcome at Pondicherry. For several days Dupleix would not allow him to appear in his presence. On March 8 Clive wrote that he

> "was then encamped on the ground where Nazir Jung was cut off, in commemoration whereof a very fine Choultry was erected, and a Village, which Monument of Villainy he designs destroying and expected to be here the 11th." [5]

[1] Orme MS.: India, Vol. II., p. 301. [2] Madras MS. Records.
[3] *Ibid.* [4] *Ibid.* [5] *Ibid.*

Orme converts the village into "a rising town projected by the vanity of Mr. Dupleix to commemorate that detestable action, and called Dupleix-Fateabad or the town of Dupleix's victory." He adds: "It is said that he was preparing a column with a pompous inscription in the French, Malabar, Persic and Indostan languages, which he intended to erect in the middle of the town, where he had already caused coins struck with symbols of the victory to be buried." Macaulay in his essay on Clive omits the important words "it is said," the column becomes a "stately pillar," "coins struck with symbols of the victory" become "medals stamped with emblems of his successes," they "were buried beneath the foundations of this stately pillar," and "round it arose a town." From the records of the time we now learn that in order to commemorate a "detestable action" won by foul treachery, Dupleix had erected a splendid Rest House for travellers on the battle-field. Both in erecting a memorial and in the nature of the memorial he was following an Eastern custom, and he did it to impress the Oriental mind as to the power of the French; and Clive levelled the splendid choultry and village to the ground, thereby altering the native impression as to the respective powers of the French and English. The work of destruction could not have been very onerous, for three days after the receipt of his last letter Clive encamped within the bounds of Fort St. David.

"11th March.—At about 5 this afternoon arrived Captain Clive with the Forces under his Command at Trivendupuram where they encamp'd, and orders were immediately issued out for bringing in all such Necessaries as were in want of Repair and to get the same done as soon as possible, also that the necessary Supplies of Ammunition, &c, for the use of the Camp be got ready with the greatest expedition." [1]

When the preparations of the detachment had been almost completed, Stringer Lawrence arrived unexpectedly at Fort St. David. He had not been two months at home when he was appointed Commander-in-Chief of all the Company's

[1] Madras MS. Records—Diary, March 9, 1752.

military forces in the East Indies, "on a salary of £500 per annum to which was added a yearly allowance of £250 in lieu of diet money, servants, houses, and all other privileges and perquisites whatever."

At a Consultation held on Monday, March 16, it was determined that

"The Military being very well refresh'd and the Stores for the Camp all ready, ordered that the Forces march to-morrow evening to join the Army at Trichinopoly, and Major Lawrence acquainting the Board that if agreeable to them he purposes proceeding with the Troops and taking upon him the Command of the whole when he gets there, the Board entirely concur therein and his instructions being accordingly draughted out are read, approv'd and ordered to be transcrib'd. Copy whereof follows:

"*To* Stringer Lawrence, Esq., *Commander-in-Chief of the Company's Forces in India.*

"Sir,—Having appointed you to the Command of the Troops at Trichinopoly, you will proceed there with the Reinforcement now put under your direction; The situation of the Nabobs as well as the Enemy's Force you will soon be acquainted with by the representation of the Officer on Command, the former must be greatly superior. We would by all means have you press an engagement as soon as possible, this we are strongly induc'd to from a certain knowledge that they have applied to Salabut Jung for a strong Reinforcement which may be reasonably expected to arrive soon as well as their Ships from Europe. Should you prove successful, very probably the enemy must abandon their Cannon, &c, which by all accounts is considerable; The passions of the Moors are ever fluctuating, their friendship and alliance not to be depended on. We therefore, after providing in a reasonable manner for the security of Trichinopoly, think it would be prudent to send them to Deve Cotah as the leaving them there might prove a disadvantage to us; Should the enemy have address enough to secure a Retreat, you will be mindful that our Garrisons here and at Fort St. George are weak, and take such measures as may prevent them doing harm to our Districts; The Nabob's allies consisting of several Countries whose Customs are greatly different from ours, we must particularly recommend you as much as possible [to] promote a harmony. Write us constantly the material that we may give you the proper assistance. On your departure from Trichinopoly you will leave such a Force as you judge necessary for the security of that place."

Dupleix had in vain implored Law to storm Trichinopoly while Clive was at Arcot; he had planned the raid into the

British territory around Madras in order to keep Clive employed away from Trichinopoly. He had supplied Rezza Sahib with reinforcements, but he had no intention that Rezza should fight; but Rezza had fought, and was totally routed. The manner in which Dupleix bore misfortune was, however, worthy of his great ambition. His cool courage never failed, his high energy never diminished. The relieving column must be crushed. He sent Law every soldier he could spare, and wrote to him:

"*Veillez sur la route que suivent les Anglais; vous avez été averti à temps; il est de votre honneur de détruire le secours. . . . Tout dépend de ce coup. Ne négligez rien pour réussir. Je vous laisse carte blanche.*"

The weak, vacillating Law determined to wait till it reached the vicinity of Trichinopoly, and Dupleix added to him:

"*Il sera pourtant difficile de persuader en France que trente mille hommes en aient laissé passer deux mille, embarrassés d'un charroi et d'un transport effroyables. . . . Quand cesserez-vous de remettre d'un jour à l'autre pour aller au-devant du convoi?*"

But neither taunts nor commands had any effect on Law.

On March 17 Stringer Lawrence, as commander of the troops at Trichinopoly, accompanied the relieving force, which consisted of 400 Europeans and 1,100 sepoys with eight field-pieces. It escorted a large convoy of military stores. There has been some weak, watery talk of Clive's disappointment at being superseded by Lawrence. "The young and successful soldier," says Malcolm, "placed himself under the veteran, whom he never ceased to regard with attachment and respect."[1] Young soldiers do not place themselves under a commander-in-chief. Macaulay writes:

"From the waywardness and impatience of control which had characterized Clive, both at school and in the counting-house, it might have been expected that he would not, after such achievements, act with zeal and good humour in a subordinate capacity. But Lawrence had early treated him with kindness; and it is bare justice to Clive to say that, proud and overbearing as he was, kindness was never thrown away upon him. He cheerfully placed himself under the

[1] "Memoirs of Lord Clive," Vol. I., p. 103.

orders of his old friend and exerted himself as strenuously in the second post as he could have done in the first." [1]

Clive was the junior of all the young captains, and when he reached Trichinopoly he would be under the command of Gingens, whose incapacity in the field he had witnessed. The arrival of his old capable commander must have afforded Clive considerable relief and pleasure. Clive's own splendid success and rapid rise had aroused considerable jealousy, and many of the officers fresh from England objected to a lad of twenty-six, recently given the rank of captain, being appointed second in command. Lawrence tells us that "the uncommon success" which attended the Arcot expedition "some people were pleased to term fortunate and lucky," but he considered it was due to "an undaunted resolution, a cool temper and a presence of mind which never left him in the greatest danger." [2]

Most beautiful and attractive is the father-like interest that Stringer Lawrence took in fostering the glory and advancing the fortunes of the young soldier. It is refreshing to turn from the paltry jealousies and spiteful detractions of this time to the frankness and simplicity of the official communications between Lawrence and Clive. In their desire to win distinction by fighting their country's battles there was no alloy of selfishness, no feeling of rivalry. The brave veteran, a master of the art of command, and the young soldier, fearless, strong, self-dependent, but always loyal, working together, were the forces which mainly contributed to the success of the campaign.

When Madras was restored to the English the authorities at Fort St. David wrote to the Court: "As Fort St. George is much better situated for despatch of business of all kinds than this place, we take the liberty of recommending it to Your Honours to make that place again the Presidency." [3] Their Honours, after some delay, acted on the suggestion.

[1] Macaulay's Essay on Lord Clive ("Essays," Vol. III., p. 134).
[2] Lawrence's Narrative (Cambridge: "War in India," p. 14).
[3] Fort St. David MS. Records.

At a Consultation held on Monday, March 30, 1752, we find the following: "By the Company's Orders receiv'd per ship *Dunnington*, the Presidency is now remov'd to Fort St. George." The President also laid before the Board for their perusal two letters from Major Lawrence, the contents of which were summarised as follows:

> "That he had sent Captain Clive, on his being near Tanjour, to wait upon the King [of Tanjore] who treated him very handsomely, gave him great assurance of his regard for the Company and heartiness in the present alliance and expressed a desire to continue always upon the same good terms with the English. That he had been inform'd Chunda's camp was reinforced with a hundred Europeans, seven hundred Seapoys and four Camels loaded with money, which addition he is of opinion does not yet make them formidable. That he should make what haste he could to Trichinopoly when he shall give his opinion of the enemy's situation and the designs on them." [1]

On March 27, 1752, Stringer Lawrence arrived within eighteen miles of Trichinopoly. "I was met," he says, "by the commanding officer of artillery who brought me intelligence that the enemy had posted a strong force at Koyladdy [Coilady] within cannon-shot of the road I was to pass the next day." Lawrence at once dispatched his guides to find out another road. He deposited in the neighbouring fort of Tricajapoly, "belonging to the King of Tanjore," a part of his "very large quantity of ammunition and stores," in order that "it might not retard my march next day." [2] Next morning Lawrence continued his march along the strip of land between the two southern branches of the Caveri with the intention of crossing the southernmost branch before coming in touch with Coilady.

"By some mistake of my guide we were led within reach of the very post I wanted to avoid." To draw off the fire of their battery, which among the baggage created considerable confusion, he ordered some guns from his rear to answer

[1] *Ibid.*

[2] Cambridge: "War in India," p. 22. Orme states that they arrived "on the 26th of March" at Coilady and the next day passed Coilady. This does not agree with Lawrence's Journal. Clive in a Letter, dated Fort St. George, 14th (*sic*), 1752, states they arrived "near Coilady" March 28. "On the 29th in the morning we pursued our march" (Orme MSS.: India, Vol. II., p. 475).

them, and he left a guard of 100 Europeans under Clive to support them. The main body moved on slowly "inclining to the left, which with a small loss brought us out of reach of their guns, upon which we halted till the party and guns came up."[1] But the loss cannot be considered "small" when we remember the few Europeans engaged. "In this affair," wrote Clive, "we had about 25 Europeans killed and wounded, besides blacks: the enemy who were under the protection of the fort would not venture to follow us into the plain, tho there was little or no difference in the point of numbers."[2] After he had been joined by the rear division Lawrence continued his march, crossed the southernmost branch of the Caveri, and halted within ten miles of Trichinopoly.

During the night Lawrence was joined by 100 Europeans and 50 dragoons from the garrison. At break of day he advanced towards Elimeseram, where the French had mounted cannon. He had not advanced far when an officer, who had ridden from the town across the broken plain, informed him that the enemy's left was drawn up between Elimeseram and the French Rock, and their right extended from the latter height to their encampment on the Caveri. Soon Lawrence came in sight of their vast host, and earnestly surveying their position, he saw that if he passed north of Elimeseram, the direct route to the town, they would sweep home on him and coil his small army up rear and front. Prompt were his orders: "March south;" and at noon, half-way between Elimeseram and the Sugar Loaf Rock, he found Dalton, who had stolen forth during the night from the city with 200 Europeans, 400 sepoys, and four field-pieces. The heat was now intense, and Lawrence ordered his troops to halt and take their breakfast. They had hardly sat down when the scouts came at good speed and reported that the whole of the enemy's army was advancing, and their cannonade had put the Mahratta horse to flight. The enemy soon galloped up, and forming with the rest of the native allies in the rear of the Europeans and

[1] Cambridge: "War in India," p. 22.
[2] Orme MSS.: India, Vol. II., p. 475.

sepoys, followed them slowly. Clive having reconnoitred the enemy, reported that there was a large choultry (caravanserai) with some stone buildings not far from the front of the French battalion. Lawrence ordered him to advance with the first division of artillery and the grenadiers and seize it. Clive did as bidden; the enemy opened a heavy fire and pushed forward their French battalion. But they had not advanced 800 yards when Clive reached the choultry, and his guns opened fire. Then

"A cannonade ensued, without doubt, for the time it lasted, the hottest that had ever been seen on the plains of Indostan, for the French fired from 22 pieces of cannon and the English from nine. Such of the English troops as were not employed at the guns found shelter behind the choultry and the buildings near it, whilst the whole of the enemy's army stood exposed on the open plain, suffering in proportion to this disadvantage." [1]

For half an hour the French battalion bore it; they then began to waver, and withdrew their guns. Clive continuing to advance with his artillery, the French retreated to their camp, "and left us," says Lawrence, "to finish our march to Trichinopoly."

Clive, in his letter written in 1752, gives a brief account of what took place that day, but he makes no mention of the important part he and Dalton played in the action:

"On the 29th in the morning we pursued our march: at the distance of 6 miles from Tritchenopoly we were met by our allied army consisting of near 12000 horse; they were in the utmost confusion having been put to the route by Chunda Saib who had advanced upon them with all his forces and a heavy Train of artillery, luckily we had been joined by 300 Europeans, 2 field pieces, and some Seapoys, this junction strengthened our detachment to 600 Europeans, 1200 Seapoys and 8 pieces of cannon: with this force we threw ourselves between the enemy and our scattered horse, and after about one hours brisk Cannonadement, obliged the enemy to retire into their Camp and entrenchments: all the french in general were there, but concealed in such manner behind a ditch or high bank that we could see nothing of them till they retreated: on the plain lay dead 1 Elephant and 297 Horse, Allam Cawn the 2d in command was killed with abundance of Seapoys, besides the number of wounded is

[1] Orme, Vol. I., p. 220.

very considerable. Our loss was trifling and not worth the mentioning." [1]

Lawrence was desirous to attack the French camp without delay; but the Mohammedan and Hindu allies insisted on waiting for a lucky hour. Thus precious time was thrown away. "On the second of April," Clive says, "400 Europeans & 800 Seapoys were detached in the night time to attack the Enemy's Black Camp. This design miscarried through the timorousness of the guide, but whether the enemy had intelligence of the scheme and dreaded its consequences in another attempt, or were too much dispirited by the battle of the 29th March, they decamped the next day and took possession of Syringham Island and its Pagodas." [2] It was a fatal move; and Lawrence and Clive, with the instinct of good commanders, took advantage of it. They determined to divide their forces, as Clive says, "that we might have it in our power to cut off the enemy's supplies and communications with Utatoor, Volgonda and Pondicherry." Lawrence in his narrative states: "Promising myself great success from the activity and vigilance of Captain Clive, I detached him with 400 of my best Europeans, 1200 seapoys and 4000 [3] horse to take post on the other side. He crossed the two rivers about seven miles below Seringam." [4] Clive was the junior captain of the battalion, and his seniors had to be reconciled to his being appointed to an independent command. The matter, however, was soon settled: "The Nabob, the Marattas, and Mysoreans demanded Captain Clive to command the army sent to Sumiavaram." [5]

On the night of April 4 Clive took possession of that village, "in which are two pagodas about a quarter of a mile distant from each other, one on each side of the high road leading to Utatoor: these were allotted for the quarters of the Europeans and Seapoys; ravelins were immediately flung up before the gates, and a redoubt capable of receiving all the cannon

[1] Letter from Captain Clive to Mr. Schoning, Fort St. George, 14th [?], 1752.—Orme MSS.: India, Vol. II., pp. 475–8.
[2] *Ibid.*
[3] Clive gives the number as 3,000 (letter quoted *supra*).
[4] Cambridge: "War in India," p. 24.
[5] Orme MSS.: India, Vol. II., p. 301.

was constructed to command the road to the north and south. The Morattoes and Tanjorines encamped round the pagodas." [1] On the 6th the enemy made an attempt to dislodge them, "but were repulsed to their Camp," says Clive, "with considerable loss." The following day Lawrence wrote to Clive:

TRICHENOPOLLY *April 7th* 1752
5, *Evening.*

DEAR SIR,—I have received yours & congratulate you on your success. Mr. de Vareille is arrived and on talking with him I have altered my mind as to sending my disposition and intend to be with you myself as soon as you let me know you have received this. I am
Dear Clive
Your most humble Servant
STRINGER LAWRENCE.

On the following day Lawrence visited Clive to concert further measures. "We agreed that he should make an attack on Pitchunda, a place which they had fortified, situated on the banks of the Coleroon, opposite to Seringham, and commanding the pass of that river. But it was first necessary to storm Lalgoody, a mud fort where the enemy had a large magazine of grain." [2] Three days later the sepoys stormed the fort of Lalgoody, "and found here a quantity of grain sufficient for ten thousand men for two months." [3] On the 13th Lawrence wrote: [4]

TRICHINOPOLY *April 13th* 1752
½ *past* 10 *morn*

DEAR CLIVE,—I have just received two letters from you . . . I shall send you all your supplies as soon as possible and the party of seapoys marched off this morning to join you and I shall send immediately Carriages and Cooleys for the Paddy & would have you withdraw your party from Lolgoody leaving a careful Serjeant and six Europeans with such a garrison as you think proper to defend the place. In answer to your second Letter you'll easily reflect that it will be of full as bad consequence for me to divide my men as you yours, and I assure you Dalton's Company are the greatest part of our Strength, so I would have you to be certain of Chunda's son's motions before you leave your post as perhaps on their hearing Lolgoody is taken they may halt at Coiladdy: if you hear they proceed you can then march to intercept them leaving the force you

[1] Orme, Vol. I., p. 225.
[2] Cambridge: "War in India," p. 24.
[3] Orme, Vol. I., p. 226.
[4] Orme MSS.: India, Vol. II., p. 458.

mention in your post which if I judge right of the matter is capable of defending it against any the enemy can send: for the rest I leave it to your discretion as you won't be so far from your post but you'll be able to support it on occasion and I'll watch their motions and be on their backs if they attempt to disturb you: I shall send you two Guns with ammunition for the fort and beg to hear from you often that I may be able to assist you with every thing you want. I approve entirely of your sentiments that the effects found in the fort belong to your party & every thing they may hereafter get while divided from me. But remember that Arms or warlike Stores of any kind are no plunder for which reason it is ordered here & you'll immediately give it out That all Arms that shall be taken belong to the Company, and for every firelock & bayonet the men bring off they shall receive a Pagoda and that no one after victory presume to plunder till ordered by his officer on pain of death, but the Effects are to be sold at outcry & equally divided. My compliments to all the Gentlemen and I am very sincerely

Dear Clive
Yours
S. LAWRENCE.

That same afternoon Lawrence wrote a letter to Clive [1] which he concludes as follows: "I am highly satisfied that you take every prudent method of distressing the enemy and discovering their designs and God grant you success." He signs himself "Dear Clive: Your most sincere Friend." On "April 14th, 1 morning," Lawrence wrote to Clive: [2] "I have just advice that the enemy are marching down the island. Watch their motions & protect Lalgoody & endeavour to protect their escape by a forced march when you know their design; we are under arms and prepared to follow." He added in a postscript: "I am not certain the whole party is marched. If the French are not I shan't move; nor do you quit your post intirely till you hear again. I leave all to your discretion." Clive had to quit his post and act on his own responsibility. That same day, April 14, he discovered from an intercepted letter to Law why the French on the island were in motion.

When Dupleix heard that Law had carried out his long-cherished design of taking up a position on the island of Seringham, where he would be "*dans une belle concentration*" and security, his heart bled because he thought it was due to

[1] Orme MSS.: India, Vol. II., p. 459. [2] *Ibid.*, p. 460.

some grave calamity. He was in transports of rage when he discovered that Law had taken the step without consulting his officers and against the wish and advice of his allies. He divined that the outcome of the move would indeed be far-reaching. He knew that Lawrence was an able commander and Clive a dashing war-captain, and he foresaw that they would cut off Law's communication with Pondicherry. Without reinforcement, without supplies, Law would be forced to surrender.

But obstacles both military and political only aroused the energy of Dupleix. He at once got together and dispatched a substantial force and 5 field-pieces, with a large convoy of provisions and stores. He superseded Law. No amount of energy could, however, create a capable commander. He had to appoint d'Auteuil, disabled by age and gout. In the letter announcing to him his supersession, Dupleix wrote to Law with cruel irony: "*Je suis persuadé que cet arrangement va faire plaisir à madame votre femme, qui ne désire que le moment de vous tenir dans ses bras.*" On April 14 d'Auteuil arrived "at the streights of Utatoor," and intended by making a large circuit to avoid Clive's position, gain in the night the river, and join the force on the island. When Clive discovered d'Auteuil's intention, he saw at a glance the whole importance of the crisis. He had no time to consult with Lawrence. He decided that the most daring course was the best to follow. The story of his great exploit and romantic escape is well told by the hero in his simple narrative:[1]

"Dauteuil was now advanced as far as the streights of Utatoor with 100 Europeans, 500 horse & as many Seapoys, with a large convoy of military stores, provisions & money: all these were intended to reinforce the army in the Island of Seringham which now began to be in great distress. The intercepting this convoy was of the greatest consequence; the fate of the two armies in a great measure depended upon

[1] "Attack made by the French in the Night on the Camp at Samiavaram, and Clive's Escapes."—Orme MSS.: India, Vol. II., pp. 302–5.

its arrival or non-arrival. Captain Clive was aware of this . . . his force was too small to attack this party & at the same time leave a sufficient force to oppose Captain Laws who might have attacked Summiavaram and Carried it before Major Lawrence could have come to his assistance. Therefore the success of this attempt depended upon secresy and expedition; accordingly Captain Clive quitted his strong situation with the greatest part of his force leaving his Camp &c. all standing to deceive the enemy, the instant it was dark & made a forced march of about 14 miles & [? arrived] within about 3 miles of Uttatoor when he received advice the enemy did not intend to move that night upon which he returned to Sumiavaram & got there a little after day break. To explain this matter more fully it is necessary to observe that one of the two Pagodas was much larger and stronger than the other. At the large one was placed the whole body of Europeans with the greatest part of the Seapoys; the entrance into the gate was fortified with a strong ravelin. The other Pagoda being much smaller only a party of Seapoys was placed which served as a body guard to Captain Clive who slept in a Choultry adjacent. Between the two Pagodas as was said before ran the great road from Tritchanopoly to Pondicherry. On this Road was erected a battery with dry ditch, parapet & Glacis. The enemy in the afternoon of the same day, and not before, received advice of Captain Clive's march, but none of his return. In consequence of which a party of 80 Europeans & 500 Seapoys were ordered to take possession of this strong post on a supposition that Capt. Clive was absent and had not left force sufficient to make any resistance. In this error the enemy continued till they approached the camp when their spy informed Captain Colhier he had just received advice the party was returned. This Intelligence the french officer disbelieved & attributing all to the cowardice and apprehension of the conductor pursued his march. It happened of this party near 40 men were English deserters with an English officer at their head. Upon being challenged by the advanced guard of Seapoys the English officer advanced & in English told the Seapoy officer he was sent by

Major Lawrence with a party to reinforce Captain Clive. This being likewise confirmed by all the deserters who spoke English also, so far convinced the Seapoy officer of the truth that he omitted asking the counterword and sent one of his Seapoys to shew the party the head quarters where Captain Clive slept, and the enemy continued their march through part of the Maratta Camp without the least disturbance till they came to the small pagoda when challenged by the centries who were at the gate & at the choultry, they returned the challenge by a volley into each place. This immediately awakened Captain Clive who jumped up in his shirt, got out of the choultry and made the best of his way to the great Pagoda where upon the alarm he found all the Europeans & Seapoys under arms. Captain Clive not having the least conception that the enemy could get into the middle of the camp without his knowing it, concluded as he was marching down at the head of his troops it was only some alarm at the outskirts of the camp & that the firing he heard was from his own Seapoys who are always greatly alarmed upon night attacks & fire, whether they see any one to fire at or not. His conjecture was the more confirmed in this persuasion when he approached nearer from observing the firing still continued & that the party firing had their backs towards the camp & their faces towards the enemy. Fully convinced of this after having drawn up 200 Europeans within 20 yards of the Seapoys he went among them and made them cease firing, upbraiding them with cowardice & striking several of them. But one of the Officers who understood something of the french language found out Captain Clive to be an enemy and cut him in two places with his sword & then ran into the little Pagoda where Captain Clive immediately followed him to the entrance of the gate, when to his very great astonishment he found himself in the midst of six french. He made use of presence of mind upon that occasion & told them if they would look out they would find they were all surrounded and would certainly be cut to pieces if they did not surrender immediately. This had such an effect that 3 of the men ran into the pagoda to give the intelligence and the other 3 surrendered to Captain Clive who was returning with a full design to demolish the Seapoys whom he now knew for the first time to be enemies, but they finding out their error likewise had stolen off. During this time of ignorance and darkness we had made prisoners of 8 or ten frenchmen between the ranks; these with the other three were put under charge of a Serjeants party who not knowing the french were in possession of the pagoda conducted them there and found the place full of frenchmen. Such was the confusion and ignorance of the french also that they suffered the Serjeant & his party to return who reported to Captain Clive this matter & that the Pagoda was full of French. This Captain Clive then knew and was making the proper disposition for the attack of the Pagoda. Accordingly Captain Clive judging it of the utmost consequence to dislodge the enemy before they could be reinforced perhaps from the whole french army resolved to storm the Pagoda, but the entrance of the gateway being so narrow that not even two men could enter abreast an Officer & 12 or 15 men were killed in the attempt which proved impracticable. This being the case Captain Clive ordered a Platoon to watch the entrance of the gate and was making a disposition to keep the enemy within the walls of the Pagoda & at the same time oppose the enemy in case they should come to the relief of their party when the french commander finding the desperate situation made a sally at the head of his men, who was killed with the like number of men by the platoon stationed there for that purpose. After this Captain Clive went to the gate of the Pagoda and being weak with loss of blood leaned upon two souldiers shoulders with his body projected & summoned the officer to surrender on pain of having no quarter. The English officer made no answer, but immediately fixed [*sic*, ? fired] his piece at Captain Clive which luckily missed him but shot the two men who supported both through the body. The other Officer as well as the men seeing the desperateness of their situation oblidged the English officer as well as the rest of the English with themselves to surrender at discretion. Thus ended this affair. The unfortunate Seapoys who had so fortunately escaped the late danger were overtaken by the Moratta horse before they could get back to their camp and every one cut to pieces. Captain Clive found two Musket balls lodged in his hand escrutore at the foot of his bed and the servant who slept on the ground by him killed."

On April 16 Lawrence wrote to Clive:[1] "I rejoice at your success, as your wounds are not dangerous, and if they spoil the beauty of your face they raise your fame in having served your country when you got them." The same day he sent to him the following official communication:[2]

TRICHINOPOLY *April* 16 1752
No. 3.

SIR,—As Kelsall was taken in arms against us after he had deserted our service, no commission of any kind whatsoever from any nation can be a protection to him; so let him be hanged immediately for an example and keep the other English deserters strictly guarded as I intend they shall soon share the same fate. Hancock will tell you the rest I have to say, & I am

Dear Clive
Yours very sincerely
STRINGER LAWRENCE.

The gunner who deserted yesterday & shewed the enemy the way to the Pagoda you will likewise order to be hanged immediately.—S. L.

Clive states in a note:[3] "Kelsall had been a pay serjeant in the Independants and deserted to Pondicherry with the pay of his company. This man Dupleix made an officer. He with three other Englishmen were hanged the next day."

Lawrence directed[4] that the other prisoners should remain with Clive,

"till I appoint a time for fetching them with my whole force, which can't be till the day after to morrow: my scheme in it is that it may probably draw out their whole force to attack us: if so you know what we have to do. If they give us no disturbance, yet carrying them in open day light will have a great Effect on the minds of the people. I shall send my watch to you & fix an hour for you to march that we may meet on the Coleroon together. I believe the remains of the enemy are too sick to attempt any thing against you. For

[1] Orme MSS.: India, Vol. II., p. 462.
[2] *Ibid.*, p. 461.
[3] *Ibid.*, p. 305.
[4] *Ibid.*, p. 462.

your prisoners, if you pinion them all, their late behaviour to ours will warrant it, so that you need not be over complaisant if necessity requires your doing otherwise."

Clive, however, did not think that the enemy were so decidedly worn out and shaken by recent events. The two French commanders might fall upon him by a concentrated movement while Lawrence, owing to the swollen state of the river, could render him no timely assistance. He therefore considered that the greatest part of the forces should be on his side. Lawrence did not agree with him. If he diminished his force, the enemy might cross the river Caveri and the road to the sea would be open to them. He wrote on the 20th:[1]

"But do you think if I should make such a removal they are so stupid as not to pass the Covry which is a matter of less difficulty, and then the road is open to Caricawl. Your force is now superior to mine so that I don't know how to think of making any farther division or quitting my present post. If they are ignorant of your strength that's our advantage and the passing over a rapid and wide river, should you have notice of their designs, may be opposed with a few men against all their force. I need not sum up more particulars as your own judgment will best point out to you what may be done but shall conclude with assuring you that it's my opinion you are more than a match, considering the Situation you are in, for all their force weakened and dispirited as they are. Pray let me hear from you with your farther thoughts on this subject and as an interview [*sic*, ? interchange] of letters is endless I should be glad you'll give me your firm opinion."

On the following day, April 21, the fort of Coilady surrendered to the Tanjore general "on terms for the garrison to march out with their arms to Pondicherry."[2] Law was now cut off from communication with the east, and a contemporary writer states: "From this time Chunda, the French Nabob, began to suffer much by the desertion of the black troops and want of provisions."[3] Clive sent a friend to headquarters to explain his plans, and Lawrence wrote to him:[4]

"But that we may thoroughly understand each other I should be glad that on the receipt of this you'll leave the command of your

[1] Orme MSS.: India, Vol. II., p. 463.
[2] "Dates of Several Events from the 20th of March to 3rd June, 1752." —*Ibid.*, pp. 313-14. [3] *Ibid.* [4] *Ibid.*, p. 464.

party with Captain Chase, and come over to me bringing with you an estimate of everything you can possibly want for which you can consult your train officers."

There is an indication of the nature of the scheme on which they agreed. Lawrence wrote: [1]

TRECHINOPOLY *April 27th* 1752
No. 13.

DEAR CLIVE,—I crossed the river this morning as I proposed which I had no sooner done but a very heavy rain fell; however the Coffry's and Grenadiers marched to their posts & took them without any loss, but the rain continuing and the powder which I was obliged to carry over in barrels being wet, add to this the uncertainty of having it in our power to give a second fire, I thought it prudent to defer the prosecution of our scheme & returned without losing a man. A certain instance of the cowardice of the enemy. As soon as we have our things in order I'll let you know what I intend next which possibly may be the attack of Pitchundah Pagodah, if so I'll be on the island to sustain you. Let me know you have received this and any thing else that may occur to you. If it's fair weather to morrow I'll send the stores you want, and I am

Dear Clive
Yours very sincerely
S. LAWRENCE.

PS.—After we left the Island there was a long fight between the enemy and our allies but I believe as usual with very little harm done on either side.

D'Auteuil, however, remained at Utatoor. If Clive besieged the Pitchandah pagoda, d'Auteuil would certainly take the opportunity to make his way good to Seringham. He must first be driven from Utatoor. Not a man could be spared from Samiaveram. It was Clive's presence of mind and pluck which had prevented a terrible disaster on the night of the 16th. Lawrence now saw that he must do what Clive had suggested—strengthen the force on the other side of the river. On April 28 he sent Dalton across the stream with 150 Europeans, 400 sepoys, 500 Mahratta horse and four guns to attack d'Auteuil. At 5 o'clock the next evening Dalton arrived at a caravanserai within two miles of Utatoor. Here he intended to pass the night, as his troops were much fatigued. Some distance in front of the choultry lay a village from which he

[1] Orme MSS.: India, Vol. II., p. 465.

might be attacked. Dalton sent some dragoons to reconnoitre. They brought back word that it was occupied by the enemy, and Dalton straightway pushed forward a body of Europeans and sepoys to dislodge them. "This they effected with so much ease, that, flushed with success, they pursued the enemy beyond the village." Suddenly they saw in full view d'Auteuil's whole force marching out of Utatoor. No time to form—a party of the enemy was upon them. The English officer was mortally wounded and they fell back on the village, "where they remained and sustained the fire of the enemy's cannon until the rest of the troops came up." It was now almost dusk. A bold and clever stratagem entered Dalton's mind. In the fading light the enemy might think they were attacked by the whole of Clive's force. He therefore kept only a few Europeans with the guns near the village, who played vigorously, while at the same time he divided his small detachment into two bodies, who marched to attack each flank of the enemy's line. On seeing this movement d'Auteuil became completely convinced that it was Clive's whole force, "and retreated with great precipitation pursued within a few yards of the walls of Utatoor."[1] "The same night," says Clive,[2] "Mr. Dauteuil took the advantage of its darkness to quit Utatoor likewise, retreating to Volgondah and leaving behind him a large quantity of ammunition and store of good claret." A few days after his success Dalton wrote to Clive as follows:[3]

Dear Clive,—I had the pleasure of yours last night and have received the 2 Tumbrils, Camels & about 40 Cooleys; I am going to send you back the 12 pounder as it can be of no sort of service here & with it the french ammunition. I send you 12 baskets of Claret each containing 15 bottles to rejoice the hearts of your Lads of war; the 14 other baskets please to forward immediately to Trichenopoly; 10 are for the Major—there is likewise 2 bottles of Rappee snuff & a ham: Likewise one for yourself to make the wine relish: the arrack I shall keep for the people.

I would have wrote the letter as you advised me but you never sent me a person to do it. The Braminy promised me faithfully he would send

[1] Orme, Vol. I., pp. 230–1. [2] Orme MSS.: India, Vol. II., pp. 475–8.
[3] *Ibid.*, pp. 478–9.

me a Canicoply [native clerk], but he never thought more of it when my back was turned. I shall leave here 20 Europeans, 100 Seapoys and 500 of the Toroor punes [peons], with ammunition and all the paddy that is in the place, which is but a small stock. The Torroor [Tirur] Chah has never been near me yet; I find the Enemy have got into Volconda, and am afraid that should I march that way, as in all probability I should not be able to get 'em out, it would be a sort of discredit to us. Tis true they are damnably frightened, and perhaps might not [*sic* ? run] off tho' a deserter that came this morning tells me they expect a reinforcement from Europe to proceed to their army: I am getting every thing in readiness to march, as soon as ever I get a Line from the old gentleman: perhaps he may be offended if I move without it. Mr. Bodginrow has a mind to trot to Trichenopoly; I don't find he has sent 300 horse to make their appearance near Volconda as he promised me he would. If he had pursued briskly instead of staying to plunder we might have destroyed their whole command. My compliments to Innis, Chase, &c. and believe me

Dear Clive

very sincerely yours

J: DALTON.

WOOTATOOR, *May 5th.*

P: S:—Upon second thoughts I won't send the 12 pounder till I hear from the Major. You'll receive the wine Per Bearer. I expect news from Volconda this evening. Send back the Cooleys directly.

On the morning of April 29 Law saw from the lofty gateway of Seringham Pagoda a long line of troops marching across the plain towards Utatoor. As he had not heard of Dalton's movement, he thought it was a part of Clive's force, and he determined to cross at once the Coleroon, "with all his Europeans and Sepoys and a large body of cavalry," and attack Samiaveram. Clive, on hearing that the enemy were crossing the river, set out with the greater part of his force to oppose them. He came in sight of them just as their rear had reached the northern bank.

"Mr. Law, startled at the appearance of a force which exceeded his expectation, halted and formed his troops in a strong situation along the bank of the river. Both armies remained in order of battle until evening, each having advantages which the other respected too much to venture to attack. Some skirmishes passed between the advanced Sepoys, and in the night the French recrossed the river."[1]

[1] Orme, Vol. I., p. 232.

Dalton now got orders from "the old gentleman" to rejoin him. But on his return to Samiaveram he found that the Coleroon had suddenly risen and cut off all communication with Lawrence. The French post of Pitchandah could not receive any support from the island, and Clive had determined to seize the opportunity to renew his attack on Pitchandah. "I therefore ordered him to continue with Mr. Clive," says Lawrence.[1] Dalton was Clive's senior, and Orme states that he put his detachment under Clive's command, "and to prevent the disputes which might arise from the superiority of his rank, resolved to act himself as a volunteer."[2] It was an action worthy of a brave soldier of warm heart, full of honesty and simplicity.

While the batteries for the attack on the pagoda were being erected, Clive placed the guns on a lofty mound close to the Coleroon. Beneath them within gun-shot thousands of tents stretched their canvas, from the Royal red to the white cotton cloth on two sticks. Multitudes of camp followers and servants, with women and children, were camped on the brown plain. Every horseman had two servants, one to take care of his horse and the other to procure him forage, and prince, general, soldier, and servant were accompanied by a harem or a single spouse. Vendors of provisions, dealers in luxuries plied their trade in the bazaars assigned to them, "a movable town of shops where everything is to be sold as in their cities." Elephants, camels, horses and oxen were picketed among the tents in different quarters of the camp.[3] With the first light of the morning the six guns on the mound opened fire. A horrid din arose in the air. The trumpeting of elephants, the neighing of horses, and the lowing of oxen were mingled with the cries of the women. The tents were swiftly struck, and the frenzied mass of men and women and beasts swayed to and fro and then slowly rolled away between the pagodas out of the range of the shot. It was only a brief respite. As the crowd approached the river

[1] Cambridge: "War in India," p. 26. [2] Orme, Vol. I., p. 232.
[3] *See* Wilks: "History of Mysoor," Vol. I., p. 292.

Caveri the guns of Trichinopoly opened on it, and, seized with a fresh panic, it made its way down the island and took refuge below the Jumba-kistna temple.

During the day the battery was finished and the next morning two heavy guns opened a lively cannonade on the walls of the pagoda. They soon began to crumble away. The continuous strain was, however too much for one of the great guns: it burst, killed three Europeans, and wounded Dalton. The other gun continued the cannonade, and by 4 P.M. the breach was practicable, and it was determined to storm and escalade at the same time.

> "The enemy, seeing the preparations for the assault, were discouraged and beat the chamade.[1] The Sepoys, mistaking this signal of surrender for a defiance, fired a volley, which killed the drummer, and then, giving a shout, ran to plant the colours on the breach."[2]

Before they could be restrained by their European officers they killed several of the garrison. The rest surrendered. The joy of Lawrence at the capture of the temple was great. He wrote to Clive:[3]

> "I have just received the joyful news of your success against Pitchunda by yours of last night, tho I was on the rock when you took it. I heartily congratulate you on this glorious success as it has opened the way for us to join and put an end to the war, and you'll hear a salute before this reaches you."

The fate of Chanda Saheb's army was sealed. Law's communication with the north was severed, and the Indian camp was again exposed to artillery. Clive tells us that he "began to fire at the enemy on the Island of Seringham with all the artillery, 10 or 12 Ps., he could mount on the walls of Pitchunda."[4] The renewal of the cannonade and the increasing want of provisions led the greater part of Chanda Saheb's chiefs and officers to the determination to quit his service. They went in a body and informed him of this resolution. The blow was indeed a heavy one. But Chanda Saheb behaved like a Mohammedan gentleman. He received their address graciously. He assured them that he himself intended

[1] Inviting to a parley. *See* N. E. D. *s.v.*
[2] Orme, Vol. I., p. 234.
[3] Orme MSS.: India, Vol. II., p. 467.
[4] *Ibid.*, pp. 305–6.

to propose that they should retire. He was deeply sorry that he could not pay them the whole of their arrears, but he promised them that he would punctually acquit himself of all his obligations whenever his better fortune should return. "As a proof of his sincerity he offered to deliver up to them the greatest part of his elephants, camels, horses, and other military effects which they received at a valuation in part of what he was indebted to them."[1] On May 14 Chanda Saheb's commanders sent into the English camp offering their services or requesting a free pass through their posts. The allies strongly objected: "the Morattoes particularly, who do not rate the life of a man at the value of his turban were averse to the granting of any terms which might hinder them from exerting their sabres to get the spoil."[2] The English, however, insisted that the passport should be given. On May 17 Lawrence wrote:[3]

Dear Clive,—I have this instant received yours and I believe you know you can't do me a greater pleasure than keeping strictly up to your promises and I beg you'll give Coop Saib and his people your protection against any body that attempts to hurt them. I have sent to the Nabob to let him know his baseness and that of his allies & am extremely sorry we have any thing to do with people of so vile a character.

I sent two of your horses over this morning before I returned to this Camp. I intend to go to Chercorapollum again to night and if it's by any means convenient I shall be glad to see you in the morning as I have a great many things to talk to you about.

I am Dear Clive
Yours sincerely
S. Lawrence.

Two thousand of Chanda Saheb's best horse and 1,500 of his foot joined Clive, some the standard of the Mysoreans, and the troops of the independent chiefs followed them to their respective dominions. By May 18 not a tent was standing on the island. Chanda Saheb occupied the first and second courts of the Pagoda of Seringham with 2,000 horse and 3,000 foot, all that was left of his vast host. The French occupied the other pagoda, for Clive states that, knowing the extreme

[1] Orme, Vol. I., p. 235. [2] *Ibid.*
[3] Orme MSS.: India, Vol. II., p. 469.

veneration which the Indians owe to the sanctity of Seringham, they "had given preference to Jambakkistna for the reception of all their battalion, and had avoided all occasion of frequenting the Pagoda of Seringham." [1]

On May 18 Lawrence's main body crossed the Coleroon and encamped to the east of the pagoda occupied by the French, "where some days after," says Lawrence, "we threw up an entrenchment quite across from river to river, intending to wait there till we could get up heavy cannon from Davecotah; having but one 18 and one 12 pounder, artillery not sufficient to make a breach." [2] Clive's force encamped along the southern bank of the Coleroon and the troops of the allies also drew closer the ring round the quarry. The circle was, however, a wide one, and Law might have broken out of it if he had made a vigorous dash. He was urged by Chanda Saheb, an adviser more able and more bold than himself, to try a vigorous course. But he clung sullenly and obstinately to the belief that d'Auteuil would relieve him, and that he would be able to defend the pagoda until reinforcements from France reached Pondicherry.

D'Auteuil, pressed by the repeated and urgent solicitations of Law, quitted Volconda in the vain hope of relieving the island. On the evening of May 27 Clive again stole out of his camp with 100 Europeans, 1,000 sepoys, 2,000 Mahratta horse, and six field-pieces to intercept him. Before daybreak he reached Utatoor and remained in the fort "all that day and the ensuing night, in hopes that Mr. d'Auteuil would inadvertently come near enough to give them an opportunity of falling upon him on the plain before he could reach Volkondah." [3] D'Auteuil arrived within seven miles of Utatoor, and hearing that the British were there in force he fell back.[4]

[1] Orme MSS.: India, Vol. II., p. 307.
[2] Cambridge: "War in India," p. 27.
[3] Orme, Vol. I., p. 238.
[4] Orme continues: "Either from some rumour, or suspicion, his heart failed him on a sudden, and he took the resolution of returning in great haste to the place from whence he came." This is hardly fair to d'Auteuil. His force, as Orme tells us, consisted of 100 Europeans, of which 35 were English deserters, 400 sepoys, and 340 horse. Clive had 100 Europeans, 1,000 sepoys, and 1,000 Mahratta horse. D'Auteuil's artillery was only three pieces; Clive had six.

Clive, on discovering d'Auteuil's route, at once sent forward small parties of Mahratta horse to harass and detain the enemy until his main body reached them. Forming his men in a column with two field pieces in front, d'Auteuil made his way across the plain while the Mahratta came surging around him. Between the mud walls of the town of Volconda and a dry river he drew up his small force. Six hundred of the English sepoys had, when in the enemy's service, gallantly stormed the breaches at the assault of Arcot. Clive had enlisted them after the battle of Arni, disciplined them, led them in several actions, and by his power of command and his courage won their confidence and devotion. "These men no sooner came within cannon-shot of the enemy than they ran precipitately to attack them, without regarding any order. They received the fire of the enemy's cannon and musketry, which killed many of them but did not check the rest from rushing on to the push of bayonet."[1] After a short tussle the enemy retired within the walls of the town. Clive tells us that he "now gave orders for storming the pettah,"[2] which after some resistance was effected. "During the storm Mr. D'auteuil was informed the Governor had shut the gates of the lower fort, & determined not to be disappointed of a retreat of so much consequence, sent a party with scaling ladders who got into the lower fort and opened the gates, which now received all the fugitives who were now retiring from before the storm of the suburbs. These fugitives were pursued so closely that the English had like to have got into the fort along with them. Captn. Clive now ordered the field pieces to be brought up to batter the gate, at the same time, a constant fire of musketry which suffered nothing to appear on the walls."[3]

Here Clive's memorandum abruptly ends. D'Auteuil, as the last resource, attempted to get into the fortifications of the adjacent mass of rock, but the governor threatened to fire upon them if they used any violence, and as the English pieces

[1] Orme, Vol. I., p. 238.
[2] Orme MSS.: India, Vol. II., p. 306.
[3] *Ibid.*

THE GREAT PAGODA, TRICHINOPOLY

From "Oriental Scenery. 24 Views in Hindoostan. From the Drawings by Thomas Danieli" (1797)

were bound to batter in the gate, he hung out the white flag and surrendered with his whole force. On May 30 Lawrence wrote to Clive:[1]

Before SYRINGHAM *May* 30th, 1752.

DEAR CLIVE,—I have just received yours with a great deal of joy at your excellent situation and hope a few hours will bring me word that we have conquered the enemy. I hope you'll be troubled with but few prisoners and leave those at Outatoor under a guard of the Nabob's Sepoys assisted by an officers command of ours, to whom give special directions & God bless you. Dear Clive make haste here with the rest of your Command for I expect the great Guns to morrow and have every thing ready to open ground so I shall want your people for a covering party as ours must be employed in the trenches and at the battery. I gave your Hircar 5 rupies and hope soon to pay another better: let me hear from you as often as you can and above all things take care of making any terms with the Enemy. I am Dear Clive

Your sincere friend
S. LAWRENCE.

Clive was troubled with few prisoners, as "the horsemen and Sepoys were, as usual, disarmed and set at liberty."[2] Clive returned to his camp with the European prisoners on May 30. The following day the battering cannon arrived from Devicotah and Law received a summons to surrender at discretion. He replied defiantly that he would defend the pagoda to the very last extremity unless he was permitted to march away with all the troops under his command. Lawrence refused to accede to his proposal. That night Chanda Saheb attempted to make his escape through the Tanjore lines. He had paid the Mahratta commander of the Tanjore troops a very large sum, and had promised him a much larger sum if he had him conveyed to a place of safety. At dusk Chanda Saheb set forth on the perilous road, and on drawing near the Tanjore lines he sent one of his officers to the commander's quarters who demanded an important hostage for his master's safety. The Mahratta calmly replied that no hostage would be a check to treachery if it were intended. To send an important hostage would reveal the secret. Escape would then be impracticable.

[1] Orme MSS.: India, Vol. II., p. 470.
[2] Orme, Vol. I., p. 239.

"He, however, took an oath, the most sacred of all to an Indian soldier, on his sabre and poniard, wishing they might be turned to his own destruction if he failed in his engagements, which were to send away Chunda-saheb as soon as he came into his quarters, with an escort of horse, to the French settlement of Karical. At the same time a Tanjorine officer assured Chunda-saheb's that he was appointed to command the escort, and shewed the pallankin and other preparations which were intended for the journey. The two officers then repaired to a choultry, where Chunda-saheb himself, with a few attendants, waited the result of the conference. As soon as he had heard it related, he proceeded with the Tanjorine to Monackjee's quarters, where, instead of the escort he expected, he was met by a guard patroling for him, who carried him with violence into a tent, where they immediately put him into irons." [1]

Next day, June 1, a conference of the native chiefs was held regarding the disposal of this important prisoner. Lawrence, who was present, states in his narrative that Mohammed Ali and Monakji, the Tanjore commander, "judged it very dangerous to let out of their hands a man who had already given them so much trouble." The Mysore Regent and Morari Rao, the Mahratta chief, "were for having him in their possession." He adds: "Finding they could not agree, I proposed that we should have the care of him and keep him confined in one of our settlements: this was by no means approved, and we parted without coming to any resolution." [2]

Immediately after the meeting of the chieftains, Lawrence sent another summons to Law, more peremptory than the former. But the obstinate Law was even then unable to realise that the sands were fast running out. He had heard a rumour of the French defeat at Volconda, but he would not credit how serious it was. He refused to believe (Clive tells us) that d'Auteuil was a prisoner till he was sent to him. "On seeing him he immediately desired a personal conference with Major Lawrence." [3] The conference was held, and Law put forward the plea that the peace which existed between the two nations entitled him to expect from the English

[1] Orme, Vol. I., pp. 241–2.
[2] Cambridge: "War in India," p. 28.
[3] Orme MSS.: India, Vol. II., p. 307.

every mark of consideration for the French troops. Major Lawrence replied "that he acted in the conference only as the interpreter of the Nabob's intentions, with whom the English were in close alliance; and as a justification of the Nabob's conduct, produced a letter in which Mr. Dupleix had declared that he would never cease to pursue him while a single Frenchman remained in India."[1] After some discussion a capitulation was signed in the Nawab's name. On the morning of June 3 Law came out of the great pagoda with some of his officers and conducted Dalton's detachment of 250 men into it, "where they formed with their backs to the gate opposite to the French troops who immediately flung down their arms in a heap and surrendered." Thirty-five commissioned officers, 725 Europeans, "battalion men bearing arms," besides 60 sick and wounded in the hospital and 2,000 sepoys, became prisoners of war. Four 13-inch mortars, eight cohorns, and thirty-one pieces of cannon, besides large quantities of ammunition, stores, and carriages "of all sorts in very good condition,"[2] fell into the hands of the victors. The Pagoda of Seringham was soon after delivered up and the remnant of Chanda Saheb's force, who were quartered there, were suffered to leave it without molestation. The Rajpoots illustrated their race. Clive wrote: "The Raspoots in Chunda Saheib's army amounting to about 1000, on hearing that Mr. Law was about to surrender to the English took the resolution of not quitting the Pagoda of Seringham, and of not suffering any others to enter it. They acquainted Mahomed Ally and his allies that they were not there in the intention of resisting hostilities as Enemies of war but that they were determined to fight to extinction in defence of their gods & the sanctity of this place which would be defiled by the intrusion of strangers."[3]

When the British troops took possession of the pagoda, the Rajpoots refused to quit the temple "and threatened their victors to cut them to pieces if they offered to enter within

[1] Orme, Vol. I., p. 243. [2] *Ibid.*, p. 244.
[3] Orme MSS.: India, Vol. II., p. 307.

the third wall: the English, in admiration of their enthusiasm, promised to give them no occasion of offence." [1]

So ended with the blaze of victory the first contest for the city of Trichinopoly, the key of Southern India. It also terminated with a tragedy which was at once most piteous and most inevitable. The aged head of Chanda Saheb fell under the sword of the executioner. After the conference held in Lawrence's tent, every one of the confederates attempted to get possession of the prisoner by bribes or threats. The Mysorean promised money, Mohammed Ali threatened resentment, and the Mahratta free lance "swore plainly that he would pay him a visit at the head of 6,000 horse." [2] The Mysorean was terrified by these threats; the English had also proposed that they should have the care of him, and they might insist on compliance with their proposal. The same morning that the pagoda surrendered he had a conference with Lawrence "which convinced him that the English were his friends, and that they were resolved not to inferfere any farther in the dispute." On returning to his camp Monakji ordered the head of Chanda Saheb to be struck off.

> "The executioner of this deed was a Pitan, one of Monack-jee's retinue, reserved for such purposes. He found the unfortunate victim an aged man, stretched on the ground, from whence the infirmities of sickness rendered him unable to rear himself. The aspect and abrupt intrusion of the assassin instantly suggested to Chunda-saheb the errand on which he was sent. He waved his hand, and desired to speak to Monack-jee before he died, saying, that he had something of great importance to communicate to him: but the man of blood giving no heed to his words, proceeded to his work, and after stabbing him to the heart, severed his head from his body." [3]

Dupleix, in his Memoirs, asserts that Lawrence himself ordered the death of Chanda Saheb, "which," to use the words of Mill, "it is difficult to suppose Dupleix must not have known to be untrue." Mill, however, adds:

> "But it is true, that Lawrence showed an indifference about his fate which is not very easy to be reconciled with either humanity or wisdom. He well knew that his murder was, in the hands of any

[1] Orme, Vol. I., p. 244. [2] *Ibid.* [3] *Ibid.*, p. 245.

of them, the probable, in those of some of them, the certain consequence, of their obtaining the charge of his person. He well knew, that if he demanded him with firmness, they would have all consented to his confinement in an English fort." [1]

Lawrence had made the suggestion that Chanda Saheb should be confined in an English fort and the confederates had rejected it. He, acting as an ally of Mohammed Ali, had neither the right nor the power to dictate to the confederates. If he had the power, any attempt to use it was bound to lead to the execution of Chanda Saheb. He well knew that Mohammed Ali would never consent to so powerful and dangerous a rival being in the hands of the English. Wilks states, with the support of native authority, that Chanda Saheb was slain at the instigation of Mohammed Ali.

"It is a fact of public notoriety," he writes,[2] "that his head was immediately sent to that personage, and after being subjected to unmanly insult, was delivered to Nunjeraj [the Mysore Commander-in-Chief] and by him sent to Seringapatam; where it was suspended in a cheenka[3] over the southern or Mysoor gate, to be gazed at by the multitude during three days, as a public trophy of the victories in which the troops of Mysoor had certainly as yet borne no very distinguished part. The death of Chunda Saheb is hardly ever mentioned by a Mussulman, without noticing, as a visible manifestation of Almighty vengeance, that he was treacherously murdered in the same choultry, in which, sixteen years before, he had profaned the holy Koran by a false and treacherous oath to the Ranee of Trichinopoly."

[1] Mill: "History of India," Vol. III., pp. 123–4.

[2] Wilks, Vol. I., p. 285.

[3] *Cheenka*—"a sort of open net of small rope, in which natives usually suspend food to preserve it from the rats. Mr. Orme has been informed that the head of Chunda Saheb has never been carried out of the Carnatic (Drauveda)."—Wilks, Vol. I., p. 285 (footnote).

CHAPTER XI

1752: CLIVE'S "GLORIOUS CAMPAIGN"

TRICHINOPOLY was relieved, the besiegers were beaten, and their candidate for the throne of the Carnatic was put to death. Lawrence now thought that he had only to place the Nawab "in quiet possession of his territories to the northward, where many places still remained with the French."[1] He considered Gingee "was the only fort of consequence which could give us any trouble." He was, therefore, not a little surprised, when he pressed Mohammed Ali to march with his allies in order to reduce the rest of his province, to find him most unwilling to move. The explanation of the mystery was a thunderstroke to Lawrence. He discovered for the first time that Mohammed Ali had promised to "the Mysorean" the possession of Trichinopoly and its dependencies as the price of his assistance. Nanj Raj refused to march until the Nawab fulfilled his engagement. Mohammed Ali pleaded that the Mysorean could not but know that such a promise was never made to be fulfilled. He also advanced the more substantial plea that he should be prepared to carry out the agreement when Nanj Raj had assisted in the recovery of the rest of his dominions.[2]

"The Maissoreans, seeming satisfied," says Lawrence,[3] "promised to march and remove this objection. In confidence that they would

[1] "Cambridge: "War in India," p. 29.

[2] "The Nabob, by giving up Trichinopoly and its dependencies, without being in possession of the rest of the Arcot countries, quitted for ever that part which alone, of all his pretensions, he was actually in possession of. The King of Maissore's friendship and alliance was of great consequence, but it also might be purchased too dear; for however he might promise to assist the Nabob in the recovery of his other countries, when he was once in possession of the place, if he should refuse to fulfil this part of the engagement, who could force him? Other compensations were proposed, and the Nabob even offered to give him a promise under his hand, to deliver Trichinopoly in two months, if he would but march with and assist him."—*Ibid.*, p. 30.

[3] *Ibid.*, p. 30.

follow, we marched with our Europeans to Outatoor the 16th of June, but not finding our allies, or the Nabob follow us, we returned the 18th of June, hearing that Morarow with his Marattas intended putting a stop to the Nabob's march."

Lawrence endeavoured to reconcile the chiefs, but he found that Morari Rao, the Mahratta leader, wanted to get Trichinopoly once more into his own possession.

"An agreement therefore between the two contending parties never could procure it him, wherefore he separately advised both not to give up their pretensions, hoping a breach would give him an opportunity to effect what he saw was not to be obtained by another method." [1]

The Madras Government determined they would take no part in the dispute unless an attack was made on the Nawab. Then as auxiliaries—not mercenaries, as Wilks states—they were bound to interpose. If they allowed the Mysore chief or the Mahratta captain to gain possession of Trichinopoly, they would lose all the advantages for which they had spent blood and treasure. The return of Lawrence to Trichinopoly led to an agreement. The Mahrattas and Mysoreans wanted the English to quit the neighbourhood, for both hoped that then by strength and stratagem one of them would gain possession of the city.

"The Nabob made over to the regent the revenues of the island of Seringham, and of several other districts, impowering him to collect them himself; promised again to deliver up Tritchanopoly at the end of two months; and in the mean time agreed to receive 700 men, provided they were not Morattoes, into the city." [2]

The Regent of Mysore with his force was to accompany the rest of the combined army and assist the Nawab in reducing the Arcot or northern province. Neither side had any intention of keeping the fresh agreement.

On June 28 Lawrence again set forth with 500 Europeans and 2,500 sepoys, accompanied by the Nawab at the head of 4,000 horse, but, in order to frustrate any attack on Trichinopoly, he left a garrison of 200 Europeans and 1,500 sepoys under the command of Captain Dalton. The Tanjorines and Poligars

[1] Cambridge: "War in India," p. 30. [2] Orme, Vol. I., p. 250.

returned home. But "the Mysoreans and Morattoes remained in their encampment to the west of the city, placing a detachment in Seringham Pagoda, which the Nabob had permitted them to take possession of."[1] They "every day talked of following the Nabob." On July 7 Lawrence arrived before Trivadi (Tiruvadi), about fifteen miles from Fort St. David, and found a garrison of French sepoys in the pagoda, who surrendered on the first summons. The troops encamped in the neighbourhood, and Lawrence left the army under the command of Captain de Gingen, "being in so bad a state of health that I could not keep the field."[2] Clive's health had also been broken by the strain of the defence of Arcot, followed by the brilliant but toilsome operations before Trichinopoly at the hottest season of the year, and he, too, left the field and proceeded to Madras.

Lawrence and Clive had good reasons for considering that further important operations would be suspended for a time. "Our forces were not very considerable; we had lost a great many men; there was a strong garrison left in Trichinopoly and we had but few recruits that year."[3] Lawrence was therefore surprised when he heard that the Governor of Madras had, at the earnest request of the Nawab, determined to lay siege to Gingee and vainly hoped to complete the discomfiture of the French by capturing the only important fortress that remained in their hands. "Ill as I was, at that time with the fever," says Lawrence, "I set out from Fort St. David for Madras, to see the governor, and try if I could dissuade him from the attempt." But Saunders was hard to dissuade. He listened to the reasons put forward by the military commander and merely replied "that he had ordered a party and it must go."[4]

On July 23 Major Kinneer, who had lately arrived from Europe, left the camp with 200 Europeans, 1,500 sepoys, and 600 of the Nawab's cavalry. The next day he reached the fort of Villuparam, twelve miles north of Trivadi, which

[1] Orme, Vol. I., p. 250. [2] Cambridge: "War in India," p. 31.
[3] *Ibid.*, p. 32. [4] *Ibid.*, p. 33.

surrendered without resistance. Continuing his march, he rapidly passed through the flat country and reached the foot of the mountains which girdle Gingee for ten miles. A few strong passes pierce them. Kinneer made his way through one of them without opposition and encamped before the fortress on the 26th. He summoned the garrison to surrender. The commander answered with civility that he kept the place "for the King of France" and was determined to defend it.[1] Kinneer could not compel him to yield, for he had neglected to wait for two pieces of battering cannon, together with ammunition and carriage, which had started from Fort St. David under an escort of 150 Europeans.[2]

The catastrophe at Trichinopoly was a grave blow to Dupleix and his plans. But the vain, passionate nature of the man could defy despair. He was always ready to grapple with the last disaster. His magnificent talents, his extraordinary energy, enabled him to frame and carry out fresh expedients for the removal of the perils which threatened his wide aspirations. The instant he heard of the surrender of Law he began to intrigue through his wife with the Regent of Mysore and the Mahratta chief to gain them as allies. He promised the Regent of Mysore not only Trichinopoly, but gave him hopes that the kingdom of Tanjore might be added to it. When Chanda Saheb's fortune was on the decline Bussy persuaded Salabat Jang, who had assumed the office of Viceroy of the Deccan, to issue a commission appointing Dupleix governor from the River Kistna to Cape Comorin. The commission, "with several other pompous patents, was sent to Pondicherry and Salabat-jing promised they should soon be followed by an embassador from the Great Mogul." [3]

[1] Orme, Vol. I., p. 257.

[2] Cambridge: "War in India" (Lawrence's narrative), p. 33.

[3] Orme, Vol. I., p. 256. Lawrence writes: "The supposed messenger from Delly was received with all the honour and ceremony usually paid to an ambassador from the Mogul; and that nothing might be wanting to compleat the farce, Mr. Dupleix himself, in the country manner, with musick and dancing-girls before him, mounted on an elephant, received with due reverence from the hands of the pretended ambassador, his commission from the Mogul, and in consequence of his appointment, gave out all orders from that time as such; he even kept his Durbar or court, sat on a sofa, and received presents from

On the death of Chanda Saheb, Dupleix published these mandates, held his durbar, and exhibited on all occasions the oriental pomp and marks of distinction which he assumed as the Mogul's Viceroy. The *sanad* from the Emperor was forged, but in virtue of the authority supposed to be derived from it Dupleix proclaimed Rajah Saheb, the son of Chanda Saheb, Nawab of the Carnatic.

The surrender of Trivadi increased the gloom and anxiety at Pondicherry, but it merely roused the ire of Dupleix and made him eager for the French troops to take the field. They were few in number. It was the season of the year for the ships to arrive from Europe with reinforcements. The horizon was anxiously scanned. On July 16 two broad sails were seen; [1] they were the *Bourbon* and the *Centaure*, and they brought the greatly-desired reinforcement. It consisted of 500 raw recruits badly armed. As soon as they disembarked, Dupleix proceeded to "sort out" the best of them to form the corps destined to operate in the Carnatic. The process of selection furnished him with 200 men; the remaining 300 he sent at once to Bussy and gave orders that they should be drilled on the march and bent to discipline. In order to increase the strength of the Carnatic army corps, he landed 150 sailors and replaced them by Lascars.[2] Dupleix appointed his nephew, the Chevalier de Kirjean, who had distinguished himself by Bussy's side, to command the Carnatic force, and he was busy completing with characteristic energy the arrangements for their taking the field when he heard that Kinneer's detachment had marched for Gingee. Two courses

his council as well as the natives, like a Prince of the country; and thus endeavoured to support the character of Subah of the Deckan."—Cambridge: "War in India" (Lawrence's narrative), p. 31.

[1] "Dupleix," by Tibulle Hamont, p. 216. The discrepancy to be seen in the dates given by Hamont, Lawrence, and Orme is due to the change in the calendar.

[2] *Ibid.*, p. 217. Lawrence (Cambridge: "War in India," p. 31), writes: "The surrender of Mr. Law happened at that season of the year, when the ships arrived from Europe, and brought a large reinforcement, to which Mr. Dupleix added all the sailors from the Company's ships, sending Lascars on board to navigate them to China." Orme (Vol. I., p. 256) converts this into: "The annual ships from France arriving at the time Mr. Law surrendered, brought a large reinforcement to Pondicherry which he increased by taking the sailors, and sending Lascars on board to navigate the ships to China."

were now open to him. He might attack the force left at Trivadi, or he might cut off communication from the base of Kinneer's operations by placing De Kirjean somewhere in his path. Dupleix chose the second course. He sent orders to Bernier, who commanded at Gingee, to defend himself to the last extremity, and he dispatched De Kirjean with 300 Europeans and 500 sepoys and seven field-pieces. He instructed him to choose a strong position between the three routes from Pondicherry and Trivadi to Gingee, and he suggested the town of Vikravandi. De Kirjean followed the suggestion and took possession of the town, which was on the high road "and not far distant from the pass through which the English had marched."

Kinneer, finding that without battering guns he had no prospect of taking Gingee and that the French were attempting to cut off his communication, immediately repassed the mountains. Having been reinforced by troops from Trivadi, he marched on July 26 "with 300 Europeans, 500 sepoys, a company of Coffrees, and 2,000 horse to give the enemy battle," [1] and found them posted in a strong position. The greater part of the town was surrounded by a stream whose bank was lined with old ruined houses which acted as a parapet. The opposite bank was as high as the houses. The French were drawn up beyond the outwork bank; but as soon as the English field-pieces began to play, they poured across the stream "with precipitation, and the appearance of fear." The ruse was successful. The English, leaving their field-pieces, advanced rapidly to the bank and opened a fire of musketry. A fearful storm of missiles came upon them from the line of old houses.

"The company of English Coffrees were first flung into disorder by carrying off their wounded as they dropped, and soon after took flight; they were followed by the Sepoys; and Major Kineer in this instant receiving a wound which disabled him, the Europeans began to waver likewise. The enemy perceiving the confusion, detached 100 of their best men, amongst which were 50 volunteers, who, crossing the rivulet briskly, advanced to the bank. The

[1] Orme, Vol. I., p. 258.

vivacity of this unexpected motion increased the panic, and only 14 grenadiers, with two ensigns, stood by the colours: these indeed defended them bravely, until they were rejoined by some of the fugitives, with whom they retreated in order; and the French, satisfied with their success, returned to the village, having, with very little loss to themselves, killed and wounded 40 of the English battalion, which suffered in this action more disgrace than in any other that had happened during the war: Major Kineer was so affected by it, that although he recovered of his wound, his vexation brought on an illness, of which he some time after died." [1]

Dupleix, greatly elated by this success, reinforced the Carnatic corps with all the men he could send into the field. After taking the fort of Villuparam, De Kirjean with 450 Europeans, 1,500 sepoys, and 500 horse marched on Fort St. David and encamped to the north of it "close to the bounds." The English and the Nawab's troops quitted Trivadi and encamped at a redoubt "in the bound hedge" three miles to the west of Fort St. David. They remained inactive. They had no commander competent to lead them to victory. Lawrence and Clive were at Madras. On the receipt of the unwelcome information of Kinneer's disaster and the threatened attack on Fort St. David, Saunders determined to dispatch at once to its relief one of the two Swiss companies which had recently arrived at Madras from Europe; and in order to avoid the risk and delay of a march by land he determined to send them by sea. He thought as peace subsisted between Great Britain and France, Dupleix would not dare to violate the English colours on the high seas. He therefore had the force embarked immediately in the light boats of the country. Dupleix, on hearing of their embarkation, "sent a ship out of Pondichery road, and took Captain Schaub and his whole company, and carried them into Pondichery, and there detained them prisoners of war." In Madras and in England the capture raised the most hostile feeling. Lawrence considered it "an action against the law of nations, and an open violation of the peace then subsisting between us and the French; sacred here, as well as in Europe, though we were allies in different causes." Dupleix, however, "insisted that the capture was as

[1] Orme, Vol. I., pp. 258–9.

justifiable as that which had been made of his own troops at Seringham."

As soon as the news reached Madras of the capture, Lawrence, "ill as I still continued," embarked with the other company of the Swiss on board the *Bombay Castle* and arrived at Fort St. David on August 16. The next day he took command of the force consisting of 400 Europeans, 1,700 sepoys, and 4,000 of the native troops with eight field-pieces. De Kirjean, discovering that he was about to be attacked, broke up his camp and fell back on Bahur two miles from the fort. Lawrence followed; De Kirjean again went back and encamped between the bound hedge marking the limits of Pondicherry and Villanur. "I attacked their advanced post at Villenour," says Lawrence, "but as they would not support it I could do no more than drive out that party, my orders not permitting me to follow them into their bounds." Seeing that they had no intention of leaving their bounds, Lawrence now affected fear and retreated precipitately to Bahur. The impetuous Dupleix fell into the trap. He

> "ordered De Kerjean to follow us, conjuring him to improve the minute, and make the proper use of our fears. De Kerjean, suspecting it might be otherwise, represented his thoughts of our retreat, which only procured him a more peremptory order, to march after us immediately; for Mr. Dupleix told him he was convinced we would not fight, that he expected the *Prince*[1] every hour with Mr. De la Touche, who should instantly supersede him."[2]

De Kirjean yielded to the threat, and, leaving the bounds, marched within two miles of Bahur. Lawrence determined to attack him next morning. On August 26, at 2 A.M., his little force was under arms, the sepoys in front in one line; the European battalion formed the second with the artillery divided on the flanks. A high bank on the left flank extended to the French camp. Behind it was posted the Nawab's cavalry "with orders to march as we did." The force advanced,

[1] "The *Prince* was a very large French company's ship, with 700 men, and presents from the French king for the Mogul, Salabatzing, and Chunda Saheb; she was burnt on her passage to India, and scarce a man saved."—Cambridge: "War in India," p. 35, note.

[2] *Ibid.*, p. 35.

and the sepoys placed in the front line to ascertain the strength and position of the French European battalion were challenged a little before the break of dawn by the enemy's advanced post, and not answering, received their fire and returned it, still marching on. When the light came, Lawrence saw the French battalion five hundred strong drawn out a little upon his left.

"On their right was the bank I mentioned before, and on their left a tank or pond of water, which obliged us to incline, to make our front equal to theirs." As the English force advanced they were saluted by a brisk fire from the enemy's cannon. "The small arms soon began," says Lawrence, "our men advanced firing, and the French stood their ground, till our bayonets met." After a rough death wrestle the English grenadiers broke the enemy's centre, and their whole line became a ruin. "They then threw down their arms, and ran for it." [1] This is the battle of Bahur, famous in Indian military annals as one of the very few actions on record where bayonets were fairly crossed. More than a hundred of the French fell by "the queen of weapons" alone. Three commanders and fifteen officers were made prisoners. Their artillery, with all their ammunition, tumbrils and stores, became the spoil of the victors.

The victory was followed by far-reaching results. Lawrence had struck so severe a blow that Dupleix could not take the field until reinforcements should arrive from France. The fame of the British arms, which had been tarnished by the failure of the Gingee expedition, was restored, and the intrigues which Dupleix had carried on with the Regent of Mysore and Morari Rao with success were shattered at a critical moment. They had sent ambassadors to Pondicherry, a treaty had been concluded, war resolved, 3,000 Mahrattas, "commanded by Innis Cawn, the next in rank to Morarow," [2] were on their way to join the French, when they heard the news of the British victory at Bahur. Innis [Yusus] Khan halted on receiving instructions from Morari Rao:

[1] Cambridge: "War in India," p. 36. [2] *Ibid.*, p. 37.

"he joined the Nabob, with great protestations of friendship and seeming joy at the late event, pretending to lament that he had not come up in time to have a share in it; and in order to accomplish his intention of getting money, he did not hesitate to take the oath of fidelity to the Nabob."[1]

On September 18 Lawrence marched to Trivadi with the intention of devoting the time before the north-east monsoon began to the reduction of the country northward from Pondicherry to the Palar. Within half a mile of the northern bank of that river, about thirty miles from the coast and forty north-west of Madras, was situated the strong fort of Chingleput. North of Chingleput on the coast was the fort of Covelong, "called by the Moors Saudet Bunder," about twenty miles south of Madras. They were both regularly garrisoned by French troops, European and native. In the hands of the French Covelong was a perpetual danger to Madras, and Chingleput a grave obstacle to Lawrence establishing the authority of the Nawab in the centre of the Province. Governor Saunders therefore determined to capture both these strongholds before the reinforcements from France, which were daily expected at Pondicherry, arrived. On August 31, 1752:

"The President acquaints the Board that he had concerted with the Nabob measures for reducing Saudet Bunder Fort and Changleput to his obedience which they are of opinion will greatly contribute to the tranquility of the Country about us, as these places give the enemy opportunities of making frequent incursions into our Villages of Poonamallee, St. Thomé, &c., and that the Nabob had promis'd (if the Plan be approved) to send a Detachment of his Troops to join what Forces we can assemble without weakening the grand Army and attempt the enterprize, whereupon it is debated how far we can be assisting therein, as the French Colours are hoisted on the former, and it being considered that although these places are now in possession of the French, yet as they hold them only by right of Conquest, without any Cession, Legal Grant or Phirmaund, the Nabob's natural claim to them as Governour of the Carnateck Country remains unimpeach'd and in this light we are of opinion that we may agreeable to the Law of Nations or rather the custom of Europe (not to mention the example shew'd us by the French in attacking Arcot and Coiladdy, where our Colours were flying),

[1] Orme, Vol. I., p. 265.

without infringing the late Treaty of Peace between our Sovereign and the French King, assist the Nabob, in consequence of our alliance with the Circar in recovering these places. It is therefore agreed that Captain Clive with what Forces can be spared from this Garrison and such as can be drawn together from Poonamallee, &c., proceed to join a Detachment of the Nabob's Troops and in conjunction with them undertake the Seige of Saudet Bunder Fort." [1]

At seven-and-twenty Clive came again to Fort St. George with the honour which he had won. The defence of Arcot was really a brilliant and romantic piece of work, and the battle of Coverepauk and the operations before Trichinopoly brought fresh glory on the hero of the hour. In his great manœuvres and operations he had shown that he was gifted with the quick eye and intuitive powers of command, and in repairing an error or meeting the blows of fortune he showed coolness and tenacity and a strongly tempered soul. What Napoleon said of Frederick the Great was true of Clive: "He was especially great at critical moments." Like Cæsar, Cromwell, or Napoleon, Clive had great administrative ability united to a genius for war. Like them, he won victories and perfected his command of the instruments and means by which he won them. However wild and degenerate the young recruits might be, he discovered the sound stuff that was in them and by discipline converted them into effective soldiers. He had a wonderful understanding of the nature and humours of Orientals; and the sepoys, elevated by the confidence he placed in them, rivalled their European comrades in many a gallant deed. He had not a gracious person, he possessed no ornament of discourse, nor any of those talents which win the affections of acquaintances, but no man was more beloved by his friends. Lawrence, Dalton, Maskelyne, Repington, all the signal men of the time, show by their letters how greatly they esteemed his spirit, generosity, and sincerity. His purse and his influence were always at the disposal of a friend. During his ten years' service he had amassed by private trade, batta, and prize money a moderate fortune. In December, 1750,

[1] Selections from the Letters, Despatches and other State Papers preserved in the Madras Secretariat (Clive Series), edited by George W. Forrest.

Robert Orme of Calcutta "made Ordain'd Authoriz'd Constituted and Appointed . . . and in my stead and place put Mr. Robert Clive of Fort St. David to be my true Certain and Lawful Attorney."

Eight years before, Robert Orme had arrived in Calcutta; he became an assistant in the house of Jackson and Wedderburn, at that time the first English mercantile firm in India—Mr. Jackson being one of the Council, and Mr. Wedderburn ("of the same family as the late Earl of Rosslyn") a free merchant. While with them young Orme made a voyage round the Peninsula to Surat in one of the freight ships, "as they are termed"; and it was on his return to Calcutta in 1743 that he found he was appointed from England to be a writer in the Company's civil service, in which he continued between nine and ten years, becoming, after the first five, a factor. As writer and factor, Orme, in accordance with the Company's regulations, exercised the right of internal trade. Clive became his partner, The firm at Madras was entitled "Robert Orme and Clive," and, according to a mass of accounts and receipts, they carried on a very lucrative trade between Bengal and the Coromandel Coast. They were successful as merchants because they studied "at all convenient seasons the institutions, manners and customs of the native inhabitants." Clive also had the contract for supplying the troops with provisions. At the close of the campaign, Repington wrote to him that the Governor and Council had written to Stringer Lawrence desiring his opinion

> "whether the men may not be dieted on easier Batty[1] to which he answered that they were better judges than he, however proposed the giving a handsome salary to the Steward for the future instead of contracting, and he to give in his accounts upon Oath, by which the Company would pay no more than is necessary."

Repington added:

> "You have deserved your money Clive, and every honest Englishman will think so; besides I could prove that no man unless a soldier beloved by the country People and either in Command himself or

[1] Batty, Batta—"subsistence money." Hence, extra pay given to E.I. regiments when on a campaign.—N. E. D.

highly in favour with the Commander Can ever make half so much of the Employ as you have done on the same terms."

Clive amassed wealth, but he was the least sordid-minded of men. He had more the soul of a prodigal than that of a usurer. After enduring for two years the hardships of a trying campaign, Madras was to the young man a climax of comfort as well as a centre of convivial companions. He plunged into the trivial pleasures of the small society of exiles to which the ships of the season had brought some fair recruits. When Clive was in the field his friend Boddam wrote to him from Fort St. David, May 30, 1752 : [1]

> "I have heard the following Europe news, the King of Sweden is dead, the Queen of Denmark also, and the Prince of Orange too, the Princess of Orange is made Stadtholdress. The Duke of Bolton has married Polly Peacham, his Duchess being dead. There are Eleven Ladies coming out vizt. Mrs. Keene and Mrs. Edwards, two young ladies to Mrs. Ackell, Miss Eliot and Miss Austin, Miss Ross a Scotch Lady, and a prodigious fine Girl it's said, and Miss Maskelyne Your Friend's sister. The others I have not heard the Names of but However I would advise you to guard your heart well against these, when you think of the time of seeing us, as I don't doubt but after such a campaign as you have had, these beauties will have a wonderful effect upon you."

There is a romantic tradition regarding the meeting of Miss Maskelyne and Clive. It is said that Clive saw and was fascinated by a miniature of a young woman in Maskelyne's room. He asked about the subject of the delicate and spiritual features—gracious, intelligent, and sweet. Maskelyne told him she was one of his sisters. He begged his friend to invite his sister to come to Madras. The other tradition is that Maskelyne read to his chum his sister's letters, and he was so struck by them that he asked him to invite her to come to Madras. What substance there is in these legends it is impossible to tell, but in a packet of old letters whose white tape had not been unbound since they were tied together at Madras there was discovered the following letter from Maskelyne to his sister Margaret : [2]

[1] Powis MSS. [2] *Ibid.*

DEAR PEGGY,—I was Favoured with yours of the 20th August 1751: by the *Donnington*, on the 14th Instant, and hope your declining my Proposal for tripping it this Way, proceeds from some more agreeable views at Home, as otherwise I can't but blame you for it; Matches in this Country generally proving so vastly Superior to what are made in Europe.

I am Extremely Glad you left our Uncle Nevil in good Health; whom I do myself the Pleasure of writing to by this Conveyance; and hope Mrs. Fowke who Quitted us in October last is so too.

As I have given you my Advice, Supported by the most Solid Reasons I could urge; I leave it Entirely to you to determine for yourself, only begging Your Assurance that whenever We have the Happiness of meeting you will find

a Sincerely Affectionate Brother in

DEVICOTA, *March* 28*th* 1752: EDM[D] MASKELYNE.

P.S.—You leave me quite in the Dark as to where the young Astrologer Nevil is.

As a voyage to Europe in those days took seven or eight months, Peggy must have sailed from England before she received this letter, for she arrived at Madras about the end of June. To her the East was no unknown land. She came, like Clive, from the strong middle-class stock which had the privilege of providing the East India Company with its most successful soldiers and its most able administrators. Her uncle had served in the East India Company and died at Fort Marlborough on the west coast of Sumatra, a settlement of the East India Company which was founded, as York Fort, in 1684. Her aunt Elizabeth married at Fort St. George Joseph Walsh, Governor of Fort Marlborough, and her aunt Alice Maskelyne married at Calcutta Captain Kelsall. Their brother, Edmund Maskelyne, was for many years clerk in the Secretary of State's Office, Whitehall. He had three sons. Two of them had the high honour of being elected Fellows of Trinity College, Cambridge. Nevil, the "young astrologer," afterwards became Astronomer Royal, and did an invaluable service to humanity by establishing the Nautical Almanac.[1] It was through the influence of the Duke of Newcastle that the third brother, Edmund, obtained a writership at Madras.

[1] "Maskelyne, Nevil, Astronomer Royal, 1765, established the Nautical Almanac, 1766, F.R.S. 1758."—"Dictionary of National Biography," Vol. XXXVI., p. 414.

Peggy and her fair companions on their arrival at Fort St. George were looked at, observed, talked about and written about. On July 1 Dalton writes to Clive from Trichinopoly:[1]

DR. BEAUTY,—By this time I reckon you are able to give one an Account of the new arrived angels—by god it would be a good joke if your countenance was to smite one of them, and you were to commit matrimony—I should however be concerned at it as it would put me out of all hopes of the pleasure I propose myself in company with you in Covent Garden &c.

On July 26 Dalton again wrote:[2]

TRICHINOPOLY *July 26th*

DEAR CLIVE,—What can be the meaning I can never have the pleasure of a line from you; you now & then favoured me with one when you had infinity of business on your hands & now you neglect me when you have no other employ than gallanting the Ladies, and jovially entertaining your friends. I hear that you keep one of the best houses in Madras—not in the least resembling our Bandipolem Oeconomy—however recollect at a leisure hour that you have a friend at Trichinopoly to whom the news of your health and welfare will always give infinite satisfaction & I'm sure you'll write me a Line. A rascal of a Vaquil that came from Pondicherry entertained the King & Morari with a plausible account of your being clink'd and Trivedy retaken, which made us uneasy tho' it had not the colour of the truth; however these reports only serve to do you honour, as it is manifest by 'em, how sensible the enemy are of how much consequence your life is to the cause.

The Batta for this month will come to upwards of 4000 Rups. for the french and my people. I have already drawn on you for 3600. I sent you last months account a good while ago, as I shall also this in a few days. I beg you'll order Boddam to answer my Bills at sight for I should be sadly off if Buckangy did not supply me.

I am absolutely astonished the Nabob's people stay with him at all, paid in the manner they are; I am obliged to keep spies on his sepoys the same as the Misoor Punes[3] since the late affair, tho I'm convinced the people would serve him well if they had but enough to support nature. There was a Company wanted to go out of the gate yesterday who assured me they had 5 months pay due and had received but 8 fans. each this month, those under me have had but 3 rupees. However, I promise high to keep up the poor devils spirits. These lads in Camp must shortly move if the rain continues; they are in a shocking condition. Do Clive write me a line and believe me with the utmost sincerity

Your most affectionate friend and servant

J. DALTON.

[1] Orme MSS.: India, Vol. II., pp. 488–99. [2] *Ibid.*, pp. 490–1. [3] Mysore Peons.

The man who owned your great grey horse is here a prisoner. He assures me he is the finest beast India ever saw: I imagine you are by this time acquainted with his qualities. Remember me to Maskelyne.

Clive, under the warmth of youth, increasing fortune, and success, entered into the social life of the settlement—which was the social life of the eighteenth century transplanted from England to the Coromandel Coast. Society, owing to the increase of English ladies, had grown since he entered Fort St. George a friendless and penniless lad. The factor and merchant considered it enhanced their importance if they imitated the luxurious splendour of the Indian nobles, and a luxurious style of living came to be regarded as a necessity. Ives, who visited Madras in 1755, remarks, "Many of our countrymen residing there, to maintain their dignity among the natives, live in all the magnificence of the East." They introduced the miscellaneous socialities of the West. They were unusually fine and brilliant in their costumes; they paced their minuets, they flirted, they drank their claret and their madeira at the tavern, they toasted the beauty of the hour, and they exchanged shots on the beach. The letters afford glimpses of bright scenes in which Clive mingled with all the gay audacity of youth. His nature was like many others, open alike to cheerful and gloomy impressions, and when the fits of despondency did not attack him, there was no pleasanter companion than the fearless, open-hearted soldier.

The time for sport, however, soon passed. Clive had been three months in Madras when Governor Saunders determined to turn the French out of the two strong forts of Covelong and Chingleput. The troops which could be spared from this garrison were 200 European recruits and 500 untrained sepoys.

"It could hardly be expected," says Orme, "that any officer, who had acquired reputation, would risque it by taking the command of them; but Captain Clive, whose military life had been a continued option of difficulties, voluntarily offered his service on this occasion, notwithstanding that his health was at this time much impaired by the excess of his former fatigues." [1]

[1] Orme, Vol. I., pp. 265–6.

Orme, who was at Madras at the time, had already begun to gather material for his History, and among the many memoranda which Clive sent him there is one of the "Siege of Cobelong & Chinglapet," which Orme extended, embellished, and incorporated in his work. Every reader will be pleased to see it printed in its original state: [1]

"SIEGE OF COBELONG & CHINGLAPET.

"Captain Clive at the request of the Governor took the command of about 200 Europeans, & 500 Seapoys destined for the siege of Covelong; the Europeans consisted of European recruits just arrived from Europe, not one of which had ever seen service & were very indifferently disciplined. The Seapoys were no better, being raised on the occasion. On the [15th] Septr. Captain Clive began his march towards Covelong, & the next day arrived at a rising ground at about 2 miles distant from the fort. Over night Captain Clive ordered Lieutenant Cooper before day break with one half of the forces to take possession of a garden very advantageously situated at the distance of about 500 yards from the fort; on receiving advice from Lieut: Cooper that he had taken possession of the garden without any opposition from the enemy, Captain Clive began his march at day break to join him. As he approached the garden he perceived the forces were broken and running away in great confusion; it was with great difficulty they were rallied and with the assistance of the other forces the enemy were drove back into the fort and the garden repossessed again with several other advantageous posts necessary to keep the enemy within their garrison. It seems upon the enemy receiving notice of this party being in possession of the garden [they] sallied [out] with about 30 Europeans & 100 Seapoys & having killed the commander Lieut: Cooper the rest of the troops took to flight and were found in that condition when Captain Clive came to their assistance. The next day Captain Clive summoned the fort to surrender, in answer to which the governor com-

[1] Orme MSS.: India, Vol. II., pp. 309–10.

manded Captain Clive to retire from a fort belonging to the King of France & where the french colours were flying & assuring him at the same time he would defend the place to the last extremity. Upon this Captain Clive began to erect a battery of two 24 pounders at the distance of about 300 yards to batter in [the] breach. During the erection of this battery which took up three days Monsr. St. Germain the Governor of Chengalaput being reinforced from Pondicherry arrived within about 4 miles with 30 Europeans, 2 field pieces & 700 Seapoys but upon a party being detached towards him retired with great precipitation towards Chengalaput. By this time the battery was up and no succour arriving the governor instead of performing his promise to defend the place desired to capitulate which was granted on condition of the whole being made prisoners of war & the fort being surrendered in the afternoon which was taken possession of about 4 o'clock. In the morning Captain Clive received intelligence the Chengalaput party was again approaching towards Covelong but concluded they would immediately retreat on receiving advice the place was up early in the morning Captain Clive discovered them.

"This party came a second time upon receiving a letter from the governor that if they did not come immediately he should be obliged to surrender the place. And approaching near the place at dawn of day mistook the Nabob's colours the ground of which was white bordered with green for french Colours, & having received no other intelligence marched confidently on to the relief of the fort. Captain Clive perceived by the motion of the enemy their ignorance of the surrender ordered the greatest part of the troops to conceal themselves behind the Rocks, bushes and houses which lay in their way. Mr. St. Germain the commandant of Chengalaput with 25 Europeans & 2 field pieces were either killed or taken prisoners. The taking of Covelong & Chingalaput put the Nabob in Possession of all the Carnatic to the North of the Punniar."

Clive's own modest account is too terse to do him sufficient justice. As in his former campaigns, he had been foremost in the charge and fought in the thickest press. He had at Covelong converted disaster into victory by the hardihood with which he rallied his broken troops, and with "even violence" compelled the cowards to return to the fight. Orme records,[1] what Clive omits, that at Covelong, when Clive began to erect the breaching battery at the distance of 300 yards from the wall, he at the same time placed a strong guard on a rock about a hundred yards to the left of the battery.

> "The enemy brought many of their guns to bear upon the face of attack, and fired smartly; whilst it was with the greatest difficulty the English troops could be kept to their posts, both Europeans and Sepoys taking flight on every alarm: an unlucky shot, which struck the rock and with the splinters it made, killed and wounded fourteen men, frightened the whole so much, that it was some time before they would venture to expose themselves again, and one of the advanced centries was found several hours after concealed in the bottom of a well.
>
> "Captain Clive judging that shame would avail more than severity to reclaim them from their cowardice, exposed himself continually to the hottest of the enemy's fire, and his example brought them in two days to do their duty with some firmness."

The fort of Covelong having fallen and the detachment being advancing to its relief having been defeated, Clive followed up his success by pushing on to Chingleput, which surrendered as soon as its walls had been breached—the garrison marching away with the honours of war to Pondicherry.

It is recorded at a Consultation of the 9th October, 1752, that "Captain Clive complained of want of health, and desired to return, which, as he had executed his plan, was granted."[2] So ended what the President in his letter to Lawrence calls Clive's "glorious Campaign."

[1] Orme, Vol. I., p. 267.

[2] Madras Records.

CHAPTER XII

1752–5: MARRIAGE AND RETURN TO ENGLAND

WHEN Clive returned to Madras after the relief of Trichinopoly, his health broken completely, and with no prospect of immediate service, he must have mentioned to his father his intention of returning to England, for we find Mr. Richard Clive writing to his son on December 15, 1752, as follows:[1]

DEAR SON,—I was at Dinner at S[r] Philip Chetwoods our Nieghbor in the Country when I reced Your welcome Letter which gave me Joy not to be express[d]. Since then now I am come to London the Pleasure is repeated by the aplause every one gives to your Gallant Actions and Behaviour, and the Success that hath attended you and you are compar[d] to no less than some of those brave Generals who are gone but left their names upon Record to their Glory and Honour. The Directors of the Company you have so faithfully Served I hear at a Publick Entertainm[t] drank Your Health by the name of General Clive, and are pleas[d] to Say they are Under great Obligations to you, I waited on the three principal Direct[rs] last week in order to find out if I could what they propos[d] for you but perceive they are desirous to have the Acc[t] the next Ships bring before they give me any positive answer other than a general one that they are very desirous to do you any Service in their power. Your freinds amongst which is one of the princip Direct[rs] and my intimate Acquaintance advise that you Should not leave Madrass before you know how the Direct[rs] propose to Reward you, but this will be for your owne determination who can best Judge in the Situation you are in what is most propper to be done. You may be Shure Your Mother and my Self shall think the time long till wee See you. I have seen Mr. King but twice since I came to Town and once he Dined with me with the late Govern[r] Floyer. Mr. King tells me that he finds great dificulty to put off the Diamonds that only £300 worth are yet disposed of and the rest are sent to Holland and that he do's not beleive they will make more than £700 of the whole Cargo, this is bad encouragem[t] to make Remittances in Diamonds—Mr. Vere and I are not quite so intimate as when you left England and I could have wisht you had put Mr. W[m] Belchiers name in your power of

[1] Powis MSS. A portion of this letter is printed in Malcolm's Life of Clive.

Attorney in his Stead as the latter is my very good freind and Yours but tis only for form and so not very material.

I hope you receiv^{d} the £500 which I gave you an Acc^{t} of in my last Letter and doubt not but you will make the most of it, Your 5 Sisters that are now most of 'em grown Women & two little Bro. the one 11 and the other 7 all Rejoyce at Your Welfare and are not a little proud of their Relation, I hear that Duplex on behalfe of himself and the French in India hath made large Remonstrances to Govr Saunders and that he has remitted them to the Direct^{rs} and at the same time tis Said that France hath Sent Some Remonstrances of the Same nature (complaining of the Usage they have met wth in India) to Our Secretary of State, this the Direct^{rs} seem pleas^{d} with that those who carried it wth So high a hand very lately are now oblig^{d} to make Remonstrances. I hope this will meet you before you leave Madrass. I have but one word more & Conclude. As Your Conduct and Bravery is become the Publick talk of the Nation and this is the time to encrease Your fortune, make use of the present Opportunity before you quit the Country Remembering that the Intrest of 20,000 in this Country is no more than £500 p^{r} Ann. May Heaven direct and prosper you in all Your Undertakings and bring you safe to your Native Country where with transporting Pleasure you'll be reced by

Your Affectionate Father,

RICH^{D} CLIVE.

SWITHEN LANE LONDON *Decemb^{r}* 15*th* 1752

I send this by Mr. Hulls who will see you if possible & with whom I am well acquainted.

The following day his mother wrote to him: [1]

LONDON *December the* 16 1752

DEAR SON,—I Cant express the joy yours to your Father gave me your brave Conduct and Success which providence has blesst you with is the talk and wonder of the publick the great joy and Satisfaction of all your friends: but more peculiarly So to me has it gives me hopes of Seeing you much Sooner then I could possible have expected: I finde Some of your friends [? omission] which your longer Stay in india but I earnestly entreat you will lett no motive induce you except your honour and the peace of the Country require it: your relations are all well 4 of your Sisters are with me the youngest and your 2 Brothers are at School: your Cousin Ben has no employ his onely in half pay as a lieutenant lives with his Father I believe wishes himself with you: we are removed to a large House in Swithens lane near the post House and hope to See you in it: may a kind

[1] Powis MSS. This letter is printed in Malcolm's Life of Clive, but the spelling and punctuation have been altered.

providence attend and bless you and bring you Safe to your native Country is the most Sincere wish and prayer of your

Ever affectionate mother

REB CLIVE.

Before these letters could meet Clive at Madras he had embarked for England. He had volunteered to take the field before his health was re-established, and the fatigues of the campaign during the worst season of the year had worn out body and mind. He was again attacked by the nameless and inscrutable disease which tormented and embittered the greater part of his too short days. Stringer Lawrence writes to him:[1]

FORT ST. DAVID.
Novr. 30*th* 1752.

DEAR CLIVE,—I'm greatly concerned to find your Fits continue which I sincerely hope will be removed by a change of Climate and shall be glad that you'll tell me yourself The last has not done much mischief and you are on the mending Hand. As I'm perswaded however distant we are from each other Our Friendship is unalterable I shall be always anxious for your welldoing and the oftner I hear from you the more real satisfaction it will give to

Dear Clive

Your Affectionate friend

S. LAWRENCE.

To CAPT. CLIVE *at Fort St. George.*

On his return to Madras Clive resumed the office of steward, but his health rendered the habits and responsibility of business almost an impossibility. He was, however, unwilling to leave India, for the prospect of active service in the field was again before him. On December 14 the President laid before the Board two letters from the Governor of Fort St. David advising "that the Morattas plunder burn and destroy wherever they come and that the French have taken the Field." Lawrence had, owing to Saunders' constant interference in military details, resigned the command and requested permission to return to Europe if he could not be serviceable in the other settlements. The Governor and Council, in a conciliatory but firm letter, state:

[1] Orme MSS., Vol. I., p. 37.

"At a time when the Honour of our Nation, the Welfare of our Honble Masters Affairs, perhaps the Happiness or Misery not only of Ourselves in general, but those that may come after us (for certainly on the Success of Affairs at this Critical Juncture depends the good or ill Fate of the Settlements on this Coast) is at Stake, at a time when an Enemy is in Sight and you know that Major Kinneer is dead, that Captain DeGingins (who has very honourably staid two Years 'till an Officer came out) is going home, that Captain Clive's Health is so bad that he must probably do the same, and that there is no Commanding officer but yourself; At this Juncture we cannot think it honourable in you to ask, nor can we grant your Request of laying down the Service and going to Europe; We have no power to annul the Contract you have made with the Company, but desire that you take the Command of the Army as the present Occasion renders it much more necessary than your Presence can be at any other Settlement." [1]

The old soldier resumed command of the army, and in January again took the field, but Clive found that his constitution had been so completely shattered that he would never be fit for active service without a complete change of climate. He took the advice of his friends, resigned the office of Steward, and prepared to embark for England. In a bundle of old receipts we find the following:

To CAPT^{N}. EDMUND COOKE *of ship Admiral Vernon.*

SIR,—The President and Council having Granted Captain Robert Clive leave to take his Passage for England on your Ship. You are hereby permitted to receive him and his Necessaries on board. Dated in Fort St. George this 13th day of February 1753.

Signed By Order of the President &

C. H^{s}. BOURCHIER Sec^{y}.

CAPTAIN ROBERT CLIVE *Dr.*

To the Honble Company for permission of Passage to England on the *Admiral Vernon*	£12 or Pags.	30
To Secretaries Fees		1
	Pagodas	31

FORT ST. GEORGE 13*th Feb*^{y}. 1753.

C. H^{s}. BOURCHIER Sec^{y}.

On Sunday morning, February 18, 1753, five days after he had leave to take his passage for England, Robert Clive was

[1] Records of Fort St. George, Diary and Consultation Book, Military Department, 1752, pp. 88, 89.

married to Miss Margaret Maskelyne in the small, picturesque church within the walls of Fort St. George. His bride, besides grace and beauty, combined practical sagacity with a love for music and letters. During his stormy career he sought confidence and counsel from her to whom all things might be safely confided, and from whom he found comfort in the black hours of gloom. Some of her letters to him are extant,[1] and with their assistance we form a good conception of her accomplishments and strong devotion to the heavy-laden intrepid genius, brave and much-suffering man. During all their married life they wisely kept their honeymoon.

Many were the congratulations which Clive received on his marriage with Peggy, who seems to have won all hearts in Madras. His old commander wrote:

> " I now oblige myself by taking this opportunity of wishing you and Mrs. Clive much Happiness on your marriage. I always thought her a worthy and deserving Young Lady and am sincerely rejoiced you both have met with such good fortune."

A few days later, in reply to a communication from Clive, Lawrence writes: [2]

> " For God's sake why do you mention obligations to me. I never thought you under any and the Proof you have given me that I was not deceived in my opinion of you from the beginning affords me much satisfaction: May you have health to enjoy the fortune your merit has gain'd."

In one of the letters which passed between them Lawrence requests Clive to take home for him letters to be sent to the "Indian house . . . as they are of great consequence to me," and "two Runts[3] for Mr. Mabbott." "I beg you'll take care of them and fee the Butcher to use them well by promising him two Guineas if they get safe which you'll give him on their Landing and I'll pay you again when we meet in England if you'll trust me so long." [4]

Clive cancelled the passage for England he had taken in the *Admiral Vernon* owing to the lack of suitable accommo-

[1] Strachey MS. [2] Orme MSS., Vol. I., p. 49.
[3] An ox or cow of a small breed or size.—N. E. D.
[4] Orme MSS., Vol. I., p. 45.

dation. He writes to Lawrence that the two "Runts" had arrived with the "Paddy Straw." "They are now grassing on shore. In a day or two I shall send them on board the *Bombay Castle*, and will try all in my power to carry them safe to Lady Delver." He adds:

A few days ago I deliverd in a polite Letter to the Board but as I received no other Answer than a Note for 30 Pagodas Passage Money & an Order to the Captain to take me on Board I think in Justice to the Military in General I cannot leave this Coast without leaving a Paper behind me representing the little Notice taken of People of our Profession I hope the World will not accuse me of Vanity or be of Opinion that I think too highly of my own Successes as I seldom or ever opend my Lips upon the Subject all that I ever expected was a Letter of Thanks and that I am informed is usual upon such Occasions.

A few days ago the Governor sent for & informed me the Nabob had made me a present of 40,000 Rupees I sent a Note for that Purpose, but by all the Enquiries I have made since can learn nothing further, if there should be any such thing & the Nabob should after my Departure be in peaceable possession of the Promise I must request the favor of You to stand my Friend in this Affair. Mrs. Clive desires to be remembered to You in the most Affectionate Manner we shall both think ourselves extreamly happy and your Correspondence which we desire may be as frequent as Opportunity will permit. May perfect Health & the greater Success attend You and may I always have the Pleasure of subscribing myself Dear Major

Your Affec[t] Friend and hum Serv

R. C.

There is no date to this letter, but it must have been written after March 12, 1753, for in the Minutes of Consultation of that day we find a letter from Captain Clive desiring "to have an error in his account rectified" and leave for himself and family to go to Europe on the *Bombay Castle*. At a Consultation held on March 16, a letter was read from Mr. Orme, desiring passage to England per the *Bombay Castle*.[1] On March 31, 1753, Clive wrote as follows:

To MESS[RS]. WALSH VANSITTART & MASKELYNE

GENTLEMEN,—I have left in the Hands of Mr. Levi Moses the Sum of fifty thousand Arcot Rupees, to be invested in Diamonds, should a part or the whole remain uninvested, at the Dispatch of the last Ship, I desire it may be let out if possible on good Security

[1] Madras Public Consultations (India Office Records), 1753, pp. 141, 156.

at Land Interest with all other Moneys in Your hands belonging unto me, till another Opportunity of investing it offers, so as to be sent next September.

If Mr. Levi Moses will give it as his Opinion in writing that the purchasing of Diamonds is likely to turn out to my Advantage, I not only direct that the above Sum be made over to him for that purpose but likewise every farthing belonging to me in your Hands—but if on the contrary Diamonds are not procurable upon advantagious Terms I then desire that the whole of my Estate remaining in India may be sent to Bengal, paid into the Compys Cash Bills taken out in my Name and transmitted me by the first Opportunity.

Mr. Levi Moses hath my Consent to take up at Respondentia at 9[s] the Pagoda, as far as one half the Money of mine in his Hands, on Condition that he concerns me jointly with himself to the amount of the Sum lent him and consigns the Diamonds to me and his Brother Mr.

Should you have reason to apprehend the Death of Mr. Levi Moses through Sickness or any Accident, I then direct that you immediately withdraw any Sum or Sums of Money belonging to me in his Possession, as I would not on any Account whatever have my Affairs blended with those of Mr. Levi Moses after his Decease, and should your Apprehensions prove true you will then send the whole as before directed to Bengal, if not the before-mentioned Instructions are to take place. I am

Gentlemen

Your most Obe[t] hum Serv

ROBERT CLIVE.

FORT ST. GEORGE, 21*st March*, 1753.

On the evening of March 23, 1753, Clive and his bride sailed from Madras on board the *Bombay Castle*.[1] Of this homeward voyage we know little except that the *Pelham* "spoke" the *Bombay Castle* off the Cape on June 10, 1753, and on June 14 "came on board Captain Clive and Mr. Oram (*sic*) Passengers from The Bombay Castle."[2] Maskelyne, writing to Clive from Madras (October 27, 1753), says:[3]

"I had the Pleasure of learning by Peggy's Letter of the 20th June, that You had made a considerable Progress in Your Passage, and tho' removed to the *Pelham* partly on Account of Your Health, partly Your Confidence in Captain Lindsay's superior Assiduity, yet that the former was in no such Condition as to alarm us."

[1] Log (India Office Marine Records, 125 C.). Malcolm writes: "He embarked at Madras in February 1753." This error has been copied by subsequent biographers.

[2] Log (India Office Marine Records, 607 C).

[3] Orme MSS., Vol. I., p. 145.

We learn from the log of the *Pelham* that on July 12 Clive and " Oram " (Orme) went ashore at St. Helena. On October 14 the *Pelham* anchored at Erith, and " most of our people went ashore." Ten years had passed since Clive, a lad of seventeen, had left England. Great was the happiness in the " large house in Swithens Lane " on his return.

Clive soon discovered that the establishment was beyond his father's means, and the first use which he made of the fortune he had brought home was to apply a part of it to place his parents in a state of independence, and to redeem the debt with which the family estate of Styche was burdened. He also gave freely to his relations, and there was no limit to the happiness which he spread around him. But his welcome was not confined to his family circle. The splendid services he had rendered were known not only to his masters, but also to his countrymen at large, and he was received with every mark of popular honour. The Court of Directors had written to the Governor of Fort St. David " of the great regard they had for the merit of Captain Clive, to whose courage and conduct the late turn in our affairs has been mainly due; he may be assured of our having a just sense of his services." They had, as his father informed Clive, toasted him at a public entertainment as " General " Clive, and they now received him with every mark of respect. Shortly after his arrival Clive went, according to custom, to pay his respects to the Court, and in the Court Minutes[1] we find the following:

" 31*st October,* 1753.—Robert Clive Esqr late a Commander of the Companys Forces, under the Presidency of Fort St. George, being returned from thence on the *Bombay Castle,* and paying his Respects to the Court.

" The Chairman in the name of the Court, congratulated him on his Arrival, and returned him thanks for the Signal Services he had done the Company, hoping he would afford such further Attendance and Assistance, with his Opinion on Affairs in those parts, as the Court or any Committee thereof may advise with him upon.

" Captain Clive then made his Acknowledgments for the Courts favors, and desired leave to assure them, he should with the greatest

[1] Vol. 65, p. 189 (India Office Records).

readiness, offer any experience he may have gained, and embrace every opportunity for furthering their Service.

"Whereupon a Motion being made

"Order'd That it be referr'd to the Committee of Correspondence, to consider of a proper present, to be made to Captain Clive, as a Token of the Courts sense of his singular Services in the East Indies, and to report."

Clive settled in a house in Queen Square, and was soon drawn into the whirlpool of London fashionable life. The foremost statesmen of the day were anxious to meet and converse with the hero of Arcot and the young commander who had materially helped to humble Dupleix and his ambitious policy. From Lord Hardwicke, Murray—soon after Lord Mansfield—Lord Barrington, and Lord Sandwich he received marked attention. Henry Fox was introduced to him, and, by the force of his personal attractions, won Clive's confidence and attachment. Clive always regarded him as "the patron of the East India Company." Lord Holderness, one of His Majesty's Secretaries of State who was negotiating with two French deputies as to the best means of putting a stop to the hostilities in India, sought Clive's opinions concerning the military and political relationship of the English and French companies.

Both the English Company and the French Government found the burden of the war too great. The East India Company had, about 1751, represented to the Ministry that they were little able with their own resources to continue the war against the French Company strongly supported by the administration of France. They stated in clear and emphatic terms that the object of Dupleix was the complete destruction of the English establishments in India, and they solicited the Government either to terminate or carry on the war. The trade of the English nation in the East was a national concern. The Ministry now began to make frequent remonstrances with the French Government with regard to the continuation of hostilities in India when the two countries were at peace in Europe. At the same time the French Company and the King's Minister began to lose faith in Dupleix.

His early successes and acquisitions lost their glamour. Stories were circulated regarding his pride, ambition, and cupidity. The merchants and officials who returned from Pondicherry spoke of the large jaghires, the money and the jewels bestowed on Mr. Corfe and his followers. The Directors reminded Dupleix in 1750 that officials were forbidden by Royal Ordinance to receive gifts from native princes. But the remonstrances and commands of his masters merely aroused the pride, temper and arrogance of the man. Their servants were growing fabulously rich, but the Company had drifted into the shoal of bankruptcy. They held that peace was essential to the progress of commerce, and they ordered Dupleix to make a peace and withdraw Bussy from the Deccan. But the idea of a permanent peace was never in the mind of Dupleix. He would never abandon his great project to render France in effect the Dictator of Southern India and to shut out England from all interference in its politics. If he had kept Bussy and his splendid French corps in the Carnatic, he would by mere superiority in numbers have been able to capture Trichinopoly. The miserable end of that ill-projected enterprise blasted his hopes and sealed his fate. About the close of the year 1752 news reached Paris of the surrender of Law. The surrender of French troops touched the pride of a sensitive and gallant nation. All the former services of Dupleix were effaced, and men began to consider that the statements made by his old rival, La Bourdonnais, in his "Mémoires," recently published, that he was a vain, ambitious, grasping ruler without prudence or judgment, might be true. Delaître, one of the Syndics, and Silhouette, one of the Royal Commissioners, who had been inspired by La Bourdonnais, had prophesied disaster, and disaster had come to pass.

When France was in this temper a Director of the East India Company proposed to the correspondent of the French Company in London that the best way to stop the fighting between the two companies in India would be to have the matter discussed either at the Court of St. James or Versailles. The French Minister of Foreign Affairs adopted the suggestion.

Duvelaer, one of the Directors of the French Company, and his brother des Lude, were going to England on private affairs, and it was determined to give them a general power to settle the preliminary negotiations. In March, 1753, Duvelaer and his brother arrived in England charged with the mission to conclude a treaty of neutrality between the two companies. Three months passed before negotiations with the Ministry began. Then sundry conferences were held in London between the Earl of Holderness and the two deputies. Months passed, and no progress was made towards a definite settlement. On October 25, 1753, Louis XV. signed a decree appointing M. Godeheu the Managing Director of the Compagnie des Indes' naval establishment at L'Orient, Commissioner of his Majesty and Commander-General of the French establishments in the East. He had been a factor at Chandernagore when Dupleix was Governor. By this decree Godeheu was commanded to arrest Dupleix, keep him under a safeguard, and place him on board the first vessel sailing to France. At the same time secret and supplementary instructions were given Godeheu that he was to show the letter of recall to Dupleix and then make it public. If Dupleix calmly faced his dismissal that portion of the decree ordering his arrest was not to be put in force; but if he resisted his fall, Dupleix, his wife and daughter were to be arrested and sent to France.[1]

The English Ambassador at Paris informed the Ministry of the appointment of Godeheu and also of the more important fact that the French Company were raising 2,000 men to send to India with him. The dispatch of so large a force seemed to contradict the statements that Godeheu had powers and orders to make peace. The Earl of Holderness informed the French Ambassador that the King had resolved to support the East India Company in all their rights and privileges, and that a regiment would be sent to Madras. Early in January, 1754, the French Ambassador was told that a squadron of men-of-war, on which the regiment would embark, were pre-

[1] "Dupleix," by Tibulle Hamont, p. 283.

paring to sail in a fortnight for the East Indies. The attitude of the English Government produced the desired impression on the French administration, "and they consented that the disputes of the two companies should be adjusted by commissaries in India, on a footing of equality; without any regard to the advantages which either the one or the other might be in possession of, at the time when the treaty should be concluded."[1]

In February Godeheu set sail in the *Duc de Bourgogne*, and two ships with 2,000 French troops on board followed him. In March, 1754, a naval squadron consisting of six line of battle ships under Admiral Watson, sailed for the East Indies. The squadron had on board the 39th Regiment, of 700 men, under the command of Colonel Adlercron, 40 of the King's artillerymen, and 200 recruits for the Company's force. In the commissioned ranks of the 39th were Eyre Coote, Forde, and Carnac.

The Court of Directors refused to send out a commissary, but they invested Mr. Saunders and some of the Madras Council with authority to treat with Mr. Godeheu. They also sent out Orme, who had been in communication with Lord Holderness, to be a member of the Council at Fort St. George. Clive, in a letter to a friend at Madras, makes the following comments on Orme's appointment:

"There is no doubt by the Station he goes out it must be disagreable to every one under him. It is very natural yet you will allow that Dear Self gets the better of every other Consideration, make his Case Your own would not you and every one else gladly have ascended the Ladder by the like means. I find *by Experience* that a man is not the farther from Preferment by paying a Visit to his Native Country this is not wrote out of any particular regard or Attachment to Orme. I declare he has not had any Interest his own Merit in a particular Way has done the Thinking (I mean his History,) my Lord Holderness to whom he first shew'd it, is so pleas'd with the Author that he has made a Point of Serving him.

"What ever the World may think I am no Stranger to Orme, it is in his Power to make himself as agreable or Disagreable as any man in India if he pleases so he is going to be an Inhabitant of Madras I hope he'll study to make himself more and more acceptable in

[1] Orme, Vol. I., pp. 367–8.

future he has had my Advice freely upon this Subject so much for business."

He adds:

"My Health will/would not permit me to accept the Offers that have been made me of going abroad this Year If I can have the same next I shall very happy in the thought of seeing again all my old Friends & Accquaintance."

At a meeting of the Court held on February 6, 1754, the Minutes of the Committee of Correspondence, who had been asked to "consider of a proper present to be made to Captain Clive," were read, and it was unanimously

"Resolved That a Sword sett with Diamonds to the value of £500 be presented by the Court to Capt Robert Clive as a Token of their Esteem for him and sense of his singular Services to the Company, upon the Coast of Choromandel.

* * * * * * *

"Order'd That it be referr'd to the Committee of Correspondence to provide those presents and give such further directions thereupon as they shall see fit." [1]

Clive objected to receiving this mark of distinction unless a similar compliment was paid to Stringer Lawrence. He wrote as follows to his old and gallant friend:

DEAR MAJOR,—I could not let any more Ships sail for India without writing. I have taken the Opportunity of Mr. Orme's return to make him the Bearer.

I deliver'd Your Letters safe to the Secretary, & your two Runts in good Health to My Lady Delves she returns you many thanks & is vastly pleas'd with them, at the same time wishes for the Sake of the Breed they had not been both of the Female kind. You know her Ladyship is a Quicksighted Woman in these Cases.

It is natural to imagine that many Questions would be ask'd about the Indies and especially of the Dispute between You and Mr. Sanders, I gave my Opinion with sincerity & I must do many of the Directors, especially the principal, justice to say that they spoke highly in Your favour at the same time that they express'd their Concern least something prejudicial to their Affairs through your Disagreement. I assured them to the Contrary & that your Zeal for the Publick would not suffer private Animosities to interfere with their Interest.

I must refer you to Orme who is a Master of the Subject for an

[1] Court Minutes, Vol. 66, p. 60 (India Office Records).

Acc[t] of what is carrying on in England, I sincerely wish Peace may be the thing at last, the Directors have and are still [*illegible in original*] all ways and Means to make every thing as agreable to You as possible they have always express'd the highest Sense of Your Services and Mine & as I am informd are going to make You a Present of a Sword set with Diomonds of £700 Value & me another of £500.

I give You Joy of the Mutiny & Desertion Bill which will be most certainly past, & made perpetual it is the best thing that has happen'd for the Company these many Years, our Goven[rs] will now be no longer afraid of the Consequences of signing a Death Warrant when it [is] for the Publick Good.[1]

The Compy have made me some advantagious Offers in a Civil Way I am sorry my Health will not permit me to accept them however I hope the next Year the same Opportunity will offer again & that I shall have the Pleasure of seeing You & my Friends a second time in India—Mr. Pigot who is appointed Mr. Saunders' Successor I am sure will make India more agreable to You than it has hitherto been & I enjoy/have great Pleasure in the thoughts of spending a few more Years there in Harmony & Peace my best Wishes attend Mess[s] Paulk Rippington & all my Brother Officers &

I am Dear Major

Your Affec[t] Friend & hum[l] Serv

ROBERT CLIVE.

Three months passed before the Committee of Correspondence provided the presents. On May 29, 1754:

"A Gold Hilted Sword enrich'd with Diamonds being provided agreeable to the Resolution of the 6th February last and Robert Clive Esq[r]. waiting upon the Court was called in when the Chairman in their name presented him therewith as an acknowledgment for the eminent Services he had done the Company in the East Indies and a further mark of the Courts esteem for him.

"Whereupon Cap[t]. Clive express'd his grateful sense of this Instance of the Courts favor as well as for the obligations he was under to them while in the East Indies, adding his Assurances of the readiness with which he shall embrace every occasion of shewing how sincerely he has the promotion of the Companys Interest at heart."[2]

Clive had now secured a seat in the House of Commons. On March 6, 1754, Henry Pelham, who had been almost uninterruptedly Prime Minister since the fall of Walpole, died, and his brother, the Duke of Newcastle, became the head of the Government. A month later (April 8, 1754) Parliament was dissolved,

[1] In 1754 Mutiny Act (27 Geo. II., c. 9) was passed for Indian forces.
[2] Court Minutes, Vol. 66, p. 60.

and in the general elections which followed immediately Clive stood for the borough of "Midsholl otherwise Mitchell," in the County of Cornwall, which then returned two members. Lord Sandwich, as Walpole tells us, "had long dictated there upon the interest of his nephew Courtney, a minor," and he was no doubt pleased to bring forward as a candidate the hero of the hour who had brought home a fortune. The Duke of Newcastle encouraged the families of Edgecumbe and Boscawen to oppose him.[1] Sandwich carried his candidates, the numbers of the poll being:

For Robert Clive, Esq. ,, John Stephenson, Esq.	30	For Simon Luttrell, Esq. ,, Richard Hussey, Esq.	25

Petitions against Clive and Stephenson were lodged. Sandwich applied to all parties for supplies. He "worked so artfully as to engage the Chancellor[2] on his side; and having once engaged him pleaded his countenance, as a proof that it was a private affair unconnected with party." But Newcastle was too great a master of political intrigue to be deceived. He entertained grave doubts of support from any member returned by the intrigues of Sandwich. "The Duke of Newcastle at first did not appear in it," says Walpole, "but Lord Lincoln,[3] pretending to espouse the Edgecumbes, commanded all their dependents to vote against Lord Sandwich." The Earl tried to defer a hearing, but was defeated by a majority. "The second hearing," Walpole says, "was on the 28th [of February 1755] when Mr. Fox attacking and attacked by the law of which body was Hussey,[4] one of the petitioners, beat four lawyers and Nugent,[5] and carried a division by 26;

[1] Horace Walpole: "Memoirs of the Reign of King George the Second," Vol. I., p. 407. Macaulay writes: "Newcastle had set his heart on returning two members for St. Michael, one of those wretched Cornish boroughs which were swept away by the Reform Act in 1832."

[2] Horace Walpole: "Memoirs of the Reign of King George the Second," Vol. II., p. 11.

[3] Henry Fiennes Clinton, ninth Earl of Lincoln (1720–94), was nephew of the Duke of Newcastle, and succeeded him in the dukedom, 1768.

[4] Hussey, Richard (1715–70), a prominent barrister and formidable in debate. He was counsel to the East India Company.

[5] Robert, Earl Nugent (1702–88). *See* Walpole Memoirs.

in which he was aided by Potter,[1] one of the tellers who counted five votes twice." [2] The Tories who had promised their votes indiscriminately "as their affections led them," now perceived that "this election was to decide whether Fox or Newcastle should carry the House of Commons," and that at least in this affair the numbers were nearly balanced, "came to a sudden resolution of giving their little body importance, and at once, as if to add to their weight, threw all their passions and resentments into the scale." Then sixty-two of them met on March 7, "and determined to vote according to their several engagements, on previous questions, but not on the conclusive question in the Committee." On March 12, after evidence had been taken upon the whole matter, the Committee came to the following resolution, viz.:

"*Resolved.* That it is the Opinion of this Committee that Robert Clive Esquire is duly elected a Burgess to serve in this present Parliament for the Borough of Midsholl otherwise Mitchell in the County of Cornwall."

The Tories, however, now took "the shameless resolution," says Walpole, "of cancelling all their engagements in order to defeat Fox." When the resolution was reported to the House on March 24, 1755:

"Only twelve of them stood to their engagements; the Duke of Newcastle assisted by the deserters, ejected Lord Sandwich's members by 207 to 183; the House by a most unusual proceeding, and indeed by an absurd power, as the merits are only discussed in the Committee, setting aside what in a Committee they had decided." [3]

[1] Thomas Potter (1718–59), "wit and politician"; associate of Wilkes.

[2] Macaulay converts the above into the following: "Fox put forth all his rare powers of debate, beat half the lawyers in the House at their own weapons, and carried division after division against the whole influence of the Treasury."

[3] "And a Motion being made, and the Question being put, That the House doth agree with the Committee in the said Resolution—That *Robert Clive* Esquire is duly elected a Burgess to serve in the present Parliament for the Borough of *Midsholl* otherwise *Mitchell* in the County of Cornwall:

The Houses divided
The Noes went forth

Tellers for the Yeas	Mr. Yorke Mr. Ellis	183
Tellers for the Noes	Mr. Townshend Mr. Nugent	207

So it passed in the Negative."—"Journals of the House of Commons," Vol. XXVII., 1754–7, p. 263.

So ended Clive's first experience of borough-mongering and the black arts of politics. The very day after the House rescinded the resolution of the Committee he signed an agreement with the Company which "Received and entertained him the s^{d} Robert Clive into their service as their Council and Covenanted Servant at Fort St. George in the East Indies to serve them for the term of five years." Macaulay states: "Ejected from Parliament and straitened in his means, he naturally began to look again towards India." [1] Considering that Clive signed the agreement the day after the decision and sailed seven or eight days later, he must have begun to look again towards India before he was ejected from Parliament. In fact, it became known, before the resolution was reported to the House, that he was returning to India, and that the Court of Directors had asked that he should have a Commission in the British Army. Lord Sandwich wrote to him:

QUEEN STREET, *March* [2]

DEAR SIR,—I heard last night for the first time that you was to have a Lieut: Collonells commission which surprized me greatly, as your seat in Parliament would thereby be vacated; I take for granted you are not aware of this circumstance otherwise you could not have given in to it, & therefore will I flatter myself immediately prevent anything farther being done in it.

If you would write me a letter in answer to this to tell me that you are determined not to vacate your seat, by communicating that letter in proper places I might possibly retrieve some of the ground this report may have made us lose

I am
Your most obedient and most Humble Servant
SANDWICH.

I am in very good spirits and not at all diffident of success. You must observe that the instant the King signs your commission your seat is vacant.

The statement that during his first stay in England Clive was lavish in his private expenditure and became straitened in his means is based on a very slender foundation. When Clive returned to India his household goods and chattels were

[1] Macaulay: "Essays" (Lord Clive), Vol. III., p. 140.
[2] No date of day in the original.

sold by auction, and his father sent him an account of the sale. The coach fetched £40, a pair of horses £40, and a grey riding horse £12 12s. "From this statement of property," says Malcolm, "we infer that Clive while in England must have lived very expensively." Macaulay converts this into the following: "He lived splendidly, dressed gaily even for those times, kept a carriage and saddle horses, and not content with these ways of getting rid of his money resorted to the most speedy and effectual of all modes of evacuation, a contested election followed by a petition." The expenses of the election were no doubt great, and Malcolm states, "It would seem from his agents letters that he had not, when he returned to India, more than three thousand pounds of money, the interest of which, together with a small annuity he had purchased, he directed to be given to his father." It is quite possible that his cash balance in England was not more than three thousand pounds, for he had not only acquired Styche, but purchased another small estate, and the bulk of his money was in India. Ambition and generosity made Clive profuse, but he was never reckless and heedless in money matters. He kept his accounts with the greatest precision, and he filed his bills with the utmost care. We have the receipt for the thousands he paid for Walcote Park, the receipt for 12 pagodas paid to the official warehouse keeper for Medley cloth and flannels he bought when he returned from the defence of Arcot, and his hairdresser's account when he resided in Queen Square:

"July the 30: 1754

——CLIVE ESQ. *Dr.* to WM BEDDINGFIELD

To 28 weeks Shaving	£2 2 0
To a cutt Bob Wigg	1 1 0
To a bobwigg for your black boy . .	18 0
	£4 01 0

Recd. the contents in full and all demands

M WM BEDDINGFIELD."

Clive returned to India at the call of glory and duty. He had regained health; he was appointed to a high office "in the civil way," and he saw the prospect of obtaining fresh renown as an independent commander in the field. War between England and France was impending, and if it broke out in Europe it was certain to extend soon to India. Clive told the Court of Directors that "so long as there was one Frenchman in arms in the Deccan or in India, there could be no peace. For his own part he desired nothing better than to dispute the mastery of the Deccan with M. Bussy."

Bussy had not only made himself supremely powerful at Hyderabad, but he had obtained from the Nizam, on account of the great services he had rendered during the wars with the Mahrattas and the personal courage he had shown in the field, a grant of the extensive district of Condavid on the right bank of the Kistna not far from where it falls into the Bay of Bengal. Dupleix was always desirous to obtain possession of the district on account of its proximity to Masulipatam, and Bussy now generously handed it over to his nation. In December, 1753, he further obtained from the Nizam an assignment for the payment of his French corps of four northern provinces lying along the eastern coast, commonly called the Northern Sircars (Sarkars). These provinces, with Masulipatam and the adjoining district previously ceded, made the French masters of a seaboard extending about 450 miles along the Bay of Bengal, from the mouths of the Kistna to the far-famed Temple of Juggernaut in Orissa. The breadth of this tract, rich in natural productions and manufactures, was from fifty to eighty miles, and it was protected from any Oriental invasion from the interior by woods and mountains, but a European Power who was master of the sea coast could employ all the resources of European warfare to attack it and also to invade the Deccan.

Clive thoroughly realised the strategical value of these provinces. The Ministry and the Court of Directors, having full confidence in his penetration, sagacity, and sound judgment, accepted his view that French influence in the Deccan must be destroyed. It could not be done by an invasion from the Carnatic. Bombay was, however, within two hundred miles of Aurungabad, the Nizam's capital, and the Mahratta territory stretched to his borders. Between the Mahrattas and the Viceroy of the Deccan there were frequent collisions. It was determined to assist at the first opportunity the Peshwa, the head of the Mahratta Confederacy,

> " with a force of Europeans the first time he should march against Salabad-jing, who it was hoped would be so much alarmed by this measure as to consent to dismiss the French troops from his service, on condition that the English retired from the banners of the Morattoes: and if he persisted in his attachment to the French, it was determined to weary him into a compliance by vigorous hostilities, in conjunction with the Morattoes." [1]

The Directors settled that before Clive proceeded to Fort St. George to assume office as a Member of Council he should land in Bombay with a European force and conduct this military operation. But the Duke of Cumberland insisted that Colonel Scott, who had gone out to India in the previous year as Engineer-General, should command the expedition. The Directors, however, adhered to their resolution to send Clive to Bombay in the hope that some unforeseen occurrence might give him the command.

On March 26 they wrote: [2]

> " The Court of Directors having appointed Mr. Clive, one of the Council at Fort St. George in rank next below Mr. Pigot, and as We have reason to believe Mr. Saunders has resigned the Government, in which case Mr. Pigot is Governour of Fort St. George, and Mr. Clive, Second and Deputy Governour of Fort St. David, you are to show him the same respect, and order the same Honours to be paid to him as are usually paid to the Second of Bombay, and during the Progress of the Expedition, he is not to be otherwise employed, than of his own free Choice, except the Command of the Expedition devolve upon him and unless it be to give his Advice, whenever called upon by the Commander-in-Chief, or that he may think proper to give it, though not called upon, he is therefore, during the whole Course of the Expedition, to be regarded in a manner suitable to his rank as Deputy Governour of Fort St. David accompanying the Expedition, as Second of the Council belonging to it, and as a Lieutenant Colonel appointed to take the Command upon him, in case of accident or necessity as abovementioned, and on his arrival on the other Coast, if not in the Chief Command, he will be at liberty

[1] Orme, Vol. I., p. 399. [2] Madras Records, 1755.

to quit the Army to repair to his Government. If he should happen to go by Vizagapatam, or any other Subordinate Factory on that Coast, he must be respected in his said Rank."

Four days later Clive addressed to Robert James, Esq., at the East India House, the following letter to the Secretary to the Court of Directors:

Sunday Morning March 30th, 1755.

Sir,—I am this Instant setting out: as my Affairs requir'd a day to settle I could not conveniently go before.

Yesterday morning I was with Mr Fox who enquired the Name of the Ship I went on Board, and where it lay, and promised he woud get the Commission ready by Monday and send it to me: but for fear of Disappointment I think it woud be proper to send to the Earl of Holderness to be certain whether it will be so or not. I am

Sir
Yr. most Obedt. Servt.
Robert Clive.

Addressed:—
To Robert James Esq[r]. *at the East India House.*

The next day Lord Holderness signed a commission appointing Clive, not as Lieutenant-Colonel in the King's Army, as so often stated, but as Lieutenant-Colonel of Foot in the East Indies only.

> " George the Second, by the Grace of God, King of Great Britain, France and Ireland, Defender of the Faith, &c. To Our Trusty and Welbeloved Robert Clive Esq., Greeting: We, reposing especial Trust and Confidence in your Loyalty, Courage and Experience in Military Affairs, do by these Presents, constitute and appoint you to be Lieutenant Colonel of Foot in the East Indies only. And do give and grant you full power and Authority to take your Rank as Lieutenant Colonel of Foot, in the East Indies only; You are therefore to take upon you the said Charge and Command of Lieutenant Colonel of Foot, in the East Indies only, as aforesaid, and carefully and diligently to Discharge the Duty thereof, by doing and performing all, and all Manner of Things thereunto belonging; And We do hereby, Command all Officers and Soldiers to obey you as Lieutenant Colonel of Foot, in the East Indies only; And you are to observe and follow such Orders and Directions, from time to time, as you shall receive from Us, Our Captain General of our Forces, or any other your superior Officer, according to the Rules and Discipline of War, in Pursuance of the Trust we hereby repose in You. Given at our Court at

St. James's the Thirty first Day of March 1755 in the Twenty Eighth Year of our Reign.

BY HIS MAJESTY'S COMMAND
(sgd) *Holdernesse.*

Entered with the
Secretary at War.
(Sgd) *Thos Sherwin*
ROBERT CLIVE, ESQ., Lieutenant Colonel in the East Indies only."

On April 5, 1755, Captain Clive and "his lady" were saluted with nine guns "at their coming on board" the *Stretham.*[1] On April 18 his father wrote him a letter which must have been the last he received from England:

DEAR SON,—I was glad to hear from you last post and tho' you banter me ab[t] the Election at Dover I think as you are so near and the Elect[rs] so well disposed to oppose the M . . y you have a fair Opportunity to disapoint the D of N and after you are Elected you may proceed on y[r] Voyage. S[r] James went wth me Yesterday to dine with the ArchB. at Croydon who Drank y[r] health & Success with great pleasure and gave us reason to beleive he will Soon provide for Georges Father which will be more than he deserves. It's now agreed the King goes to [*blank in original*] this day Sevenight every thing is getting ready for his Departure. Yet preparations are making for Warr J wrote Ben an Angry Letter for Loitering in the Country and this day J wrote me that he's on the Road & will be with us to morrow,

Set him agoing in Some Ship or other if the Wind do's not change I think to come & take another farwell my Love to my Daughter who diverts us every day and the rest of y[r] Company & am

Y[r] affect Father
R[D] CLIVE

April 18*th* 1755.

On April 23, 1755, the *Stretham* "weighed" with the *Pelham, Doddington,* and other ships,[2] which carried under the conduct of Clive three companies of the Royal Artillery and three or four hundred of the King's troops. When he sailed for the East a second time Clive had no conception that an Empire was waiting to be created under his hand: he and his wife went forth with heavy hearts at leaving behind them two infant sons.

[1] Log, Marine Records 605 I. (India Office). [2] *Ibid.*

CHAPTER XIII

1755–56 : FALL OF DUPLEIX

At the close of October, 1755, the *Stretham* and companion ships anchored in the harbour of beautiful sun-girt Bombay, and the troops were immediately landed. Between the time that Clive left the surf-beaten coast of Coromandel and his return to the East important changes had been occurring in Southern India. These must be briefly taken into account because the greatness of the issues then arising affected the policy of Clive and the foundation of British dominion in India.

When Clive sailed from Fort St. George, in 1753, Lawrence was encamped at Trivadi, while the French had formed entrenchments on the banks of the Penner, "which with the usual dexterity of that nation in works of this kind, were soon compleated, and rendered little inferior to the defences of a regular fortress." [1] Late at night, on April 20, Lawrence received a dispatch from Dalton, who had been shut up in the fort at Trichinopoly, stating that he was in urgent need of provisions. On the 22nd instant, in the morning, he set forth for Trichinopoly and arrived there on May 6, "much decreased in numbers through fatigue; and notwithstanding we frequently sent the sick back to our settlements, the hospitals were filled at our arrival. We had even left our tents behind, and took only with us what baggage was absolutely necessary, that nothing might retard our relieving Trichinopoly, which, indeed, was of so great consequence that everything was to be risked for it." [2] Lawrence's whole force, including the original garrison, consisted only of 500 Europeans, 2,000 sepoys, and 3,000

[1] Orme, Vol. I., p. 281.
[2] R. O. Cambridge: "War in India" (Lawrence's Narrative), p. 44.

of the Nawab's horse. His artillery consisted of ten field-pieces and one or two eighteen-pounders.

The day after Lawrence's arrival at Trichinopoly M. Astruc, who had been sent in hot haste by Dupleix, reached Seringham, which was held by the Mahrattas and Mysoreans. Astruc, a brave and capable commander, brought with him 200 Europeans, 500 sepoys, and four guns. "Nanderauze was on the island and had with him 10,000 cavalry, 6,000 Black infantry and about 100 Europeans with a good train of artillery." Inferiority in numbers never deterred Lawrence. After giving his men "two days refreshment," [1] he crossed the river to Seringham, the scene of his former triumph, with the intention of attacking the enemy if he found a favourable opportunity, but their superiority in numbers and advantage in situation made it impracticable. Recrossing the river he encamped at the Fakeers' (Faqirs') Tope or Beggars' Grove, a mile and a half S.S.W. of the city. Owing to his health he had to go into the fort, and the officer in command, neglecting his orders, allowed the French to gain possession of some high hills called the Five Rocks, about a mile to the south, between him and the Tanjore country. In order that his communications might not be quite cut off, he ordered two companies of sepoys to occupy the Golden Rock. On June 26 the French commander attacked it with his grenadiers and a large body of sepoys. But the resistance of the English sepoys was so gallant that he had to send his whole army to support them.[2]

Lawrence, on hearing of the attack, dispatched a messenger to order a European picket to support the sepoys. Then, galloping to the camp, he perceived the whole French army had begun to move. He swiftly ordered all the troops under arms, and leaving 100 Europeans to protect the camp, he hastened with the rest of his force to reach the rock before

[1] Cambridge: "War in India," p. 45. Orme (Vol. I., p. 287) states: "Major Lawrence, having allowed the men *three* days to refresh themselves," etc.

[2] *Ibid.* Orme (Vol. I., pp. 287–9) gives a long account of the battle. He states the French were prepared to retreat when the grenadiers were ordered to return.

B. F. M. DE LA BOURDONNAIS

JOSEPH FRANÇOIS, MARQUIS DUPLEIX

the main body of the enemy. The French, perceiving his approach, made a vigorous effort, "and before the Major had got half way, the sepoys who defended the rock were all either killed or taken prisoners, and the French colours immediately hoisted."[1] Lawrence halted his small force. It was a critical moment. The French battalion had arrived behind the rock, and their guns from right and left poured forth at a murderous rate their shot. The French sepoys, supported by their grenadiers, covered the rock. The whole Mysore army was drawn up in one great body at the distance of cannon-shot in the rear. The Mahratta horse in small bodies charged in flank and rear the English battalion. The officers agreed with their stout old general that to retreat before such numbers was impossible. The soldiers "seeming much delighted at this opportunity of having what they called a fair knock at the French men on the plain,"[2] Lawrence ordered the grenadiers to carry the rock with fixed bayonets, whilst he himself with the rest of the troops wheeled round the foot of it to engage the French battalion. "The soldiers received the orders with three huzzas, and the grenadiers setting out at a great rate, though at the same time keeping their ranks, paid no attention to the scattered fire they received from the rock, nor made a halt till they got to the top of it, whilst the enemy, terrified at their intrepidity, descending as they were mounting, without daring to stand the shock of their onset."[3] Grenadiers and sepoys poured down their fire upon the French troops, drawn up within pistol-shot below. Lawrence, wheeling his corps round the base of the hill, formed up in line directly opposite to the enemy at the distance of twenty yards. The gallant Astruc did his utmost to make his men keep their ranks. But it could not be. The hot fire from the rock above, grape from a field-piece, and a well-levelled discharge from the battalion threw them into irreparable disorder, and they fled. The Mahratta horse made a gallant effort to cover their retreat by flinging themselves behind, "and some of the grenadiers who had run forward to seize

[1] Orme, Vol. I., p. 294. [2] *Ibid.*, p. 295. [3] *Ibid.*

the field pieces fell under their sabres." [1] Animated by this success, the Mahrattas again and again charged the battalion up to the very bayonets, but were received with so much steadiness and with so severe a fire that, after losing many horses and men, they galloped out of shot. Amongst their dead was Ballapah, brother-in-law of Morari Rao.

> "He commanded the Marattas, as their chief was yet in the Arcot province. I had known this young man when he was on our side—a youth of great spirit and courage, and an excellent horseman. His body being found in the field, was sent back in my pallankeen to his friends: a respect I thought justly due to so gallant an officer; and they were very thankful for the favour. He was shot by one of our grenadiers, being advanced so near us that he cut one of our men in the ranks, though accompanied by only four horsemen." [2]

Lawrence remained three hours at the foot of the rock in order to give the enemy an opportunity of renewing the fight; but on their showing no inclination to do so, he placed the prisoners and three captured guns in the centre of the column, and set out towards his camp. The rear had scarcely got clear of the Golden Rock into the plain, when the Mysore and Mahratta cavalry, 10,000 horsemen, shouting and waving their swords and spears, pressed on at full speed from all sides, resolved to exterminate the handful of men that opposed them—scarcely 400 Europeans and 1,300 sepoys, guarding seventy European prisoners and three captured guns. "But the enemy had to deal with Veterans equal to any who have done honour to the British nation." [3] They halted, formed square, and calmly waited for the enemy. When they had come sufficiently near, the signal was given, and the eight six-pounders sent showers of grape through the advancing masses of horsemen. They suddenly drew rein, "and stood a while like men astonished by the fall of thunder." Seeing their ranks wasted by every discharge of grape, and that the English battalion and sepoys, with unyielding spirit, reserved their fire "with recovered arms," they broke and fled. [4] The

[1] Orme, Vol. I., p. 296.
[2] R. O. Cambridge; "War in India" (Lawrence's Narrative), pp. 47-8.
[3] Orme, Vol. I., p. 297. [4] *Ibid.*, p. 297.

English troops returned quietly to their camp. Thus by the victory of the Golden Rock was Trichinopoly saved. "But the numbers of the enemy were so great," says Lawrence, "that a victory or two more would have left all my men on the plains of Trichinopoly."[1]

The Mysore and Mahratta cavalry had so laid waste the country that Lawrence was now mainly occupied in marching and counter-marching through the land in order to get supplies for his troops and the garrison. On August 9, as he was returning to Trichinopoly with a convoy of some thousands of bullocks laden with provisions, Dalton signalled to him from the rock that the enemy were preparing to oppose him. "And by the same signals we were enabled to judge of their disposition, which we soon discovered more plainly as we advanced." They had extended themselves from the French Rock to the Golden Rock, at each of which some of their infantry was posted. "At the Sugar Loaf, as between both, and readiest to oppose us if we attempted to pass, was their battalion, with the artillery planted to advantage. All the cavalry was between these rocks."[2]

Lawrence, wishing to avoid an engagement on account of his large convoy, determined to go round by the Golden Rock. The French, on discovering his intention, sent a party of their European battalion to seize first that post. But the British troops pressed forward, and driving the enemy from the rock, planted their colours on the top of it. Seeing this, the French party halted, and also the main body which had advanced a little way to support them. The former were nearer the English than their own men. So favourable an opportunity was not to be lost. Lawrence promptly sent the picket, grenadiers, and four platoons to attack them, and he himself with the main body followed, "either to support, if repulsed, or to join and push the advantage to their main body, by driving on them their beaten party."

The artillery were on each flank to keep in check the enemy's cavalry. The officer appointed to lead the attack, instead

[1] R. O. Cambridge: "War in India," p. 48. [2] *Ibid.*, p. 49.

of following his orders, which directed him to come "to the push of the bayonet without hesitation," sent word that he could not advance without guns. Lawrence, on receiving the message, galloped from the main body, and putting himself at the head of the attacking party, led them on, "the line keeping in admirable order in spite of a very smart fire from the enemy's artillery." Several fell, and amongst them Captain Kirk, "at the head of his favourite grenadiers. The brave fellows, by whom he was much beloved, could not see his death without some emotion. Captain Killpatrick, who saw him fall, and his men at a stand, immediately put himself at their head, and desired them if they loved their captain to follow him and revenge his death. . . . The fellows roused in an instant, swore after their manner they would follow him to hell; and in that disposition attacked the enemy, who were unable to stand the shock."[1]

The main body coming up pursued the blow, and the French retreated in great haste round the Golden Rock and away to the Five Hills. On September 1, owing to sickness among his troops, Lawrence moved his camp to the French Rock; the enemy at the same time moved, and encamped with the Sugar-Loaf Rock on their right and the Golden Rock on their left. On September 16 Lawrence again attacked the enemy. A wing of the British sepoys stormed in gallant style the Sugar-Loaf Rock, and the French battalion was broken by a bayonet charge of the grenadiers. After an action of two hours, "the three camps of the enemy, with all their baggage and ammunition, were taken."

The success of the battle of the Sugar-Loaf Rock was great, but for a year active operations were carried on around Trichinopoly. Lawrence won victories, but also had, like every general, to endure severe reverses, partly due to fortune, partly to the errors of his subordinates. In February a detachment, consisting of two captains, six officers, the grenadier company, 100 strong, and eighty other Europeans, four pieces of cannon, and 800 sepoys, was surprised by a large

[1] R. O. Cambridge: "War in India," p. 50.

body of the enemy, and after a hand-to-hand struggle had to surrender. One hundred and thirty Europeans, of whom 100 were wounded, were made prisoners; fifty were killed on the spot; of eight officers, five were killed and the other three wounded. "And what still [more] added to the misfortune," writes Lawrence, "our brave company of grenadiers, who had ever behaved well and successfully, were amongst them."[1] Lawrence met his misfortunes with a stern resolution that he would win at any cost, and his confidence never abated.

But his steadfast mind was sorely tried. The difficulty of obtaining supplies greatly increased. They had been brought by the traders to a place eighteen miles east of Trichinopoly, whence they were escorted in by detachments from Lawrence's camp. But having now only 500 Europeans and a large number of French prisoners to guard, he could not spare a detachment of sufficient strength which he could safely send so far. He was therefore entirely dependent on the provisions brought from the barren and sparsely cultivated Tondiman's[2] country to the Tondiman's woods twelve miles from the city. They were scanty, and day by day the situation grew worse. To add to his misfortunes, Lawrence fell dangerously ill. Weeks of grave anxiety passed. Provisions must be obtained; convoys must be escorted. On May 23, at four in the morning, a detachment consisting of 120 Europeans, 500 sepoys, and two field-pieces was sent to escort a large convoy of stores hourly expected from the Tondiman's country. The detachment was to march to an old dry tank surrounded by a lofty mud bank two miles to the south of the Sugar-Loaf Rock. Here it was to halt until the convoy emerged from the wood. The small force proceeded stealthily

[1] R. O. Cambridge: "War in India," p. 62.

[2] "The Tondiman's country," or the Pudukkottai State in Madras. It is bounded on the north and west by the Trichinopoly District, on the south by Madura, and on the east by Tanjore. It measures fifty miles from east to west and forty miles from north to south. It is called after its chief town the name meaning "new fort." The State was formerly known as the Tondiman's country from the family name of the ruling chief.—Imp. Gaz. of India new ed., Vol. XX., pp. 230–1.

in the darkness before the dawn. Mohammed Yusuf of Nellore, a gallant native soldier, rode at some distance before the advanced guard. Of him Lawrence said, " An excellent partizan . . . brave and resolute, but cool and wary in action. He was never sparing of himself . . . born a soldier, and better of his colour I never saw in the country. He always prevents my asking, by offering himself for everything, and executes what he goes about as well and as briskly as he attempts it." It was owing to Lawrence that Mohammed Yusuf was granted a commission as commandant of all the sepoys in the Company's service. On approaching the place of meeting, Yusuf, whilst ascending a little mound, was surprised by his horse neighing and being answered by several others. " When he got to the top of the bank," says Lawrence, " he discovered a part of the enemy posted ; the French troop in particular who mounted on his appearing, first discharging their carbines, on hearing which Captain Caillaud halted, formed his party, and rode up to his advanced guard." [1] He met Yusuf, who told him that he thought the French had taken post in the choked-up tank. Caillaud determined to attack them at once. He ordered Yusuf with the sepoys to attack them on the right whilst he with the Europeans fell on the left flank. The two divisions dashed forward, almost stormed the mud bank, and drove the enemy from the tank. They quickly rallied, and when daylight spread over the place, they commenced a sharp cannonade, " which was answered with the disparity of two to four." Caillaud now also discovered how superior the foe were to him in numbers. Grave was the danger which threatened. But the sound of the firing had been heard in Trichinopoly.

Lawrence had been obliged by illness to leave the camp and go into the town the previous day, and Captain Polier, an intrepid soldier, commanded in his absence. No sooner did Polier hear the firing than " the little army being under arms " he marched to Caillaud's assistance. The rest of the confederate force at the same time crossed the river, but " as

[1] R. O. Cambridge : " War in India " (Lawrence's narrative), p. 65.

our distance was less than that of the enemy we were first joined." The British force now amounted only to 360 Europeans, 1,500 sepoys, 11 troopers with five guns, and the united force of the enemy determined to intercept their return to camp amounted to 700 Europeans, 50 dragoons, 5,000 sepoys, 1,000 horse, "of which fortunately none were Morattoes," and ten guns. Caillaud had employed a native to slip through the enemy and order the provisions to return. He and Polier now agreed to go back to camp. The English battalion defiled out of the enclosure and formed a column. The sepoys followed and formed a line touching the rear of the column at right angles and extending to its left. Thus making two sides of a quadrilateral, the little detachment moved forward. The French sepoys, getting to their rear, plied the English line of sepoys with musketry. Polier himself was wounded. On the small force tramped for almost a mile, when it reached another tank, also surrounded by a mud bank. Just as they got into the enclosure Polier received a second wound, and Caillaud again assumed command. The sepoys and cavalry of the enemy closed round the tank on three sides of it, the French battalion on the fourth. Caillaud placed two field-pieces in front of the English battalion which blazed out in the face of the advancing French, and in a few moments a hundred of them lay on the ground. "Never, I believe," says Lawrence, "were two pieces better served. They were of the short six-pounders that take in a large quantity of grape." [1] The French, surprised and galled, halted and began to waver in spite of the efforts of their officers. Caillaud improved "the lucky minute"; the English battalion advanced and delivered so hot a fire that the French gave way in panic. The sepoys and Mysore cavalry, which had been kept at bay by the English sepoys, then joined in the retreat. The English detachment continued its march to its camp. But many were left behind. The killed and wounded on their side is put down at a little more than two hundred, of whom rather more than a third were Europeans,

[1] R. O. Cambridge: "War in India," p. 66.

while the French lost two hundred of their battalion and three hundred sepoys killed or wounded.

Lawrence, although very ill, ordered himself to be carried to the top of one of the city gates, and watched the dread fray as it swayed this way and that across the plain. It was the last of the stern Homeric combats fought beneath the walls of Trichinopoly.

Foiled in their attempt to intercept the convoys, the French determined to destroy the supplies at their source. They marched into the country of the Poligars with the intention of destroying everything they could. The country people, alarmed, quitted their villages, drove their cattle to the woods, and left their homes to be burned by the enemy.[1] The French troops proceeded to devastate the Tanjore frontier, and they "cut through the great bank which, preventing the waters of the Cauvery from running into the channel of the Coleroon, may be called the bulwark of the Tanjore country."

Lawrence, leaving half his force to defend Trichinopoly, marched to Tanjore. On his arrival there he was joined by a reinforcement from the coast consisting of 150 Europeans and 500 sepoys. After a stay of some weeks he again entered the plain of Trichinopoly on August 17, with a force comprised of 1,200 English and Topasses, 3,000 English sepoys with 14 field-pieces, 2,500 Tanjorean cavalry, and 3,000 infantry with some field-pieces. He intended to pass between the Sugar-Loaf and the French Rocks. Maissin, the French commander, whose force consisted of 900 European infantry 400 Topasses, a number of sepoys, 8 guns, and 10,000 Mysore horse under Hyder Ali, "the best officer of the Mysoreans," advanced from his camp at the Five Rocks on hearing of Lawrence's approach. His plan was to make a brisk demonstration of attack, then a strategic retreat, and, if the enemy followed him rapidly and placed a wide interval between their troops and their baggage, Hyder was to sweep round the French Rock with his cavalry and cut off the convoy.

[1] R. O. Cambridge: "War in India," p. 67.

The design very nearly succeeded. The action began with an artillery duel. Lawrence's gunners dealt the French a punishment more tremendous than they expected. They drew their cannon off and began to retreat regularly. Lawrence was on the point of following them when he heard that Hyder Ali had attacked his rear. The Mysore commander had fallen too soon on the baggage. Lawrence ordered the rear guard to march back to their station, and Hyder had only time to secure and carry off about thirty-five carts, some of them laden with arms and ammunition. A party of 500 Topasses and sepoys with two guns had crossed the river to cover Hyder's operation, but a sally from the garrison drove them back to the island. After the scattered bullocks and coolies had been gathered together, the force continued its march, encamped near the city, and supplied it with a stock of provisions.[1] By the end of the first week in September all the French troops had been forced from the plain into Seringham, the grave of French glory and ambition. On September 23, the rainy season having commenced, the greater portion of the English force went into cantonments in some pagodas, and while there Lawrence heard in October that a three-months' truce had been concluded.

On August 1, 1754, the *Duc de Bourgogne* anchored in the road of Pondicherry, and Godeheu landed on the following day, accompanied by some of his troops. Dupleix went down from Government House to the landing-place to meet his old acquaintance, the former factor at Chandernagore. After a few polite words of greeting, Godeheu handed to Dupleix the King's warrant depriving him of the office of governor. Dupleix read it, and replied that he "only knew to obey the King and submit to all." They then proceeded to Government House, where Godeheu read the orders of the Company and of the Court, and assumed the administration of the Government, which M. Dupleix resigned to him with an appearance of composure and serenity, and was treated by his successor with all imaginable respect.

[1] Orme, Vol. I., pp. 370–1.

The following day "Mr. Godeheu was acknowledg'd at the Head of the Troops Commissary General & Governour General for the King, of the French Nation in India."[1] Dupleix was permitted "to continue the exhibition of those marks of Moorish dignity, which both Murzafa-jing and Salabad-jing had permitted him to display, when they appointed him Nabob of the Carnatic. These were of various flags and ensigns, various instruments of military music, particular ornaments for his palankeen, a Moorish dress. . . . In this equipage he went . . . to dine with Mr. Godeheu on the feast of St. Louis."[2] The fact that after having been deprived of all power he should rejoice in an exhibition of this kind shows the weak side of his nature. The better side is illustrated by his writing to entreat Bussy not to allow the change of governor to diminish his zeal for the service. He entreated Godeheu to send reinforcements to Trichinopoly. But Godeheu had been sent out for the express purpose of substituting pacific for warlike relations between the two companies. He knew how low were the French finances, and he also knew that the English were sending out a fleet with a large number of troops. He therefore lost no time in making overtures for peace. On August 5:

"The President lays before the Board a Letter from Monsr. Godeheu at Pondicherry dated the 1st Instant advising his Arrival there with full Power from the King and the French Company in Quality of Commander General of all the French Settlements on both sides the Cape of Good Hope, that he is come with a Sincere Intention to Endeavour to pacify the Troubles in India, that as an Example of his Sincerity & moderation he sets at Liberty the Troops which Mr. Dupleix caused heretofore to be stopped in their Passage from Madrass to Fort St. David. That as Nothing is more uncertain than the fate of Arms, & new Acts of Hostility on which side soever the Advantage may turn will only serve to inflame he proposes a Suspension of Arms during which each Nation is to remain in their present Condition & that a Day be agreed on for publishing the same at the head of the Troops of both Nations, which will afford a proper Opportunity for Exchanging the Prisoners."[3]

[1] Diary and Consultation Book, Military Department, 1754, p. 180.
[2] Orme, Vol. I., p. 369.
[3] Madras Records.

The Board in their "General Letter" to Lawrence wrote:

"There is a great Finesse in sending back Captn Schaub & such of his Party as Remain at Pondicherry, it has an Air of Frankness & Sincerity whilst the Satisfaction offered is no way equal to the Injury & Indignity receiv'd, perhaps not above one third or ½ of the Men who were seized are now at Pondicherry the rest have been inveigled into the French Service & are now with de Bussy, We propose to write Mr Godeheu that We have directed Captn Schaub to deliver him a Roll of all his Men who were unjustly seized by Mr Dupleix & if he will return us the whole Number or make up the Deficiency out of the English Prisoners We then shall consider this Action as a real mark of his good Intentions & shall be ready to take the most effectual Measures for restoring of Tranquility." [1]

On the morning of August 12 "arriv'd the Ship *Galatea* from Pondicherry with Captain Schaub and the remainder of his detachment." On September 2 the President lays before the Board two letters from Mr. Godeheu "by which it is very plain to be observ'd that at the same Time he speaks in the most pacifick State he endeavours to evade his own Proposal of a Suspension of Arms." Seven days later they heard that the *Britannia*, one of the tenders of the squadron, had arrived at Fort St. David with part of His Majesty's troops. On September 12 they received the following letter from Admiral Watson:

GENTLEMEN,—I this Morning arriv'd here with his Majesty's Ships Kent and Salisbury, in which Ships are about two hundred Soldiers, who in Consequence of your Opinion dated the 11th July last, (which I have just receiv'd) will be landed to morrow Morning, and Join Lieutenant Colonel Bagshaw.

The remaining part of the Regiment are on board his Majesty's Ships Bridgwater & Kings Fisher (*sic*) Sloop & three of the Company's Ships; The Bridgwater & Sloop I parted with two Days ago off the North end of Ceylon, but expect to see them to morrow or next Day at farthest, & hope very soon to see all the India Ships, and to get the whole Regiment Landed, that they may be ready to act upon the very first Occasion.

I must own, I very readily Concurr with you in regard to your Opinion relating to the Station of the Ships, & think this by much the most adviseable Place to remain in, in the present Circumstances of Affairs, and if Nothing material happens to cause any Alterations in this Disposition, I shall remain here 'till I am forced to retire on

[1] Madras Records.

Account of the Monsoons setting in, but you may depend I shall exert my utmost Endeavours to continue on this Coast as long as Possible, & to do every thing that will promote the Benefit & Advantage of our Possessions in this part of the World.

I am Gentlemen Your most Obedient Servant

CHA[s] WATSON.

FORT ST. DAVID'S ROAD
10th *Sept[r]* 1754.

P.S. Inclos'd I send you four Packets from the East India Company.

Watson very soon saw all the ships anchored in Fort St. David's road, and the whole of Adlercron's regiment, 700 strong, 40 of the King's artillerymen, and 200 recruits for the Company's service, were sent ashore. The French had also received a reinforcement of 1,200 men, half of which were hussars, under the command of Colonel Fitscher, a German partizan of some reputation: but the rest were only raw recruits. The arrival of the English fleet and troops, better disciplined than his own, induced Godeheu to propose terms more reasonable, and on September 29, 1754, "Articles for a Suspension of Hostilities between the English & French Nations in the Carnateck" were "Signed in the English Copy Tho[s] Saunders in the French Copy Godeheu." They were "to begin from the 11th October the Day on which the Suspension of Arms shall be published to all the Troops in all the Forts and actual Possessions of the two contracting Nations in the Carnateck."

The day after the signing of the suspension Dupleix and his wife embarked on board *Le Duc d'Orleans*. The high officials, factors, and clerks, and a multitude of the native population, moved with a deep sense of admiration and regret, went to the seashore to bid farewell to the departing ruler. His temper, pride, and arrogance, which had offended so many, were forgotten; his kindly actions and profuse generosity were remembered. He had spent a princely fortune to exalt the French name. His whole career as a ruler through ten years of stress and storm shows the single-handed courage with which he met every blow of fortune, the infinite skill with which he would cover over disaster and the audacious self-reliance with which he worked to promote the ultimate advantage of his nation. But with many splendid gifts he was defective in plain judgment. The plans which he formed were well imagined, but the course which he pursued was never cautious and definite. He never put a bound to his aspiring spirit and his love of pomp. He did not, like Clive in Bengal, attempt to quiet the minds of the natives by leaving the country in the hands nominally of the native princes, but he claimed to be recognised as Nawab of the Carnatic by doubtful patents. This claim aroused the jealousy of the country powers, and could never be acknowledged and recognised by the English. His ostentatious parade of sovereignty, his intrigues with the Indians were miserable blunders, because a European governor ought to govern on European principles and by European forms. But his resort to other principles and other maxims was due in a large measure to his Oriental wife. Madame Dupleix was fond of intrigue and avaricious of power and money, because that was her Eastern nature. It was her corrupt native agent who became the real administrator of the Carnatic and pillaged the districts and cruelly imprisoned and tortured the inhabitants whose treasure he seized. The Frenchman who opposed the native agent was a ruined man. It was the abuse of the powers vested in him that led the way to the state in which the Company's affairs stood when Godeheu was sent for the purpose of reforming it. Godeheu found a corrupt and chaotic administration, a bankrupt treasury and troops mutinous for want of pay. The ill-success of these troops in the four years was in a great measure due to the perpetual interference of Dupleix in the details of the campaign and his constant removal of commanders. It is true that he had no able captain except Bussy, and the English had some of the most splendid officers who ever graced an army—Clive, Lawrence, Dalton, Kilpatrick, and Caillaud. The French soldiers fought with all the gallantry of their race. But they could not support a fabric whose foundation had never been properly laid. This was the cardinal mistake of Dupleix. In writing about him we, however, feel what Bolingbroke felt about Marlborough: "He was so great a man that I have forgotten his faults."

Poor Dupleix! All who have read the story of his career must regret that there was not a less melancholy end for that brilliant and vehement nature. His life had been a long battle to enrich his nation, and to fulfil his work he had sacrificed his own fortune and the fortunes of his friends. His claims may have been exaggerated, but from the French Government and the French East India Company he was entitled to generous treatment. But they would not do him bare justice. He sought it by a law process. The Ministry exercised their despotic right, and put a stop to the proceedings. A few days before the mournful settling he published his final appeal: "*Je me suis soumis à toutes les formes judiciaires; j'ai demandé comme le dernier des créanciers ce qui m'est dû. Mes services sont traités de fables; ma demande est dénoncée comme ridicule; je suis traité comme l'être le plus vil du genre humain. Je suis dans la plus déplorable indigence; la petite propriété qui me restait vient d'être saisie; je suis contraint de demander une sentence de delai pour éviter d'être trainé en prison.*"

On the night of November 11, 1763, Dupleix died. After a century of neglect France determined to erect at Pondicherry a monument to one of the most famous of her sons. Near the beached verge of the tumultuous surf, on a pedestal constructed from old fragments of temples brought from Gingee, stands the statue of Dupleix. The sculptor has succeeded in giving the magnificent head, lofty and wide forehead, and the intellectual face, full of energy and power, of the great French patriot and statesman.

Two months after Dupleix left the East a provisional treaty was concluded[1] between "Thomas Saunders Esqr President for the Honourable English Company on the Coasts of Choromandel and Orixa Governour of Fort St. George &c^{a} and Charles Robert Godeheu Esqr Commissary for his most Christian Majesty, Commander General of all the settlements of the French Company on both Sides the Cape of Good Hope and

[1] Done at Fort St. George, December 31, 1754.

at China, President of all the Councils there Establish'd and Director General of the India Company of France." The first Article was a counsel of perfection : " The two Companies English and French shall renounce for ever all Moorish Government and Dignity and shall never interfere in any Difference that may arise between the Princes of the Country." All places in their possession except those which should be stipulated in the treaty should be given up to the Moors. In Tanjore the English should retain Devecotah and the French Karikal " with their present Districts " : on the Coromandel Coast the English should retain Fort St. George and Fort St. David with their respective districts and the French Pondicherry, " the Districts of which are to be specified (*sic*) in the definitive Treaty." The districts of Pondicherry were, however, to be made equal to those of the other two.

In the Northern Sircars Masulipatam and Divi were to remain " neuter," leaving to the two companies the choice of making a partition. " Each Nation shall have a House for Commerce at Mazulipatam, with an equal Number of Soldiers to guard it ; in case this Town should remain Neuter, Divi shall be deliver'd to the English if the French reserve Mazulipatam, and if the French keep Divy, the English shall have Mazulipatam ; In these two last Cases equal districts shall be annex'd to the Possessions." Northward of Masulipatam and within the Northern Sircars each Company should have four or five subordinate factories merely as places of trade without any district attached to them, and so situated as not to interfere with each other. Till the district was made definite by its ratification in Europe, " Neither Nation shall be allowed to procure during the Truce any new Grant or Cession or to build Forts for the Defence of new Establishments, It shall only be lawful to Rebuild and Repair the Fortifications now subsisting in the Establishments they possess at this Time in order to prevent their entire Ruin." The indemnities due to each nation were to be " amicably adjusted in the Definitive Treaty."

By a separate convention signed the same day, December 31, the truce was extended from January 11 until it was known whether England and France would accept the treaty. James Mill writes: "By this treaty everything for which they had been contending was gained by the English; every advantage of which they had come into possession was given up by the French." But, as Orme points out, before the decision of the two companies was known eighteen months would pass, and "there was no positive obligation on either of the companies to adopt the opinions of their representatives expressed in the conditional treaty." During that time the French would draw annually the revenues of all the territories acquired during the war, amounting to £855,000 sterling,[1] while the English would draw only £100,000 derived from land mortgaged by the Nawab to reimburse the large sum of money they had spent on his account in military expenses. If the treaty was accepted by both parties, the French would make the larger sacrifice; but this was a substantial reason for the French Company not accepting it. The important advantage gained by the English was the tacit acknowledgment of Mohammed Ali as Nawab of the Carnatic.

The omission of any direct mention of Bussy and his connection with the Deccan in the treaty has been often discussed.[2] But the solution is simple. The French could not possibly agree to withdraw their troops from the Deccan because that meant restoring the Northern Sircars to the Viceroy. The Madras Government knew it would be useless to press this point, and therefore, as Orme states, all mention

[1] Orme states: "In all 6,842,000 rupees equal to 855,000 pounds sterling."—Orme, Vol. I., p. 377-8.

[2] James Mill writes ("History of British India," Vol. III., p. 140, note): "Col. Wilks must have read the treaty very carelessly, to imagine that 'the substantial Moorish government and dignity of the extensive and valuable provinces of the Northern Circars were not noticed in the treaty,' when the very first article of the treaty says, 'The two Companies, English and French, shall renounce for ever *all* Moorish government and dignity, and shall never interfere in any differences that arise between the princes of the country.' Mr. Orme, too (so easily is the judgment warped of the best of men when their passions are engaged), imagined it would have been no infringement of the treaty, to assist the Mahrattas with English troops from Bombay for the purpose of compelling Salabut Jung to dismiss Bussy and the French, and deprive them of the Northern Circars."

of the French troops seems to have been studiously avoided. The main object of the provisional treaty was to secure for at least some time peace in the Carnatic. The truce was, however, badly kept by both parties. The English early in February assisted Mohammed Ali to reduce Madura and Tinevelly, and M. de Leyrit, who had succeeded Godeheu as Governor of Pondicherry, sent a force to collect rents for the Rajah of Mysore.

CHAPTER XIV

1755–6: THE GHERIA EXPEDITION—THE BENGAL EXPEDITION

SUCH was the condition of affairs in Southern India when Clive reached Bombay.

On the *Stretham* entering Bombay harbour, Clive saw Admiral Watson's squadron lying anchored in front of the grey walls of the old Castle. On landing he learnt that Colonel Scott was dead, and he therefore became commander of the expedition. But he was at the same time informed of the provisional treaty, and that the Bombay Government intended to abandon the expedition, not because they considered it a violation of the treaty, as it has been so often stated, but for other reasons which Clive mentions in the following letter:

SIR,—My last was from St Jago and the *Pelham* being now under dispatch for Europe gives me an opportunity of addressing you a second Time, it may suffice, without being particular to acquaint you that the Troops which embark'd on board the 4 Ships are safely arriv'd at this place with the loss only of 6 or 7 private men.

Tho we have recd news from the other Coast so late as the 6th of last Month we have no account as yet of the arrival of the *Doddington* she cannot surely be gone to Bengal the most probable conjecture is that being too late to venture on the Coast she may have stood for [*illegible*] intending to stretch over to Madrass sometime in December when the Danger of the Monsoon is over however at all events I hope no very ill fortune hath attended her.

It would be needless to expatiate on the Truce by this Time so well known in England Copy of which and of the private Articles have been transmitted to this Place by the select Committee on the Other Coast who have recommended in the strongest Terms the entring into an immediate Treaty with the Morattoes, the joining them in the Field and even coming to action if necessity should require the Gentlemen of this place are of opinion that acting by halves or making a

Cats paw of the Morattoes may ruin the Company's Affairs in these parts they urge that if after having joined and put them to a very great Expence in assembling an Army a peace shou'd be concluded in consequence of the private articles carried home by Mr. Saunders that the withdrawing the Forces may cause an Evolution greatly detrimental to this Island at present in a very flourishing Condition: that even the very treating with them without being at a Certainty of fulfilling the articles of such treaty, will not only publish the Scheme to all the world but likewise deprive the English of that Reputation for Equity and Justice, which at present they are so fam'd for—at the same Time they have agreed to make all necessary preparations, for the carrying this Scheme into Execution when they are assured it may be done to the purpose. I must confess that I join Issue with the Gentlemen here on this Subject (as do the two admirals who were present upon the Occasion). I should not be over-Scrupulous or wanting in a little chicanery towards a nation who never made any treaties at all but with a view of breaking them, but really at present I think any Infringement whatever would not be agreeable to the Maxims of Sound Policy: it is not only the welfare of the other Coast but this likewise that comes under Consideration, they on the other side have no connection at all with the Morattoes, therefore any step towards weakening or removing the French Influence from Golcond is the grand point gaind to them even tho' it be at the Expence of the Moratta Friendship the loss of which may cause us ill Effects there whereas a failing in our Engagements may occasion the whole weight of the Moratta Resentment to fall on this side; in short I can only remark that if no such Truce had subsisted the Scheme which was design'd at the India House might have been carried into Execution with a prospect of great Advantage to the Company and great Credit and Honor to the Gentlemen who plann'd it. I hope the first Ship that comes from England will either enable us to put the intended plann in Execution or to enjoy the great Benefits arising from Peace, Trade and Plenty.

At present an affair of the like nature tho not of the like Consequence seems to engross the Attention of this place I mean the Attack of Gueria, if a perfect Harmony subsisting between the Sea & Land Forces can add anything to the prospect of our Success I am sure such Harmony will not be wanting. Mr. Watson ever attentive to the good of his Country hath undertaken this Expedition by Sea the Command by Land devolves on me who upon this occasion have offer'd my Service and indeed I cou'd not do less both in Justice to those to whom I owe everything as in Justice to my own Reputation. I hope Mr. Drake will believe that I ever carry in my remembrance a thorough conviction of his Friendship and that without dwelling too much upon so tender a point I cannot take a better method of shewing my Gratitude to him than by proving myself a faithful and honest Servant to the Company, whenever I cease to be such I am sure I shall very deservedly cease to enjoy the least Share of his Esteem.

Mrs. Clive joins with me in best wishes to Mrs. Drake and all the Family and I am

Dear Sir

Your most affect: and most obed[t] Serv[t]

ROBERT CLIVE

BOMBAY *Jan[y]* 31st 1756
To ROGER DRAKE ESQ[R]

About the same time in a letter without date Clive writes:

DEAR SIR,—I flatter myself you will be greatly pleased to hear of the safe arrival of all the Troops at this place. I wish I could add and in readiness to put in Execution the Plan you intrested yourself so much about in England nothing but the Truce could have prevented so glorious an undertaking The Gentlemen on the other side seem very desirous of carrying this Scheme into Execution even at the Risque of infringing the Treaty but the committee here differ greatly in opinion, affirming that deceiving the Merattas will ruin the Company's Affairs in these parts which would certainly be the Case if in consequence of the private articles carried home by Mr. Saunders a peace should be concluded: however everything is making ready for joining the Merattoes the instant a fitting opportunity offers: on this Subject I have been more particular with Mr. Drake to whom I beg leave to refer you.

At this place the Subject of Discourse has been chiefly about the Attack of Gueria I thought it a duty incumbent on me to offer my Service on the Occasion, and hope in a very few days to embark with 1000 Men ready to act by land or Sea as may be most for the Comp[s] Interest: it would be vain and presumptuous to insure success but if we may credit Report and compare that Report with the Forces carried against the Place, we have the most sanguine hopes of sending home agreeable news by the next Ship: I am sure nothing has been wanting on my part to forward this Expedition and Major Chalmers every way qualified for the command of the Train has been very assiduous in what concerns his Branch; the treating on this Subject leads me to a few Remarks which by some may be deem'd ill-naturd ones and yet I cannot pass them over in Silence without Injustice to you and the rest of my Employers. The Preparations for Gueria did naturally induce me to be more inquisitive concerning Military Affairs than otherwise I should have been, and upon such Enquiry I cannot say I have found Capt. DeFinck so equal to the command of the Train as I could wish: his method of proceeding fell so far short of Expectation that I was obligd to take everything out of his hands relating to the present Expedition, a refractory jealous way of thinking, not at all calculated for the good of the Service, seems to have possessed him and I have been at last reduced to the Necessity of writing him a Letter couchd in pretty severe Terms in which I have taken notice of this Complaint.

I am under some concern to find most of the Officers of the 3 Companies of Artillery to be Forreigners for without mentioning the many Inconveniences that may attend the employing those in the Train who cannot speak one word of our Language it may be in their power to destroy at one Blow what all the Wisdom or Caution of man cannot guard against.

I do not mean by the above to reflect on Capt. De Finck as an Engineer, it woud be folly in me to give my opinion on a Subject in which I am not sufficiently versd. I can only observe that the Fortifications go on very slowly as indeed they do in all parts of India, and notwithstanding the Gentlemen at Home have shewn an uncommon attention in what relates to their Fortifications abroad, by sending out able and experienc'd Engineers yet that fatality which has attended them (and I much fear) a want of Zeal even in the Company's Servants themselves have left two of the principal Settlements (perhaps at the Eve of war) in a Condition scarce defensible I mean Madras and Bombay, as to the latter there is cover for 5000 Men within twenty paces of the Counterscharp the Ground just without the Walls is crowded with buildings which shoud be pulled down immediately a Glacis and cover'd way made which is the greatest & most Expeditious strength that can possibly be added to a Fortification in this Country. It would put it out of the Enemies power to batter in Breach the Body of the Place till in possession of the coverd way, and of consequence of the Edge of the Counterscharpe ; this was the Plan which was pursud by the French when in possession of Madras but enough of what does not come within the Compass of my Knowledge and Experience.

By the last advices from Madras Colo[l] Herring notwithstanding great Favour shewn him by the Courtmartial was broke with Ignominy and is since escapd to Sadrass : It seems he was detach'd sometime ago with a strong party to the Madera and Trinovelly Countries to gather the Nabobs Revenues on the Company's Account where he was guilty (even by his own confession) of most notorious and illegal Practices in consequence of which he was suspended from his seat in Council and afterwards prosecuted by Mr. Dupree the Secretary in the Company's name at the General Court Martial, I thought proper to transmit you this advice as thinking it not unlikely but the *Pelham* or *Stretham* may arrive in England before any ship from the other Coast.

I am sorry so little Harmony reigns on the other side, and yet I am so far partial to the Gent[n] in Council as to think they have done everything (if not more than in their power) to satisfy his Majesty's Officers Advices coming round of this grant has occasiond the Officers here to apply for the same Allowance which has been given them to put them on a footing with the Gent[n] at St. Davids and in consideration of their going into immediate Service, when this Allowance was first propos'd I should certainly have voted against it as being persuaded when the Gentlemen gave orders his Majesty's Officers should be put upon a footing with the Companys they meant in point of pay only, not cloathing, a perquisite they coud not possibly have without a Foundation for such Perquisite, the Companies not being cloathd by the Captains but by the Colonels.

I coud wish that both Civil and Military wd. cooperate in what is for the good of their Country ; it has been my good fortune hitherto to agree with all parties, and I am sure it will be so during this Expedition. I hope the Obligations I am under to the Company will so far inspire me with a grateful sense of them as to withstand all selfish considerations when their welfare is at Stake. I am sure Mr. Mabbot woud never have shewn himself so firm a Friend if he had thought otherwise ; a Friendship on which I have very great dependance, yet great as it is I am confident that Friendship will cease whenever I cease to deserve it.

It is with Regret I think on the Loss of Lady Delve's and Miss Cotes's agreeable company I shall not easily forget the Honor done us at Swithin's Lane I hope the Time will come when that Favour may be repeated I desire my best Respects to them and to Mrs. Mabbot being

Dear Sir

Your affectionate & obliged humble Servant

ROBERT CLIVE.

To WM. MABBOT ESQ[R].

Gheria,[1] built on a craggy promontory almost surrounded by the ocean, was the stronghold of Tulaji Angria, the chief of the pirates who infested the west coast of India. The founder of the family was Kanoji Angria, who was appointed Admiral of the Mahratta fleet in 1698, and proved himself a brave and daring commander. His ships crept along the coast, plundering every vessel and sailing up every fiord to sack every undefended town. Shivaji had fortified every creek with a fort, and these fell into the hands of Kanoji, who became the founder of a piratical empire, which extended from Goa to Bombay. The fleets of the Angrias consisted of fast sailing vessels of small burden and rowing boats of forty or fifty oars and crowded with daring and desperate men. From the wik or creek in which their fleet lay the Vikings or creekmen pounced upon their prey. When they drew near

[1] Vijayadrug or Gheria, 170 miles south of Bombay, is one of the best harbours on the western coast.

they gathered astern of their victim and fired into her rigging until they succeeded in disabling her; the rowing boats then closed with her, and the crew, sword in hand, boarded her from all sides. A heavy merchant vessel lay completely at the mercy of the pirates, and the Company had to spend a large sum annually in protecting their growing trade.

At length, in 1755, the Bombay Government determined, in alliance with the Peshwa, to make a vigorous attempt to crush the pirates. On March 22 Commodore James, who commanded the Company's marine force in India, as gallant a sailor as ever trod a deck, sailed from Bombay with a small squadron, consisting of his flag-ship the *Protector*, the *Bombay*, twenty-eight guns; the *Swallow*, sixteen guns; and the *Triumph* and *Viper*, bomb vessels. He was found at Chaul[1] by the Mahratta fleet, consisting of seven grabs[2] and sixty gallivats,[3] having on board 10,000 soldiers. It was intended that the Mahratta army should besiege the forts of the enemy and the English fleet blockade the harbours. Commodore James was not to lend any of his people, except a few of the train, "which you may lend them to point their cannon."

Captain James, both in his letter to the Board and in his diary, gives a graphic account of Suvarnadrug. "Suvarnadrug, the golden fortress, is built on a low, irregular island situated about a quarter mile from the mainland. The fortifications are cut out of the solid rock, here and there supple-

[1] Chaul (Cheul), a town on the coast about thirty miles from Bombay.

[2] *Grab* (Ar. *ghorab*), a galley. "The grabs have rarely more than two masts, although some have three; those of three are about 300 tons burthen; but the others are not more than 150: they are built to draw very little water, being very broad in proportion to their length, narrowing, however, from the middle to the end, where instead of bows they have a prow, projecting like that of a Mediterranean galley" (Orme, Vol. I., p. 401). The grabs carried a number of guns, two of them from nine to twelve pounders, placed on the main deck so as to fire through port holes over the prow, and the rest usually six to nine pounders fitted to give a broadside.

[3] *Gallivat*. "The gallivats are large row-boats built like the grab, but of smaller dimensions, the largest rarely exceeding 70 tons. They have two masts, of which the mizen is very slight: the mainmast bears only one sail, which is triangular and very large. . . . In general, the gallivats are covered with a spar deck, made for lightness of bamboes, split; and those only carry petteraroes fixed on swivels in the gunnel of the vessel: but those of the largest size have a fixed deck, on which they mount six or eight pieces of cannon from two to four pounders. They have forty or fifty stout oars, and may be rowed four miles an hour" (Orme, Vol. I., p. 402).

mented by blocks of large red stones of near four feet square, so hard that many of our shot split by striking against them." Opposite the island commanding the narrow channel was Fort Goa, called by James, Fort Gova, and on a peninsula of land joined to it Fattedurg and Connoidurg. Suvarnadrug, James informs us, had fifty guns, Fort Goa about forty-four, and the two others twenty guns each. On April 2 James opened fire on Suvarnadrug from the seashore, but "found their walls too thick and solid to beat down." He asked the Mahratta commander for the loan of 800 or 1,000 of his people to enter the fort by storm, "but could not prevail on him." Next morning James discerned that the water was deep enough for him to go further in and bombard both Fort Goa and Suvarnadrug. "They fired pretty briskly upon us from the inner and outer forts," he writes, "but by returning the compliment of the former with the lower deck, of the latter with the upper deck guns, two or three at a time, and by that means keeping an incessant fire upon them, they were very silent in three hours, and afterwards fired a shot only now and then." A shell blew up the magazine, and a general conflagration ensued. Next morning James renewed the bombardment, and "at 10 [on April 4] three of the forts struck their colours, on which [I] sent Lieutenant Young on shore with English flags, which were hoisted, manned ships, and gave three cheers." On landing James discovered that the Governor of Fort Goa and some of his followers had escaped to Suvarnadrug, and "was resolved to maintain it some time in hope of receiving succour from Dabul." He therefore next day opened fire on it from the ships and shore, and "landed a number of people under the cover of it," who "cut and broke open the wicket of the door and entered without much opposition."

Thus, as Orme remarks, Commodore James by his determination and pluck "destroyed the timorous prejudices which had for twenty years been entertained of the impracticability of reducing any of Angria's fortified harbours." [1]

[1] Orme, Vol. I., p. 406.

Tulaji Angria, after the capture of Suvarnadrug,[1] took refuge in the fort of Gheria about a hundred miles lower down the coast. As the expedition into the Deccan was abandoned, the Bombay Government considered that the Royal squadron under Watson and the detachment of King's troops under Clive might be employed with advantage in destroying the pirate in his den. A large Mahratta force was to proceed by land to Gheria in order to assist in the operations. Admiral Watson consented on certain conditions to employing the King's ships in reducing the fastness, and Colonel Robert Clive tendered his services. Commodore James was sent with three ships to reconnoitre the fortress, which was believed "to be at least as strong as Gibraltar, and like that, situated on a mountain inaccessible from the sea." He, however, reported that the place was not high nor nearly so strong as it had been represented. On the 7th February, 1756, the fleet sailed from Bombay. It consisted of twelve men-of-war, six of the royal and six of the Company's, five bomb vessels, four Mahratta grabs and fifty gallivats. On board this squadron to co-operate with it on the land side was a force of eight hundred Europeans, a company of King's artillery and six hundred native troops. Before the fleet sailed, the chief officers met to determine how the prize money should be divided. According to the King's proclamation, Clive was entitled only to the same share as the captain of a ship, but Watson generously consented "to give the Colonel such a part of his share as will make it equal to Rear Admiral Pocock's."

On the 11th the squadron arrived off Gheria and found the Mahratta force camped against it. Tulaji Angria, terrified at the strength of the British fleet, left the fortress in charge of his brother and took refuge in the camp of his own countrymen. The Mahratta general came on board the admiral's ship and Captain Hough, in his diary, informs us he told the admiral that if he should have " a little patience the fort

[1] The island fortress of Suvarnadrug, or " the golden fortress," was eighty miles south by east of Bombay.

would surrender without our firing a gun." He promised to bring Tulaji the next morning "to treat with us in regard to giving up the place, though at the same time he had the assurance to offer me any sum of money I could name on condition I could persuade the Admiral to desist commencing hostilities till they should deliver up the fort." Next morning the Mahratta general did not appear according to promise, and the admiral determined "to run in and begin the attack as soon as the sea and wind would permit." The ships and bomb-ketches sailed straight into the harbour, anchored abreast of the fortress, and opened a fire that in the course of a few hours silenced the enemy's guns. A shell set on fire one of Angria's ships and the whole of his fleet was burnt. Late in the evening Clive landed and occupied the ground between the Peshwa's army and the fort. Next afternoon, the morning having been spent in fruitless negotiations, the ships warped in to within two hundred yards and opened fire on the walls with only the lower-deck guns. In a couple of hours the fort capitulated. One officer with sixty men marched into it and took possession, and "at 36 minutes past 6 English colours were hoisted at the fort." Next morning Colonel Clive, with all the land forces, entered the citadel. This was a bitter disappointment to the Mahratta general, who, the diary informs us, "made use of all the methods he could think of for the place to be delivered up to him without any regard to us, and when he found he could not obtain his ends he even tempted our own officers, (who were lodged with a party of men within a hundred and fifty yards of the fort,) by offering them a lakh of rupees to let his people pass our sentinels in order to get into the fort before us, which they rejected in a proper manner, and told him they would immediately fire upon him and his people if they did not retire, which they thought proper to do upon our people being ordered to present their fire-locks." [1]

[1] "Selections from the Letters, Despatches, and Other State Papers Preserved in the Bombay Secretariat" (Mahratta Series), pp. 89–115. Edited by George W. Forrest.

As there remained nothing more to do on the western coast, Clive wrote the following letter, requesting permission to be allowed to proceed to Fort St. David:[1]

HON'BLE SIR AND SIRS,—As the men-of-war will sail in four days for the other coast I am very desirous of your approbation and consent to take my passage for Fort St. George on one of them. It will be needless to explain the Secret Committee's intentions in sending me first to Bombay. Your Honour and Council being sufficiently acquainted therewith, I would only represent that, as the truce on the other side hath at least suspended all thought of carrying into execution the proposed plan till further advices from England, my absence may be dispensed with without detriment to the Company.

If your Honor and Council think my undertaking the expedition against Golconda absolutely necessary, my going to the other coast I apprehend, can occasion no loss of time or be any impediment thereto. The same conveyance which brings round the detachment ordered from home may bring me likewise.

The approach of the rainy season, if I am not misinformed, will make it impossible to take the field before next October, by which time I may be returned to Bombay; and as the success of the undertaking will greatly depend upon the train of Artillery, Major Chalmers (whose particular province it is) is very well qualified to give directions relating thereto. The expedition against Gheria has put the train in great forwardness, and I make no doubt but what remains to be done will be accomplished long before the month of October.

The above reasons will, I hope, induce your Honor and Council to think that as I cannot be of immediate use in a military capacity, I may be allowed in the meantime to look after the Company's interest and my own at Fort St. David.

By offering my service against Gheria at a time when success could not be ensured or private advantages foreseen, will, I flatter myself, be deemed a proof of my zeal and attachment to the Hon'ble Company's service, and indeed my obligations are of such a nature that I can have no choice when their interest is at stake, and though I much suspect both want of abilities and constitution to command so great an undertaking, yet, if called upon, I shall cheerfully exert myself in that service to which I owe every thing.

Hon'ble Sir and Sirs,

Your most obedient humble Servant,

ROBERT CLIVE.

BOMBAY, 21st *April*, 1756.

Dated three days later, Clive wrote another letter[2] in which he complains of the way in which he had been treated

[1] "Selections from the Letters, Despatches, and Other State Papers Preserved in the Bombay Secretariat" (Mahratta Series), p. 10. Edited by George W. Forrest.

[2] *Ibid.*

regarding a court martial on an officer which had been lately held :

"Neither do I complain against your Honor and Council," he writes, "for ordering the general court-martial, but against the Governor only, who never thought proper to ask my advice or opinion, or even to inform me himself or by any other person whatever with one syllable relating thereto ; and considering the rank I bear of Lieutenant-Colonel in his Majesty's service, of Deputy Governor of St. David, and of a member of the committee of this place, I do not think I have been treated by the Hon'ble Richard Bourchier, Esq., agreeably to the intentions of the Hon'ble the Court of Directors, who, I flatter myself, will do justice herein when they come to hear thereof."

Mr. Daniel Draper, Secretary to Government, was instructed to reply that the Government do not pretend to instruct Colonel Clive in military duty, " but judge it necessary to put him in mind of something so generally known that no body can be supposed ignorant of them except such as willfully shut their eyes." The fact generally known was that a particular rank commenced when it was conferred for a particular service, and " expired of course when that service was no more needed." Mr. Draper was also further directed to acquaint Colonel Clive " that the Board had no intention to insult or affront you, and that they can likewise answer the same for the President, but that they do not think him in the least obliged to be accountable to any officer of whatever rank, or the Governor of any other settlement, for what he shall think proper to lay before the Board, and that they as readily as you refer the whole of this affair to the determination of the Hon'ble Company."

On April 27, 1756, Watson and his squadron left Bombay and once more sailed for the Coromandel Coast. " We touched at Geriah in our way, and on the 14th of May got to Fort St. David's road." Eleven days later Clive reached Madras and took his seat as second in council.[1] Clive did not hold this office long. A Consultation held on June 1 " Ordered that a Commission be drawn out Constituting Robert Clive Esq Deputy Governour of Fort St. David, and that he be

[1] Madras Records Pub. Cons., Vol. LXXXV., pp. 186–92.

paid the Company's Allowance as Deputy Governour for seven months past which have elapsed since his arrival in India."[1] It is stated by Malcolm[2] and accepted by subsequent biographers that Clive took charge of the Governorship of Fort St. David "on the 20th June, 1756, the very day by a remarkable coincidence, on which the Nabob of Bengal took Calcutta." But we find that at a Consultation held on Monday, the 28th, 1756:[3]

"No. 84, from Robert Clive, Esqr Deputy Governour, &^ca Council at Fort St David, dated 23rd Instant acquainting us of the arrival there of Robert Clive, Esqr on the 22^d when agreeable to Our Orders of the 18th he was receiv'd with the usual Honours, and Richard Starke, Esqr the late Deputy Governour deliver'd over to him the Charge of the Settlement, who intends to proceed to the Presidency so soon as he can settle his private Affairs."

On July 14, 1756,[4] evil tidings reached Madras. Roger Drake, Governor of Fort William, informed them in a letter dated June 4 that:

"they had been & are still involved in a dispute with the Country Government occasioned by the Nabobs taking Umbrage at their repairing and strengthening their line of guns towards the River and that by letters from Cassimbuzar (copies of which they send us) they are afraid matters will be carried to extremities the Nabob having stationed a party of Horsemen round the Factory and seeming much Exasperated."

In a postscript to a letter dated June 7, Drake informed them of the surrender of Cossimbazar (Kasimbazar), and entreated them to send a reinforcement without the least delay.[5] The Madras Government had few men they could spare. Salabat Jang had applied for assistance to sever his connection with the French, and the Madras Government were preparing to send an expedition into the Deccan. They had heard from England that a war with France seemed inevitable, and "that the French were preparing to send a fleet of 19 ships of war with

[1] *See* [2], *infra*. [2] Vol. I., p. 136. [3] *Ibid.*

[4] Orme (Vol. II., p. 84) states: "The letters advising the surrender of Cossimbuzar did not arrive until the 15th of July." They were read at a Consultation held on July 14.

[5] "Selections from the Letters, Despatches, and Other State Papers Preserved in the Madras Secretariat" (Clive Series). Edited by George W. Forrest, C.I.E.

3000 regular troops from Brest to Pondicherry." They therefore determined not to send Watson's squadron nor to weaken it, but finding the Company's trading ship *Delawar* "alone can carry as many men as can be spared it is agreed that the *Delawar* only be despatched as expeditiously as possible . . . and that two compleat Companys of Military be sent on her."

"The Board then proceeded to the Nomination of Officers to Command the said Detachment, when Colonel Lawrence very readily offer'd to proceed with the Command, but the Board thinking his Service necessary here, and judging also from an Indisposition which constantly attends him that the air of Bengal especially at this Season of the year might prove fatal to him, it is therefore on these considerations thought more adviseable to desire Major Killpatrick to take upon him the Command of the Detachment. Major Killpatrick being thereupon desired to attend the Board and being informd of the circumstances of Affairs at Bengal & the resolution of sending a Reinforcement thither, acquaints the Board that tho' he had resign'd the Service and resolv'd on going home, yet being ready and desirous at all times to show his inclination to serve the Company, as well as Gratitude for the favours receiv'd, if the Board think proper he will proceed with the said Command. It is thereupon Agreed Major Killpatrick Command the said Detachment." [1]

On July 20 the *Delawar* sailed for Bengal.

On August 3 the Board resolved to send a further detachment to Bengal, and approved of a general letter to Admiral Watson "acquainting him of the state of affairs at Casimbazar, and desiring a supply of a number of ships of his squadron for the conveyance of the relief now ready for dispatch to Bengal, and the freighting of the *Sea Horse* for a lading of arms and ammunition for Bengal." Three days later we learn from the records of the Council's resolution to send a further reinforcement to Bengal upon the news of the danger of Calcutta, and to suspend the prosecution of the designed expedition to Salabat Jang's camp. [2] On August 16, 1756,

[1] "Selections from the Letters, Despatches, and Other State Papers Preserved in the Madras Secretariat" (Clive Series). Edited by George W. Forrest, C.I.E.

[2] Orme states that after the news of the capture of Calcutta: "Nevertheless there prevailed in some of the members of Council a strong propensity at all events to assist Salabadjing," and that it was due to that the Council determined to send a strong force of the whole squadron.—Orme, Vol. II., pp. 86–7.

intelligence was received "of the taking of Calcutta by the Moores on the 20th June." On the following day a general letter from Messrs. Watts and Collett advising of the surrender of Fort William to the troops of the Moors, and "giving a graphic account of the occurrence," was read and discussed by the Board. On the 18th the Board passed resolutions:

"ordering the whole Squadron and all the land forces to the relief of Calcutta under Governor Pigot of Fort St. George who volunteered his services for the purpose—Mr. Clive to repair to Fort St. George from Fort St. David—Mr. Stringer Lawrence to proceed to Fort St. David to take charge of the garrison there till Mr. Clive's return, and the approval of orders to Admiral Watson to proceed to the relief of Bengal with his whole Squadron."

The following day at a Consultation:

"John Adlercron Esq., Colonel of His Majesty's 39th Regiment of Foot and Commander-in-Chief of the Land Forces in India also Present at the request of the Board . . . the following letter from Admiral Watson [was read]:—

"GENTLEMEN,—I have receiv'd your Letter of the 18th Instant and am much concern'd to find the Company's Affairs in so bad a situation at Bengal, I shall very readily give them all the Assistance in my power and will proceed with the whole Squadron as far as Ballisore Road, where I shall be able to consult the Pilots on the Practicability of my getting there, I shall with the utmost cheerfullness put every thing in execution that can be proposed for their Service.

"The time of my Sailing wholly depends on you, as the Ships can't proceed to Sea till their Provisions and Water is compleated, which will take up a considerable time, if some better method is not pursued in the management of the Boats, than is now followed.

"As I propose sending a Frigate before me, in order to have the Pilots ready at Ballisore Road at my arrival. If you have any Troops or Stores you would send by her I will give the Captain Orders accordingly.

"I am Gentlemen,
"Your most obedt. humble servant,
"CHARLES WATSON.

"FORT ST. GEORGE,
"19*th Augt.* 1756."

On August 24 "arrived the *Boneta* Ketch John Edwards from Batavia, last from Fort St. David with Lieutenant-Colonel Robert Clive, Deputy Governour of Fort St. David, Passenger."

That afternoon Clive took his seat at the Board. Watson had written to the Board pointing out the danger of sending the whole squadron to Bengal in case of a French war: and he stated that if the large ships could not proceed up the river he would not land the troops.

"Is it not very probable, if the French Squadron should arrive here, which you have reason to expect, that they having intelligence where I am gone to, will, under the presumption of the largest Ships not being able to get higher than Ballasore Road, come there in search of me? how then should I be able to defend His Majesty's Ships without men? would they not become an easy capture to the French, and thereby contribute to heap Ruin on your Affairs instead of being of any service?"

He also expressed the opinion that "the Fifty and Twenty gun ships would be as much force as there would be occasion for."[1] The Board replied that "the retaking this, so valuable a settlement of the Companys should not be put to the Hazard this expedition would be subject to if undertaken by one Ship only, And are therefore to request that you will permit the *Tyger* and *Salisbury* to proceed." Watson wrote the following day that if more were thought necessary he would "send the sloop with them," but he could "never think of separating two ships of the Line from only four, till some certain advices arrive from Europe." He also considered that if the expedition was postponed till the last week in September it would have a far better chance of success "than if the Ships were to proceed immediately, as they will then escape the rainy Season, which is allow'd by every body to be the most unhealthy part of the year, and in all appearance if the Ships were to go now, one-third of their Men would fall sick before there would be an opportunity to do any Service."

After considerable discussion:

"It is unanimously Resolved that Admiral Watson be desired to send the Fifty and Twenty Gun Ships down to Bengal, with about two hundred and forty Military, with the intent to retake Calcutta only, without attempting any thing more untill join'd by further

[1] "Selections from the Madras Records" (Clive Series). Edited by G. W. Forrest, C.I.E.

succours, and that all necessary preparations be made, as expeditiously as possible, to send all the Forces that can be spared from hence with the remainder of the Squadron, if in the interim the expected Advices from Europe should not make it necessary to alter these Measures."

Two days later, after another long debate, it was resolved:

"That the Survivors of the President & Council of Bengal do still retain their Powers as such, and consequently that whatever Expedition do proceed thither must fall under their Direction: the Board are now of Opinion (in consequence of that Resolution) that it is neither necessary nor proper for either the President or Colonel Clive to proceed."

It was at the same time determined:

"That Admiral Watson be desired to suspend any Orders he may have given for the departure of the Fifty & Twenty Gun Ships and that the Embarkation of the Men intended to be sent on them be also Countermanded. That in case the expected Ships from England should not bring the News of a War with France, Admiral Watson be then desired to proceed down to Bengal with the whole Squadron at once. That Colonel Adlercron be desired to proceed on the Squadron with his whole Regiment and Train of Artillery, And That all preparations of Stores and Necessaries be made with all possible Expedition, in the same manner they would be, were it peremptorily Resolved such an Expedition should proceed at all Events."

On September 19 two of the expected ships from England anchored in the road of Madras. They were the *Chesterfield* and the *Walpole*, and they brought a general letter from the Court of Directors, but no news of a war with France. The Select Committee at Madras also received a letter from the Court stating that:

"In the present dangerous Situation of Affairs we have thought it highly necessary to appoint a Select Committee at Fort William with Similar Powers to those you and the Select Committee at Bombay are invested with, to transact Affairs and take such measures as shall best conduce to the Protection and Preservation of the Company's Estate, Rights & Priviledges."

On September 21 the Council discussed "whether upon the news receiv'd from Europe it is proper to undertake the expedition to Bengal," and it was unanimously decided that the expedition be undertaken. It was also agreed that "the present expedition be put under the command of an officer in the service of the Company," and "as Colonel Clive has before offer'd his Services, he is now desired on many considerations to accept the Command which he very readily does." It was also resolved that Messrs. Smith and Walsh, Council members, should be sent, "join'd with Colonel Clive," as Deputies "from this Board for conducting the expedition."

At a Consultation held on September 30,

> "The President acquaints the Board that the Secret Committee think it necessary & therefore desires that the Board will grant a Commission appointing Robert Clive, Esqr., Commander-in-Chief of all the Troops sent and to be sent on the Expedition to Bengal, and in case of his Death or Absence, that Major James Killpatrick succeed him in the said Command.
>
> "Order'd that a Commission be drawn out accordingly."

The appointment of Clive gave satisfaction to the troops, but not to Colonel Adlercron, who as senior officer claimed the command, but would not bind himself to obey orders from Madras nor to repay the Company's losses out of the expected booty. He now refused to allow any of the King's troops to proceed to Bengal. "Surely gentlemen," he wrote to the Board, "you are not so unreasonable as to expect that I will send away any part of His Majesty's train or regiment (who are so immediately under my direction) and leave to you the nomination." He demanded that His Majesty's artillery with the stores be immediately disembarked. The Select Committee agreed "to order immediate landing of the King's train but to request of Colonel Adlercron to spare the train appurtenances, stores, &c. for the present expedition, upon the Committee's promise to replace the same for the use of His Majesty's train." But the sullen and perverse Adlercron refused to spare the King's stores unless he were satisfied of the Committee's ability to replace them, and the Committee ordered the Company's stores to take the place of the King's stores.[1]

The following day the Select Committee resolved, against the strong opposition of Orme and Clive, to alter the resolution

[1] Military Consultations, Vol. VI., pp. 789–913.

of September 21 appointing Deputies. But they agreed to appoint a Select Committee for Bengal who were to act jointly with Clive, and provisions were to be made empowering Colonel Clive to act independently of the Select Committee in certain urgent cases. On October 5 Clive wrote to his father:[1]

HONOURED SIR,—The expedition to Bengal which I am upon the point of undertaking will not allow me to write a long letter. I hope to write you fully and to your satisfaction by the next conveyance.

I have desired my attorneys to pay you the interest arising from all my moneys in England and the Bishop of Clonfert annuity which is all in my power at present, having lost over £3,000 on the *Doddington* and I fear a greater sum at Bengal. This expedition if attended with success may enable me to do great things. It is by far the grandest of my undertakings. I go with great forces and great authority.

I have desired Mrs. Clive, who has nothing else to do, to write you all particulars and I am with duty to my mother and affection to my brothers and sisters,

Honoured Sir,—Your most dutiful and obedient son,

ROBERT CLIVE.

The following day Clive wrote to William Mabbot, Chairman of the East India Company, as follows:[2]

DEAR SIR,—I have received your Favors by the *Marlboro* and have desired Mr. Pigot that Mr. Fitzpatrick may be stationed at St. Davids which he very readily consented to Your Recommendation added to Mr. Fitzpatricks own Merit will entitle him to all the Services in my power.

Providence who is the disposer of all Events Has thought proper to inflict the greatest Calamity that ever happened to the English Nation in these parts I mean the loss of Calcutta attended with the greatest Mortifications to the Comp^y & the most barbarous & cruel Circumstances to the poor Inhabitants.

This Unhappy News has calld me to the Presidency & the Gentlemen thereof have thought proper to put me at the Head of this Expedition for the recovery of Calcutta the Companys Losses Rights & Priviledges I have that Sense of my Duty to my Country & of my Obligations to the Company (be the Event what it will) there is no Hardship or Risque consistant with common prudence I will not undergo to obtain the wished for Success.

I am not so apprehensive of the Nabob of Bengal Forces as of being [recalled] by the News of a War or checkd in our progress by the Woods & Swampiness of the Country which is represented as

[1] Powis MSS. [2] *Ibid.*

almost impassable for a train of Artillery Be assurd I shall endeavor to merit that good Opinion you have entertained of me.

My best wishes attend Lady Delves M^rs. Mabbot & Miss Coates and I am with real Esteem

Dear Sir

Yours most obliged humble Servt

ROBERT CLIVE.

FORT S^T. GEORGE, 6th *October* 1756

To W^M. MABBOT ESQ^R

On October 11, Clive's commission appointing him Commander-in-Chief was signed, and the same day he wrote to "The Honourable Gentlemen of the Secret Committee London":[1]

HONBLE GENTLEMEN,—From many Hands you will hear of the Capture of Calcutta by the Moors & the Ghain of Misfortunes & Losses which have happened to the Company in particular & to the Nation in General. Every Breast here seems filled with Grief Horror & Resentment indeed it is too sad a Tale to unfold & I must beg leave to refer you to the General Letters, Consultations & Committees wch will give you a full account of this Catastrophe.

Upon this Melancholy Occasion the Govr & Counsel tho^t proper to summons me to this Place ; as soon as an Expedition was resolv'd upon I offer'd my Service which at last was accepted & I am now upon the point of embarking on board His Majestys Squadron with a fine Body of Europeans full of spirit & Resentment for the Insults & Barbarities inflicted on so many British Subjects.

I flatter myself that this Expedition will not end with the retaking of Calcutta only : & that the Companys Estate in these parts will be settled in a Better & more lasting Condition than ever.

There is less Reason to apprehend a Check from the Nabobs Forces than from the Nature of the Climate & Country. The news of a War may likewise interfere with the Success of this Expedition ; however, shoud that happen & Hostilities be committed in India, I hope we shall be able to dispossess the French of Charnagore & leave Calcutta in a state of Defence.

" I have a true sence of my Duty to my Country & the Company & I beg leave to assure you that nothing shall be wanting on my part to answer the Ends of an undertaking on which so very much Depends.

Success on this Occasion will fill the Measure of my Joy ; as it will fix me in the Esteem of those to whom I have the Honor to subscribe myself with great Respect,

Their most obliged & humble Servt

R. CLIVE.

FORT ST. GEORGE

11th *Octo^r* 1756.

To The Honble Gentlemen of the Secret Committee London.

[1] Powis MSS.

The expedition to be sent from the coast of Coromandel to restore English authority in Bengal and discover the high road to British dominion in India was now almost ready to start. The squadron consisted of five of His Majesty's ships of war—the *Kent*, of sixty-four guns, bearing Admiral Watson's flag; the *Cumberland*, of seventy, bearing Admiral Pocock's flag; the *Tyger*, of sixty; the *Salisbury*, of fifty; the *Bridgewater*, of twenty guns; and the *Blaze* fireship, were to convoy the following transports: the *Protector*, *Walpole*, *Marlborough*, Indiamen, and the *Lapwing*, *Snow*, and *Boneta*, ketch, also belonging to the Company. A large supply of military stores and provisions for six weeks was laid in, and the water-casks were filled. A few field-pieces were embarked. Men and officers of a detachment of land forces were on board. It consisted of "528 military, 109 train, 940 sepoys and 160 lascars."[1] This did not include three companies belonging to H.M.'s 39th Regiment. Adlercron had refused to let any of the King's troops form part of the military force, but, as the corps had served as a marine battalion previous to their going to India, he had most reluctantly to consent to their serving as marines on board the fleet. The three companies were commanded by Captain Archibald Grant of that corps, with whom were Captains Weller and Eyre Coote. The Company's Europeans consisted of five companies of the Madras European Battalion with a detachment of artillery under Lieutenant William Jennings. Captain Briggs of the Madras European Battalion was appointed aide-de-camp to Clive, and Mr. Walsh paymaster to the detachment.

On October 13 Clive went on board the admiral's ship *Kent* and received his final instructions. He was to assist the Select Committee for Bengal with his best advice, and was to endeavour "to preserve a good harmony throughout." But he was empowered "to pursue such measures as you shall judge most conducive to the Company's benefit." If they received news of war with France it was their intention imme-

[1] Letter from Council, Fort St. George, to Colonel Clive, dated October 13. 1756. (Fort St. George Select Committee Consultations.)

diately to recall him and the greater part of his troops. Upon the receipt of such orders he was "to leave so many men as you judge necessary for the immediate defence of Calcutta and proceed hither with the rest without loss of time."[1] The same day the Select Committee, Fort St. George, wrote to the Select Committee, Fort William, that:

"The mere retaking of Calcutta should we think by no means be the end of the undertaking; not only their settlements and factories should be restored but all their priviledges established in the full extent granted by the Great *Mogul*, and ample reparation made of them for the loss they have lately sustained; otherwise we are of opinion it would have been better nothing had been attempted, than to have added the heavy charge of this armament to their former loss, without securing their colonies and trade from future insults and exactions."[2]

It is now necessary that the origin, progress, and loss of the settlements and factories in Bengal should be traced, in order that the subsequent narrative may be intelligible and instructive.

[1] Letter from Council, Fort St. George, to Colonel Clive, dated October 13, 1756.

[2] Letter from the Select Committee, Fort St. George, to the Select Committee, Fort William, October 13, 1756.

CHAPTER XV

FOUNDATION OF BRITISH RULE IN BENGAL

On March 22, 1632–3, Master Norris, the agent at Masulipatam, having learnt "that all kinds of provisions for subsisting the Company's factories on the Coromandel coast could be purchased in Bengal, and an indefinite quantity of fine white cloth," resolved to send two merchants into Bengala for the settling of a factory, and six Europeans besides, who were then at Masulipatam, were to accompany the merchants and carry a present from the agent to the Nawab or king of that country. On April 1 they set sail, "and in much various weather, with many difficulties and dangers (which to relate here would be tedious and impertinent to my intended discourse); the twenty-first of April being then Easter-day, we were at anchor in a bay before a town called Harssapoore; it is a place of good strength, with whom our merchants hold commerce with correspondency." At Hariharpur, on the Orissa coast, the party hired a house for a factory, and whilst some of them remained to build, Mr. Cartwright, one of the merchants, travelled towards "Ballazary" (Balasore), at the mouth of the Hugli estuary, and a small agency was established there. From Balasore the Company's servants made their way round the Gangetic delta, and so up its south-western channel to Hugli, "the principal port of the province, lying about one hundred miles from the sea, on the river to which it gives its name."

Seven-and-twenty years rolled on, and the Company, besides having a small establishment at Hugli, had crept up the river and founded a trading station at Cossimbazar, near Murshidabad, the modern capital of Bengal, containing about 200,000 inhabitants, and farther north at Patna, famous for its raw silk, saltpetre, and opium, where two great rivers meet the Ganges. In 1658 Job Charnock, of whose early career we know but little, was appointed first member of Council at Cossimbazar, with a salary of £20. In 1664 he became chief at Patna. Eleven years later his "hon. employers," thinking that Job Charnock had done them "good and faithfull service, and it being his right," appointed him (January 3, 1679) "to be Chief of Cassumbazar and 2 of Council in the Bay, and consequently to succeed in the Chiefship at the Bay according to our Rules." But Job Charnock could not leave Patna until he had started the saltpetre cargoes, a material much wanted at the time in England, and Streynsham Master, governor and agent at Madras, deprived him of the appointment. The Court greatly resented this treatment "of our old and good servant, Mr. Job Charnock, who had the right indisputably of succession (as you call it), beside our express order to be chief of Cassumbazar. A person that hath served us faithfully above 20 years, and hath never, as we understand, been a prowler for himselfe, beyond what was just and modest: Who therefore We are resolved, shall not live unrewarded by us." But they twice in succession appointed other men to be chief of the Bay.

It was not till August, 1685, on the death of the chief agent at Hugli, that Job Charnock succeeded him, but the factory at Cossimbazar was boycotted because he had stoutly fought against the exactions and extortions of the native officials, and it was closely watched by soldiers to prevent his leaving. He, however, managed to slip through the cordon, and reached Hugli in April, 1686.

The East India Court had now come to the conclusion that if their trade in Bengal was to prosper, they must shake off the exactions of the Nawab and his officials. To do this they must increase and discipline their troops, and have a fortified settlement. On January 27, 1685/6, they wrote to "our President and Council at Fort St. George":

"You must not forgett to send to Bengall some of ye bookes of military discipline & Martiall Law, now in use in his Maj^{tys} Army, & to give them strict orders for keeping all our land officers and soldjers constantly to live & Lodge in Hutts or Barracks w^{th}in our Fort, according to y^e usage of y^e modern Garrisons in Europe, and that they may know how the more decently & conveniently to contrive them, we have induced all our $Comand^{rs}$ and Lieutenants bound for Bengall before theire going to sea to take a view of that regular Fortification of his Maj^{ty}, ye Block House at Gravesend."

In a letter written on December 21, 1683, the Court state that some

"of our Captains tell us there is noe way to mend our condition but by seizing and fortifying one of these pleasant Islands in the Ganges about the Braces"; but "some others have propounded to us the seizure upon a Toune called Chittagong in the easternmost mouth of the River Ganges, upon or near the coast of Rackan [Arakan]."

Years later, having obtained the permission of James II., they determined to send an expedition to capture Chittagong, a port of considerable importance in the sixteenth century, which was known familiarly to the Portuguese as Porto Grande. Chittagong had belonged to the Mogul Emperor, and the Court wrote:

"But you must always understand that th^o we prepared for and resolve to enter into a warr wth ye Mogull (being necessitated thereunto) our ultimate end is peace, for as we have never done it, soe our natures are averse to bloodshed & Rapine, wch usually attend the most just warrs, but we have noe remedy left, but either to desert our Trade, or we must draw the Sword his Maj^{ty} hath Intrusted us wth to vindicate the Rights & $Hono^r$ of the English Nation in India."

The fleet sent to "enter into a warr wth y^e Mogull," and "to vindicate the Rights & $Hono^r$ of the English Nation," was the most formidable armament ever dispatched to India—the *Beaufort*, with seventy guns and 300 seamen, commanded by John Nicholson; the *Nathaniel*, with fifty guns and 150 seamen, commanded by John Mason; and the *Rochester*, with sixty-five guns; three "Frygatts so contrived for the Sea that they may as well goe about the Cape as the best ships we have," armed with twelve guns and twenty seamen. They carried six companies of English soldiers, recruited for the purpose, with subaltern officers, but without Captains, for the Court write:

> " We have appointed noe Capt of our sixe Comp^{a} of Soldiers, because we resolve to keep to our ancient well-grounded custome of keeping always our Soldiers under ye Command of our Chiefe and Councill, & therefore we doe appoint, y^{t} our Agent for the time being be always Lieut^{nt} Genn^{l} & Command^{r} in Chiefe of all our Forces by Sea or Land in or near ye provinces of Bengall & Oriza, and in all Seas, Harbours, Creeks, and places near unto those provinces or either of them, & that he be Collonell & Capt of ye first Company of English Soldiers in Bengall, that ye 2^{d} of our Councill be always Lieut^{nt} Collonell & Capt of our 2^{d} Comp^{a} of Foote Soldiers, y^{t} the 3^{d} of our Councill be Major of our Regiment & Capt of o^{r} 3^{d} Comp^{a}, & that all the rest of our Councill, according to theire station in Councill, be respectively Capt of the succeeding Comp^{a} of Foote Soldiers."

Royal commissions were granted by His Majesty to Captain Nicholson and the other commanders; Nicholson was appointed admiral, and Mason vice-admiral. The fleet was to be joined by the Company's other vessels in Bengal, and orders were to be sent to Madras to dispatch to the Bay all the vessels they could spare. Enclosed in the instructions to the agent was a letter to the Nawab demanding £620,000 damages "for this great Fleet and Force," for loss "sustained by his beseidging our Factories and obstructing our trade"; "Yett," they add, "we are not only soe desirous but fond of peace" that if he would agree "to leave us ye Inheritance of Chettegam and ye small Territories thereunto belonging," they "were willing to relinquish all our forementioned demands and resettle in his Country in our old Factorys & upon our old privileges." If on the arrival of Nicholson the Nawab had not agreed to these hard terms, they were to proceed "wth all y^{or} forces to Chyttegam both by Sea and land and take ye Towne." But if "ye said Towne or Fort was peaceable delivered," they were to give the inhabitants "faire Quart^{r}, and not to kill any of them or to take anything from them, but to suffer them to remaine in theire owne houses."

> " You are to allow ye Natives ye liberty of theire sev^{ll} Religions as these Subjects to ye Comp^{a} have at Fort St George. Above all things we would have you very carefull that noe Violence or Injury

be offered to women, children, or any innocent people, that doe not hastily oppose you, & particularly that you suffer noe prejudice to be done to Churches, Pagodas, or other public places where God is worshipped or said to be worshipped."

From the day on which it sailed the fleet was pursued by misfortune; the winds were unpropitious, and detained it; when it set out to sea a storm dispersed it. One vessel was lost, and two of the largest ships, having a very considerable number of troops on board, could not make the passage. It was not till October, 1686, that the *Rochester* and her frigate anchored at the mouth of the Hugli. They had 108 men on board, who were sent up the river in small vessels to the English factory. The *Beaufort* and her frigate with 200 men arrived soon afterwards. The arrival of these ships with troops roused the fear and anger of the Nawab. On November 24 Job Charnock and his Council wrote to Surat: "The arrivall of our Forces (tho Small) soe alarumed the country" that the Viceroy "ordered doune for the guard of this towne two or three hundred horse & three or four thousand foot." The local governor now "became very insolent in denying us all manner of necessaries for trade and forbidding us Victualls in the Buzar to prevent our Souldiers resorting thither." On October 28 three soldiers went out to purchase "Victualls in the morning," and news reached the factory "that two Englishmen were sett upon by the Governors Penos [guards], desperately cut and wounded, and lying dying in the Highway." Charnock immediately sent Captain Leslie with a company of soldiers "to bring in their bodies dead or alive but to offer violence to noe man except they were assaulted." They were attacked on their way by a body of the Nawab's horse and foot, whom they repulsed, killing and wounding seven. The inhabitants took alarm and set fire to the houses near the English quarters, and the old factory was burnt. "At the same time they began to display their great gunns from a battery consisting of Eleven Gunns that they had lately raised to command our Shipps in the Hole." Charnock immediately summoned reinforcement from Chandernagore, "three miles from towne," and sent a detachment under Captain Richardson to attack the battery. They had to retire with the loss of many wounded.

"Whereupon Capt. Arthburtnot [Arbuthnot] went out with a fresh recruite, made an assault upon the battery, took it, and maintained it while they spiked and dismounted all the gunns, carried the battle on beyond the Governor's House, burneing and driveing all before them, upon which, it was reported, the Governor himselfe fledd in disguise by Water—leaveing the towne in this desolated condition."

Thus, for the first time it was proved in Bengal that numerical superiority was of no avail against the courage and discipline of English troops. "The skirmish we have had with the Government," writes Charnock, "mightily startles them, & has made them mightily afraid of us. The Nabob knows not what to think of it." The Nawab showed what he thought by directing all the English factories in Bengal to be seized, the factors to be made prisoners, and a large body of troops to be dispatched to Hugli. Charnock's garrison did "not number 400 fighting men," and the shallows in the river prevented large ships from coming up to his protection.

The Court had given repeated instructions that a spot nearer the sea and more defensible should be found for their establishment, and Charnock now determined to comply with their wishes. On December 31, 1686, he wrote to Sir John Child, General, and Council at Surat:

"On the 20th instant we all withdrew & left Hugly, bringing off all the Rt. Honb[le] Company's Concerns, and our own. Our coming off was very Peaceable, and no less Honourable, having (as formerly advised) continued the Cessation of arms on both sides hitherto, for the conveniency of getting of the Rt. Hon[ble] Company's Estate."

Charnock's letter was addressed from Chuttanuttee. The site of future empire was occupied by three hamlets, the chief of which was Chuttanuttee (literally, *Satanati Hath*, Cotton Thread Mart); the other two were Kalikata (Calcutta) and Gobindpur, where the present Fort William stands. It was situated on the east bank of a reach of the river, about seventy miles from the sea, and accessible at high tide to heavily armed ships. Charnock proceeded to erect some huts as temporary residences, and began to negotiate with the Viceroy's agent for permission to build a factory; but the Viceroy did not forget the skirmish at Hugli, and sent an army to destroy the rising settlement. "The country all up in armes round us," wrote Charnock, "and without any hope of peace or ffurther treaties about it, Warr broke forth"; and the English having burnt down "the King's salt houses" and captured his "ffort at Tanna" on the right bank of the river below Satanati, sailed seventy miles farther down the river to Hijili, a low, flat island, separated from the mainland by a narrow channel. They placed their

"small shipping at severall stations round the Island to hinder the Enimies landing, in the most probable places, and also began to raise breastworks & to Digg trenches round our main Fort, which was but ffalcely so Tearmed, it being but a small weake house and a thinn wall about it, with 2 or 3 points, not nigh so strong as our ffactory at Hughley, and scituated among a Grove of Trees and a thick Towne of mudd houses about 500 (yards) distant from the Water Side where was raised a battery of Gunns. The upper Fort had Gunns also mounted where they Could doe Service."

The Viceroy's army of 12,000 men followed Charnock and his small band, and at once erected batteries where the channel was narrowest,

"thereby so Annoying our Shipping that they placed every Shot, & our men, Souldiers, Sailors, and others ffell doune every day sick of the Generall Distemper of the Island, Feavour and Ague, which was by this time Epidemicall, so that wee had buried almost 200 men of all sorts and Scarce 100 men remained to keepe the Fort and those very weake."

On May 28, 1687, the besiegers landed "700 Horsemen and 200 Gunnmen," and capturing a battery, marched "with their fforces & our ffeild-peeces to the maine Forte in the Towne." They arrived as "our Intelligences," and surprised Lieutenant Richard Frances, his wife, and child, who were sick in a house in the town. "Himm they cutt in Peeces, his wife & child they Carryed away Prisoners." The enemy seized the outer trenches, and all that night a fierce fight raged, " but the Mogull's Courage, as their Nature is, going out of them with their Bang [opium]; Next morning were soon ffeazed [harassed] out from thence." The condition of the garrison was most desperate " by reason of sickness and death, not having but one officer, of 6 Lieuts. and 8 Ensigns, to command under his Worshipp at that time in the Fort, and of 26 Sergeants and Corporalls, not above 4 alive and all to do duty." The admiral's ship sprang another " desperate Greate Leake," and " not one of the others was half manned." If Charnock surrendered the fort, the Company's ships expected from home would be lost. He held out the next day, " notwithstanding they Landed a greate many more men upon us and battered us with their field-peeces, and beseidged us $\frac{3}{4}$ round." A flat-roofed masonry house on which Job Charnock had planted two guns and a guard prevented a complete investment. It stood half-way to the water-side, and by holding it, and a battery of two guns at the landing-place, the garrison kept that passage to their shipping open, and were able to procure ammunition and provision.

All that day and the next night the firing continued on both sides. Heavy rain fell during the night, " which with constant duty much disabled our men." A great many had to be sent aboard, and the small shipping that kept guard round the island were ordered into the river to be ready to receive the scanty remnant. One of them, the *Revenge*, grounded upon a sandbank by the way, and the vessel was deserted by her crew and possessed by the enemy. But in face of all trials and misfortunes, Job Charnock held out. Four days drove on, the garrison " growing very thinn, not having above 100 ffighting men it, and the 2 Batteryes." On June 1 the sentinels on the ramparts saw the sails of a ship from Europe coming up the Hugli, and the garrison received a recruit of seventy men, " who cheerfully sallied out the Next Day, and beate the Enemy ffrom their Gunns, burning their houses & returned with the Loss of a Manne."

On June 3 Job Charnock resorted to a bold and clever

stratagem. He dropped all the sailors out of the fort by one and two at a time to the under battery at the water-side, "when being all drawne up in arms, marched up to the Fort with Drums beating and Trumpetts Sounding and the men hazaing as two daies before." The garrison lost about sixteen men, the enemy "a very greate number." Thinking that Charnock was supplied with constant recruits from the shipping, the enemy "grew Dull upon it," and "on the next day in the morning, being the 6th day, held forth a flagg of Truce in order to a Treaty." After three days' negotiations, a treaty was signed. On the 11th day, Job Charnock having given the Mogul commander "full possession," went forth "with our Ammunition and Artillery, drums beating and Collours flying." So ended the siege of Hijili. It lasted only a few days, but it displayed all the patience, courage, and stubbornness of resolution of our race. In "that direful place" many died, and great numbers fell afterwards victims to the disease they contracted there. "Wee have buried," wrote Job Charnock, "the last Yeare from the Shipps and the military nigh 500 men, amongst which are 14 of the Rt Honoble Company's Servants and 6 women. Of 6 Lieutenants only 2 Left, and those miraculously recovered—8 Ensigns fell, 10 Sergeants and about as many Corporalls, with 250 Sentinells and as many Seamen; and Very few or Scarce any that Escaped a fitt of Sickness upon that infected Island." So our Indian Empire was built.

And now, peace having been established, Charnock spread his sails, and once more held his course up the Hugli. He dare not return to Chuttanuttee, so he cast anchor at Ulabarea, sixteen miles below it. He obtained permission to remain there, and began making docks for careening his ships; but after remaining there three months he found it not suited to the inland trade, and returned to Chuttanuttee about November, 1687. Here he and his factors lived for about a year. On June 27, 1688, Charnock wrote to the Governor of Fort St. George and the city of Madras:

"Wee are in great hopes of obtaining Chutanuttee to settle in with three or four other adjacent townes which doubtless may be in some years so improved as to be very proffitable to the Right Hono'ble Comp[a] & possibly may be gradually improved to a considerable strength; for when once we came to be settled thoroughly, the country people will flock to us to live under our Government, the nature of which they are well acquainted with, and soe a vast disparity between the lenity of ours and the tyranny of their own, of the which we have a pregnant instance in their present flocking to us such abundance as they dayly do."

Charnock's good hopes were soon wrecked. In September there arrived the *Defence*, 64-gun ship, commanded by Captain Heath, accompanied by a small frigate having on board 160 soldiers. Heath had positive orders "that in any case our Servants in the Bay have not already fortified themselves in some considerable place," they were "to prepare to come on board our ship in three days' time," and he was to proceed with them against Chittagong. Heath had an extraordinary commission, which superseded Charnock in his chief command of the forces in the Bay. Charnock objected to leaving his rising settlement, and he knew that the attack on Chittagong was a vain adventure; but the old sailor exercised his authority, and ordered all the Company's servants to embark on board the fleet, and on November 8 he proceeded down the river to Balasore. After sacking and burning that town he set sail for Chittagong. But Heath found the works stronger than he expected, and 10,000 men ready to defend them. After a month of fruitless negotiations with the native governor, he abandoned the enterprise, and on February 17 he set sail for Fort St. George, "giving orders for every ship to make the best of her way."

At Madras Job Charnock remained fifteen months. In January, 1690, Aurangzib, finding how important the commerce of the Company was to the wealth and prosperity of his empire, and that the Company's cruisers prevented pilgrims from going to Mecca, authorised his representative to make peace with Sir John Child, the Governor of Bombay and Director-General of the Company's settlements. On

February 18 the President of Fort St. George wrote to the Court: "For confidence whereof (i.e. of peace) we are resolving to send doune Agent Charnock to Bengall to the Bay upon the Princess when she arrives, . . . which we are the more encouraged to by the kind invitation of the now worthy good Nabob Ebrahim Cawne." On the arrival of the *Princess*, Charnock with his Council and factors, accompanied by an officer and thirty soldiers, went on board, and on Sunday, August 24, at noon, she anchored off Chuttanuttee.

From the deck of a giant steamer as she anchors off Calcutta a noble prospect now meets the eye, which is the delight of visitors from all quarters of the globe. Vessels of all sizes and descriptions gliding over its waters animate the vast river with varied life. Stately ships lie at anchor by the bank, and their lofty spars tower up black into the air. In the far distance, beyond a wide green plain, rise into sight tower and dome and spire of the City of Palaces.

Charnock saw from his small vessel a different scene. A stretch of rising ground along the river, with mat-covered lodges strewn around; beyond it all a vast, green, malarious swamp, girded by a dense jungle like a mighty hedge. Job Charnock found the place in a deplorable condition, "nothing being left for our present accommodation, and the rain falling day and night. We are forced to betake ourselves to boats, which, considering the season of the year, is unhealthy." On Thursday, August 28, at a consultation:

"*Present.*—The R[t] Worshipful Agent Charnock, Mr. Francis Ellis, Mr. Jere. Peachie. In consideration that all the former buildings here are destroyed, it is resolved that such places be built as necessity requires and as cheap as possible—viz., 1, A warehouse; 2, A dining-room; 3, The Secretary's Office to be repaired; 4, A room to sort cloth in; 5, A cook-room with its conveniences; 6, An apartment for the Company's servants; 7, The Agents and Mr. Peachie's house to be repaired, which were part standing, and a house to be built for Mr. Ellis, the latter being totally demolished; 8, The guard-house. These being done with mudd walls and thatched till we can get ground whereon to build a factory."

The mud huts rose, the swamp around was reclaimed, the jungle was cleared away, but many succumbed to the cruel fever. The growth of the infant settlement was slow, and accompanied by much suffering. Nine months after its birth the President at Fort St. George wrote that "they were in a wild unsettled condition at Chuttinuttee, neither fortifyed houses nor goedowns, only tents, hutts, and boats, with a strange charge of near 100 soldiers, guardships, &c." The Nawab of Bengal would "neither permit building or Factory, nor merchants to settle or trade with them." But Job Charnock, the Madras President complains, "continues contrary to all reason or consent of the Government." It is by "divine madness," contrary to all reason or consent of Government, that empires are made. Charnock's far sight saw that it needed only courage and perseverance to make the enterprise a success. But the whole weight of the task fell on the sturdy old man, who had served thirty years in India, and the burden proved too heavy. He fell into deep dejection, and during his last years his stubborn will was no longer a law to his followers. His race of glory run, on January 10, 1693, Job Charnock was with them that rest.

It is the lot of the pioneer to plough and to sow, and for others to reap. Job Charnock was no mere money-making trader, no wild daring speculator, but an old English merchant, with the high character, calm judgment, and cool courage of his order. He felt responsible for the merchandise and credit of his "Honble. Masters." He was, they said, "always a faithful man to the Company." He had, no doubt, the faults born of unrestricted power and isolated stations of command. But his career attests that Job Charnock was a valiant and true servant, who for the good of his country set at naught all risks and sufferings. By working in the same spirit his countrymen have won for England a vast and stable dominion.

The settlement which Job Charnock formed was improved by degrees into a valuable possession. The English began to build walls and bastions round their factory, and so created the original citadel of Fort William. Under the protection of the English flag and of English law, a large population of native and foreign traders settled on the Company's estate, and Calcutta became not a miserable trading fort, as Burke described it, but a prosperous town, a mart and seaport of considerable importance. In the year 1716 the English obtained from the Mogul an important firman or imperial order, "That all their mercantile affairs, together with their gomashtas (agents), have free liberty, in all subahships (provinces), to pass and repass to and fro, either by land or water, in any part or district through the several provinces above said. And know, they are custom free; that they have full power and liberty to buy and sell at their own pleasure." The liberty was abused by the servants of the Company. Captain Rennie, a mariner, in his "Reflections on the Loss of Calcutta" (June, 1756), states:

"The injustice to the Moors consists in that, being by their courtesy permitted to live here as merchants, to protect and judge what natives were their servants, and to trade custom free,—we under that pretence protected all the Nabob's subjects that claimed our protection, though they were neither our servants nor our merchants, and gave our *dustucks* or passes to numbers of natives to trade custom free, to the great prejudice of the Nabob's revenue; nay more, we levied large duties upon goods brought into our districts from the very people that permitted us to trade custom free, and by numbers of their impositions (framed to raise the Company's revenues, some of which were ruinous to ourselves)—such as taxes on marriages, provisions transferring land property, &c.—caused eternal clamour and complaints against us at Court."

In 1742 Alivardi Khan, an Afghan adventurer, won for himself by the sword the rulership of Bengal. He was a good soldier and a strong administrator. He maintained friendly relations with the authorities of the European factories, and, in return for the subsidies which he exacted from them, he gave them protection and enforced good order. At the close of his long reign he, however, regarded with suspicion the strong indomitable race whose ships commanded the sea and whose forts protected their rising settlements. When his chief commanders urged him to expel the English and seize their property, he said: "It is now difficult to extinguish the fire on land; but should the sea be in flames, who could put them out ?" Three years before his death Alivardi Khan, who was stricken in age, appointed his favourite nephew and adopted son, Mirza Mahmud, to be his successor, and invested him with considerable power. On his appointment Mirza Mahmud received the name of Siraj-ud-Daula, signifying "the Lamp of the State," by which he was afterwards called; but he is known to history as Surajah Dowla. Richard Becher, chief of the subordinate factory at Dacca, describes him as "a young man, violent, passionate, of great ambition tinctured with avarice."

Surajah Dowla suspected (and he had good grounds for his suspicion) the Company's servants of corresponding with a widowed daughter of Alivardi Khan, who had adopted a probable rival to the throne; and he was greatly irritated when they gave a cordial welcome to Kissendas (Kishn Das), the son of her Hindu lover and principal adviser, who, under pretence of a pilgrimage to the sacred shrine of Jugernath (Jagannath), had proceeded to Calcutta with his family and an immense amount of treasures. Kissendas took up his residence with Omichund (Aminchand), a banker of great wealth. Macaulay speaks of him as "the artful Bengalee," but he was a trader from the north of India who had for forty years resided in Bengal. His commerce extended to every part of the province, and he had provided most of the Company's investments. But three years before the arrival of Kissendas, Omichund was excluded from any participation in the Company's affairs, and this vexed his pride and avarice. It was stated at the time that he was an active party in bringing Kissendas to Calcutta, with the intention of ruining the English by embroiling them in quarrel with Alivardi or of regaining his former influence by acting as mediator.

The reception of Kissendas at Calcutta has been assigned as one of the main causes of the war, but it was due to a deeper and more remote foundation. Captain Rennie states that "the principal cause of the war was the knowledge of what had happened on the coast of Coromandel, for many

Moors (and some of distinction among them) have come lately from thence and declared that the English and French have divided the country, while their respective Nabobs are not better than shadows of what they should be." The news of the capture of the great stronghold of Gheria on the Malabar coast by Clive confirmed the impression that the Europeans intended to claim the whole as their own. Soon after the receipt of the intelligence of the taking of Gheria, Alivardi died, and Surajah Dowla took quiet possession of the government. He at once sent a written order to the Governor of Calcutta to deliver Kissendas up, his property, and his followers. The messenger, a man of considerable importance, who entered Calcutta in the disguise of a European, "was turned out of the factory and off the shore with derision and insolence."

When our Hindu agent at his Court represented the suspicions which had induced the authorities at Calcutta to treat the messenger as an impostor, Surajah Dowla listened, armed with the true impenetrability of an Oriental. He showed no emotion or displeasure—news had reached him of a more serious and exasperating nature than an affront to his messenger. His spies at Calcutta had often informed him of the small strength of its fortifications and garrison, and before the death of Alivardi Khan "the easy capture of it was the Publick discourse of the city and Durbar"; Surajah Dowla was now informed that the English were busy raising strong fortifications. The report was in a certain measure true. He had just been proclaimed when a letter from the E.I. Court reached Calcutta stating that war with France was inevitable, and "in consequence of these advices the line of guns towards the river was repaired and strengthened and some other trifling works erected particularly a Redoubt at Perrin's Garden." Surajah Dowla at once wrote to the President "that he did not approve of our carrying on these works without his permission, and ordered Mr. Drake to desist immediately, and destroy what he had already done." The French having strengthened their fort by an additional bastion, also received an order to the like effect. They discreetly replied that "they had not built New Works, and had only Repaired One of their Bastions, which had been injured by Lightning, with which answer he appeared satisfied." The English President, on the other hand, stated:

> "That in the late War between our Nation and the French, they had attacked and taken the Town of Madras Contrary to the neutrality We expected would have been preserved in the Mogull's Dominions; and that there being at present great appearance of another War between the Two Crowns, We were under some apprehensions they would act in the same way in Bengal, to prevent which We were only repairing our Line of Guns to the Water-side."

The indiscreet answer increased the wrath and suspicion of Surajah Dowla. It seemed to him an evasion of his clear demand. "Upon what pretence," he wrote, "will the French attempt to attack them on the river? which they have never done since the settlement of Europeans in the Country." If the English began the struggle he feared it would lead, as it had done in the Carnatic, to the ascendancy of the conqueror and the destruction of the power of the native princes. Surajah Dowla felt that if he were to maintain his supremacy he must take some open and decided action. Now was the time. He had firmly established himself on the throne, and had collected a large army to chastise a rebellious cousin. On May 28 he sent the principal merchant of the province, who resided at Hugli, a letter stating:

> "It has been my design to level the English fortifications raised within my jurisdiction on account of their great strength; as I have nothing at present to divert me from the execution of that resolution, I am determined to make use of this opportunity; for which reason I am returning from Ragahmaul, and shall use the utmost expedition on my march that I may arrive before Calcutta as soon as possible."

He added at the bottom in his own hand:

> "I swear by the Great God and the prophets that unless the English consent to fill up their ditch, raze their fortifications, and trade upon the same terms they did in the time of Nabob Jaffeer Cawn, I will not hear anything on their behalf, and will expel them totally out of my country."

On June 9 Surajah Dowla, having seized the factory at Cossimbazar, near his capital, bent his march towards Calcutta. On June 7 news reached Fort William that Cossimbazar had surrendered, and "that the Nabob was determined to march to Calcutta with his whole army, estimated then at 50,000 men, besides a large train of artillery." The English, when they fortified their settlement, had never meant that it should be able to stand a regular siege, and had contented themselves with throwing up work sufficient to protect the inhabitants against "an irruption of the Moors" and an inroad of the Mahratta horse. Orme, in a "Narrative of the Loss of Calcutta, composed at Madras, October 1756," which has never been printed, speaks of Fort William as "a building which many an old house in the country exceeds in its defence":

> "It is situated a few paces from the river-side, on the bank of which runs a line of guns the whole length of the fort from North to South, and this the only formidable part, as it is capable of annoying ships on the river. The ends of this line are joined to the two bastions of the fort nearest the river by a garden wall and a gate in each, which would resist one shot of a six-pounder, but which would be forced by the second. Opposite to the two bastions mentioned are two others placed to the Eastward, but within thirty yards to the North and fifty yards to the South the bastions are commanded by large houses. To the Eastward inland the top of the church commands the whole of both the Northern and Eastern Ramparts."

The curtains of the fort were only four feet thick, and terraces which were the roofs of the chambers formed the top of the ramparts. Nine years before the siege a range of warehouses had been built on the inside of the southern face occupying the space between the flanks of the adjacent bastions, and consequently rendering, as Holwell states, "your too southerly face of the fort, which could not be flanked by a single gun from either bastion." Holwell's account of the condition of the fortifications illustrates how ancient is the English prerogative never to prepare in the time of peace for the exigencies of actual war.

"The ruinous state of the lines to the Westward of the fort," he writes, "had been a reproach to our settlement, and to everything bearing the name of fortification, for more than two years. The whole easterly curtain had been for many years in so ruinous a condition as not to bear a gun; one we fired from it, a three or four pounder, as I remember, which made its way through the terrace."

The ammunition, like the fortifications, was impaired by neglect.

"'No cartridges,' writes Captain Grant, the adjutant-general, 'of any kind ready. The small quantity of grape in store had lyen by so long that it was destroyed by worms; no shells fitted nor Fuses prepared for small or great. The few that were thrown at the siege burst half way. There were 2 Iron Mortars, one of 13 and the other of 10 inches, sent out about 3 years ago. The 10-inch Mortar we had just finished the bed for it, but the 13-inch one lay by useless for want of one; tho' there was upwards of 300 shells sent out for both, all that could be prepared was not above 20, and such as was thrown of them burst some after quitting the mortar, other half way. We had but a small quantity of powder, and the greatest part of that damp.'"

The regular force of the garrison amounted only to 264 men, of whom a portion were native Portuguese and Armenians. "Of these Handfull of Troops in Garrison there were not five who had ever I believe seen a Muskett fired in Anger." The officers, however, commanding the regular companies—Minchen, Clayton, Buchanan, Grant, and Wetherington—had all except Clayton seen service either in Europe or on the Coromandel Coast. Captain Minchen was the chief commander. Of him Holwell writes, and the other narratives confirm the justice of his criticism:

"Touching the military capacity of our Commandant I am a stranger. I can only say we were unhappy in his keeping it to himself if he had any, as neither I, nor, I believe, any one else was witness to any part of His Conduct that spoke or bore the appearance of his being the Commanding Military Officer in garrison."

When the news that Surajah Dowla was advancing on them reached Calcutta, a council of war, consisting of the military captains and the engineer joined to the ordinary Council, was held. It decided that the militia should be called out. That same evening the Governor "by beat of drum, caused all the inhabitants of Calcutta fit to bear arms to be assembled." The next morning, June 8th, two companies of militia were enrolled, consisting of the European, Portuguese, and Armenian inhabitants, amounting to 250 men. If they had been regularly trained to arms according to the repeated orders of the Court, they might at this juncture, as Holwell states, have

"been a most seasonable supply, but this essential regulation, I am sorry to say, was totally neglected, so that when We came to action there was hardly any amongst the Armenians and Portuguese inhabitants, and but few among the European Militia, who knew the Right from the Wrong end of their pieces."

Holwell commanded the 1st Company of the militia and William Mackett the 2nd Company,

"and the following gentlemen were appointed officers under them —viz., Robert Mapletoft (a clergyman, Chaplain of the Presidency), Captain-Lieutenant; Richard Court, H. Wedderburn, T. Holmes, and Wm. Summer, Lieutenants; C. Douglas, T. Coates, and R. H. Baldick, Ensigns; and William Dumbleton, Adjutant."

The council of war, instead of repairing and strengthening the fortifications of the fort, determined that the "Batterys should be erected in all the roads leading to the fort at such distances as Cou'd be anywise defensible with the small number of Troops We had." The resolution was a capital error. The troops were few in number and the ground covered a considerable area. Captain Grant supplies the reason which led the Council to come to so unwise a decision. No one thought, "even to the very last day, that the Nabob would ever venture to attack us or offer to force our lines."

Orme enables us by plan and description to ascertain exactly where the three batteries which the besieged constructed and mounted were situated. The eastern battery was erected near the present Scotch church, "opposite to the Eastern gate of the fort, at the distance of 300 yards on the principal avenue, which continued in a straight line to the rearward as far as the Merattoe ditch." This battery adjoined to the left the gateway of an enclosure, in which, at the distance of a few feet, stood a very spacious house of one floor in which the mayor's court and assizes used to be held. The north battery must have been situated at the foot of Clive Ghat Street; the third battery at the corner where Hastings Street, Council House Street, and Government Place meet. The fort occupied a site now comprised between Coilah Ghat Street and Fairlie Place. The chief gateway looked out upon an avenue, which was skirted on the north side by a large enclosure called "the Park," and Orme's plan gives in the enclosure the tank which forms a prominent feature in Dalhousie Square. To the south of the Park was the Rope Walk, at whose eastern extremity was the east battery. Beyond the Rope Walk there were three large English houses, and a short distance from them, on the edge of the avenue, was the gaol.

On June 13 a letter was intercepted from the chief of the Nawab's spies to Omichund. The banker was arrested and imprisoned in the fort. And Omichund, who was "implacable in his resentments," never forgave the insult and injury. His endeavours to mitigate things, when he really found they were coming to extremities, Holwell states, were sincere enough,

"until his imprisonment by the President, an Act of his power and sole authority, for which the pretence made use of was in my judgment by no means sufficient: the correspondence detected between him and Rajaram Harkarah (the Suba's Head Spy), which was read in the presence of many of us, contained in our opinions nothing to vindicate it, nor had your President even the consent or approbation of his Council for this step, or that I ever remember acquired it."

When Omichund was arrested his brother-in-law concealed himself in the women's apartments. The next day a body of peons were sent to arrest him and Kissendas. The latter, who had gathered around him a large number of armed retainers, vigorously defended his house, drove the peons away, "and took some of them prisoners, whom he treated very barbarously." Lieutenant Blagg was now sent with thirty

Europeans, who stormed the house and "took him with all his arms, which was a very large quantity." At Omichund's house the resistance was equally desperate. When further defence was hopeless the head of his followers,

"who was an Indian of a high caste, set fire to the house, and in order to save the women of the family from the dishonour of being exposed to strangers, entered their apartments, and killed, it is said, thirteen of them with his own hand, after which he stabbed himself, but, contrary to his intentions, not mortally."

Kissendas was taken a prisoner into the fort: "Juggernaut Sing, the Jemmautdar or Head Peon, was conveyed away by his followers."

Meanwhile, Surajah Dowla was marching in hot haste towards Calcutta. Many of his troops died of fatigue, many more were struck down by the sun, but he pushed on. On June 15 he reached Hugli, and his army crossed the river in a vast fleet of boats, which had accompanied him on his march. Early in the morning of June 16 the inhabitants of Calcutta were alarmed by the tidings that he was close at hand. The Englishwomen left their houses and retired to the fort; the Portuguese or black Christians—men, women, and children—about 2,000 in number, also sought shelter within its walls. The natives fled from the town. About noon the booming of guns confirmed the news. The advanced guard of the royal army had reached Chitpur, the northern suburb, and had opened a brisk cannonade on the *Fortune* ketch and *Chance* sloop, that had been sent up the river to assist the garrison of the redoubt at Perrin's. It consisted of only twenty Europeans, commanded by Edward Piccard,[1] ensign. The ships, by keeping a quick fire, maintained their station, "upon which the enemy turned their whole force upon the redoubt, and accordingly brought up their cannon on elephants to the edge of a small wood, to the northward of the fosse," over which there was a drawbridge. Six guns were playing on the redoubt and the sloop when Lieutenant Blagg, with 40 Europeans, an 18-pounder, and two brass

[1] Also spelt Picard, Paccard, and Pischard.

field-pieces, arrived. Under the fire of their cannon and small-arms the enemy, 4,000 strong, made several attempts to force a passage across the bridge, but " our little troop " checked them by a constant platoon fire, " as likewise by playing smartly the two three-pounders." For hours the unequal contest raged. It was half-past six when the enemy, seeing the picquet advancing, retired into the grove.

> " At midnight nothing was moving in the thickets; for every man, after eating his meal, had as usual betook himself to sleep; which Ensign Piccard, who had served on the coast of Coromandel, suspected from their silence, and crossing the rivulet at midnight with his party, seized and spiked the four pieces of cannon, beat up and drove all the troops out of the thicket, and returned without the loss of a man."

The enemy must have sustained a considerable loss in their attack, " for seventy-nine of their dead were found the next morning, most of them killed with cannon-shot at the corner of the wood where they had brought up their artillery."

The main body of the enemy, on desisting from their attack, " directly drew off their artillery and filed off in very large columns towards Dum Dum plains." This movement was due to the advice of Omichund's head peon, who, in spite of his wounds, was put upon his horse and led to Surajah Dowla, " whom he informed of the transactions relating to his master's imprisonment; and when the enemy was repulsed at Baagbazar he led the van of the army to the eastward, and directed them to the avenues by which they could enter our bounds." During the night the enemy reached Cow Cross Bridge, where they encamped " behind the brick-kilns, and stretched from the bungalows as far as Govinderam Metre's Garden on the Dum Dum road." At Cow Cross Bridge were posted 1,000 peons and *buxerries* (hired match-lock men), who deserted to the enemy. Next morning (June 17) Monsieur Le Beaume, " who was a French officer, and left Chandnagar on a point of honour, requested permission to take possession of the gaol, about 200 yards advanced before the Battery A (eastern battery), and where three roads terminated into the place." He was sent with 12 military and militia, 40 *buxerries*, and 2 cannon, to take possession of it. "He broke embrasures through the gaol-house for the cannon, and made loopholes all round for the musquetry." The enemy, however, did not appear in sight of the batteries that day, "but they entered the skirts of the town, plundering and burning all they met on their way, especially the Black merchants' houses." Many of them were taken prisoners. Their accounts of the Nawab's situation and strength varied so much that little dependence could be placed on them.

> "Our own Intelligence all along from our spies was equally so. These Prisoners in general told us that he had all the Cossinbuzar's cannon, and 10 or 15 pieces, which he brought from Muscadabad, of a larger size, besides numbers of swivels and wall pieces mounted on camels and elephants. That his troops consisted of 20,000 to 30,000 Horse and Foot."

The garrison was also advised by their spies and prisoners that the Nawab's artillery "was commanded by a French Renegade who had been an officer at Pondicherry, and gave himself the Title of Marquis de St. Jaque,[1] and had under his command 25 Europeans and 80 Chittygam Fringees." By evening the enemy had set fire to the great bazaar and many parts of the Black Town and the English, all the bazaar, and native huts to the eastward and southward, "which burnt till morning, and being so very extensive and near, formed a scene too horrible for language." That night the peons and matchlock-men, to the number of 500, deserted to the enemy, as the lascars and coolies had done some days before.

> "That we had not a Black Fellow to draw or work a gun, not even to carry a cotton bale or sandbag on ye Ramparts; and what work of that kind had been done was by the Military and Militia. This want of workmen at last and Scarcity at ye beginning harras'd us Prodigiously, and prevented our doing several works that would have been necessary."

Early on the morning of the 18th the enemy appeared in all quarters of the town, and the tactics they intended to

[1] Marquis de St. Jacques.

pursue soon became apparent. They meant to force their way into the lines, not by attacking the batteries, but by creeping into the different houses. The garrison "accordingly fortified some of the houses which they thought commanded the batteries with as many as could possibly be spared." But they had very few to spare. The fighting men of the garrison were so small a number that they found it difficult to perform their ordinary duties and also guard the crowd of prisoners. "The same morning," writes William Tooke, "orders were issued out that no quarter was to be given to the enemy, the prison being but a very small place, was full, and among other prisoners was Omichund." About eight o'clock a large body of the enemy took possession of the houses adjoining the southern battery, whence they opened a destructive fire of musketry and wall-pieces. The guns of the battery were turned against these houses, but they had little effect on the hard Indian mortar. However, Buchanan, who was in command, and his gallant men fought on strongly and sent small bodies of men to hold the houses to the left of the battery, so that their flank might not be turned through any of the avenues in that direction.

An hour later a column of the enemy rushed up the narrow street leading to the northern battery, commanded by Lieutenant-Captain Smith. The guns opened fire with grape, and "smote them with such effect that they went to confusion." Many took shelter in the adjoining streets, "from whence they came out in small parties and continued a desultory fire." A platoon with a field-piece was detached to drive them out of the cross-streets, which was easily effected. They then proceeded along the southern street, until they lost sight of the battery. The enemy, seeing their error, returned through the cross-streets to cut off their retreat, "but yielded again to the field-pieces and the fire of the platoon." Soon after the whole body went away and joined those who were employed against the eastern battery.

About eleven o'clock the enemy brought two cannon to bear on the gaol, "one of them an 18 lb. by the size of the balls." Ensign Carstairs with twenty men and two field-pieces was sent to reinforce Le Beaume. "But the walls of the gaol-house were so weak that they were hardly any defence against their cannon." However, the gallant garrison held it till about two, "when Le Beaume and Ensign Carstairs, being both wounded, and numbers of their men killed, had liberty to retire within Captain Clayton's Battery." The enemy instantly took possession of the gaol and all the adjacent houses.

"Tho' our men from the tops and windows of the houses kept a constant fire on them as they advanced, and our cannon from the Fort and our Batterys played on every house they cou'd see them in possession of, and endeavour'd, tho' with little success, to fling shell amongst them (which had they been properly fitted for service would have been of more use than our cannon), yet the superiority of their numbers under cover of the Houses at all quarters made it impossible for our people to withstand such showers of small shott as they fired into the houses we had possession of."

At one o'clock Captain Clayton recalled all his out-parties. He had been reinforced with an 18-pounder "to endeavour to demolish the houses round about," but all their endeavours proved ineffectual. From the three houses on the right and two on the left the enemy poured a murderous fire into the east battery. Only those who were working the guns remained; the rest took shelter in the mayor's court, from whence a soldier came forth to face the storm of cannonade and musketry when a comrade fell at the guns. At four o'clock a large body of the enemy forced the palisade at the farther or western end of the Rope Walk, and made a rush down the lane to take the battery. The gunners got one of the 18-pounders to bear on them, and "stopped their career with much slaughter, the Fort at the same time keeping a warm fire upon them from the Bastions." For an hour the hurricane raged. The enemy "had now possessed the Houses in all quarters of the town in Multitudes, and by their superiority obliged most of the men to quit the Houses they occupied." They threatened to attack the battery in flank, and cut off their retreat. About five o'clock Captain Clayton ordered Mr. Holwell, who, "as Captain of the first company of militia, was stationed under him at this Battery with a detachment of militia, to go down to the Fort and represent the state of the Battery, and receive orders whether it should be withdrawn or maintained." He hastened to the fort and

"the orders were to withdraw it immediately and spike up the cannon we could not bring off. I returned with these orders, and to my astonishment found the two 18-Pounders and one of the 6-Pounders on the Battery spiked up, and the Post in such confusion as bars all description. There was nothing could have prevented their bringing off the cannon and making the most regular and soldier-like retreat, had we been commanded by an officer of Resolution and Judgment, but as it was, our Retreat had more the appearance of a confused Rout, bringing off only one Field-Piece, and the cannon spiked with so little art that they were easily drilled and turned against us."

At the southern battery Captain Buchanan, finding himself pressed in front and his communication with the fort threatened, fell back upon an inner battery close to the Park gate, leaving one of his field-pieces at the corner of the Park wall to cover his retirement. To the east of the southern battery was a palisade which was overlooked by two large houses, one on each hand. A sergeant and sixteen soldiers were posted on one of them. Lieutenant Blagg "and ten of our volunteers (8 of them your covenanted servants)" were dispatched from Captain Buchanan's post to sustain them, "and they threw themselves into the other house (Captain Minchin's), from the top of which they made a great slaughter of the enemy." About three o'clock Captain Clayton withdrew the garrison from the neighbouring house. Soon after the sergeant and sixteen men who defended the palisade deserted. The enemy broke it down, and rushing in, took possession of all the houses around—"nay, even of that house itself, and barricaded the doors up to the very top of the house, which passage to the top being very narrow, they did not dare to attempt." Deserted and begirt by enemies, Blagg and his ten volunteers held the house resolutely. A destructive fire was poured on them from the neighbouring houses, and "they were in no small danger from our own guns at the factory, who were at that time playing very smartly on the enemy." At seven o'clock their ammunition was exhausted. An attempt had been made to relieve them, and had failed. Nothing was left but to sally forth. The door was burst open, and they made for a lane at the back of the house, "in the hope of getting under shelter of our guns." They found the avenue crowded with the enemy. "Messrs. Smith and Wilkinson, two of the party, having imprudently advanced a little too far, were cut to pieces, though the first killed 4 or 5 of the enemy before he fell; the remainder, by making good use of their bayonets (not having a single charge left), gained the front gate of the house." By this time the enemy had taken possession of the whole square. Blagg and his eight comrades fighting gallantly, ran the gauntlet of their fire till they reached the field-piece at the corner of the Park wall, "which, playing upon the enemy, drove them to a greater distance."

Captain Buchanan was ordered to post a lieutenant and thirty men at the Company's House, and to march the rest into the factory, "which he did, having made a very fine retreat by securing all his ammunition, and without the loss of a gun except an 18-pounder which was sent to the inner battery, and upon his being ordered away so abruptly he eft it spiked up." As the inner battery was within pistol-shot of the walls, and commanded two out of the three roads of the place, its abandonment was a grave error. Orders were now sent to Lieutenant-Captain Smith to withdraw from the northern battery, and boats were dispatched which brought away Piccard and his twenty men from Perrin's redoubt. When darkness fell, all three batteries had been abandoned, "and most people said that the fall of them would be attended with fatal consequences."

That night was one of great tumult and confusion in the fort. The native Portuguese women filled the passages with loud clamour, and crowded the back gate in order to force their way on board the ships. At nine o'clock a council of war was held, and "the European women were ordered on board the ships, and Colonel Manningham and Lieutenant-Colonel Frankland permitted to see them safe there." The detachment in the Company's House having been much galled by the enemy's fire from the next house to the south, "thought their situation too dangerous to be maintained on ye approach of Day," and were withdrawn. At midnight the enemy were heard approaching to escalade the terraces of the warehouses. Every man of the garrison was so harassed and fatigued for want of rest by constant duty for two days, "that it was impossible to rouse them even if ye enemy had been scaling ye walls. Three different times did ye Drums beat to arms, but in vain, not a man could be got to stand to their arms, tho' we had frequent Alarms of ye enemy's preparing ladders under our walls to scale them." The enemy, however, hearing the drums beat, thought the garrison prepared, and retreated.

About one o'clock in the morning a second council of war was held.

"The majority of the military officers gave it as their opinion, that it was impracticable to defend the fort with so small a garrison and so unprovided with stores for a siege, against the numerous army of the enemy; the artillery officers reported we had not enough powder and shot for three days; our bombs and grenades were of no use, the fusees being spoiled by the dampness of the climate owing to their being filled some years, and never looked into afterwards."

It was therefore unanimously agreed that a retreat to the ships was the best step to be taken. A dispute arose "whether that retreat ought to be made immediately, under favour of the night, or deferred till the next day, and in what manner to conduct a general retreat without confusion or tumult." Mr. Cooke adds: "It was at least resolved to defer the retreat till the next night, and that all the next day should be employed in embarking the Portuguese women and our most valuable effects, by which means we should avoid the disorder we dreaded."

At break of day the enemy renewed their attack and cannonaded the fort very briskly from two or three different batteries, besides keeping up a hot fire from the houses they had occupied. They had, however, neglected to take possession of the Company's House, "and Ensign Piccard having offered to maintain it with twenty military, his proposal was readily agreed to." But to hold it was an impossible task. From the house-tops, ensconced behind the walls of the enclosure, the enemy sent their bullets fast. Every loophole was a target for them, but the fire was returned with steadiness and not without effect. But though many of them fell, "their loss in so great a multitude was scarcely felt and immediately supplied." At nine o'clock Ensign Piccard was brought in wounded from the Company's House, and by noon the garrisons had been withdrawn from all the houses inside the walls. The courage of the enemy increased with their success, whilst confusion and terror prevailed more and more in the garrison. Then from the ramparts they saw a sight which filled them with despair. The ships were floating down the river.

Early in the morning the embarkation of the women had begun. But as no orders for the general retreat had been issued, "many of the inhabitants imagined every body was to shift for himself," and "every one endeavoured to get on board such vessel as he could, and to be the first to be embarked." The boats were filled with more than they could carry, and several were upset. "Most of those who had crowded into them were drowned, and such as floated with the tide to the shore were either made prisoners or massacred; for the enemy had taken possession of all the houses and inclosures along the bank of the river, from which stations they shot fire-arrows into the ships and vessels, in hope of burning them." The Captain of the *Doddalay*,[1] fearing that she would be burnt, hoisted anchor, and between nine and ten o'clock dropped down to Surman Garden. Then every ship and sloop followed the example, and weighing anchor floated down the stream. The spectacle of the ships creeping away increased the confusion and uproar on the bank. One who was present writes:

[1] Also spelt Doddaly, Dodalay, and Dodley.

"The moment it was observed many of the gentlemen on shore (who perhaps never dreamt of leaving the factory till everybody did) immediately jumped into such boats as were at the factory stairs and rowed to the ships. Among those who left the Factory in this unaccountable manner were the Governor, Mr. Drake, Mr. Mackett, Captain-Commandant Minchen, and Captain Grave."

Drake attributes his desertion to a momentary act of panic. It is admitted that he had freely exposed himself to danger when visiting the fortifications. But when the supreme test came, an evil conscience and love of life prevailed. For Mackett there is some excuse. He had the previous night left his wife on board the *Doddalay*, "dangerously ill as she was, and returned to the Fort, though the strongest persuasions, I am well informed," says Holwell, "were used to detain him on Board."

The spirit of the soldiers swelled up high and fierce against the dastards who had deserted them. Nothing was heard for some time but execrations against the fugitives. No sooner, however, had the first burst of rage at their cowardice spent itself than the garrison, "one and all," called upon Mr. Holwell to assume the command. A Council was hastily summoned, and the senior member of Council on shore was told that the garrison had elected Mr. Holwell their governor. On assuming the chief civil and military command Holwell exercised his authority with resolution. He locked the western gate in order to prevent further desertion. The whole force which he could muster in defence of the fort, including the militia, amounted only to 190 men, but he might be able to hold it until the ships could be made use of. They lay a mile distant. "Signals were thrown out from every part of the fort for the ships to come up again to their stations. But there never was a single effort made to send a boat or vessel to bring off any part of the garrison."

Meanwhile the enemy pressed on their attack with great vigour. From the church they galled the garrison in a terrible manner, and killed and wounded a prodigious number.

"In order to prevent this havoc as much as possible, we got up a quantity of broadcloth in bales, with which we made traverses along the curtains and bastions; we fixed up likewise some bales of cotton against the parapets (which were very thin and of brick-work only) to resist the cannon-balls, and did everything in our power to baffle their attempts."

But by no expedient could they hold out much longer. In the heat of the fight a gleam of hope appeared. The *Prince George* (a Company's ship employed in the country) had been ordered up to Perrin's to assist that redoubt, and when the garrison had been withdrawn from it the *Prince George* was directed to fall down to her station opposite the south-eastern bastion of the fort. About noon her sails were seen. Two of the garrison were immediately sent on board with positive instructions to the commander to bring his ship as near the fort as he could. As she bore down with the sails set all were filled with the expectation of a safe retreat that night. "But it was otherwise determined by Providence; for by some strange fatality the *Prince George* run aground a little above the factory (owing to the Pilot's misconduct, who lost his presence of mind) and was never got off." Death now stared them in the face.

The enemy suspended their attack as usual, when it grew dark, says Cooke,

"but the night was not less dreadful on that account; the Company's House, Mr. Cruttenden's, Mr. Nixon's, Doctor Knox's, and the marine yards were now in flames, and exhibited a spectacle of unspeakable horror. We were surrounded on all sides by the Nabob's forces, which made a retreat by land impracticable; and we had not even the shadow of a prospect to effect a retreat by water, after the *Prince George* run aground."

On the Sunday morning, June 25, the besiegers renewed their cannonade, and pushed the siege with much more warmth and vigour than ever they had done. About eight o'clock they attempted to break into the fort by means of some windows in the eastern curtain which the besieged had neglected to brick up. Every man rushed to the spot, and there was stiff fighting to keep them out. At this moment an alarm was spread that the enemy were scaling the north-west bastion, and to defend it a stubborn conflict ensued. For above an hour the hottest fire "that we had yet seen" continued on both sides. "The besiegers at length gave over their efforts, and retired with great loss; but they continued to cannonade very briskly from the batteries, and with their wall-pieces and musquetry did us infinite mischief." About fifty Europeans perished on the bastion.

Early in the morning Holwell, "to quiet the minds of everybody as much as lies in my power," had a letter written by Omichund to Manikchand, the Governor of Hugli, who commanded a considerable body of the enemy's troops, requesting him to "use his influence with the Suba to order his Troop to cease Hostilities; that We were ready to obey His commands, and persisted only in defending the Fort in preservation of our Lives and Honours." An Armenian undertook to carry the letter to Manikchand, and was suffered to pass. About noon the enemy, after their mortifying repulse, ceased to fire. For two hours not one of them was to be seen. Men began to hope that Omichund's letter had reached Surajah Dowla, and had produced the desired effect. But no answer ever came. At two o'clock the enemy appeared again, but they did not resume their attack with any vigour. "About four afternoon word was brought me," says Holwell, "that some of the enemy was advancing with a Flagg in his Hand, and called us to cease firing, and that We should have quarter if We surrendered: this was judged a favourable juncture to answer it with a Flagg of Truce." Accordingly Holwell repaired with the flag to the original south-eastern bastion, where Captain Buchanan was posted, and ordered firing to cease.

"I had a letter prepared with me addressed to Roy Doolub, the General of the Forces, Importing an overture to cease hostilities until the Suba could be wrote to and His pleasure known. This Letter I threw over the Ramparts and Hoisted the Flagg of Truce on the Bastion. The Letter was taken up by the Person who advanced with the Flagg, who retired with it. Soon after multitudes of the Enemy came out of their hiding-Places round us and Flocked under the Walls; a short Parley ensued. I demanded a Truce to Hostilities untill the Suba's pleasure could be known. To which I was answered by one of His officers from below that the Suba was there, and His pleasure was that we should have quarter. I was going to reply when at that Instant Mr. William Baillie, standing near me, was slightly wounded by a Muskett-ball from the enemy on the side of the Head, and Word was brought to me that they were attempting to force the South-West Barrier and were cutting at the Eastern Gate."

The enemy had treacherously made use of the truce not only to crowd in multitudes under the walls, but with ladders and bamboos they scaled the north-west bastion and the wall to the southward, which was low. The gallant Blagg defended the bastion till he and his men were cut to pieces. "Many were slain on the walls: all who wore red coats without mercy." As soon as it was known that the enemy had driven the besieged from the walls, "a Dutchman of the Artillery Company," says Cooke, "broke open the back door of the factory, and with many others attempted to escape." Holwell, on hearing that the western gate was forced by our own people, and betrayed, instantly sent Ensign Walcott with orders to see if there was no possibility of securing it again. "He returned and told me it was impossible, for the Locks and Bolts were forced off." Holwell now saw that the courtyard below was thronged with the enemy, who had entered by the open gate. Thinking "that further opposition would not only be fruitless, but might be attended with bad consequences to the garrison," he and Captain Buchanan "delivered up their swords to a Jemmautdar (native officer) that had scaled the walls and seemed to act with some authority among the Moors." The few troops who had survived surrendered prisoners of war.

So ended the siege of Calcutta. For three days a few soldiers and a motley gathering of civilians held a range of fragile buildings, encircled by a mouldering wall, against an army furnished with guns and Europeans trained to use them, and a vast host of armed men inspired by hatred and fanaticism. It ended in disaster, but the men who did the fighting showed at the siege of Calcutta English courage at its very best.

Immediately after the few troops who had survived the siege of Calcutta had surrendered prisoners of war, the Company's factory was filled with the enemy, who began to plunder it.

> "We were rifled of our watches, buckles, buttons, &c.," says Cooke, "but no further violence offered to our person. The Bales of broad cloth, chests of coral, Plate and Treasure laying in the apartments of the gentlemen who resided in the factory were broke open, and the enemy were wholly taken up in plundering till the Subah entered the Fort, which was a little after five in the afternoon carried in a kind of Litter; his younger brother accompanied him in another. Surajah Dowlah seemed astonished to find so small a garrison, and immediately enquired for Mr. Drake, with whom he appeared much incensed."

But Mr. Drake, fearing with good reason the vengeance of Surajah Dowla, was at the time sailing down the Hugli. Orme, in his "Narrative of the Loss of Calcutta, composed at Madras, 1756," says:

> "The Nabob entered the fort in the afternoon and admired the building, adding that the English must be fools to oblige him to drive them out of so fine a city. He ordered Mr. Holwell, who had been put in irons, to be freed from them, and that the English in general who were become his prisoners should be treated with humanity."

Cooke states that Holwell was brought before the Nawab "with his hands bound, and upon complaining of that usage the Nabob gave orders for loosing his hands, and assured him, upon the faith of a soldier, that not a hair of our heads should be touched." Cooke's statement is confirmed by Holwell, who writes:

> "The Suba and his troops were in possession of the fort before six in the evening. I had in all three interviews with him: the last in durbar before seven, when he repeated his assurances to me, *on the word of a soldier*, that no harm should come to us; and I believe his orders were only general, that we should for that night be secured."

After mentioning the promises of Surajah Dowla that the prisoners should not be molested, Cooke adds: "The Nawab then held a kind of durbar in the open area, sitting in his litter, where Kissendas (who had been kept a prisoner by us during the siege) was sent for and publicly presented with a *surpaw* or honorary dress." Orme, in his history, also mentions the important fact that the Nawab "immediately ordered Omichund and Kissendas to be brought before him, and received them with civility." Drake in his "Narrative of the Succession of Surajah Dowla and of the Siege of Calcutta," mentions that "Mr. Holwell was conducted to him with his hands bound. Omichund and Kissendas were released and permitted to pay their respects to the Nawab, and it is reported that the former's houses were, during the siege, guarded and protected by the enemy's force from plunder." Orme further relates that Surajah Dowla

> "having bid some officers go and take possession of the Company's treasury, he proceeded to the principal apartment of the factory, where he sat in state and received the compliments of his Court and Attendants in magnificent expressions of his prowess and good fortune. Soon after he sent for Mr. Holwell, to whom he expressed much resentment at the presumption of the English in daring to defend the fort, and much dissatisfaction at the smallness of the sum found in the Treasury, which did not exceed 50,000 rupees. Mr. Holwell had two other conferences with him on the subject before seven o'clock, when the Nabob dismissed him with repeated assurances, on the word of a soldier, that he should suffer no harm."

The reception of Kissendas and Omichund with honour by Surajah Dowla tends to confirm the suspicion felt at the time that the true nature of the visit of Kissendas to Calcutta was to embroil the English with Alivardi Khan, and it clearly proves that they must have rendered him a signal secret service. The Nawab, says John Cooke, after ordering the Armenians and Portuguese to be set at liberty, between six and seven left the fort, and Manikchand, the Governor of Hugli, was put in charge of it. After the departure of the Nawab his troops searched every part of the factory to prevent treachery, "and in the dusk of the evening the Mussalmen sang a thanksgiving to Allah for the success they had met with." Hitherto the prisoners had fared extremely well, as Cooke states, "and had been left unmolested in person so long," that they even entertained hopes "not only of getting our liberty," but of being suffered to re-establish their affairs and carry on their business upon the terms the Nawab had indicated when he captured Cossimbazar on his way to Calcutta. "But these hopes and expectations were very soon changed into as great a reverse as human creatures ever felt." When Holwell returned to his unfortunate companions, darkness had begun swiftly to fall, and they were ordered by their guard to collect in one body and sit down quietly under "the arched veranda or piazza" to the south of the eastern or main gateway. The piazza was of arched masonry, and along the inner pillars ran a small parapet wall, forming with the curtain (or outer wall) of the fort a long chamber known as "the barracks." A wooden platform for the soldiers to sleep on was fastened along the curtain wall, but owing to the pillars being low, in order to protect the soldiers from the sun and rain, little light or air entered the barracks from the parade which it faced. Standing on the parade and looking towards the east, on the right of the inner gate, one saw the court of guard, and adjoining it the low, narrow barracks stretching to the south-eastern bastion, and in front of them the piazza, with its double row of arches. A small portion of the barracks abutting this bastion had been converted into a cell, "where our soldiers," says Cooke, "were usually confined in the stocks." And it had been always called by them "the Black Hole." James Mill, the historian, who never wearies of fouling the fair fame of his countrymen, writes :

> "The atrocities of English imprisonment at home, not then exposed to detestation by the labour of Howard, too naturally reconciled Englishmen abroad to the use of dungeons—of *Black Holes.* What had they to do with a *black hole?* Had *no black hole* existed (as none ought to exist anywhere, least of all in the sultry and unwholesome climate of Bengal), those who perished in the Black Hole of Calcutta would have experienced a different fate."

The Black Hole was not a dungeon. It was an ordinary cell, to be found in every garrison, where two or three drunken soldiers could be confined till they recovered their carouse.[1] Cooke states it was "about 18 feet long and 14 wide, with only two holes, barricaded with iron bars, to let in air, which opened into a low piazza." Holwell describes it as "a cube of about eighteen feet, shut up to the eastward and southward by dead walls, and by a wall and door to the north, open only to the westward by two windows." Besides the guard at the barracks,

> "another was placed at the foot of the stairs at the south end of this veranda, leading into the south-east bastion, to prevent any of us escaping that way. On the parade (where you will remember the two twenty-four pounders stood) were also drawn up in a line four or five hundred gun-men with lighted matches."

As the prisoners sat under the arches of the veranda they saw a red glare in the sky. Various were the conjectures at its appearance. Then flames were seen dancing up in the dark night, and the sinister crackling of fire was heard. The factory was burning to the right and left of them—"to the right the Armoury and Laboratory, to the left the Carpenter's yard"; and "as the fire advanced with rapidity on both sides, it was the prevailing opinion that they intended suffocating us between two fires." The fearful meaning seemed to be confirmed by the appearance of some officers and men with lighted torches in their hands, who went into all the apartments under the easterly curtains—to the right of the miserable assembly. They intended to fire them, to carry out more swiftly and certainly their dark resolve. "On this we presently came to a resolution of rushing on the guard, seizing their scimetars, and attacking the troops upon the parade rather than be thus tamely roasted to death." At the request of some of his companions Holwell advanced to see if they were really setting fire to the apartments, and discovered that their worst fears were not well founded. They were only searching for a place in which to confine the prisoners. At this moment the brave Holwell had an opportunity

[1] The Black Hole was the *official* designation down to 1868, when it was formally abolished. *Vide* Army Ord. and Reg., 1868.

to escape, and there occurred an act of genuine chivalry which places the name of Leach, the Company's smith, and clerk of the parish, high in the splendid calendar of England's heroes. To him Holwell had in many instance been a friend.

> "This man had made his escape when the Moors entered the fort, and returned just as it was dark, to tell me he had provided a boat, and would ensure my escape, if I would follow him through a passage few were acquainted with, and by which he had entered. (This might easily have been accomplished, as the guard put over us took but slight notice of us.) I thanked him in the best terms I was able; but told him it was a step I could not prevail on myself to take, as I should thereby very ill repay the attachment the gentlemen and the garrison had shown me; and that I was resolved to share their fate, be it what it would; but pressed him to secure his own escape without loss of time, to which he gallantly replied, that 'then he was resolved to share mine, and would not leave me.'"

Holwell had scarce time to answer Leach when he saw part of the guard drawn up on the parade advance towards them. They were accompanied by the officers who had been viewing the room, and "they ordered us all to rise and go into the barracks to the left of the court of guard." The prisoners went more readily, as they were pleased "with the prospect of passing a comfortable night on the platform." Short-lived was their joy. No sooner had they entered the barracks than the guard advanced "to the inner arches and parapet wall" and ordered them to go into the Black Hole. A body of men with clubs and drawn scimitars from the court of guard enforced the command by pressing upon them.

> "This stroke was so sudden, so unexpected, and the throng and pressure so great upon us next the door of the Black Hole prison, that there was no resisting it; but like one agitated wave impelling another, we were obliged to give way and enter; the rest followed like a torrent, few amongst us, the soldiers excepted, having the least idea of the dimensions or nature of a place we had never seen; for if we had, we should at all events have rushed upon the guard and been, as the lesser evil, by our own choice cut to pieces."

The door was immediately locked. It was eight o'clock "on a close sultry night in Bengal." "The number of souls," says Cooke, "thrust into this dungeon were near 150. Among which was one woman: and twelve of the wounded officers."[1] The instant the miserable survivors of the siege cast their eyes round and saw the size and situation of the room, they knew that they had escaped the shot and the sword only to perish by a more cruel death—suffocation. "Many unsuccessful attempts were made to force the door; for having nothing but our hands to work with, and the door opening forward, all endeavours were vain and fruitless." The baffled victims began to rave and utter curses. Holwell commanded silence, and speaking to them

"in the most pathetic and moving terms which occurred, I begged and intreated, that as they had paid a ready obedience to me in the day, they would now for their own sakes, and for the sakes of those who were dear to them, and were interested in the preservation of their lives, regard the advice I had to give them. I assured them, the return of day would give us air and liberty; urged to them that the only chance we had left for sustaining this misfortune, and surviving the night, was the preserving a calm mind and quiet resignation to our fate; intreating them to curb, as much as possible, every agitation of mind and body, as raving and giving a loose to their passions could answer no purpose, but that of hastening their destruction."

The ferment subsided. Holwell, who had been amongst the first to enter the cell, had got possession of the window nearest the door, "and took Messrs. Coles and Scot into the window with me, they being both wounded (the first, I believe, mortally)." Amongst the guards posted at the window Holwell observed an old native officer "who seemed to carry some compassion for us in his countenance." He called him and begged him to get the prisoners separated into two chambers. For this service he promised him a thousand rupees in the morning. In a few minutes he returned and said it was impossible. "I then thought I had been deficient in my offer, and promised him two thousand. He withdrew a

[1] Holwell states the number to be "a hundred and forty-six wretches exhausted by constant fatigue and action." Captain Grant writes: "Prisoners to the number of about 200 Europeans, Portuguese, and Armenians were at night shut up in ye Black Hole." Captain James Mill states: "But most of those who remained in the fort were put in the Black Hole, to the number of 144 men, women, and children."

second time, but returned soon, and (with, I believe, much real pity and concern) told me it was not practicable: that it could not be done but by the Suba's orders, and no one dared awake him." By "Suba" the man on duty must have meant the Governor, for Surajah Dowla, according to Cooke, had left the fort.

The heat and stench rapidly grew intolerable. Everyone fell into a profuse perspiration. "This consequently brought on a raging thirst, which still increased in proportion as the body was drained of its moisture." Various expedients were thought of to give more room and air. It was moved to put off their clothes. In a few minutes every man was stripped except Holwell, "Mr. Court, and the two wounded young gentlemen by me." Every hat was put in motion. Then it was proposed that all should sit down on their hams.

> "As they were truly in the situation of drowning wretches, no wonder they caught at everything that bore a flattering appearance of saving them. This expedient was several times put in practice, and at each time many of the poor creatures whose natural strength was less than others, or had been more exhausted, and could not immediately recover their legs, as others did, when the word was given to rise, fell to rise no more; for they were instantly trod to death or suffocated. When the whole body sat down, they were so closely wedged together, that they were obliged to use many efforts before they could put themselves in motion to get up again."

Before an hour passed away every man's thirst grew intolerable and respiration difficult. Another attempt was made to force the door, but in vain. Then the captives heaped insults on the guard, to provoke them to fire on them. Kindly death relieved some of them. Some went mad. "Water! Water!" became the general cry. The old native officer, taking pity on them, ordered some to be brought—"little dreaming, I believe," says Holwell, "of its fatal effects." The water appeared. There was, however, no means of conveying it into the prison "but by hats forced through the bar." Holwell, Coles, and Scot at the window brought it in as quickly as possible. But "though we brought full hats within the bars, there ensued such violent struggles and frequent contests to get at it that before it reached the lips of any one there would be scarcely a small teacupful left in them. These supplies, like sprinkling water on fire, only served to feed and raise the flame."

Those at the back of the cell cried and raved and implored, "calling on me by the tender considerations of friendship and affection." Several quitted the other window, "the only chance they had for life," to force their way to the water. "The strength and force upon the window grew greater and greater. Many forcing their passage from the further part of the room, pressed down those in their way who had less strength, and trampled them to death." Holwell's friend Baillie and several others lay dead at his feet,

"and were now trampled upon by every corporal or common soldier, who, by the help of more robust constitutions, had forced their way to the window, and held fast by the bars over me, till at last I became so pressed and wedged up, I was deprived of all motion."

Holwell begged them, "as the last instance of their regard," that they would relax their pressure and allow him to leave the window or to die in quiet.

"They gave way, and with much difficulty I forced a passage into the centre of the prison, where the throng was less by the many dead (then, I believe, amounting to one-third) and the number who flocked to the windows; for by this time they had water also at the other window."

He strode over the dead bodies to the platform, and seated himself opposite the second window.

"Here my poor friend Mr. Eyre came staggering over the dead to me, and, with his usual coolness and good-nature, asked me how I did; but fell and expired before I had time to make him a reply."

But Holwell's thirst and the difficulty of breathing greatly increasing, he determined to push his way to the window opposite him,

"and by an effort of double the strength I ever before possessed, gained the third rank of it, with one hand seized a bar, and by that means gained a second, though I think there were at least six or seven ranks between me and the window."

The difficulty of breathing ceased, but the thirst grew intolerable. He called aloud for "*Water, for God's sake!*" They thought he was among the dead. But as soon as they heard his voice these poor creatures, who had fought for every drop of water, "had still the respect and tenderness for me to cry out, '*Give him water! Give him water!*'" And never did Englishmen bear themselves more nobly than this. "Nor would one of those at the window attempt to touch it till I had drunk." The water, however, afforded Holwell no relief. It only increased his thirst.

"So I determined to drink no more, but patiently wait the event; and kept my mouth moist from time to time by sucking the perspiration off my shirt-sleeves, and catching the drops as they fell like heavy rain from my head and face: you can hardly imagine how unhappy I was if any of them escaped my mouth."

Then was brought about an incident with a touch of grim humour.

"Whilst I was at this second window I was observed by one of my miserable companions on the right of me, in the expedient of allaying my thirst by sucking my shirt-sleeves. He took the hint and robbed me from time to time of a considerable part of my store; though after I detected him, I had ever the address to begin on that sleeve first, when I thought my reservoirs were sufficiently replenished; and our mouths and noses often met in the contest. The plunderer I found afterwards was a worthy young gentleman in the service, Mr. Lushington, one of the few who escaped from death, and has since paid me the compliment of assuring me he believed he owed his life to the many comfortable draughts he had from the sleeves."

Before he hit upon this expedient Holwell, in an ungovernable fit of thirst, had adopted a more horrible one, "but it was so intensely bitter there was no enduring a second taste, whereas no Bristol water could be more soft or pleasant than what arose from perspiration."

It was now half-past eleven. A large number of the poor wretches living were wild with delirium; some were beyond all control. "Few retained any calmness but the ranks next the windows." "Air! Air!" was the general cry. Fresh torrents of abuse were poured on the guard. Every foul epithet was applied to their sovereign to rouse them to fire

—"every man that could, rushing tumultuously towards the windows with eager hopes of meeting the first shot." Then there arose a general prayer to Heaven that the flames would consume them. "But these failing, they whose strength and spirits were quite exhausted, laid themselves down and expired quietly upon their fellows." Those who had any energy left made a last effort to reach the windows. A few succeeded in scrambling over the backs and heads of those in the first ranks and got hold of the bars, from which there was no removing them. Many sank beneath the pressure and were suffocated. Holwell sustained the weight

"of a heavy man with his knees in my back and the pressure of his whole body on my head. A Dutch serjeant, who had taken his seat upon my left shoulder, and a Topaz (a black Christian soldier) bearing on my right; all which nothing could have enabled me long to support, but the props and pressure equally sustaining me all around. The two latter I frequently dislodged, by shifting my hold on the bars, and driving my knuckles into their ribs; but my friend above stuck fast, and as he held by two bars, was immovable."

An hour slowly crept away. Then, seeing no hope of relief, Holwell thought it better to "leave God and die." He remembered he had a small clasp penknife in his pocket. He determined to open his arteries. "I had got it out when Heaven interposed, and restored me fresh spirits and resolution, with an act of abhorrence of the act of cowardice I was just going to commit." It was now two o'clock. And Holwell was quite exhausted in vainly attempting to shake off the human load. He must quit the window or sink where he was. He determined to quit the window and meet death calmly.

"In the ranks behind was an officer of one of the ships, whose name was Carey, who had behaved with much bravery during the siege (his wife, a fine woman, though country born, would not quit him, but accompanied him into the prison, and was one who survived). This poor wretch had been long raving for water and air. I told him I was determined to give up life, and recommended his gaining my station. On my quitting he made a fruitless attempt to get my place, but the Dutch serjeant who sat on my shoulder supplanted him."

Carey thanked Holwell, and said that he, too, was prepared to give up life. With the utmost labour they forced their way from the window. Then the brave sailor laid himself down to die. "And his death, I believe, was very sudden; for he was a short, full, sanguine man. His strength was great; and I imagine, had he not retired with me, I should never have been able to have found my way." Holwell, finding a stupor coming on, also laid himself down "by that gallant old man the Reverend Mr. Jervas Bellamy, who lay dead with his son the lieutenant hand in hand near the southernmost wall of the prison." He had lain there some little time when athwart his delirious brain there came the dread that he should be trampled upon when dead, "as I myself had done to others." With a supreme effort he raised himself, and gained the platform a second time, when he soon became senseless. "The last trace of sensibility that I have been able to recollect, after my lying down, was my sash being uneasy about my waist, which I untied and threw from me."

Three more hours wore away in misery. When the dawn came the miserable wretches at the windows again implored the guard to release them. But they asked in vain. Then it occurred to one of them to make a search for Holwell, as he might have sufficient influence to obtain their removal from the cell. After a search they discovered him by his shirt under the dead upon the platform. Seeing some signs of life, they carried him to the window.

> "But as life was equally dear to every man (and the stench arising from the dead bodies was grown intolerable), no one would give up his station near the window, so they were obliged to carry me back again. But soon Captain Mills (now captain of the Company's yacht), who was in possession of a seat in the window, had the humanity to offer to resign it. I was again brought by the same gentleman and placed in the window."

Shortly after there came a gleam of hope. A native officer sent by Surajah Dowla arrived. The Nawab had heard of the havoc death had made among the prisoners, and he had dispatched him to inquire if the chief was alive.

> "They showed me to him; told him I had appearance of life remaining, and believed I might recover if the door was opened very soon. This answer being returned to the Suba, an order came immediately for our release, it being then near six in the morning."

The door was thrown open, but it was some time before the survivors could leave that small cell.

> "The little strength remaining amongst the most robust who survived, made it a difficult task to remove the dead piled up against the door; so that I believe it was more than twenty minutes before we obtained a passage out for one at a time."

About twenty-three came out alive. The rest, one hundred and twenty-three persons, "mostly gentlemen and men of hopes," perished through suffocation.

Holwell, on reaching the open air, found himself "in a high putrid fever," and not being able to stand, threw himself on the grass wet with the rain of the monsoon, without the veranda. A message reached him that he must immediately go to the Subah. Supported under each arm by a stalwart sepoy, he limped along, till he came into the Nawab's presence. Surajah Dowla, seeing his condition, ordered a large folio volume, which lay on a heap of plunder, to be brought for him to sit on. "I endeavoured two or three times to speak, but my tongue was dry and without motion. He ordered me water. As soon as I got speech I began to recount the dismal catastrophe of my miserable companions." Orme, in his Narrative, written in 1756, states that Holwell

> "complained loudly to the Nabob of the inhuman barbarities which had been inflicted on his countrymen the preceding night, and added that it was inconsistent with the character of a soldier, as the Nabob was, to see him, a soldier too, in irons for no other cause than having done his duty. The Nabob disavowed any knowledge of the horrors of the preceding night, and seemed, as much as a man naturally cruel could be, affected with what had passed."

Holwell, however, affirms that Surajah Dowla stopped him short with telling him he was well informed of great treasure being buried or secreted in the fort, and that Holwell was privy to it, and that if he expected favour he must discover it.

"I urged everything I could to convince him there was no truth in the information; or that if anything had been done, it was without my knowledge. I reminded him of his repeated assurances to me the day before; but he resumed the subject of the treasure, and all I said seemed to gain no credit with him. I was ordered prisoner under Mhir Muddin, General of the Household troops."

Holwell proceeds to relate that he was taken to the camp of the general's quarters

"within the outward ditch something short of Omychund's garden (which you know is about three miles from the fort), and with me Messieurs Court, Walcot, and Burdet. The rest who survived the fatal night gained their liberty, except Mrs. Carey, who was too young and handsome. The dead bodies were promiscuously thrown into the ditch of our unfinished ravelin, and covered with the earth."

The majority of the survivors at once left the fort and proceeded towards the ships, "which were still in sight"; but when

"they reached Govindpore, in the southern part of the Company's bounds, they were informed that guards were stationed to prevent any persons from passing to the vessels, on which most of them took shelter in deserted huts, where some of the natives, who had served the English in different employments, came and administered to their immediate wants. Two or three, however, ventured, and got to the vessels before sunset."

And so it was a hundred years later, in the dark days of the Mutiny. Many a native who had served the English came at the risk of his life and administered to the wants of his old master. William Lindsay states that

"Cooke and Lushington set out and arrived on board of the ships the same night, we then laying above Buggee Buggee. We had a very warm fire upon us as we passed Tanna's fort, and several of the ships received damage as they passed Buggee Buggee."

Holwell and his three companions were conveyed in a bullock-cart to the camp, "and soon loaded with fetters." They were stowed all four in a sepoy's small tent. All night it rained severely.

"Dismal as this was, it appeared a paradise compared with our lodging the preceding night. Here I became covered from head to foot with large painful boils, the first symptom of my recovery, for until these appeared my fever did not leave me."

The following morning, June 22, they were marched to the town in their fetters under the scorching beams of an intensely hot sun, " and lodged at the Dockhead in the open small veranda fronting the river." " Here the other gentlemen broke out likewise in boils all over their bodies (a happy circumstance which, as I afterwards learned, attended every one who came out of the Black Hole)." On the afternoon of the 24th they were put on board a large boat to carry them to Murshidabad.

> " Our bedstead and bedding were a platform of loose unequal bamboos laid on the bottom timbers; so that when they had been negligent in baling, we frequently waked with half of us in the water. We had hardly any cloaths to our bodies, and nothing but a bit of mat, and a bit or two of old gunny-bag, which we begged at the Dock-head to defend us from the sun, rain, and dews. Our food only rice, and the water alongside, which you know is neither very clean nor very palatable in the rains: but there was enough of it without scrambling."

On reaching the fort at Hugli, Holwell wrote a letter to the native governor (" by means of a pencil and blank leaf of a volume of Archbishop Tillotson's Sermons given us by one of our guard, part of his plunder ") informing him of their miserable plight. The governor " had the humanity " to send three several boats " with fresh provisions, liquor, cloaks, and money " after them, none of which reached them. " But whatever is, is right! Our rice and water were more salutary and proper for us." The river grew too shallow for the large boat, and on the last day of June they were transferred to a small open fishing craft with two of their guard.

> " Here we had a bed of bamboos, something softer, I think, than those of the great boat; that is, they were something smoother, but we were so distressed for room that we could not stir without our fetters bruising our own or one another's boils."

The monsoon having burst, they were exposed to one regular succession of heavy rain or intense sunshine with nothing to protect them.

> " But then don't let me forget our blessings, for by the good-nature of one of our guard, Sheike Bodul, we saw and then latterly

got a few plantains, onions, parched rice with *Taggree* (Molasses), and the bitter green called Carella; all of which were to us luxurious indulgences, and made the rice go down deliciously."

On the morning of July 7 they came in sight of the French factory at Cossimbazar. Holwell persuaded the friendly guard to put in there, and sent a letter to Mr. Law, the chief, who came down to the riverside to see them.

"He gave the Sheike a genteel present for his civilities, and offered him a considerable reward and security, if he would permit us to land for an hour's refreshment; but he replied, his head would pay for the indulgence. After Mr. Law had given us a supply of cloaths, linen, provisions and liquors, and cash, we left his factory with grateful hearts and compliments."

About four that afternoon they landed at Murshidabad, and were led like felons through the streets, "a spectacle to the inhabitants of this populous city," to an open stable not far from the Nawab's palace. Here they were kept in close confinement. Two days later Surajah Dowla returned to his capital, and the prisoners were removed to an open bungalow belonging to a native officer, Bandu Singh, who had commanded their guard when they left Calcutta. They were treated with much kindness and respect by him, "who generally passed some time or other of the day with us, and feasted us with hopes of soon being released." On July 15 the prisoners were taken to the Nawab's palace in the city in order to have an interview with him "and know our fate." But Surajah Dowla could not see them that day, and they were marched to their former lodgings, "the stables, to be at hand, and had the mortification of passing another night there." Next morning a female attendant on the Dowager Princess (grandmother to Surajah Dowla) visited their chief custodian and had a long talk with him. Overhearing a part of the conversation, and finding it was favourable to them, the prisoners elicited from their friendly jailor the whole story. At a feast the preceding night the Begum had solicited their liberty, and the Subah had promised he would release them on the morrow. Great was their joy. But even yet misfortune had not tired of persecuting them. At noon their friend Bandu Singh, the native officer, told them that an order was prepared " and ready to pass the seal " for sending them back in irons to Manikchand, the Governor of Calcutta. They gave up all hope of liberty. They knew they would never get alive out of the hands " of that rapacious harpy, who is a genuine Hindoo in the very worst acceptation of the word." But men in this state of mind, says Holwell, are generally pretty easy; it is hope which gives anxiety. "We dined and laid ourselves down to sleep; and for my own part I never enjoyed a sounder afternoon's nap." Towards five the native officer awoke them with the news that the Nawab would presently pass by on his way to the palace. Rousing themselves, they begged the guard to keep the view clear for them. " When the Suba came in sight we made him the usual salaam; and when he came abreast of us, he ordered his litter to stop, and us to be called to him." The wretched prisoners, laden with fetters, advanced, and Holwell made a short speech, setting forth their sufferings, and petitioning for their liberty.

> " He gave no reply, but ordered a Sootapurdar and Chubdara immediately to cut our irons off, and to conduct us wherever we chose to go, and to take care we received no trouble nor insult; and having repeated this order distinctly, directed his retinue to go on. As soon as our legs were free we took boat and proceeded to the Tanksall (the Dutch Mint near Murshedabad), where we were received and entertained with real joy and humanity."

So ends Holwell's story. His tale of horror called forth the execrations of the civilised world, and even after the lapse of one hundred and fifty years it excites emotions which make it difficult to reason calmly. As the event, however, can never sink into insignificance or oblivion, it is proper that the contemporary evidence should be subjected to a strict and fair scrutiny, in order to enable us to form an impartial opinion of the actors and their motives. It is almost a hopeless task to arrive at a final judgment as to the motives which have prompted actions. We can only discuss authentic testimonies. William Lindsay states: " At first they used the gentlemen very well, but some of the soldiers getting drunk, they were all ordered into the Black Hole." According to Orme: "The indiscretion of one or two drunken men served for a pretext to the Nabob's officers to commit the most despicable act of cruelty that has for many years, if ever, been the lot of British subjects." Stewart, in his "History of Bengal," a work of considerable research, printed in 1813, however, writes:

> "The prisoners were at once ordered to draw up in the veranda, but the officer commanding the guard, not thinking they would be sufficiently secured there, inquired where was the prison of the fort; and one of the chambers before mentioned, which was used as the Black Hole, to confine disorderly soldiers, being pointed out to him, he, without examining the extent of the apartment, forced them all into it."

This statement is, in a measure, supported by Holwell, who mentions that few amongst the prisoners themselves had the least idea of the dimensions or nature of a place they had never seen; and it is therefore highly probable that the native officer, who had entered the fort for the first time, had no idea of the extent of the apartment. On the other hand, if the prisoners had been confined in the Black Hole merely by the order of a native officer, "the old Jemmautdaar" would not have told Holwell, "with, I believe, much real pity and concern," that the prisoners could not be released "by the Suba's orders." Stewart adds:

> "For the credit of human nature we would fain believe the assertions of the native historians, who say the Nawab knew nothing of this transaction; and that the conduct of the officer who confined them proceeded entirely from stupidity, and not from malevolence and cruelty."

The most favourable construction we can put upon their conduct is that the number of deaths was due to crass stupidity and physiological ignorance; but the fact remains, as Holwell states, "that this scene of misery proved entertainment to the brutal wretches without."

The rhetoric of Macaulay has created a widespread belief that the cruelty and baseness of Surajah Dowla was the main cause of the tragedy. Macaulay describes him seated, "on the eve of the battle of Plassey, gloomily in his tent, haunted—as a Greek poet would have said—by the furies of those who had cursed him with their last breath in the Black Hole." The evidence of the survivors, however, indicates that Surajah Dowla was not answerable for the confinement of the prisoners in the Black Hole. Orme, no favourable critic of Surajah Dowla, states that on entering the fort "he ordered Mr. Holwell, who had been put in irons, to be freed from them, and that the English in general who were become his prisoners should be treated with humanity." Holwell affirms: "I believe his orders were only general—that we should for that night be secured." Cooke further states: "Between six and seven Surajah Dowla left the fort, the charge whereof was given to Moneckchund as Governor." Macaulay writes: "The day broke. The Nabob had slept off his debauch, and permitted the door to be opened." There is no authority for the statement that the Nawab had a debauch. He must, at any rate, have quickly slept it off, for Cooke states that he left the fort at 7 P.M. and was back at 6 A.M. On his arrival he was told of the tragedy that had occurred, and at once sent a messenger to inquire if the chief was dead. As soon as the messenger returned, he ordered the prisoners to be released. When Holwell complained to him of the inhuman barbarities which his countrymen had suffered, the Nawab, Orme states, "disavowed any knowledge of the horrors of the preceding night, and seemed, as much as a man naturally cruel could be, affected with what has passed." If we consider his surroundings and his education, it is highly probable that Surajah Dowla was prone to cruelty, the common vice of despots. If, however, we judge him by his conduct to the prisoners after the capture of Calcutta, no monarch appears less disposed to persecution nor less inclined to avenge himself. Orme informs us that the Nawab immediately ordered Holwell to be freed from his chains, "but was persuaded by his officers that it was necessary such a man should not be set at liberty." If the chief was released and went on board the ships, all hope of finding the treasure was gone. Surajah Dowla, acting on the advice of his officers, "ordered Mr. Holwell and two other gentlemen of the Company's servants," says Orme in his Narrative, written at the time, "to be carried to Muxadabad, *but to be well treated.*" Orme also affirms that "the orders of Surajah Dowla were perverted in regard to the captivity and the release of Mr. Holwell by that spirit of revenge which had been roused in his officers for the great loss sustained by the Moors in their attacks on the English." When Surajah Dowla returned to Hugli he made an inquiry for Holwell and his two companions "when he released Watts and Collett and the prisoners he had taken at Cossimbazar," and he expressed "some resentment at Mhir Mhuddon for having so hastily sent us up to Muxadabad." On arriving at his capital the prisoners were, Orme tells us, "released by the repeated and peremptory order of the Nabob, as soon as he was acquainted that his first order had not been obeyed." On the very morning of their release the Nawab's Prime Minister and some others had, according to Holwell, taken no small pains to convince the Subah

"that, notwithstanding my losses at Allynagore,[1] I was still possessed of enough to pay a considerable sum for my freedom; and advised the sending of me to *Moneckchund*, who would be better able to trace out the remainder of my effects. To this, I was afterwards informed, the Suba replied: 'It may be; if he has anything left, let him keep it: his sufferings have been great; he shall have his liberty.' Whether this was the result of his own sentiments, or the consequence of his promise the night before to the old Begum, I cannot say; but we believe we owe our freedom partly to both."

It was not Surajah Dowla who was at the time pronounced to be the original author of the tragedy of the Black Hole. Holwell gives us a clue to the man who was considered to be the arch-conspirator. He mainly attributes the severity with which he was treated to the instigations of Omichund,

"in resentment for my not releasing him out of prison as soon as I had command of the fort; a circumstance which, in the heat and

[1] Orme writes: "To perpetuate the memory of his victory he ordered the name of Calcutta to be changed to Alinagore, signifying the Port of God." It means the City of Ali (the saint).

hurry of action, never once occurred to me or I had certainly done it, because I thought his imprisonment unjust."

Holwell proceeds to add:

"But that the hard treatment I met with may truly be attributed in a great measure to his suggestions and insinuations, I am well assured from the whole of his subsequent conduct; and this further confirmed me, in the three gentlemen selected to be my companions, against each of whom he had conceived particular resentment, and *you know Omechund can never forgive.*"

It was, indeed, a common belief at the time that the English owed their sufferings to the intrigue and resentment of Omichund; and letters in the old records show that when, after the battle of Plassey, the money sent to Calcutta as compensation was about to be distributed, a vigorous protest was raised against any restitution to Omichund "in common with the other Gentoo merchants, because it is well known he was the chief instigator of the massacre of the Black Hole."

CHAPTER XVI

1756–7: DEFEAT OF SURAJAH DOWLA

On October 16, 1756, the fleet sailed out of Madras. The elements were against them on their start. During the first twelve days they were driven down as far as Ceylon[1] by strong currents from the north. It was now the time when the north-east monsoon blows hardest down the Bay of Bengal and the waves are the highest. In order to avoid a direct and tremendous encounter, vessels for Bengal steered across the Bay to the Tenasserim coast, and thence beat over to Balasore roads and assured the entrance into the River Hugli. Admiral Watson followed this course. But he was badly knocked about by the monsoon gales and could make little way. On the night of November 13

"the *Salisbury* sprung a leak, which kept all her pumps going to free her, and after making the signal of distress, the carpenters of the *Kent* and other ships were sent on board, who found out the leak and in some measure stopped it, so that she was able to proceed on the voyage under an easy sail upon her foremast, as the leak was discovered to be in the wooden ends forwards." [2]

Two days after, "the seamen and military were put to half allowance of provisions, and two-thirds allowance of water. The scurvy began to appear in the fleet, particularly amongst the seamen." It was not till December 1 that six ships arrived in the soundings off Point Palmyras.

"About 8 P.M. the 2nd, *Cumberland* struck upon the reef off Point Palmiras, but was soon got off without any damage; the ship came to an anchor and lay till daylight. After making the signal of distress the fleet came to an anchor, some in seven, some in five and others in four fathoms water upon the edge of this dangerous shoal."

[1] Ives, Voyage, p. 95.

[2] Journal of the expedition to Bengal from October 13, 1756, to February 18, 1757, kept by one of Colonel Clive's family.

The following day the *Kent*, the Admiral's flagship with Clive on board, the *Tyger*, and *Walpole* rounded the shoal and reached the road of Ballasore, but the other ships could not weather the point.

"As soon as the *Kent* arrived in Ballasore road, two English pilots came on board us, who gave the admiral a further account of the miserable situation of affairs in Bengal; as, that since the reduction of Calcutta, almost every inhabitant who survived the attack of the place, or the dreadful catastrophe of the Black Hole prison, had made their escape to Fulta, a despicable village on the river's side; that some families lived in tents on shore, while others continued on board the same ships and vessels in which they had escaped from Calcutta." [1]

The squadron was now in sore distress for water and provisions, "having only eight days' water on board and numbers down with the scurvy." On December 8 the pilot sloop put on board the *Walpole* some rice, "she being in the greatest want of provisions." The *Walpole* carried only sepoys, and when the supply of rice failed, there was "nothing to serve out to them but beef and pork; but though some did submit to this defilement, yet many preferred a languishing death by famine to life polluted beyond recovery." [2]

The pilot guided the vessels over the dangerous shoals at the mouth of the Hugli, then an almost unknown river, and Clive told the Select Committee of the House of Commons that he considered that attempt to go up the river "to be as daring and meritorious an attempt as was ever made in his Majesty's sea service." On December 9 the pilot, taking advantage of the spring tides, entered the river. On December 15 the *Kent* "anchored at Fulta[3] in company with the *Tyger* and *Walpole*, where we found riding at anchor the *Kingsfisher* sloop, the *Delaware*, Indiaman, and about twelve sail of country ships, snows." [4] Here they found the fugitives from Calcutta and other parts of Bengal, and the military under Major Kilpatrick

[1] Ives, p. 96. [2] Scrafton, "Reflections," p. 12.

[3] A village on the left bank of the River Hugli, twenty miles in a straight direction below Calcutta, but more than double that distance by the winding of the river.

[4] Journal by one of Clive's family.

who had arrived there on August 2. The civilians, except some few families who were in tents, lived on board the country ships, and the military were cantoned ashore. The majority of their companions had died—died of cruel fever due to scanty food, bad water, and the pestilential air of the swamps.[1] Great was the joy of the survivors at seeing the long-expected squadron.

> "For almost five months they had been surrounded by sickness and disease, which made strange havoc among them," says Ives, "and yet, when we saw them first, to our great surprise, they appeared with as chearful countenances, as if no misfortunes had happened to them."

On arriving at Fulta Clive learnt that Mr. Drake had received dispatches from England appointing him and three of his former council a committee for the conduct of the Company's affairs in Bengal. They had already associated Major Kilpatrick, says Orme, and they now added Watson and Clive to their board. But neither the admiral nor Clive had any intention of abandoning their separate authority. The same day that Clive reached Fulta he exercised that authority by writing to Rajah Manikchand, Governor of Calcutta:

> "Upon my arrival in these parts from Madras I was informed that you had shown a great friendship and regard for the English Company, for which I write to return you thanks. I doubt not but as you have hitherto professed a desire to serve the Company, you will at this time, when their affairs must require it, retain the same disposition in their favour."[2]

The Rajah sent the following reply, dated December 23, 1756:

[1] Orme states "that of the whole detachment, which was 230 when sent, one half were dead, and of the remainder not more than thirty men were able to do duty when Admiral Watson arrived."—Orme, Vol. II., p. 120. Ives states that to the best of his remembrance not above thirty remained alive and not above ten fit for duty.—Ives, p. 99. Broome writes: "The remnant of the Bengal Military force, from being more accustomed to the climate, appears to have fared better, and was now able to join the force, strengthened by the Company of Volunteers formed from amongst the civilians and respectable European inhabitants who had escaped from Calcutta and the out-factories, which Company now mustered upwards of 70 officers and men."—Broome, p. 79. Clive states that the few effective Europeans at Fulta, including the volunteers, did not amount to more than one hundred.

[2] Orme MSS.: India, Vol. XI., p. 2702.

"I have had the pleasure to receive your most friendly letter. To hear you are in good health gives me the sincerest pleasure. Your sending a copy of your address to the Nabob enclosed in your letter to me for my perusal I esteem as an instance of your friendship. Finding in it many improper expressions and concluding that by sending me the copy you desired to know my sentiments upon it, I have, therefore, made some alterations in it and return it entrusted to Radakissen Mullick, who will deliver it to you. You will write your letter after that form and dispatch it again to me, and I will forward it to the Nabob. You write that you are desirous of peaceable measures. I likewise am as desirous, as nothing is better than peace. To take away every cause of ill-will or contention, this is the part of a good man." [1]

On December 25 Clive answered as follows:

"I have received your letter with the form enclosed for a letter to the Nabob. I am very sensible of your friendship and kind intentions in sending me the latter, which I have read, but am sorry I cannot, consistently with my duty to the Company or their honour, accept of your advice in writing to the Nabob a letter couched in such a stile, which, however proper it might have been before the taking of Calcutta, would but ill-suit with the present time, when we are come to demand satisfaction for the injuries done us by the Nabob, not to entreat his favour, and with a force which we think sufficient to vindicate our claim. Anaverdi Cawn's letter went by a former conveyance which I have taken notice of in mine to the Nabob." [2]

Clive, however, did slightly modify his attitude, and Watson also wrote a letter to the Nawab in which he stated:

"As you must be sensible of the benefit of having the English settled in your country, I doubt not you will consent to make them a reasonable satisfaction for the losses and injuries they have suffered, and by that means put an amicable end to the troubles and secure the friendship of my king, who is a lover of peace, and delights in acts of equity. What can I say more?"

The Nawab was not sensible of the benefit of having the English settled in his country, and he ordered the whole of his army to assemble at his capital preparatory to marching towards Calcutta, and Manikchand took measures to strengthen Fort William as well as the neighbouring forts on the river. On December 16 "the Company's troops and seapoys on the *Kent*, *Tyger*, and *Walpole* landed at Fulta," and six days after

[1] Orme MSS.: India, Vol. XI., p. 2703. [2] *Ibid.*, p. 2704.

"the Grenadiers and Artillery Companies from the *Salisbury* and *Bridgwater* joined the battalion in camp." The malarious swamp around them produced fever, and Clive fell a victim. On December 23 he wrote to Major Kilpatrick:

> "A violent Cold and Slight Fever has reduced me to the necessity of committing to writing what otherwise I should have been glad to have executed in Person, and by word of Mouth.
>
> "The time now draws near for the quitting of Fulta, previous to which many necessary steps are to be taken, Boats, Sloops, &c should be in readiness for the Embarkation of all our Military, Lascars and Seapoys, as likewise all our Stores, Provision &c I think it would be gaining of time, if all the baggage Stores &c were embarked immediately on large Boats, excepting what the Service on Shore absolutely requires, I would have all our Military and Seapoys supplied with 36 Rounds pr Man, and the rest of the Ammunition disposed of in such a manner as to be at hand when called for, I would have the 2.6 prs & 2.3 prs well supplyed with Ammunition and in readiness to Land at a Moments warning, for I take it for granted, we shall march from Budjee Budjee to Calcutta by Land, it would save us the Trouble of Embarking, if we could do the same from Fulta, please to speak to the Governor to give Orders that the Vessel which has the 100,000 Musket Cartridges on Board accompany the Squadron.
>
> "I am very anxious for the return of the Man who is sent to examine the Situation of Budjee Budjee; a good account from him would save a World of Trouble, pray make enquiry if there be any other road to B.B. except the foot Path between the two Fortifications.
>
> "There are many other things which do not occur to me, which may fall within your Knowledge, in short I leave every thing to your Prudence and Discretion for the present; dispose of the Troops in such manner that they may be in readiness to March overland to Calcutta, and, if necessary, to attack Budjee Budjee, Tana Fort, &c
>
> "It would be of singular service could you prevail upon the Bazar people to follow us to Budjee Budjee.
>
> "Having applied to the Governor for the *Delaware* India-man to serve as a Hospital Ship have as yet received no Answer; it will be necessary to apply again to him that it may be executed." [1]

On December 27 the fleet proceeded up the river, having re-embarked the Company's troops and artillery pursuant to the resolution of a Council of War held on board the *Kent*, "but the *seapoys* marched over land keeping the ships in view and Captain Barker following in boats with 80 of the Train

[1] Powis MSS. No. I.: Letters from the Hon. Colonel Clive, from October 11, 1756, to April 16, 1757.

and two field pieces properly compleated." [1] The following day the ships reached Mayapur, and about three in the afternoon the troops and two field-pieces were disembarked and joined the sepoys.[2] According "to the plan concerted at the Council of War," the ships were to bombard the Fort of Budge Budge,[3] which stood on the river, while Clive marched with the troops northwards in order to lay an ambuscade for the garrison as they retreated along the Calcutta road. Clive did not agree with the plan concerted by the majority at the Council of War.[4] He wished to convey the troops by water to Budge Budge, but he had to follow the decision of the majority.

At four o'clock Clive set forth with the troops for Mayapur, the two field-pieces with a tumbril of ammunition being drawn by the men. The native guides,

"in order to prevent discovery, led the troops at a distance from the river, through a part of the country, which was uninhabited indeed, but full of swamps, and continually intersected by deep rivulets, which rendered the draught and transportation of the three carriages so tedious and laborious, that the troops did not arrive until an hour after sun-rise at the place of ambuscade." [5]

The spot chosen for the ambush was the dry bed of an ordinary Indian tank about ten feet below the level of the plain. It lay about a mile from the river, a mile and a half north-east of Budge Budge, and half a mile east of the high road to Calcutta. Clive proceeded to post his small force.

"Kessersing,[6] commander of the *seapoys*, was detached from hence with 200 *seapoys* to reconnoitre, and was followed by Captain Pye at the head of the Grenadier company and the rest of the *seapoys*; Captain Gauppe was likewise advanced with his company and the

[1] Journal of the expedition to Bengal from October 13, 1756, to February 18, 1757, kept by one of Colonel Clive's family.

[2] Orme states: "All the men of Adlercron's regiment who were arrived, being 120, remained on board the ships of war. The rest of the battalion, 500, with all the Sepoys, and two field-pieces, landed, and at sunset marched from Mayapore, under the command of Colonel Clive, and under the conduct of Indian guides."

[3] Orme spells it Buz-buzia; Ives, Bougee Bougee; Elphinstone, Bujbuj.

[4] It has always been stated that Watson alone insisted on the troops marching northwards, but we now know it was according to a decision of a Council of War.

[5] Orme, Vol. II., p. 122.

[6] Keshar Singh.

volunteers in the Calcutta Road to give timely notice of the approach of any of the enemy that might come that way. Captain Pye had orders to take possession of the suburbs and send an immediate report when he had effected it, but not to attempt any thing further without order."[1]

Captain Pye, finding the suburbs deserted, joined the party of sepoys "under the bank, and put himself under the orders of Captain Coote who was landed with the King's troops; they had just struck a flag on one of the advanced batteries, and were reconnoitring from behind it, when Keshar Singh was ordered back with the *seapoys;* Captain Waller landing soon after from the *Salisbury,* and, hearing that the Colonel was attacked by the enemy, ordered the whole to march to his assistance." The European battalion under Clive's immediate command, "consisting of 260 rank and file," had been attacked by the main body of the enemy under Manikchand from the surrounding houses and thickets.

"The skirmish lasted about half an hour, in which time we had Ensign Kerr with nine private men killed and eight wounded. The enemy's loss must have been somewhat considerable as their number of horse and foot appeared to be about 2,000 and several of them exposed themselves pretty freely at first; but were much alarmed at the briskness of our fire and startled at the first appearance of cannon which they thought impossible for us to transport over the ground we had marched the preceding night; 'tis said that 200 of inferior note were killed and wounded, four *jemidars*, an elephant and the Commander shot through his turban, besides about forty who perished in their confusion on passing a creek."[2]

[1] Journal by one of Clive's family.

[2] *Ibid.* Orme's account of the skirmish differs materially from that given in the Journal and the Logs. He writes: "The rest of the troops remained with Colonel Clive, and concealed themselves, some in the hollow, and others in the adjoining village, and the two field-pieces were placed on the north side of the village. The troops being excessively fatigued, were permitted to quit their arms, in order to get rest; every man laid himself down where he thought best, some in the village, others in the hollow; and from a security which no superiority or appearances in war could justify, the common precaution of stationing centinels was neglected. In a few minutes they were all asleep." It is difficult to believe that, after 200 sepoys had been sent to reconnoitre and a company with the volunteers had been posted in the Calcutta Road to give timely notice of the approach of the enemy, the battalion of Europeans under Clive, who were in ambush ready to cut off the enemy, would be found an hour later asleep. With regard to stationing sentinels, Clive had taken, as we now learn, all the precautions he considered necessary for giving timely notice of the approach of the enemy. Clive did know the elements of the business of war, and, if the statement be true that he did not post sentinels,

Clive, in a letter to Mr. Pigot, dated January 8, 1757, gives the following account of the engagement:

"You will find by the return, that our loss in the skirmish near Budjee-Budjee was greater than could well be spared, if such skirmishes were to be often repeated. You must know, our march from Moidapoor to the northward of Budjee-Budjee was much against my inclinations. I applied to the Admiral for boats to land us at the place we arrived at after sixteen hours' march by land in which the men suffered hardships not to be described. It was four in the afternoon when we decamped from Moidapoor, and (we) did not arrive off Budjee-Budjee till past eight next morning; at nine, the Grenadier company and all the seapoys were despatched to the fort, where I heard Captain Coote was landed with the King's troops. At ten, Monichaund, the Governor of Calcutta, attacked us with between two and three thousand horse and foot, and was worsted. The people of the country raise fabulous reports about the killed and wounded; but there is reason to believe, from the smartness of the fire while it lasted, and the nearness of the enemy, some of which were within twenty yards, one hundred and fifty might be killed and wounded, and with them four of the principal *jemidars* and an elephant. Monichaund himself received a shot in his *turban*. Our two field-pieces were of little or no service to us, having neither tubes nor port-fires, and wrong carriages sent with them from Fort St. David; indeed we still labour under every disadvantage in the world, for want of the *Marlborough*. It seems the enemy were encamped within two miles of us, and we ignorant of the matter; so much for the intelligence of this country."

An hour before Clive began his northward march "the squadron weighed and came to sail and at 6 anchored off Pengal's Point." At 7 A.M. the squadron again weighed and came to sail for Budge Budge, and half an hour after the enemy opened fire at the *Tyger*,[1] who returned it. A few minutes later the *Kent* began to fire, and, having anchored, made the signal to engage. The fire of the enemy soon slackened,

the nature of the country or some other sound reason must have prevented him from departing from this ordinary military practice. Orme further states: "Had the cavalry advanced and charged the troops in the hollow, at the same time that the infantry began to fire upon the village, it is not improbable that the war would have been concluded on the very first trial of hostilities." Sir John Malcolm, a soldier acquainted with war, writes: "In answer to this remark, there is one single fact to be stated—the thick jungle which concealed the approach of the infantry was impervious to cavalry, who had no means of advancing except through openings, where they must have been seen, and the possibility of surprise defeated."—Orme, II., 122.

[1] Not the *Kent*, as Orme states.

and all the King's troops were disembarked and took possession of an abandoned battery. Captain Eyre Coote was desirous of storming the fort, but Captain Weller, "who was my senior, . . . thought it necessary to desist from my project and to go to the Colonel whom we knew to be very weak."

After Clive had repulsed the enemy, he went on board the flagship to consult the admiral. On his return Eyre Coote learnt that a body of sailors was going to be sent ashore to join them, and that they were to storm the fort when night fell.

"When night came on," says Eyre Coote, "400 sailors came on shore under the command of Captain King; the Colonel and Major Kilpatrick were retired to rest, as they had had a very fatiguing march all the night before, and Captain Weller was gone sick on board; so that I then had the command, and as my opinion was all day for storming the place, I was in hopes then to have the honour of doing it, but the Colonel sent me word he'd have nothing done till the morning." [1]

During Eyre Coote's absence

"one *Strahan*, a common sailor belonging to the *Kent*, having been just served with a quantity of *grog* (arrack mixed with water), had his spirits too much elated to think of taking any rest; he therefore strayed by himself towards the fort, and imperceptibly got under the walls; being advanced thus far without interruption, he took it into his head to scale at a breach that had been made by the cannon of the ships; and having luckily gotten upon the bastion, he there discovered several *Moor-men* sitting on the platform, at whom he flourished his cutlass, and fired his pistol, and then, after having given three loud huzzas, cried out, '*The place is mine.*'" [2]

He was immediately attacked, and then began a deadly tussle. Strahan's cutlass broke off near the hilt, and the moments of life were fast running out when the advanced guards, who were in the village and had heard his shouts, quitting their post, joined him on the rampart.[3] The enemy had been moving out of the place ever since dusk, and those

[1] Journal of Captain Eyre Coote.

[2] Ives' Journal, p. 100. Eyre Coote's Journal.—Orme, Vol. II., p. 124.

[3] Ives writes: "*Strahan*, the hero of this adventurous action, was soon brought before the admiral, who, notwithstanding the success that had attended it, thought it necessary to shew himself displeased with a measure in which the want of all military discipline so notoriously appeared. He therefore angrily enquired into the desperate step which he had taken: 'Mr. *Strahan* what is this that you have been doing?' The fellow, after having made his bow

that remained were quickly driven out or killed. Eyre Coote assumed command of the fort, and at dawn a salute was fired. Eighteen pieces of cannon from 24-pounders downwards, and forty barrels of gunpowder with ball in proportion, were found in it.

The following evening, after disabling the guns, carrying off the powder and demolishing the parapets of the fort and batteries, the European troops re-embarked. The sepoys remained ashore, "taking their route along the bank of the river with the fleet in view, and the artillery following again in boats."[1] On December 31 the squadron weighed "and dropt up the river." The next day at twenty minutes past 10 A.M., the *Tyger* made the signal and anchored. Twenty minutes later the *Kent* anchored. "A French ship saluted with nine guns and was returned five."[2] Shortly after noon the *Tyger* and *Kent* again set sail, "and at 2 P.M. came abreast of Tanna and Aleghur which is a new mud fort erected by the enemy opposite to the former." The enemy abandoned both forts as the ships approached, and the boats' crews of the squadrons landed and took possession of them without firing a shot. They found in them "about forty guns, some twenty-four pounders, and all mounted on good carriages, most of them the company's."[3] They also discovered some ammunition.

"In the night," says Watson, "I sent the boats manned and armed up the river, to set fire to a ship and some vessels that lay

scratched his head, and with one hand twirling his hat upon the other, replied 'Why, to be sure, Sir, it was *I* who took the fort, but *I hope there was no harm in it.*' The admiral with difficulty was prevented from smiling at the simplicity of *Strahan's* answer; and the whole company were exceedingly diverted with his awkward appearance, and his language and manner in recounting the several particulars of his mad exploit. Mr. *Watson* expatiated largely on the fatal consequences that might have attended his irregular conduct, and then with a severe rebuke dismissed him; but not before he had given the fellow some distant hints, that at a proper opportunity he should certainly be punished for his temerity. *Strahan*, amazed to find himself blamed, where he expected praise, had no sooner gone from the admiral's cabin, than he muttered these words: *'If I am flogged for this here action, I will never take another fort by myself as long as I live, by G——d.'*"

[1] Journal of the expedition to Bengal from October 13, 1756, to February 18, 1757, kept by one of Colonel Clive's family.

[2] Minutes taken aboard His Majesty's ship *Kent* at the attack of Budge Budge Fort, at Tana, and at the attack on Calcutta.

[3] Letter from Admiral Watson, dated H.M.S. *Kent*, off Calcutta.

under a fort, which was executed without opposition. That was a necessary piece of service, as I heard they were filled with combustibles in order to be set on fire when the ebb made, to burn our ships."

Early on the morning of January 2 Clive landed at Aligarh with the Company's European troops and, joined by the sepoys, marched on Calcutta. The *Kent* and *Tyger*, together with the twenty-gun ship and sloop, weighed and stood up following the line of the well-wooded shore of the broad Hugli.[1] No forest of masts then rose into the blue azure. A few country boats with their large broad sails filled with sunshine were flying away. As the *Tyger* approached, the batteries on the bank opened fire, but the enemy deserted them on the approach of the fleet and Clive's force.

"At 10 A.M. the ships coming abreast of Fort William (by the Moors called Alinagor) were fired upon pretty warmly as they lay becalmed, sheering round in the eddies of the tide; but soon, after coming to an anchor close in with the western line of guns on the river side, they drove the enemy from their batteries, who fled through the eastern gate before the military or *seapoys* could come up with them; in this action three of the King's soldiers and six sailors were killed."[2]

When the enemy deserted the fort some of the old inhabitants of the town waved their hands from the shore, and one of them hoisted an English pendant on a tree.[3] The admiral immediately sent Captain King, R.N., to take possession for the Crown, and a few minutes after it was garrisoned with a detachment of Adlercron's regiment under Eyre Coote. At the same time a party of sepoys reached the fort, entered it, and, Clive states, were ignominiously thrown out.

"Upon coming near the fort myself I was informed that there were orders that none of the Company's officers or troops should have entrance. This, I own, enraged me to such a degree that I

[1] January 1st, 1757. "About 2 in the afternoon came abreast of *Tanna Forts*, which were found evacuated, the enemy retiring as the ships advanced. At 3 the boats of the men-of-war landed with the seamen and took possession of the Fort of Tanna and Aligur, a mud fort raised opposite in which were found 31 pieces of cannon of 24 and 13 of a smaller size, some shot, and a small quantity of gunpowder."—Selections from the Letters, Despatches, and other State Papers preserved in the Madras Secretariat (Clive Series), edited by George W. Forrest, C.I.E.

[2] Journal of the Expedition to Bengal, from October 13, 1756, to February 18, 1757.

[3] Ives, p. 102.

was resolved to enter if possible which I did, though not in the manner maliciously reported, by forcing the sentrys, for they suffered us to pass very patiently upon being informed who I was."[1]

At Clive's entrance Eyre Coote presented him with the following commission from Admiral Watson:

"By *Charles Watson*, Esq.; Vice-admiral of the blue squadron of his majesty's fleet, and commander in chief of his majesty's ships and vessels employed in the *East Indies*, and of the marine forces of the united company of merchants trading to and in these parts.

"You are hereby required and directed to garrison the fort of *Calcutta* with his majesty's troops which you have now on shore, and take care to post sentinels and guards so as not to be surprized by the enemy. In the evening I shall be on shore; and you are not to quit your post, or deliver up your command till farther orders from me. During your continuance on shore, you are to take care that no disorders be committed by his majesty's troops, or any other people, but to treat the natives with humanity, and take particular care that there is no plundering, as such offenders may depend on the severest punishment. Given under my hand on board his majesty's ship the *Kent*, off *Calcutta*, 2d *Jan.* 1757.

"CHARLES WATSON.

"*To* CAPTAIN EYRE COOTE, *of his majesty's* 39*th regiment of foot.*

"By command of the admiral.

"HENRY DOIDGE."

Clive denied any authority that Admiral Watson had to appoint an inferior officer in the King's service governor of the fort, and told Eyre Coote if he disobeyed his orders he would place him under arrest. Eyre Coote assented, and desired leave to acquaint the admiral with these particulars. Clive consented.[2] Watson, on hearing what had taken place, sent Captain Speke on shore to know by what authority Clive had assumed command of the fort. "I answered, by the authority of his majesty's commission, as being lieutenant-colonel and commander in chief of the land forces." Speke went on board with the message, and wrote the following letter to Clive:

"I am extremely sorry to find by your Letter and by what I know of the Admiral's Sentiments that things are tending to an

[1] Letter from Colonel Clive to Mr. Pigot, dated Fort William, January 8, 1757. Clive in his evidence before the Select Committee of the House of Commons stated that "he entered the Fort at the head of the Company's troops."

[2] Clive's Evidence, Ives, p. 102.

Extremity which cannot but be hurtful to the Company's Affairs—I will not pretend to give you my Sentiments on a Subject in which, as a King's Officer I cannot but be a Party; & on which I own I am so unhappy as to differ with you in Opinion I mean if you are in truth of that, by which you seem to Act—I hoped for a better ending of this Affair when I parted from you—and was much surpriz'd to find you denyed to Major Kilpatrick having forc'd the Sentinels—when to me you not only acknowledged it, but upon my taking the Liberty to ask if it was a Soldier-like Action, you said much more so, than Capt. Coot's making Mr. Court a Prisoner, & driving out the Sea-Poys. As you was then in heat, I have no Doubt you did not much consider what you said, but it was the first Question I ask'd You, & upon your owning it, my 2[d] was do you defend it? To which you likewise answered in the Affirmative, adding that you was a King's Officer as well as Mr. Watson—I shall be glad to think this was as I said the Language of Passion—but you must pardon me, if I say it was yours." [1]

Speke returned to the fort, and must have conveyed to Clive the following letter from the admiral:

"SIR,—After what I said to Major Killpatrick, I am extremely surprised to find you have not withdrawn the Company's Troops, which puts me under a necessity of acquainting you, If you still persist in continuing in the Fort, You will force me to take such methods as will be as disagreeable to me, as they possibly can be to you. I hope yet, after you have prudently consider'd this Affair, you'll not drive me to the Extremities I should be sorry to be urg'd to, for the Plea you make of being Commanding Officer of the Land Forces, gives you not the least Authority to enter a Place (forcibly) conquer'd by me, and garrison'd by Troops under my immediate Command." [2]

Speke informed Clive that if he did not abandon the fort "he should be fired out." In answer, "I said I could not answer for the consequences, but I would not abandon the Fort." [3] Speke returned to the admiral, and the following letter was sent to Clive:

"DEAR SIR,—I have talked with the Admiral on the late disagreeable Subject of our Conversation, & have related to him your Offer of evacuating the Fort provided you may have Assurances of your commanding there. He has commanded me to tell you, that as, neither in this Affair, nor any other he ever meant you any Dishonour, he is disposed to give you any reasonable Proofs of it; but as by forcing the Guards placed in the Fort by his Orders you have offered him a Personal Affront, & thro' him to his Ma'ties Authority; the

[1] Powis MSS. [2] *Ibid.* [3] Clive's Evidence.

Duty he owes to himself as an Officer trusted with the Care of his Ma'ties honour, in supporting that of his Forces, will not admit of his promising any thing 'till you have first by withdrawing the Troops under your Com'and, acknowledged the Insult you have so unadvisedly offered—That done, if You will give yourself the trouble to Step aboard, I dare promise you, you will receive clear Proofs how very unwilling Mr. Watson is to disagree with a Man for whom he has always had an Esteem."

Clive refused to "step aboard." The admiral now sent Captain Latham, who commanded the *Tyger*, and "was in a strict intimacy with him," to confer with Clive.

"They talked the affair over with calmness, and soon settled a dispute which otherwise might have ended greatly to the prejudice of the public cause. The colonel's messages to Mr. Watson implied, that if the admiral would come on shore and command in person, he should have no manner of objection to it: And on Admiral Watson's going on shore the next day, the colonel delivered the keys of the garrison into his hands, and then the admiral delivered them to the late governor, Mr. Drake, and his council. And these gentlemen, persuaded by Colonel Clive of the necessity of the step, immediately published a declaration of war against the Nabob, in the name of the East India company, as did Admiral Watson in that of the king his master." [1]

Clive and Watson decided to press the war promptly and vigorously. As it was found that some time must elapse before the Nawab could reach Hugli, a town of considerable strategic importance owing to its proximity to Calcutta, it was determined to send a detachment by water to attack it without delay, and destroy the large stores of grain and rice collected for the use of the Nawab's army. The expedition, the admiral states in his dispatch, was

"to be executed by the twenty-gun ship and sloop, the boats of the squadron mann'd and arm'd, assisted by all the King's troop

[1] Ives, p. 103. Clive in his Evidence stated: "I was sent to Madrass with a power independent of the governor and council of Calcutta. I commanded in Bengal as the King's officer and the Company's both. The King's troops, when on shore, were under me. I was commander-in-chief of the Company's forces in Bengal, by a commission from the governor and council of Madrass, on my setting out on that expedition. The governor and council of Madrass looked on the government of Calcutta as annihilated. They thought, if I had not the independent command, the governor and council of Bengal would retain the troops which they thought necessary should return to Madrass. I took the command as a military officer. The governor and council of Calcutta put their troops under my orders."

amounting to one hundred and seventy, the Company's Grenadiers and two hundred Seapoys which were to be landed under the command of Major Killpatrick. Several sloops were procur'd to embark them, and there being a proper vessel for carrying two mortars, which being judg'd of great consequence to the success of the expedition, the committee offered her to go upon this service, if I would appoint a proper officer to take the command of her. I accordingly gave my first lieutenant, Mr Warrick a commission as Captain, and appointed a Lieutenant and Surgeon to her, which I hope their Lordships will approve of." [1]

The expedition proceeded up the river on January 5, and hoped to reach Hugli at one time, but the *Bridgwater*, the twenty-gun ship,

" by not having a good pilot, stuck on a sand bank where he lay forty-eight hours in great danger, but got off without receiving much damage, and by the assistance of a Dutch Pilot, who he took on board in his passage up, he proceeded agreeable to his orders."

The Dutch chief, however, complained that the Dutch pilot was one of their quartermasters who had been forcibly removed from their brigantine lying before their settlement of Barnagore. On the 9th

" at noon the ships came to an anchor off Hughly and began firing in order to dislodge the enemy from the banks and houses where they might annoy us in landing. At 4 in the afternoon the troops landed about 700 yards below the Fort under cover of the ships which immediately after moved farther up the river and anchored close to the fort." [2]

They began at once to cannonade it, which they continued doing till about 12 o'clock, when Major Kilpatrick sent Eyre Coote, who had embarked with the King's troops (the 39th Foot), to examine the breach, which Eyre Coote enters in his journal:

" I found practicable to enter, on which we formed two attacks, one of 50 men went to the main gate and kept a great noise with continual firing, whilst we entered privately at the breach; the sailors under Captain King, that were on shore with us, put up our scaling ladders and assisted us in getting in, which we did without

[1] Selections from the Letters, Despatches, and Other State Papers preserved in the Madras Secretariat (Clive Series), edited by George W. Forrest, C.I.E.

[2] Journal of Military Transactions in the Expedition to Hughley. Selections from the Letters, Despatches, and Other State Papers preserved in the Madras Secretariat (Clive Series), edited by George W. Forrest, C.I.E.

any loss, for the enemy (as we had imagined) went all to the place where our false attack was made, and ran away through one of the gates; we found the Fort much stronger than we at first imagined and the garrison consisted of 2,000 men; we had some of our men killed and wounded before we stormed." [1]

On the 12th Eyre Coote was sent with 50 soldiers and 100 sepoys to burn a great granary about three miles from the fort. He was to be joined on the march by some sailors. On arriving in the neighbourhood he took possession of a Portuguese convent, where he was informed that between 3,000 and 4,000 of the enemy were encamped behind the village. "However as it was a very great granary I knew it must be of very great service could I succeed." He marched into the village, set fire to it, and on returning through the narrow lane was attacked by the enemy in force, and with difficulty fought his way back to the men-of-war boats. On January 20, after disabling the enemy's guns ("carrying on board such as were serviceable") and demolishing the walls and bastions of the fort, the King's and Company's troops went on board the sloops and returned to Calcutta, leaving behind the sepoys. The intention was to send an expedition to Dacca, "to be carried on by 400 sailors in boats under the command of Captain Speke." "The surprize of this place," says Clive, "may be of great consequence to the Company's affairs." But the surprise of Dacca never took place, as the Nawab appeared at Hugli with his army the very day the European troops embarked on the sloop to return to Calcutta. [2]

Meanwhile, Clive had addressed himself to repairing and strengthening the fortifications of Fort William. But, as he wrote, he "could not make it more than barely tenable against a Country enemy for to all its former defects when taken from us, the Moors have broken down part of the Curtain

[1] Journal of Captain Eyre Coote.

[2] "But our attention was called off from this very desirable and tempting object, by the alarming intelligence we received, that the *Nabob*, incensed at the loss of all his late conquests, and alarmed at the rapidity of ours, had raised a formidable army, and was marching at the head of it from his capital *Muxadabad* towards *Calcutta*, fully determined to drive the *English* out of all his territories, and take ample vengeance for the disgraces we had brought upon him."

to make room for a mosque they were erecting." The work was, however, pushed forward with such energy that at the close of the month Clive was able to state, "I may assure you Fort William can never be taken again by the Moors but by Cowardice." Clive, however, knew that Calcutta was now threatened with a graver danger than an attack by the Moors. During the expedition to Hugli news arrived from Aleppo that war had been declared between Great Britain and France in the preceding month of May.[1] At Chandernagore the French had 300 Europeans and a train of field artillery, and it was expected they would strengthen the Nawab's considerable mass. Clive could now expect no further reinforcements from Madras. He and Stringer Lawrence had, by drilling the Madras sepoys and teaching them to fight "in the European manner," created a body of brave, disciplined, devoted soldiers. Clive now determined to raise a battalion of sepoys in Bengal: and he found willing recruits among the soldiers of fortune—Pathans, Rohillas, Jats, Rajputs, and even Brahmins, who had followed the Mohammedan conquerors into Bengal. Having enlisted some two or three hundred, he formed them into a corps and furnished them not only with arms and accoutrements, but with the British military uniform of the day somewhat modified. He appointed a British officer to command the new corps and British non-commissioned officers to drill and discipline them as regular troops. The First Regiment of Bengal Native Infantry was called from its equipment the "Lal paltan" or "Red Regiment," a name which it long maintained.[2] This was the origin of the Bengal Native Army—an army to whose bravery and devotion the expansion of British dominion in India from the swamps of Bengal to the Himalayas is mainly due.

Menaced by an overwhelming force, Clive decided that the best strategic plan was to protect Calcutta in the field and to prevent as long as possible a direct attack on the

[1] Orme, Vol. II., p. 127.

[2] An Historical Account of the Rise and Progress of the Bengal Native Army, by Captain Williams, pp. 4 and 165, 166. Pultun—Hind. *paltan*, a corruption of *Battalion*, possibly with some confusion of platoon or péloton.—Hobson-Jobson.

fort. He therefore occupied a position a mile northward of the town and half a mile from the bank of the river. It was well chosen, as the salt water lake then came up to within a mile of the Mahratta ditch, and an enemy coming from the northward could not pass round to invest Calcutta except through that interval, and consequently within sight of the British camp.[1] Ives mentions an incident which illustrates the condition of what is now a populous and prosperous portion of the City of Palaces:

"While the colonel was in search of a proper place for an encampment, a wild buffalo ran at his guard; and although the *Sepoy* it attacked, discharged his musket ball into its body, and received it on his bayonet, yet the creature killed the man, and made off. The wild buffaloes are here very large; they exceed the largest ox in *England*, and have legs remarkably thick and strong." [2]

On January 28, 1757, Clive wrote from "Camp on Barnagut Plain" to Select Committee, Fort St. George:

"We have fortified a great tank near Barnagut with high banks which command a very extensive plain; we have likewise erected two batteries, one advanced towards Dum Dum Bridge and another to the river side to keep our communication open with the river; in short we are in a very good condition to act defensibly against his whole army, and when the other forces arrive hope to finish everything by a decisive stroke." [3]

He was looking forward to the arrival of the troops from Bombay. In the same letter he mentions that the *Marlborough*, which had been so long missing, had arrived with the Field Artillery and stores on board. Eight days before Clive had written to Watson:

"You are very sensible, Sir, that with sickness and other accidents how far this force falls short of what was intended to act offensively against the Nabob of Bengal; indeed at present nothing but our strong situation can enable us to act against him at all. I must therefore request the favour of you, Sir, to land the King's forces and to lay your commands on the officer who commands them to put himself under my orders; assuring you at the same time that whenever you think it for the good of the service to recall them, upon signification thereof to me by letter, they shall be returned." [4]

[1] Orme, Vol. II., p. 128. Broome, p. 92.
[2] Ives, p. 110 (note). [3] Powis MSS.
[4] Letter from Colonel Clive in Camp to Admiral Watson, January 20, 1757. Powis MSS.

Next day the Admiral wrote:

"I have received your favour of yesterday's date, enclosing me a return of your little army, and desiring the King's forces may be sent to join you. I cannot help thinking the number of your own troops are too few even to act defensively against the Nabob, therefore I have given orders to the captains of the several ships to discharge their troops, and have directed Captain Weller to join you, and put himself under your command until further orders." [1]

Writing to Mr. Pigot on January 25, Clive says:

"At last the King's troops are put under my command during the Admiral's pleasure (or rather during mine if I insist upon my right). It had been better for the service they had never come and I had the like number of Company's in their room." [2]

Clive knew how to humour the brave and generous sailor and to deal with his pretensions to interfere with the land operations. But for the weak and disunited Select Committee, whose chief object was to possess themselves of the independent power with which he was invested, he could feel nothing but contempt. On January 18 the Select Committee informed him that they considered it

"our duty to require you as follows:

"That you recede from the independent powers given you by the Committee of Fort Saint George as Commander-in-Chief of their land forces, and subject yourself to the orders of this Presidency.

"That you strictly comply with and follow whatever plans of military operations the Select Committee of Fort William may judge proper to point out, and that you do not think of making any treaty of peace or accommodation with the *Subah* without their concurrence and approbation.

"That you remain in Bengal with the troops under your command until honorable and advantageous terms can be obtained from the *Subah*, and that when circumstances will admit of your leaving us, the number of men necessary for our defence be submitted to our determination, in which we shall give due attention to the exigencies of the gentlemen at Fort Saint George." [3]

[1] Letter from Admiral Watson to Colonel Clive, dated H.M.S. *Kent*, January 21, 1757.—Orme MSS.

[2] Letter from Colonel Clive to Mr. Pigot, dated Camp, January 25, 1757.—Powis MSS.

[3] Letter from Select Committee, Fort William, to Colonel Clive, dated January 18, 1757.

Clive in his reply says:

"What I have had the honor to represent to the Board, I now take an opportunity of repeating in writing, that I do not intend to make use of my power for acting separately from you without you reduce me to the necessity of so doing, but as far as concerns the means of executing those powers you will excuse me, Gentlemen."[1]

Though eminently and decisively firm, Clive was never obstinate. He saw his goal with a vision steady and clear, but he had likewise the faculty which enabled him with rapidity and boldness to alter his design and adapt it to the circumstances of the hour. He realised "the immense consequence of Bengal to the Company," and he determined to conclude matters either by a treaty or by war. But there were strong reasons why war was undesirable. Clive considered it most hazardous to engage with his slender force the vast host of the enemy. And there was every probability of the French co-operating with the Nawab. An offer "of neutrality in the Ganges" had been made to them on the condition that they joined the English against the Nawab, but this had been declined. They and the Dutch, however, were willing to act as mediators. But Clive was strongly averse to accepting the French proposition. The admiral was inclined to accept the mediation of the French, but not that of the Dutch. He wrote:

"I own I am not so very averse to our putting some confidence in the French, who I think would be glad at this juncture not to embroil themselves, but endeavour to make matters up between our Company and the Nabob; and should it appear necessary to choose a mediator, most certainly the French ought to be preferred to the Dutch, who are only a Republic, and I am persuaded will not have the same weight, neither can it be so honourable to ourselves."[2]

On January 21 two Frenchmen, deputed by M. Renault, Director of the French in Bengal, arrived at Calcutta. They stated that they were not accredited agents, but were willing to act as mediators and to forward to the Nawab the terms on which the Council were willing to make peace. They

[1] Letter from Colonel Clive to the Select Committee, Fort William, dated Camp, January 20, 1757.

[2] Letter from Admiral Watson to Colonel Clive, dated H.M.S. *Kent*, January 22, 1757.

were told the terms had already been sent to Coja Wajed (Khwaja Wajid), a wealthy Armenian merchant resident at Hugli and Chandernagore, who was employed by the Nawab in his negotiations with the European powers. On the 26th Clive informed Pigot that the Nawab's "private Minister" had sent a messenger to him "desiring that I would send a trusty person with our proposals intimating that the Nabob was desirous of settling matters in a private manner without the mediation of the French." Clive asked the Select Committee to send their proposals fully explained, that they might be laid at once before the Nawab. He was desirous of returning to Madras, the field of his former triumphs, and striking again his old foes. "Be persuaded," he wrote, "I long most earnestly to have the Peace concluded, and, if in time, shall desire the Admiral to call at Vizagapatam that we may have a slap at Bussy if near at hand." At the close of a postscript he says:

> "Ten thousand men under the command of the Nabob's brother crossed the river the day before yesterday. They are at a place called Cowgauche about 18 miles from our camp. They have 30 pieces of cannon, which we probably may give a good account of if they come near enough." [1]

On January 30 the Nawab's army began to cross the river about ten miles above Hugli. The same day he wrote "to the greatest of merchants, the model of true friends, M. Renault, Director-General of the French Company," that if he would aid him and send the ships of war "to punish this faithless people and chase them from this country he would load him with marks of his good will."

> "I abolish for ever the annual imposts on your commerce, and I give you the right to establish a mint at Chandernagore. I will demand a *firman* for this from the light of the presence, the greatest and purest, the Emperor of Delhi, and will send it to you. Until the arrival of the *firman* I will give you a *parwana*, with my seal, so that you may exercise these two privileges with perfect tranquillity of mind."

But fortunately the model of true friends did not assist the Nawab, and the French lost a good opportunity of crippling,

[1] Letter from Colonel Clive to Mr. Pigot, dated Camp, January 25, 1757.

if not crushing, their rivals. On February 1 Clive wrote "To the Honble Secret Committee for affairs of the Honble United Comp[y] of Merchants of England trading to the East Indies" that

"A second offer has been made to the French of a neutrality in the Ganges and without the condition we formerly insisted upon of their joining us against the Nabob. As yet we have had no answer from them, but I think the proposition too advantageous for them to decline, unless indeed the Gentlemen of Chandernagore should not be vested with powers to enter into engagements of such a nature, which I sometimes suspect." [1]

Two or three days after, Clive wrote to his father: [2]

"I wrote you last by the *Chesterfield*, and acquainted you with my being just ready to set out upon the expedition to Bengal. I have now the pleasure to inform you that we all are safely arrived, and that success has attended our arms hitherto by sea and land. Calcutta is retaken and fortified; and some time ago, the second city in this province[3] was taken by storm and plundered.[4]

"We are encamped with our little army; and the Nabob is at the head of forty thousand men to give us battle. I am in hopes everything will be concluded to the Company's advantage, though not in so glorious a manner as I could wish. For more particulars I must refer you to Mr. Mabbot.

"It is not possible to describe the distresses of the inhabitants of this once opulent and great town. It must be many years before it is restored to its former grandeur. It is computed the private losses amount to upwards of two millions sterling.

"I enjoy my health better than could be expected, and think my nervous complaint decreases. Mrs. Clive was very well when I last heard from her, which was the fourth of last month.

"Colonel Lawrence is Governor of St. David's during my absence. I believe it would be no difficult matter to get appointed from home Governor of this place; but it would be neither agreeable to me nor to my advantage. I heartily wish in these perilous and uncertain times all my money was in England; for I do not think it safe here; no one knows what the event of war may be in these parts. My loss by the capture of Calcutta is not less than £2,500; so that hitherto I am money out of pocket by my second trip to India. I hope the end may crown all."

[1] Letter from Colonel Clive to the Secret Committee. London, dated Camp on Barnagore Plain, February 1, 1757.

[2] Powis MSS.

[3] Hugli.

[4] Clive estimated the value of all that was taken as a lac and a half of rupees —£15,000.

On February 3 the advanced guard of the Nawab's army was seen marching in the direction of Calcutta. Small parties entered the northern part of the town and began plundering and burning.[1] About noon Le Beaume, who had been given a captain's commission for his gallantry at the siege of Calcutta, was sent with a small force to drive them out, which he effected with rapid success.

> " In the evening the major part of the troops advanced towards the enemy to discover their situation and whether they were making any lodgment that could disturb us: whereupon a cannonading ensued which was soon discontinued as night came on, when both parties returned to their respective camps." [2]

That evening Clive received a letter from the Nawab stating

> " This place being unfit for encamping my army, for this reason my forces have marched forward and are encamped in Omichund's garden. Let not this give you any uneasiness. Your business is with me. Rest contented and send me your relation and the other person whom you shall depute to settle affairs with me as soon as possible. I swear by God and His Prophet that no evil shall happen to them."

Clive determined to dispatch Messrs. Walsh and Scrafton to him with the proposals of the Select Committee. The deputies started the next morning, and on reaching Nawabgang, a village six miles to the north, which was the appointed place of meeting, they found that the Nawab had followed his army and established his headquarters in Omichund's garden within the Mahratta ditch. They went after him, and in the evening they arrived at his camp. Scrafton wrote at the time an account of what took place:

> " Febr. 4, 1757, at seven in the evening, the Soubah gave them audience in Omichund's garden, where he affected to appear in great state, attended by the best looking men amongst his officers, hoping to intimidate them by so warlike an assembly. After the first compliments, they were desired to retire, and acquaint his ministers with their proposals. Prior to any accommodation, they insisted on the Soubah's returning to the place from which he had first offered to treat; but finding the minister shuffled with them, they desired a private conference with the Soubah: but his Excellency, judging

[1] Admiral Watson to the Nawab, dated February 4, 1757.

[2] Extract from " A Journal of the Proceedings of the Troops commanded by Lieutenant-Colonel Robert Clive on the Expedition to Bengal."

from his own treacherous disposition, was so firmly persuaded that they had private arms about them and wanted to assassinate him, that he could by no means be brought to trust himself alone with them; so that, finding the Soubah only intended to amuse them he expected their return in the morning, with full powers to finish every thing; and desired, before they quitted the camp, they would go to the tent of Jagutseat's agent,[1] who had something to communicate to them that would be very agreeable to the Colonel." [2]

Surajah Dowla had, however, given orders to detain them there, as he intended to assault the fort next day, "but suspecting his design they put out their lights, pushed forward, and soon gained the camp." They at once reported to Clive what had taken place, and they assured him they thought the Nawab was not sincere in his intentions for peace, and that he meant treachery. Clive acted with his usual energy and decision. "I went immediately on board Admiral Watson's ship, and represented to him the necessity of attacking the Nabob without delay; and desired the assistance of four or five hundred sailors, to carry the ammunition and draw the artillery; which he assented to. The sailors were landed about one o'clock in the morning. About two the troops were under arms, and about four they marched to the attack of the Nabob's camp." [3] The troops under arms numbered "470 rank and file, 800 seapoys, six field-pieces, one howitzer and 70 of the Train, besides the above body of seamen (600) half of whom were employed in drawing the guns, while the other half bore arms." [4] The Nawab's force consisted of 40,000 men, including 18,000 cavalry, 40 guns, and 50 elephants.[5]

[1] *Jagutseat's agent*, Jagat Seth, Merchant of the World, the title of a great firm of Hindu bankers at Murshidabad.

[2] "Reflections on the Government of Indostan: with a Short Sketch of the History of Bengal, from MDCCCXXXVIII. to MDCCLVI.; and an Account of the English Affairs to MDCCLVIII., by Luke Scrafton, Esq." The title of the other imprint runs: "Reflections . . . from the year 1739 to 1756; and an Account of the English Affairs to 1758," etc.

[3] Clive's Evidence—First Report of the Committee of the House of Commons.

[4] "A Journal of the Proceedings of the Troops commanded by Lieutenant-Colonel Robert Clive on the Expedition to Bengal." Eyre Coote in his Journal states, February 5: "About one in the morning we were joined by 600 sailors from the squadron under the command of Captain Warwick, and soon after marched to attack the Nabob's camp, our force being 500 rank and file in battalion, 800 seapoys, 600 sailors, six field pieces, one cohorn and 60 artillery men."

[5] Scrafton states that "the Soubah's army consisted of at least eighteen thousand horse and sixty thousand foot with forty pieces of heavy cannon," p. 68.

His best troops and his battering train lay in Omichund's garden.

Clive's plan of operation, bold as it was skilful, was first to attack the enemy's camp, which was scattered over a great extent of ground to the eastward of the Mahratta ditch, march through it, until they reached a high causeway leading through some swampy rice-fields across the ditch. Clive knew the causeway was barricaded, but he determined to carry the barricade by assault, and then counter-march on the inner side of the Mahratta ditch, attack Omichund's garden in the rear and, having spiked the enemy's battering train, capture the tent of the Nawab. Orme expressed a decided opinion, which has been accepted by biographers and historians, that the column

"ought to have assembled at Perring's Redoubt, which is not half a mile from Omichund's garden, to which they might have marched from the redoubt, in a spacious road, capable of admitting 12 or 15 men a-breast, on the left exposed indeed to the annoyance of matchlocks from some enclosures, where, however, cavalry could not act; but their right would have been defended by the rampart of the Morattoe ditch, contiguous to which the road lies; and their only danger would have been in front, from onsets of cavalry, and the discharge of what pieces of cannon the enemy had got near the garden." [1]

The answer is obvious. If Clive had followed this route he would have left the Nawab an ample outlet to withdraw his cannon and troops and join his main body. Clive's object was by his daring conception to gain a decisive victory. The plan demanded instant action, and about an hour before dawn he put his force in motion.

"One half of the Sipahis were in advance, then followed the European Battalion, the Grenadiers of the King's and Company's detachments leading; after them came the Artillery, the guns drawn by the sailors, and the ammunition carried by the Lascars,—and to prevent the latter from throwing away their loads, they were guarded all round by the remainder of the sailors, who also formed a protection to the guns; the rear was brought up by the remaining half of the Sipahis." [2]

[1] Orme, Vol. II., pp. 134–135. Orme makes two strange errors. If the troops marched inside the ditch their left would have been defended by the rampart and their right exposed to the matchlock men.

[2] "History of the Rise and Progress of the Bengal Army," by Captain Arthur Broome, p. 97. Orme, Vol. II., p. 131.

Eyre Coote marched at the head of the grenadiers immediately in the rear of the sepoys, and Clive himself took post by the European battalion. The column began its march at 4 A.M., and at 6 A.M. it approached the enemy's camp and struck some of their pickets, who opened a brisk fire of matchlocks and rockets. A rocket struck a sepoy's cartouch-box,

"which blowing up, communicated the mischief to several others, and the dread of catching this fire threw the whole division into confusion: fortunately none of the enemy were at hand to take advantage of it, and Captain Coote, who marched at the head of the grenadiers, immediately in the rear of the Sepoys, rallied them, and restored the line of march." [1]

The column pressed onward, but though morning had broken, one of those thick mists which prevail at that season of the year in Bengal, and are peculiar in their intensity, shrouded the place. For more than an hour the troops tramped slowly forward. The fog grew more intense, and rendered objects at the distance of two or three yards as invisible as in a dark night. The guides lost their way, and instead of leading the troops on to the Nawab's headquarters, as Clive intended, they turned too much to the left and took them on to the southward into the midst of the enemy's camp.[2] Knowing not where they were going, they had come in line with Omichund's garden when they heard the thunder of many hoofs, and they saw through the dense mist a large body of horse, "almost within reach of bayonet." It was the Nawab's guard, a select body of Persian and Mogul horsemen, who were stationed near his quarters, but outside the ditch. "They were received with so much coolness and such a regular fire that few of them escaped."[3] The darkness grew more intense and broken only by the flashes of the muskets of the platoon firing to the right and left, and of the field-pieces firing out-

[1] Orme, Vol. II., p. 132. Eyre Coote in his Journal states: "A shower of arrows came among us with some fire-rockets, one of which unfortunately fell on one of the Company's grenadiers (who were in my rear) and blew up almost the whole platoon." Ives says: "We lost upwards of fifty men in this action; a platoon of the company's grenadiers being blown up before day by a shower of the enemies arrows with fire-rockets falling upon them, which set fire to the powder that they carried in their pockets."

[2] Ives, p. 112. Orme does not mention this important fact.

[3] "Journal of the Expedition to Bengal, from October 13, 1756, to February 18, 1757," kept by one of Colonel Clive's family.

wardly and forward in order to clear their front. After a tramp of about a mile, the detachment reached the causeway. The leading sections of the sepoys clambered up the ascent, and, facing to the right, were on the point of rushing the barricade when some round shot came crashing through their ranks and killed several of them. The gunners in the rear not knowing of this change of front had continued their fire. The foremost sepoys sought shelter by jumping into the ditch the other side of the causeway, and those in the immediate rear followed their example. When Clive heard what had taken place he ordered the whole line to continue crossing the causeway, but to halt immediately they had passed it.[1] In descending into the ditch they lost all semblance of cohesion. While Clive was re-forming them into a column of attack to storm the barricade, two heavy guns from a small bastion on the ditch revealed their position by opening suddenly with canister shot, which swept through the mass. Twenty Europeans fell. A second discharge, and more fell. The situation had changed. It was useless to attempt to storm the barricade. Clive gave the order to march forward to a high road a full mile and a quarter to the south, which, running parallel to the causeway, also crossed the Mahratta ditch. Between the causeway and the road the land was laid out in small rice fields, divided by embankments. About 9 A.M., the sun growing stronger, the mist rose and the enemy saw a small body trudging across a muddy, naked plain. Swarms of their horse followed them and hovered about on all sides of them. Fresh guns opened on them. Clive, who had his aide-de-camp and secretary killed by his side, bravely rallied his men. He sent platoons to the right and left, which kept the horsemen at a distance, and he had the field-pieces hauled over the banks by the sailors to give them a salute. Two field-pieces broke down and had to be abandoned. The troops marched on slowly. At 10 A.M. the road was reached. The foremost files formed column to force the passage of the ditch, which was defended by a strong body of horse and foot posted in front of it. For a time the attack was checked.

[1] Orme, Vol. II., p. 132.

The enemy's troopers pressed hard upon one of the field-pieces, it being at some distance from the battalion. Ensign York, with a platoon of Adlercron's regiment, was sent to rescue it. When he arrived on the scene, "he drew up his platoon in the rear of it, and by keeping a constant fire secured the gun till it was drawn to the front." [1] With its arrival the leading platoons opened fire, the enemy's force dispersed in flight, and the British detachment crossed the Mahratta ditch. Clive's first objective was to surprise the Nawab's headquarters. But this design, like Colonel Wellesley's attack on Tippoo's outpost, was frustrated by the troops being led, owing to the darkness, in the wrong direction and getting into confusion in the gloom. Far too much has been made of both incidents.

After crossing the Mahratta ditch, for Clive to change the direction of his advance and to attack the Nawab's quarters was out of the question. He would have had to march along the Mahratta ditch for more than a mile with his flanks exposed to the fire of guns on its parapet. His small force, fatigued by its long tramp through the mire, and weakened seriously by continuous fighting, could not make certain of decisive victory. Clive therefore marched his troops along the broad road which led directly to Fort William, where they arrived a little after eleven. "In the afternoon we set out for the camp, which we reached by 7 in the evening." [2] The enemy's loss in the action was

"by the best accounts 1300 killed and wounded including twenty-two officers, some of which were of great distinction; upwards of 500 horse were counted upon the spot with four elephants and a number of camels, cattle, etc. The loss on our side amounted to twenty-seven killed in the battalion and seventy wounded, twelve seamen killed and as many wounded, eighteen *seapoys* killed and fifty-five wounded."

The British loss, considering the smallness of the force, was heavy—27 soldiers, 12 sailors, and 18 sepoys killed; 70 soldiers, 12 seamen, and 55 sepoys wounded. "It was the warmest service I ever yet was engaged in," Clive wrote

[1] Journal of Eyre Coote. [2] Journal of the Expedition to Bengal.

to his father. "The attack failed in its main object, owing to a natural event which could not be anticipated; but the boldness of design and vigour of execution terrified the Nawab, who the following day moved out into the open plain and expressed his readiness to negotiate."

On February 6 Clive, in a brief note to the Secret Committee announcing the engagement, stated:

> "The Nabob has decamped with his whole army, has wrote me a letter that he will comply with all our demands except a sum of money for the inhabitants, *viz.* that he will put us in possession of everything granted by the royal *phirmaund*, liberty to fortify Fort William as we please, and the liberty of a mint. He concludes with desiring me to sign these proposals, and that he will sign and seal them inmediately, that he will send me a *seerpah*,[1] elephant and jewells."

Clive also informed Watson of the Nawab's letter. The following night the admiral wrote:

> "I am now fully convinced the Nabob's letter was only to amuse us, in order to cover his retreat and gain time till he is reinforced, which may be attended with very fatal consequences. For my own part, I was of opinion that attacking his rear when he was marching off, and forcing him to abandon his cannon, was a most necessary piece of service to bring him to an accommodation; for till he is well threshed, don't, Sir, flatter yourself he will be inclined to peace. Let us therefore not be overreached by his politics, but make use of our arms, which are more to be depended on, and I dare say will be much more prevalent than any treaties or negotiations."

Two days passed, and Clive, fearing that the admiral's suspicions might prove correct, wrote a peremptory letter to Ranjit Rai, Jagat Seth's broker, who had accompanied the Nawab and was conducting the negotiations:

> "I am surprised that the Nabob and you trifle. I observe that you are not inclinable to agree to our proposals. God is my witness that my actions have been open and generous, and that my inclinations are for Peace. I now send you the articles wrote fair. Let the Nabob sign 'agreed' to each separate article in the manner that I have upon the copy. If this is done there shall be Peace, if not, do not concern yourself further in this affair. War must take its course."

The letter had the desired effect. On February 9 the Nawab wrote to the Admiral:

[1] *Sarāpā*—robe of honour.

"The articles which were sent to me I have returned, signed by myself, the King's *duan*,[1] my own *duan*, and the *Bukhshi*[2] of my army. I should be glad if you would confirm this treaty by a paper under your hand and seal, as the Colonel has done. I have in the most solemn manner called God and the Prophets to witness that I have made Peace with the English. As long as I have life *I shall esteem your enemies as enemies to me*, and will assist you to the utmost of my power whenever you may require it."

The Admiral replied: "The paper of agreement to the treaty on my part I send you herewith, done in the manner you desired it, signed with my hand and sealed with my seal."[3]

By the terms of the treaty signed on February 9 the Nawab agreed to restore to the Company all their factories, and to confirm all privileges granted by the Imperial Court at Delhi; to hand over to them the villages, thirty-eight in number, which they had been allowed to purchase by the Emperor Farokshah (Farrukhangar), but of which they had not received possession;[4] to permit them to fortify Calcutta and to coin money; also to permit goods with their *dustuck* (dastak) or permit, to pass free throughout Bengal, Behar, and Orissa. By the third article it was proposed that not only all the effects belonging to the Company, their servants and tenants should be restored, but "what has been plundered and pillaged by his people shall be made good by the payment of such a sum of money as his justice shall think reasonable." The Nawab, however, agreed only "to restore whatever has been seized and taken by my orders and accounted for in my Sincanny," or books of his government.

The omission in the treaty of any mention of compensation for the loss of private sufferers, some of whom had been ruined by the pillaging of Calcutta, created great dissatisfaction

[1] The king's *duan* or *Diwan*—chief officer appointed by the Mogul Emperor.

[2] *Bakhshi*—paymaster.

[3] "I, Charles Watson, etc., etc., in the name of His Britannic Majesty, and in the presence of God and Jesus Christ, do solemnly declare, that I will faithfully observe and maintain the Peace concluded on the 9th of February, 1757, between the Soubahdar, etc., and the English in every part and article thereof. And that so long as the Soubahdar, etc., shall abide by his promises, and the articles signed by him, I will always look upon his enemies as the enemies of my nation, and when called upon, will grant him all the assistance in my power." —Ives, p. 117.

[4] Their purchase was part of the privileges granted to the English on account of Mr. Hamilton, the surgeon, having cured the Emperor.

and led to the treaty being severely criticised. Clive was charged with having been guilty of undue haste in concluding it. But those who criticised Clive did not realise how difficult and complex were the problems which now confronted him. In a private letter to the Chairman of the Court of Directors he stated the grounds on which he acted with great force and clearness.

"If I had consulted the interest and reputation of a soldier, the conclusion of this Peace might easily have been suspended. I know, at the same time, there are many who think I have been too precipitate in the conclusion of it; but surely those who are of this opinion never knew that the delay of a day or two might have ruined the Company's affairs, by the junction of the French with the Nabob, which was on the point of being carried into execution. They never considered the situation of affairs on the Coast, and the positive orders sent me by the Gentlemen there, to return with the major part of the forces at all events; they never considered that, with a war upon the Coast and in the province of Bengal at the same time, a trading company could not subsist without a great assistance from the Government; and last of all, they never considered that a long war, attended through the whole course of it with success and many great actions, ended at last with the expense of more than fifty *lacs* of rupees to the Company." [1]

The policy and letter were alike statesmanlike. It marks a period in the career of Clive. The commanding temperament and far-seeing vision which made him a great Captain were now to enable him to effect brilliant triumphs of policy and legislation. Clive's critics, as he stated in the letter, had not considered the situation of affairs on the coast. England and France were at war, and the Madras Government was urgently pressing him to return with the force under his command. But the troops could not return to Madras until Calcutta had been placed beyond danger from the French at Chandernagore. If he left Bengal, the government of the province would be left in the feeble hands of Mr. Drake and the Select Committee. The violent friction between the Select Committee and the Madras Government caused him to recognise the need of a central authority. There was no bond which held together the three Presidencies, and the absence of a supreme executive power boded grave danger

[1] Letter from Colonel Clive to Mr. Payne, February 23, 1757.

to the Company. The Governor of Pondicherry was Director-General of the East Indies, and Clive wrote to his father: "I am desirous of being appointed Governor-General of India if such an appointment should be necessary."

To his father:

23 *February* 1757.

HONOURED SIR,—Since my last I have the pleasure to acquaint you the Nabob with 20,000 horse and 30,000 foot appeared in sight of our camp at the distance of about a mile and a half and encamped near Calcutta Town. His situation obliged me to attack him, which I did at daybreak in the morning. Our success was very great, being in his camp upwards of two hours, in which time we killed 1,300 men and between 5 and 6 hundred horse with 4 elephants. This blow has obliged the Nabob to decamp and to conclude a peace very honourable and advantageous to the Company's affairs, by which means they have a more promising prospect than ever. The Nabob sent me a jewel, Moorish dress and an elephant—the same to the Admiral.

As this success has probably saved the Company, this is a proper time to push my interest. I have written to my Lord Chancellor, the Archbishop, Mr. Fox, and my Lord Barrington, Secretary at War, to desire their interest. I have likewise wrote to Messrs. Mabbot, Drake and Payne. I am desirous of being appointed Governor-General of India if such an appointment should be necessary. I have opened myself a little to Mr. Mabbot; however I would have you manage this affair with great prudence and discretion and not mention the word Governor-General without you find it hinted at by other hands. Consult Mr. Belchier and don't make the contents of this letter known to anyone else but the Judge[1] and Mr. King. Consult them.

This expedition is attended with nothing but reputation; the last attack was the warmest service I ever yet was engaged in. 200 men were killed and wounded, of which number our battalion, consisting of 500 men, had 85 killed and wounded; my secretary and aide-de-camp killed by me. I shall send you a journal of our military proceedings, and I enclose you the letters to Great Men under flying seals for your perusal and for your delivery, and beg you will not be too sanguine in your expectations or expressions. I have enclosed journals to Mr. Fox and Lord Barrington.

I expect to return very shortly to the Coast, as all is over here. I have executed the conveyance you sent me, which you will receive by the *Delawar*. Make an apology to my friends for not writing them. I really have not time. My warmest wishes attend my mother, brothers and sisters, and I am,

Your dutiful and affectionate Son, ROBERT CLIVE.

[1] "Probably refers to Lord Hardwicke," says the editor of "Bengal in 1757"; but it is far more probable that the judge was Clive's uncle Sir Edward Clive, J. Common Pleas, 1753–1770.

To The Archbishop of Canterbury: [1]

May it please your Grace,

The countenance your Grace was pleased to shew me when in England, has emboldened me to address a few lines to your Grace, on the subject of the East-India Company.

No doubt your Grace has been acquainted with the capture of the town of Calcutta, and of Fort-William, by the Moors, the principal settlement in the kingdom of Bengal, and of the utmost consequence to the East-India Company. To give your Grace some idea of the richness of the place, the loss of private property only is valued at more than two millions sterling.

When this unfortunate news arrived at Madras, the President and Council applied to Vice-Admiral Watson, for his assistance in recovering the Company's rights, privileges, and possessions, in the province of Bengal; and for the purpose, ordered a large body of land-forces to embark under my command; and I have the pleasure to inform your Grace, this expedition, by sea and land, has been crowned with all the success that could be wished.

The town of Calcutta and Fort-William were soon retaken, with several other forts belonging to the enemy; and, last of all, Hughly, the second city in the Bengal Nabob's dominions. This news brought down the Nabob, or Prince of the country, at the head of twenty thousand horse, and thirty thousand foot, twenty-five pieces of cannon, with a great number of elephants. Our little army, consisting of seven hundred Europeans, and twelve hundred blacks, armed and disciplined after the English manner, lay encamped about the distance of five miles from the town of Calcutta. On the 3rd of February the Nabob's army appeared in sight, and past our camp at the distance of a mile and a half, and encamped at the back of the town, about the like distance from Fort-William. Several parties of horse passed within four hundred yards of our advanced battery, but as we entertained great hopes of peace from the Nabob's promises, we did not fire upon them.

On the 4th, agreeably to the Nabob's desire, I dispatched two gentlemen to wait upon him, in hopes everything might be settled without drawing the sword; but the haughtiness and disrespect with which he treated them, convinced me that nothing could be expected by mild measures. This determined us to attack his camp in the night-time; for which purpose I applied to Vice-Admiral Watson for five hundred sailors, to draw our cannon, &c. which he very readily complied with; and, at three o'clock in the morning, our little army, consisting of six hundred Europeans, eight hundred blacks, seven field-pieces, and the sailors above-mentioned, set out for the

[1] The letter to Lord Hardwicke is word for word the same as the letter to the Archbishop. But it closes as follows: "As your Lordship heretofore honoured me with your favour and protection, I flatter myself with the hopes of a continuance of it, and that if your Lordship thinks me deserving, your Lordship will recommend me to the Court of Directors."

attack. A little before daylight we entered the camp, and received a very brisk fire. This did not stop the progress of our troops, who marched through the enemy's camp, upwards of four miles in length. We were more than two hours passing, and what escaped the van was destroyed by the rear. We were obliged to keep up a constant fire of artillery and musketry the whole time. A body of three hundred horse made one gallant charge and were received with so much coolness by the military, that few escaped. Several other brisk charges were made upon our rear, but to no manner of purpose. We returned safe to camp, having killed, by the best accounts, thirteen hundred men, and between five and six hundred horse, with four elephants. The loss, on our side, amounted to two hundred men killed and wounded, including soldiers, sailors, and blacks. This blow had its desired effect; for the next day the army decamped, and the Nabob sent me a letter, offering terms of accommodation.

I have the pleasure of acquainting your Grace, a firm peace is concluded, greatly to the honour and advantage of the Company. The Nabob has entered into an alliance, offensive and defensive, and is returned to his capital of Muxadavad.

CHAPTER XVII

SIEGE AND CAPTURE OF CHANDERNAGORE

AFTER the conclusion of a definite treaty the Nawab, according to Oriental custom, sent not only to Clive but to the Governor and Admiral a jewel, a robe of honour, and an elephant.[1] Drake and Clive accepted the gift as representatives of the Company.

> "Mr. Watson, as representative of the King, refused to accept the present; but received the Soubah's officers who brought them in a very polite manner on board the *Kent*, and displayed to them his lower tyre of thirty-two pounders, of which they made a dreadful report to their master, who not conceiving any great liking to his new friends, marched with all haste to the capital, happily for his subjects, somewhat humbled by his late defeat."

Ranjit Rai, the active agent of the great bankers, was the head of the mission. The French had given no answer to the offers of neutrality made to them, and Clive's policy was to prevail on the Nawab to suffer him to attack Chandernagore at once. War between England and France had been proclaimed at Bombay, and he had a legitimate right to attempt the reduction of that fortified settlement.[2] The powers of the French in Bengal having been crippled, he intended to return with some of the British troops to Madras, where the French squadron was daily expected. He discussed the subject with Ranjit Rai, "but he had reason to think that he met with no advocate in him with regard to this point," and he selected another agent.

[1] Scrafton says: "An elephant dress, and head jewel."

[2] James Mill states: "In return to the French for that neutrality of theirs which had saved the English, Clive at the very moment of making peace with the Nabob, sounded him to know if he would permit the English to attack the settlement at Chandernagore, for which there still would be time before the setting in of the southern monsoon." As the French had given no answer to the offer of neutrality, the English had no cause to be grateful for their forbearance.

Omichund was, as Holwell said, vindictive and implacable, but he was still more grasping and avaricious. He had taken ample revenge on the English for the indignities he had suffered, and their expulsion from Calcutta appealed to his avarice. When he was living under the protection of the English he kept up a treasonable correspondence with the Nawab, but when Fort William was captured, a large amount of treasure was taken away from his house. As "an eminent merchant of Calcutta," the restoration of peace and the revival of the trade of the port was greatly to his interest. Omichund therefore opened up communications with the fugitives at Fulta, and did all in his power to encourage them to renew their intercourse with the leading Indian magnates. He was desirous of again winning the good will of the English, but when rumours reached him that they were about to return he thought it prudent to proceed to Murshidabad, where, first ingratiating himself with Mohun Lal, the chief favourite of Surajah Dowla, "he soon acquired a degree of confidence and intimacy with the Nawab himself; who nevertheless restored with a very sparing hand his effects which had been siezed in the general plunder and confiscation of the English property."[1] Omichund accompanied Surajah Dowla in his advance on Calcutta.

On January 19, 1757, the Nawab's army arrived a little above Hugli; on January 20, "at a Consultation," the following resolution was passed:

OMYCHUND his Behaviour during the Siege of Calcutta, his Conduct since, and the universal Notion that prevails of his having been aiding in the Councils of our Enemys giving great room to suspect his having been directly or indirectly concerned in involving the Settlement in the late Troubles.

AGREED that all his Tenures Grounds and Effects be for the present attached and sequester'd and that all his perishable effects be sold by our Agents and the Amount deposited in the Treasury till some determination is come to concerning Omychund.[2]

On January 28 Omichund wrote to Clive:

"God be praised that Calcutta is again restored to its former splendour by your arrival. Most fortunate is their lot who serve you, but how unhappy is mine who am secluded from your presence

[1] Orme, Vol. II., p. 128.
[2] Bengal Public Proceedings, Range I., Vol. XXIX., pp. 19–20.

by my confinement, which you must be acquainted with. I hope that when I shall have the honour to be called to attend you I shall be able to find means to procure my liberty. At present I understand I lie under your displeasure by means of some evil persons who have misreported me to you." "I have made it," he added, "the subject of my constant devotion that God would bring back my masters into the country. God has granted my prayers. How little I am deserving of blame will be evident when I appear before you, and then I shall have justice done me."

Whether Omichund was confined by the English or the Nawab, or whether it was a fable invented by him to justify his presence with the hostile army, there is no means of ascertaining. But from Orme we learn that he was present at the Nawab's durbar on February 3. "As the deputies were going out," says Orme, "Omichund, who had been present at the audience, advised them to take care of themselves; adding with a very significant look, that the Nabob's cannon was not yet come up." In truth the depths of Omichund's knavery are unfathomable. It is impossible to say which of his treasons were single treasons and which double treasons. Orme writes: "Messages of negotiation continued, brought and carried by Omichund and Rungeet Roy; and, on the 9th of February a treaty was concluded." The negotiations were conducted by Ranjit Rai, but that messages were brought and carried by Omichund before the treaty was concluded is not in accord with what Clive wrote to the latter on February 9, "I desire greatly to see you, and have many things to impart to you. If you can come to me for a short time you may do it with safety. No harm shall happen to you, and you shall be at liberty to return whenever you please, in security." Omichund evidently accepted the invitation, for he accompanied Ranjit Rai on his mission, and bland, clear-headed, and imperturbable, he ingratiated himself with Clive as he had with Surajah Dowla. Clive tells us that Omichund accompanied Ranjit Rai "back to the Durbar and had particular instructions to sound the Nabob on the subject" of attacking Chandernagore. Omichund returned with the following letter from the Nawab, dated February 14:

"I have imparted to Omichund several particulars which he will fully acquaint you with. I desire that when you despatch Mr. Watts to Muxadavad you will send me 25 artillery soldiers with him, and write upon a separate paper their monthly allowance, which they shall duly receive from my Treasury with an additional gratuity when I give them their dismission. What more shall I write ? "

The particulars were :

" that he had been informed that Monsieur Bussy with a large army was coming and that some French men-of-war were likewise expected, and that he desired we would prevent the French from entering his kingdom by land or water. As this was construed in some measure a permission for attacking the French in Charnagore, a proper answer was wrote to the Nabob, and Mr. Watts accompanyed by Omichund was sent to urge the point." [1]

Many points without which the treaty was of very little consequence had to be adjusted, and the Select Committee selected Mr. Watts, " being well versed in the country language and in their politics and customs," [2] to accompany the Nawab as their agent at his Court.[3] Watts was accompanied by Omichund, " whose conduct in the late negotiations had effaced the impression of former imputations, insomuch that Mr. Watts was permitted to consult and employ him without reserve."

On February 18 the British troops crossed the river and encamped opposite to Barnagal. The same day Watts wrote, from " Coss above Hughly," [4] that " Omichund is returned from Hughley and has had a meeting with Nuncomar, who is duan, and in the place of Phousdar of Hughley." [5] This is the first notice of one who has played so notorious a part in that great drama—the rise of British Dominion in India. It is strange that biographers and historians who have discussed the most conspicuous incident in the respective careers of two chief villains in that drama should not have attempted to form their judgment by a study of their whole official life.

[1] Letter from Colonel Clive to Secret Committee, London, dated " Camp opposite to Barnagul, 22 February, 1757."

[2] Scrafton's Reflections, p. 72.

[3] Orme states that the Nawab " recommended that Mr. Watts might be appointed the Company's representative at his Court ; choosing him from a persuasion that he was a meek man without guile." The Nawab soon discovered that Watts, being a diplomat, was not a simple child of nature.

[4] *Coss*—in the greater part of Bengal about two miles.

[5] *Phousdar, Foujdar*—properly a military commander (*P. fauj*, a military force ; *fauj-dar*, one holding such a force at his disposal), or a military governor of a district.—Hobson-Jobson.

Omichund, the Punjabee banker, and Nuncomar (Nandkeemar), the Bengali Brahmin, were well matched in ability, cunning, and treachery, but the Panjabi was the bolder scoundrel. Omichund learnt from Nuncomar that messengers had arrived the day before from the Nawab

> " with a present of a *lack* of rupees from the Nabob to the French Company, with orders to Nuncomar to assist the French with all his force, in case the English should attack Chandernagor, or if the French should attack the English, to assist them in the same manner, that there may be no quarrels or disputes in this country."

Watts adds :

> " Omichund upon this advises the attacking of Chandernagor immediately, and not to be apprehensive of the Nabob, and says he is certain that there is not above three hundred matchlockmen in Hughley, that he has concerted measures with Nuncomar, who has engaged to delay matters, so as to prevent any assistance coming to the French from the Nabob for these fourteen days or more, and he says you may depend on it when you are once engaged with the French no one will come to the assistance of either party. Further Omichund has promised in behalf of the English that if Nuncomar keeps neuter, and by his policy prevents any assistance arriving from the Nabob to the French, that we will then make him a present of ten or twelve thousand rupees, and use our interest to continue him in the government of Hughley. If you approve of giving this present, all that you have to say to the bearer of this letter is, *Golaub que Foul*, or ' a rose flower ' ; with which message Nuncomar will be satisfied that you comply with the agreement made by Omichund, who says that it is not pleasing to him to acquiesce in such demands, but he thinks the necessity of our affairs require it to prevent our intentions being misrepresented or further jealousies of us instilled into the Nabob, as this is such a venal Government in which nothing is to be effected without money or a very superior force. Omichund and I are of opinion that this money, if the man proves faithful (and not till then is it to be paid) will be well laid out. If you think otherwise give the bearer no answer and do not mention the *Golaub Foul*. Omichund says that the French are indebted to Juggutseat's house upwards of thirteen *lack* of rupees, which will of course I imagine prevent their engaging themselves in our interest. Omichund likewise says, that Monickchund and Coja Wazed have obtained this favour for the French in his absence, but he hopes when we arrive in camp to overset their schemes. Pray write me by express *cossids*, and if you agree to the terms proposed above, the Bramin who brings this, will carry in future the messages to and fro between you and Nuncomar. I have wrote these particulars to you and no one else, therefore you will make what use of them you think proper."

The word "Rose" was given and conveyed to Nuncomar. The Governor of one of the most important towns in Bengal, whose annual emolument was over £30,000, betrayed his sovereign for the paltry sum of a little more than £1,500.

On February 21 Watts and Omichund came within reach of the Nawab's camp, about forty miles south of Murshidabad. Surajah Dowla sent at once for Omichund and told him he had heard that the English had broken their agreement and were marching up the river. Omichund answered: "From whom, Sir, did you get this information, and what part of the agreement is broken?" The Nawab in return wished to know "if such an unprecedented act as fighting among the Europeans in the river had ever before been known. If any complaints were made to him was he not obliged to redress them?" Omichund, with the ready tact of his race, answered that the English had heard that the Nawab had given Hugli to the French. This Omichund knew was a false rumour, but he then proceeded to mention the proposals which the Nawab had so secretly made to the French. The English, he said, had also heard that he had given the French a lac of rupees and had promised to allow them to establish a mint. The English, he proceeded, were much concerned at what they heard. They wanted to discover what the French had done for the Nawab to merit such favour. When the Nawab wanted their assistance they had refused it, while the English had agreed to aid him and would always render him assistance to the utmost of their power. Then he proceeded to a delicate subject which demanded cautious and careful handling. The English were surprised, he said, that the Nawab did not consider and reflect on what were the motives and reasons for Bussy coming into this country with a large land force. Then, "with persuasion sweeter than honey on his lips," Omichund told the Nawab

"that he had lived under the English protection these forty years, that he never knew them once to break their agreement: to the truth of which Omychaund took his oath by touching a Bramin's foot: and that if a lie could be proved in England upon any one, they were spit upon and never trusted. Upon this the Nabob was (so) well pleased that though before he had ordered Meir Jaffeir himself to the assistance of the French, and proposed returning himself, he countermanded that order and sent a message by Omychaund to me to write to you that what men he had already sent down was only to garrison Hughley, and that he would give orders we should not be molested." [1]

The Nawab had written to Clive peremptorily forbidding an attack on Chandernagore. On February 22 Clive wrote to the Secret Committee of the Court: [2]

"We were in expectation of receiving very soon further encouragement from Mr. Watts for attempting the enterprise, but yesterday arrived letters from the Nabob absolutely forbidding hostilities against the French and declaring that he should consider all attempts against them as a violation of the treaty, and that he would assist them in such case with his utmost force. At the same time came in a request from the Governour and Council of Charnagore for a neutrality within the Ganges, which the Select Committee taking into consideration thought it advisable to accede to rather than risque a rupture with the Nabob. Accordingly an answer was returned them that if they were duly impowered to conclude such an act, and could get it guaranteed by the Nabob, we would come into it on our part. I wrote at the same time to the Nabob acquainting him of our submission to his orders, but that if by this means the French should hereafter be in such a state as to disturb his country he must lay the blame on himself."

On February 25 three deputies from Chandernagore attended a meeting of the Select Committee at Calcutta, and

"they were asked whether the Director and Council at Chandernagore have power to conclude a neutrality which shall be binding on all Frenchmen within the prescribed limits, whether they can restrain the ships of the French navy from attacking us, how far they extend the limits of the Ganges, whether the Council will immediately send one of their own body to the *Darbar* to get the *Nabob's* sanction, whether they will, until this is obtained, refrain from fortifying their town; to these questions they asked time to reply in writing."

The deputies Fournier, Nicolaas, and Le Conte sent an answer the same day from Calcutta Roads:

"Stating, in reply to the queries of the Council, that all the Councillors at Chandernagore are members of the Council at Pondicherry

[1] Letter from Mr. Watts to the Select Committee, dated near Agadeep February 21, 1757, 2 P.M. P.S.—"The Nabob is 12 miles off. As I have wrote this under a tree in a hurry you will (I flatter myself) excuse any little errors."

[2] Letter from Colonel Clive to The Honble Secret Committee for Affairs of the Honble United Company of Merchants of England trading to the East Indies—Camp, opposite to Barnagul, February 22, 1757.

and hence are able to conclude such a treaty, which moreover is conformable to the orders of the Nawab, that the Council will order Mr. Law, the French Chief at Cossimbazar, to obtain the Nawab's guarantee if Mr. Watts will do the same on the part of the English, that as the English can only protest if any of their commanders break the engagement so will the French, that they cannot suspend the works at Chandernagore, these being absolutely necessary for defence in case of any revolution."

The articles of a proposed treaty were drafted and explained to the French deputies:

"(1) Neutrality to be observed throughout Bengal during the present war between England and France, (2) this neutrality to extend to Cape Palmyras, (3) each party to send a copy in Persian to the Nawab who shall guarantee the treaty, (4) the French will send a copy to Pondicherry to be ratified by the Commander-General of all the French Settlements, (5) the English shall give in exchange a copy signed by Admiral Watson, (6) until these have been exchanged no act of hostility shall be committed."

On March 2 it was "Agreed to write to Admiral Watson sending a copy of the treaty, explaining our reasons, asking his opinion and whether he will agree thereto on behalf of His Majesty and lodge with us a confirmation of the treaty on his part." The day after the Admiral wrote to the Select Committee that he could not confirm the treaty until it had been sanctioned by the Supreme Government at Pondicherry. The objections were perfectly sound, and Watson gives an adequate reason for not raising them sooner.[1]

"I did suppose the Committee at Chandernagore was invested with proper powers, to make and confirm such a treaty of themselves, otherwise I should not have listened to them as much as I did: But since I have been assured by the present deputies, they have not those powers, but that the articles must be sent to Pondicherry, to be there ratified and confirmed, I can by no means think of agreeing to such a neutrality, whereby it is so evident, the French will have every advantage, and we subject to every uncertainty. Will they not reap immediate benefit by the neutrality as it now stands? And further, shall we be certain of its being complied with, till it is returned from Pondicherry, ratified and confirmed by the Governor and Council there? This appears to me, to be giving so sensible an advantage

[1] Elphinstone writes: "These objections were perfectly well founded, but they ought to have been brought forward before the terms were agreed to." —Elphinstone, p. 293.

to the French, without even a possibility of benefiting by it ourselves, that, with regard to myself, I cannot think of giving my consent to its taking place, till such time we are certain it will be agreed to by the Governor and Council of Pondicherry."

The Select Committee "Agreed to request the Admiral either to reconsider his objections to the treaty or to assist us with his squadron to attack Chandernagore without delay."[1] But Watson was obdurate, and at a meeting of the Select Committee on March 5 a letter was read from him

"repeating his belief that no Frenchman in India has power to conclude a binding treaty and that therefore he cannot consent to the treaty, also saying that he cannot break his engagements with the Nawab by attacking Chandernagore until he has full assurance that the Nabob does not intend to carry out his promises."

Clive was indignant at the want of regard shown by Watson for the promises made by himself and his colleagues to the French and the Nawab. He wrote to the Select Committee:

"If the neutrality be refused, do but reflect, gentlemen, what will be the opinion of the world of these our late proceedings. Did we not, in consequence of a letter received from the Governor and Council of Chandernagore, making offers of a neutrality within the Ganges, in a manner accede to it, by desiring they would send deputies, and that we would gladly come into such a neutrality with them? And have we not since their arrival, drawn out articles that were satisfactory to both parties; and agreed, that such articles should be reciprocally signed, sealed, and sworn to? What will the Nabob think, after the promises made him on our side, and after his consenting to guarantee this neutrality? he, and all the world will certainly think, that we are men without principles, or that we are men of a trifling insignificant disposition. It is therefore incumbent on us to exculpate ourselves, by declaring the real truth, that we were intirely ignorant of Mr. Watson's intentions to refuse the neutrality in the manner proposed, and settled by us, and that we always thought him of a contrary opinion, to what his letter declares. I am persuaded, these must be the sentiments of the gentlemen of the Committee, or they never would have gone such lengths, as must expose them to the censure of all reasonable and conscientious men."

Clive pointed out "the situation of the Company's affairs on the coast," the positive orders he had received to return to Madras with a great part of the forces under his command"; the near approach of the monsoon, which would render return

[1] Proceedings of the Select Committee, March 4, 1757.

impossible; and he insisted that if the treaty was not signed an immediate attack should be made on Chandernagore.

"You may be assured, the instant the French find their offers of neutrality refused, they will immediately assist the Nabob in all his designs against us, if he has the least intentions of not complying with the late articles of peace; it may then be too late to wish Mr. Watson had been pleased to pay more attention to our representations.

"Give me leave, gentlemen, further to represent, that though Mr. Watson has done every thing that could be expected from a brave and gallant man, and has been greatly instrumental towards settling the affairs of this province, that our future operations against the Nabob will chiefly depend upon the land forces; and the officers of such forces must certainly be the best judges of what can be effected by land; and I do take upon me to give it as mine and my officers' opinions, that success against the Nabob and French together will be very precarious, notwithstanding the arrival of the Bombay troops, which fell short in real strength of the detachment on board the *Cumberland*. I must therefore request you will join with me, in desiring Mr. Watson a third time to ratify the neutrality in the manner agreed upon; and if he refuses, to desire he will attack Chandernagore by water immediately, as I am ready to do by land with the forces under my command; and if he refuses this likewise, he becomes responsible for every misfortune that may happen to the East India Company's affairs.

"This done, I propose leaving all the forces I can possibly spare for the defence of the Company's settlements, rights, and privileges, in Bengal, and return with the rest immediately to the coast, agreeable to the positive orders received from the President and Committee of Madrass; and I must request you will order proper conveyances for that purpose."

The arrival of the Bombay reinforcement Clive considered did not diminish the immediate necessity of concluding the treaty. The choice lay, as he persistently stated, between an immediate attack on Chandernagore and an armistice with the French. But he warned his colleagues that if they adopted the former alternative, war with Surajah Dowla was bound to follow. "If," he wrote, "you attack Chandernagore you cannot stop there, you must go farther. Having established yourselves by force and not by the consent of the Nabob, he by force will endeavour to drive you out again." This was the main consideration which induced Clive to favour the immediate conclusion of a treaty with the French. He had, however, no sooner given his warning when he received a letter from the Nawab which altered his opinion, for it led him to suppose that he would be able to convince Surajah Dowla that it was for his interest and safety that he should consent to Chandernagore being attacked.

At a meeting of the Select Committee held on March 6 :

" Present : The Honourable Roger Drake, *President*, Robert Clive, *James Killpatrick*, Richard Becher.

" Approved Proceedings of the 5th instant.

" Letter from *Mr. William Watts*, dated the 3rd instant, intimating the *Nabob's* disposition in regard to our attacking Chandernagore and his request for our assistance against the *Pytans.*[1]

" *Colonel Clive* presents a translation of a letter from the *Nabob*. As this letter shows that we may possibly get the *Nabob's* permission to attack the *French* if we make it a condition of assisting him against the *Pytans*, the question of writing again to the *Admiral* is raised. *Mr. Becher* is strongly in favour of establishing a neutrality and telling the *Admiral* that the treaty was commenced with his consent, and that he is responsible for the results if he now refuses. *Colonel Clive* and *Major Killpatrick* are in favour of advancing on Chandernagore on the chance of getting the *Nabob's* permission. The *President* thinks that all the advantage of the neutrality will be with the *French*, that neither the *French* nor the *Nabob* are to be trusted, that without the *Admiral's* consent we cannot conclude a peace, so, though we should wait for the *Nabob's* consent if obtainable, we should attack Chandernagore as soon as possible. Agreed to postpone the treaty till we have tried again to get the *Nabob's* consent and to write to the *Admiral* explaining why unless we get it the peace must be ratified." [2]

At the close of the letter, a translation of which was laid before the Select Committee, Surajah Dowla wrote in his own handwriting as follows :

[1] In the ancient documents " Pytans " is written for Pathans, and, as in this case, often used for the equivalent of Afghan. " Puttán, Pathán, Hind. Pathān. A name commonly applied to Afghans and especially to people in India of Afghan descent. The derivation is obscure.—Hobson-Jobson, p. 746.

[2] The Official Record of the proceedings differs materially from Clive's account of the debate in his evidence before the Parliamentary Committee of 1772. Clive said : " That the members of this Committee were, Mr. Drake, himself, Major Kilpatrick and Mr. Becher :—Mr. Becher gave his opinion for the attack of the place ; Mr. Drake gave an opinion that nobody could make anything of : Major Kilpatrick then asked him, Whether he thought the forces and squadron could attack Chandernagore, and the Nabob's army, at the same time ?—he said, he thought they could : upon which Major Kilpatrick desired to withdraw his opinion, and to be of his Lordship's. They voted Mr. Drake's no opinion at all ; and Major Kilpatrick and he, being the majority, a letter was wrote to Admiral Watson, desiring him to co-operate in the attack on Chandernagore." Clive " Approved Proceedings of the 6th instant." His evidence was given fifteen years after the event.

"The advanced forces of the new King are endeavouring to make an eruption into Bengal and I purpose marching to Azimabad.[1] If you will join me upon this occasion and go with me, I will allow you every month a lakh of rupees (£10,000) during the time you continue with me for the maintenanee of your army. Write me speedily an answer to this."

The new king was the terrible Ahmad Shah, Chief of the Abdali tribe of Afghans and ruler of Afghanistan, who had invaded India for the second time, sacked Delhi, and was now said to have marched from the Imperial capital with the intention of conquering Bengal. The Nawab had made the same offer to the Admiral on February 22, and asked for an immediate answer.[2] Watson, so jealous of his authority, evidently did not inform Clive of the offer, and he did not send an answer till March 4, the very day that the Nawab was writing to Clive requesting his assistance. The Admiral informed the Nawab that he had invited the French to enter into a treaty of neutrality, but after the terms had been settled the French deputies, to his great surprise, owned they had no power to secure its observance.

"You are too reasonable not to see, that *it is impossible for me to conclude a treaty with people who have no power to do it; and which besides, while it ties my hands, leaves those of my enemies at liberty to do me what mischief they can.* They have also for a long time reported that Monsieur Bussy is coming here with a great army. Is it to attack you? Is it to attack us?"

He added:

"You are going to Patna. You ask our assistance. Can we with the least degree of prudence march with you, and leave our enemies behind us? You will then be too far off to support us, and we shall be unable to defend ourselves. Think what can be done in this situation. I see but one way. Let us take Chandernagore, and secure ourselves against any apprehensions from that quarter, and then we will assist you with every man in our power, and go with you even to Delhi if you will. Have we (?) not sworn reciprocally that the friends and the enemies of the one should be

[1] Azimabad—Native name of Patna.

[2] The Nawab wrote: "The van of the King of Delhi's army is advancing towards these provinces. Upon this intelligence I design marching towards Patna to meet them. If at this critical juncture you will be my friend and send me assistance I will pay your forces a *lack* of rupees monthly, while they remain with me. Send me an immediate answer."

regarded as such by the other? And will not God, the avenger of perjury, punish us if we do not fulfill our oaths? What can I say more? Let me request the favour of your speedy answer."

No speedy answer came, and definite proof having been obtained that the Nawab was inviting Bussy to advance to his aid, the Admiral wrote again in a different strain. He demanded that the Nawab should fulfil every article of the treaty in ten days, and he closed his letter with a menace:

"As I have always acted the open, unreserved part in all my dealings with you, I now acquaint you that the remainder of the troops, which should have been here long since (and which I hear the Colonel told you he expected), will be at Calcutta in a few days; that in a few days more I shall dispatch a vessel for more ships and more troops; and that I will kindle such a flame in your country as all the water in the Ganges shall not be able to extinguish. Farewell: remember that he promises you this, who never yet broke his word with you or with any man whatsoever."

Two days after the dispatch of Watson's fiery epistle, Clive sent a calm diplomatic reply to the Nawab's request for assistance. He stated that, like Watson, he was very inclinable to enter into a neutrality with the French, "but I found upon endeavouring to treat with them, they had no powers to make a peace with us till it was confirmed at Pondicherry, which could not be effected in less than three months"; and that it gave him great concern to find the Nawab so strongly insist on the neutrality with the French, which was attended with all the advantage on their side and most prejudicial to ours. "What we agree to will be immediately binding, but what they agree to will be of no signification till ratified by the Governor of Pondicherry, and whilst all our forces are employed in assisting you against your enemies, Monsieur Bussy may come and attempt to destroy our Settlement." He added, with a sort of naïveté which, when it suited him, Clive could well assume, "To give you a convincing proof of my sincerity, by that time you receive this letter, I shall be as far on my way as Chandernagore, where I will wait without committing any hostilities against the French, till I receive your letter, which I hope will be satisfactory."

Clive realised that the Nawab's request for assistance was

a call to a decisive action. On March 5 "Lieutenant Molitur, with 8 sergeants, 8 corporals, 2 drums, and 53 privates besides 43 topasses, in all 114, arrived at camp from Bombay." [1] Clive, strong and prompt, determined to advance at once. He had told the Committee that the Bombay troops "fell short in real strength of the detachment on board the *Cumberland*." A strong body of troops would have been a welcome addition to his small force. But the political situation demanded an immediate move. It was uncertain when the *Cumberland* would arrive. On March 7 she reached the mouth of the Hugli too late for Clive to hear of her arrival before his advance. But if he had delayed, the arrival of the *Cumberland* would have added but little to the strength of his force. She had, as Clive knew, embarked when the expedition left Madras 300 infantry. But when Admiral Pocock was forced to leave the fleet and bear away to Vizagapatam he found, on arriving there, the factory in great fear and anxiety, expecting to be attacked by Bussy. He accordingly, at the request of the local authorities, landed one company of the Madras Battalion. The currents being still opposed to his progress he returned to Madras, where, at the request of the Madras Government, he re-landed the remainder of the Madras Battalion.

"There now only remained on board the Company of H.M.'s 39th, amounting to about 90 men, and with these he arrived at the mouth of the Hooghly, in time to take part in the capture of Chandernagore, but not to admit of the troops being employed;—they were moreover in a very sickly condition, having suffered greatly during the protracted voyage."

The statement made by numerous writers that the arrival of the *Cumberland* influenced Clive's decision to advance on Chandernagore is not in accordance with the facts. [2]

[1] Colonel Clive's Military Journal, March 2 to March 25, 1757. Eyre Coote enters in his Journal: "March 4th.—The first division of the Bombay troop consisting of 150 men, joined us under the command of Captain Buchanan."

[2] Broom, p. 118. Orme, Vol. II., pp. 142–3. Mill, misled by Orme, states: "The very same day on which the letter of the Nabob reached Calcutta, the arrival was announced of three ships with troops from Bombay, and of one of the ships, also bearing troops, which sailed with Clive from Madras, but was compelled to return." "With such additions," says Mr. Orme, "the English force was deemed capable of taking Chandernagor, although protected by the Nabob's army. Colonel Clive therefore immediately dismissed the French

On March 8 Clive broke camp and moved his troops northwards, the infantry proceeding by land, the artillery by water. The force advanced slowly, "so as to give the Bombay detachment time to join them before entering the French boundary." On March 9 the force "marched and encamped near Serampore, a factory belonging to the Danes."[1] The French Council had written to Clive demanding an explanation of his advance, and Clive replied on the 9th: "I very sincerely declare to you that at this present time I have no intention to attack your Settlement. If I should alter my mind, I shall not fail to advise you of it." At the close of the letter he reiterates the statement: "I have no intention of acting offensively against your nation at present; whenever I have, you may be assured I shall frankly acquaint you with it." Clive had not received the Nawab's consent to attack Chandernagore, and without it he had no intention of acting offensively against the French settlement. He, however, continued his advance. On March 10 he "marched and encamped about two miles from the French Gardens." At the northern extremity of the French gardens was the country house of the governors of Chandernagore. It was a splendid mansion, situated in a large park with trees. L. de Grandpré describes it as the finest building in India.

> "The front towards the garden is in the taste which the Europeans have adopted in this part of the world, being ornamented with a peristyle of the Ionic order, after the Grecian manner. The inside of the place is splendid, the hall spacious, and the ceiling and cornice are painted by the hand of a master. The front towards the court is entirely in the French taste, with no peristyle. It represents three buildings, each adorned with a pediment, in which are the cartouches for bas-reliefs, which have not been executed. The court is circular, and in a good taste, and the entrance is by an avenue, that opens majestically upon this beautiful edifice."[2]

deputies, who were then with him waiting to sign the treaty, which was even written out fair, and which they supposed had been entirely concluded."—Mill, Vol. III., pp. 126–7. The Bombay troops arrived some days before the Nawab's letter asking for the co-operation of the English. The *Cumberland* reached the mouth of the Hugli some days later. The articles of the treaty were "explained to the French deputies," but they could not suppose the treaty had been "entirely concluded" until it had been signed by the Chandernagore government and confirmed by Admiral Watson.

[1] Eyre Coote's Journal.

[2] "A Voyage in the Indian Ocean and to Bengal undertaken in the Years 1789 and 1790." Translated from the French of L. de Grandpré, an officer in the French Army, Vol. II., p. 85.

A few crumbling ruins in the midst of a dense jungle mark the site of the splendid mansion, often compared by travellers of old to the Château of Versailles. In the French gardens the force rested the following day, and "the second division of the Bombay troop consisting of 150 men" joined them. While at the gardens, Clive's spies having given him timely and true notice that the French had erected batteries in the principal streets of the town leading from the south to the fort, in order to stop his advance from that direction and from the river side, he determined to make a detour. On March 12 he "marched and encamped about two miles to the west of Chandernagore."[1] On the 13th the Admiral received a letter from the Nawab which settled the fate of the French settlement.

The anger of Surajah Dowla waxed hot on the receipt of the Admiral's menace. It is stated that he sent at once for Omichund and demanded to know why the Admiral had refused to sign the treaty. Omichund replied that he had been enraged at the duplicity of the French in pretending to negotiate a treaty which they had no authority to sign. The Nawab "had already sent a large body of troops to assist the French; had returned the two laacks of rupees taken from them the year before; and had entered into some private negociation with the French governor, wherein he promised him the government of Houghly, a mint, and other advantages."[2] Surajah Dowla was a faithless ally. Unlike his warrior ancestors, he was a coward, and he was sore afraid of the terrible Afghan Abdali. It was in this temper of mind that Surajah Dowla had an audience with Watts, who represented in the strongest light "the Condescension shewn him by the *British* by accepting, and the Indignity offered to him by the *French* in rejecting his Expedient."[3] Watts made skilful "use of the Nawab's dread of the Afghauns and observed to him that we could never think of leaving our settlement to be attacked by the French,"[4] in case he

[1] Colonel Clive's Military Journal. [2] Scrafton, p. 74.
[3] "Memoirs of the Revolution in Bengal," p. 42.
[4] The full account given by Law, who was present at the interview, differs from the brief statements of Watts and Scrafton.

required our assistance against the Afghans. The Nawab, a victim to chagrin at the treaty not being signed, and in alarm at the prospect of losing the assistance of the British, directed a letter to be written to the Admiral. Watts bribed, or, as it is euphemistically stated, "added a hansome present" to, the Nawab's secretary, "to pen this important Epistle in a proper stile, so as to permit the Attack immediately, and to despatch it without delay." To the letter the Nawab's seal was attached, and it was sent off at once. The Nawab thus communicated his views on March 10:

"Your obliging answer to my letter I have received, wherein you write that your suspicions are at an end, and that on the receipt of my letter you forbore attacking *Chandernagore*, and sent for their people to make peace, and wrote out the terms of agreement; but when they were about signing them, they declared that if they signed the articles, and any other commander should arrive, they could not be answerable for his adhering to them: and that on this account there was no peace. You also write many other particulars, of which I am well acquainted. It is true, if it is the custom of the *French* that if one man makes an agreement, another will not comply with it, what security is there? My forbidding war on my borders was because the *French* were my tenants, and upon this affair desired my protection: on this I wrote you to make peace, and no intentions had I of assisting or favouring them.

"*You have understanding, and generosity: if your enemy with an upright heart claims your protection, you will give him his life, but then you must be well satisfied of his intentions; if not, whatever you think right, that do.*"

The Admiral and Clive regarded the last paragraph, couched in characteristic Oriental phraseology, as a permission to attack Chandernagore.[1] Moreover, Watts wrote to Clive the same day that the Nawab's letter was dispatched, that he had just returned from visiting him, and "the Nabob said he could not write, but desired I would inform you that if you was determined to attack the French, he would not intermeddle or give them the least assistance, he only requests to be informed of your sentiments three or four days before you begin upon action." In the "Memoirs of the Revolution in Bengal" it is stated that the Nawab's letter arrived

[1] "It was this paragraph that encouraged the Admiral and Colonel to proceed in their attack of Chandernagore."—Ives, p. 125, *n*.

"in the most critical conjuncture. For, notwithstanding the *French* had avowed their Want of Power to conclude an effectual Neutrality, yet so much were some afraid of recurring again to Arms, that they were still for accepting of this Expedient, however precarious. Upon this, Admiral *Watson* held a Council of War, to consider what was most proper to be done; and it was while this Council was actually sitting, wherein those who argued yet for a Neutrality insisted chiefly upon the Suba's Repugnancy to see the Flame of War, so lately extinguished, again rekindled in his Dominions, that this Letter was brought, which cut the Gordian Knot, and put an End to the Debate." [1]

Watson's scruples with regard to attacking Chandernagore had been removed by the receipt of official notice of the war with France, "accompanied by orders" from the Admiralty. "The Declaration of War," Watson held, "is an order to all officers under the King to distress the enemy as far as it is in their power." On March 12 the Admiral wrote to the Select Committee:

GENTLEMEN,—I have received your favour of this day's date, acquainting me with your motives and reasons for altering your sentiments in relation to your conduct with the French, and now desire the assistance of His Majesty's squadron to attack Chandernagore.

You may be assured that I shall most readily give you all the assistance I can in this enterprise, and am heartily glad, in the present circumstances I am in of having received His Majesty's Declaration of War against France with orders from the Right Honourable the Lords Commissioners of the Admiralty to put the same in execution, that this step is judged a right measure.

The moment the pilots think it safe to move the large ships I shall proceed up the river, and am, Gentlemen, your most obedient,

CHARLES WATSON.

On the 13th Clive wrote to M. Renault, Governor of Chandernagore:

SIR,—The King of Great Britain having declared war against France, I summons you in his name to surrender the fort of Chandernagore. In case of refusal you are to answer the consequences, and expect to be treated according to the usage of war in such case.

I have the honour to be, Sir,

Your most obedient and humble Servant,

R. CLIVE.

Since the departure of Dupleix from the settlement, the foundation of whose wealth and commerce was due to his

[1] "Memoirs of the Revolution in Bengal," p. 43

far-seeing and vigorous administration, Chandernagore had continued to prosper. French vessels from Jedda Moka, Bassorah, the Maldwer, China and Pegu, steered through the reefs and quicksands of the Hugli by the "*pilotin du Gange*," brought their rich cargoes to the quay. The country vessels dropping down the river brought to it corn, opium, silk, and the fine muslins of Bengal. It was, says Clive, "a most magnificent and rich colony." The year after the departure of Dupleix tacit permission was given to fortify the factories on the banks of the Hugli, and the French, wiser than the English, who thought the slightest rampart might prevent a surprise, erected a fort called Fort D'Orleans, situated almost in the middle of the colony and about thirty yards from the river. It was a square of about 120 yards with a bastion mounting ten guns at each corner, and several guns were also placed on the connecting curtains. On the north was the gateway, Porte Royale, which gave access to the high road to Chinsura; on the east was the Ganges Gate,[1] and beyond it a ravelin extending to the bank of the river, and on this outwork eight guns were mounted. These guns were chiefly 24- and 32-pounders. The best buildings within the fort were the warehouses almost facing the Ganges or Water Gate, and directly west of them was the factory; on the north of the warehouses were the official quarters, and along the northern curtain the barracks; along the southern curtain the director's quarters, or Government House, and the Church of St. Louis overlooking the eastern walls facing the river. On its flat terrace six small pieces were mounted. The fort was surrounded on three sides by a ditch, and on the western side, "beyond the Ditch, a great Tank only two fathoms away from it which prevented any precipitate attack of the enemy on this side."[2] The most populous quarter of the town lay south of the fort. Here were situated the markets, and in front of them were the great white villas of the opulent merchants, with luxurious gardens stretching down to the

[1] Ganges Gate. The western delta branch of the Ganges has been long known from the town of Hugli as the Hugli River.

[2] "Revolution in Bengal." "Bengal in 1756–1757," edited by S. C. Hill, Vol. III., p. 232, Brit. Mus. Add. MSS., 20, 914.

margin of the stream. Behind the markets was the Dutch Octagon.[1] The houses on the south extended beyond the south-western bastion (St. Francis) to the road which led to the Company's gardens. They then stretched northwards to the southern extremity of the tank. Directly west of the tank was the Company's hospital, and near the north-western bastion (Des Anges), the house of the Jesuits, and a church.

Renault, the Governor of Chandernagore, tells us that when the English recaptured Calcutta and positive information reached him by an express from Surat of the declaration of war, he thought it wise to set about putting the outworks in a defensible condition:

"Accordingly I began pulling down the Church, the House of the Reverend Jesuit Fathers, and all those to the north. I would have done the same to those on the south if I had had time and workmen, and if, at the first hostilities between the English and the Moors, all the country people had not taken alarm and entirely deserted our Colony." [2]

The wood of the débris he utilised to construct palisades to protect the northern curtain which, he states, was falling down from mere age.

"I also had built before the Porte Royale, the weakest side of the Fort, a platform on which we put 3 guns, and we worked at digging out and enlarging the ditch, but had not time to put it in a condition to serve for the defence of the place. A warehouse for goods, on which I had put bales of *gunny*[3] to prevent the bombs breaking the vaults, served it as a casemate."

Renault also informed the Council at Pondicherry that:

"The ships of war being, in case of a siege, what we had most to fear from, we erected close to the Ganges a battery of six guns, of which four defended the entry to the harbour. From the foot of this battery was begun a screen 22 feet thick running from the river to the Fort to protect the whole of the curtain on this side from the fire of the ships, but it could not be finished, the Settlement also needing attention. It was decided whilst we were working at all the above mentioned defences to try and put the Settlement in safety against a surprise, as it was not possible to do anything better. Con-

[1] The Dutch Octagon—the quarters of the Dutch East India Company.

[2] Letter from M. Renault to M. the Marquis Dupleix, September 4, 1757, "Bengal in 1756–57," Vol. III., p. 245. Bibliothèque Nationale MSS., Paris.

[3] A fibre used for rough materials like sacking.

sequently we barred all the streets with ditches and barricades, at which we established guards."

Besides the battery before Porte Royale, the gate leading to Chinsura, and the battery close to the river commanding a narrow part of the channel, Renault erected three batteries in the principal streets in the south of the town leading to the fort and one of four guns on the road which led from the Company's garden to the north. He states that after the outposts had been abandoned the forces in the fort numbered "237 soldiers (including 45 French pensioners and the sick), 120 sailors, 70 half-castes and private Europeans resident in the Settlement, 100 individuals—as Councillors, Company's servants, officers of the Indiamen, and other principal inhabitants, 167 sepoys, 100 topasses." [1] The Nawab had also left at Chandernagore two thousand of his troops under the command of the French Governor, in case the English attacked the settlement.

On the night of the 13th the French, having taken no notice of the affront of a summons, Clive ordered the Company's grenadiers[2] under Captain Lin "to join the picquet with orders to take possession of the French Bounds, and to annoy and alarm the enemy at their out-batteries, which accordingly they did, and took possession of a battery to the north-west of Chandernagore Fort, which was abandoned by the French." At 6 o'clock the next morning the 3rd Division of the Bombay troops having reached the camp, Clive ordered Major Kilpatrick with half the troops, including Eyre Coote and his

[1] Eyre Coote states that "the number of the enemy in the garrison were 500 Europeans and about 500 blacks."—Journal of Captain Eyre Coote. Orme writes: "The garrison consisted of 600 Europeans and 300 Sepoys; but only 300 of the Europeans were regular troops, the rest being inhabitants of the town and sailors."—Orme, Vol. II., p. 141. Clive wrote on March 29, 1757: "The garrison consisted of more than five hundred Europeans and seven hundred blacks all carrying arms." Malleson, whose figures are taken from the old records of Chandernagore, says: "The French garrison consisted of a hundred and forty-six French troops and three hundred sepáties; but the European population and the sailors of the merchant vessels, to the number of about three hundred, had been hastily formed into a kind of militia and had been armed. These, however, had but little training."—"Life of Lord Clive," p. 203.

[2] The Company's Grenadiers consisted of 1 captain, 3 lieutenants, 1 quartermaster, 11 non-commissioned officers, 2 drummers, and 65 Europeans.—A General Muster of the Troops under the Command of Colonel Clive in Camp near Chinsurah, April 7, 1757.

company of grenadiers, to advance to the post which the grenadiers had taken possession of the night before.[1] It was situated near a gateway spanning the road leading from the Company's gardens to the northern face of the fort. From the enemy's deserted battery Major Kilpatrick and his men could see the 4-gun battery within a hundred yards of the north-western bastion. In order to check their advance the enemy from this battery "played down an avenue with two field-pieces and musketry, but did little execution on account of the too great distance."[2] Some detachments of sepoys were now ordered to advance under cover of the thickets on each side of the avenue with an intention of flanking the enemy's battery. The King's grenadiers, under Eyre Coote, and the Company's, under Captain Lin, followed to support them. The enemy opened a smart fire, but the sepoys and Europeans continued their advance and took possession of some houses within fifty yards of the battery. "We continued firing at each other in an irregular manner till about noon."[3] Eyre Coote informs us that Clive then ordered him to hold the advanced post with his grenadier company and about 200 sepoys while he returned with the rest of the troops to the gateway, which was about a mile back. About 2 o'clock word was brought to Eyre Coote that the French were making a sortie, and soon after he saw the sepoys returning from their post. He at once sent a message to Clive, informing him that the French were advancing. "I was then obliged," says Eyre Coote, "to divide my company, which consisted of about fifty men, into two or three parties (very much against my inclination), to take possession of the ground the *sepoys* had quitted; we fired pretty warmly for a quarter of an hour from the different parties at each other, when the French retreated again into their battery."

The firing then ceased on both sides. It had been a trying day for the brave garrison whose strength had been seriously diminished. The troops which the Nawab had sent, some two thousand in number, deserted the houses in which

[1] Colonel Clive's Military Journal, March 2 to March 25, 1757.
[2] *Ibid.*
[3] Journal of Captain Eyre Coote.

they were posted, at the firing of the first shot, "and did not again reappear." The outposts were soon surrounded by burning buildings, and in the midst of the conflagration their defenders were harassed by long and incessant attacks "made in the greatest heat" of an Indian March day.[1] When under cover of the fast-falling darkness the British got possession of the houses adjacent and to the rear of the north-west battery, Renault saw there was nothing left but to abandon it. This entailed withdrawal from the other outposts. The French Governor states:

> "The loss of this would have occasioned that of seven others in the Settlement by the ease with which they would have cut off their communication with the Fort, and the troops, which already consisted of three-quarters of our garrison, could not during the night, at so great a distance, be relieved from the Fort without putting the latter in danger. The outposts were therefore abandoned at 9 P.M. and each retired in good order, after having spiked such of the guns as they could not bring back with them."

The French not only abandoned their batteries to the northward but they deserted

> "that night all their works to the southwards, among the rest a strong Moon on the river side mounting heavy metal, and a battery of 3 guns playing down the Channel, both of which must have annoyed our ships greatly in their passage up."[2]

On the 15th Clive occupied the abandoned outworks and the houses on the southern esplanade to within a hundred yards of the fort, "and the same evening began to bombard the place from five small mortars and a cohorn." On the 16th the British force was employed in bringing up the artillery and the stores, and "this evening the 13-inch mortar began to play upon the Fort, and several small parties by way of alerts advanced under the walls to keep the enemy constantly awake."[3] During the 17th the mortars and cohorns continued to throw their shells into the fort, and the assailants opened a heavy fire of musketry from the tops of the houses. At

[1] Letter from M. Renault to the Superior Council at Pondicherry, dated Pondicherry, October 26, 1758.

[2] Letter from Colonel Clive, camp near Chandernagore, to the Select Committee at Fort St. George, March 30, 1757.—Powis MSS.

[3] Colonel Clive's Military Journal.

the approach of night a French doctor states the besieged found on the bastions a number of arrows, round the steel points of which little slips of papers were rolled. On them was written: "Pardon to deserters who will rejoin their colours, and rewards to officers who will come over to us." On the 18th Clive wrote to Watson: "The only artillery officer at Chandernagore is come over to us. He gives a very favourable account of matters. He shall wait on you when you think proper." The deserter was Monsieur Terraneau, a man of considerable ability, who had quarrelled with the Governor of Chandernagore. Renault writes:

> "Cossart de Terraneau, Sub-Lieutenant of this garrison, who had lost an arm in the wars on the (Madras) Coast in the service of France, and who commanded the artillery, deserted to the enemy on the evening of the 19th, and the same night by the improved direction of the besiegers' bombs, I had no doubt that he had done us a bad service."

On the 19th the besiegers began to erect a battery of five 24-pounders behind the wall of a house that was close to the glacis and opposite to the south face of the south-east bastion. They likewise turned a battery of the enemy's on the south flank of the north-east bastion and mounted three 24-pounders. The next day the enemy silenced this battery and almost demolished the work. On March 21, "Continued making the five-gun battery, and almost finished the three; when the enemy began firing warmly again at it and knocked down a veranda close by the battery, the rubbish of which choked up one of our guns, very much bruised two artillery officers, and buried several men in the ruins." [1] On March 22 the battery was finished, "but got no more than four guns in it." In the evening the enemy opened a warm fire. The batteries were, however, completed during the night and were ready to open at daybreak, when the fleet lying at anchor about two miles below Chandernagore [2] moved up the river.

On March 12 the Declaration of War with the French having been read on board the *Tyger*, the *Bridgwater* and *Kingsfisher* sailed up the river to cover the landing of the artillery and

[1] Eyre Coote's Journal.
[2] Letter from Admiral Watson—*Kent*, off Chandernagore, March 31, 1757.

the ammunition. On the 15th the *Kingsfisher* anchored three miles below Chandernagore. The same day Admiral Watson, taking advantage of the flood tides, sailed from Calcutta with his flagship the *Kent* (Captain Speke), the *Tyger* (Captain Latham), and the *Salisbury* (Captain Martin). Three days later, turning the point of Chandernagore reach, they anchored off the Prussian Octagon,[1] "from whence we had a full view of the town and fortification."[2] Watson wished to get up the river at once, but the tides rendered it impossible. The French had also neglected no means of obstructing the passage which directly above where the fleet had anchored was very narrow, owing to an extensive sandbank. They had sunk "two ships, a ketch, a snow, a hulk, and a vessel without masts," all directly in the Channel within gunshot of the fort, and had laid two booms moored with chains across the river.[3] Above the fort three large French vessels lay at anchor. The Admiral learnt that they were prepared as fireships to be sent down with the tide to burn our vessels, and he resolved that something must be done at once. At 8 P.M. Saturday, March 19, he dispatched the boats manned and armed up the river, and three hours later they returned, having cut the cables of the three vessels. The crews belonging to them had been taken to reinforce the garrison, and all drifted on the sandbank.[4]

The following morning the Admiral sent Lieutenant Hey, the third lieutenant of the *Kent*, with a flag of truce, to the fort to demand its surrender. Renault writes:

"Not having had time to fortify the Fort completely on the river side, and having equal cause to fear from the depth of the water in the place where the vessels were sunk in the narrowest point of the Road that the English men-of-war (the fire of which I foresaw we could not resist) would come and anchor broadside on to the Fort, I determined to write to the Vice-Admiral and try to persuade him to content himself with a ransom. Mr. Watson refused this offer, always insisting that I should give up the Fort, though promising, it is true, to leave to the inhabitants the enjoyment of their property. The fact that he insisted upon conditions so unfavourable

[1] The Prussian Octagon, the head-quarters of the Agent of the Prussian Company, a little south of French territory.

[2] Ives, p. 126.

[3] Letter from Admiral Watson, *Kent*, off Chandernagore, March 31, 1757.

[4] Ives, p. 127.

to the Company when the land force had obtained such slight advantages was our reason for the recommencement of hostilities."

Hey, intelligent and trustworthy, observed as he rowed between the masts of the sunken vessels that their hulls were not deep under water, and he concluded that they had not been sunk in their proper place. On the night of the 20th Mr. John Delamotte, master of the *Kent*, "a brave and active officer," was sent to sound around them, and regardless of a heavy cannonade from the fort, he did his work and brought back the pleasant tidings that there was sufficient room for one vessel to pass between them with safety.[1] The following day there appeared an unexpected arrival. When at Ballasore Admiral Pocock heard that the fleet was about to start immediately on an expedition against Chandernagore. He knew that, owing to the intricacies of the winding river, it was impossible to get the *Cumberland* up in time. He therefore, "with a spirit worthy of an English Admiral," took his barge, strongly manned, and rowing night and day joined Watson on the 21st, and the next night, a few hours before the coming attack, he hoisted his flag on board the *Tyger*. The same evening the King's detachment was ordered on board the three vessels.

On March 23, before daybreak, Clive marched with the

[1] The author of the "Seir Mutaqherin" states that Admiral Watson "was incited to this enterprise by Moosher-terno who, forgetting what he owed to his own nation, pointed out to him a particular passage which the French had left open in the Bagrati [Bhāgirathī] for their own ships to pass, in case of need; for they had spoiled the whole breadth of the river by sinking a number of vessels. The Amiral Dilir-djung, under such a guide, advanced up with his ships of war, and took by force the French fortress."—"Seir Mutaqherin," p. 760. Monsieur Raymond, the translator of the "Seir Mutaqherin," appends the following note: "*Terrano*, a French officer, who, dissatisfied with Renaud, the governor of the fort, went over, not to the Admiral, but to the Colonel, to whom he became of some use. This man, who had some merit, having made money in the English service, sent, a few years after, a supply to his father in France, promising to take care of him henceforward. The old man returned the money, with a letter, in which he protested against holding any correspondence with a traitor to his country; and the son, in despair at the style of the letter, hanged himself at his own door, with his own handkerchief. He was a tall, stout man, who, having lost his right arm by a ball of cannon, had found means to write legibly with the left, and what is more, to write a pamphlet on Artillery, in good English. The officers at first would not admit him in their corps; but the Colonel remonstrated, and he observed that his word was engaged to the man on that article, and that a failure on his part would preclude any further desertions." Bhāgirathī—one of the delta branches of the Ganges which forms the Hugli River.

Company's troop from the camp into the town and posted them in the batteries and houses that overlooked the bastions of the fort. When the dawn brought the first light the ships hoisted the white sails and moved slowly upwards with the tide. The *Tyger* with Admiral Pocock's flag led, the *Kent* with Watson's flag quickly following, and the *Salisbury* bringing up the rear. In a few minutes they were through the sunken ships. Clive watched them sailing on, and when they came within reach of the enemy's guns he opened both his batteries and raked the ramparts with a sharp fire of musketry from the tops of the houses. The gallant French stood by their guns and returned the fire with rapidity and accuracy. Meanwhile, the three vessels, moving majestically upwards with the tide, continued to approach the fort under a warm cannonade. Not a shot was returned, nor was it till the *Tyger* came opposite to the ravelin before the Ganges Gate that she opened her broadside and cleared that defence. Sailing slowly on, she anchored at her station fifty yards opposite to the north-east bastion. A few minutes later the *Kent*, with Admiral Watson's flag flying, came to before "the middle of the curtain."[1] The tide of the ebb now making down the river, occasioned her to drag, "so that before she brought up, she had fallen abreast of the S.E. bastion, the place where the *Salisbury* should have been, and from her mainmast aft, she was exposed to the flank guns of the S.W. bastion also."[2]

[1] Letter from M. Renault to the Superior Council at Pondicherry, dated Pondicherry, October 26, 1758.

[2] Ives, p. 128. Eyre Coote, who was on board the *Kent*, states, "And a few minutes after the *Kent* came to opposite the south-east, both of which bastions consisted of five guns in face and three in flank; they fired very warmly and with a good deal of success; the *Kent* very unfortunately dragging her anchor exposed her quarter to the fire of the flank of the south-west bastion." In "The Extracts from the Log of the *Kent*" it is stated: "At 7 anchored abreast the south-east bastion and began the attack." In "Remarks from on board His Majesty's ship *Tyger*" we find the following: "At 5 minutes past 6 the *Kent* came to an anchor abreast of the south-east bastion." Ives says: "Before she could reach her proper station" she had drifted abreast of the S.E. and "from her mainmast aft she was exposed to the flank guns of the S.W. bastion also." Orme writes: "The *Kent* soon after let go her anchor opposite to the ravelin, but in this instant, the fire from the fort killed and wounded several of the sailors appointed to manage the ship, and a shot unfortunately disabled the commander, Captain Speke; who not being able to continue the directions he intended to give, so much confusion ensued, that the cable, not stopped in time, ran out to its end; and the ship, instead of anchoring opposite to the ravelin, fell back so far, that her poop appeared beyond the S.E. bastion, exposed likewise to a flank of the bastion on the S.W."

Owing to the drifting of the *Kent*, the *Salisbury* had to anchor lower down the river, and remained out of the action. The *Kent* and *Tyger* now saluted the fort with their broadsides, and from their tops opened a warm discharge of musketry. The two batteries on shore continued to batter the southern bastions, and the troops from the housetops kept up their constant raking fire. Monsieur Devignes, the gallant commander of the French Company's ship *Saint Contest*, had charge of the guns of the bastions, and so telling was his fire that an officer who was on board the *Kent* states that one hundred and thirty-eight shots were lodged inside, and several of the shot at close range went through and through her, "all her masts wounded and rigging very much cut." Her "quarter deck was cleared." Most of her officers were killed or wounded. "All this while Admiral Watson was very cool and very unconcerned, in regard to himself; and when he was told an officer with a glass was giving directions to point a gun at him, and that the gun was traversed for that purpose, he answered, 'Why then they shall have a fair shot'; stood still, smiled, and went on after the ball had passed just by him." A shot entered the *Kent* near the foremast and ignited two or three 32-pound cartridges. They exploded and set fire to the wad-nets and other loose articles between the decks. The ship was so soon full of smoke that a cry was raised that she was on fire in the gunners' store-room. Some seventy or eighty men jumped out of the portholes into the boats that were alongside. The gunners on the bastions seeing what had taken place from front and flank poured a heavier fire. The flames were soon quenched by a few brave men, and Lieutenant Brereton, who commanded the lower-deck battery, rushing to the ports, exhorted the men in the boats to return. They hesitated. He cried aloud, "Are you Britons? You Englishmen, and fly from danger? For shame—for shame!" "This reproach had the desired effect; to a man they immediately returned into the ship, repaired to their quarters, and renewed a spirited fire on the enemy." [1]

For about three hours the brave garrison endured, their

[1] Ives, p. 129.

parapets being torn to pieces, their guns dismounted, and the merlons destroyed by cannon shot. The batteries were covered with dead and wounded. No one could appear on the bastions. Clive had a body of troops ready to storm the shattered walls. Renault saw that further resistance was useless. "Accordingly I ordered the drum to beat a parley." Lieutenant Brereton[1] and Captain Coote were sent with a flag of truce to the fort, and "in about a quarter of an hour," says Coote, "I returned to the Admiral with the Governor's son and a letter concerning the delivery of the place." After some hours spent in discussion, Articles of Capitulation were settled, and on the part of the British signed by the two admirals and also by Clive, in spite of the strong opposition of Watson. The most important terms were that—All officers of the garrison should be prisoners on their honour, but the soldiers were to be prisoners of war so long as hostilities continued. The sepoys had leave "to return to their own country on the coast." By the ninth article—"The directors, counsellors, and those employed under them shall have leave to go where they please with their cloaths and linen." Soon after 3 P.M. Eyre Coote took possession of the fort with a company of artillery, his own company of grenadiers, and the Company's grenadiers.[2]

The siege and defence of Chandernagore derives its importance from the immense and far-reaching effect it had on the extension of British dominion in India. It dealt a blow which shook the faith of the native princes and chiefs of Western India in the French power. The capture of the Fort D'Orleans secured the safety of Calcutta, our base on the sea, and it made us masters of the gate of the great water-way which led to the rich provinces of Bengal, Behar, and Orissa, and from thence further northwards to the great central plain which stretches to the foot of the Himalayas. The rout at Plassey was a corollary of the conquest of the fortified station of Chandernagore. The success was, however, not won without heavy losses on both sides. In the last tremendous day

[1] "The only commission officer on board the *Kent* that was not killed or wounded."—Ives, p. 129.

[2] Eyre Coote's Journal.

the French lost two captains and 200 other men killed and wounded. The numbers of the British force on land were not seriously reduced, owing to Clive's deliberate and well-planned attack. It was on the *Tyger* and the *Kent* the full fury of the storm burst. On board the former 13 men were killed and 50 wounded.[1] Among the wounded was Admiral Pocock. An officer on board writes: "Mr. Pocock is still very lame and swelled about the legs but not greatly hurt; the splinters flew so thickly about him, that he was scratched most shockingly and covered with blood from head to foot." In the *Kent* the casualties amounted to 19 killed and 49 wounded. Every commissioned officer but one was hit or killed. Among the wounded were the captain and his son, an "aid-de-camp or, rather, as we call them on board, the people that pass the word."

> "One shot took off Captain Speke's calf of his left legg, and struck off Billy Speke's thigh; as soon as one got up he saw the other, and a shocking sight it was. Billy bore it very courageously, and the other was no more concerned for himself but said, 'Father and son at one time and with one shot is hard indeed.' One would have staid on the deck, and the other wanted to be dressed in the Admiral's cabbin, but the Admiral insisted on their being taken down to the surgeon."

Ives, the surgeon, tells us how Billy refused to be touched until his father's wound had been attended to, and after being assured that this had been done, he exclaimed, pointing to a fellow sufferer, "Pray Sir look to and dress this poor man who is groaning so sadly before me." When he had been assured that this had already been done, he submitted to his wound being examined, and calmly observed, "Sir I fear you must amputate above the joint." Ives replied, "I must." The operation was performed above the joint of the knee. "During the whole time the intrepid youth never spake a word or uttered a groan that could be heard at a yard distance." The next day the son was removed to the house of a friend. For the first eight or nine days young Speke's symptoms were favourable. A change took place. The

[1] Letter from Admiral Watson—*Kent*, off Chandernagore, March 31, 1757.

night before he died the lad sent the following incoherent note, written in pencil, to Ives:

"*If Mr.* Ives *will consider the disorder a son must be in, when he is told he is dying, and is yet in doubt whether his father is not in as good a state of health. If Mr.* Ives *is not too busie to honour this chitt,*[1] *which nothing but the greatest uneasiness could draw from me. The boy waits an answer.*"

"Immediately on receipt of this note, I visited him," says Ives, "and he had still sense enough left to know who I was. He then asked if his father was dead. 'No,' I replied, 'nor is he in any danger, I assure you; he is almost well.' '*Thank God!—then why did they tell me so? I am now satisfied, and ready to die.*' At that time he had a locked-jaw, and was in great distress, but I understood every word he so inarticulately uttered: he begged my pardon, for having (as he obligingly and tenderly expressed himself) disturbed me at so early an hour, and before the day was ended, surrendered up a valuable life."

The sparks of human excellence appear in the dark clouds of war.

[1] *Chit*—a letter or note.

CHAPTER XVIII

1757: CLIVE AND OMICHUND

After the fall of Chandernagore Admiral Watson returned with the squadron to Calcutta, and Clive encamped about a mile to the northward of the town. He intended, as he says, by this small advance northwards "to strike some awe into the Nabob and facilitate our business at the Durbar." [1] The moods of Surajah Dowla varied as the wind. He had no sooner sent the letter implying his consent to an attack on Chandernagore than he repented of the act. He now desired Watts to write to Clive that he would not have war made in his country. The Nawab himself wrote to Clive on March 15 that he had received friendly communications from the dreaded Afghan, and had therefore abandoned the idea of marching to Patna. He added:

> "I look on this blessing as the effect of my friendship with you. I therefore write that you need not give yourself the trouble of coming. I have great pleasure in your friendship. Since on a single letter of mine you were ready to come to my assistance I make no doubt that whenever I shall desire you to come and assist me, you will be ready to join me. I now write that you need not give yourself the trouble of coming."

Clive continued to be bombarded with letters from the Nawab, and is said to have received no fewer than ten of them in one day, and these in very opposite styles, "which the Colonel answered punctually with all the calmness and complacence imaginable."

The Nawab, prompted by vanity and fear, sent an envoy to Clive to act as a mediator and compose the differences between the contending powers. But the time for mediation had passed. The French had sent glowing accounts of fictitious

[1] Letter from Colonel Clive to the Secret Committee, London, dated Camp near Chandernagore, April 16, 1757.

successes to the Nawab. But when the envoy discovered that the French outposts had been driven in, he "extolled the English highly and threw all the blame upon the French." On the 17th news reached the Nawab that a town two miles west of Chandernagore was in the hands of the English, and that his troops had been withdrawn from it. Nuncomar, who had received a fresh bribe, wrote to the Nawab: "That as the French were unable to resist the English, he had therefore ordered his troops to Hughly, lest his victorious colours should be involved in their disgrace." [1]

Surajah Dowla was greatly disturbed by the news from Chandernagore, but he recovered his courage when he heard from his spies that the English batteries had not damaged the fort. He gave orders that a division of his armies under the command of Rai Dulab should advance towards Chandernagore. He lived in the vain hope that this show of force would induce Clive to raise the siege. But Clive was not so easily deterred. The day before the capture of Fort D'Orleans he wrote to Rai Dulab, with that tone of self-confidence which distinguishes his letters:

> "I hear you are arrived within 20 miles of Hughly. Whether you are come as a friend or an enemy I know not. If as the latter, say so at once, and I will send some people out to fight you immediately. If as the former, I beg you will stay where you are, for we can conquer the enemies we have to deal with here if they were ten times stronger."

He added:

> "I now declare to you the French are our greatest enemies, and I will destroy them."

The same day he wrote to the Nawab with animation and some irony:

> "If you are determined to march this way I cannot forbid it, but I should be very sorry to see the troubles renewed. As I persuade myself you will have pleasure in hearing good tidings from me, I therefore write this to inform you that hitherto I have only made use of musketry against the French, but to-morrow early I shall open my batteries, and the ships will begin their fire, so that by the blessing of God I hope the place will be our own to-morrow.

[1] "But another well-applied bribe to Nuncomar, the Governor of Houghly, removed all obstacles."—Scrafton, p. 71.

I this day heard of Roy Dullub's march. I am much obliged to you, but in this case have no occasion for assistance. I pray that Your Excellency may be ever victorious over your real enemies, and that God may bless you with health and prosperity."

As soon as Fort D'Orleans surrendered Clive sent a special note to the Nawab informing him of the event and ascribing his success to the blessing of the Almighty, " and the influence of your favour." He added :

" As I am perswaded you will be pleased at my success, therefore I thought proper and necessary to send you the particulars of this victory. My heart is earnest in your interest, and shall be always ready with my own life and that of my whole army to drive away your enemies. I hope that by Your Excellency's favour all our enemies in your country will fall into our hands."

The rage of the Nawab when he heard that Chandernagore had been taken was great, but the fear of an Afghan invasion dominated him, and six days after the receipt of Clive's letter he replied :

" The particulars of your victory at Frankedongy which I had long been impatient to hear, gave me inexpressible pleasure. I thank God that your enemies so easily fell into your hands, and that their great place is fallen into your hands. You have no longer any uneasiness on their account. It has pleased God to make you and all your friends happy in this great victory."

Clive forwarded to Watts duplicates of his letters to Surajah Dowla, with instructions as to his future policy towards the Nawab :

" The Bent of our Politicks hitherto has been by haughty and by submissive Letters such as the Occasion requir'd to persuade him to abandon the French to us, We must in persuit of that system now endeavour to convince [him] that what we have done is best both for him and us ; the Argument that will best serve that purpose must be drawn from their Actions on the Coast of Choromandel, compared with ours on the same, that as soon as they had made themselves Masters of Dekan they would not have scrupled attempting the same here. Represent to him in the strongest Light what a State they have reduced Salabut Jung to ; that they have extorted whole provinces from him. While the Man that we support is immensely indebted to us, that by our last Advices from the Coast they have exhibited a new piece of Treachery in the Murder of Rajah Vizeramroy whom they had invited to a Feast, and conclude the whole with assuring him that our sole View is to stop the ambitious

Progress of the French, to effect which he must enter into a strict Alliance with us; That we shall always be ready to support him against his Enemies, and that we desire in Return only a strict Compliance with his Treaty with us and free Currency for our Trade; that we do not aim at any further Possessions than what our Phirmaund has given us; that we shall henceforwards act as Merchants, but shall always keep up a Force sufficient to support him against all his Enemies. Tell him with such an Army as I now command the French would not fail to raise Disturbances in his Country and never lay down their Arms till they had extorted at least a province from him, But that our whole Aim is to have the Treaty made with him strictly complied with. That it is absolutely necessary that the good Work now begun should be compleated and that he give up to us the French and their Property wherever they are found."

The key of Clive's policy was the expulsion of the French from Bengal. By the capture of Chandernagore the danger of the past had by no means vanished. Bussy at the head of a force of Europeans and sepoys was said to be at Cuttack, about two hundred miles from the banks of the Hugli. A junction between his disciplined troops and the vast host of the Nawab was no imaginary peril. As long as the French had a factory at Cossimbazar near the capital, the court of Murshidabad would be a focus of intrigue against the English. M. Law, the chief of Cossimbazar, who had shown himself to be a better diplomatist than general, had obtained an ascendancy over the Nawab. The garrison of the fortified factory under his charge had been increased by fugitives from Chandernagore.

Clive, in spite of the earnest entreaties of the Madras Government, had delayed returning to the coast with his troops until he had secured the safety of Calcutta by the capture of Chandernagore, and he now determined by a vigorous policy to complete the extinction of the French power in Bengal before the season of the year would permit him to transport his troops back to Madras. Six days after the fall of Fort D'Orleans Clive wrote to Pigot:

"I make no doubt but the forces are impatiently expected at Madras. It is a very great blow which has detained them—no less than the attack and taking of Chandernagore: of more consequence to the Company, in my opinion, than the taking of Pondicherry itself."

He proceeded to state:

"Our stay till August, which is now become unavoidable, will, I hope, settle everything here in the most advantageous manner for the Company, and perhaps induce the Nabob to give up all the French Factorys. This will be driving them out root and branch. I am well informed, without Chandernagore, the Islands[1] must starve, and Pondicherry suffer greatly.

"My inclinations always tend towards the Coast; and I hope to be with you, with a very considerable force, in September. The lateness of the season makes the passage very uncertain; and the length of it would certainly cause the loss of a great part of our forces."

In order to induce the Nawab to give up all the French factories, Clive wrote to him on March 29 as follows:

"It is almost impossible that there can be a lasting peace in your kingdom while there are two such powerful nations in it, because whenever a war breaks out between our two Kings they would not fail to extend the effects of it to these parts, endeavouring to drive each other from their Settlements in Bengal. . . . All these circumstances make it absolutely necessary that Your Excellency should deliver up to us the persons and effects of the French at Cossimbazar, and their out-Settlements, as being our enemies. We shall then be without rivals, and our whole force ready to obey your commands, and assist you in punishing all those who dare to molest the peace of your kingdom."

The Nawab, however, had no desire that the English should be without rivals, and he was not quite certain that the whole British force would always be ready to obey his commands. As Chandernagore had already been taken, he made a virtue of necessity, and sent Clive one of his happiest compositions:

"If you want the French Factory it is well. Whatever they paid into the treasury, write to Mr. Watts to make good here, and it is very well; then you keep possession of the Factory. But if it be agreeable to you, it will be showing yourself a man of a great mind to give it up to them that they may carry on their trade as before."

Clive did not adopt the Nawab's suggestion. On the contrary, the two admirals, also Clive and Kilpatrick, thus communicated their views to the Select Committee on the following day:

"Having taken into consideration the disposal of the Fort of Chandernagore, we imagine it will be for the interest of the Com-

[1] The islands of Mauritius, etc.

pany and of the nation that it be demolished. For should the Nabob from the capriciousness of his disposition once again turn his arms against [us], or should the French be able to send a force into this Province, two garrisons will be more than we can well maintain, especially after the departure of the squadron and return of the Madras troops. We should be glad to know your sentiments on this subject."

The Select Committee concurred, and a few months later Fort D'Orleans was demolished.

A more immediate danger embarrassed Clive from the action of M. Renault and his Council. After the surrender of Fort D'Orleans some of the most important Frenchmen of the settlement went to Chinsura (the Dutch station), where they had sent their wives and children before the siege. Previous to their departure they gave their parole. Clive now received definite information that M. Renault and his Council had not only harboured the French prisoners who had escaped from Chandernagore, but furnished them with money, guides, and even arms for their march to Cossimbazar. They had also begun to assemble as a governing body, and "by their correspondence kept up the spirit of Law and his party and intimidated the Nabob with reports of Bussy's army being near." Clive promptly met the new danger. On April 12 he sent the following letter "to Peter Renault Esq., and French gentlemen who have given their parole."

"Gentlemen,—Give me leave to represent to you, that I think a *parole* of honour, either given verbally or in writing, to be the most sacred thing on earth; such who receive this indulgence are always esteemed gentlemen of unquestionable reputation, who, being actuated by principles of honour only, will not make use of the liberty granted them of being prisoners at large in any shape to the disadvantage of that nation whose prisoners they are. Now I am informed you have meetings and carry on a correspondence with the country Government and your Subordinate Factories. If there be any truth in this report, that you make use of that liberty granted you in any shape to the disadvantage of the English nation, you will be no longer looked on as men of honour or entitled to the advantage you now enjoy. I could wish, gentlemen, to give satisfaction on that head, that you would separate, some go to Serampore, the Danish Settlement, some to Calcutta, and some may have liberty to stay in the town of Chinchura and in Chandernagore."

As the Frenchmen on parole declined to accept his suggestion, Clive wrote the next day the following peremptory note " to Peter Renault late Governor of Chandernagore and to the gentlemen late of Council there " :

> " Gentlemen,—By virtue of your *parole* of honour I summon you in the name of His Britannick Majesty to render yourselves at Chandernagore the 14th April at 10 o'clock in the forenoon.
> " Dated at the English Camp the 13th April 1757."

Clive also sent an officer to the Governor of Chinsura to demand the surrender of the Frenchmen who had given their parole " in the Admiral's and my name, and I flatter myself that you will be kind enough to have them escorted out of your bounds where proper persons will be ready to receive them." Renault and his Council represented to the Dutch Governor that they were not prisoners of war, as he could see from the capitulation, and so not under the orders of Clive. Renault informed the British officers that their parole had been extorted by force, and was therefore not binding on them. Alfred Bisdom, the Dutch Governor of Chinsura, stated their case in a letter to Clive, who replied :

> " Persons on their *parole,* such as the French gentlemen at Chinchura in general are, must surrender themselves whenever formally required. What they pretend as to the Capitulation having been made in the name of Admiral Watson is nothing to the purpose. They surrendered the Fort themselves to an officer of His Britannick Majesty, and gave their *parole* conformably, by virtue of which any officer belonging to that Crown can afterwards call upon them to deliver themselves up. I have already summoned them as an officer belonging to His Britannic Majesty, and in his name shall do it again : if they still refuse to comply, I must consider and treat them as enemies at open war with us, and flatter myself you will afford them no kind of protection, but order them immediately to leave your bounds. You will please to observe, that it is on their *parole* of honour, and that only, that I call upon them to surrender themselves. Let me repeat that the Capitulation has nothing to do in this case."

Clive enforced his arguments by a display of force. He sent a body of sepoys to Chinsura, who surrounded the houses where the French were residing. The Dutch director " told us," says Renault, " that this business did not concern him in any way, and the English could do as they liked. The

Director pushed the indignity so far as to tell me personally to leave his settlement." Renault adds that "fear of the violence which the English *sepoys* might use towards their women" induced them to go to the British camp. Clive wrote to Watson the same evening as follows:

"A few Days ago I informd you of my Suspicions that some of the Gentlemen on Parole had been acting a very base Part, which Suspicions I have now brought to Proof. The enclosd is the Report of a Frenchman whom we took in Chinchura, he is not a deserter and declard every Thing of his own free will. Part of his Evidence is confirm'd by two of the Governour's own Servant(s) who affirms that 5 Days ago 6 Frenchmen who escapd came to the Governour and stayd with him some Time, that on coming out they had Money in their Hands, and that the Governour orderd him one of the Servants to conduct the 6 Men to La Vigne the Europe Captain's House which he accordingly did and that In the Evening 6 more Prisoners came, whom the French Governour orderd to be carried to La Vigne's likewise; there are many other Particulars too tedious to mention which shall appear hereafter. The above base Behaviour of Mr. Renault and some others occasioned my taking the Steps which will appear by the enclos'd Papers. It was with some difficulty Mr. Bisdom could be prevail'd upon to order all the Gentlemen on parole out of Chinchura, which he at last after many Consultations did. This Evening the Governour and Council came to my Quarters when I acquainted them that Tomorrow Morning they must set out for Calcutta, with which I have acquainted Mr. Drake, that he may get Accommodations ready for them. I hope my Proceedings in this Affair will meet with your Approbation. I have consulted Capt: Martin in every Thing who approves of all that has been done. Be assured Sir that without this Step our business would have been but half done, a Governour and Council, which you will observe they call themselves in their Letter to me, must always have great Influence with the Nabob, and be capable of doing many things highly detrimental to the Companys Service, and I really think if some of them were sent Home by the *Kings Fisher* it is no more than they deserve, Laportre and Le Count in particular. The Inhabitants are to be with me tomorrow; the lowest of them and such as are no Gentlemen and have no Pretensions to a Parole I shall send to prison; the others I will quarter to the Southward and exact such a parole as will leave it out of their power to do any more Mischief."

On April 15 Watson informed Clive that the Frenchmen had arrived, and would be detained unless they could clear themselves. "Would Clive come down and bring the proofs of their assisting prisoners to escape, as the matter was delicate?" Renault in his appeal to the Admiral stated that they had been compelled by force to sign the parole, and that Clive's charge against them was based on the worthless evidence of a deserter. Clive wrote to Watson to say that "the critical situation of the Companys affairs will not permit of my quitting the camp on any consideration," and he emphatically contradicted the statements of Renault.

"I have this instant recd your Favour. as to what Mr. Renault says about the Testimony of a Deserter, it is intirely false, the Man has a wife & family & 'twas the latter Consideration which induced him to refuse Mr Renault when he insisted upon his going to Cossimbuzar; he came of his own accord & gave the Evidence before related and never ask'd to be entertained in our Service till some time after.

"What M Renault alledges about being obliged to sign the Parole is entirely false; he & every one else signed the parole of their own Free will; I am sure it was never meant either by you or me that the Companys Servants should be free to go where & do what they pleased: they broke thro' the Articles of Capitulation by suffering so many men to Escape out of the Fort, & setting fire to sundry Goods at a time when Captn Buchanan desired they would give him admittance which was absolutely refused.

"Their having kept their parole in not leaving Chinchura is another Falsity; for Monsr St Martin a French officer who gave his Parole and receivd his Effects, went to Cossimbuzar and is now with Mr Law as are I am persuaded many more. To have a good opinion of Mr Renault would be doing him more Justice than his Countrymen ever did; his suffering the Inhabitants to enter the Ware Houses & look out a Number of Gold watches & conceal them in their Chests was a very dirty Action & an Infringement of the Capitulation."

The Admiral refused to have any further correspondence with the French, and they were kept as prisoners at Calcutta until after the victory of Plassey, when they were allowed to return to Chandernagore.

While this episode was in progress the English difficulty with the Nawab was fast coming to a point. They pressed him to expel the French from his dominion and to fulfil all the articles of the treaty. Surajah Dowla played the game of diplomacy with considerable skill. He wanted time. He hoped that when the monsoon was over Clive would return with his troops to Madras, and then Calcutta would again be at his mercy. He wrote at the end of March "to the

Distinguished of the Empire, the Sword of Riches, the Victorious in War, Monsieur Busie Bahadur:

"I am advised that you are arrived at Echapore, this news gives me pleasure, the sooner you come here the greater satisfaction I shall have in meeting you. What can I write of the perfidy of the English? they have without ground picked a quarrel with Monsieur Rennault and taken by force his Factory. They want now to quarrel with Monsieur Law your Chief at Cassimbuzar, but I will take care to oppose and overthrow their proceedings. When you come to Ballasore I will then send Monsieur Law to your assistance, unless you forbid his setting out. Rest assured of my good will towards you and your Company."

He lived in daily hope that Bussy would come to his aid, and until he could gratify his consuming desire of expelling the English out of Bengal he determined to temporise with them. He informed Clive that as the French had by a grant of the Mogul Emperor built their several factories in his kingdom, he could not without injuring his character deliver up these factories and goods unless he had an order from them. If Clive would only obtain an order from M. Renault there would be no further trouble. Clive replied:

"Now that I have granted terms to Mr. Renault, and that he is under my protection, it is contrary to our custom after this to use violence, and without it how would he ever of his own will and pleasure write to desire you to deliver up his master's property? Weigh the justice of this in your own mind."

The Nawab next stipulated that the English should indemnify the Mogul Emperor for the loss of the duties paid by the French. To this Clive immediately agreed. He wrote on April 10 to the Nawab:

"Be satisfied with my engaging to make good to Your Excellency the King's customs arising on the French trade, and taking care that the Empire suffer nothing by the taking of Chandernagore, and the delivery of the French, their Factories and effects. This I promise to do as long as they are kept out of your country."

He added:

"It gives me great concern to find there is so much delay in fulfilling the Articles of Peace. It is a long time since Your Excellency promised to fulfil every thing in fifteen days; twice that time is passed, and most of the material Articles as far from being put into execution as ever. Every day I receive complaints on this subject."

He called upon the Nawab in the most emphatic and solemn manner to fulfil the several important articles of the treaty still not executed. The Nawab, moved by Clive's determined tone, adopted a stratagem. He wrote to him on the 14th that he had ordered " Mr. Law & his people " out of the province. He also wrote to the Admiral :

" YOUR letters at several times, I have received, with the news of your health, which has given me great pleasure. The purport of them I have duly understood ; and for your satisfaction, and in observance of the agreement between us, to look upon each others enemies as our own, I have expelled Mr. Law with all his adherents from my country, and have given strict orders to all my *Naibs* and *Fougedars* not to permit them to remain in any part of my dominions. I am ready upon all occasions to grant you my assistance. If the French ever enter the province with a great or small force, with a design of making war upon you ; God and his Prophets are between us, that whenever you write to me, I will be your ally, and join you with all my force. Rest satisfied in this point, and be assured of my resolution to remain inviolably by the promises which I have made in my letters, and in the treaty concluded betwixt us "

On April 14, the same day that Surajah Dowla wrote to Clive and Watson, Watts wrote to Clive's private secretary that the Nawab had ordered the French out of his dominions and promised to support the English with his whole force, but that he had heard that the Nawab had actually taken the French into his service, and they were going to Patna. He also mentioned that the Nawab had recently again threatened him with personal violence. On the 16th Watts informed Clive that " the French left their Factory and marched through the city to-day." Two days later he states that the Nawab replies that he has ordered the French out of his dominions, but will do nothing further. " If we pursue them he declares that the agreement will no longer subsist, and if I have sure intelligence that forces are being sent, I must depart." [1] The Nawab's subterfuge kindled the rage of the honest sailor, and Watson wrote to him on the 19th :

" I have already told you, and I now repeat it again, that while a Frenchman remains in this kingdom I will never cease pursuing him."

[1] Watts to Clive, Moorshedabad, April 18.

He added:

"If you will reflect upon the oath you have taken, you cannot but join with me in what follows: As soon as Cossimbuzar is properly garrisoned, to which place our troops will speedily begin their march, I desire you will grant a *dustuck* for the passage of two thousand of our soldiers by land to Patna."

Watson's demand increased the fierce wrath of the Nawab against the English. Watts, as his letters show, was timid, and he vacillated. At one time he suggested that Clive should dispatch at once an armed force; he then urged in turn that Clive should take no decisive steps unless he thought it worth while. He informed Clive's private secretary on the 20th that the Nawab swears that his patience is at an end, and he will march against us. "Pray consider the loss to the Company if war broke out at this juncture. Surely we should be quiet." [1] Clive, seeing that Watts lacked firmness, ordered Luke Scrafton, a younger and stronger man, to stop at Murshidabad on his way to Dacca. Scrafton in a letter to the private secretary describes the stormy scene that was enacted in the Nawab's court on April 19:

"Young minds cannot keep resentment long concealed; his heart broke out to-day. When our *vacqueel* went to him, the instant he saw him he ordered him to be turned out of the *Durbar;* as the fellow was going he overheard him say, 'I will destroy them and their nation.' Meer Jaffer was ordered to march and he would follow himself; when asked the reason he said 'they are always writing me to deliver up the French; I will receive no more of their letters.'" [2]

Surajah Dowla's hot mood was quickly followed by a cold fit. Scrafton informs Walsh that the next day the Nawab countermanded Meer Jaffier's (Mir Jafar) march and sent for the Vakil or British agent "and gives him beetle." [3] Surajah Dowla had, after the bombardment of Chandernagore, a haunting dread of the British men-of-war, and Scrafton writes: "He is cutting down Placy grove to stop the river that way, and

[1] Watts to Walsh, April 20, 1757.

[2] Scrafton to Walsh, Moorshedabad, April 20.

[3] "Beetle," generally called "Pawn." "The betel leaf, Hind. *pan*, from Skt. *parna*, 'a leaf.' It is a North Indian term, and is generally used for the combination of betel, areca-nut, lime, etc., which is politely offered (along with otto of roses) to visitors."—Hobson-Jobson.

he is flinging up the sand to prevent the water entering this river, at any rate least our ships should come up. Oh the fool." Clive, writing two days afterwards to Watts, states:

"The Nawab's behaviour makes it very difficult to pursue such Measures as may not in their Consequence be approved or disapproved of according to our Success, his late Transactions carry with them the Appearance of an Amendment in the Situation of his Affair. Surely he has rec^d. some Hopes of Bussy's Approach or has accommodated Matters with the Patans. If they were approaching I think he would never put us at Defiance which I think he has done by his Message to you."

At the close of his letter he says:

"After the Nabob's last Message I cannot depend upon his Friendship, and therefore shall get every Thing ready for a March. I shall consult the Committee and not willingly undertake any Thing which may occasion a Rupture without I am obliged to it; notwithstanding I shall write the Nabob in high Terms."

On the following day Clive wrote in his own hand to the Nawab:

"Your behaviour to our *vacqueel* has given me great uneasiness; however that is over and forgotten. Trust me and I will be faithful unto you to the last, but remember that if you have given ear to my enemies and are resolved to break through the Articles of Agreement, you will become responsible for all the blood that shall be spilled, and all the mischief that shall be done."

On April 26 the Nawab in his reply disclosed that Clive's surmise as to the cause of the change in his attitude was correct.

"By the favour of God," he wrote, "peace has been agreed upon betwixt Achmud Shah Abdally and me. By repeated advices I am informed of his returning by continued marches from Delhi to his own country, and that he had got as far as Paniput and Suniput. As I look upon Abdally's returning at this time in the light of a victory, for your pleasure and satisfaction I have acquainted you with it."

In the official communication was enclosed a brief note, which ended as follows:

"As by your army's marching this way the treaty must be infringed and the Kingdom suffer; on this account I write you, so that if you do send an army this way, it is you who break the treaty, and I am blameless. I have directed my generals, when they receive accounts of your having begun your march, to set out to meet you."

At the same time the Nawab ordered Meer Jaffier, with a force estimated at 15,000 men, to march to Plassey, where the troops under Rai Dulab which had been sent to relieve Chandernagore were stationed. Clive determined to waste no more time in argument or persuasion. He had discovered that the grave quarrel with the Nawab admitted of a different solution.

It is not an English chronicler, but a contemporary Indian historian whose testimony is of great weight, who tells us that Surajah Dowla, by his fiery and choleric temper, by his cruelty, by his treachery, by his avarice, provoked the resentment of his Court and camp. Ghulam Husain Khan, the author of "The Seir Mutaqherin, or View of Modern Times," states that Surajah Dowla insulted his Mohammedan chiefs "and thoroughly estranged them from him by his harsh language and his shocking behaviour; nor were the principal citizens of Murshidabad better used, Djagat-Seat (Jagat Seth) especially." [1] The Indian historian proceeds to mention that "all these were tired of living under such an administration and wished no better than to be rid of such a government," and when they perceived any symptom of active discontent they "sent secret agents to the party with exhortations to contrive some mode of deliverance; under promise of their being heartily and effectually supported." On Law leaving Murshidabad all trace of French power in Bengal vanished, and, as the Nawab could not rely on their aid, the old chiefs and ministers approached Jagat Seth, "and all these joined together in the scheme of oversetting Seradj-ed-doolah, whose character of ferocity and thoughtlessness kept them in continual alarms, and whose fickleness of temper made them tremble." And "every one (was) firmly persuaded that the concurrence of the English was a necessary piece to the completion of his wishes." The conspiracy to get rid of Surajah Dowla was formed amongst the Mohammedan officers and Hindu capitalists who were his own subjects. When Clive,

[1] "Seir Mutaqherin," p. 763.

and the English Council acting under his strong influence, were made aware of their designs they lawfully and rightfully entered into them.[1]

Surajah Dowla had struck Jagat Seth, the great Hindu banker, on the face, and according to the native historian had mortally affronted him "by some times threatening him with circumcision."[2] It was Jagat Seth who first approached the English. Scrafton in his letter to the private secretary (April 20), describing the stormy scene at the Nawab's Court, mentions "that Omichund is gone to Juggutseat. I know the intent of his sending for him before hand; it is to communicate to him his desire that we should set up Lattey."[3] Two days afterwards Watts wrote to Clive as follows:

> "Since writing the above, Omichund has by my desire had a meeting with Meir Godau Yar Cawn Laitty, who has engaged that whenever the Nabob breaks with us he will join us as soon as possible with his whole force on condition of our making him Nabob; in recompense for which he will grant the Company a large extent of country near Calcutta, and a sum of ready money sufficient to satisfy the navy, military, and all the inhabitants of Calcutta; that we shall enter into a league together, offensive and defensive, against all enemies whatever. He requests you will write a soothing letter to the Nabob, which may entirely allay the apprehensions he has of us and induce him to march northward, which he will the moment his fears of us cease. Omichund and Godau Yar Cawn Laitty both assure me the Nabob will break his agreement with us, that he has entertained the French in his service, and that they will not go beyond Patna. All that we have to do is to lull him into security, and by that means induce him to march northward. You must be sensible what great honour will accrue to you from this project and how much secrecy is necessary."

On April 26 Clive wrote to the Admiral:

> "I have not reced a Letter from him (the Nawab) this many Days. In short there is such Confusion and Discontent at Muxadavad, from the Nabobs weak Conduct, & Tyranny, that I have recd certain advice of several great Men, among whom are Juggut Seat & Meer Jaffeir, being in League together to cut him off & set up Murgodaunyer Cawn Luttee, a Man of great Family, Power & Riches, supported Tooth & Nail by Juggut Seat."

[1] "The British in India," by the Right Hon. Sir William Melbourne James, Lord Justice of Appeal.

[2] "Seir Mutaqherin," p. 759.

[3] Yar Luty Khan.

The same day Watts wrote to Clive informing him that Meer Jaffier, supported by two chief men of the Court and others,

"are ready and willing to join their forces, seize the Nabob and set up another person approved of."

He added:

"If you approve of this scheme, which is more feasible than the other I wrote about, he (Meer Jaffeer) requests you will write your proposals of what money, what land you want, or what treaties you will engage in."

Watts enclosed a copy of a letter from Nuncomar in which he informed the Nawab that he was present at a review of the whole British force at Chandernagore, and that Clive had informed him that he intended to "begin my march to-morrow towards the Nabob and do you acquaint him with it." The statement was absolutely false. It was an act of revenge because the British had failed to obtain for the traitor the confirmation of his appointment as Governor of Hugli. Before he received this letter Clive wrote to Watts:

Sir,—I wrote the Nabob a letter a few days ago which I hope will reconcile him and calm his resentment. I have sent Captain Grant to bring down the money, the Gentlemen being in want of it to carry on the investment. The military we ordered down likewise. I observe the contents of your letter of the 23rd.

If the Nabob is resolved to sacrifice us, we must avoid it by striking the first blow. You should enquire if Luttee be a man of interest. Is he a Moorman? May not all be overset by the Afghans if they come? Has Luttee any interest there? You should consider the honour of the nation, and if possible avoid engaging us in any executions.

I hear Meer Jaffier wants to get rid of the Nabob. I hope it is true.

The military from Cossimbuzar are deserters and cannot be trusted. If I hear the plot thickens, I shall slip some of the King's best men in their room with ammunition &c. All is ready for marching.

Remember me to Omychund.

Watts ordered Grant and his party to return, as "there is orders gone that if any ammunition is found in our boats, to cut off the nose and ears of the soldiers and people belonging to them. Boats are strictly searched." He informed Clive that the French are kept at Rajamahal and the "Pytans" are returned. "Upon this the Nabob is very uppish. The three fourths of the Army are his enemies. When the agreement with Meer Jaffeer is settled we cannot have a man more powerful. There is none equal to him." He implored Clive to keep what he wrote "an inviolable secret and talk of nothing else but merchandize": and he concluded with the following significant advice: "I request you will order your army to Calcutta and keep only a garrison in Chandernagore, and appear to give up all thought of war, and send your people no where but keep quiet." [1]

Clive had been corresponding directly from his camp with Watts, Scrafton, and the Nawab. This aroused the jealousy of the Committee, and on April 28 they wrote to him desiring that all letters concerning the Company's affairs might be answered by the advice of the Select Committee and not by Clive himself. They did not object to Scrafton remaining in Murshidabad, but maintained that in all affairs concerning their employers Mr. Watts was the person to whom application should be made. They expected that the large expenses for troops would cease at the end of the month. [2] Clive replied promptly:

"I have just received your letter of the 28th. The stile and purport of which I must confess to you surprised me. You surely forgot, Gentlemen, that at a Committee held here so late as the 23rd I laid my letters before you, consulted with you on the general measures to be taken in the conduct of our affairs with the Government, and was desired to manage a certain secret correspondence at the *Durbar*. What has since come to my knowledge I have communicated to the President, and indeed I cannot think I have ever been deficient in acquainting you with all particulars, and advising you whenever the subject was important enough to require it.

"It will not be improper to send an European of capacity and secrecy, as you observe, to Mr. Watts, but if you mean thereby that nothing on so nice a subject is to be committed to writing, you may have occasion to despatch many such persons before the negotiation is concluded. Let me observe to you a correspondence by cyphers as now practised is not less secret, and doubtless it is much more expeditious, which is of great moment in particular conjunctures." [3]

[1] Letter from Mr. Watts to Colonel Clive, dated April 28, 1757.
[2] Powis MSS.—Letters, April to June, 1757.
[3] Selections, Vol. II., pp. 367–8.

On the following day, May 1, 1757, Clive went down to Calcutta and laid before the Select Committee the whole correspondence.

"The Committee then considered whether they could accept the offers of *Meer Jaffier* and decided that as the Nabob cannot be relied upon, a revolution will be for the interest of the Company, on the following grounds, (1) his dishonesty and insolence show that the recently made treaty was concluded by him only to gain time, (2) the almost absolute certainty of his intention to break the peace, as shewn by his intrigues with the *French*, (3) the hatred felt for the *Nabob* by everybody makes it probable that there will be a Revolution whether we interfere or not, and it would be a mistake not to assist his probable successor and so obtain the exclusion of the *French*."

On these grounds it was agreed to support Meer Jaffier, and certain terms were drafted on which they promised their alliance. It was "Agreed that *Colonel Clive* transmits these terms to *Mr. Watts* and urge him to expedition." On May 2 Clive wrote to Watts as follows:

Sir,—Yours of the 29th is come to Hand. Every thing is settled with the Committee; enclosed are the proposals: and if there be any other Articles which you and Omychund think necessary to be added, you have full Liberty so to do, or leave out any which you think may hurt our Cause or give Disgust. as for any Gratuity the new Nabob may bestow on the Troops, is left to his Generosity & to your & Omychunds Management.

Now for Business

Tomorrow morning we decamp part of our Forces return to Calcutta, the other will go into Garrison here, and to take away all Suspicion I have orderd all the Artillery & Tumbrels to be embarkd in Boats & sent to Calcutta. I have wrote the Nabob a soothing Letter, this accompanies another of the same kind & one to Moon Lol agreeable to your Desire. Enter upon Business with Mier Jaffier as soon as you please. I am ready & will engage to be at Niesaray in 12 Hours after I receive Your Letter, which place is to be the rendezvous of the whole Army. The Major who commands at Calcutta has all ready to embark at a Minutes Warning & has Boats sufficient to carry Artillery Men & Stores to Niesaray I shall march by Land & Join him there and we will then proceed to Muxadavad or the place we are to be joined at Directly.

Tell Mur Jaffeir to fear nothing, that I will join him with 5000 Men who never turn'd their Backs and that if he fails seizing him we shall be strong enough to drive him out of the Country assure him I will march night & Day to his Assistance and stand by him as long as I have a Man left. I am in great want of Draft Bullocks you must send some at all Events when you hear I am upon the March.[1]

The contest now resolved itself into a trial of diplomatic skill between Clive and the Nawab. Clive, in his soothing letters to the Nawab, stated:

"Yesterday my army broke up their camp; more than half is gone to Calcutta, the rest remain at Chandernagore. Calcutta is become a place of such misery since your army has almost destroyed it, that there is not room for more soldiers without endangering their lives by sickness. However, farther to satisfy you, I shall order down to Calcutta all my field cannon. I expect to hear that your army has retired likewise to Muxadavad, and that you have been as expeditious in performing what you promised as I have."

The closing sentence contained a delicate hint: "I shall reside at the French Garden, a very convenient and pleasant house to the southward of Chandernagore."

The Nawab was not soothed. He kept his army at Plassey, he sent money to Law and told him to remain quiet at Rajamal. "When Monsieur Bussie Bahaudur &c comes on this side of Cuttack I will then send for you." On May 4 Law wrote: "I have just received a letter from the Nabob

[1] *Proposals.*—1. An Alliance Offensive and Defensive against all Enemies Country or European. 2. The French fugitives to be taken and deliverd up to us. All their Factorys to be deliverd up to us in order to be destroy'd. The French never to be permitted to resettle in this Subah Ship. In Consideration of which the English Company will annually pay the Amount of Duties usually paid into the King's Treasury on the French Trade or a sum not exceeding 50,000 Rs annually. 3. Restitution of the Companys whole Loss by the taking of Calcutta & their Out Settlements, also Restitution for the Losses of all Europeans by Ditto as may be fairly stated by Adml. Watson, Governor, Colonel Clive, Wm Watts Esqr. Major Killpatrick, & Becher. Blacks & Armenians are not included. 4. That the whole of our Phirmaund be compli'd with and all other Grants ever made to us particularly in the Treaty with Sei Rajah Dowlet. 5. That the Bounds of Calcutta to extend the whole Circle of the Ditch dug upon the Invasion of the Morattas also 600 Yards without it for an Esplanade. The Inhabitants dwelling within our Bounds to be entirely subject to the English Laws & Governmt. 6. That we have Liberty to fortify & Garrison our Factorys of Cossimbuzar & Dacca as we think proper and a sufficient Esplanade be granted us round each. That Convoys too & fro from our Settlement to another be permitted to pass without Interruption or Molestation. 7. That the Moors shall erect no Fortifications within 20 Miles of the River side from Hughley to Ingelee. 8. That a Tract of land be made over to the English Compy whose Revenues shall be sufficient to maintain a proper Force of Europeans & Seapoys to keep out the French and assist the Government against all Enemies. 9. That whenever the English Troops are called to the Assistance of the Government that the Extraordinary Expences of the Campaign be made good by the Government. 10. That an English Gentleman in Quality of Envoy be permitted to reside at Court, have audience whenever required & be treated with due Respect.

by which he orders me to return to Moorshedabad. He wishes, he says, to join us in order to fall upon the English." If the vacillating Law had carried out the wishes of the Nawab and marched to Murshidabad with his detachment, it is open to question whether the English would have gained a decisive victory at Plassey. Clive's aim was to bring matters to a crisis before the appearance of Bussy or Law on the scene, but he was heavily weighted. He had to quiet the fears of the feeble Government. He had to win the support of the Admiral, who did not wish to involve himself in an enterprise which he considered was entirely an affair of the Company and of the success of which he was in doubt. He had unaided and alone to watch and guide the details of an intricate intrigue. Scrafton went down to the French Gardens to reveal to Clive its numerous complicated threads. On May 5 Clive wrote to Watts:

> "Since my last Mr. Scrafton is arrived, from whom I have learnt many particulars. . . . Omichund in consideration of his services should have all his losses made good by an express Article of the treaty."

Clive's letter must have crossed a note which Watts wrote to him on the following day:

> "I have let Omychund into the scheme, and am afraid he will startle when he hears it, as he has no opinion of the *Gentoos*. However I will conclude nothing without consulting Omychund and hope soon to have a meeting with Meer Jaffier and finish everything."

By "Gentoos" Watts meant the Hindu Bankers, and the Seths had no opinion of Omichund. Meer Jaffier was a protégé of theirs, and Omichund did not approve of the change from Rai Dulab to Meer Jaffier because he knew he would have no control over that powerful prince. He could not oppose the new arrangement with success, but he could gratify his two ruling passions—avarice and revenge. Surajah Dowla had agreed, when the treaty with the British was made, to pay Ranjit Rai, the agent of the Seths and Omichund, two lacs of rupees, a half of which was to go to the former and "20,000 gold muheers more, which they told the Nabob was to be given among the leading men in Calcutta for assenting to the treaty." Ranjit Rai was now pressing the Nawab hard to pay these two sums. "This Omichund observed," wrote Watts to Clive:

> "and in order to gain favour at a proper time he told the Nabob that if Runjeet Roy was suffered to interfere in our affairs the Nabob would be obliged to pay the above sums, but if he disgraced him he would save the money." [1]

The foolish young Nawab followed the advice of Omichund. He disgraced Ranjit Rai, and issued orders that Omichund should "have his money, goods and effects delivered up." The disgrace of their agent increased the wrath of the Seths against Omichund. Watts heard of his intrigue with the Nawab. Scrafton wrote to Watts that Clive agreed to give Omichund 5 per cent. "on whatever money he may receive on the new contract." Watts replied that: "As I by no means think he merits such a favour or has acted so disinterested a part as I once imagined, I have not mentioned the 5 *per cent.* to him." But if he had mentioned it to Omichund it would have fallen short of the expectations he had formed. In the same letter, dated May 14, Watts informs Clive:

> "I showed the Articles you sent up to Omichund who did not approve of them, but insisted on my demanding for him 5 *per cent.* on all the Nabob's treasure, which would amount to two *crore* of rupees, besides a quarter of all his wealth, and that Meir Jaffier should oblige himself to take from the *zemindars* no more than they paid in Jaffeir Cawn's time. To secure Roy Dolub to his interest he proposed giving him a quarter part of whatever they could dupe Meir Jaffeir out of. These and many other Articles, in which his own ambition, cunning, and avaricious views were the chief motives, he positively insisted on and would not be prevailed upon to recede from one Article."

Watts estimated that the value of the Nawab's treasure was forty millions sterling, and that Omichund's demand, therefore, amounting to two millions sterling, independent of the jewels, was excessive. But it was the common estimate of the hour. Omichund's demand, however, at the lowest estimate formed of the treasure at the time would, with "all

[1] Letter from Mr. Watts to Colonel Clive, dated May 14, 1757.

his wealth," have fallen little short of one million of pounds sterling.[1] Watts wrote to Clive:

"Perceiving his (Omichund's) obstinacy would only ruin our affairs and that we should alarm the jealousy and lose the good opinion of all people, and that the accomplishment of his treaty (if agreed to) would take some years, Meir Jaffeir likewise having expressed an utter distrust and disgust at his being anyways concerned in the treaty, and as delays are dangerous, I therefore with Petrose[2] had a meeting with Meir Jaffeir's confidant,[3] who sets out to-day with the accompanying Articles, which he says he is sure Meir Jaffeir will comply with."

Watts, contrary to the wish of Meer Jaffier, inserted among the proposed Articles of Agreement one for £300,000 to Omichund. The agent reached the camp on the 16th. Clive had to come to a conclusion at once on a complicated and momentous matter—not a conclusion in the abstract, but a conclusion in the concrete. He had a choice of difficulties. If he rejected Omichund's terms, Omichund threatened to reveal the whole conspiracy to the Nawab.[4] Watts and all the Europeans up the country would be murdered. But this would not be all. The Nawab, assisted by French troops, would attack and destroy the British settlements in Bengal. If Clive allowed himself to be blackmailed by Omichund, and complied with his terms, the Seths and Meer Jaffier, he had every reason to think, would, according to Watts's letter, refuse to agree to the treaty and the enterprise would have to be abandoned. The abandonment of the enterprise meant massacre and the destruction of the British settlements in Bengal. Clive had to resort to a device in

[1] Orme states: "The common people, to whom numbers give no distinct ideas, rated these (treasures in money) at 45 millions of pounds sterling, which nothing but idiotism could believe; but better enquiries supposed them to be four millions and a half; on which Omichund's share would have been 675,000 pounds sterling." His jewels were afterwards valued at one million sterling, of which Omichund's fourth would be £250,000.

[2] Khwaja Petrus, an Armenian.

[3] Omar Beg. Letter from Mr. Watts to Colonel Clive, dated May 14, 1757.

[4] Orme writes: "Whether he would have betrayed it, if refused, is uncertain; for part of his fortune was in the power of the English and he had the utmost vengeance of Jaffeir and his confederates to fear." The part of his fortune in the power of the English was comparatively small. He knew he had already every reason to fear the anger of Meer Jaffier and his confederates. The Nawab with his large army could protect him and amply reward him.

order to avoid civil bloodshed and to save a province from destruction.

A recent biographer of Clive[1] has endeavoured to show that there is no evidence that Omichund used any such threat, and that in the circumstance it is very improbable that he would use any such threat in speech or writing. "The positive assertions," he writes, "rest upon rumour, and upon rumour only. There is not a particle of proof to support them. Those of Malcolm, of Macaulay, and of Gleig have no other foundation than the historian Orme's 'It is said.'"[2] Mill and his careful annotator are omitted. Orme writes: "The audacity of the pretension implied malignant art;[3] but it is said he threatened to reveal the conspiracy to the Nawab if not complied with. If so, the boldest iniquity could go no further. Mr. Watts in his letter on the subject intimated that he had some apprehensions of such a consequence if Omichund were not satisfied."[4] However, in a later part of his history Orme makes the following positive statement: "Grounded on his importance, by knowing the secret, he held out the terror of betraying it to secure his own advantages."[5] Clive, in his evidence before the House of Commons, said:

> "That when Mr. Watts had nearly accomplished the means of carrying that revolution into execution, he acquainted him, by letter, that a fresh difficulty had started; that Omichund had insisted upon 5 per cent. on all the Nabob's treasures, and 30 lack in money; and threatened, if he did not comply with that demand, he would immediately acquaint Serajah Dowla with what was going on, and Mr. Watts should be put to death:—That when he received this advice, he thought art and policy warrantable in defeating the purposes of such a villain."

The evidence of Mr. Sykes is more explicit. He said:

> "That in the year 1757 he was stationed at the subordinate factory called Cossimbuzar, in council; but being on a visit to Mr. Watts, he found him under great anxiety; that he took him aside, and told him Omichund had been threatening to betray them to

[1] "Lord Clive," by Colonel G. B. Malleson, C.S.I., 1882.
[2] *Ibid.*, p. 230.
[3] These words are omitted by Colonel Malleson.
[4] Orme, Vol. II., p. 151.
[5] *Ibid.*, p. 182.

Surajah Dowla, and would have them all murthered that night, unless he would give some assurances that the sum promised him (by Mr. Watts) should be made good ;—that upon this visit Mr. Watts further said, That he was under the greatest anxiety how to counteract the design of Omichund ; the witness could so far say, on his own part, that Omichund's conduct in the whole scene of that business was always suspected, and that he had spies upon Mr. Watts's conduct—he apprehends that nothing was reduced to paper at that time ; that it was only talked of between Omichund and Mr. Watts, and believes it was only a verbal promise ; he further said, that Serajah Dowla was at Muxadavad at that time, and was visited frequently by Mr. Watts—that he (the witness) was in the service about 20 years, from 1749 to 1769."

The proof then that Omichund threatened to reveal the conspiracy if his exorbitant demands were not complied with does not rest upon rumour, and rumour only, but on substantial evidence and other circumstances auxiliary to this evidence.

Clive acted promptly. He received Watts's letter on May 16, and went down to Calcutta. On the following day, at a meeting of the Select Committee, the terms proposed by Mr. Watts were accepted, with some modifications, except : "The Article in favour of Omichund, the Committee think should be totally left out, as his behaviour rather merits disgrace and punishment at our hands than such a stipulation in his behalf."

The day after the Select Committee met, Clive wrote to Drake as follows :

To THE HONBLE ROGER DRAKE ESQ[R.]
&c. GENTLEMEN OF THE SELECT COMMITTEE

GENTLEMEN, — Enclosed you will receive the real & fictitious Articles of Agreement which you will please to sign, the Admiral promised me to do the same by the real one, but not the fictitious one ; if he makes any scruple send it without, & we will sign it for him in such a manner that Omichund shall not discover it ; you will see dispatch is necessary by Mr. Watts's last letter, Copy of which I now enclose you. There is no alteration made excepting leaving it to Mr. Watts's discretion either to insert 100 or 50 Lack on Account of the Company, as he finds Meer Jaffier's inclinations, & adding another Article which is as follows.

On Condition Meer Jaffier Cawn Behauder solemnly ratifies and swears to fulfill the above Articles we the undermentioned do for

& on behalf of the Honble East India Company declare upon the Holy Evangelist & before God that we will assist him Meer Jaffier Cawn Behauder with our whole force to obtain the Subahship of the Provinces of Bengal Bahar & Orixa & further that we will assist him to the utmost of our Power against all his Enemies whatever, whenever he calls upon us for that purpose provided that when he becomes Nabob he fulfills the above Articles.

I am
Gent[n.]
Your most Obed. Hble Serv[t]
(signed) ROB CLIVE.

French Gardens
18 *May* 1757.

The drafts were dispatched; the real treaty, drawn out on white paper, was signed by Admiral Watson, but he refused to sign the fictitious document written on red paper, and it was signed for him. Mill writes: "The Committee forged his name." [1] Macaulay says, in an Essay which has been read wherever our English is spoken: "But another difficulty arose. Admiral Watson had scruples about signing the red treaty. Omichund's vigilance and acuteness were such that the absence of so important a name would probably awaken his suspicions. But Clive was not a man to do anything by halves. We almost blush to write it. He forged Admiral Watson's name." [2] If Clive forged Watson's name, Macaulay ought to have done more than "almost blush." But Macaulay did not stop to test motives and actions, nor to analyse the evidence which is essential to a right understanding of the matter. Clive informed the Parliamentary Committee that he himself formed the plan of the fictitious treaty, to which the Committee consented:

"it was sent to Admiral Watson, who objected to the signing of it; but to the best of his remembrance gave the gentleman who carried it (Mr. Lushington) leave to sign his name upon it:—That his Lordship never made any secret of it; he thinks it warrantable in such a case, and would do it again a hundred times: He had no interested motive in doing it, and did it with a design of disappointing the expectations of a rapacious man."

Lord Clive further said, in regard to the fictitious treaty:

"That he did not recollect whether Mr. Lushington brought it back with Mr. Watson's name to it; to the best of his remembrance,

[1] "History of British India," Vol. III., p. 136 *n*.
[2] "Essay on Lord Clive" (January, 1841).

Mr. Lushington told him, that Admiral Watson gave him leave to sign his name to the fictitious treaty; he did not recollect whether Mr. Watson's seal was put to it, but believes that Mr. Watson's name and a seal were put to both the treaties before they were dispatched to Mr. Watts, he is not certain whether Mr. Lushington signed in his presence at Calcutta or the French Gardens."

In a later part of his evidence Clive also observed:

"That he certainly should not have declared that Admiral Watson had consented to have his name put to the fictitious treaty, if he had not understood so from Mr. Lushington, but that he would have ordered his name to be put, whether he had consented or not."

The next witness was John Walsh, who was at the time Clive's private secretary. He said:

"That he and Mr. Lushington went together to Calcutta, with the treaty; a letter from Colonel Clive was carried by him and Mr. Lushington from the French gardens, where the army then lay, to the Committee, and he returned with the treaties signed in the evening; that he cannot recollect whether he went to Admiral Watson, nor now recollect the whole transaction:—He only recollects that the treaties were sent and brought back again: That his idea had always been, that Mr. Watson refused to sign the fictitious treaty, but permitted Mr. Lushington to do it for him."

The next witness called upon was Captain Brereton, who was with Admiral Watson in the *Kent* at the capture of Chandernagore. He was a most hostile witness. A great deal of his evidence is at second-hand, as Elphinstone points out, and it is inaccurate in many particulars. On being asked whether he had heard Admiral Watson make any declaration concerning the fictitious treaty, Brereton said:

"That he had often heard the Admiral speak of it; that it was proposed to him to sign a fictitious treaty to deceive Omichund of 30 lack, which he refused to do, as dishonourable to him as an officer, and an affront to propose it to him: That it was then proposed somebody should sign it for him, which he also refused, and said, he would wash his hands of it, he would have nothing to do with it, he was a stranger to deception, they might do as they pleased."

Being further questioned whether he had ever heard Watson say that he had authorised any person to sign the treaty for him, Brereton replied: "He believed not; that he had often heard him say, he had not; and would not authorize any body to do it." But though Brereton declared that he had often heard the Admiral speak of not signing the fictitious treaty, yet on being further questioned if he knew whether Admiral Watson before his death had ever heard of his name being put to the fictitious treaty, he said :

"He had ; it was communicated to him by Captain Martin, on his death bed ; and that the secret Committee had agreed to share the 30 lack, stipulated in the agreement for Omichund, among themselves, and excluding the Admiral of his share, because he had not signed the treaty :—The Admiral said, that he always thought the transaction dishonourable, and as there was so much iniquity among mankind, he did not wish to stay any longer among them ; this was just before his death, which he believes was the 16th of August 1757 :—The witness said, He was not present at this conversation, but in the next room ; and that it was communicated to him by Captain Martin (who is now dead) the moment he came out of the room."

It was on the 12th that "Captain Martin paid the Admiral an occasional visit at his country house and found him a little indisposed."[1] The statement that Watson did not hear of his name being put to the fictitious treaty until he was on his death-bed did not bear the test of cross-examination. Brereton being further questioned,

"whether, between the report of the Admiral's name being put, and his taking to his bed, was not nearly two months, and whether he believed that the first time the Admiral heard of it was in the conversation referred to with Captain Martin ? he said, He believed it was about two months, and that the Admiral might know it before that conversation, but then he was sure he knew it : That it is impossible he can recollect for 15 years distance the precise time of the conversation, when the Admiral said he knew his name had been put to the fictitious treaty."

On Brereton being further cross-examined,

"whether when he used the words of the Admiral, that he declared he always thought the transaction dishonourable ; he meant that it was dishonourable to make a false treaty to deceive Omichund, or to use the Admiral's hand and seal to the treaty when he did not put it himself ? he said, He understood it that it was dishonourable to make a false treaty to deceive Omichund. And being further asked, whether before Captain Martin communicated the subject of Admiral

[1] Ives, p. 176.

Watson's name being put to that treaty, it was not a matter of suspicion only? said, He believed it might."

On being asked

"what he understood the Admiral to mean when he said 'he was a stranger to deception, they might do as they pleased'? he said, In the transaction of the Company's affairs:—And if he understood Admiral Watson to mean by those words that they might put his name to the fictitious treaty if they pleased, he said, He did not; he could not conceive that the Admiral would give his consent to any transaction that he held dishonourable, that should insinuate his approbation of deception."

The next witness summoned before the Parliamentary Committee was John Cooke, who had been Secretary to the Select Committee in Bengal in the year 1757, and the simplest and clearest piece of evidence is supplied by him. He informed the Parliamentary Committee that after the battle of Plassey he waited upon Admiral Watson with a message from the Select Committee.

"Among other things this fictitious treaty was mentioned in conversation; that the Admiral said he had not signed it, (shrugging up his shoulders) but had left them to do as they pleased, alluding, as the witness supposed, to Colonel Clive and the select Committee."

He further said

"that he had no doubt that the Admiral knew his name was to it; and he understood, from what dropped from him, that he had secretly permitted his name to be used; he believed he did not publicly give his consent, but had known of it, and made no objection; he did not conceive his name could have been put without his permission: The conversation was only between the Admiral and himself; the Admiral, in that conversation, certainly did not express any resentment or surprize that his name was put. And being questioned again, as to the purport of that conversation? he said, If he remembered right, when the circumstance of the fictitious treaty was mentioned, he shrugged up his shoulders, and said (laughingly) that he had not signed it, but that he had left it to them to do as they pleased."

Being further questioned

"whether it was from this circumstance that he collected the Admiral knew of his name being put? he said, it was, and from this circumstance only: And he further said, It gave him no surprize that an officer of Admiral Watson's rank had agreed to have his name put to a treaty he could not sign, because he was convinced the Admiral knew the motives for which such a fictitious treaty was made ; and that, though he would not sign it, he had no objection to Omichund being lulled into a security, and preventing the whole design from being discovered and defeated."

Cooke merely expressed the general feeling of the time when he said it gave him no surprise that an officer of Admiral Watson's rank had agreed to have his name put to a treaty he could not sign. "All classes of people," says Ives, "from their knowledge of Omichund's avarice and treachery applauded the artifice by which he was so deservedly outwitted." Clive himself felt it needed no justification. He told the Parliamentary Committee it was warrantable in such a case, and he would do it again a hundred times. It is remarkable that one most important matter should have been omitted in their evidence by Clive, Walsh and Cooke. The two admirals were present at the meeting of the Select Committee held on May 17, when "As *Omichund* is a dangerous man and yet not likely to be of any use to us, decided to deceive him by a double treaty." The presence of the two admirals is not recorded in the Minutes of Proceedings, as they were not members of that body, and it is due to this that the matter has not been noticed by historians and biographers. It is mentioned by Clive in a letter to Watts written two days after the meeting. He says :

"I have your last Letter including the Articles of Agreement, I must confess the Tenor of them surpriz'd me much. I immediately repaird to Calcutta and at a Committee held, both the Admirals and Gentlemen agree that Omichund was the greatest Villain upon Earth, and that now he appears in the strongest Light what he was always suspected to be, A Villain in Grain ; however to counterplot this Scoundrel, and at the same Time give him no Room to suspect our Intentions, enclos'd you will receive two Forms of Agreement, the one real, and to be strictly kept Up to by us, the other fictitious, in short this Affair once concluded Omichund will be treated as he deserves—this you will acquaint Meer Jaffeir with."

Clive had hitherto advocated Omichund's cause and defended his character, and his treachery excited surprise and unbounded indignation. Watson was at first reluctant to involve the King's forces in a matter which he considered only concerned the Company's affairs, and he was doubtful of its success. But it is evident that he afterwards became convinced of the necessity of a revolution. Brereton declared in his evidence "that he had heard Admiral Watson say he thought it an extraordinary measure to depose a man they had so lately made a solemn treaty with." The statement is difficult to believe, as Watson was a party to the measure by signing the real treaty. That he approved of it is also illustrated by what he wrote to Clive:

> "I am glad to hear that Meer Jaffier's party increases, I hope everything will turn out in the expedition to your wishes and that I may soon have to congratulate you on the success of it."

Watson was, as we now know, present at the meeting of the Select Committee when the fictitious treaty was discussed, but he refused to sign it. Dr. Ives states

> "that a strict principle of delicacy, which in him was superior to any point of policy, operated too strongly on his mind to permit him to join even in a necessary deception of this nature he manifested no displeasure against the actors."

"A strict principle of delicacy" prevented Watson from signing the fictitious treaty, but his scruples did not extend so far as to his objecting that the actors in "a necessary deception" should do as they pleased. The manly, frank testimony of Cooke supplies an intelligible explanation of the matter. When Lushington and Walsh brought the fictitious treaty to him, Watson refused to sign it, but said they might do as they pleased. They came to the conclusion, and not, surely, an unnatural one, that this amounted to a permission to sign his name, and they informed Clive. Watson's feeling of honour and of duty did not permit him actually to sign the sham treaty, but he did not feel the same misgivings of conscience when he claimed to benefit by it. On a settlement being made of Meer Jaffier's donation to the Select Committee Admiral Watson demanded, in addition to his large share of the prize-money as senior naval officer, an equal share with those members of the Select Committee who had signed the sham treaty. He thus assumed the responsibility of his signature having been attached to it.[1] Such is the unvarnished tale of a famous incident. Clive did in his heart believe that what he did was right, and he never shrank from stating his belief. Everybody at the time thought the same.

Clive, after informing Watts that he was sending two forms of agreement, proceeded to state in his letter of May 19:

"As it is for the Interest of the Company, and for Calcutta in general, that Meer Jaffeir may conceive a good Opinion of our Moderation a blank is left for the Company's Demand, and the rest is moderated, as you will observe, and as Delays are dangerous I am to acquaint you it is determind that there be no Alteration in the enclos'd Articles, unless Meer Jaffeir thinks them too extravagant, in that Case they must be moderated. The Committee having taken the Oath of Secresy upon the Bible have agreed that Meer Jaffeir's private Engagements be obtaind in writing to make them (the Committee in which you are included) a present of 12 Lacks of Rupees, and a present of 40 Lacks to the Army and Navy over and above what is stipulated in the Agreement. Having very maturely consider'd the Approach of the Rains and the little prospect there is of your seeing Meer Jaffeir to concert about a Plan of military Operations, the Committee & self have unanimously agreed to send Scrafton to endeavour at getting a private Conference with Meer Jaffeir; The Plan we propose pursuing to avoid the Nabobs Suspicions is this. I shall write the Nabob a Letter informing him I have sent Scrafton to him on an Affair of the utmost Consequence, and therefore I request he will give instant Orders to Roydulub & Meer Jaffeir not to detain him a Moment; as soon as he arrives he is to acquaint the Nabob with the proposals the Mahrattoes have made us. In his Way he will pursue the Rout of Meer Jaffeirs Camp where in all probabilty he will be stopt till the Nabobs Order comes, and by that means may get a personal Conference with Meer Jaffeir, when a plan of Operation may at once be determind on; however if he should not succeed, probably in his Return he may, when I am persuaded the Nabob will be induc'd to put more Confidence in us by the important News we have communicated to him. I desire that in this you will be persuaded that there is not the least Intent to take from you any part of the Reputation of conducting this Affair, Mr. Scrafton having Orders to follow your Instructions, the Shortness of the Time as well as many other Considerations require that we bring this Affair to a speedy Conclusion.

"Flatter Omichund greatly tell him the Admiral and Committee and self are infinitely oblig'd to him for the pains he has taken to aggrandize the Company's Affairs, and that his Name will be

[1] Brereton informed the Parliamentary Committee, "That he never heard that Admiral Watson applied to the Select Committee for a part of this money; but that after his death his executors did." The matter was a general subject of discussion at the time.

greater in England than ever it was in India if this can be brought to bear to give him no Room for Suspicion we take off 10 Lacks from the 30 demanded for himself, and add 5 pr Cent upon the whole Sum receiv'd which will turn out the same Thing."

Meanwhile, Omichund had extracted a large sum of money from Surajah Dowla. The story, as it has come down to us, illustrates the dexterity of the insatiate extortioner. He was well aware that a visit by him to the palace would become known and create suspicion. He therefore thought it a wiser and safer course in appearance to take Watts and the agent of Meer Jaffier into his confidence. They advised him positively against going to the palace and attempting the stratagem he proposed.[1] But Omichund went to the palace, and had an interview with Surajah Dowla. According to the tale he told Watts, he first aroused the Nawab's fear and curiosity by saying to him: "I have a secret of great moment to tell you. If it were known my life would be in danger." Surajah Dowla promised secrecy. Omichund afterwards declared that he then unfolded the fable, which he had invented, that the English had sent two gentlemen to Bussy, and the French and English had agreed to unite their forces and divide Bengal between them. By this lie he stated he had so gained the favour of Surajah Dowla that he had granted him a *párwan*, or letter under royal seal, to the Burdwan Rajah to pay him the forty thousand pounds which he owed him, as also express orders for the payment of the ready-money the Nawab had taken from his house at Calcutta—estimated at forty thousand pounds—and for the delivery of the remainder of his goods. So far as the magnificent reward was concerned, Omichund's story was true. The money that was taken from his house at Calcutta he took care to have paid him that night. "He was till ten o'clock at night receiving them," Watts wrote to Clive. Watts told Clive the story as it was told him by Omichund, but he afterwards suspected that Omichund never told the Nawab the lie about the alliance with the French, but that he divulged to him so much of the alliance between the English and Meer Jaffier as might be

[1] Letter from Mr. Watts to Colonel Clive, May 17.

confided to his ears without danger. Surajah Dowla, who was in constant correspondence with Bussy, and knew the aim of the French was to drive the English out of Bengal, would not have believed in such a clumsy fabrication as a secret alliance between the two powers. And Omichund was far too clever to tell him such a story. The revelation of a secret alliance between the English and Meer Jaffier against Surajah Dowla would, however, meet with ready credence and be handsomely rewarded.

Clive in his letter to Watts mentions " certain proposals the Mahrattoes have made us," which Scrafton was to lay before the Nawab. About May 10 a messenger arrived at Calcutta with a letter to Mr. Drake purporting to come from Balajae Rao the Peshwa.[1] The writer stated that the misfortunes of the English had been told him. They were only to send their proposals, and a hundred and twenty thousand Mahratta horse would enter Bengal. " Besides there are other forces shall be ready at your call if you need them." The terms offered were the most generous. " Whatever goods and riches you have lost in Bengal, the double of its value shall be restored by me. Do not on any account make peace with the Nabob. In a few days my forces shall enter Bengal, and the trade of that province shall be entirely yours. The French shall not remain in Bengal: Your forces shall keep them out by sea, mine by land." Clive, on being informed of the arrival of the messenger and the contents of the letter, wrote to Drake on May 11:

> " The more I consider of this the more I am convincd the Man is a Spy sent by the Nabob to discover our Sentiments & who possibly may have recd some distant Hints of our Designs. By no means give the least Encouragement of entering into his Proposals. I have had some Dealings with the Morattas lately ; if you send him to me I can find out by proper Questions Whether he is a Counterfeit."

The messenger was sent, but Clive discovered nothing definite. The letter was laid before the Committee and discussed. The other members agreed with Clive that it was a forgery intended to test their sentiments. They knew that a Mahratta invasion meant the devastation of the land, and

[1] " Ballajeerow Seeho Bajeroy, Vizir to Ram Rajah brother to Rajah Sehoo, from Hydrabad to Roger Drake, Governor of Calcutta."

they had no desire to see a host of Mahrattas again enter Bengal. But the Peshwa was most powerful, and if the letter was proved to be genuine they would offend him by not sending a reply. A most diplomatic answer was drafted and dispatched. They were on good terms with the Nawab, they said, but that if he did not fulfil his promise they intended to renew the war after the rains. Clive saw in the Mahratta letter the means of playing an adroit game. He sent a copy of it to Watts to be shown to Meer Jaffier as a proof of their loyalty to him. "Tell Meer Jaffier," he wrote on May 12, "the English have no opinion of the Moratta Government. If he will be bold and firm I will stand by him to the last. Let him see this letter and make what use he pleases of it." The Committee and Clive also determined (as Clive states in his letter to Watts of May 19) to send the letter by Scrafton to the Nawab, "when I am persuaded the Nabob will be induc'd to put more confidence in us by the important news we have communicated to him."

But Surajah Dowla's suspicions had been aroused, and a past-master in statecraft was not easily deceived. Scrafton wrote to Clive on May 25, 1757:

> "It is with much concern that I acquaint you that after having got within a few miles of Meir Jaffeir's camp I was stopped by a guard of *harcarrahs* and obliged by them to turn off to Plassey. I arrived here the night before last and this morning had audience of the Nabob. The effect these letters have produced is quite different from what was expected; the answer he made to them was that he would immediately order Meir Jaffeir in, and, as soon as you had wrote to him that you would use no treachery towards him, he would withdraw his army under Roydulub, and he has wrote to all his commanders in the different countrys to be on their guard against the Marrattoes. To counterplot this scheme of his to withdraw Meir Jaffeir only, which would be very bad for us, Mr. Watts proposes sending to him by no means to come, and I propose to get my letters from the Nabob for you to-morrow night, (see) Meir Jaffeir the next night, settle everything, carry down the papers, and Mr. Watts is content for his own safety to fling himself into Meir Jaffeir's camp."

Scrafton had another interview with the Nawab, and pointed out to him that the English could not rely on any of his professions as long as the greater portion of his army was encamped at Plassey. "The Nawab meditated some time on this argument and then starting as a man agitated by suspicion and dismay, said eagerly, 'But should the Colonel deceive me.'"[1] Scrafton seems to have in some degree allayed his fears and suspicions, for Surajah Dowla wrote to Clive on May 27 informing him that he had ordered the three chief commanders to return at once with their armies to Plassey.

> "They will accordingly speedily be with me. It becomes you on your part to act agreeable to our treaty, to endeavour that there may not be the smallest deviation from it, and that our friendship may encrease. With confidence also go on with the Company's business so that the merchants as well as the poor may be benefited thereby."

Meer Jaffier returned to Murshidabad on the 30th and had an audience with the Nawab, who received him with marked distrust and displeasure. The suspected chief dare not afford Scrafton a private interview, but he received him that afternoon in the audience hall of his palace.[2] Scrafton left Murshidabad that evening, accompanied by Omichund. Watts's belief in the treachery of the extortioner had grown stronger every day. It was, however, no easy task to get "the crafty old man" away from Murshidabad. It was represented to him that it would be difficult for a man of his age to escape on horseback at the last moment. But he refused to leave until he had got from the treasury all the money the Nawab had promised him. Scrafton assured him that, after the revolution, he would be appointed the principal agent of the English at the capital, and that the emoluments of the office would compensate him for any present loss. At length Omichund consented.[3] They set forth in palanquins, but

[1] Orme, Vol. II., p. 156.

[2] *Ibid.*, p. 158. Scrafton, however, states that he saw him on the morning of the 31st.

[3] Orme states: "It was necessary and seemed difficult to obtain the Nabob's consent to his departure as he relied chiefly on him for intelligence concerning the proceedings and views of the English. But Omichund himself solved the difficulty, by advising Mr. Scrafton to demand of the Nabob the present which he had intended to give to the English commanders at the conclusion of the peace in February; in consequence of which, the Nabob suspecting the secret had been disclosed by Omichund, would immediately hold him in as much detestation, as he had hitherto regarded him with favour. Accordingly, this scene was acted. The Nabob denied the promise. Omichund pretended to be terrified; and the Nabob being really irritated, told Mr. Scrafton that he might carry him wheresoever he pleased."

when Scrafton reached Cossimbazar his companion was missing. Messengers were sent to the city, and they found the old man in the treasury endeavouring to extract more money from the treasurer. Finding the attempt was hopeless he returned with the messengers. The journey was resumed. On waking in the morning Scrafton found that Omichund had again disappeared. He waited on the high road till three in the afternoon, when Omichund again joined him. He had been to the camp at Plassey, where he had a long interview with Rai Dulab. On June 8 they reached Calcutta. The suspicions of Omichund had been aroused, and he bribed the Persian Moonshi of the Committee "to inform him if any deceit to his detriment should appear in the treaty when ratified by Meir Jaffier in the Persian language."

Meer Jaffier, however, refused to sign the treaty until he had consulted Rai Dulab, who, as the Nawab's treasurer and commander of a large part of his army, was a most important member of the conspiracy. On June 2 Rai Dulab arrived at the capital, and the following day Watts wrote to Clive: "Our scheme with Meir Jaffeir is upset and there is reason to believe that Omichund's four hours' visit to Roydulub at Plassy has been the cause of it." The State treasurer objected to the enormous pecuniary demands, "saying there was but a small sum in the treasury."[1] He proposed as a compromise, says Watts, "giving us half of what might come into his and Meir Jaffier's possession after the Nabob's death." Watts adds: "This proposal of Roydulub's is much the same as what was made me some time ago by Omichund; therefore, if you'll strictly examine him I imagine you will find it a concerted scheme between him and Roydulub." On June 4 Watts wrote to Clive:

"I left it to Meer Jaffeir and Roydulub's opinion either to give us half of what they might get, or stand to the old agreement; they have chose the latter, and give me the strictest assurances of getting the contract to-morrow morning, when if there should be no more delay (as there is no such thing as hurrying these people) I shall swear Meer Jaffeir to them and despatch Mirza Omar Beg with the utmost expedition."[2]

[1] Letter from Mr. Watts to Colonel Clive, dated June 3, 1757.
[2] Orme's account differs from Watts's letter. Orme, Vol. II., p. 158.

The same day the Nawab removed Meer Jaffier from his high office and command. He surrounded his palace with spies and posted guards on all communications with it.

Meer Jaffier had signed the treaties, but it was necessary that he should take an oath to observe them. It was, however, difficult for him and Watts to have a meeting without great risk of discovery. A clever but dangerous expedient was arranged. Khwaja Petrus the Armenian had provided for Watts "a covered palankeen such as the Moor women are carryed in, which is inviolable, for without previous knowledge of the deceit no one dare look into it." [1] The bearers carried the palanquin unchallenged by the guards into one of the apartments of the seraglio, where Watts was received by Meer Jaffier and his son Meeran. After certain explanations Meer Jaffier "gave his full assent to the terms of the real treaty and to whatever other donations had been stipulated," and signed it. "Then placing the Koran on his own head, and his hand on the head of his son, whilst Mr. Watts held the papers open before him, he swore with great solemnity that he would faithfully perform all he had promised." [2] The following morning Omar Beg set out with the treaty and delivered it to the Select Committee at Calcutta on June 11.

The fictitious treaty contained a clause securing to Omichund £300,000. Along with the treaty a private engagement of the Committee was obtained from Meer Jaffier by which he promised in writing to give as a donation 12 lacs of rupees (£150,000) to the Committee (in which Watts was included) and 40 lacs (£500,000) to the army and navy.[3] The donation to the Committee was in accordance with a general custom of the period in India. It was also in accordance with the policy of the Company, who paid their servants inadequate salaries and allowed them to enrich themselves by trade on their own account and out of perquisites. Even after Lord Corn-

[1] Letter from Petrus Arratoon to the Court of Directors, dated January 25, 1759.

[2] Orme, Vol. II., p. 159. Letter from Mr. Watts to Colonel Clive, dated June 6, 1757, 9 A.M.

[3] Letter, May 19, 1757. Mr. Becher in his evidence with regard to the actual payments stated: "What I know of was to the governor two lacks and 80,000 Rupees (£35,000) to Colonel Clive the same and to the rest of the gentlemen two lacks & 40,000 rupees (£25,000) each."

wallis had adopted the only practical method of making public servants honest—the payments of an adequate wage—similar donations were regarded as legitimate. On the conclusion of the peace with Tippoo thirty lacs of rupees (£375,000) were demanded and given as *darbar kharach*, or durbar expenses, to be distributed among the officers concerned in settling the treaty.[1] The sums demanded from Meer Jaffier were excessive, but they were calculated on "a fond and literal belief of Oriental exaggeration" that their partner in the enterprise would obtain forty millions sterling deposited in the palace at Murshidabad, whose owner had vanished. In an Oriental kingdom the money in the treasury does not belong to the State, but is the personal property of the sovereign. The critics of Clive and the Committee have judged them by the standard and ideas of their own time, and not by the standard and ideas of "those slovenly times,"[2] to use Lord Morley's euphemistic phrase.

[1] Malcolm, "Political India," Vol. II., p. 245. "Memoirs of Lord Clive," Vol. I., p. 304.

[2] "There is no positive evidence that either the First Lord or the other Commissioners of the Treasury received anything out of the Fee fund, though it may possibly have been a practice in those slovenly times for a First Lord to enrich himself out of perquisites."—Walpole, by John Morley, p. 136.

CHAPTER XIX

1757: PLASSEY

On May 28 Clive wrote to Watson as follows:

To Charles Watson Esq[r]

Sir,—Enclos'd you will receive Copys of two Letters the last from M[r] Scrafton whom I sent to the Nabob, with Views and Designs, which you are well acquainted with.

You will perceive by his Letters that Affairs are drawing to a Conclusion and as you have throughout the whole shewn the utmost Zeal for the Company I am persuaded a Continuance of that Zeal and Assistance will not be wanting on this necessary important Occasion, and I must request the Favour of you to spare 200 Sailors, 100 to accompany and assist us in our March, the other to garrison Chandernagore; there are between 50 and 60 Sailors formerly belonging to the *Walpole & Marlborough*, which have been train'd up by us, and would be of great Service. As the Fate of this Expedition must be decided in a few Days, the Sailors cannot be detain'd long, and you may be assur'd of there being returnd the Instant the Affair is over.

I must further request it as a particular Favour that you will assist Major Killpatrick with the Boats of the Squadron if he has not sufficient for the Transportation of his Troops

I have the Honour to be

Sir

Your most obedient humble Servant

Robert Clive.

French Gardens

28 *May* 1757.

The next day Watson replied as follows:

" I have just received your favour of yesterday's date . . . and as you desire two hundred seamen I will use my best endeavour to collect such a number . . . but I must desire that those who accompany you on your march may not be made use of as *cooleys*, for I have too much reason to fear it would occasion a mutiny among the seamen, who made great complaints at the fatigue they underwent when they marched through the Nabob's camp. . . . I do not think your letters carry the most promising appearance of success; you cannot therefore be too cautious to prevent a false step being taken, which might be of very fatal consequence to our affairs.[1]

The same evening Clive wrote to the Admiral:

To Charles Watson Esq[r]

Sir,—I have receiv'd your Favour & am greatly obligd to you for your promise of assisting us with 200 Seamen you may be persuaded nothing shall be requested of them but fighting our Artillery or making Use of their small Arms as Occasion may require, nothing but meer Necessity oblig'd us to make Use of them before in the Manner you mention which is now entirely remov'd by the Number of Draught Bullocks we are in possession of.

I hope when M[r] Scrafton returns he will bring with him such a plan of Operations as may be satisfactory, and give us the fairest Prospect of Success, at present you know, Sir, nothing of this Kind is settled, and until it is, the Day of the Military's Departure cannot be known when it is I will give you early Notice that the Sailors may set out with the Major, where I have sent such Assistance of Boats as will I hope be sufficient.

The News of Patna is certainly true, the Nabob is very uneasy about it, and wants of all Things to send a part of his Army there but his Apprehensions of us torments him. I much fear he will send Meer Jaffeir that Way if he can. I hope you enjoy your Health this hot Weather.

We have discoverd a great Scene of Villany among several of the Military; it seems a Boat has constantly come in the Night Time from Chinchura to receive stolen Goods, & at last one Frenchard was catchd in the fact of stealing a small Coehorn, one had been missing before and a small brass Field piece. A General Court Martial has sentencd two of them to be hang'd which is to be put in Execution on Friday Morning. One belongs to the Kings, the other to the Company.

I have the Honour to be

Sir

your most ob[t] Hum St

Robert Clive.

French Gardens

29th *May* 1757.

[1] The same evening Admiral Watson wrote to Clive that all he could do was to send men to garrison Chandernagore; but from a letter from Clive, dated June 10, it appears Admiral Watson changed his mind, and gave him at least fifty-sailors to accompany his army.

On June 10 Clive wrote to Watson:

To CHA[s] WATSON ESQ[r]

SIR,—I send you the enclosd Letters from M[r] Watts by which you will observe every Thing is concluded. I expect Mirza Aumee Beg [1] with the Articles this Evening and propose beginning our March early on Monday Morning. I shall therefore be oblig'd to you if you'll send the 100 Sailors those who are to march with us, sometime on Sunday Evening. I have desird Major Killpatrick to wait on you and acquaint you with further particulars

If you can spare the 20 Gun Ship to lay off Hughly she will awe the Phousdar of Hughly greatly and prevent his stopping our Communication by Water.

I have the Hon[r] to be S[r]

Your most ob. Ser[t]

ROBERT CLIVE.

FRENCH GARDENS
10 *June* 1757.

Watson complied with Clive's request, and on Monday morning, June 12, the troops stationed at Calcutta, accompanied by 150 sailors of the squadron, crossed the river and marched to join the force at Chandernagore. A few invalid Europeans and some native troops were left behind to protect the town and guard the French prisoners; a few artillerymen manned the guns on the ramparts. Chandernagore was reached that evening. The following morning, June 13, Clive, leaving behind him 100 seamen to garrison the place, began his hazardous march with a weak force. It consisted of 613 European infantry, 48 Bengal topasses, 43 Bombay topasses, 171 artillery (including 50 sailors and seven midshipmen under the command of Lieutenant Hayter). The Native infantry consisted of 2,100 men, partly the Madras sepoys, partly the newly raised Bengal battalion and a company of Bombay sepoys who had gone with troops from Madras to Bengal.[2] The artillery train was composed of 10 field-pieces, viz. 8 six-pounders and 2 small howitzers. The European infantry consisted of a detachment from Adlercron's regiment, the 39th Foot, now the Dorsetshire Regiment,

[1] Omar Beg.

[2] Broome, p. 142. Sir John Malcolm states: "A company of Bombay sepoys who had gone with troops from Madras to Bengal were present at the victory of Plassey."

which bears on its colours the word "Plassey" and the proud motto *Primus in Indis*, and from the Bengal, Madras,[1] and Bombay battalions. The Europeans, with all the artillery, ammunition and stores, were towed up the river in boats; the sepoys moved in a parallel column along the right bank of the river by the high road which had been made by the Mogul Government from Hugli to Patna.[2]

On the afternoon of the 14th the force arrived at Culna, fifteen miles north of Hugli, where it was joined by Messrs. Watts, Collet, and Sykes. The preceding day Watts rode with the Nawab's consent from his house in the city to the country residence of the factors at Cossimbazar, about two miles south of the factory. Here he found Messrs. Collett and Sykes, the second and third of the factory. "In the evening," says Mr. Sykes, "they set out from the country seat, attended by a *Mogul* servant, a few *peons*, and their greyhounds, having

EXTRACT FROM AN EXACT RETURN OF THE TWO BATTALIONS UNDER THE COMMAND OF LIEUTENANT-COLONEL CLIVE, JUNE 15, 1757:—

Detachments	*Officers*	*Volunteers*	*Non-commissioned Officers*	*Drummers*	*Europeans*	*Topasses*	*Train*	*Total of Columns 3, 4, 5, 6 and 7*
1st Battalion—								
King's troops ..	9	—	15	6	194	—	—	215
Bengal troops ..	21	3	21	11	120	48	—	200
Train	9	—	8	2	—	—	84	94
Total	39	3	44	19	314	48	84	509
2nd Battalion—								
Madras troops ..	19	7	40	14	218	—	—	272
Bombay troops ..	8	1	17	4	81	43	—	145
Train	8	—	8	1	—	—	87	96
Total	35	8	65	19	299	43	87	513
Grand total ..	74	11	109	38	613	91	171	1,022

N.B.—The Sepoy Sergeants are not returned in the above Return.—JOHN FRASER, *Major of Brigade*.

[1] Now The Royal Munster and The Royal Dublin Fusiliers.

[2] Sufficient credit has not always been given to the Mogul Government for the great roads they constructed.

previously left directions with their servants to provide a supper, telling them they should return and entertain the Dutch that evening."[1] It was dark before they arrived at Daudpur, about six miles from Plassey.

"On the plain near that place was encamped Roydulub, an officer of the Nabob's, with a very large force. Here they were exposed to imminent danger, falling unawares on the outposted guards, but the darkness of the night favoured their escape. By striking off into the plain and taking a circuit of the whole camp they regained the road and arrived about one o'clock in the morning at Augadeep, where a second misfortune threatened their destruction. They unexpectedly found themselves in the midst of a body of horse, which had been stationed there to prevent the passing or repassing down or up the country of any Europeans. The first notice they had of this danger was the neighing and kicking of the horses about; their riders luckily were asleep. At this place they quitted their horses, and embarking on two open boats which they had the good fortune to seize, proceeded down the river. Next day about three in the afternoon they met Lord Clive at Changdack, which is near ninety-five miles from Cossimbuzar."[2]

On the 17th Clive's force reached Pattlee, a town on the western bank of the Cossimbazar river, and the following day he sent Major Coote with 200 Europeans, 500 sepoys, and two field-pieces "to possess himself of Cutwa, town and fort about fourteen miles distant, and a post that might have proved extremely advantageous to us, not only from its situation, it lying just by the high road to Muxadavad, and a quantity of grain which we were informed was there, but also the assistance which the Fort would have afforded to our boats and the troops in case either of a retreat or their continuance there."[3] On the 19th the remainder of the force proceeded to Cutwa, "and had an account from Captain Coote while on our march that he was in possession of town and Fort." The following is the brief note from Eyre Coote handed to Clive on the march:

[1] Mr. Collet, in replying to certain questions sent to him by Orme, states: "I am ashamed to say I cannot recollect the gentlemen for certain who were with us, but I think Mr. Batson and Mr. Hastings were of the party, but won't be positive. Mr. Watts, myself, Mr. Russell, surgeon, and the Mogull or Tartar I am certain of."

[2] Mr. Sykes's Account of his Escape from Mandepur in June, 1757. Orme MSS.

[3] Journal of Military Proceedings on the Expedition to Muxadavad.

SIR,—We have this Moment enter'd the Fort by Storm they Kept firing at us—Last night & this morning, I must remark to you Mr. Lewis, neither brought up the Six Pounder nor Houbits

I am

Sir

Your H Ser[t]

EYRE COOTE

The Place all on fire round us.

The troops on their arrival at Cutwa pitched their tents on the plain which surrounded the fort, but the monsoon burst with tremendous violence, and in order to escape the thick rain the men were obliged to shelter themselves among the huts and villages near.

The situation with which Clive had now to deal was beset by grave difficulties. The ground would soon be rendered impassable by the rains for marching, and the deep, wide, and rapid river which lay between him and the enemy would not be fordable. On the other hand, to cross it with his handful of men without delay and without some certainty of being assisted by Meer Jaffier, who commanded 10,000 men, would involve the most serious risk. The slightest disaster meant the destruction of his force—for retreat was impossible. At Cutwa he expected to be joined by Meer Jaffier, but advices received from him contained nothing but excuses for not acting. On June 16 Meer Jaffier wrote to Clive:

"On the news of your coming the Nabob was much intimidated, and requested at such a juncture I would stand his friend. On my part, agreeable to the circumstances of the times, I thought it advisable to acquiesce with his request, but what we have agreed on must be done. I have fixed the first day of the moon for my march. God willing I shall arrive."

To this ambiguous epistle Clive sent the following reply, dated Pattlee, June 18, 1757:

"I have received your letter which has given me the utmost satisfaction after the great pain I have suffered by your silence. I have sent a party to possess themselves of Cutwa fort and town, and shall move with my whole army there to-morrow. I believe I shall march from thence the next day and hope to be at Moncurra in two days, but my motions will in a great measure depend on the advices I receive from you. Write me what you intend to do and what is proper for me to do. On mutual intelligence depends the success of our affairs, so write me daily and fully. If I meet the Nabob's army, what part will you act, and how am I to act? This you may be assured of, that I will attack the Nabob within twenty-four hours after I come in sight of his army. Of all things take care of yourself that you be not undone by treachery before my arrival."

In the next of these letters, dated June 19, Clive expresses clearly to Meer Jaffier what he felt regarding his conduct:

"I wrote yesterday that I should march to Cutwa, and accordingly am now arrived there with my whole force, the fort having been taken by the detachment sent against it. It gives me great concern that in an affair of so great consequence to yourself in particular that you do not exert yourself more. So long as I have been on my march you have not yet given me the least information what measures it is necessary for me to take, nor do I know what is going forward at Muxadavad. Surely it is in your power to send me news daily; it must be more difficult for me to procure trusty messengers than you; however the bearer of this is a sensible intelligent man, and in whom I have great confidence. Let me know your sentiments freely by him. I shall wait here till I have proper encouragement to proceed. I think it absolutely necessary that you should join my army as soon as possible. Consider the Nabob will encrease in strength daily. Come over to me at Plassey or any other place you judge proper, with what force you have. Even a thousand horse will be sufficient, and I will engage to march immediately with you to Muxadavad. I prefer conquering by open force."

Clive thought it his duty to intimate the same day his very serious apprehensions to the Select Committee:

"GENTLEMEN,—The party I sent has taken Cutwa town and fort. Both are strong, notwithstanding which I feel the greatest anxiety at the little intelligence I receive from Meer Jaffeir, and if he is not treacherous, his *sangfroid* or want of strength will I fear overset the expedition. I am trying a last effort by means of the Braminy to prevail upon him to march out and join us. I have appointed Plassey the place of *rendezvous*, and have told him at the same time without he gives me this or some other sufficient proof of the sincerity of his intentions, I will not cross the river. This I hope will meet with your approbation. I shall act with such caution as not to risque the loss of our forces, and whilst we have them, we may always have it in our power to bring about a revolution, should the present not succeed. They say there is a considerable quantity of grain in and about this place; if we can collect 8 or 10,000 *maunds* we may maintain our present situation during the Rains, which will greatly distress the Nabob, and either reduce him to terms which may be depended on, or give us time to bring in the Beirboin [1] Rajah, Marattas, or Gazoody Cawn.[2] I desire you will give me your sentiments freely how you think I should act, if Meer Jaffeir can give us no assistance."

Clive, having no cavalry, wrote on the following day, June 20, to the Rajah of Burdwan asking him to send some of his horse to his aid:

"By continued marches I have reached Cutwa, and the fort, which had a great force in it, by the blessing of God fell into my hands in a very short time. If you are firmly inclined to join me call God and your Prophet to witness your sincerity, and send 2 or 300 good horse to march day and night to join me in the time of battle, and I shall look upon your affairs as my own, and end them happily for you; and your country shall not be injured, nor shall any collector be put over you; and whatever may be the charge of the forces you send me I will make the Government pay you. My real meaning is that I will content you, if your people arrive in time. Send me an immediate answer."

That evening two letters arrived from Meer Jaffier, dated June 19. One was written to Omar Beg, his confidential agent:

"By the blessing of God I shall pray on the Eade [3] day at Cutlee mosque, and shall then join the army, and shall be a mile to the right or left; then I shall know the situation the different commanders are in. I have sent an answer to the Colonel sewed up in slippers."

The letter to Clive was as follows:

"Your note from Colsannie is arrived. I have perused the contents. To-morrow the day of the Eade by the blessing of God I shall march. I shall have my tent fixed to the right or left of the army. I have hitherto been afraid to send you intelligence. After I am arrived in the army mutual intelligence will be easier, but here the Nabob has fixed *chokeys* on all the roads. Your letters come too open to me. I hope that till our affairs are publicly declared you will be very careful."

These letters were not sufficiently explicit, and increased Clive's distrust of Meer Jaffier. He acknowledged in his

[1] Rajah of Burdwan.

[2] Gazoody Cawn, Ghazi-u-dur, the powerful Vizier who had deposed and blinded the Mogul Emperor Ahmad Shah and placed the reigning sovereign Alamghir II. on the throne.

[3] The great Mohammedan festival of the Bukra Eed which, according to the history of Islam, commemorates the day when Abraham intended to sacrifice Ishmael.

letter to Omar Beg that there had been an interview with the Nawab and that some reconciliation had taken place. "At this time intelligence was received through another channel that the whole affair had been discovered and that the Nabob and Meer Jaffier were one." [1] Clive had not resigned the settled purpose of his own mind either to the advice of those around him, or to any combination of opposing circumstances. There was now no "shrinking from the fearful responsibility of making a decision." [2] Clive had quite decided that he would not advance unless he had full assurance of support. He assembled a Council of War on June 21, when the following question was proposed by him :

"Whether in our present situation without assistance and on our own bottom it would be prudent to attack the Nabob, or whether we should wait 'till joined by some Country Power." [3]

[1] Memorandum on Mr. Bolts's book, "Consideration on Indian Affairs." The Memorandum was written by Clive, or under his supervision. Some pages are wanting—Powis MSS. The intelligence came through Omichund.

[2] Macaulay's "Essay on Clive."

[3] The following is an exact transcription of the original record of the Proceedings of the Council of War signed by the *Officers present* and now in the Powis MSS :—

At a Council of War held at Cuttawa, June 21st 1757 :

Colonel Clive *President*		
Major Kilpatrick	Memrs.	Major Grant
Major Coote		Capt. Gaupp
Capt. Armstrong		Capt. Grant
Capt. Rumbold		Capt. Cudmore
Capt. Mieur		Capt. Fisher
Capt. Corneille		Capt. Palmer
Capt. Campbell		Capt. Hater
Capt. Lieut. Passhaud		Capt. Castiers
Capt. Lieut. Jennings		

When the following question was proposed by Colonel Clive

Whether in our present Situation without assistance & on our own bottom it would be prudent to attack the Nabob, or whether we should wait 'till joined by Some Country Power & was carried in the Negative

Robert Clive	Eyre Coote
James Kilpatrick	G. Alexr. Grant
Archd. Grant	G. Muir
George Fredrich Gaupp	Chr : Palmer
Andrew Armstrong	Robert Campbell
Thos. Rumbold	Peter Carstairs
S Cudmore	W. Jenings
Christian Fischer	
John Corneille	
J S Paschoud	

John Power aid du Camp

Clive voted for delay and was supported by Kilpatrick, one of the best officers in the service, and by five other senior officers who are entered in the original proceedings of the Council of War as "Members." Eyre Coote and Captain Alexander Grant, the only two senior officers entered as "Members," supported by five others, voted for an immediate attack.[1] Eyre Coote had at that time acquired very little experience of Indian warfare. On being asked by the Parliamentary Committee what were the reasons he gave for that vote, he replied:

"Having hitherto met with nothing but success, which consequently had given great spirits to our men, I was of opinion that any delay might cast a dampness; 2dly, that the arrival of Monsieur Law would not only strengthen the Nabob's army, and add vigour to their councils, but likewise weaken our force considerably, as the number of Frenchmen we had entered into our service after the capture of Chandernagore would undoubtedly desert to him (Law) upon every opportunity; 3dly, our distance from Calcutta was so great, that all communication from thence would be entirely cut off, and therefore gave us no room to hope for any supplies, and consequently that we must be soon reduced to the greatest distress. For these reasons, I gave it as my opinion that we should come to an immediate action; or, if that was thought entirely impracticable, that we should return to Calcutta; the consequence of which must

[1] Orme states: "Contrary to the forms usually practised in councils of war, of taking the voice of the youngest officer first, and ascending from this to the voice of the president, Colonel Clive gave his opinion first." Eyre Coote, in his evidence before the House of Commons, said: "The question then being put, began with the president and eldest members whose opinions were against coming to an immediate action." Eyre Coote does not mention that this was contrary to the usual forms.

Clive in his evidence stated: "Every member gave their opinions against the attack till they had received further intelligence except Captains Coote and Grant." When Clive was recalled he "observed, that in a former part of his evidence he had made a mistake in respect to the number of the Council of war, who on the 21st June voted for the immediate attack of Serajah Dowla, and said, he might very easily have been led into that mistake, the event having happened 15 years ago, and he not having consulted a single record from that time to this."

If Clive had consulted the original record he would have found that his first statement that "every member" except "Captains Coote and Grant" had given their opinions against the attack was correct. But he ought to have added, "and five other officers." Eyre Coote in his evidence before the Select Committee gives a list which differs from the list in the original record, and the list in Malcolm's "Life of Clive," which is said to be transcribed from the Original Document, is not accurate with regard to the spelling of the names. Broom, who gives the list to be found in Coote's evidence, introduces some additional errors of his own.

be our own disgrace, and the inevitable destruction of the company's affairs."[1]

The only success the English force had obtained was the surrender of Cutwa after a brief resistance. There was no real reason to suppose that Law's army would strengthen the Nawab's army before Clive could attack it: the English had command of the water communication, and therefore could not be entirely cut off from Calcutta. Clive never proposed to return to Calcutta, but what he did propose was to occupy the strong fortress of Cutwa until he received some trustworthy assurances of assistance from Meer Jaffier. This point Eyre Coote did not discuss, and he did not realise the political situation. His evidence shows, as Clive says, that "he did not even then understand the subject upon which he delivered so peremptory an opinion at the Council of War." [2]

Eyre Coote informed the Parliamentary Committee that:

"About an hour after the Council broke up, Colonel Clive informed him, unasked (Captain Robert Campbell, to the best of his recollection, was with him at the time), that, notwithstanding the resolution of the Council-of-war, he intended to march the next morning, and accordingly gave orders for the army to hold themselves in readiness, leaving a subaltern officer's command in the Fort of Cutwa."

Orme writes:

"The sanction of this council in no wise alleviated the anxieties of Clive; for, as soon as it broke up, he retired alone into the adjoining grove, where he remained near an hour in deep meditation, which convinced him of the absurdity of stopping where he was; and acting now entirely from himself, he gave orders, on his return

[1] Orme writes: "He said, 'that the common soldiers were at present confident of success; that a stop so near the enemy would naturally quell this ardour, which it would be difficult to restore; that the arrival of the French troops with Mr. Law would add strength to the Nabob's force and vigour to his councils; that they would surround the English army, and cut off its communication with Calcutta, when distresses not yet foreseen might ruin it as effectually as the loss of a battle. He therefore advised, that they should either advance and decide the contest immediately, or immediately return to Calcutta."—Orme, Vol. II., p. 170.

"The common soldiers were at present confident of success" instead of "our men," "would naturally quell this ardour" for "might cast a dampness," "might ruin it as effectually as the loss of a battle" for "reduced to the greatest distress," are striking examples of Orme's habit of embellishing a quotation.

[2] Memorandum, Powis MSS.

to his quarters, that the army should cross the river the next morning."[1]

Prosaic documentary evidence destroys the picturesque scene. After some hours Clive decided to do what he always intended to do, push forward, if he had sufficient assurance of support. In his evidence before the Parliamentary Committee he states: "That although he might have informed Captain Coote of his resolution to attack Serajah Dowla, notwithstanding the opinion of that Council-of-war, he did imagine that he had not concluded upon the whole plan till twenty-four hours after, because the troops did not cross the river to make that attack till the 22d of June in the evening, and the discourse between Captain Coote and him was the 21st in the morning." After the Council of War had dispersed, Clive wrote to the Select Committee, Fort William:

"Enclosed are copies [2] of two letters received last night. I likewise transmit the sentiments of a Council of War held this day, whether or not it was proper without the assistance of some country Power to attack the Nabob. I wait only for some encouragement from Meir Jaffeir to proceed, which must be the issue unless the Nabob makes very fair offers of accommodation."

Later in the day he informed the Committee that he had learnt from a messenger that since his last another letter had been delivered to Meer Jaffier and no answer returned in writing. The prospect was gloomy. Clive wrote to the Select Committee:

"I am really at a loss how to act at the present situation of our affairs, especially should I receive a confirmation by letter of Meir Jaffeir's resolution to stand neuter. The Nabob's forces at present are not said to exceed 8,000 men but a compliance with their demands

[1] Eyre Coote, in his Journal: "June 22nd. At 6 o'clock in the morning, the army crossed the river and marched to a large *tope* about two miles' distance."

Journal of Military Proceedings, written at the time, June 22nd: "At 5 in the evening crossed the river, leaving a subaltern's party and 100 seapoys in the Fort and about 12 at night we arrived at Placis after a very long and fatiguing march." On July 2, 1757, nine days after Plassey, Clive wrote: "The 22nd in the evening we crossed the river and landing on the island (the island of Cossimbazar) marched straight for Plassey where we arrived by 1 in the morning." On July 26 Clive in a letter repeated the statement: "The 22nd in the evening we crossed the river."

[2] Meer Jaffier's Letters, dated June 19.

may easily encrease them. If we attack them it must be entrenched, and ourselves without any assistance. In this place a repulse must be fatal, on the contrary success may give the greatest advantage. The Nabob's apprehensions at present are great, and perhaps he may be glad to grant us an honourable Peace. The principle of fear may make him act much against his private inclination and I believe that has been the case ever since the capture of Chandernagore. There still remains another expedient of sending an embassy either to Gazoody Cawn or the Morattoes to invite them in. I beg you will let me have your sentiments how I ought to act at this critical juncture."

The night passed and morning broke, and no answer from Meer Jaffier. It was three o'clock in the afternoon ere a messenger came that brought glad tidings to Clive. Meer Jaffier informed Clive that he had marched from Murshidabad and collected his people. The Nawab had pitched his tent at Muncarra, a village six miles to the south of Cossimbazar, and he added :

" The Nabob's intention is to have his intrenchment at Moncurra, therefore the sooner you march to fall on him the better before his design can take place. As yet you are now only designing, but it is not now proper to be indolent. When you come near I shall then be able to join you. If you could send two or three hundred good fighting men the upper road towards Cossimbuzar, the Nabob's army would of themselves retreat. Then the battle will have no difficulty. When I am arrived near the army I will send you privately all the intelligence. Let me have previous notice of the time you intend to fight."

Clive considered the letter contained a sufficient assurance of support to justify a bold course being adopted. He wrote to Meer Jaffier :

" I am determined to risque everything on your account, though you will not exert yourself. I shall be on the other side of the river this evening. If you will join me at Placis, I will march half way to meet you, then the whole Nabob's army will I know fight for you. Give me [leave] to call to your mind how much your own glory and safety depends upon it. Be assured if you do this you will be *Subah* of these Provinces, but if you cannot go even this length to assist us I call God to witness the fault is not mine, and I must desire your consent for concluding a Peace with the Nabob, and what has passed between us will never be known. What can I say more than that I am as desirous of your success and welfare as my own."

Clive at once ordered the force to march, and at five in the evening the river was crossed.[1] An hour later he sent the following scrap of paper to Meer Jaffier: "Upon receiving your letter I am come to a resolution to proceed immediately to Placis. I am impatient for an answer to my letter by the trusty man." The advance now continued, and "after a very fatiguing march and through a whole night's rain" Plassey Grove was reached "about 12 at night."[2] Clive from Meer Jaffier's last letter expected to find the Nawab entrenched at Muncarra. He now learnt that the Nawab's vanguard, consisting of 6,000 men, was within three miles of him.[3] "He ordered our advanced guard of 200 Europeans and 300 sepoys, with two field pieces, to post themselves at Plassey House and several videts at proper distances from each other round the grove."[4] Plassey House, situated on the bank of the river, was a substantial shooting-lodge of the Nawab's, built of brick and surrounded by a high wall. Here Clive fixed his headquarters. About fifty yards from the river, a little to the south of the house, was a mango orchard known as the Laksha Bagh, or orchard of one hundred thousand trees. In the Laksha Bagh, protected by a mud-bank and a ditch, bivouacked the main body of the English force.

A little more than a mile to the north of the orchard, Surajah Dowla lay in his tent disheartened by many anxieties. The day that Clive marched from Chandernagore he dispatched a long letter to the Nawab, upbraiding him on account of his connection with the French:

[1] Scrafton writes: "On the twenty-second of June the Colonel received a letter from Meer Jaffeir which determined him to hazard a battle, and he passed the river at five in the evening."—Scrafton, p. 85, *see* note, p. 446.

[2] Journal of Military Proceedings, Eyre Coote's Journal: "After a fatiguing march of twelve or fifteen miles the van arrived at Plassey Grove (twenty miles from Muxadavad) at 11; the rear hardly came up before 3 in the morning." "A Narrative of the battle near Muxadavad," dated "Cossimbazar, 29 June, 1757."—Orme MSS.

[3] Orme, fond of the picturesque, states: "The army immediately took possession of the adjoining grove, when, to their great surprize, the continual sound of drums, clarions, and cymbals, which always accompany the night watches of an Indian camp, convinced them that they were within a mile of the Nabob's army."

[4] "From the narrative of an officer at the time a captain in the army."

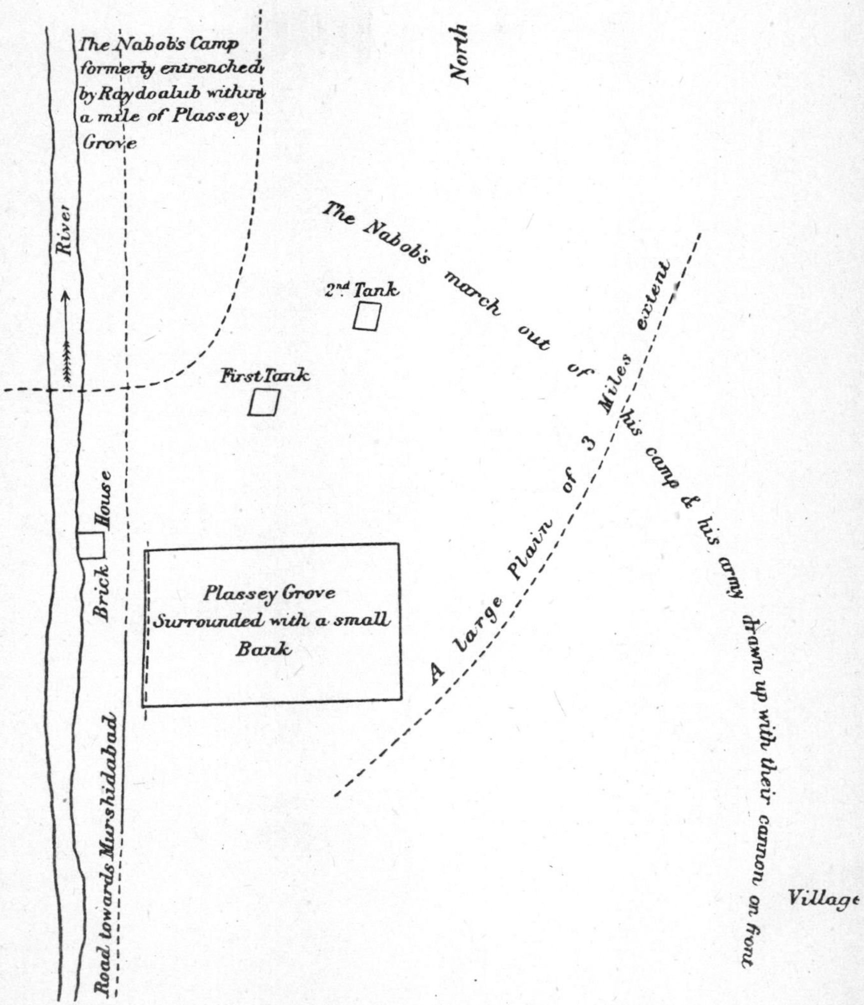

PLAN OF THE PLASSEY GROVE (ASCRIBED TO CLIVE)

(By permission of the India Office)

"It was agreed between us that your enemies should be mine and mine yours. When Your Excellency called me to your assistance against the Patans, I swear before God that it was my firm intention to assist you with my whole force, and that I esteemed it the greatest happiness to have such an opportunity of testifying my friendship for you, whereas Your Excellency chose your friends from among my enemies as evidently appears from this, that we have certain knowledge from Decan of the letters you have wrote to our enemy Monsieur Bowsie. I refer you to the copies of your own letters. If you do not chuse to shew me your copies, I will wait on (you) with those I have."

He reproached him for all the injuries he had inflicted on the Company, and the non-fulfilment of his engagements:

"You have discouraged the Company's business beyond what I am able to express, but I will only touch on a few particulars. Four months are elapsed since the treaty, and many times that you have fixed on for the full execution of the treaty passed by, yet very little advance is made towards fulfilling it. Of the great sums paid into your Treasury taken at Calcutta you do not consent to pay me above a fifth part, and yet expect I should send you a full discharge."[1]

He enumerated the injuries and insults to which the English had been subjected, and he announced that it was "the sentiments of all who have charge of the Company's affairs" that he should

"go to Cossimbuzar, put our disputes to arbitration before Juggut Seat, Rajah Mohun Lal, Meer Jaffeir Khan, Rajah Roy Dulub, Meer Murdun and the rest of your great men, and if it shall appear that I have deviated from the treaty I bind myself to give up all my demands. But if it should appear Your Excellency has deviated from it, I shall demand satisfaction for all our losses, and all the charges of the navy and army."

He concluded with a startling announcement:

"The Rains being daily encreasing, and it taking a great deal of time to receive your answer, I therefore find it necessary to wait on you immediately, and if you will place confidence in me no harm shall come from it. I represent this to you as a friend. Act as you please."

[1] "Selections from the Letters, Despatches, and other State Papers preserved in the Madras Secretariat (Clive Series)," edited by George W. Forrest.

On the morning of June 14 Surajah Dowla heard of the flight of Watts, and the intelligence greatly alarmed him. It seemed to confirm the rumours which had reached his ears regarding a dark conspiracy of which Meer Jaffier was the head. A few hours later the war-breathing epistle from Clive arrived. The Nawab realised it meant his destruction. He had intended that morning to attack Meer Jaffier's palace and seize the traitor. He now wavered. The next day the young Nawab, proud and arrogant, went to his powerful minister's palace in order to conciliate one who might be a terrible enemy. Both men were wary, and both felt alike that they were engaged in an intricate game.

> "The Koran was introduced, the accustomed pledge of their falsehood; the Soubah swore he would never attempt his life; Meer Jaffier that he would be his faithful soldier, and fight for him to the last drop of his blood. They parted with smiles on their countenances, and treachery in their hearts; each happy in the thought of over-reaching the other: And now we were the grand object of their attention."[1]

The Nawab, taking Meer Jaffier at his oath, sent a letter of defiance to Clive. He inveighed bitterly against Watts's secret flight, "which appears to be done with a very deceitful design and intention to break the treaty." The closing sentence clearly showed his intention:

> "It was the consideration that something of this kind was contriving that hindered me from recalling the army from Plassy, for I know some trick was intended. I thank God, however, the treaty has not been broke on my part, and as it was so solemnly sworn to before God and His Prophet He will doubtless punish him who has first violated it." [2]

The letter dispatched, Surajah Dowla ordered his troops to march towards Plassey, and he wrote to M. Law bidding him to come to his assistance with the utmost expedition. But the troops refused to move until all arrears had been discharged. For three days Murshidabad was in a state of tumult, and the mutinous soldiers only consented to advance to meet the enemy after a liberal distribution of money. On

[1] Scrafton, p. 90.
[2] Letter from the Nawab to Colonel Clive, dated June 15, 1757

June 18 the Nawab's force marched out to the village of Muncarra, a few miles south of Cossimbazar, where, as Meer Jaffier stated in his letter to Clive, the Nawab intended "to have his entrenchment." But on hearing that Clive had not crossed the river he renewed his march. On the evening of the 21st he arrived at the small village of Daudpur within four miles of the entrenched position which Rai Dulab had constructed before the siege of Chandernagore; it had been held by a part of the Nawab's army for some time. The position was by no means ill adapted for defence. The banks of an Indian river are continually shifting, and here the stream, making a wide curve in shape like a horseshoe, enclosed a peninsula about three miles in circumference, the neck of which was, however, less than a quarter of a mile in breadth from stream to stream. The entrenched line, starting from the river bank a little below the southern neck, ran for about two hundred yards nearly parallel to the north side of the grove, until it reached a redoubt on which several guns were mounted. From the redoubt the entrenchment turned north-east and continued in that direction for about three miles. About three hundred yards to the east of the redoubt, but outside the entrenchment, stood a hillock covered with trees: half a mile south-west of this hillock was a small tank, and farther south-west, nearer the river, almost facing the centre of the northern side of the grove, was a larger artificial pond. They were both surrounded by bunds or embankments of earth obtained by their excavation.

Between the village of Daudpur and the southern front of the entrenchment, and partly in the peninsula itself, the Nawab's vast force encamped.[1] The royal tent was pitched a little behind the front line facing the grove. The big moment had come, and many melancholy considerations did not escape the Nawab. He had 35,000 infantry, 15,000 cavalry, with

[1] Orme writes: "Within this entrenchment encamped the whole army of which a part likewise occupied the peninsula."—Orme, Vol. II., p. 173. Broome referring to the plan says: "The Nawab's Army was encamped partly in the peninsula and partly in rear of the entrenchment." An Oriental army consisting of 50,000 troops accompanied by a large number of elephants, camels and oxen, and the usual host of camp followers, could not have been held in the space mentioned by Orme.

53 guns, chiefly of large calibre. His opponent had no more than 3,200 men with 10 light field-pieces. But the English, though small in numbers, had before defeated him. His army was strong in numbers, but his generals were a source of anxiety and doubt. There was none upon whose steadfast loyalty he could depend. The most respectable men of his Court had in his insane fits of temper been spat upon, beaten, imprisoned, and had narrowly escaped death. A trifling circumstance which he took for an ill omen, says Scrafton, confirmed him in his fears :

> " As he was sitting in his tent, the evening before the battle, revolving in his mind the doubtful issue, his attendants imperceptibly left him one by one till he was alone ; when a fellow entered, unperceived by the Soubah, and carried off the gold top of the hookah he was smoking, and cut off some of the broad-cloth of his tent. It shocked his soul to think, that he, whose frowns were death but in the morning, should now be so little feared : He called for his attendants, and cried, with great emotion, ' Sure they see me dead.' "

At dawn, June 23, 1757, Clive climbed to the roof of the hunting lodge and saw below him a wide green plain lit up with the broken lights from a blue sky across whose face drove dark masses of monsoon clouds as they rolled up from the Indian Ocean. When the sun rose in Eastern splendour the enemy appeared marching out of their entrenchments at different points, " and what with the number of elephants all covered with scarlet cloth and embroidery ; their horse with their drawn swords glittering in the sun ; their heavy cannon drawn by vast trains of oxen ; and their standards flying, they made a most pompous and formidable appearance." [1] They advanced in dense columns of cavalry and infantry interspersed with batteries of guns of different strength. Marching in this order, the divisions under Rai Dulab, Yar Lu'f Khan, and Meer Jaffier soon formed a crescent line from the hillock to within half a mile of the southern angle of the grove, the last two divisions encircling and outflanking the English. Some fifty Frenchmen under M. St. Frais had accompanied the Nawab. They pushed forward with four field-pieces and took post at the larger tank, distant from the

[1] Scrafton, p. 91.

British about two hundred yards. Farther to the right, near the river, two heavy guns under the command of a native officer were posted. In support of these two batteries were 5,000 horse and 7,000 foot, the best of the Nawab's army, under the command of Meer Murdeen (Mir Madan), a loyal and brave leader.

This display of great military force did not disturb Clive's equanimity. The daring genius, always desirous of anticipating the attacks of an enemy, determined him to withdraw his few troops from the shelter of the grove and draw them up in a single line with their front facing the French. The thin line extended only about a thousand yards from the hunting lodge on the left to some distance beyond the right of the grove. About two hundred yards in front of the hunting lodge and the left division of sepoys were a couple of brick-kilns, and here a small party was posted in advance with the remaining two six-pounders and the two howitzers.

Clive expected every moment a communication from Meer Jaffier, but no messenger came with it. At 7 A.M. Clive sent him the following short note:

> "Whatever could be done by me I have done, I can do no more. If you will come to Daudipore I will march from Placis to meet you, but if you won't comply even with this, pardon me, I shall make it up with the Nabob."

An hour after the French guns at the large tank opened fire,[1] and the field-pieces at the brick-kilns replied promptly and effectively. Soon after the enemy's guns of heavier calibre were dragged up by trains of oxen and opened with vigour at a short range. They were answered by the six-pounders of the line, and a fierce duel of artillery ensued. The British light guns could make little impression upon the heavier weight of the Nawab's artillery, but great gaps were

[1] "The first shot was fired by the enemy at eight o'clock from the tank; it killed one, and wounded another of the grenadier company, which was posted on the right of the battalion."—Orme, Vol. II., p. 174. In a letter describing the action, written six days after the event, we read: "We were scarcely drawn up in this manner, when a 24 lb. shott from their camp, bounding along, and carrying off the arm of one of the King's granadiers, convinced us that their cannon was come up."—"A Narrative of the Battle near Muxidavad," dated "Cossimbazar, 29 June, 1757."

opened in the masses stationed behind them. The guns of the enemy swept the thin line before them, and in half an hour ten Europeans and twenty sepoys were struck down. Clive, alive to the necessity of husbanding his small force, ordered the Europeans and sepoys " to retire and lye upon their arms within the bank of the Grove, fronting the enemy as before and drawn up in the same order. Our houbitz was advanced about half-way to the first Tank, and our eight guns properly divided in the intervals, betwixt the battalions and *sepoys*, but advanced a little distance without the banks of the Grove." [1] The enemy's cannon moved slowly forward, and " their heavy mettle continued to play briskly on the Grove." [2] The round shots shattered the branches of the lofty mango trees, but the British infantry, lying under the shelter of the bank, had very few disabled. The howitzer and field-pieces advanced in front played with great success among " those that were of the first rank." Meer Murdeen, a fine soldier, was mortally wounded.[3] The movement of a large body of the enemy's horse on the right creating an impression that " they intended an attempt on the advanced field pieces and hawitzes, they were both ordered back." [4]

It was now about noon, and the cannonade had been in progress nearly four hours, when were heard volleying thunders, and the rain came down in tropical torrents. " We had some apprehension that the enemy would take advantage of this opportunity and make a push with their horse, but our guns

[1] " A Narrative of the Battle near Muxidavad," dated " Cossimbazar, 29 June, 1757." Orme states : " The troops were ordered to sit down, whilst the field-pieces alone answered the enemy's cannon from behind the bank." Broome converts the sentence into the following : " The troops were well protected by the embankment and were directed to sit down so as to be little exposed ; holes were made in the bank to serve as embrasures."—Broome, p. 145. Scrafton states : " Our little army was at first drawn up without the bank which surrounded the grove, but we soon found such a shower of balls pouring upon us from their 50 pieces of cannon (most of which were 32- and 24-pounders), that we retired under cover of the bank, leaving two field pieces without ; whilst the other four kept playing through the breaches in the bank." —Scrafton, p. 92.

[2] " Journal of Military Proceedings on the Expedition to Muxadavad."

[3] " One great cause of our success was, that in the very beginning of the action, we had the good fortune to kill Meer Modun, one of the Soubah's best and most faithful officers."—Scrafton, p. 93.

[4] " Journal of Military Proceedings on the Expedition to Muxadavad."

continuing to play very briskly, prevented any such motion. The enemy's guns during the rain, which lasted half an hour, did not fire a shott."[1] When the rain ceased the cannonade was resumed. About 3 P.M. the enemy was seen returning "without confusion to their old camp, their artillery marching first."[2] At this time a large corps on the extreme left of the enemy's crescent line was seen moving in such a manner as to create a doubt whether their aim was to gain possession of the village of Plassey, about a mile south of the grove, or whether they were friends and wanted to join the British force. The village was strategically important because it commanded the passage of the river, and by moving up the stream the enemy could attack the British baggage and boats, The corps, which proved afterwards to be that of Meer Jaffier, was kept at a distance by our artillery.

When the enemy retired to their entrenchments, Clive, drenched to the skin, went into Plassey House to change his clothes. He had determined to maintain his position in the grove during the day, and at night to force with his handful of men a passage through the vast camp of the enemy. He had learnt from past experience in the Carnatic campaign that the darkness, the suddenness and violence of the attack, would throw an enemy lacking drill and discipline into confusion and so make victory more certain. He left orders with

[1] "A Narrative of the Battle near Muxidavad," dated "Cossimbazar, 29 June, 1757." "The enemy's fire now began to slacken and soon after entirely ceased."—Journal of Military Proceedings. "About noon a very heavy shower covered the plain, and very soon damaged the enemy's powder so much, that their fire slackened continually; but the English ammunition served on."—Orme, Vol. II., p. 175. Broome states: "About noon a very heavy shower commenced, which lasted for nearly an hour, and completely deluged the plain, at the same time that it damaged nearly all the enemy's ammunition, which was much exposed; the consequence was that their fire materially slackened. A party of the enemy's horse, anticipating a similar result as regarded the English Artillery, advanced boldly towards the grove, to take advantage of it; but the English arrangements were so much better in this respect, that their ammunition had received little or no injury—and this body of Cavalry were received with so warm a fire as to induce them to retire with some precipitation. In this affair Meer Moodeen was mortally wounded by a shot from one of the six-pounders." "In this situation both armies remained till 12 o'clock, when a heavy shower of rain falling, the enemy's horse advanced as if to take advantage thereof; but when they found our field-pieces continued firing notwithstanding the rain falling, the enemy's horse were checked in their ardour."—Narrative of an Officer.

[2] From the Narrative of an Officer.

Major Kilpatrick that, if the enemy made any fresh movement, it was to be immediately reported to him.[1] Great, therefore, was his surprise when he learnt that, without his sanction, a detachment of the force with some field-pieces was marching towards the large tank which the French had abandoned.[2] He immediately hastened after the detachment and joined it as it was on the point of reaching the tank. He now found that it was commanded by Major Kilpatrick, his old and favourite comrade. In the fire of wrath, "he at first ordered him under arrest for such unmilitary conduct, but was pacified on receiving an apology." He sent Kilpatrick back to the grove and assumed the direct command. As an advance had been made, he knew to fall back would be disastrous, so he resolved with his usual promptness to renew the action and by attacking to make it decisive. He sent to the grove for another detachment, upon which

[1] From the Narrative of an Officer. "Memoirs of the Revolution in Bengal." Orme states: "At eleven o'clock Colonel Clive consulted his officers at the drum head; and it was resolved to maintain the cannonade during the day, but at midnight to attack the Nabob's camp."—Orme, Vol. II., p. 175. Eyre Coote enters in his Journal: "In this situation we cannonaded each other till 12 o'clock, when the Colonel came from Plassey House which was close to the river side and called the captains together in order to hold a Council of War, but changing his mind returned without holding one."

[2] Orme was the first to give currency to the unfounded statement that Clive was asleep, and he tries to emphasise the statement by a shallow apology. He writes: "Major Kilpatrick, impatient to seize the opportunity, advanced from the grove with two companies of the battalion, and two field-pieces, marching fast towards the tank, and sent information of his intention and the reason of it, to his commander, who chanced at this time to be lying down in the hunting-house. Some say he was asleep; which is not improbable, considering how little rest he had had for so many hours before; but this is no imputation either against his courage or conduct."—Orme, Vol. II., p. 176. Walsh, who "was present at the battle of Plassey and constantly near the person of the Commander-in-Chief during the whole engagement," published a letter in 1763 to the "Proprietors of East India Stock," and forwarded a copy to Orme. He stated: "The English Commander-in-Chief made the disposition of the troops himself, and was at the head of them during the whole of the action until the enemy had retreated back to their entrenched camp, the attack of which he had then determined to defer till night. The field being now clear, he retired into an adjacent building, for no tents were pitched, to shift his cloaths wet with rain, but before he could change them word was brought him that a part of his troops were marching out of the Grove towards a small eminence on which the corps of French in Suraja Dowlet's Army had been posted. Surprized that such a motion should be made without his orders, he instantly hastened to the party, at the head of which he found Major Kilpatrick, whom he reprimanded for his unsoldierlike conduct and ordered him back to the Grove, and then, taking the command of these advanced troops himself, remained at the head of them during the second action which ended with our storming the enemy's camp two hours afterwards."

Eyre Coote marched out and joined him with his division.[1] Clive then ordered the King's Grenadiers and a grenadier company of sepoys to lodge themselves behind a bank that was close upon the enemy's lines. From their entrenchment and from the wooded mound near their redoubt the foe kept up a smart fire of musketry, to which the detachment at the large tank, with four field-pieces, replied. Clive's object was to draw the enemy from their entrenchment a second time, and he was successful. Their infantry and cavalry poured forth from their lines, " but in attempting to bring out their cannon they were so galled by our artillery that they could not effect it, notwithstanding they made several attempts." [2] Regardless of the hot artillery fire, they advanced over the naked plain, and " by their motions made as if they intended to charge us, two or three large bodies being within one hundred and fifty yards." Clive, fearing that his small isolated post would be overwhelmed by numbers, twice or thrice ordered the remainder of his force in the grove to join him, " and that order as often countermanded on account of the movement of a large body of horse towards the Grove whom we had often fired upon to keep at a proper distance." [3]

For some time the enemy faced with no abatement of courage the brisk fire of the field-pieces. Men and horses fell rapidly. Among the slain were four of their principal commanders. Confusion now began to prevail in their ranks, and it was observed " that their elephants grew very unruly." [4] Clive, with his usual decision and boldness in battle, took advantage of the critical moment. He ordered Eyre Coote to attack the mound and a party to storm the redoubt, " which we carried at the same instant with little or no loss ; though the latter was defended (exclusively of blacks) by forty French and two pieces of cannon ; and the former by a large body of blacks, both foot and horse." [5] The redoubt was taken with little or no loss because the French had

[1] Eyre Coote's Journal.

[2] *Ibid.* : " This encouraged us to take possession of another advanced post within three hundred yards of the entrance of the enemy's camp."—Journal of Military Proceedings.

[3] Journal of Military Proceedings.

[4] Narrative of an Officer.

[5] Letter to the Honble. George Pigot.

received orders from the Nawab to retire, and they soon afterwards learnt that he had fled.

Meer Murdeen, on being mortally wounded, was carried into the Nawab's tent and died in his presence. The young prince, overcome at the sight of the death of his most loyal military commander, lost his presence of mind. He knew Meer Jaffier was a traitor. He sent repeated messages and pressing solicitations to him to come to his tent. Meer Jaffier came, accompanied by his son and strongly guarded.

> "Seradj-ed-doulah spoke to him in the humblest strain, and at last descended to the lowest supplications; he even took his turbant from off his head, (at least this was the report) and placed it before the General; to whom he addressed these very words; 'I now repent of what I have done; and availing myself of those ties of consanguinity which subsist between us, as well as of those rights which my grandfather, Aaly-verdy-qhan, has doubtless acquired upon your gratitude, I look up to you, as to the only representative of that venerable personage; and hope therefore, that, forgetting my past trespasses, you shall henceforward behave as becomes a Seyd, a man united in blood to me, and a man of sentiments, who conserves a grateful remembrance of all the benefits he has received from my family; I recommend myself to you: take care of the conservation of my honor and life.' Meer Jaffier coldly replied that the day was now drawing to its end: and that there remained no time for an attack; 'send a counter-order to the troops that are advancing,' said he; 'recal those engaged; and to-morrow, with the blessing of God, I will join all the troops together, and provide for the engagement.' Seradj-ed-doulah observed, that they might be attacked by the enemy in the night: this also the General took upon himself to provide against, and he promised that the enemy would not form a night attack."[1]

The traitor rode back to his troops and promptly sent a messenger to Clive. Surajah Dowla's fear increasing every moment, he sought the counsel of Rai Dulab, another traitor, who advised him to withdraw his troops within the entrenchment. The fatal advice was adopted. Orders were sent to Mohun Lal to fall back. At first he refused to obey them, but after repeated imploring orders and pressing messages had reached him, he yielded and withdrew his force. It was their retirement which Kilpatrick saw from the grove. When

[1] "Seir Mutaquharin," Vol. I., p. 767–768.

Surajah Dowla learnt that the British force was attacking the entrenchment and that some of his troops had begun to retreat, he mounted a fleet riding camel and fled in the direction of Murshidabad.

By 5 o'clock the English were in possession of the whole entrenchment and camp, which they found had just been evacuated. An enormous mass of baggage, stores, camp equipage and cattle was scattered around them. Clive sent at once a detachment under Major Eyre Coote to follow the flying foe. The pursuit was continued for upwards of six miles, "which for want of horse answered no other purpose than that of taking all their artillery consisting of five pieces of cannon." [1] The detachment halted at Daudpore, "where the rest of the arms under Major Kilpatrick joined us." [2]

So ended the battle of Plassey. The Nawab's army, according to Clive's calculation, lost 500 men; the victors lost only 4 Europeans and 14 sepoys killed, and 9 Europeans and 36 sepoys wounded and 2 European sentinels missing. But it is not wise to estimate victory by its cost. Plassey was a great victory because it was conclusive in result. For a force of 800 Europeans, 8 pieces of cannon and 2,100 sepoys, and no cavalry, to advance against an army of 20,000 horse and 40,000 foot, with a large number of guns, was the height of daring. By well-conducted operations and by perfect coolness of nerve Clive gained his last great battle. It has been stated that Plassey can "hardly be called a battle"; it was a rout.[3] But it was a rout because Clive, after exercising the highest of all military virtues, patience, hurled his small force at the right moment against the entrenched lines and ended the contest by a vigorous pursuit.

That evening (June 23, 1757) Clive sent the following brief note to "Charles Watson and the Gentlemen of the Committee of Fort William":

GENTLEMEN,—This morning at one o'clock we arrived at Placis Grove, and early in the morning the Nabob's whole army appeared

[1] Journal of Military Proceedings.
[2] Eyre Coote's Journal.
[3] "The rout of Plassey, for it can hardly be called a battle."—"British Dominion in India," by Sir Alfred Lyall, p. 132.

in sight and cannonaded us for several hours, and about noon returned to a very strong camp in sight, lately Roydoolub's, upon which we advanced and stormed the Nabob's camp, which we have taken with all his cannon and pursued him six miles, being now at Doudpoor and shall proceed for Muxadavad to-morrow. Meer Jaffeir, Roydoolub and Luttee Cawn gave us no other assistance than standing neuter. They are with me with a large force. Meer Muddun and five hundred horse are killed and three elephants. Our loss is trifling, not above twenty Europeans killed and wounded.

APPENDICES

I

When I was in Pondicherry a learned French lawyer, who took most patriotic interest in the history of his countrymen in India, told me that there was in the archives some important evidence as to La Bourdonnais having taken a bribe. He also, with the characteristic generosity of his race, gave me the following authenticated copy of the document. The translation was made by Mr. Markheim, Fellow of Queen's College, Oxford, whose death deprived that University of one of her brilliant sons.

"21 *August*, 1747. This day, twenty-first of August 1747, at four o'clock in the afternoon, I was summoned by Mr. Dupleix to act as interpreter between him and Mr. Savage, formerly Councillor at Madras and now ready to leave on parole for Ceylon. Mr. Savage asked me to make his best thanks to the Governour for all the civilities which he had received from him, and on his own part to assure him of his everlasting gratitude. The Governour, after making response to this compliment, requested him as a proof of friendship to tell him how much Mr. Morse and the Madras Council had given privately to Mr. de La Bourdonnais, and to declare to him there and then, in a friendly way, and in secrecy, how the business had been done. Mr. Savage, very much surprised by this unexpected request, appeared to hesitate in his answer. I consented, he said, to all that was done, and I signed. What will Mr. Dupleix think of me if I myself reveal operations at which I should be the first to blush. Never mind, replied Mr. Dupleix, anybody would have done the same in your place; you did your best to extricate yourself, and to get out of the hands of the victor whose overtures you were obliged to accept, however inconsistent they might appear to you with straightforwardness and with your honour able sentiments which are known to me.

"This answer cleverly given reassured Mr. Savage. After several long-winded compliments he required of Mr. Dupleix his word of honour that he would not mention the matter and made the same request of me. Mr. Dupleix insinuated that he did not ask him the question with intent to use his name, but simply and solely, in order to get a clue; that he knew already a great deal, but in a confused way, and without being positively sure.

"Your Madras Council must have already written to you fully

about it, said Mr. Savage, for our English gentlemen of the hill have revealed to them the whole mystery. Mr. Dupleix answered that nothing had been told them. Pardon me, replied Mr. Savage, I was present when some of our gentlemen took Mr. Morse to task for this matter. They blamed him for the way in which he had practised upon them, but (added) that he would not take advantage of it, since they had revenged themselves by the exposé they had made of all his secret manœuvres to the gentlemen of the Pondicherry Council then at Madras. I am surprised, he continued, that so public a matter and which has been in the mouths of so many malcontents, is not known to you in all its circumstances; you know the public treaty of the eleven lacs; the secret article was that we were to give privately to Mr. La Bourdonnais one lac down, to save the town from pillage and secure private property from aggression.

" Did he receive the whole lac? asked Mr. Dupleix.

" No, but to my knowledge he received in gold and silver as well as in diamonds eighty-five to ninety thousand pagodas, and if he had but waited a day longer the whole sum would have been paid.

" From whom was the sum levied? From the English residents? Were the Malabars made to contribute? I have not been able to clear up this point, but they complain loudly. And as to the Armenians what was extracted from them before they were let loose from prison?

" I do not believe that till then anything had been got out of them, but if the town had remained in our possession, they would have been compelled to do as the others did.

" Who were those malcontents who cried out so much against Mr. Morse and his Council?

" They were Messrs. Fawkes Junior and many others, because after contributing to the payment of this lac with their most clear and portable property, they saw by the way matters were going that their goods were going to be confiscated, nothing less than that. Don't ask me more about it, he continued, you will see all these underhand dealings in the English public papers next year; there have been so many complaints that they cannot fail to be noised about in Europe. I wish that all that has passed at Madras could be forgotten, I can only think of it with abhorrence.

" I asked him how many boxes of piastres there were in the Treasury the day when the town was taken.

" I cannot recollect the exact number, he said. But, Sir, I answered him by the minute of the deliberations, which is in your handwriting, there were in the last days of August eighteen boxes. This record goes as far as the sixth or seventh of September. Your . . . and no mention is made in it that piastres had been taken out of the Treasury. I have noticed in all this record that as soon as they were drawn, and even before, you did not fail to make an entry of it.

"Yes, he said, there must have been eighteen boxes, and no doubt they were there.

"He was much surprised when I told him that there were only six.

"This is the gist of what passed in that conversation. On leaving Mr. Dupleix asked me to put it down in writing, so that he might be the better able to remember it. Which I did as accurately as possible before seven o'clock in the evening this twenty first of August 1747.

"(*Signed*) FRIELL.

"I the undersigned certify on my soul and conscience that the contents of this document are true and were told me by Mr. Savage in English which I interpreted in French to the said Mr. Dupleix at Pondichery, at half past seven in the evening, this twenty first of this August 1747.

"(*Signed*) FRIELL.

"I the undersigned Councillor in the Higher Council and commandant of Karikal, certify that the present document was presented to me by Mr. Dupleix, commandant general of India at the very moment when it was completed by Mr. Friell, and that I read it after having previously given my word of honour to the said Mr. Dupleix to keep a profound silence on its contents, in consequence of the same pledge which had been required of those two gentlemen by Mr. Savage at Pondichery at half past seven in the evening, this twenty first of August 1747.

"(*Signed*) PARADIS.

(*Copy*). "*Pondichery*, 10 *April*, 1876.

"*The Conservator of the Library and of the Old Records.*

"(*Signed*) DE GACON.

"*Stamp of the Old Records of Pondichery.*"

II

Archives des Affaires Etrangères. Mémoires et Documents. A sie, Vol. 12, ff. 142–143.

Gingy fut pris en 1750 par les François sur les Maures.

C'est une forteresse qui a 4600 toises de circuit. Elle renferme 7 forts, dont quatre sont autant de montagnes qui se communiquent par des courtines très étendues. La plus considérable a 900 toises de long et n'est flanquée que par une espèce de tour saillante et qui n'est pas protégée par ses flancs.

Cette place extraordinaire est très foible par differens endroits, les montagnes seules sont de difficile accès, mais si éloignees les unes des autres, qu'elles ne peuvent se proteger mutuellement.

L'aldée ou village qui dépend de Gingy est très considérable et très peuplée. Elle est située dans la plaine au pied de la courtine principale dont on vient de parler.

Tous les militaires ont pensé que la communication entre Pondichery et Gingy étoit très difficile à garder, parce que le pays qui est entre deux n'est que plaine. Il faudroit construire beaucoup de redoutes et des lignes qui ne pouroient être gardées que par un nombre de troupes trop considérables pour une compagnie de commerce.

Gingy luy même en demande beaucoup pour sa sureté et celle des récoltes qui en dependent. L'air y est très mauvais et l'eau n'y vaut rien.

Gingy, à 18 lieues dans les terres, n'est d'aucune utilité pour le commerce des Européens.

On peut s'engager à rendre Gingy aux Maures, si cette place entre nos mains fait quelqu'obstacle au succès des negociations.

Mais, comme les Anglois n'y ont aucun droit, if faut bien se garder de la leur céder. Nous ne ferions un ennemy du nabab d'Arcatte, à qui cette place apportient, et peut être même des Marattes, qui y ont des droits, car anciennement ils en étoient les maîtres ; mais il vaut mieux favoriser le nabab d'Arcatte que les Marattes, dont l'expulsion de toute la côte, si elle est possible, est plus avantageuse au commerce.

III

Archives des Affaires Etrangères.
Mémoires et Documents.
A sie,
Vol. 12,
ff. 192–197.

Relation de la Bataille donnée le 1er F[bre] 1750, entre les trouppes françoises commandées par M[r] d'Auteüil et celles de Nazerzingue, commandées par Mahamet Ali Kan, près de Ciravady.

MONSIEUR,—

Je vous ecrivis deux mots sur le champ de battaille pour vous apprendre l'heureux succès de notre entreprise, me reservant de vous en faire le détail à tête reposée.

Je joignis, selon vos ordres, l'armée de M[r] de La Touche, campée à Ciravady le 31 du mois dernier à onze heures du soir. Je trouvay tout le monde dans la joye qu'avoit causé la reussitte d'une affaire (qui n'estoit d'abord qu'une escarmouche) et qui devint generale par l'execution des ordres que M[r] de La Touche avoit donné à M[r]. de Bussy, qui partit vers les trois heures après midy avec sa compagnie, Puymorin et ses grenadiers et Mr de Caix pour ayde major. Cette petite troupe pouvoit composer environ cent blancs. Elle estoit suivie de quelques centaines de cipayes à pied et à cheval, commandés par Chek Assem, et quelques Caffres.

Mr de Bussy avoit ordre d'engager une affaire generale s'il en trouvoit l'occasion et qu'il le jugeat à propos. Mr Puymorin n'avoit d'abord été envoyé que pour degager Mrs Durouvray et Garanger, qui avoient arrêté un convoy, et qu'on disoit être entourés par toute l'armée. Le Convoy, par la protection de ces Messieurs, ce rendit au camp malgré les efforts des ennemis.

Mr de Bussy prit sur la droite, Mr Puymorin estoit sur la gauche, et, à une demie lieüe au dessus de l'aldée de Panerouty, ils trouverent l'ennemy. Il n'y avoit pour lors que de la cavalerie, que de Bussy chassa devant luy. Puymorin et les dragons, après en avoir fait autant de leur côté, joignirent les volontaires. Toute l'armée ennemie sortit pour lors de son camp. Mr de Bussy, qui connoissoit les intentions de Mr de la Touche, fit ferme, et envoyoit des petits pelotons de dix à douze hommes pour les attirer. Cela eut le succès qu'il en esperoit. L'ennemy, voyant peu de monde, s'avança assez pour que le Sr Picciny, qui commandoit une pièce de canon, pût tirer à mitraille sur un corps de cavalerie. Pendant ce tems, toute l'infanterie ennemie s'avançoit. Bussy, voyant la chose au gré des desirs de Mr de La Touche, se retira à quelques cinquante toises de l'endroit où il estoit. Il fit entrer sa petite troupe dans un ravin, mit son canon sur une hauteur, et fit fasse à toute l'armée par un feu continuel. Mrs Garanger et Durouvray avoient mis leurs dragons sous des arbres, d'où ils faisoient feu sur ce qui se presentoit. Mr. de Bussy envoya un dragon à Mr de La Touche pour luy faire part de sa scituation, mais ce courrier fut pris. La Touche, qui avoit son dessein, n'en attendit pas un second, il marcha avec tout son monde et toute l'artillerie, et fit la plus grande diligence. Mrs Puymorin et de Caix, qui découvrirent nos troupes les premiers, firent crier un : Vive le Roy ! Bussy, alors, poussa les ennemis de son côté et La Touche culbuta tout ce qui se trouva du sien. Mr. de Sabadin, qui commandoit l'artillerie, la seroit avec vivacité.

La Touche eût bien voulu pousser jusqu'au camp, mais il fit reflexion qu'il y avoit encore près d'une lieüe, qu'il faisoit presque nuit, que son monde étoit fatigué ; et d'ailleurs, sçachant que je devois arriver, il prefera le certain à l'incertain, et jugea à propos de rester sur les avantages d'une assez belle journée. La perte des ennemis fut considérable. Il n'y eut de notre côté que deux soldats de blessés et un Caffre, et le pauvre Mr Deligny, qui reçut dans les reins un coup dangereux de notre propre feu, par l'étourderie et l'ardeur d'un canonier qui mit le feu à sa pièce avant d'avertir. Cet officier se trouva malheureusement devant, et un morceau du volet le toucha.

Voilà, Monsieur, dans quel état j'ay trouvé les choses. Cette belle journée n'estoit que le prélude de la victoire la plus complette et la plus heureuse qu'on puisse desirer. Tout étoit sy bien disposé pour une affaire generale, qu'il ne restoit qu'à donner l'ordre de bataille et à faire la disposition de Messieurs les officiers.

Les grenadiers, commandés par Mrs Puymorin et Dugrez, avoient avec eux les Dragons, qui ont à leur tête Mrs Garanger et Durouvray ; cecy estoit l'avant-garde. Le corps de bataille étoit formé des pelotons commandés par Mrs Villeon, Verry, Hemart, Legris, Boulaine, Sornay. Les estrangers estoient conduits par Mr Vansandeyk. La compagnie de Bussy formoit l'arrière-garde et estoit conduite par Mrs St George et Le Normand. Mrs Sabadin, Gallard, et Picciny commandoient l'artillerie. Mr de La Touche devoit conduire la droite, and Mr Bussy la gauche, lorsqu'on se mettroit en bataille. Mr Law, major general, avoit pour ayde major Mrs de Caix et Demons.

Nous sortîmes ainsy de notre camp le premier de ce mois, à deux heures après midy, et marchâmes sur trois colonnes avec nos cipayes droit à l'ennemy. Une heure et demie après, nous decouvrîmes le camp de Mahamet Ali-Kan, qui s'estendoit le long de la riviere de Poniar, qu'il avoit à dos ; la droite et la gauche estoient appuyés à deux petits vilages brûlés. Ce camp estoit retranché par intervalle. L'infanterie occupoit ce retranchement, la cavalerie estoit à cheval par gros corps en seconde ligne. Les tentes estoient presque toutes debout. Trois grands pavillons flottoient dans le milieu du camp. Je dis alors à Mr Law de mettre l'armée en bataille, ce qu'il executa avec tout l'ordre possible, secondé par Mrs de Caix et Demons, qui se donnèrent tous les mouvemens nécessaires.

Nos François occupoient le centre ; les cipayes de Mouzaferkan la droite, ceux de Chek Assem la gauche, la cavalerie noire sur les ayles. Notre artillerie fut distribuée sur tout le front de l'armée, les chariots de munition estoient en ligne derrière nous. Le terrain nous permettant de marcher dans cet ordre, nous allâmes à l'ennemy. Quand je fus à porter le canon, je fis faire alte. Mrs de La Touche et de Bussy prirent leur poste, le premier le commandement de la droite, et de Bussy à la gauche. Je priay pours lors le père Thomas de donner la benediction. Cet aumônier, qui joint à la qualité de bon prêtre, celle d'homme de valeur, fit une bonne et courte exortation et assura sa benediction d'un coup de pistolet. Je donnay le signal à l'artillerie, qui fut servie dans l'instant avec une telle vivacitée que l'ennemy abbandonna presque ses retranchemens de cette première salve. Me tournant alors du coté du soldat, je leur dis : Enfans, qui m'aime me suive ! Sa bonne volontée qui, estant soutenue par la fermetée de Mrs les officiers, se manifesta par un cry de : Fonssons. Je fis mettre l'artillerie en route ; je contins mon centre avec l'ayde des braves officiers qui y estoient. Je n'étois nullement embarrassé des deux ayles, j'y avois La Touche et Bussy. Puymorin et les dragons faisoient toujours l'avant-garde à la droite de tout.

Nous marchâmes dans un ordre admirable. Les commandants des deux ayles, les officiers majors, les commandants d'artillerie, et tous les officiers des pelotons contribuerent à se bon ordre. Je vis alors des mouvemens chez l'ennemy qui paroissoient plus être de confusion qu'autre chose. Je fis faire alte une seconde fois et donnay le signal à l'artillerie, qui fit des merveilles (ce qui ne pouvoit être autrement) ayant de bons chefs. Mrs Gallard et Sabadin avoient l'œil partout.

Il y avoit déjà quelque tems que nous essuyons les salves du canon de l'ennemy, qui estoit repandu sur tout le front de l'attaque, et en grande quantitée. Nous n'avions qu'un soldat de blessé, lorsqu'une fusée, qui partit de la droite de l'ennemy, donna dans deux chariots de munition, qui sautèrent à vingt pas derrière nous, et qui, par le plus grand bonheur du monde, ne blessèrent aucun blanc. Je vis avec plaisir que cela n'avoit fait qu'animer le soldat, au lieu de luy faire la moindre impression. Les fuzées, quelques decharges de mousqueterie dont les balles venoient à nous, m'annoncèrent qu'il étoit temps d'entrer dans le camp. J'en donnay l'ordre, qui fut executé sur le champ, chaque officier contenant sa troupe au mieux.

Il se trouva quelque difficultée à la gauche, où étoient Bussy et Law qui l'avoit joint. L'ennemy avoit coupé un ruisseau, qui avoit inondé le passage ; mais, les officiers marchant toujours, le soldat ne s'apperçut qu'à peine de ce petit obstacle, il le franchit et se trouva dans le camp en même tems que le centre et la droite ! Nous fûmes dans un instant maîtres de tout. Les officiers menoient leurs troupes en si bon ordre, que le soldat ne pensa qu'à suivre son ennemy, et laissa le pillage.

Nous poussâmes la victoire aussy loin que nous pûmes. Les fuyards se precipitoient dans la rivière avec confusion. Il y en eut beaucoup de noyés. Quelques corps de cavalerie qui avoient pris la plaine, sembloient avoir envie de faire un coup de valeur, mais l'artillerie, qui avoit pour soutien Villeon et Puymorin, les mit bientôt en desordre, et les força à prendre comme les autres le party de la fuitte. Ainsy, nous eûmes le plaisir de voir près de quinze mille cavaliers en deroute, et quatre à cinq mil fantassins se precipiter en désordre dans la rivière, après avoir passé sous le feu d'une partie de notre mousqueterie.

Je ne puis vous dire la quantitée de munition de guerre et de bouche qui se trouva dans ce camp ; elle est inconcevable. Je fis sauter toutes les poudrières, et dans un instant cet amas de tentes et de paillotes fut embrasé. J'emmenay ce que je pus d'artillerie, et je sortis du camp à minuit pour retourner à Ciravady. Je laissay dans le camp ennemy quelques centaines de cipayes, et dès la pointe du jour j'envoyay cent blancs et toutes les troupes noires pour s'emparer des vivres et des munitions de guerre. Le tout s'apporte continuellement à notre camp.

Nous avons trente pièces de canon de differens calibres, deux petits mortiers de fonte marqués aux armes du Roy d'Angleterre avec leur munition. Une quantité prodigieuse de balles et de boulets. Quant aux vivres, la prise n'est pas moins considérable et consiste en bled, ris et plusieurs autres sortes de grains, chevaux, chamaux, et grand nombre de differents effets, tant bons que mauvais ont étés trouvés dans ce camp.

Je ne puis vous dire au juste le nombre des morts du côté de l'ennemy ; nous aurions tous souhaitté qu'ils eut tint plus long tems pour en faire un plus grand carnage. L'on a trouvé dans la rivière beaucoup d'hommes et femmes noyez, beaucoup de chevaux et d'autres bestiaux et une grande quantité de differents grains abbandonnés de l'autre côté.

Une victoire aussy complette ne nous a couté que quatre blancs de blessés par le feu de l'ennemy et dix-huit noirs brûlés par l'accident de nos chariots.

Lors que tout le monde prenoit part à la joye que causoit cet heureux evenement, il arriva un accident qui nous affligea tous ! Le pauvre Mr Sornay, voulant détourner avec la crosse de son fusil un cheval qui barroit son passage, le coup partit qui luy perça le cœur. Il mourut sur le champ. Je le fis enterrer le lendemain avec les honneurs accoutumés.

Voila, Monsieur, le détail de deux journées qui ne font pas peu d'honneur à la nation. M^rs les officiers, dont la conduite meritte les plus grands eloges, seront toujours charmés de travailler à la gloire du nom françois, et executeront toujours avec zele les projets que vous conduisés sy sagement et dont la reussitte et l'honneur vous appartiennent.

Je suis avec respect, Monsieur

Votre, &^a Signé,

D'AUTEIÜL, LE PREVOST DE LA TOUCHE, DE BUSSY, PUYMORIN, VILLEON, LAW, SABADIN, VERY S^T ROMAIN, GALLARD, GARANGER, DE S^T GEORGE, F^s THOMAS CONWAY, DEMONS, BOULAINE, DE CAIX, DUGREZ, DUROUVRAY, PICCINY, LE GRIS, DE S^T MARS, VANSANDEYK, LE NORMAND.

IV

Archives des Affaires Etrangères.
Mémoires et Documents.
A sie
Vol. 12,
ff. 199–203

Relation de la bataille donnée près de Gingy sous le commandement de Mr de Bussy et la prise de cette place et tous ses forts par escalade par toute l'armée françoise sous les ordres de M^r D'Auteuil le 12 F^bre 1750.

J'avois suivant vos ordres detaché Mr de Bussy après la bataille de Ciravady avec le nombre de trouppes que vous m'aviés prescrit. Il marcha vers Gingy par la routte que vous luy aviés donné. Quelques jours après son départ, je le suivis avec le reste de l'armée observant de laisser toujours son camp volant à quelques lieues devant moy, comme vous me l'aviés ordonné. Nous marchions depuis sept jours, et nous avions, Bussy et moy des nouvelles differentes des debris de l'armée de Mahamet Alikan. Les plus vraisemblables estoient l'envie qu'on nous disoit que ce chef avoit de se jetter avec ses forces dans Gingy, que nous semblions par nos marches vouloir attaquer.

Bussy arriva avec sa petite armée le neuviesme jour de sa marche à Moustakgory, d'où l'on decouvre Gingy, qui n'en est qu'à une lieue. L'on sçait que cette place est une des plus fortes de l'Inde. La ville est entourée d'un beau mur, la citadelle est une pièce imprenable aux Asiatiques deffendüe par des Européens. Il y a de plus sept montagnes d'un accès difficile, sur le haut desquelles il y a des citadelles très bien construites. Toutes ces fortifications sont garnies de canons de fer et de bronze depuis 4 £ de balles jusqu'à 36 £ et en grand nombre.

Bussy campa à la vüe de cette place à neuf heures du matin. Peu de tems après, on luy vint dire que Mahamet Alikan, qui avoit ramassé sept à 8 mil cavaliers, deux mille pions et mille cipayes anglois avec huit pièces de canon, devoit l'attaquer et profiter de notre separation. Mr. de Bussy avoit d'autant plus de peine à croire ce qu'on luy disoit que ses espions l'avoient assuré de l'eloignement de l'armée ennemie à son approche. Cependant, il ne negligea pas cet avis. Il se prepara à recevoir l'ennemy et envoya quelques cavaliers à la decouverte, qui vinrent luy dire que l'armée s'avançoit en bon ordre. Il ne fut pas long tems luy même à la decouvrir. Il y avoit un petit village brûlé que Bussy se mit à dos et dans lequel il plaça un peloton d'infanterie pour garder ses bagages. Il se mit en bataille en avant de ce hameau, ses cipayes, commandés par Chek Assem (qui fit bien) sur la droite et sur la gauche, et plaça son artillerie de façon qu'il pût faire face partout. Connoissant la manœuvre des ennemis à qui il avoit affaire (qui est d'entourer) il detacha Mr. Le Normand avec un peloton pour s'emparer de quelques cases qui étoient à la portée du mousquet de sa droite, et dont il tira grand party.

L'ennemy, pendant ces preparatifs, s'avançoit toujours. Il commença à canoner. Mr. Gallard commandoit l'artillerie, qui consistoit en 4 pièces, la fit servir avec toute la vivacitée possible. L'ennemy, contre son ordinaire façon de combattre, ne se rompoit point et eut la hardiesse de venir à la portée de la mousquetterie. Il paya cher cette demarche. Bussy, qui estoit en bataille, avoit pour officiers Mrs. de St. Georges, Very, Pradeau, Le Normand et de Caix, ayde major. Secondé par ces braves gens, il mit bientôt l'ennemy en desordre. La plaine fut en un moment jonchée d'hommes et de chevaux. L'infanterie s'estoit un peu eloignée et canonnoit toujours. Leurs canons estoient servis par une vingtaine d'Européens, dont plusieurs furent tués, entr'autres un Allemand blessé qu'il fit prisonnier, et qui mourut quelques heures après.

Aux premiers coups que j'entendis, je fis battre la generale. Je fis toute la diligence possible. Je ne fus pas long tems à me trouver à portée de canonner les corps qui s'estoient mis entre l'armée avancée et moy. Ils furent bientôt obligés de repasser sous le feu de Bussy, qui en abbatit un bon nombre. Pendant ce tems, il avoit eu une pièce de canon de demontée, quelques soldats de blessés. Mrs de Caix et Pradeau estoient de ce nombre, le dernier dangereusement.

Bussy, nous voyant à peu de distance de luy, rappella M^r Le Normand, qu'il avoit envoyé pour dégager six braves soldats, qui, quoyque blessés, deffendoient depuis long tems deux mortiers à grenades, qui eussent été pris sans ce secours et cela par la faute de quelques soldats d'artillerie à qui ils avoient été donnés en garde. Bussy poussoit devant luy l'ennemy qui perdoit beaucoup de monde par notre artillerie. Mrs Villeon, Puymorin et Dugrez avec les dragons que j'avois detaché joignirent bientôt Bussy, qui, avec ce renfort, poursuivoit Mahamet Alikan sans relâche. Il estoit deja sous les canons des forts que l'on tiroit sur luy, quand je priay M^r de La Touche de prendre le commandement du reste de l'armée, qui s'avançoit toujours en bon ordre. Je joignis Bussy pour prendre avec luy le parti le plus convenable. Je sentois bien comme luy qu'il falloit profiter de la terrein où l'ennemy estoit. Je le laissay le maître d'entrer dans la ville avec sa trouppe, ce qu'il executa sans perte de tems, et fut se placer à cinquante toises de la citadelle. M^r de La Touche avoit decouvert quelques corps des ennemis qui paroissoient vouloir en venir aux mains. Il fit faire alte et m'en donna avis ; Mr Law fut detaché avec sa compagnie, mais l'ennemy se retira à son approche. Nous attendions des nouvelles de Bussy, qui vint bien tôt nous faire part de la situation des choses. Pendant tout ce tems, le canon des citadelles faisoit grand feu. Bussy n'avoit eu neantmoins qu'un soldat de blessé à son passage. La Touche, qui marchoit à la tête du reste de l'armée que j'avois fait mettre en colonne, vit les soldats de son premier rang emportés d'un coup de canon. Nous entrâmes dans la ville vers les 7 heures du soir, ou, après avoir fait placer les chariots de munitions dans les rues de traverses, je distribuay les trouppes et je fis border en dehors la place par les cipayes. Je fis placer l'artillerie et les deux mortiers, qui furent servis par Mr Gallard avec toute l'activité imaginable. M^rs de St George, Very et Le Normand furent commandés pour donner l'escalade à un des forts au couché de la lune, ce qu'ils executèrent avec beaucoup de valeur. Puymorin et les Dragons estoient destinés à soutenir ceux qui devoient attacher les petards aux portes du fort principal, et que je devois forcer avec De La Touche et de Bussy. Pendant ce tems, l'ennemy faisoit grand feu de mousqueterie et de canon et jettoit quantité de fouquettes. Nous avions déjà six hommes de tués et quelques (uns) de blessés, lorsque j'envoyay M^r Du Rouvray reconnoître la porte. Ce brave officier, en se retirant, reçut un coup de fusil au travers du corps, dont il est mort le lendemain, avec le regret de tous ses camarades.

Mr Law m'ayant rendu compte des dispositions, nous restâmes dans cette sçituation jusqu'au coucher de la lune, qui estoit le signal pour agir de tous côtés. Cependant, Mr Gallard accabloit l'ennemy de grenades. Vers les 4 heures du matin, j'entendis crier Vive le Roy sur une des montagnes. C'estoit M^{rs} de St George, Very et Le Normand, qui avoient executé ce dont ils avoient été chargés.

Je fis pour lors petarder les portes de la citadelle principale, qui renferme une assés belle ville. L'ennemy prit l'epouvente et, après quelques mousquetades, la fuite. Dans moins d'une heure, nous fûmes maîtres de tout. Les fuyards se retirèrent dans deux forteresses placées sur deux hautes montagnes que nous avions à dos et se deffendirent encore quelque tems. Ils nous avoient deja blessés plusieurs soldats. Mr Kine, officier de la Compagnie etrangere, estoit du nombre des blessés.

Mais Mr Law, avec les dragons, obligea bientôt ce reste d'ennemys à fuir, et nous fûmes tranquiles possesseurs de Gingy et de tous ses forts.

Je fis mettre pavillon et garnison partout. On a trouvé sur tous ces forts des munitions de guerre en quantité, l'artillerie très nombreuse et très belle, beaucoup d'autres armes à feu. Il ne falloit pour deffendre ces postes que des braves gens qui roulassent seulement des pierres, tant ces forts sont redoutables et de difficile accès. Il y avoit une quarantaine d'Européens répandus dans tous ces postes ; les vingt deserteurs de la Compagnie angloise estoient du nombre.

Il faut que l'ennemy ait raccommodé les endroits que le S^r La Roche vous a dit être tombés. Cependant, nous n'avons rien vu de neuf, et tout est innaccessible. L'on ne revient point de sa surprise de se trouver dans de telles places à si bon marché. Il eut fallu des écheles de quarante pieds pour escalader le fort dont nous avons petardé les portes. Cette citadelle a un grand fossé bien revêtu, et communique à toutes les autres montagnes par des courtines pratiquées dans les roches. Ceux qui vous ont dit, Monsieur, que ces forts estoient accessibles dans certains endroits, n'en avoient nulle connoissance. Tous les cipayes de l'Asie n'eussent jamais osé se presenter devant de telles pièces.

Tout est tranquile. J'ay reçu le salamy du rajah du vieux Gingy. Nous sommes occupés à ramasser les provisions de guerre et de bouche qui sont en grand nombre. Il ne nous a pas été possible d'empecher le pillage, qui, au reste, est assez juste, dans une place prise d'escalade. Je l'ay fait cependant cesser le plus tôt que j'ay pu. Je travaille à rassurer l'habitant. Je vous envoye prisonnier celuy qui commandoit en l'absence du gouverneur, qui est à Arcatte depuis quelque tems.

Une bataille gagnée sous les murs d'une place que l'on emporte d'escalade dans la même nuit ne nous coûte que dix hommes de tués, dont le pauvre M.r Du Rouvray, onze blessés, du nombre desquels sont M.rs de Caix, Pradeau et Kine.

La perte des ennemis a été plus considérable que jamais dans la bataille. La plaine en étoit couverte. L'on a passé au fil de l'épée tout ce qui s'est trouvé en armes dans les differents endroits qu'on a escaladés. Le soldat, conduit par d'aussi braves officiers, a marqué dans toutes ces differentes actions, un intrepidité digne de toutes sortes de louanges.

La gloire de toutes ces victoires vous est deub, Monsieur, puisqu'on ne fait qu'executer vos ordres. M.rs les officiers vous remercient de leur procurer des occasions de se distinguer et de travailler à la gloire du nom françois. Ils vous presentent toutes ces conquêtes en signe de leurs reconnoissances, et ne cesseront de vous donner des preuves de leur zèle.

J'ay l'honneur d'être avec respect,

Monsieur,

Votre très humble et très obéissant serviteur,

(*Signé*) D'Auteuil.
Le Provost de La Touche.
De Bussy et Law.

A Gingy, ce 14 F.bre 1750.